ROMAN COINS AND THEIR VALUES

DUPONDIUS OF 241-222 B.C.
(No. 41 in catalogue)

Photo: Raymond Gardner

ROMAN COINS

AND THEIR VALUES

by

DAVID R. SEAR

Revised Edition
1970

SEABY

AUDLEY HOUSE
10 & 11 MARGARET STREET, LONDON, W1N 8AT

CATALOGUE OF ROMAN COINS, H. A. Seaby, 1936
A CATALOGUE OF ROMAN COINS, Gilbert Askew, 1948
ROMAN COINS AND THEIR VALUES, H. A. Seaby, 1954
ROMAN COINS AND THEIR VALUES, David R. Sear, 1964
ROMAN COINS AND THEIR VALUES, Revised edition, 1970

PRINTED IN ENGLAND BY ROBERT STOCKWELL LTD., LONDON, S.E.1

INTRODUCTION TO THE 1964 EDITION

INTEREST in Roman coins has increased so much since the publication of our 1954 catalogue that it was felt that a somewhat more detailed work was now called for. Accordingly, I took it upon myself to produce this new volume, and sincerely hope that all who use it will approve of the result.

The object of this catalogue is to provide the collector with a fairly comprehensive introduction to the Roman coinage. As Mr. H. A. Seaby stated in his introduction to the 1954 catalogue, it is intended to be more of a general guide to the subject than merely a list of our stock. Gilbert Askew's articles on denominations, reverse types and mint-marks have again been included in this work, but they have been considerably revised and somewhat lengthened.

Roman coins, particularly the Imperial series, reflect the life and record the historical events of their period more precisely than the coinage of any other era of history. A catalogue of this series would, therefore, be incomplete without biographical notes for the various emperors, providing an historical background to the coinage. Such biographical notes were included in the last two Roman catalogues, but in this present work these have been entirely rewritten and, in certain deserving cases, considerably lengthened.

Concerning the coinage itself, an attempt has been made in this catalogue to explain the various monetary reforms which some of the emperors carried out, particularly in the later period. Obverse legends, which are of prime importance for the identification of Roman coins, are also given in a fuller form than before, and for many of the commoner reigns the most frequently encountered legends are given in a tabulated form, similar to that employed in H. A. Seaby's *Roman Silver Coins*. In addition, the actual lists of coins have been entirely rewritten and somewhat extended, with the object of presenting to the reader a more comprehensive selection from this vast series.

It must be emphasized, however, that this catalogue contains only a small number of the known varieties, for if all were listed, the work would run into a dozen volumes instead of just one.

Illustrations in the text are far more numerous than in previous catalogues, and the half-tone plates are also new: these were specially photographed by Frank Purvey from coins, most of which were very kindly loaned by Brian Grover. My thanks are also due to H. A. Seaby and Lieut.-Col. J. Kozolubski, both of whom read the proofs and offered much useful advice, and to Peter Seaby who drew the map.

In conclusion, I should like to express the hope that to both collectors and students alike this new version of this popular work will prove to be of even greater use than its predecessors.

Pinner   DAVID R. SEAR

December, 1963

INTRODUCTION TO THE REVISED EDITION

THE half decade that has elapsed since the publication of the 1964 edition of this catalogue has seen a number of notable advances made in the study of Roman coins. Foremost amongst these were the publication of two important volumes of the *Roman Imperial Coinage*—Vol. VI, Diocletian to Maximinus, in 1967 and Vol. VII, Constantine and Licinius, in 1966. Only two volumes (VIII and X) remain to be published to make the *R.I.C.* complete, and although some of the earlier volumes are seriously in need of revision the importance of this work as the standard reference book on the Roman Imperial series cannot be over-estimated.

In this revised edition of *Roman Coins and Their Values* I have added *R.I.C.* and *B.M.C.* (British Museum Catalogue) references to those of Cohen already given. I hope that in later editions I may be able to produce a work based on *R.I.C.* and *B.M.C.* rather than on Cohen, with more emphasis placed on mintage and the chronological sequence of issues.

For the present, however, my revisions have been confined mainly to the front part of the catalogue, and these are as follows:

1. The section on deities and personifications has been thoroughly revised and extended, and many new illustrations have been added to show most of the personifications.

2. Coverage of reverse types has been greatly extended to include representations of the emperor, types of military conquest and victories, legionary types, geographical types, architectural types, etc., etc., and not merely deities and personifications as in the original edition.

3. A new section on countermarks has been added.

4. A new section on mints has been added covering the period from the Early Empire to the reform of the coinage by Diocletian.

5. Mints and Mint-Marks of the Later Roman Empire has been extensively revised, with details given of the periods of operation of the late Roman mints.

6. A new section on dating Roman Imperial coins has been added, based on my article in the October 1962 *Bulletin*.

In the main body of the catalogue, a list of the mints issuing pure Roman currency for that particular emperor has been given at the start of each reign: in addition, tables of titles and powers have been inserted before those reigns where they will be of most use in dating the coins. The eight half-tone plates of Imperial coins used in the first edition have been retained, and in addition Frank Purvey has prepared four plates of Republican coins from pieces which were very kindly made available by the Coin and Medal Department of the British Museum.

The value of Roman coins has increased very considerably since 1964, and in repricing this edition a survey has been made of prices realized at recent auction sales in order to achieve a realistic set of valuations for the rarer pieces. It should also be noted that really superb specimens of otherwise common types have been realizing prices dramatically higher than the value given for an average piece. For example, an *as* of Agrippa, priced at £12·50 in "F" condition in this catalogue, fetched nearly £200 in superb state in a Swiss sale at the end of 1968. More recently, in London, a *denarius* of Vespasian with a common reverse type fetched £75, whereas similar pieces are priced at £4 in this catalogue for "F" condition.

As a result of this trend, I feel that I must advise new collectors not to set themselves too high a standard when forming their collections. The average collector, working on a limited budget, would be hard-pressed to assemble even a small group of the commoner rulers if he confines himself to "EF" and better coins. A similar group, however, in "VF" condition for silver, and "F" for brass and copper could be assembled comparatively easily and for only a fraction of the cost.

Prices in this edition are being expressed in the new decimal currency, in line with the most recent volumes of *Roman Silver Coins*.

In conclusion, I should like to thank Frank Purvey for his work in preparing the new plates of illustrations; and H. A. Seaby, Peter Seaby and Helen Webster who all very kindly read through the proofs and offered much constructive criticism. I am also indebted to Peter Jones, head of our Publications Dept., for assembling the new list of Books on Roman Coins, and to Michael Dickinson for his valuable help in preparing the survey of auction prices. My wife, Margaret, gave me great assistance in the laborious task of checking all the *R.I.C.* and *B.M.C.* references, as well as being very tolerant of the moods of a numismatic writer.

Pinner   DAVID R. SEAR

November, 1969

COLLECTING ROMAN COINS.

(Being part of the Introduction to the 1948 catalogue)

WE are sometimes asked "How does one begin collecting Roman coins?" The usual way is by building up a series of portrait coins of the various emperors; and this was the basis on which the F. J. Hansen "No. 1" Collection was formed. The late Mr. Hansen's object was to amass the finest portrait series of Roman emperors and members of the Imperial families in large bronze coins wherever possible, and from 1926 to 1939 he acquired specimens from the principal auction sales in Europe, always trying to improve his collection by the addition of finer pieces. Having obtained as good a series of portraits as financial considerations will permit, the collector can then turn his attention to the reverse types or perhaps the various denominations. Some people, indeed, prefer to select a certain type, such as SALVS, and attempt to obtain a coin of each emperor who used it.

We would advise the beginner never to buy a poor specimen of any coin unless it has the recommendation of rarity. Set a reasonable standard for the commoner pieces, and adhere to it: it is better to acquire one VF specimen than two or three which can only be assessed as "fair," although, of course, in this as in most other matters, financial considerations may be the ultimate determining factor. If advice is required, our experience is at your service.

The science of numismatics covers an immense field, and can only be comprehended by careful study of both the coins themselves and the various text books dealing with them; but let no beginner be deterred by difficulties which are more apparent than real. A very small collection of well-chosen pieces, properly studied with regard to their historical background, can give much pleasure and instruction.

Finally, I should like to quote some remarks of the late Stanley Casson,* the well-known archaeological writer. "In coins . . . there is almost always some historical information or some allusion, political or religious. They therefore contain much and varied information. From the purely artistic point of view, as well, they mirror in a microcosm the prevailing artistic tendencies of their day, and, since they can often be arranged in a chronological order that depends upon evidence other than that of their style, they can be used to contribute to the study of style itself in art. As evidence for the illustration of contemporary life at the period of their issue, they are of inestimable value. Cults, notable events, traditions, social and political changes, and artistic achievements are faithfully recorded in their inscriptions and on the designs and the types that they bear . . . But the uses of numismatics are too manifold and the information which is provided by a study of coinage is so vast and fertile that it would be idle to do more than hint at it."

GILBERT ASKEW.

---

* In *Archaeology*, Ernest Benn Ltd., 1930.

THE DENOMINATIONS OF THE ROMAN COINAGE.

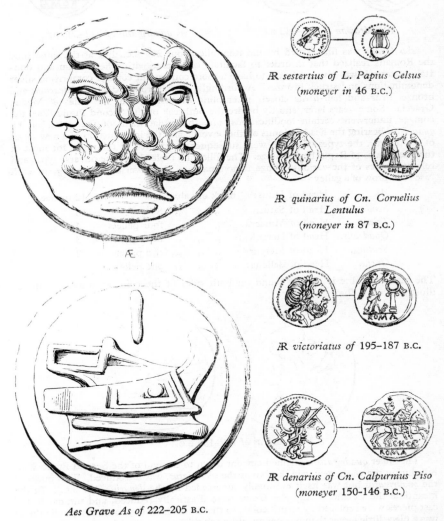

Æ sestertius of L. Papius Celsus
(*moneyer in* 46 B.C.)

Æ quinarius of Cn. Cornelius
Lentulus
(*moneyer in* 87 B.C.)

Æ victoriatus of 195–187 B.C.

Æ denarius of Cn. Calpurnius Piso
(*moneyer* 150-146 B.C.)

Æ

Aes Grave As of 222–205 B.C.

The earliest coinage of Central Italy was of bronze, the various pieces being cast and not struck: this class of coinage is known as "Aes Grave." Previous to the currency of these, rough pieces of bronze, known as "Aes Rude," and oblong bronze castings bearing types in relief ("Aes Signatum") were in use, although these may have been used as bullion exchangeable by weight rather than as money.

Æ didrachm of 269–242 B.C.   *Æ quadrigatus of* 222–205 B.C.

Aes Grave was first issued by the Republic about 269 B.C., but at the same time the Romans realized that in order to facilitate commerce with other Italian and non-Italian states it was also necessary to have a more convenient coinage comprising silver denominations and struck bronzes. Accordingly, they introduced silver *didrachms* and bronze *litrae* and half-*litrae* closely resembling the coinages of the cities of Magna Graecia. Some years later, shortly before the outbreak of the Second Punic War, the coinage underwent certain modifications, *viz.* the replacement of the *didrachms* by *quadrigati* bearing the head of Janus on the obverse, and the introduction of a new series of *Aes Grave*, the types of which were subsequently adopted as the norm for most of the later issues of Republican bronze. The following table shows the obverse types and relative values of the various bronze denominations, the reverse type being, in each case, the prow of a galley:—

As.	Head of Janus:	mark of value, I		= 12 unciae.
Semis.	Head of Saturn:	,, ,, ,, S		= 6 ,,
Triens.	Head of Minerva:	,, ,, ,, four pellets	= 4 ,,
Quadrans.	Head of Hercules:	,, ,, ,, three pellets	= 3 ,,
Sextans.	Head of Mercury:	,, ,, ,, two pellets	= 2 ,,
Uncia.	Head of Bellona:	,, ,, ,, one pellet.		

The mark of value is usually found on both sides of the coin, as shown on the *as* illustrated on *p.* 9.

Struck as of 167–155 B.C.

The silver *quadrigatus* remained current down to the end of the Second Punic War, but during the war a new coin, known as the *victoriatus*, was introduced. This outlived the *quadrigatus* but was itself eventually superseded by the *denarius* (187 B.C.). In the meantime the weights of the *Aes Grave* were drastically reduced, and ultimately the cast pieces were replaced by struck coins, so that in the later days of the Republic the *as* was a piece little larger than our penny, although thicker and clumsier.

The *denarius* was the chief coin of the Republican period and was originally equal to ten *asses*, but in 133 B.C. it was retariffed at sixteen *asses*. There was also a silver *quinarius* (half-*denarius*), although this was only coined at intervals, and still scarcer was the silver *sestertius* (quarter-*denarius*).

Æ *aureus of Brutus*   Æ *quinarius of Tiberius.*

Gold coins were very seldom issued and formed no part of the regular coinage in the Republican period. They were struck for military and similar emergency purposes, and all types are now rare. In the period of civil strife which followed the assassination of Julius Caesar, gold was issued by and for the various contestants: such a coin is illustrated above, being an *aureus* bearing the name and portrait of Brutus and struck, as the coin tells us, by Casca Longus, the "envious Casca" of Shakespeare's play.

No Republican bronze was issued after about 80 B.C., except for a brief emission under Julius Caesar, but as soon as Augustus had achieved supreme power and restored peace to the Roman world, he resumed the regular issue of *aes* as part of his re-organization of the coinage. The minting of gold and silver he kept under his own control, but the copper and orichalcum coins were issued by the Senate, and bear the letters S.C. ("Senatus Consulto") as evidence of this. These Senatorial coins begin in 23 B.C., and at first the names of the responsible moneyers form part of the legends, but not after about 4 B.C.

Gold now became a regular issue, and the various denominations of the re-organized coinage, in all metals, with their relative values, are listed below:—

Gold *aureus*	=	25	silver *denarii*
Gold *quinarius*	=	12½	silver *denarii*
Silver *denarius*	=	16	copper *asses*
Silver *quinarius*	=	8	copper *asses*
Orichalcum *sestertius*	=	4	copper *asses*
Orichalcum *dupondius*	=	2	copper *asses*
Copper *as*	=	4	copper *quadrantes*
Orichalcum *semis*	=	2	copper *quadrantes*
Copper *quadrans*	=	¼	copper *as*

The *dupondius* and *as*, though of similar size, could be distinguished by the colour of the metal (yellow orichalcum, red copper), the radiate head of the emperor only coming into use as a regular feature of the former coin at a later date.

Ɍ *cistophorus of Augustus.*   Æ *semis of Nero.*

At certain Asiatic mints Augustus and his successors continued to strike the large silver pieces, equal to three *denarii*, which are usually termed *cistophori* or *tetradrachms*. Coins of this size and value, bearing as one type the "cista mystica" from which the name derives, had been the chief coinage of Asia Minor from the 2nd century B.C., and although in the Imperial period the types were more in accordance with the general style of Roman issues, the coin was substantially the same and readily passed current.

Æ *quadrans of Domitian.*   Æ *dupondius of Antoninus Pius.*

The emperor Nero, who with all his faults was a man of considerable artistic talent, took an interest in the Imperial coinage which led him to institute an *as* and a *quadrans* struck in orichalcum in addition to those of copper. Whether his ultimate intention was to discard copper altogether is not certain, but in any case these pieces did not survive his own reign, with certain small exceptions such as the orichalcum *asses* struck by Trajan and Hadrian.

Æ *sestertius of Hadrian.*

The *sestertii* of the first and second centuries A.D. are amongst the most attractive of all the Roman series, bearing interesting types very often most artistically portrayed. These coins, when in the finest condition, are much sought after and always realize high

Æ *as of Antoninus Pius.*   Æ *quinarius of Julia Domna.*

prices. The *asses* and *dupondii* also, though their smaller flans do not give the scope offered by the larger denomination, are often beautiful examples of the moneyer's art.

Æ *denarius of Nerva.*   N *aureus of M. Aurelius.*

Nero lowered the weight of the gold and silver coins and reduced the fineness of the latter. Successive emperors, always pressed for money, carried on the evil process, until by the reign of Caracalla the *denarius* was barely 40% of silver. This emperor further debased the coinage by introducing a new coin of similar metal which, although only equal in weight to 1½ *denarii*, was probably tariffed as being the equivalent of two. The new piece, which we know by the name *antoninianus* (after Caracalla's official name, Antoninus), always shows the emperor wearing a radiate crown, as opposed to the laurel-wreath of the *denarius*. In the case of empresses, this denomination is distinguished by a crescent placed beneath the bust.

Æ *antoninianus of Pupienus.*   Æ *antoninianus of Aurelian.*

The *antoninianus*, which drove the *denarius* out of circulation towards the middle of the third century, became more and more debased until, by the reign of Gallienus, it was reduced to a mere copper or bronze piece, often of very small module, with a slight silvery wash. Aurelian, in his reform of the coinage, restored the *antoninianus* to something like its original size, but did little to improve its silver content. The *antoniniani* of Claudius Gothicus, and of the Gallic usurpers Tetricus Senior and Junior, were largely imitated by unofficial mints, and these contemporary forgeries are frequently found in British hoards. Although sometimes reasonably good copies of the originals, many of them are grotesque in the extreme as well as being much smaller than the officially minted coins. To this class of coin the name "barbarous radiate" has been given, and the exact dating of the various types and classes is still a matter of dispute.

Thus the Imperial coinage was reduced to a very low level, except for the gold which continued to be of fine quality although fluctuating in weight. The *sestertius*, *dupondius* and *as* were issued more or less regularly, but fell out of use when the *antoninianus* became itself only a bronze coin. The last *sestertii* of the old style were issued by Postumus, who also struck the two lower denominations.

An innovation by Trajan Decius (A.D. 249–251) was the *double sestertius* bearing a radiate bust. This fine piece, which is actually very little heavier than the *sestertii* of the early emperors, is rare, and was not continued by the successors of Decius.

Æ *follis of Maximianus.*   Æ *argenteus of Galerius.*

Diocletian, who towards the end of the third century devised a new constitution for the empire, also regularized the coinage. This great reform was probably not one decisive act but rather a series of changes covering a period of about ten years. The most important of these changes were the introductions of two new denominations, the *argenteus*, a silver coin of approximately the same fineness and weight as the *denarii* of Nero, and the *follis*, a coin of silver-washed bronze resembling the *as* of the earlier empire. The issue of the *antoninianus* was discontinued, but a similar coin was still struck for about a decade following the reform. This piece was of the same size as the *antoninianus* and had the familiar radiate crown on the obverse, but it no longer bore the mark XXI on the reverse and it contained no trace of silver. These coins are referred to in this catalogue as *post-reform radiates*.

    Æ 3 of Licinius II.   *Æ siliqua of Delmatius.*

Constantine the Great made further changes in the monetary system. In place of the *aureus* ($^1/_{60}$ lb. of gold) he introduced a new coin called the *solidus* which was struck at 72 to the lb. The *solidus*, which was first struck in 312, soon superseded the *aureus* as the standard gold coin of the Empire. Other gold denominations introduced by Constantine were the *semissis* ($\frac{1}{2}$ *solidus*) and the $1\frac{1}{2}$ *scripulum*, a smaller coin about which very little is known at present.

  Æ centenionalis of Constans.   *Æ miliarense of Valentinian I.*

Later in his reign, Constantine resumed the issue of silver coins, which appears to have almost ceased after the large output under the Tetrarchy. There were two main denominations in this metal, the *miliarense* ($^1/_{18}$ *solidus*) and the *siliqua* ($^1/_{24}$ *solidus*). The latter was of the same weight as Diocletian's *argenteus* ($^1/_{96}$ lb. of silver) but Constantius II reduced its weight to $^1/_{144}$ lb.

              Æ 1 of Julian II.

The bronze coinage of the fourth century presents many problems. The *follis* soon began to decline in size and weight and this process was allowed to continue for nearly half a century until, by the time of Constantius II and Constans, the only bronze coins in issue were tiny pieces of about 15 mm. diameter and 20-25 grains weight. As the standard of the bronze coinage was thus continuously changing, it is impossible to establish its relationship to the gold and silver denominations.

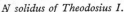

Aʹ solidus of Theodosius I.   *AR siliqua of Flavius Victor.*

In A.D. 346, Constantius II and Constans introduced a heavier coin called the *centenionalis*, and later emperors also made attempts to restore the bronze coinage. Magnentius (350–353) and Julian II (360–363) both struck very large pieces (*c.* 30 mm.) and Gratian (367–383) introduced a coin closely resembling the *centenionalis*. However, all these attempts were comparatively short-lived, and after the death of Theodosius I in A.D. 395, only the small bronze denominations continued in regular issue.

As so little is known about the names of the denominations of the late Roman bronze coinage, they are usually referred to as Æ 1, Æ 2, Æ 3 or Æ 4, Æ 1 being the largest.

Aʹ tremissis of Valentinian III.   *Aʹ semissis of Galla Placidia.*

The coinage of the fifth century consisted mainly of the *solidus* and the two smaller gold denominations, the *semissis* (½ *solidus*) and the *tremissis* (⅓ *solidus*). The *tremissis* had been introduced by Theodosius I to replace the 1½ *scripulum* of Constantine's system. Very little silver was issued and the bronze, which was mostly of the tiny Æ 4 module, was only struck in comparatively small quantities. The shortage of officially minted coins was to some extent made good by another vast output of barbarous imitations, many of them copies of the "FEL. TEMP. REPARATIO" *centenionales* of Constantius II.

In A.D. 498, Anastasius I introduced a new series of bronze coins of a completely revolutionary type, each denomination bearing its mark of value conspicuously on the reverse. As the introduction of these coins marks an almost complete break with the traditions of the Roman coinage, the reform of A.D. 498 is a convenient point at which to begin the Byzantine series, at least as far as the bronze is concerned.

THE REVERSE TYPES OF THE IMPERIAL COINAGE

Although most collectors of Roman Imperial coins begin by acquiring as good a series of portraits of the various emperors as possible, it is in the reverse types that the greatest interest will be found. Moreover, a knowledge of these types will sometimes enable a coin to be correctly allocated when the legends are obscure; and this is important where coins from excavations are to be used as archaeological evidence.

I. DEITIES AND PERSONIFICATIONS

In the following notes it is proposed briefly to outline the more important types (the chief deities of the Roman pantheon and a few other divinities which achieved great popularity in the Roman World) and their customary attributes, after which the principal personifications, which constitute the majority of the reverse types, will be dealt with.

Aesculapius. The god of medicine and healing, he is shown as a man of mature years, holding a staff about which a serpent twines, and he is often accompanied by a small figure representing Telesphorus, his attendant.

His image appears on Greek Imperial coins of Epidaurus, where the great temple of **Asklepios** was situated, of Nicopolis in Epirus, and of Pergamum.

*From an
as of Caracalla.*

Apollo. The sun-god, Apollo, was also god of music and the arts, of prophecy, and the protector of flocks and herds: he is usually depicted with a lyre. Amongst his titles are CONSERVATOR, PALATINVS (as protector of the imperial residence on the Palatine), and PROPVGNATOR. He appears at intervals on the Imperial coinage from Augustus to Aurelian, after which, except for a temporary revival under Julian II, the type falls out of use.

As to Greek Imperial coins, Apollo is represented on the Alexandrian issues named Apollo Aktios or Pythios, and on coins of Ephesus with the title Embasios. On the colonial copper of Apamaea he is named APOLLO CLARIVS. Several other Greek cities adopted the god as a coin-type in the Imperial period, but name or title are seldom given.

Bacchus. Under his ancient Italian name of **Liber,** the god of wine occasionally appears as a coin-type, and is generally shown holding a wine-cup and a thyrsus, and accompanied by a panther: sometimes his head only, crowned with vine or ivy-leaves, is depicted. On a coin of Gallienus the panther alone appears, with the legend LIBERO P. CONS. AVG. Few emperors, however, adopted Bacchus as a type.

*From a denarius of
Septimius Severus.*

In the Greek Imperial series, however, **Dionysos** was a very popular type and occurs on the coins of many cities.

Ceres. In the first and second centuries A.D., Ceres appears frequently as a type, and is generally shown holding ears of corn to symbolize her functions as presiding goddess of agriculture: sometimes, however, she bears a torch. She is depicted on a number of Greek Imperial coins, as the goddess **Demeter.**

*From a
dupondius of Julia Titi.*

Cybele. Of Eastern origin, the Mother of the Gods seems rarely to have been depicted as a Roman coin-type, except in the second and early third centuries. She is usually shown wearing a turreted crown, and is either in a car drawn by lions or enthroned between lions: the accompanying legend is normally MATER DEVM or MATRI MAGNAE, or a similar variant.

From an
as of Julia Domna.

Many Greek cities have **Kybele** on their coins, as her cult was popular in Asia Minor.

From a bronze medallion
of Antoninus Pius.

Diana. The sister of Apollo, Diana was regarded as the Moon-goddess, and is sometimes represented with a crescent moon above her forehead. She was also protectress of the young, and deity of the chase: in the latter character she appears with bow and arrows, and is sometimes accompanied by a hound or a deer, but when given the title of LVCIFERA, the lightbringer, she is depicted holding a long torch. Her other titles include CONSERVATRIX, EPHESIA and VICTRIX.

The most famous shrine of Diana (or **Artemis,** as the Greeks called her) was that at Ephesus which is mentioned in the *Acts of the Apostles*, ch. 19, 27, and some of the Imperial issues of that city show the statue of Artemis Ephesia, or a temple containing the statue, as the reverse type. The cult of Artemis Ephesia was honoured in many Greek cities, some of which used a similar type. Other titles of Artemis are Astyren (at Antandrus), Klaria (at Colophon), Tyche Gerason (at Gerasa), etc.

The Dioscuri. The twins Castor and Pollux, sons of Jupiter and Leda, were a very popular type on the Republican denarii of the second century B.C. In Imperial times, however, the type very seldom appears. They are normally depicted with their horses and wearing pointed caps surmounted by stars. Occasionally Castor appears by himself, notably on gold of Commodus and silver of Geta.

The **Dioskuri** occur on the coins of a number of the Greek cities in Imperial times, notably Phocaea in Ionia, and sometimes they are represented merely by their caps with stars.

Hercules. Hercules was a popular coin-type from the first century A.D. until the time of Constantine the Great. He can always be recognized by splendid physical development and his attributes of the club and lion-skin. Commodus, who regarded Hercules as his tutelary deity and even, it is said, believed himself a reincarnation of the demi-god, struck many medallions and coins which bear the figure of Hercules. At a later date, Postumus issued a series bearing types alluding to the various "labours." The titles of Hercules are many, and include CONSERVATOR, DEFENSOR, ROMANVS and VICTOR.

From a gold
medallion
of Constantius I.

Greek Imperial coins of Erythrae and Smyrna, amongst others, bear the image of **Herakles,** and under Antoninus Pius the mint of Alexandria issued a series of bronze coins illustrating the deity's heroic exploits.

Isis. Of purely Egyptian origin, Isis, the wife of Osiris, became one of the most popular deities with the Romans, and she even had several temples in Rome itself. She rarely appears on the imperial coinage, however, but is sometimes shown in the company of Serapis. Her normal attribute is the sistrum (rattle), but on a coin of Julia Domna she nurses the infant Horus.

Isis also appears on a number of Greek Imperial issues, particularly on the coinage of Alexandria.

Æ 3 of the time of Julian II.

Sometimes her head is shown, and sometimes she is represented as Isis Pharia, holding a billowing sail and occasionally accompanied by a representation of the Pharos (lighthouse) of Alexandria.

From an as of Hadrian.

Janus. Although the double head of Janus was the regular obverse type of the Republican *as* throughout almost the whole period of its issue, the deity very seldom appears on any coins of the emperors. He was the god of beginnings, looking both to past and future, and the first month of the year was named after him. He appears at infrequent intervals as a reverse type—a full-length figure holding a sceptre—and his temple is shown on some coins of Nero. When there was peace over the whole empire the doors of Janus' temple were closed, and this was so rare a happening that Nero thought it proper to strike a special series of coins to commemorate the event.

Juno. Juno, the consort of Jupiter, is depicted as a tall matron, either seated or standing, holding a patera and a sceptre: she is frequently accompanied by a peacock. Her titles include REGINA, LVCINA (referring to her as the presiding deity of childbirth), CONSERVATRIX and VICTRIX.

She is not so often depicted on Greek Imperial coins as is Jupiter, but does appear on some, notably on a coin of Chalcis in Euboea where her Greek name, **Hera**, is also given. Her bust and name are shown on certain tetradrachms of Alexandria.

From a sestertius of Lucilla.

From a gold medallion of Diocletian.

Jupiter. Jove, or Jupiter, Optimus Maximus (the Best and Greatest), is usually depicted as a tall bearded man in the prime of life, nude or semi-nude, holding a thunderbolt in his right hand and a sceptre in his left. Sometimes standing, sometimes seated enthroned, the figure of the Father of the Gods must have been familiar to every Roman from the many statues in Rome and other cities. On some coins he is depicted holding a small figure of Victory, or his attendant eagle, instead of a thunderbolt: often the eagle is shown standing at his feet. The titles of Jupiter are numerous, and include CONSERVATOR, CVSTOS (Protector of the emperor), LIBERATOR, PROPVGNATOR, STATOR (the Stayer of armies about to flee), TONANS (the Thunderer), TVTATOR and VICTOR. One unusual representation of the god is as a child seated on the back of the Amalthaean goat, with the legend IOVI CRESCENTI, "to the growing Jupiter": this occurs on a coin of the young Caesar Valerian II.

On Greek Imperial coins Jupiter also appears, but here, of course, when his name is given it is in the Greek form, **Zeus,** usually with the addition of one of his many titles, such as Euromeus (on coins of Euromus in Caria) and Olympios (at Alexandria).

Luna. The moon-goddess is usually equated with Diana Lucifera, and only appears with her own name on coins of Julia Domna and Gallienus.

Her Greek counterpart, **Selene,** appears rather more frequently on the Greek Imperial coinage, and sometimes her head is shown conjoined with that of Helios, the sun-god.

The crescent-moon, which is symbolic of Luna, sometimes occurs as a type, usually in association with a number of stars. In the third century, the crescent is usually shown at the empress's shoulders on the *dupondius* and *antoninianus* denominations (see also under Sol, below).

Mars. The god of war, always a popular deity with the Romans, appears frequently as a coin type until the time of Constantine the Great. He is usually shown with his spear and shield, or with a trophy instead of the latter, and is sometimes nude, except for a helmet and cloak, sometimes in complete armour. When given the title of PACIFER he bears the olive-branch of Peace, although in this connection one remembers the words which Tacitus puts into the mouth of a British chieftain who, referring to the Romans, says "They make a desert and call it peace." Amongst the titles of Mars are CONSERVATOR, PROPVG-NATOR (the Champion of Rome), VLTOR (the Avenger) and VICTOR.

From a heavy aureus of Gallienus.

Mars, known to the Greeks as **Ares,** appears on certain Greek Imperial coins, but his name or titles are rarely given.

From an as of Herennius Etruscus.

Mercury. Mercury, messenger of the gods, was reverenced as the patron of artists, orators, travellers, merchants and, curiously, thieves. He is one of the least frequent of the major deities to appear as a coin-type, and he is generally depicted wearing the winged cap or petasus, and carrying a purse and a caduceus. The latter is occasionally used alone as a coin-type, notably on the smaller denominations.

On Greek Imperial coins, **Hermes** was only adopted by some half-dozen cities as a type, without name or title.

Minerva. The counterpart in Roman mythology of the Greek **Pallas Athene,** Minerva frequently appears on coins, particularly on those of Domitian. A war-like goddess, she usually bears spear and shield and is equipped with helmet and aegis; but sometimes she holds a small figure of Victory, or her attendant owl. Minerva guided men in the dangers of war, where victory is gained by prudence, courage and perseverance: she was also goddess of wisdom and patroness of the arts. Amongst her titles are PACIFERA, bringer of Peace, and VICTRIX.

From a sestertius of Clodius Albinus.

On the Greek Imperial issues she is sometimes named as Athena with perhaps an additional title such as Areia (at Pergamum), Ilias (at Ilium), or Argeia (at Alexandria).

Nemesis. The avenger of crimes and punisher of wrong-doers, Nemesis makes comparatively few appearances on the coinage. She is usually depicted holding a caduceus, with a serpent at her feet, and sometimes draws out a fold of drapery from her breast. Alternatively, she may be shown holding a purse, a sistrum, a bridle or a cubit-rule, usually with a wheel at her feet. Occasionally, two Nemeses appear standing facing each other.

On the coins of the Greek cities she is depicted rather more frequently, most often holding a bridle or a cubit-rule, and with a wheel at her feet.

Neptune. Neptune, god of the sea, appears as a coin-type from Pompey the Great intermittently until Julian II. He is usually represented holding a dolphin and a trident, but sometimes holds an acrostolium (the prow ornament of a galley) instead of the former. The prow of a galley may be shown beside him, perhaps with his right foot resting on it.

Poseidon, the Greek counterpart of Neptune, occurs very rarely as a type in the Imperial period, but does appear at Rhodes, with the name Poseidon Asphaleios, and at Alexandria as Poseidon Isthmios.

From an as of Agrippa.

Roma. The goddess who particularly personified Rome is usually represented helmeted and in armour, holding a small figure of Victory, or a wreath, and a parazonium. When the Roman Empire became Christian, the type was still used as a personification of the city or the state, much as we use the figure of Britannia today.

From a sestertius of Galba.

Serapis. A divinity of Egyptian origin, Serapis was often equated with various other gods (e.g. Aesculapius, Osiris, Jupiter and Pluto), and his true powers and attributes are difficult to define. Nevertheless, his worship achieved great popularity in Rome and the Empire, and many splendid temples were erected in his honour.

He appears intermittently on the Roman coinage from Hadrian to Claudius Gothicus, and is usually shown raising his r. hand and holding a sceptre. On his head he frequently wears a modius, and the triple-headed dog Cerberus, the guard of the infernal regions, sometimes sits at his feet (this illustrates his connection with Pluto).

From a billon tetradrachm of Domitius Domitianus

Serapis also appears on the coins of a number of the Greek Imperial mints, particularly those of Alexandria, and sometimes his bust is shown conjoined with that of the Egyptian goddess Isis.

*From an
aureus of Probus.*

Sol. The sun-god frequently appears as a type during the third and fourth centuries, and is usually depicted nude, or almost so, with radiate head, holding a globe or a whip. Sometimes he is shown in a chariot and occasionally his bust only occurs as a type. His titles include COMES and INVICTVS, and when he is styled ORIENS, a name which properly refers to the eastern or rising sun, it may be taken as alluding to the rising fortunes of the emperor using the type.

Helios, the Greek equivalent of Sol, appears on the coins of a number of Greek cities. Sometimes his head is shown conjoined with that of Selene, the moon-goddess.

The radiate crown, which the emperor is usually shown wearing on the *dupondius* and *antoninianus* denominations, may be taken as an allusion to his position as the Earthly personification of the sun-god. Similarly from the time of Julia Domna to the end of the third century, the empress is normally depicted with a crescent at her shoulders: this is a reference to the moon-goddess.

The Three Graces. The Gratiae, or Charites, Euphrosyne, Aglaia and Thalia, were minor deities who enhanced the pleasures of life by refinement and gentleness, and they especially favoured poetry and the arts. Their images appear on certain coins of the Greek Imperial series, being generally depicted as on the coin of Deultum Thraciae illustrated here: the type was also adopted by Argos, Itanus, Naxos and Magnesia ad Maeandrum. Statues of the Graces were popular throughout the Roman world, and the Museum at Cyrene possesses one of the Hadrianic period. The type was also used by Italian medallists as late as the sixteenth century.

*From a
sestertius of Julia Domna.*

Venus. The goddess of beauty and love was a favourite Roman coin-type from Republican times until early in the fourth century. Amongst her titles are CAELESTIS, FELIX, GENETRIX and VICTRIX, and she is usually depicted completely or almost completely clothed. Sometimes she holds an apple, sometimes a helmet and a sceptre, and occasionally she is accompanied by Cupid: in those instances where she is shown semi-nude, she is usually posed with her back modestly turned towards the spectator. Julius Caesar, who claimed descent from the goddess, depicted her on many of his coins, generally holding a small figure of Victory.

On Greek Imperial coins, the goddess was sometimes adopted as a coin-type because in or near the issuing city there was an important temple of **Aphrodite,** and the type had therefore a local interest: her name is seldom, if ever, included in the legend. In a few cases, such as at Corinth and Cnidus, the representation of the goddess is known to have been copied from a statue for which the issuing city was famous.

Vesta. Vesta, one of the most honoured deities of the Romans, was the goddess of the family hearth, and was worshipped as the particular protectress of family life. She is represented, on the coins of many emperors from Caligula to Gallienus, as a matron holding a patera and sceptre, or a torch, a simpulum, or the palladium. The well-known *as* of Caligula is perhaps the best example of her image as a coin-type. Her titles include MATER and SANCTA.

Her Greek counterpart, **Hestia,** appears on a coin of Nero issued at Maeonia, in Lydia.

From an as of Caligula.

From an antoninianus of Valerian I.

Vulcan. Vulcan, the god of iron and fire, was the chief deity of smiths and ironworkers, but seldom appears as a coin-type. He is usually shown with attributes appropriate to the blacksmith's calling.

As **Hephaistos,** he appears on a number of Greek Imperial issues. On some, he is depicted seated on a rock forging the shield of Achilles, as described by Homer.

We can now proceed briefly to summarize the chief allegorical personifications which appear on the Imperial coinage. In the following list, the Latin name of each is given first, followed in brackets by the Greek equivalent where used on a Greek issue. Then comes the nearest English rendering of the name, and finally the normal attributes usually associated with the type mentioned. Feminine personifications, in alphabetical order, are given first, then the masculine, which are fewer in number.

Aequitas
(*Quietus*)

Aeternitas
(*Tetrici*)

Concordia
(*Julia Paula*)

Abundantia (Euthenia). Abundance, Plenty. Holds cornucopiae and corn-ears, or is shown emptying the former.

Aequitas (Dikaiosyne). Equity, Fair Dealing. Holds scales and cornucopiae or sceptre.

Aeternitas. Eternity, Stability. Holds globe, torch, phoenix or sceptre, or the heads of the Sun and Moon.

Annona. Corn-harvest. Holds corn-ears and cornucopiae, usually with modius and prow of galley beside her. The type refers to the corn-supply which had to be imported every year for the sustenance of Rome.

Fecunditas
(*Faustina Jr.*)

Felicitas
(*Julia Mamaea*)

Fides
(*Plotina*)

Clementia. Clemency, Mercy. Holds branch and sceptre, and sometimes leans on a column.

Concordia (Homonoia). Concord, Harmony. Holds patera and cornucopiae or sceptre. As Concordia Militum, holds two standards.

Fecunditas. Fertility. Holds child, or children, and sceptre. Sometimes the children are depicted standing at her feet.

Felicitas (Eutycheia). Happiness, Prosperity. Holds caduceus and cornucopiae or sceptre. Sometimes depicted leaning on a column.

Fides. Confidence, Good Faith. Holds patera and cornucopiae or corn-ears and basket of fruit. As Fides Militum, holds two standards or standard and sceptre.

Fides Militum
(*Maximinus I*)

Fortuna
(*Didius Julianus*)

Hilaritas
(*Didia Clara*)

Fortuna (Tyche). Fortune. Holds rudder, sometimes resting on a globe, and cornucopiae; a wheel may be shown beside her. Sometimes her attributes include an olive-branch or a patera.

Hilaritas. Mirth, Rejoicing. Holds long palm and cornucopiae, sceptre or patera: is sometimes accompanied by one or two children.

Indulgentia. Indulgence, Mercy. Holds patera and sceptre.

Justitia. Justice. Holds olive-branch, or patera, and sceptre; sometimes, though rarely, a pair of scales.

Laetitia. Joy, Gladness. Holds wreath and sceptre, or occasionally rudder on globe in place of the latter, or may rest her left hand on an anchor.

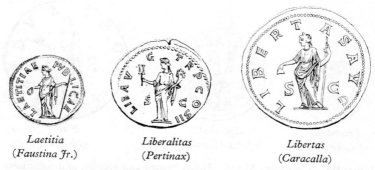

Laetitia
(Faustina Jr.)

Liberalitas
(Pertinax)

Libertas
(Caracalla)

Liberalitas.   Liberality.   Holds tessera (tablet) and cornucopiae.

Libertas (Eleutheria).   Freedom, Liberty.   Holds pileus (pointed cap of Liberty) and sceptre.

Moneta.   Mint, Money.   Holds scales and cornucopiae.   Sometimes represented as the Three Monetae, each with a pile of metal, or coins, at her feet.

Nobilitas.   Nobility, High Birth.   Holds palladium and sceptre.

Ops.   Wealth.   Holds corn-ears or sceptre.

Three Monetae
(Probus)

Nobilitas
(Geta)

Pax
(Elagalabus)

Patientia.   Endurance, Patience.   Holds sceptre.

Pax (Eirene).   Peace.   Holds olive-branch and sceptre, cornucopiae or caduceus.

Pietas (Eusebeia).   Piety, Dutifulness.   Often veiled, holds patera and sceptre: sometimes shown sacrificing at altar and holding box of perfumes.

    "*Roman piety unites in one whole, reverence for the gods, devotion to the Emperor, affection between the Augusti or between the Augustus and the people, tenderness of parents to sons, respect or affectionate care of the latter for their parents, and in general, love of one's neighbour, or in one word Religion.*"—Gnecchi.

Providentia (Pronoia).   Providence, Forethought.   Holds baton, with which she sometimes points to a globe at her feet, and sceptre.   In the third century she is often shown holding the globe.

Pietas
(*Julia Maesa*)

Providentia
(*Caracalla*)

Pudicitia
(*Otacilia Severa*)

Pudicitia. Modesty, Chastity. Holds sceptre and is usually veiled.

Salus (Hygieia). Health, Safety, Welfare. Holds sceptre and patera from which she feeds a serpent coiled round an altar; or holds the serpent in her arms and feeds it from a patera.

Securitas. Confidence, Security. Holds patera or sceptre, and may be depicted leaning on a column, legs crossed; sometimes sits back at ease in a chair.

Salus
(*Aelius*)

Securitas
(*Macrinus*)

Spes (Elpis). Hope. Holds flower, and is usually shown walking and slightly raising the drapery of her dress.

Uberitas *or* **Ubertas.** Fertility. Holds cornucopiae and purse or bunch of grapes.

Victoria (Nike). Victory. Winged, holding wreath and palm: may be shown bearing a shield, inscribing a shield, or erecting a trophy.

Spes
(*Claudius/Titus*)

Uberitas
(*Gallienus*)

Victoria
(*Volusian*)

Bonus Eventus. Good Fortune, Good Luck. Holds patera over altar, and cornucopiae.

Genius. Genius, Spirit. Holds patera and cornucopiae, sometimes with altar at feet. As Genius of the Army he is accompanied by a military standard. In the early 4th century he sometimes holds the head of Serapis.

Honos. Honour. Holds olive-branch or sceptre and cornucopiae.

Virtus. Courage. Usually depicted in complete armour, holding Victory or parazonium and spear, or with spear and shield.

Genius of the Army   *Virtus*
(Decius).   *(Gordian I).*

It should be emphasized that the foregoing notes do not pretend to do anything like justice to the subject, about which, indeed, a lengthy book could be written without exhausting it. It is hoped, however, that the information given, although brief, will be found of interest, and may lead collectors of the series to study the subject in more complete and detailed works.

II. REPRESENTATIONS OF THE EMPEROR AND HIS FAMILY.

In addition to monopolizing the obverses of Roman Imperial coins, the emperors, empresses and princes also make frequent appearances as reverse types.

Augustus set the precedent by authorizing his representation as the Victor of Actium, in a triumphal quadriga, on the reverse of a denarius of the period 30-27 B.C. Several other types of Augustus followed during his long reign, including one of 12 B.C. which shows him crowning Marcus Agrippa, his intended successor. With the exception of Tiberius, the Julio-Claudian Emperors made increasingly frequent appearances on their coins, and Nero is depicted distributing gifts to the people, haranguing his troops, taking part in military exercises on horseback, and even singing to his own accompaniment on a lyre, dressed as Apollo.

From a   *From a*   *From a*
sestertius of Titus.   *denarius of Elagabalus.*   *sestertius of Hadrian.*

In the Flavian period, Vespasian and Titus appear most frequently in connection with two main themes—the quelling of the Jewish Revolt and the recovery of the Roman State following the Civil Wars of A.D. 68-69. Vespasian is shown raising a kneeling female (the State) on one of his *aurei*, and in the illustration on *p.* 26, Titus is shown in his procession of triumph following his victories in Palestine. Domitian is depicted as Conqueror of the Germans on a *sestertius* which shows him standing with the Rhine at his feet. This emperor's most interesting appearances, however, are in connection with the Secular Games of A.D. 88, when he is shown taking part in various ceremonies, often with the temple of Jupiter Capitolinus in the background.

The Golden Age of Trajan, Hadrian and the Antonines produced a great variety of interesting reverse types depicting the emperor. Trajan, the great warrior, is shown at full gallop thrusting his spear at a Dacian, and Hadrian's famous peregrinations all over his Empire are well recorded on the coinage—the illustration on *p.* 26 shows him arriving in Gaul. Antoninus' great stature as a statesman is suitably illustrated by a *sestertius* which portrays him wearing a toga and in the act of creating a new King of Armenia by placing a diadem on the head of the monarch. With the recurrence of frontier wars under Marcus Aurelius, he and his co-emperor Lucius Verus are usually depicted in military scenes. One type shows Aurelius standing amidst four standards, whilst on a coin of Verus the emperor spears a fallen enemy as he gallops past. The first joint reign in the history of the Empire is commemorated by a type showing the two emperors, togate, clasping right hands.

The megalomania of Commodus is quite evident on several of his reverse types, as well as on the obverses which show him wearing the lion's skin of Hercules. A type common to both *sestertius* and *as* shows him dressed as a priest and ploughing with two oxen, symbolic of his insane notion to refound the City of Rome and give to it the name of Colonia Lucia Antoniniana Commodiana.

The military anarchy which crippled the Empire for a large part of the Third Century led to a decline of the representation of the emperor in any other guise but as the Chief of the Armed Forces. Septimius Severus does appear togate, as Founder of the Peace, on one type, but he and his sons usually appear in scenes of military significance. Elagabalus, who was far from being a soldier, is often depicted in his role as Chief-Priest of the Syrian Sun-God, providing a brief interlude in this martial period. One of these types, on the reverse of a *denarius*, is illustrated on *p.* 26. Elagabalus' cousin and successor, Severus Alexander, wears the toga whilst sacrificing over a tripod-altar, but most of his other representations are military in character. For the next few decades, the Roman observing the reverses of the coins he handled only saw his emperor represented in a few rather stereotyped poses, usually standing in military costume or on horseback, with right hand raised. Few other types break the monotony, although Gallienus, whose coinage as a whole is far more interesting than those of other emperors of the period, is depicted in a greater variety of poses. In one of these, he raises a kneeling figure representing Gaul. Soon after this type was struck, however, this Province was lost by Gallienus to the usurper Postumus, and remained independent of the central government for the following 14 years.

Towards the end of the Third Century successive emperors were often shown receiving a figure of Victory from the hands of Jupiter, and this type continued into the early years of the Fourth Century. With the adoption of Christianity by Constantine and the subsequent demise of paganism, coin types in general became far more limited in number and monotonous in content. The emperor usually appears as the Champion of the New Faith, holding the labarum (Christian standard) and a figure of Victory, which had now become equated with the Christian Angel. This Victory-Angel also appears on the type illustrated on *p.* 28, where it stands between two emperors enthroned side by side (in this case, Magnus Maximus and Flavius Victor). This type occurs on gold *solidi* of many of the late Fourth Century emperors, as the Empire had become more or

less permanently divided into Eastern and Western halves by this time, and there
were always at least two emperors reigning simultaneously.

<table>
<tr><td>From a solidus
of Magnus Maximus.</td><td>From a sestertius
of Faustina Junior.</td><td>From an as
of Diadumenian.</td></tr>
</table>

Representations of empresses and princes as reverse types occur throughout most
of the period, although there were no princes after Julian II Caesar (A.D. 355-60).
In the Early Empire, the emperor's relatives appeared most often on the reverses of his
own coins, as their own coinages were very small where they existed at all. Thus, we
see Caius and Lucius Caesars on the reverse of their grandfather Augustus' most
prolific single issue in gold and silver, and the Empress Livia seated on the reverse of her
son Tiberius' commonest *aureus* and *denarius*. Caligula, on one of his *sestertii*, has a
most interesting reverse type depicting his three sisters Agrippina, Drusilla and Julia.
On the reverses of some of his *aurei* and *denarii* Claudius had the portraits of his wife,
Agrippina, and his step-son, Nero, displayed, and the short reign of Vitellius produced
two interesting family types—one showing the emperor's father, and the other, the
confronted busts of his infant son and daughter.

From the Flavian period, the princes began issuing large coinages in their own right,
and from the early part of the Second Century, the empresses also were given a much
larger share of the total output of the mint. The princes, where they appear on the
reverses of their own coins, are usually represented as "Prince of the Youth" (PRINCEPS
IVVENTVTIS), and the above illustration, taken from an *as* of Diadumenian, is quite
typical. Also illustrated above is a *sestertius* of Faustina Junior, wife of Marcus Aurelius,
on which the empress is shown seated before three military standards, in her role as
"Mother of the Camps" (MATER CASTRORVM). Another reverse type, which was particularly in vogue on the coinages of early Third Century empresses, depicted the
Augusta and the Augustus standing face to face, their right hands clasped.

Before closing this brief survey of imperial representations on reverse types, mention
must be made of the unique series of "Family Coins" issued under Septimius Severus,
and depicting his wife, Julia Domna, his daughter-in-law, Plautilla, and his two sons,
Caracalla and Geta, as well as himself. All these pieces are in the *aureus* and *denarius*
denominations, and all are very rare. The obverse usually shows one bust, though
occasionally two are represented, whilst the reverse has one, two or even three imperial
portraits. The *aureus* illustrated below was struck in A.D. 202, and shows the bust of
Severus on the obverse: the reverse displays the facing portrait of Julia between the
confronted busts of her two sons.

III. TYPES OF MILITARY CONQUEST AND VICTORIES.

In the five centuries of its existence the Roman Empire was involved in many wars and campaigns, some expansionist, some defensive, and some domestic. Many of these were commemorated on the coinage, one of the earliest instances being the type of Augustus, with crocodile reverse, which refers to the defeat of Antony and Cleopatra and the subsequent annexation of the former Ptolemaic Kingdom to the Empire of Rome. This type was issued in 28 and 27 B.C.

The commencement of the Conquest of Britain, in A.D. 43, was well recorded on the gold and silver coinage of Claudius: a silver *didrachm* of the mint of Caesarea in Cappadocia is illustrated below. The great Jewish Revolt, which began under Nero in A.D. 66, was a serious embarrassment to the Romans coming, as it did, at a time of acute political upheaval in the Empire. The Rebellion was not really crushed until four years (and four emperors) had passed, and the new Flavian Dynasty widely publicized their success on a large series of coins in all metals. The one illustrated below is a *denarius* of Vespasian showing Judaea in captivity. Domitian's German Wars are commemorated by the *aureus*, also shown below, on which a female captive is seen seated on a shield, in an attitude of distress.

*From a didrachm
of Claudius.*

*From a denarius
of Vespasian.*

*From an aureus
of Domitian.*

*From a denarius
of L. Verus.*

Trajan's expansionist policy led to prolonged campaigns in several widely separated theatres of war. His greatest achievement was the conquest of Dacia, and this received considerable publicity on the coinage, with no fewer than twelve main types directly alluding to the event. The Eastern Wars of A.D. 163-5 also received considerable notice on the coins of the joint emperors Aurelius and Verus, and the piece illustrated above, a *denarius* of the latter, shows Armenia seated amidst arms. The last decade of Aurelius' reign was taken up with almost incessant warfare, mostly on the troubled Northern Frontier, and the *sestertius* shown below, struck in A.D. 177, depicts a pile of arms, symbolic of the conclusion of the German and Sarmatian Wars.

*From a sestertius
of M. Aurelius.*

*From an as
of Maximinus I.*

Severus' numerous campaigns are well recorded, but perhaps the series of greatest interest to British students is the one which commemorates the events of A.D. 208-11. During this period Severus, Caracalla and Geta compaigned on the Northern Frontier in Britain and restored Hadrian's Wall which had been severely damaged in the troubled period more than a decade before.   Caracalla's Parthian campaign received some notice on the coinage, and even Macrinus' inglorious encounter with Artaban of Parthia was celebrated as a VICTORIA PARTHICA on coins of all the metals.   More deserving of commemoration were Maximinus' victories in Germany in A.D. 235, and the *as* illustrated on *p.* 29 shows the emperor being crowned by Victory.

From an	From a
aureus of Tacitus.	*solidus of Crispus.*

The second half of the Third Century was a disastrous period for Roman arms, with large parts of the Empire succumbing to foreign attack and much of what remained being rent by internal rebellion.   Miraculously, however, the situation was restored by a succession of short-lived, but very strong emperors, foremost amongst whom were Claudius Gothicus, Aurelian and Probus.   A coin of this period is shown above—an *aureus* of Tacitus, Aurelian's successor, celebrating a victory over the Goths.

In the Fourth Century commemorative reverse types become increasingly rare, and one of the last to be issued is illustrated above.   It depicts Alamannia in captivity, seated at the foot of a trophy, and appears on a *solidus* of Crispus Caesar issued at Trier in A.D. 319/20.   The young prince had led a successful campaign against the Alamanni in 318.   A similar type, issued at the same time, bears the legend FRANCIA instead of ALAMANNIA.

IIIa. LEGIONARY TYPES, ETC.

The legionary series forms a compact group within the Roman coinage, and most of it was issued by five rulers ranging in date from the First Century B.C. to the end of the Third Century A.D.

Those of Mark Antony and Septimius Severus are similar in that both have the same basic reverse type—a legionary eagle between two standards.   Those of Gallienus, Victorinus and Carausius are, perhaps, rather more interesting as they bear the badges of the various legions, *e.g.* a lion for the IIII Flavia, and a capricorn for the XXII Primigenia.

The reason for their issue was, in general, to inspire the loyalty of the troops whose legions were honoured; but in some cases those troops were definitely not under the command of the emperor issuing the coins, and in these cases it must be assumed that we see here a very artful use of the propaganda value of coins, *i.e.* an attempt to win over the loyalty of an opponent's army by means of flattery.

From a denarius   *From an antoninianus*
of Septimius Severus.   *of Gallienus.*

The two pieces illustrated above were issued in honour of the XIIII Gemina and the XXII Primigenia legions respectively.

In addition to the appeals for loyalty directed to specific legions, there were also pleas for allegiance made to the army in general. Thus, on coins of Nerva we see clasped hands holding a legionary eagle set on a prow, accompanied by the legend CONCORDIA EXERCITVVM. Much later, the short-lived Gallic usurper Marius used a similar type on one of his *aurei*: this time just the clasped hands were shown, and the legend which encircled them was CONCORDIA MILITVM. The Valour of the Army (VIRTVS MILITVM) was proclaimed on a large issue of *argentei* issued under the First Tetrarchy at the end of the Third Century, and the Glory of the Army (GLORIA EXERCITVS) was celebrated on a vast series of small bronzes instituted towards the end of Constantine's reign and carried on for some years after his death by his sons.

Many other types of military and naval significance appear as reverse types on the Roman Coinage. A *denarius* of Augustus displays a naval trophy, a *dupondius* of Domitian depicts two German shields crossed over a vexillum, trumpets and spears, and a coin of Trajan of the same denomination has a fine representation of a cuirass. Naval power, in the form of a war-galley, is represented on coins of the Gallic usurper Postumus and on those of the British usurpers Carausius and Allectus.

IV. GEOGRAPHICAL TYPES.

The Roman Empire was a unique association of peoples and places such as the Mediterranean World had never seen before and has never seen since. What had formerly been a patchwork of Hellenistic Monarchies, independent City States and Celtic Tribes was miraculously united into one great political entity, and held together not so much by force of arms as by the *Pax Romana*.

The multitude of Provinces are depicted on many of the coins of the Imperial period, usually in the form of a female personification, and even particular cities and rivers receive occasional notice, the latter normally appearing as a bearded male figure in a reclining attitude.

A *denarius* of Augustus shows the City gate and walls of Emerita, in Spain, a colony which was founded in 25 B.C. and populated by Roman soldiers whose term of service had expired (*emeritos*). Galba, in A.D. 68, issued a very interesting type showing three small female busts, with the legend TRES GALLIAE. These represented the three great divisions of the Province of Gaul, Narbonensis, Aquitania and Lugdunensis. Dacia, the province which was added to the Empire by Trajan, is commemorated on *sestertii* and *dupondii* of that emperor with the legend DACIA AVGVST . PROVINCIA. The type shows Dacia seated on a rock, with a child before her and another at her side.

From a denarius	*From a sestertius*	*From a denarius*
of Hadrian.	*of Antoninus Pius.*	*of Clodius Albinus.*

The coinage of Hadrian provides us with a far more complete geographical survey of the Roman World than that of any other emperor. His extensive travels all over his vast Empire were commemorated on several remarkable series of coins, mostly issued towards the end of his reign when he had finally returned to Italy. In addition to honouring most of the provinces, two cities—Alexandria and Nicomedia—receive special attention, as does the River Nile (NILVS). The following is a list of the provinces whose personifications appear on Hadrian's coinage:—Britain, Spain, Gaul, Germany (illustrated above), Italy, Sicily, Noricum, Dacia, Macedon, Moesia, Thrace, Achaea, Asia, Bithynia, Phrygia, Cilicia, Cappadocia, Judaea, Arabia, Egypt, Africa and Mauretania.

Hadrian's successor, Antoninus, also issued a "provincial" series of coins, in this case to celebrate the offering of the *aurum corollarium* to the new Emperor: these were gifts sent by the various provinces, and even, sometimes, by foreign powers. Thus we see a personification of Parthia included in Antoninus' series. A fine representation of Britannia, illustrated above, also appears on the coinage of this reign, on a *sestertius* struck in A.D. 143/4.

Coins with geographical types become much scarcer in the second half of the Second Century: Aurelius has an **as** showing the River Tiber, and Commodus a *sestertius* with Italia seated on a large globe. Right at the end of the century, Clodius Albinus, in rebellion against Septimius Severus, struck a *denarius* depicting the Genius of the City of Lugdunum, in Gaul: this type is illustrated above.

Both from sestertii of Trajan Decius.

Geographical types are few and far between in the Third Century. Septimius Severus makes mention of Italy, Africa and Carthage on his coinage, and half-way through the century Trajan Decius honours the Provinces of Dacia and Pannonia with types both of which are illustrated above. Dacia again appears on the coins of Claudius II and Aurelian, and Pannonia is commemorated by Quintillus, Aurelian and Julian. The city of Siscia receives special notice on *antoniniani* of both Gallienus and Probus, and the Rhine is depicted on coins of the Gallic usurper Postumus. Britannia makes her final appearance on the Roman Coinage clasping hands with the rebel Carausius.

In the Fourth Century, geographical types rapidly disappear from the coinage. Africa and Carthage occur on *folles* of several of the emperors in the early part of the century, and one of the last types with any geographical significance is found on a small bronze of the unfortunate prince Hanniballianus (A.D. 335-7): this shows the river-god Euphrates reclining, and is a type of remarkable interest when compared with the general dullness of the bronze coinage of this period.

V. ARCHITECTURAL TYPES.

The Romans were great builders; a fact which is attested by the many splendid examples of their architecture which are still to be seen all over the Mediterranean World. Many of the emperors took great delight in adorning the capital, and other cities, with edifices which, often, were not only useful, such as the Market-Place of Nero and Trajan's Basilica, but were also of considerable architectural merit. A number of these structures were displayed on the coins, and these reverse types form one of the most sought-after groups within the Roman Coinage.

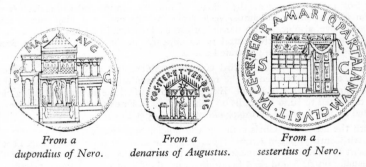

From a
dupondius of Nero.

From a
denarius of Augustus.

From a
sestertius of Nero.

Augustus issued a number of architectural types, a very early example being the Temple of Divus Julius which was represented on *aurei* and *denarii* struck *circa* 36 B.C., when the building was still under construction. The *denarius* is illustrated above. The coinage of Nero exhibits two particularly interesting types—the *Macellum*, or Market-Place, built by Augustus and restored by Nero, and the famous Temple of Janus, the doors of which were only closed when peace reigned throughout the Empire. Both of these types are also illustrated above.

The great Flavian Amphitheatre, known today as the Coliseum, appears on a *sestertius* of Titus, under whom the famous edifice was completed and dedicated. A *cistophorus* of Domitian shows the Temple of Jupiter Capitolinus together with the legend CAPIT . RESTIT.—a reference to that emperor's completion of the restoration of the Capitol following two destructions by fire in A.D. 69 and 80. Trajan's coinage has many types of architectural interest, *viz.* the Circus Maximus and Trajan's Basilica (both illustrated on *p*. 34); Trajan's Column, erected to commemorate the conquest of Dacia; the "Danube" Bridge, which is, in all probability, the Pons Sublicius in Rome; the famous Forum of Trajan; a triumphal arch inscribed I . O . M., and two octastyle temples, one of which may be that of Divus Nerva.

The Temple of Divus Augustus is shown on coins of Antoninus Pius, commemorating this emperor's restoration of the famous edifice; and the temple which Antoninus built in honour of his wife is depicted on *denarii* of Diva Faustina (the ruins of this temple are still visible in Rome today). A temple of Mercury, of very unusual form, appears on a *sestertius* of Marcus Aurelius, in company with the legend RELIG . AVG., and on a coin of Commodus, of the same denomination, a distyle shrine of Janus is represented.

Both from sestertii of Trajan.   *From a sestertius of Severus Alexander.*

The famous Arch of Severus, which still stands in all its ancient majesty in the Roman Forum, is depicted on the coinage of both Septimius and Caracalla. A representation of the Circus Maximus, very similar to the one of Trajan mentioned and illustrated above, also occurs on *sestertii* of Caracalla struck in A.D. 213. Under Severus Alexander several fine architectural types appear, one of which, the very elaborate Temple of Jupiter Ultor, is illustrated above.

For the remainder of the Third Century architectural reverses occur rather less frequently, and are confined in the main to representations of conventional temples, often containing a statue of Roma. Exceptions to this include a very interesting circular temple dedicated to Juno Martialis on coins of Trebonianus Gallus and Volusian, and a triumphal arch on *sestertii* and *dupondii* of the usurper Postumus.

With the advent of Christianity as the official State-Religion, in the early part of the Fourth Century, pagan temple types disappear entirely from the coinage: the only subsequent reverses which have any claim to be architectural are the "Camp-Gate" types, usually on Æ 3 and Æ 4 denominations, the "Plan of a Military Camp" on an Æ 3 of Thessalonica, the "Bridge over River" on an Æ 4 of Constantinople, and a distyle shrine, with arched roof, which occurs on the silver *miliarense* denomination under several of the reigns from Constantine to Valentinian and Valens.

VI. ANIMALS, ETC.

For several centuries before the rise of Rome there had been a tradition of featuring animals, birds, fish and insects (as well as various mythological beasts) on the coinages of many of the Greek States. Rome inherited this tradition, and although the representation of fauna is less frequent and less varied than in the Greek series, they nevertheless form a most fascinating group within the Roman Coinage.

From a denarius of Augustus.   *From an aureus of Augustus.*   *From an aureus of Vespasian.*

Crocodile and heifer (both illustrated on *p.* 34), bull, wild boar, lion and stag, eagle, crab and butterfly, Capricorn, Pegasus and Sphinx all appear on the coins of Augustus, but the other Julio-Claudian Emperors seem to have had no inclination to use such types at all. Under the Flavians, however, there was something of a revival, and the two *aurei* illustrated on *p.* 34 and below, one of Vespasian and the other of Domitian, show a capricorn and an eagle respectively. A particularly interesting reverse of this period depicts a goat being milked by a goat-herd, and another has a sow with its young.

In the Second Century, the Pegasus and the Griffin appear on brass coins of Hadrian; Antoninus Pius has *asses* picturing an elephant, and a sow suckling four young beneath an oak-tree, the former having reference to the celebrations on the 900th anniversary of the foundation of Rome (A.D. 147); a very attractive representation of a dove appears on an *aureus* of the younger Faustina, and the elephant occurs again on copper of Commodus and silver of Septimius Severus.

From an aureus
of Domitian.

From a sestertius
of Philip I.

From an antoninianus
of Philip II.

The "king of beasts" is depicted on the coinage of Caracalla, wearing a radiate crown and holding a thunderbolt in its jaws, and a similar representation, though without the thunderbolt, is illustrated above from a coin of Philip Junior. The elephant remained popular as a coin-type during the first half of the Third Century and appears on pieces of Caracalla, Geta, Elagabalus and Philip I (see illustration above). To celebrate Rome's thousandth anniversary Philip held magnificent games in which many wild beasts were exhibited, and a series of coins was issued picturing the lion, hippopotamus, antelope, stag, goat and she-wolf suckling the twins Romulus and Remus.

A few years later Gallienus also issued an extensive series of "animal types" on his very base *antoniniani*, but after this date such types appear far less frequently and are, in the main, restricted to the "legionary-badge" issues of Victorinus and Carausius. The latter emperor did, however, have one type featuring the milking of a cow, another depicting a griffin, and also a wolf and twins type on *aurei*, *denarii* and *antoniniani*.

In the Late Empire, the wolf and twins appear on coins of Maxentius and on small bronzes of the Age of Constantine and his successors; a Phoenix is shown on a *half-centenionalis* of Constans, and a very fine representation of a bull, sometimes accompanied by an eagle, occurs on large bronzes of Julian the Apostate. One of the last animal representations on the Roman Coinage is on a tiny bronze (Æ 4) of the Eastern Emperor Leo I (A.D. 457-74): this coin has a lion on the reverse, without inscription, and is intended as a punning allusion to the Emperor's name.

VII. TYPES OF PROPAGANDA.

From a
sestertius of Tiberius.

Both from sestertii
of Nerva.

The Emperors of Rome were fully aware of the propaganda value of their coinage, it being one of the most effective means of mass communication at their disposal. Everyone, from provincial governor down to peasant, took notice of the ever-changing reverse types on the money which he handled, and the government of the day was thus able to represent itself and its achievements in great detail to almost all of the inhabitants of the vast Empire. As it was a means of communication of which the government had the complete monopoly, the propaganda sometimes only told half the truth or was even, on occasions, a complete misrepresentation of the true facts.

A very large proportion of reverse types could be included under the heading of "Types of Propaganda", as even the Personifications were intended to proclaim the virtues of the emperor or the enlightenment of the age which was lucky enough to witness his rule. In this brief survey, therefore, mention is made only of those types which have some specific message to convey regarding the wisdom and beneficence of the emperor.

The very handsome *sestertius* of Tiberius, illustrated above, is one of the earliest examples of propaganda on the Imperial Coinage. The munificence of the Emperor is here proclaimed, in a reference to the restoration, at his own expense, of several cities in Asia Minor which had been badly damaged by a great earthquake in A.D. 17. Nero publicized his care for the annual corn supply from Egypt on a very attractive *sestertius* type which shows Annona standing before a seated Ceres, with a ship's prow in the background. The enlightenment and benevolence of Nerva's rule is well reflected in his coin-types, three of which (two above and one below) are illustrated here. The first of these, showing two mules and a cart, refers to the measure taken by Nerva whereby the cost of imperial posting on the main roads in Italy was transferred from the tax-payer to the Fiscus. The second represents a distribution scene, or *Congiarium*, depicting the Emperor bestowing gifts on the citizens; the third, which features a modius (corn-measure), alludes to a special distribution of corn to the poorer townsfolk which was inaugurated by this Emperor.

From a sestertius
of Nerva.

From a sestertius
of Hadrian.

From a sestertius
of Antoninus Pius.

Another example of the humanitarianism of this period is to be found on coins of Trajan, publicizing the *Alimenta* system: under this scheme sums of money were advanced by the Government to smallholders at low rates of interest, and the profits thus obtained were employed exclusively for the benefit of poor children. Hadrian, in an attempt to gain popularity after having come to the throne under somewhat dubious circumstances, made a grand gesture of cancelling all debts owing to his Treasury—a sum equivalent to many millions of pounds. This extraordinary act of liberality received full "coverage" on the coinage: the piece illustrated on *p.* 36 shows a lictor setting fire to a heap of papers in the presence of three joyful citizens. The notes and bonds were, in fact, publicly burned in Trajan's Forum. The orphanage for girls which Antoninus Pius founded in honour of his deceased wife (*Puellae Faustinianae*) is recorded on gold and silver of Diva Faustina. Antoninus' great stature as a statesman is advertised on the *sestertius* shown on *p.* 36, where he is depicted bestowing a new king on the Quadi, a barbarian tribe who inhabited an area on the left bank of the Danube.

There are numerous examples of this type of propaganda on the Roman Coinage, but there is not space enough here, unfortunately, to give the subject as full a treatment as it deserves. It is hoped, however, that the reader will be stimulated to pursue further this fascinating topic. In the later period, the types are generally of a less specific nature, as typified by the piece of Balbinus, shown below, the purpose of which was to try and create the impression of perfect harmony between the Emperors (the exact opposite of the true state of affairs). The other coin illustrated below was one of a series of *antoniniani* issued by Philip I in order to publicise the magnificent games with which he amused the Roman populace on the occasion of Rome's thousandth anniversary.

From an antoninianus
of Balbinus.

From an antoninianus
of Philip I.

VIII. POSTHUMOUS TYPES.

Some of the emperors and empresses were deified (placed amongst the gods) after their deaths, and in most cases commemorative coins were issued in their honour by their successors. The reverse types of these coins form a distinctive group within the Roman Coinage, and the same basic types are often repeated through many series of posthumous issues.

The commemorative pieces struck in honour of Divus Augustus have a variety of reverse types, including a thunderbolt, an eagle and a large square altar. The last two became standard types for many posthumous issues at a later date. An *aureus* and *denarius* type struck for Divus Claudius depicts an elaborate vehicle drawn by four horses, perhaps a funeral car: another type of hearse (a carpentum drawn by two mules) had already appeared on a *sestertius* struck by Caligula in honour of his mother Agrippina Senior. An unusual type on a coin of Divus Vespasian shows two capricorns supporting a shield inscribed s . c., whilst a rare *aureus* type of Divus Trajan has a representation of a radiate phoenix, the fabulous bird which was regarded as a symbol of immortality.

From a sestertius
of Diva Sabina.

From a sestertius
of Divus Antoninus Pius.

The above-illustrated *sestertius* struck by Hadrian in memory of his wife, Sabina, depicts the deified Empress in the process of being borne to heaven on the wings of an eagle. Subsequently, this type became very popular on the posthumous coinages of both emperors and empresses, though in the case of the latter a peacock usually took the place of the eagle. The other *sestertius* shown above, a coin struck by Marcus Aurelius in honour of his predecessor, has another type which was afterwards adopted as a "model" for commemorative coinages—an elaborate funeral pyre of several stages surmounted by a facing quadriga containing an effigy of the deified emperor.

Antoninus Pius had, himself, during his lifetime, issued a very extensive posthumous coinage in memory of his wife, Faustina Senior, who predeceased him by some twenty years. This coinage is in many respects unique, as it exhibits a great variety of reverse types most of which would seem to be more in keeping with the coinage of a living empress rather than a deified one. Ceres, Juno, Venus, Vesta, Pietas and several other goddesses and personifications all make their appearances in this remarkable series, and there are also some very interesting types amongst those which are more obviously connected with the apotheosis of the Empress, *viz.* carpentum drawn by mules; Faustina seated on car drawn by elephants; empty throne with peacock beneath; and Victory flying, carrying Faustina to heaven.

The type of an empty throne was revived on a *denarius* of Divus Septimius Severus, but in this case a wreath is shown on the seat representing the departed Augustus. During the Third Century the posthumous coinages settled down to a fairly regular pattern using only a few basic types—usually an eagle or a large altar for emperors, and a peacock (either standing by itself or bearing the new divinity to heaven) for empresses.

An interesting series of small bronzes, of two denominations, was issued by Constantine the Great, *ca.* A.D. 317-18, in honour of the deified Emperors Claudius Gothicus, Constantius Chlorus and Maximianus. The reverses of these coins exhibit three different types—the emperor seated on a curule chair, an eagle standing, and a lion walking. With the advent of Christianity the commemorative coinages cease completely, and the last emperor to be accorded these honours was Constantine himself. His posthumous coinage, issued only in the tiny Æ 4 denomination, was of two main types: one of these shows the Emperor standing to right, veiled and togate, whilst the other depicts him in a galloping quadriga on his way to heaven, the hand of God extended from above to receive him.

IX. OTHER TYPES.

The eight categories of reverse types which have already been covered in this brief survey comprise the great bulk of the Roman Coinage. There are, however, a number of types which do not fit very well into any of these large groups, and these are described under five subheadings here.

1. Heavenly Bodies. Objects such as stars and crecent moons make fairly regular appearances on the Roman Coinage. A more unusual representation, on a *denarius* of Augustus, is illustrated below: it shows a comet, with flaming tail, and is a direct reference to the one seen in the heavens immediately after the assassination of Julius Caesar, and

From a denarius
of Augustus.

From a denarius
of Faustina Senior.

again in 17 B.C. The type depicting a group of stars around a crescent moon was quite popular in the Second Century and appears on issues of Hadrian, Faustina Senior and Junior, Pescennius Niger, Septimius Severus and Julia Domna. The type of a single star (see illustration from a coin of Faustina) continued to appear well into the Fourth Century, the latest example being on silver of Julian the Apostate.

2. Inscriptions. It was not unusual, especially in the Early Empire, for inscriptions to appear in place of pictorial types on the reverses of the coins. A typical example, from the reign of Tiberius, is shown below: this type, with a circular inscription giving the emperor's name and titles around a large s.c., was used up to the end of the First Century. Another type, showing the inscription in several lines across the field (usually enclosed by a wreath) became popular from the time of Caligula, and continued in use

From a dupondius
of Livia.

From a denarius
of Lucilla.

right up to the end of the Roman period and even into early Byzantine times. In the First Century S . P . Q . R . P . P . OB C . S. and EX S . C . OB CIVES SERVATOS are typical examples of the legends shown in this way: the Second Century produced such inscriptions as S . P . Q . R . OPTIMO PRINCIPI, PRIMI DECENNALES COS . III. and VOTA PVBLICA (illustrated above): in the Third Century the legend VOTIS DECENNALIBVS appeared quite frequently (see illustration on *p.* 40), and in the earlier part of the Fourth Century the trend was towards inscriptions giving the emperor's name, as on the coin of Constans pictured on *p.* 40. Later Fourth Century and Fifth Century inscription types are confined almost exclusively to commemoration of the vows undertaken by the emperors, *e.g.* VOT . V., VOT . V . MVLT . X., VOTIS XXX . MVLTIS XXXX., *etc. etc.* This type

From an antoninianus
of Trajan Decius.

From a siliqua
of Constans.

of reverse extended right into the early Byzantine Coinage, the latest example being on
Carthaginian silver of Justinian I struck *ca.* A.D. 534.

3. Mythological Types. These are rare on the Imperial Coinage, except for the
representations of the she-wolf suckling the twins Romulus and Remus: this type occurs

From a sestertius
of Antoninus Pius.

From an aureus
of Maxentius.

on the coinages of many of the emperors from Vespasian to Constantine (see illustration
above). A *denarius* of Augustus depicts the death of Tarpeia, the traitor maiden, who
was said to have been crushed by the shields of the Sabine soldiers. An interesting
reverse of Antoninus Pius, also illustrated above, shows Aeneas striding, carrying
Anchises on his shoulder and leading Ascanius by the hand.

4. Nautical Types. Representations of ships are not uncommon on the Roman
Coinage, and there are even two instances of a "bird's-eye" view of Ostia Harbour, on
sestertii of Nero and Trajan. The fine ship depicted on a coin of Hadrian (see illustration
below) is a type commemorative of the Emperor's numerous voyages on his Empire-wide

From a sestertius
of Hadrian.

From a "quinarius"
of Allectus.

travels. Similar ships, though not always so finely executed, appear on the coins of
many of Hadrian's successors, and the one shown here is taken from a piece of the
British usurper Allectus whose unstable throne relied very heavily on naval power.

Even as late as the reign of Theodosius I there is a type on the Æ 2 denomination which shows the emperor standing on a galley with Victory at the helm. One other type which has claim to be included under this heading is the "dolphin entwined around anchor" reverse which occurs on *aurei* and *denarii* of Titus and Domitian.

5. Symbolic Types. These appear sporadically throughout the whole period of the Roman Imperial Coinage, and usually have some religious connotation. Exceptions to this are such types as the *pileus* (cap) on *quadrantes* of Caligula (symbolic of Liberty),

From a denarius   *From a tremissis*
of Nero   *of Romulus Augustus.*

and four young boys at play (representing Spring, Summer, Autumn and Winter) on the coins of several of the emperors from Commodus to Constantine. The thunderbolt, which sometimes appears by itself as a reverse type, is of religious significance as it is symbolic of Jupiter, the supreme deity of the Romans. More obviously of a religious nature are the types which depict various groups of pontificial and sacrificial instruments, such as the simpulum, lituus, tripod, patera, aspergillum, apex, sacrificial knife, axe and jug. The *denarius* of Nero illustrated above shows the four first-mentioned instruments, each one being symbolic of one of the *Collegia Sacerdotum* to which Nero was admitted in A.D. 51. This type of reverse, which appeared quite frequently up to the end of the Third Century, was superseded by types alluding to the new State Religion of the Roman Empire—Christianity. The first representation of the Labarum (the Christian Standard) occurs on Constantinopolitan bronzes of Constantine issued in A.D. 327, and a large Christogram appears as the main type on coins of Magnentius, Decentius and Constantius II. The supreme symbol of the Christian Faith, the Cross, became popular as a reverse type in the Fifth Century: it occurs most frequently on the gold *tremissis* denomination, and a typical example is illustrated above.

The foregoing notes can have no claim to completeness in describing the various aspects of Roman Imperial reverse types. The topic is so large that the writer can merely hope that he has stimulated his readers' interest sufficiently to encourage further study. The collector may also have found here some new themes for the formation of a collection.

With regard to the reverse types of the Republican series, it is regretted that it has not been found possible to include a survey of these in the present edition, but the reader is recommended to our publication *Roman Silver Coins, Volume* I, where nearly all of the silver types are illustrated.

Before concluding this section of the book, mention should be made of the extraordinary variety of reverse types which are to be found on the local coinages of the Roman Empire, commonly referred to as the "Greek Imperial" series. These coins, struck at hundreds of mints in Europe, Asia Minor, the Levant, Egypt and North Africa, are mainly in bronze, and they supplied the small-change needs of a large portion of the Empire for almost three centuries. The reverse types include many which make reference to topics of local interest, such as games and festivals, and the names of city magistrates also appear quite frequently.

In the present catalogue this series is only referred to briefly under the heading "Colonial and Provincial Coinage" at the end of each reign, but the writer is currently engaged in preparing a specialized work devoted entirely to these local issues. This catalogue will run into several volumes and it is not likely that any part of it will appear in print for at least another five years.

COUNTERMARKS ON THE AES COINAGE
OF THE EARLY EMPIRE.

During the Julio-Claudian period and up to the first few months of Vespasian's reign the practice of countermarking brass and copper coins was quite widespread. These overstrikings served three main purposes—to extend the area in which the coin would be accepted as currency, to prolong the life of a coin which had been in circulation for a number of years, and to denote that a new authority was converting someone else's coin into its own.

To the first category belong countermarks of the reigns of Augustus and Tiberius (intended for the Roman troops engaged on campaigns, mainly in Germany), and also of Claudius, whose conquest of Britain may have been the occasion for their use. Typical countermarks for these three reigns are A̸C, A̸, I̅M̅P̅ (Augustus); TIB, TIB I̅M̅P̅, TIB A̸ (Tiberius); and TI A̸, T C IMP, TIB CL AV IMP (Claudius).

Countermarks extending the period of circulation of old coins belong mainly to the early years of Nero's reign, when a review of the coinage seems to have taken place. The purpose of this was to withdraw those pieces which had become very worn, and to countermark (usually with "NCAPR") the coins which were still in good enough condition to remain in circulation for a few years more. A particularly interesting countermark of this period has been noted on a very worn *sestertius*: it contains the legend "DVP" which indicates that the piece was only being allowed to remain in circulation at half its original value.

In the period of civil strife at the end of Nero's reign and immediately following his death, such countermarks as S P Q R, PR and V̅I̅TE were employed. The first two of these were used by Vindex, the leader of the Gallic rebels, and the third was the mark of the Emperor Vitellius: Vindex overstruck *dupondii* and *asses* of Nero, whilst Vitellius only used the *sestertii* of this Emperor. Vespasian, the ruler who eventually emerged from the chaos of the Civil Wars as the founder of the second Imperial dynasty, also countermarked *dupondii* and *asses* of Nero, with a monogram of his name. A remarkable series of countermarks on *silver* coins of the Republic and Early Empire, probably affixed at the Antioch mint, was also the work of Vespasian: being without the facilities to produce a regular coinage to publicize his new regime he adopted the expedient of marking with the legend "IMP VESP" as many *denarii* as he could lay his hands on.

Countermarks do not normally appear on Roman coins after this period, but in the "Greek Imperial" series they occur quite frequently well on into the Third Century.

ROMAN MINTS FROM AUGUSTUS TO THE
REFORM OF DIOCLETIAN.

The monetary system which Octavian inherited on his accession to sovereign power in 30 B.C. was in a state of complete confusion—the result of decades of civil war and the eclipse of the Senate as the supreme authority in the Roman World.

In the days of the Republic the issue of coinage was entirely in the hands of the Senate, who appointed the *triumviri* of the mint. Rome itself was of course the main mint, but frequently there were other establishments at work, not always in Italy but under the direct control of the Roman Senate. Half a century before the time of Augustus, however, a new minting authority had appeared—the *Imperator*, *i.e.* the military commander in the field. Although at first these generals applied to the Senate for permission to strike money for the payment of their troops, this formality was quickly dispensed with, and "military coinages" were soon being issued in many parts of the Roman World quite independently of all Senatorial authority. As a final blow, the Senate had to flee to Greece at the time of the war between Caesar and Pompey, and the mint of Rome was left entirely in the hands of Caesar. Following the great Dictator's assassination in 44 B.C. the Senate was allowed for a few years more to issue the regular coinage from the mint of Rome; but in 37 B.C. the mint of the Capitol was closed and the Triumvirs (Antony, Octavian and Lepidus), the masters of the Roman World, continued to issue their coinages from various provincial centres.

Once Augustus had firmly established his constitutional position he turned his attention to the reorganization of the coinage, and in 23 B.C. the mint of Rome was reopened to issue brass and copper coins. A few years later coinage in the precious metals also commenced; but this was only a temporary measure, as Augustus had other plans for the creation of a new mint establishment responsible for his gold and silver issues. The city to be thus honoured was Lugdunum, the capital of Gaul, and the mint was opened *ca.* 15 B.C. It soon became the only one striking in the precious metals, succeeding in this function mints in Spain and the East, as well as Rome. Lugdunum remained the sole mint for *aurei*, *denarii* and *quinarii* until Caligula established Rome as the main coining centre for all denominations (*ca.* A.D. 38). The Gallic mint also issued *aes*, under Augustus and Tiberius, with the well-known "Altar" reverse, but this series was discontinued about A.D. 20.

Under Claudius, Rome remained the centre for the striking of all normal denominations, though Lugdunum may have issued limited quantities of gold and silver in the earlier part of the reign. There was also a large class of semi-barbarous *sestertii, dupondii* and *asses* in circulation at this period, the product of various unofficial mints in Gaul and Britain, but perhaps issued with the sanction of the Roman Government. In the East, *cistophori* (=3 *denarii*) were struck at Ephesus, the first since the reign of Augustus, and *didrachms* (= 24 *asses*) were issued at Caesarea in Cappadocia: this mint had last been active under Tiberius when *drachms* (= 12 *asses*) had also been produced.

The reign of Nero produced an important development—the reopening of the mint of Lugdunum, this time for the production of *aes* denominations from *sestertius* down to *quadrans*. Rome continued to issue all denominations, and *didrachms* and *drachms* were struck at Caesarea. The Civil Wars of A.D. 68-9 occasioned the opening of many new mints, as the various contestants for supreme power needed plentiful supplies of coined money with which to secure the loyalty of their troops. Rome, Tarraco, Narbo, Vienna, Lugdunum, Poetovio, Byzantium, Philippi, Antioch, Tyre, Alexandria and Carthage are all credited with having been Imperial mints during this period, and although some of these attributions are rather conjectural, the dramatic effect which this time of civil strife had on the mint system is indisputably obvious.

Once Vespasian had emerged as the victor from this complicated series of internal conflicts within the Empire many of these emergency mints were closed down, and the first of the Flavians issued the bulk of his coinage from Rome. Lugdunum still struck sporadically throughout the reign, and *aurei* and *denarii* were issued for several years at Ephesus. Commagene produced a series of *aes* (*dupondius*, *as* and *semis*, all in orichalcum) covering most of the reign, the first time this mint had been active since Tiberius issued *dupondii* there in A.D. 20. The coinages of Titus and Domitian belong almost entirely to Rome: Lugdunum continued to issued *aes* in small quantities but was finally closed down very early in Domitian's reign; *cistophori* were also produced at an Asiatic mint, probably Ephesus.

Throughout most of the Second Century the mint of Rome exercised a virtual monopoly in the production of the regular Roman coinage. *Cistophori* were still struck at various mints in Asia Minor down to the time of Hadrian, but apart from these no other mints appear to have been active until the time of the civil war between Septimius Severus and Pescennius Niger (A.D. 193-4). Antioch, the capital of Syria and the third city of the Empire, produced coinage in gold and silver for Niger, but following Severus' victory over his eastern rival Antioch was punished for having supported the wrong cause, and the mint establishment was transferred to Laodiceia ad Mare. Other mints, such as Emesa and Alexandria, may also have issued coins for Severus during this troubled period, but Laodiceia was the only one which continued operating well on into the reign (finally closed *ca*. A.D. 203). Rome, meanwhile, was continuing its steady output of all denominations, and the once great imperial mint of Lugdunum had a short burst of activity in A.D. 195-7 when it issued gold, silver and perhaps a few *aes* for Clodius Albinus, another rival of Severus. Needless to say the establishment was closed down immediately following Albinus' defeat and death. A final issue of *cistophori* was made during the reign of Severus, perhaps from the mint of Caesarea.

During the sole reign of Caracalla Rome was, once again, the only mint in operation, and in the opinion of the present writer this also holds true of the coinage of Macrinus, the next emperor, though in "B.M.C." and "R.I.C." many of his pieces are attributed to Antioch. Under Elagabalus and in the earlier part of the reign of Severus Alexander there certainly was a coinage being produced in the East, probably from the mint of Antioch, though there may also have been other mints at work too. After this, and until the reign of Gordian III, Rome again struck alone, but this was to be the last period of mint monopoly which the Capital of the Empire was destined to enjoy. In addition to striking all denominations at Rome, Gordian also issued some of his *antoniniani* from one, or possibly two other mints: Antioch was undoubtedly responsible for some of these coins and possibly all of them; Viminacium is the other suggested mint-place. The Antioch *antoniniani* continued in issue under Philip, Trajan Decius and Trebonianus Gallus, and Decius also inaugurated another mint, at Mediolanum (Milan). Aemilian (A.D. 252-3) issued all his coins at Rome, except for a very small class of *antoniniani* struck at some unidentified Balkan mint, but under Valerian there were some very important developments significant of the future trend towards decentralization in the Roman mint system. Lugdunum was officially reopened after 170 years of inactivity, and Viminacium also appears to have operated for a few years at the beginning of the reign: but of prime importance, perhaps, was the decision to allow all the mints to strike in gold, a precedent which was followed in varying degrees by most of Valerian's successors. This was by no means the first time that mints other than Rome had produced coinage in gold, but from this period such issues become a regular feature of the Roman Coinage and serve to emphasize the dwindling importance of the Capital as the coining centre of the Empire. The other mints striking for Valerian and Gallienus, in addition to the two mentioned above, were Rome, Milan and Antioch.

During the troubled sole reign of Gallienus the unfortunate Emperor had to revise his father's mint arrangements due to considerable losses of territory in both the Eastern and Western halves of the Empire. In the West, the rebellion of Postumus in Gaul meant that the newly-opened mint of Lugdunum was lost to the Central Government, and to take its place Gallienus opened a new mint at Siscia (Sisak, Yugoslavia). In the East, the capture of Valerian by Sapor of Persia in A.D. 260 inaugurated a period of about twelve years during which Rome exercised very little authority in the Eastern Provinces, the real power being in the hands of Odenathus and Zenobia of Palmyra. During this period it would seem that Gallienus opened the mint of Cyzicus, to make good the loss of Antioch. Claudius Gothicus, the successor of Gallienus, continued to use all the mints already in operation (Rome, Milan, Siscia and Cyzicus), whilst *antoniniani* were also struck in his name at Antioch, the Palmyrene Government having decided to adopt a more conciliatory attitude towards the new regime in Rome.

Aurelian, the great restorer of the Empire, issued coins from no fewer than eleven mints—Vienna (?) and Lugdunum (Gaul and the West having been recovered in A.D. 273), Rome, Milan, Ticinum (a creation of Aurelian and the successsor of Milan as the North Italian mint), Siscia, Serdica (also opened by Aurelian), Cyzicus, Antioch (the Empire of Palmyra having been destroyed in A.D. 272), Tripolis (in Phoenicia, another creation of Aurelian), and one other mint, issuing *antoniniani* only, the exact location of which has not yet been ascertained. Gold was issued at seven of these mints. The Gallic Empire of Postumus had pursued its own policies from A.D. 259, and at first it had used the mint establishment at Lugdunum for its coinage needs. About A.D. 265, however, Postumus transferred his mint to Cologne, and his successors Marius and Victorinus also used this establishment. There are, however, some rare coins of both these reigns which obviously are the product of some quite separate mint, as yet unidentified. The rebel Laelianus issued his small coinage from some mint otherwise quite outside the regular Gallic series, perhaps Moguntiacum. At some point in his reign Victorinus established another mint, perhaps Vienna, but undoubtedly in the South of Gaul, from which a good proportion of his coinage was issued. This mint was the only one employed by his successor, Tetricus, and it was taken over by Aurelian after his recovery of Gaul in A.D. 273. After allowing a small issue there in his own name Aurelian closed the mint and re-established Lugdunum as the sole Gallic mint.

The final two decades of the period covered by this survey (Tacitus to the Reform of Diocletian) saw few changes in the mint system established by Aurelian. A second Gallic mint, probably Arelate, operated for a short time in the reign of Tacitus, and two new mints were opened by Diocletian—Treveri and Heraclea, both shortly before the Reform. The independent British Empire of Carausius and Allectus (A.D. 287-96) brought into being three new mints, London, Colchester (or Bitterne) and Rouen. Only one of these—London—survived the re-establishment of Roman rule in Britain and found a place in Diocletian's new mint system following his great Reform of the Coinage.

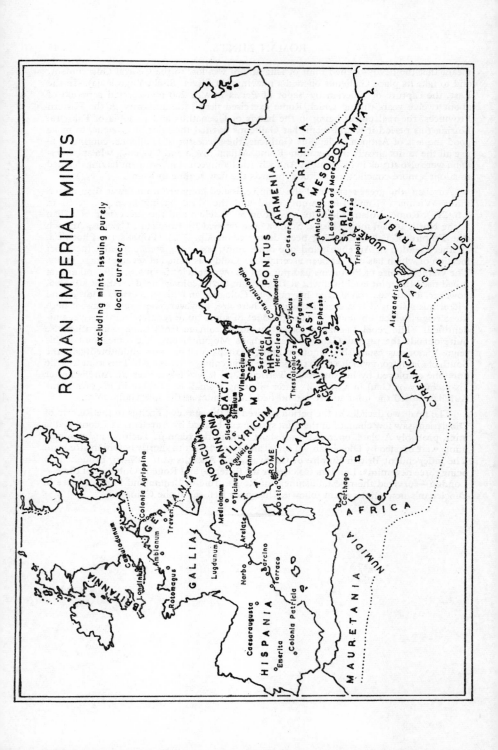

ROMAN IMPERIAL MINTS

excluding mints issuing purely
local currency

MINTS AND MINT-MARKS OF THE LATER ROMAN EMPIRE.

1   *Ostia:* follis of Maxentius from the first *officina.*
2   *Alexandria:* Æ 3 of Licinius II from the second *officina.*
3   *Sirmium:* solidus of Constantius II.
4   *Arelate:* heavy miliarense of Valens from the second *officina.*

Roman Imperial coins began to bear mint-marks about the middle of the third century, but at first the practice was not general, and the marks themselves are seldom self-explanatory. The marks were placed on the coins in order that there might be some control over the activities of the mint officials and workmen, and so that coins of less than standard weight or fineness could be traced to their originators and the culprits suitably dealt with. With the advent of the monetary reform of Diocletian unmarked coins are the exception, and the system of marking is reasonably simple and easy to understand. A mint-mark is placed in the exergual space of the coin's reverse and is normally made up of three parts: first, a letter or letters indicating "Pecunia" (P), "Sacra Moneta" (SM) or simply "Moneta" (M); secondly, there are the letters indicating the place of origin, such as LON for Londinium; and thirdly a letter indicating the *officina* or workshop of the mint producing that particular coin. Thus a coin of Alexandria may bear the mint-mark SMALB, showing that it was struck in the second *officina.* At the Western mints the *officina* letters are usually Latin—P, S, T and Q standing for *Prima, Secunda, Tertia* and *Quarta.* In the East, however, the Greek system prevailed, the comparable *officina* letters being A, B, Γ and Δ. Some Eastern mints had many *officinae:* Antioch, for example, had fifteen (IϚ) under Constantius II and Constantinople, eleven (IA). Certain mints omit the prefix letter or letters at times, an example being Trier whose commonest mint-marks are TRP and TRS. Where PTR and STR occur the prefix letters are *officina* marks placed before instead of after the mint letters. Sometimes the *officina* letter is placed in the field instead of the exergue. A small mint, such as London, may omit the *officina* letter: many of the London issues of the Constantinian period are signed PLN or PLON.

Under Valentinian I and Valens the letters PS and OB make their first appearance. These are probably abbreviations for *pusulatum* (pure silver) and *obryziacum* (pure gold) and they follow the mint letters, *e.g.* TRPS, TROB.

In addition to the mint and *officina* letters, symbols, such as a wreath, a crescent or a palm-branch, are sometimes found in the exergue or the field of a coin. These denote the issue to which the coin belongs.

Below is given a list of the mints in use at different times from Diocletian's Reform onwards. To list the various complicated mint signatures would be a task beyond the scope of this work, but it is hoped that the details given will be found of some use. Most of the commoner mint-marks are included, but all reference to symbols and *officina* letters is, of course, omitted.

Alexandria (Egypt): ALE, SMAL. *Operational for Roman currency from ca.* A.D. 294. *Finally closed under Leo I,* A.D. 457-74.

Ambianum (Amiens, France): AMB. *Operational* A.D. 350-3.

Antiochia (Antakiyah, Turkey): AN, ANT, ANTOB, SMAN. *Finally closed under Leo I.*

Aquileia (near Trieste, Italy): AQ, AQVIL, AQOB, AQPS, SMAQ. *Operational from ca.* A.D. 294. *Finally closed ca.* A.D. 425.

Arelate (Arles, France): A, AR, ARL, CON, CONST, KON, KONSTAN. *Operational from* A.D. 313 (*establishment transferred from Ostia*). *Finally closed ca.* A.D. 475.

(*In* A.D. 328, *the name of Arelate was changed to Constantina in honour of Constantine II. After his death, in* 340, *the name reverted to Arelate, but in* 353 *Constantius II changed it back to Constantina and it retained this name for the remainder of the period*).

Barcino (Barcelona, Spain): SMBA. *Operational ca.* A.D. 409-11.

Camulodunum or **Clausentum** (Colchester or Bitterne near Southampton): C, CL. *Operational* A.D. 287-96.

Carthago (near Tunis, N. Africa): K, PK, KART. *Operational* A.D. 296-307 *and* 308-11.

Constantinopolis (Istanbul, Turkey): C, CP, CON, CONS, CONSP, CONOB. *Operational from* A.D. 326 (*establishment transferred from Ticinum*).

Cyzicus (Turkey): CVZ, CVZIC, CVZICEN, SMK. *Finally closed under Leo I.*

Heraclea (Turkey): H, HT, HERAC, HERACL, SMH. *Operational from ca.* A.D. 291. *Finally closed under Leo I.*

Londinium (London): L, ML, MLL, MLN, MSL, PLN, PLON, AVG, AVGOB, AVGPS. *Operational* A.D. 287-325, *and for a very short period under Magnus Maximus,* A.D. 383-8.

Lugdunum (Lyons, France): LG, LVG, LVGD, LVGPS, PLG. *Finally closed ca.* A.D. 423.

Mediolanum (Milan, Italy): MD, MDOB, MDPS, MED. *Operational from* A.D. 364 (*or, perhaps, even earlier*). *Finally closed ca.* A.D. 475.

Nicomedia (Turkey): MN, NIC, NICO, NIK, SMN. *Operational from ca.* A.D. 294. *Finally closed under Leo I.*

Ostia (the port of Rome): MOST. *Operational* A.D. 308/9-313 (*establishment then transferred to Arelate*).

Ravenna (Italy): RV, RVPS. *Established by Honorius in the early part of the Fifth Century, and closed ca.* A.D. 475.

Roma: R, RM, ROMA, ROMOB, SMR, VRB . ROM. *Finally closed* A.D. 476.

Serdica (Sofiya, Bulgaria): SMSD, SER. *Operational ca.* A.D. 303-8 *and* 313-14.

Sirmium (Sremska Mitrovica, Yugoslavia): SM, SIRM, SIROB. *Operational* A.D. 320-6, 351-64, 379 *and* 393-5.

Siscia (Sisak, Yugoslavia): SIS, SISC, SISCPS. *Finally closed* ca. A.D. 387.

Thessalonica (Salonika, Greece): COM, COMOB, SMTS, TS, TES, TESOB, THS, THES, THSOB. *Operational from* ca. A.D. 298/9. *Finally closed under Leo I.*

Ticinum (Pavia, Italy): T. *Finally closed* A.D. 326 (*establishment then transferred to Constantinople*).

Treveri (Trier, Germany): SMTR, TR, TRE, TROB, TRPS. *Operational from* ca. A.D. 291. *Finally closed* ca. A.D. 430.

The following mints were reopened in Byzantine times:—Alexandria (*ca.* A.D. 538); Antioch (*ca.* A.D. 498); Carthage (*ca.* A.D. 534); Cyzicus (*ca.* A.D. 518); Nicomedia (*ca.* A.D. 498); Ravenna (*ca.* A.D. 555); Rome (*ca.* A.D. 552); Thessalonica (*ca.* A.D. 518).

DATING ROMAN IMPERIAL COINS.

The ability to date with some accuracy many of the coins struck under the Roman Empire gives to the collector of this fascinating and varied series yet another theme for the formation of a collection.

Some people collect Roman coins in order to assemble a "portrait gallery" of as many of the emperors and empresses as they can, others form their collections on the basis of illustrating the many different personifications, gods and goddesses which appear on the coinage, whilst a third method is the arrangement of a collection according to mints. Arrangement by dates, however, is one theme which has been very much neglected by collectors. Such a collection could take the form of a display of coins representing particular years in which events of great historical interest took place. Thus the collector might acquire a coin of A.D. 70, the year of the capture of Jerusalem by Titus, one of A.D. 79, the year of the famous eruption of Mt. Vesuvius which buried Pompeii, and so on. The scope for such a collection is, undoubtedly, very great and it will encourage the collector to read more about the history of the period in order to discover the dates of important historical events.

The cause of the neglect of this theme for the formation of a collection is, probably, a certain lack of knowledge amongst collectors on how to set about dating the coins of the imperial series. It is hoped, therefore, that the following notes and the tables of titles and powers given under many of the reigns in the catalogue will be both of interest and of practical use to collectors.

Tribunicia Potestas (the tribunician power—usually TR.P. on the coins). The Tribunes of the People were first created in the early days of the Republic to protect the rights of the lower classes (plebeians) against the powerful aristocrats (patricians). From this humble beginning the power of the tribunes gradually increased until, under the pretext of defending the rights of the people, they were able to do almost anything they pleased. This almost unlimited power was drastically reduced by Sulla and although many of their rights and privileges were restored after the dictator's death, they were again deprived of power by Julius Caesar.

Augustus realized the advantages of possessing the power of the tribunes and it had the added attraction of being a popular office with the people, in sharp contrast to the detested titles of *rex* and *dictator*. Accordingly, in 23 B.C. he had the tribunician power conferred upon him for life, thus gathering into his hands many important prerogatives previously enjoyed by the Tribunes of the People. He was now able to convene and dismiss both the Senate and the Assembly of the People and also to veto any order of the Senate. In addition, the tribunician power rendered his person sacred and inviolable.

As Augustus wished the tribunician power to be regarded as the basis of his authority, it is not surprising that he introduced the custom of dating his reign by the years of his tribunician power, as though the office was bestowed annually, as in the days of the Republic. This system was adopted by his successors and was employed extensively on the coins—thus supplying a useful means of dating accurately much of the Imperial coinage.

In the case of the earlier emperors (Augustus-Antoninus Pius) this fictitious annual renewal of the tribunician power appears to have been made on the date of its first conferment. In A.D. 147, however, Antoninus seems to have reverted to the traditional Republican date for the appointment of the tribunes (December 10th) and this practice was continued by the rest of the emperors of the Antonine Dynasty.

Septimius Severus instituted yet another system whereby the renewal was made on January 1st of each year, thus causing the tribunician year to coincide with the calendar year. Most of the succeeding emperors appear to have adopted this method, one notable exception being Gordian III, who seems to have reverted to the system of the early Empire and renewed his tribunician power on each anniversary of his accession.

Imperator (usually IMP. on the coins). There are two meanings for this title:

(a) *Imperator*—used as a praenomen of the emperor, by virtue of his supreme command over all the legions of the Roman army. From the time of Vespasian, this title was normally placed before all the other names and dignities of the emperor and at about this time also it replaced *princeps* as the popular designation of the emperor.

(b) *Imperator*—used to enumerate the victories of the emperor. Whenever a Roman army achieved some notable military success, the emperor, regardless of whether or not he was personally involved, received an imperial acclamation. The numbers of these acclamations are sometimes included in the inscriptions on coins and when they are frequent, as in the cases of Marcus Aurelius and the early years of Septimius Severus, they can be very useful from the point of view of dating.

Consul (usually COS. on the coins). The annual office of consul was established immediately after the abolition of the monarchy in 510 B.C. and was the highest of the Roman magistracies. There were two colleagues in the consulship and during their year of office they wielded an almost regal power over the whole Republic. Their authority, however, was considerably diminished by the creation of the Tribunes of the People, who were the only magistrates not subject to the consuls. Nevertheless, being the supreme magistrates of the state, their power remained very considerable as long as the Republic endured.

Under the Empire consuls continued to be appointed, but although all the grandeur of the office was retained, the holders of the consulship no longer exercised any of the political power of their Republican predecessors. Quite frequently more than one pair of consuls were appointed for each year and from the reign of Vespasian it was normal for at least five pairs to hold office each year.

Quite often the emperor himself held the consulship and if he did so frequently, and advertised the fact on his coins, it can be a very useful criterion for dating. In this respect the Flavian emperors were particularly helpful, Vespasian holding the consulship eight times in ten years, Titus eight times in twelve years and Domitian seventeen times in twenty-seven years. In marked contrast, Hadrian only held the consulship three times, corresponding with the first three years of his reign. In consequence, the inscription COS. III. for Hadrian covers the long period A.D. 119-138.

In addition to the foregoing, there are other titles appearing in the inscriptions on coins which can be of assistance for dating purposes. The most important of these are as follows:

Pontifex Maximus (usually P.M. on the coins). The *Pontifex Maximus* was the chief of the *Pontifices* (Priests of the Gods) and was the judge of everything relating to the religion and sacred ceremonies of the Romans. It was a dignity which, once conferred, was held for life and Augustus did not receive the title until after the death of Lepidus in 13 B.C. Thereafter, it became one of the titles normally assumed by the emperors at the time of their accession.

Prior to the reign of Balbinus and Pupienus the title of *Pontifex Maximus* always went to the senior emperor in the case of a joint reign, the title of *Pontifex* sometimes being bestowed on the junior partner. This title was also occasionally given to the Caesar or heir to the throne. Balbinus and Pupienus set a precedent for succeeding emperors by dividing the *Pontificatus Maximus* between them.

Pater Patriae (usually P.P. on the coins). This title of honour, meaning "Father of his Country", was conferred on Augustus in 2 B.C. and was subsequently assumed by most, but not all, of his successors at the time of their accession. Tiberius constantly refused the title and some emperors, such as Hadrian and Marcus Aurelius, only accepted it after they had reigned for several years.

Germanicus, Parthicus, Armeniacus, *etc.* These were titles given in commemoration of victories achieved over the enemies of the Empire.

The following will serve as an example in the use of the tables given in the main part of the catalogue: a sestertius of Commodus bears the legends M.COMMODVS ANT. P. FELIX AVG. BRIT. (*obv.*) and P.M. TR.P.XI. IMP. VII. COS. V. P.P.S.C. (*rev.*). Referring to the table on page 167, it will be seen that the eleventh year of Commodus' tribunician power (TR. P. XI.) extended from 10th December A.D. 185 to 9th December A.D. 186. Although it is obviously more likely that this piece was struck in 186, some title must be found on the coin to confirm it to this year before it can be said with certainty that it was not struck in 185. If we look at the *obv.* legend, we will find that the titles *Pius* (P.), *Britannicus* (BRIT.) and *Felix* were bestowed on Commodus in A.D. 183, 184 and 185 respectively and are thus of no use in confirming the coin to A.D. 186. Turning to the *rev.* legend, we see that the emperor bears the title *Pontifex Maximus* (P.M.), but according to the table it would appear that Commodus became Chief Pontif in A.D. 180. His seventh imperial acclamation (IMP. VII.) was in 184, whilst the title of *Pater Patriae* (P.P.) was bestowed on him as early as 177; this just leaves us with COS. V. It will be seen that Commodus did not embark upon his fifth consulship until A.D. 186 and so this is the one title which confirms the coin to this year.

It is not always possible to say with certainty which of two years a particular piece belongs to, but where the number of the tribunician power is stated, the date of the issue of the coin can at least be tied down to a period of twelve months. From the time of Septimius Severus, however, this difficulty does not usually arise as the tribunician year normally corresponds with the calendar year.

VALUES.

As in the case of coins of all series and periods the value of any particular specimen depends to a very great extent on its state of preservation. Rarity also plays an important part in determining the value of a piece, but it should be pointed out that often a comparatively common coin in superb condition is worth more than a rarity which is very worn or damaged.

We have endeavoured to give an average price for each coin, and as the average condition varies according to the period, the metal and the denomination, the condition for which the price is intended is marked clearly on each page.

Exceptionally fine pieces are worth very much more than the prices given in this catalogue (see Introduction, page 6), whilst poor coins are often almost valueless.

ALL PRICES ARE VALUE TO COLLECTORS, NOT THE PRICE A DEALER WOULD PAY.

At present (January, 1970) 20s. or £1 equals 2.40 U.S. dollars, 10.39 Swiss francs, 13.36 French francs, 8.84 German marks, 8.64 Dutch florins, 1500 Italian lire. For Conversion Table see page 372.

ABBREVIATIONS.

A'	= gold		dr.	= draped
AR	= silver		cuir.	= cuirassed
Æ	= copper, bronze or orichalcum		r.	= right
Obv.	= obverse		l.	= left
R or *Rev.*	= reverse		stg.	= standing
hd.	= head		ex.	= exergue
laur.	= laureate		mm.	= millimetres
rad.	= radiate		⌒	= letters are ligate
diad.	= diademed		gm.	= grammes

Abbreviations used in the text to indicate standard works of reference will be found in the list of books on Roman coins on pages 370-371.

CONDITIONS OF COINS IN ORDER OF MERIT.

Abbreviation	*English*	*French*	*German*
FDC	mint state	fleur-de-coin	stempelglanz
EF	extremely fine	superbe	vorzüglich
VF	very fine	très beau	sehr schön
F	fine	beau	schön
Fair	fair	très bien conservé	Sehr gut erhalten
M	mediocre	bien conservé	gut erhalten
P	poor		

ROMAN REPUBLICAN COINAGE

The dating of Roman Republican coins is a very controversial subject, particularly in the case of the earlier issues which are anonymous. Sydenham's book *The Coinage of the Roman Republic* (1952) presents a revised chronology of the coinage differing considerably in some places from earlier works. It is this revised chronology of Sydenham which is employed throughout the following list.

The reference "*S*" is to the afore-mentioned book of Sydenham, and the reference "*B*" to Babelon's *Monnaies de la République Romaine* (1885-6). The first part of Seaby's *Roman Silver Coins, Vol. I*, in which nearly all the Republican silver coins are illustrated, is based on this latter work.

AES GRAVE

(The figure in brackets following the denomination is the average weight in grammes.)

		269-242 B.C.	Fair
1	**As.** (321). Hd. of Janus. ℞. Hd. of Mercury l. *S.* 8		£90·00
2	**Semis.** (160). Helmeted hd. of Mars l., s below. ℞. Female hd. l., s below. *S.* 9		30·00
3	**Triens.** (106). Thunderbolt and four pellets. ℞. Dolphin and four pellets. *S.* 10		18·00
4	**Quadrans.** (80). Two grains of corn and three pellets. ℞. Open right hand and three pellets. *S.* 11		10·00
5	**Sextans.** (55). Scallop-shell and two pellets. ℞. Caduceus and two pellets. *S.* 12. **Plate 1**		12·00
6	**Uncia.** (27). Knuckle-bone. ℞. Pellet. *S.* 13		10·00
7	**Semuncia.** (17). Acorn. ℞. Σ or Ɔ. *S.* 14		10·00
8	**As.** (335). Hd. of Apollo r. ℞. Hd. of Apollo l. *S.* 15		150·00
9	**Semis.** (165). Pegasus r., s below. ℞. Pegasus l., s below. *S.* 16		45·00
10	**Triens.** (111). Horse's hd. r., four pellets beneath. ℞. As *obv.*, but hd. l. *S.* 17		35·00
11	**Quadrans.** (84). Boar running r., three pellets beneath. ℞. As *obv.*, but boar l. *S.* 18		30·00
12	**Sextans.** (57). Male hd. r., in pileus, two pellets behind. ℞. As *obv.*, but hd. l. *S.* 19		25·00
13	**Uncia.** (27). Corn-grain and pellet. ℞. As *obv. S.* 20		12·00

241-222 B.C.   Fair

14   **As.** (267).   Helmeted hd. of Roma r., I behind.   ℟.   As *obv.*, but hd. l.
S. 31   ..   ..£120·00

15   **Semis.** (134).   Helmeted hd. of Mars r., s below.   ℟.   As *obv.*, but hd.
l.   *S.* 32   ..   ..   50·00

16   **Triens.** (85).   Thunderbolt and four pellets.   ℟.   As *obv.* *S.* 33   ..   25·00

17   **Quadrans.** (66).   Open right hand and three pellets.   ℟.   As *obv.*, but
left hand. *S.* 34   ..   ..   15·00

18   **Sextans.** (44).   Scallop-shell (convex) and two pellets.   ℟.   As *obv.*,
but concave. *S.* 35   ..   ..   12·00

19   **Uncia.** (22).   Knuckle-bone and pellet.   ℟.   As *obv.* *S.* 36   ..   .. 12·00

20   **Semuncia.** (13).   Acorn and Σ.   ℟.   Acorn and Ƹ. *S.* 37   ..   .. 16·00

21   **As.** (269).   As 14, but with club behind hd. of Roma instead of I. *S.* 38 120·00

22   **Semis.** (132).   As 15, but with club behind hd. of Mars. *S.* 39   .. 45·00

23   **Triens.** (88).   As 16, but with club also. *S.* 40   ..   ..   ..   25·00

24   **Quadrans.** (66).   As 17, but with club also. *S.* 41   ..   ..   15·00

25   **Sextans.** (45).   As 18, but with club also. *S.* 42   ..   ..   12·00

26   **Uncia.** (22).   As 19, but with club also. *S.* 43   ..   ..   ..   12·00

27   **As.** (271).   As 1, but with falx (sickle) behind hd. of Mercury. *S.* 44   100·00

28   **Semis.** (135).   As 2, but with falx behind female hd. *S.* 45   ..   50·00

29   **Triens.** (91).   As 3, but also with falx on *rev.* *S.* 46.   **Plate 1**   ..   25·00

30   **Quadrans.** (67).   As 4, but also with falx on *rev.* *S.* 47   ..   15·00

31   **Sextans.** (46).   As 5, but also with falx on *rev.* *S.* 48   ..   ..   12·00

32   **Uncia.** (23).   As 6, but also with falx on *rev.* *S.* 49   ..   ..   12·00

33   **Semuncia.**   As 7, but also with falx on *rev.* *S.* 50   ..   ..   12·00

34   **As.** (284).   As 8, but smaller module. *S.* 51   ..   ..   120·00

35   **Semis.** (142).   As 9, but smaller module. *S.* 52   ..   ..   50·00

36   **Triens.** (92).   As 10, but smaller module. *S.* 53   ..   ..   25·00

37   **Quadrans.** (72).   As 11, but smaller module. *S.* 54   ..   ..   20·00

38   **Sextans.** (46).   As 12, but smaller module. *S.* 55   ..   ..   12·00

39   **Uncia.**   As 13, but smaller module. *S.* 56   ..   ..   10·00

40   **Tripondius.** (881).   Helmeted hd. of Roma r., III behind.   ℟.   Wheel
with six spokes; between the spokes, III. *S.* 57   ..   ..   350·00

41   **Dupondius.** (625).   As previous, but with II instead of III. *S.* 58.
Plate 2   ..   ..   250·00

42   **As.** (271).   As previous, but with I instead of II. *S.* 59   ..   120·00

43   **Semis.** (133).   Bull prancing l., s below.   ℟.   As previous, but with s
between the spokes. *S.* 60   ..   ..   45·00

44   **Triens.** (89).   Horse prancing l.; four pellets, two above, two beneath.
℟.   As previous, but with four pellets between the spokes. *S.* 61   .. 25·00

45   **Quadrans.** (66).   Dog running l., three pellets beneath. ℟.   As previous, but with three pellets between the spokes. *S.* 62   ..   20·00

46   **Sextans.** (44).   Tortoise.   ℟.   As previous, but with two pellets
between the spokes. *S.* 63   ..   ..   16·00

222-205 B.C.

Fair

47 **As.** (268). Hd. of Janus,—below. ℞. Prow of ship r.; above, I.
    S. 71. *Illustrated on p. 7* .. .. £60·00

48 **Semis.** (135). Laur. hd. of Saturn l., s below. ℞. As previous, but
    s above. *S.* 73 .. .. 30·00
49 **Triens.** (89). Helmeted hd. of Minerva l., four pellets beneath. ℞.
    As previous, but four pellets beneath. *S.* 74. **Plate 1** .. .. .. 25·00
50 **Quadrans.** (68). Hd. of Hercules l., three pellets behind. ℞. As
    previous, but three pellets. *S.* 75 .. .. 20·00
51 **Sextans.** (43). Hd. of Mercury l., two pellets beneath. ℞. As
    previous, but two pellets. *S.* 76 .. .. 16·00
52 **Uncia.** (22). Helmeted hd. of Bellona l., pellet behind. ℞. As
    previous, but one pellet. *S.* 77 .. .. 10·00

53 **As.** (258). Hd. of Janus. ℞. As 47, but prow l. *S.* 78 .. .. 90·00
54 **Semis.** (126). Laur. hd. of Saturn l. ℞. As 48, but prow l. *S.* 79 45·00
55 **Triens.** (83). Helmeted hd. of Minerva l. ℞. As 49, but prow l.
    S. 80 .. .. 35·00
56 **Quadrans.** (63). Hd. of Hercules l., club below. ℞. As 50, but prow
    l. *S.* 81 .. .. 30·00
57 **Sextans.** (42). Hd. of Mercury l. ℞. As 51, but prow l. *S.* 82 .. 25·00

205-195 B.C.

58 **As.** (132). As 53, but smaller module. *S.* 89 .. .. .. 100·00
59 **Semis.** (73). Laur. hd. of Saturn l., s. ℞. As 48, but prow l. *S.* 90 30·00
60 **Triens.** (53). Helmeted hd. of Minerva l.; four pellets. ℞. As 49,
    but prow l. *S.* 91 .. .. 30·00
61 **Quadrans.** (36). Hd. of Hercules l.; three pellets. ℞. As 56. *S.* 92 25·00

195-187 B.C.

62 **Decussis.** (1107-669). Helmeted hd. of Juno r., x behind. ℞. Prow
    of ship l., x above. *S.* 98 .. .. 500·00

Fair

63 **Tripondius.** (313-236).   As previous, but III instead of x.   *S.* 99   ..£300·00
64 **Dupondius.** (208-178).   Helmeted hd. of Minerva r., II behind.   R.
   As previous, but II above prow.   *S.* 100 ..   .. 200·00
65 **As.** (80-58).   Hd. of Janus.   R.   As previous, but I above prow.   *S.* 101   60·00
66 **Semis.** (46-30).   Laur. hd. of Saturn l., s behind.   R.   As previous,
   but s above prow.   *S.* 102 ..   .. 30·00
67 **Triens.** (35-27).   As 49, but prow l.   *S.* 103   ..   .. 30·00
68 **Quadrans.** (31.5).   Hd. of Hercules l., three pellets beneath.   R.   As
   56.   *S.* 104   ..   .. 20·00
69 **As.** (88).   Laur. hd. of Janus.   R.   Prow of ship r.; above, I; on r., L.
   S. 122 ..   .. 75·00
70 **Semis.** (42).   Laur. hd. of Saturn r.   R.   As previous, but s above
   prow.   *S.* 123   ..   .. 37·50

STRUCK COINAGE
269-242 B.C.   Very Fine

71   73

71 **Æ didrachm.**   Helmeted hd. of Mars l.   R.   Horse's hd. r. on tablet
   inscribed ROMANO.   *S.* 1.   *B.* 4   ..   .. 70·00
72 ROMANO.   Laur. hd. of Apollo l.   R.   Horse galloping r.; above, star.
   S. 4.   *B.* 6.   *Illustrated on p. 10 and on* **Plate 2** ..   ..   .. 100·00
73 Diad. bust of Hercules r., club over shoulder.   R.   Wolf and twins; in
   ex., ROMANO.   *S.* 6.   *B.* 8 ..   .. 65·00

Fine

74 **Æ litra.**   Diad. hd. of Apollo r.   R.   Lion walking r.; in ex., ROMANO.
   S. 5   ..   .. 9·00
75 Hd. of Hercules r., club below.   R.   Pegasus prancing r.; above, club;
   below, ROMA.   *S.* 7 ..   .. 9·00
76 **Æ half-litra.**   Helmeted hd. of Minerva l.   R.   Horse's hd. r.; on l.,
   ROMANO.   *S.* 3   ..   .. 8·00

241-222 B.C.   Very Fine

77 **Æ didrachm.**   Helmeted hd. of Diana r.   R.   Victory stg. r.; on l.,
   ROMANO.   *S.* 21.   *B.* 7   ..   .. 125·00

77   78

78 Helmeted hd. of Mars r.   R.   Horse galloping r.; above, club; below,
   ROMA.   *S.* 23.   *B.* 32   ..   .. 70·00

Very Fine

79 **Æ didrachm.** *Obv.* Similar. ℞. Horse's hd. r., sickle behind, ROMA
    below. *S.* 24. *B.* 34. **Plate 2** ..   .. £70·00
80 Laur. hd. of Apollo r. ℞. Horse galloping l.; above, ROMA. *S.* 27.
    B. 37 ..   .. 100·00
81 **Æ drachm.** As previous. *S.* 28. *B.* 38   ..   .. 110·00
82 Similar to 79. *S.* 25. *B.*— (*Seaby* 34a) ..   .. 80·00

Fine

83 **Æ half-litra.** Similar to 78. *S.* 23a   ..   .. 8·00
84 Similar to 79. *S.* 26   ..   .. 8·00
85 Laur. hd. of Apollo r. ℞. Horse galloping l., ROMA below. *S.* 29 .. 9·00
86 **Æ quarter-litra.** Helmeted hd. of Diana r. ℞. Dog walking r.; in ex.,
    ROMA. *S.* 22 ..   .. 9·00

82   89

222-205 B.C.   **Very Fine**

87 **N stater.** Hd. of Janus. ℞. Youth kneeling l., holding pig, between
    bearded warrior and soldier; in ex., ROMA. *S.* 69. **Plate 2** ..   .. 1500·00
88 **N half-stater.** Similar. *S.* 70 ..   .. 800·00
89 **Æ didrachm** or **quadrigatus.** Hd. of Janus. ℞. Jupiter and
    Victory in fast quadriga r.; below, tablet inscribed ROMA. *S.* 64. *B.* 23 30·00
90 **Æ drachm** or **half-quadrigatus.** Hd. of Janus. ℞. Jupiter and
    Victory in fast quadriga l.; in ex., ROMA. *S.* 67. *B.* 25   ..   .. 60·00

205-195 B.C.

91 **Æ double-victoriatus.** Laur. hd. of Jupiter r. ℞. Victory stg. r.,
    crowning trophy; in ex., ROMA. *S.* 83*. *B.* 7 ..   .. *Unique*
92 **Æ victoriatus.** Similar. *S.* 83. *B.* 9. **Plate 2**   ..   ..   .. 7·50

Fine

93 **Æ sextans.** Hd. of Mercury r.; above, two pellets. ℞. Prow r.;
    above, ROMA; below, two pellets. *S.* 85 ..   .. 12·00
94 **Æ uncia.** Helmeted hd. of Bellona l., pellet behind. ℞. Prow r.;
    above, ROMA; below, pellet. *S.* 86 ..   .. 10·00
95 **Æ semuncia.** Bust of Mercury r. ℞. Prow r.; above, ROMA. *S.* 87 9·00
96 **Æ quartuncia.** Helmeted hd. of Bellona r. ℞. Prow r.; above,
    ROMA. *S.* 88 ..   .. 9·00
97 **Æ triens.** Hd. of Juno r., four pellets behind. ℞. Hercules stg. r.,
    raising club to strike Centaur; on r., four pellets; in ex., ROMA. *S.* 93 75·00

Fine

98   **Æ quadrans.** Hd. of Hercules r., three pellets behind.   ℞.   Bull charging r., snake below; above, three pellets; in ex., ROMA.   *S*. 94   .. £35·00

99   **Æ sextans.**   Wolf and twins; in ex., two pellets.   ℞.   Eagle stg. r., flower in beak; behind, two pellets; before, ROMA.   *S*. 95   ..   ..

100   **Æ uncia.**   Rad. bust of Sol facing; on l., pellet.   ℞.   Crescent; above, pellet and two stars; below, ROMA.   *S*. 96 ..   .. 16·00

101   **Æ semuncia.**   Female bust r.   ℞.   Horseman galloping r., ROMA below.   *S*. 97 ..   .. 10·00

195–187 B.C.   Very Fine

102   **Æ victoriatus.**   Laur. hd. of Jupiter r.   ℞.   Victory stg. r., crowning trophy; in ex., ROMA; in field, CROT (Croton).   *S*. 120.   *B*. 36.   (*Seaby* 36*b*)   ..   .. 40·00

103   Similar, but with M͡T (Mateola ?) in field.   *S*. 117.   *Seaby* 36*i*.   **Plate 2**   .. 12·50

104   Similar, but with V͡B (Vibo) in field.   *S*. 113.   *Seaby* 36*m*   ..   .. 17·50

105   **Æ half-victoriatus.**   As previous, but also with s to r. of trophy.   *S*. 114.   *B*. 37   ..   .. 35·00

Fine

106   **Æ triens.**   Helmeted hd. of Minerva r., four pellets above.   ℞.   Prow r.; above, ROMA; below, four pellets.   *S*. 105   ..   ..   .. 12·50

107   **Æ quadrans.**   Hd. of Hercules r., three pellets behind.   ℞.   Prow r.; above, ROMA; below, three pellets.   *S*. 106   ..   ..   .. 12·00

108   **Æ sextans.**   As 93, but smaller module.   *S*. 107   ..   ..   .. 10·00

109   **Æ uncia.**   As 94, but hd. of Bellona r.   *S*. 108 ..   ..   .. 8·00

110   **Æ semuncia.**   As 95, but smaller module.   *S*. 109   ..   .. 7·00

111   **Æ quartuncia.**   As 96, but smaller module.   *S*. 110   ..   .. 7·00

187-155 B.C. **Very Fine**

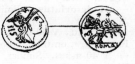

112   114

112   187-175 B.C., **Æ denarius.** Helmeted hd. of Roma r., x behind. ℞.
The Dioscuri galloping r., ROMA below. *S.* 140. *B.* 2 .. .. .. £6·00

113   — **Æ quinarius.** Similar, but with v behind hd. of Roma. *S.* 141.
B. 3. **Plate 2** .. .. 9·00

114   — **Æ sestertius.** Similar, but with IIS behind hd. of Roma. *S.* 142.
B. 4 .. .. 17·50

Fair

115   — **Æ as.** Laur. hd. of Janus, I above. ℞. Prow r.; above, I; below,
ROMA. *S.* 143 .. .. 6·00

116   — **Æ semis.** Laur. hd. of Saturn r., s behind. ℞. Prow r.; above, s;
below, ROMA. *S.* 143*a* .. .. 6·00

117   — **Æ triens.** As 106, but smaller module. *S.* 143*b* .. .. .. 6·00

118   — **Æ quadrans.** As 107, but smaller module. *S.* 143*c* .. .. 6·00

119   — **Æ sextans.** As 93, but smaller module. *S.* 143*d* .. .. 4·50

120   — **Æ uncia.** As 94, but hd. of Bellona r. *S.* 143*e* .. .. 5·00

121   — **Æ semuncia.** As 95, but smaller module. *S.* 143*f* .. 4·00

122   — **Æ as.** Similar to 115, but with anchor to r. of prow. *S.* 145 .. 10·00

123   — **Æ denarius.** Similar to 112, but with prow below the Dioscuri.
S. 146. *Seaby* 20x .. .. *Very fine* £12·50

124   182-172 B.C., **Æ sextans.** Similar to 93, but with H to r. of prow. *S.*
175*d* .. .. 10·00

125   — **Æ quadrans.** Similar to 107, but with L to r. of prow. *S.* 178*d* 10·00

126   — **Æ quincunx.** Laur. hd. of Apollo r., L behind. ℞. The Dioscuri
galloping r., ROMA below; in ex., five pellets. *S.* 179 .. .. 35·00

127   — **Æ triens.** Similar to 106, but with v to r. of prow. *S.* 186*b* .. 9·00

128   — **Æ semis.** Similar to 116, but with monogram of ROMA to r. of prow.
S. 190*a* .. .. 12·50

129   175-172 B.C., **Æ as.** Similar to 115, but with corn-ear above prow.
S. 195 .. .. 9·00

130   175-168 B.C., **Æ as.** Similar, but with cornucopiae above prow. *S.* 218 10·00

131   — **Æ denarius.**   Similar to 112, but with spear-head below the Dioscuri.
S. 222.   *Seaby* 20*aa*.   **Plate 2**   ..   ..   £9·00
132   — **Æ victoriatus.**   Similar to 91, but with spear-head in field.   S. 223.
Seaby 24*m*   ..   ..   9·00
133   167-155 B.C., **Æ 60 asses.**   Helmeted bust of Mars r., ↓x behind.   ℞.
Eagle stg. r. on thunderbolt, ROMA below.   S. 226.   **Plate 2**   ..   ..   300·00
134   — **Æ 40 asses.**   Similar, but with xxxx. behind bust of Mars.   S. 227.
Plate 2   ..   ..   250·00
135   — **Æ 20 asses.**   Similar, but with xx. behind bust of Mars.   S. 228.
Plate 2   ..   ..   150·00

Fair

136   — **Æ as.**   Similar to 115, but with dog above prow.   S. 251   ..   ..   12·50
137   — — Similar, but with star above prow.   S. 264   ..   ..   ..   9·00
138   — — Similar, but with crescent above prow.   S. 267   ..   ..   ..   9·00

139   165-155 B.C., **Æ denarius.**   Similar to 112, but with $\widehat{\text{MA}}$ below the
Dioscuri.   S. 291.   *Seaby* 32*e*   ..   ..   ..   *Very fine* £15·00
140   — **Æ as.**   Similar to 115, but with bird and rudder above prow.   S. 292   12·50
141   — — Similar, but with wolf and twins above prow.   S. 297   ..   ..   15·00

142   — — Similar, but with $\widehat{\text{MD}}$ and bull above prow.   S. 299   ..   ..   17·50

155-120 B.C.

143   155-133 B.C., **Æ quadrans.**   Similar to 107, but with CA to r. of prow.
S. 309*e* ..   ..   8·00
144   — **Æ sextans.**   Similar to 93, but with $\widehat{\text{KA}}$ to r. of prow and corn-ear
above it.   S. 310*d*   ..   ..   9·00
145   155-150 B.C., **Æ as.**   Similar to 115, but with $\widehat{\text{AV}}$ above prow.   S. 327 ..   10·00
146   150-146 B.C., **Æ denarius.**   Helmeted hd. of Roma r., x behind.   ℞.
Diana in biga r., ROMA below; wren and TOD below horses.   S. 345.
B. 35   ..   ..   *Very fine* £7·50
147   150-133 B.C., **Æ as.**   Similar to 115, but with P above prow.   S. 353 ..   12·00

Fair

148	— — Similar, but with BAL above prow. *S.* 354	.. .. ..	£9·00
149	— — Similar, but with C. SAX above prow. *S.* 360	.. .. ..	9·00
150	— — Similar, but with OPEI above prow. *S.* 363	.. .. ..	9·00
151	— — Similar, but with TVRD above prow. *S.* 366	.. .. ..	9·00

Very Fine

146   152

152 145-138 B.C., Æ **denarius.** Helmeted hd. of Roma r., x behind. ℞.
Victory in biga r., ROMA below. *S.* 376. *B.* 6 .. .. 6·00

153 — *Atilius Saranus*, Æ **denarius.** As previous, but with SAR below
horses. *S.* 377. *B. Atilia* 1. **Plate 2** .. .. 6·00

154 — — Æ **as.** Similar to 115, but with SAR above prow. *S.* 378
                                                                Fair £9·00

155 — *Pinarius Natta*, Æ **denarius.** Similar to 152, but with NAT below
horses. *S.* 382. *B. Pinaria* 2 .. .. 6·00

156 — *Q. Marcius Libo*, Æ **denarius.** Hd. of Roma r., LIBO behind, x below
chin. ℞. As 112, but with Q. MARC. below the Dioscuri. *S.* 395.
B. Marcia 1 .. .. 6·00

157 — *L. Sempronius Pitio*, Æ **as.** Similar to 115, but with PITIO above hd.
of Janus and L. SEMP. above prow. *S.* 403 .. .. *Fair* £10·00

158 137-134 B.C., *Furius Purpureo*, Æ **denarius.** Similar to 146, but with
PVR below horses and murex-shell above them. *S.* 424. *B. Furia* 13 .. 6·00

159 135-126 B.C., *C. Terentius Lucanus*, Æ **denarius.** Similar to 112, but
with Victory behind hd. of Roma and C. TER. LVC. below the Dioscuri.
S. 425. *B. Terentia* 10 .. .. 6·00

159   160

160 — *C. Renius*, Æ **denarius.** Hd. of Roma r., x behind. ℞. Juno in
biga of goats r., C. RENI below, ROMA in ex. *S.* 432. *B. Renia* 1 .. 6·00

161 — *C. Valerius Flaccus C.f.*, Æ **denarius.** Similar to 152, but with C .
VAL . C . F . below horses and FLAC. above them. *S.* 440. *B. Valeria* 7.
Plate 2 .. .. 6·00

162 — — Similar, but with XVI behind hd. of Roma. *S.* 441. *B.* 8.
Plate 2 .. .. 12·50

163   135-126 B.C., *L. Antestius Gragulus*, **Æ denarius.**   Hd. of Roma r., GRAG
behind, ✳ below chin.   ℞.   Jupiter in quadriga r., L . ANTES below
horses, ROMA in ex.   *S.* 451.   *B. Antestia* 9   ..   ..   £6·00

164   133-126 B.C., *C. Minucius Augurinus*, **Æ denarius.**   Hd. of Roma r.,
ROMA behind, x below chin.   ℞.   Ionic column, between two togate
figures, surmounted by statue; above, C . AVG.   *S.* 463.   *B. Minucia* 3   8·00

165   125-120 B.C., *M. Opeimius*, **Æ denarius.**   Hd. of Roma r., tripod behind,
✳ below chin.   ℞.   Apollo in biga r., M . OPEIMI below horses, ROMA
in ex.   *S.* 475.   *B. Opeimia* 16.   **Plate 2**   ..   ..   6·00

166   — *Sex. Julius Caisar*, **Æ denarius.**   Hd. of Roma r., anchor behind,
✳ below chin.   ℞.   Venus Genetrix in biga r., SEX . IVLI. below horses,
CAISAR in ex.; above, ROMA.   *S.* 476.   *B. Julia* 2 ..   ..   7·50

164   167

167   — *Q. Fabius Maximus*, **Æ denarius.**   Hd. of Roma r., ROMA behind,
Q . MAX. before, ✳ below chin.   ℞.   Cornucopiae and thunderbolt
crossed within wreath.   *S.* 478.   *B. Fabia* 5   ..   ..   8·00

168   — *M. Caecilius Metellus Q.f.*, **Æ denarius.**   Hd. of Roma r., ROMA
behind, ✳ below chin.   ℞.   M . METELLVS Q . F. around Macedonian
shield; all within wreath.   *S.* 480.   *B. Caecilia* 29   ..   ..   ..   8·00

169   — — **Æ semis.**   Laur. hd. of Saturn r., S behind.   ℞.   Prow r.,
inscribed M . METELLVS; on r., S; above, round shield.   *S.* 482

Fair £9·00

170   173

170   — *C. Serveilius*, **Æ denarius.**   Hd. of Roma r., lituus behind, ROMA
below, ✳ below chin.   ℞.   Horseman galloping l., spearing another
horseman before him; in ex., C . SERVEIL.   *S.* 483.   *B. Servilia* 6   ..   7·00

171   — *M. Aburius Geminus*, **Æ denarius.**   Hd. of Roma r., GEM behind,
✳ below chin.   ℞.   Sol in quadriga r., M . ABVRI. below horses, ROMA
in ex.   *S.* 487.   *B. Aburia* 6.   **Plate 2**   ..   ..   6·00

172   — — **Æ quadrans.**   Similar to 107, but with M . ABVRI . M . F . GEM.
above prow.   *S.* 488 ..   .. *Fair* £10·00

119-91 B.C.

> **From this point onwards, until the end of the Republican coinage, all coins are silver denarii, unless otherwise stated.**

Very Fine

173   119-110 B.C., *C. Aburius Geminus. Obv.* As 171. ℞. Mars in quadriga r., C . A͡BVRI. below horses, ROMA in ex. *S.* 490. *B.* 1 ..   ..   ..   £6·50

174   119-110 B.C., *P. Maenius Antiaticus.* Hd. of Roma r., ✳ behind. ℞. Victory in quadriga r., P . M͡AE . A͡NT. below horses, ROMA in ex. *S.* 492. *B.* 7 ..   ..   6·50

175   — *C. Cassius.* Hd. of Roma r., ✳ and voting-urn behind. ℞. Liberty in quadriga r., C . CASSI. below horses, ROMA in ex. *S.* 502. *B.* 1..   ..   6·50

176   — *T. Cloulius.* Hd. of Roma r., wreath behind, ROMA below. ℞. Victory in biga r., corn-ear below horses, T . CLOVLI. in ex. *S.* 516. *B.* 1   6·50

177   113-109 B.C., *L. Porcius Licinius.* L . PORCI . LICI. around hd. of Roma r., ✳ behind. ℞. Bituitus in biga r., L . LIC . CN . DOM. in ex. *S.* 520. *B.* 8 ..   ..   7·50

178   110-108 B.C., *C. Serveilius M.f.* Hd. of Roma r., wreath behind, ✳ and ROMA below. ℞. The Dioscuri galloping in opposite directions, C . SERVEILI M . F. in ex. *S.* 525. *B.* 1. **Plate 3**   ..   ..   8·00

179   — *M. Fourius Philus.* M . FOVRI . L . F. around laur. hd. of Janus. ℞. Roma stg. l., erecting trophy ; on r., ROMA ; in ex., PHILI. *S.* 529. *B.* 18..   7·00

180   185

180   — *Anonymous.* Hd. of Roma r., x behind, ROMA below. ℞. Roma seated r. on shields, Wolf and Twins at feet ; in field, two birds flying. *S.* 530. *B.* 176 ..   ..   7·50

181   *Q. Fabius Labeo* (109 B.C.) Hd. of Roma r., ROMA behind, LABEO before, x below chin. ℞. Jupiter in quadriga r., prow below horses, Q . FABI. in ex. *S.* 532. *B.* 1 ..   ..   6·00

182   *M. Sergius Silus* (109-108 B.C.) Hd. of Roma r., ROMA and ✳ behind, EX S . C. before. ℞. Horseman galloping l., holding sword and head of barbarian, M . SERGI. below, SILVS in ex. *S.* 544. *B.* 1. **Plate 3**   6·50

183   *Cn. Domitius Ahenobarbus* (108-107 B.C.) Hd. of Roma r., x behind, ROMA before. ℞. Jupiter in quadriga r., CN . DOMI. in ex. *S.* 535. *B.* 7 ..   ..   6·00

184   *M. Cipius M.f.* (107 B.C.) Hd. of Roma r., M . CIPI . M . F. before. ℞. Victory in biga r., rudder below horses, ROMA in ex. *S.* 546. *B.* 1 ..   6·00

185   *P. Licinius Nerva* (106 B.C.) Hd. of Roma l., holding spear and shield, ✳ before, ROMA behind. ℞. Two citizens voting in the comitium ; in field, P . NERVA. *S.* 548. *B.* 7 ..   ..   9·00

186   188

186   *L. Marcius Philippus* (105-104 B.C.)   Hd. of Philip V of Macedon r.,
      monogram of ROMA behind, Φ below chin.   ℞.   Equestrian statue r.
      on base inscribed L . PHILIPPVS, ✳ below.   S. 551.   B. 12   ..   ..   £8·00
187   *Mn. Aemilius Lepidus* (109 B.C.)   Laur. female hd. r., ✳ behind, ROMA
      before.   ℞.   MN . AEMILIO LEP.   Equestrian statue r., on triple arch.
      S. 554.   B. 7.   **Plate 3**   ..   ..   8·00
188   *C. Fonteius* (109 B.C.)   Laur. Janiform hd. between letter and ✳.   ℞.
      Galley l., C . FONT. above, ROMA below.   S. 555.   B. 1 ..   ..   8·00
189   *L. Memmius* (109 B.C.)   Male hd. r. wearing oak-wreath, ✳ below chin.
      ℞.   The Dioscuri stg. facing, each holding horse by bridle, L . MEMMI. in
      ex.   S. 558.   B. 1.   **Plate 3**   ..   ..   8·00
190   *Mn. Fonteius* (103 B.C.)   Conjoined hds. of the Dioscuri r., ✳ below chins.
      ℞.   Galley r., MN . FONTEI. above, letter below.   S. 566.   B. 7   ..   8·00

191   194

191   *M. Herennius* (101 B.C.)   Diad. hd. of Pietas r., PIETAS behind, letter below
      chin.   ℞.   Amphinomus advancing r., carrying his father; to l., M .
      HERENNI.   S. 567.   B. 1.   ..   ..   8·00
192   *C. Claudius Pulcher* (106 B.C.)   Hd. of Roma r.   ℞.   Victory in biga r.,
      C . PVLCHER in ex.   S. 569.   B. 1 ..   ..   6·00
193   *Appius Claudius* and *Titus Mallius* (106 B.C.)   Hd. of Roma r., uncertain
      object behind.   ℞.   Victory in triga r., AP . CL . T . MAL . Q . VR. in ex.
      S. 570.   B. 2 ..   ..   6·00
194   *L. Cornelius Scipio Asiagenus* (101 B.C.)   Laur. hd. of Jupiter l.   ℞.
      Jupiter in quadriga r., letter above, L . SCIP . ASIAG. in ex.   S. 576.   B. 24   6·50
195   *C. Coilius Caldus* (100-97 B.C.)   Hd. of Roma l.   ℞.   Victory in biga l.,
      C . COIL. below horses, CALD. in ex.; above, letter.   S. 582.   B. 2 ..   6·00
196   *C. Fundanius* (100-97 B.C.)   **Æ quinarius.**   Laur. hd. of Jupiter r., letter
      behind.   ℞.   Victory stg. r., crowning trophy at foot of which is kneeling
      captive; on r., C . FVNDA; in ex., Q.   S. 584.   B. 2   ..   ..   9·00
197   *P. Vettius Sabinus* (100-97 B.C.)   **Æ quinarius.**   *Obv.* Similar.   ℞.
      Victory stg. r., crowning trophy, P . SABIN. in field, letter on r., Q in ex.
      S. 587.   B. 1 ..   ..   7·50

198   203

Very Fine

198 *C. Egnatuleius C.f.* (100-97 B.C.) **Æ quinarius.** Laur. hd. of Apollo r.,
     C . EGNATVLEI C . F. behind, Q below. ℞. Victory stg. l., inscribing
     shield attached to trophy; in field, Q; in ex., ROMA. *S.* 588. *B.* 1   ..   £6·00

199 *Q. Minucius Thermus M.f.* (96-95 B.C.) Hd. of Mars l. ℞. Two
     soldiers fighting, the one on l. protecting a fallen comrade; in ex., Q . THERM
     . M . F. *S.* 592. *B.* 19. **Plate 3** ..   ..   8·00

200 *L. Julius L.f. Caesar* (94 B.C.) Hd. of Mars l., CAESAR behind, letter above.
     ℞. Venus Genetrix in chariot drawn l. by two Cupids, lyre below, letter
     above; in ex., L . IVLI . L . F. *S.* 593. *B.* 4   ..   ..   8·00

201 *L. Cassius Caeicianus* (93 B.C.) Hd. of Ceres l., CÆICIAN. and letter behind
     ℞. Two yoked oxen l., plough and letter above, L . CASSI. in ex. *S.* 594.
     B. 4   ..   ..   8·50

202 *M. Porcius Cato* (93-91 B.C.) Female bust r., ROMA behind, M . CATO
     below. ℞. Victory seated r., VICTRIX in ex. *S.* 596. *B.* 5 ..   ..   8·00

203 — **Æ quinarius.** Young hd. r., crowned with ivy-wreath, M . CATO
     behind, symbol below. ℞. As previous. *S.* 597. *B.* 7   ..   ..   8·00

204 100-95 B.C., *L. Thorius Balbus.* Hd. of Juno of Lanuvium r., I . S . M . R.
     behind. ℞. Bull charging r., letter above, L . THORIVS below, BALBVS
     in ex. *S.* 598. *B.* 1   ..   ..   6·50

205 — *P. Servilius M.f. Rullus.* Bust of Minerva l., RVLLI behind. ℞.
     Victory in biga r., P below horses, P . SERVILI . M . F. in ex. *S.* 601. *B.* 14   7·50

206 — *M. Serveilius C.f.* Hd. of Roma r., letter behind. ℞. Two soldiers
     fighting on foot, their horses in background; in ex., M . SERVEILI . C . F.,
     letter below. *S.* 602. *B.* 13. **Plate 3** ..   ..   9·00

204   207

207 *L. Calpurnius Piso* and *Q. Servilius Caepio* (96-94 B.C.) Hd. of Saturn r.,
     PISO and harpa behind, CAEPIO and symbol below, Q below chin. ℞.
     The two quaestors seated l. between two corn-ears; in ex., AD FRV . EMV . /
     EX S . C. *S.* 603. *B.* 5   ..   ..   9·00

Very Fine

208 *A. Postumius Albinus Sp.f.* (92-91 B.C.) Laur. hd. of Apollo r., star behind, ROMA below, x below chin. ℞. The Dioscuri stg. l. beside their horses which are drinking from fountain; in field, crescent; in ex., A . A͡LBINVS S . F. *S.* 612. *B.* 5 .. .. £17·50

209 *C. Poblicius Malleolus* (92-91 B.C.) Hd. of Mars r., mallet above, ✳ below chin. ℞. Warrior stg. l., r. foot on cuirass; on l., trophy; on r., prow and C . M͡AL. *S.* 615. *Seaby 6a* .. .. 11·00

THE SOCIAL WAR, 90-88 B.C.
The Coinage of the Marsic Confederation

210 *Anonymous.* Laur. hd. of Italia l., ITALIA behind. ℞. Youth kneeling at foot of standard, holding pig; on either side, four soldiers stg., pointing their swords at the pig; in ex., numeral. *S.* 620. **Plate 3** .. 90·00

211 — *Obv.* Similar, but Oscan legend behind. ℞. Soldier stg. facing, hd. r., holding spear; on r., recumbent bull; in ex., Oscan letter. *S.* 627 .. 90·00

212 — Helmeted bust of Italia r., crowned by Victory. ℞. Two male figures clasping r. hands; in background to r., prow of ship; in ex., A. *S.* 632 .. .. 140·00

213 *C. Papius C.f. Mutilus.* Hd. of Bacchus r., wearing ivy-wreath, Oscan legend before. ℞. Bull r., trampling on she-wolf, Oscan legend in ex. *S.* 641. **Plate 3** .. .. 175·00

90-79 B.C.

214 *D. Junius Silanus* (90-89 B.C.) Hd. of Roma r., letter behind. ℞. Victory in biga r., numeral above, D . SILANVS L . F. / ROMA in ex. *S.* 646. *B.* 15 .. .. 6·00

208   215

215 *L. Calpurnius Piso L.f. Frugi* (90-89 B.C.) Laur. hd. of Apollo r., symbol behind. ℞. Horseman galloping r., holding palm, L . PISO FRVGI and numeral below. *S.* 663. *B.* 11 .. .. 6·00

216 *Anonymous* (90-89 B.C.) Æ **semis.** Laur. hd. of Saturn r., S behind. ℞. Prow r.; above, L.P.D.A.P. (*Lege Papiria de Aere Publico.*) *S.* 678a
Fair £15·00

217 *C. Vibius C.f. Pansa* (89-88 B.C.) Laur. hd. of Apollo r., PANSA behind, symbol below chin. ℞. Minerva in quadriga r., C . VIBIVS C . F. in ex. *S.* 684. *B.* 1 .. .. 6·00

218 *Q. Titius* (88 B.C.) Hd. of Mutinus Titinus r. ℞. Pegasus r. on tablet inscribed Q . TITI. *S.* 691. *B.* 1. **Plate 3** .. .. 8·00

219 — Hd. of Bacchus r., wearing ivy-wreath. ℞. As previous. *S.* 692. *B.* 2 .. .. 9·00

Very Fine

220 — **Æ quinarius.** Winged bust of Victory r. ℞. Pegasus r., Q . TITI
below. *S*. 693. *B*. 3 .. .. £10·50

221 — **Æ as.** Hd. of Janus with long, pointed beard. ℞. Prow r.; above,
Q . TITI. *S*. 694 .. .. *Fair* £10·00

222   230

222 *L. Titurius L.f. Sabinus* (88 B.C.) Hd. of Tatius r., SABIN. behind, T̂A
before. ℞. Two Roman soldiers, each bearing a woman in his arms
(the rape of the Sabines); in ex., L . TITVRI. *S*. 698. *B*. 1 .. .. 9·00

223 — *Obv.* Similar, but palm below chin and without T̂A. ℞. Tarpeia
facing, attempting to prevent two soldiers from casting their shields upon
her; above, crescent and star; in ex., L . TITVRI. *S*. 699. *B*. 4 .. .. 9·00

224 *Cn. Cornelius Lentulus Marcellinus* (87 B.C.) Bust of Mars r., seen from
behind. ℞. Victory in biga r., CN . LENTVL. in ex. *S*. 702. *B*. 50 .. 6·50

225 *L. Rubrius Dossenus* (87-86 B.C.) Laur. hd. of Jupiter r., sceptre behind,
DOSSEN. below. ℞. Triumphal quadriga r., L . RVBRI. in ex. *S*. 705.
B. 1 .. .. 10·50

226 — **Æ quinarius.** Laur. hd. of Neptune r., trident and DOSSEN. behind.
℞. Victory advancing r., altar at feet; on l., L . RVBRI. *S*. 708. *B*. 4 .. 12·50

227 *C. Marcius Censorinus* (86 B.C.) Jugate hds. of Numa Pompilius and
Ancus Marcius r. ℞. Two horses galloping r., the nearer with rider;
in ex., C. CENSO. *S*. 713. *B*. 18. **Plate 3** .. .. 12·50

228 — **Æ as.** Similar, but with NVMA POMPILI. on l. and ANCVS MARCI. on r.
℞. Two arches; the one on l. has spiral column beneath it and the one
on r. has prow passing through it; above, C . CENSO; below, ROMA. *S*. 716
Fair £30·00

229 *Anonymous* (85-84 B.C.) Hd. of Apollo Vejovis r., thunderbolt below. ℞.
Jupiter in quadriga r. *S*. 723. *B*. 226 .. .. 6·00

230 *Mn. Fonteius C.f.* (84 B.C.) Similar, but with M̂N . FONT̂EI . C . F. behind
and monogram of ROMA below chin. ℞. Infant Genius seated on goat r.,
all within wreath. *S*. 724. *B*. 9 .. .. 7·50

231 *L. Julius Bursio* (83 B.C.) Youthful hd. r., trident and symbol behind.
℞. Victory in quadriga r., L . IVLI . BVRSIO in ex. *S*. 728. *B*. 5 .. 6·00

232 *C. Licinius L.f. Macer* (83 B.C.) Bust of Apollo Vejovis l., seen from behind,
hurling thunderbolt. ℞. Minerva in quadriga r., C . LICINIVS L . F. /
MACER in ex. *S*. 732. *B*. 16 .. .. 8·00

233 *P. Fourius Crassipes* (83 B.C.) Turreted female hd. r., AED . CVR. and
deformed foot behind. ℞. Curule chair inscribed P . FOVRIVS; in ex.,
CRASSIPES. *S*. 735. *B*. 19 .. .. 8·50

234 *L. Marcius Censorinus* (82-81 B.C.) Laur. hd. of Apollo r. ℞. The
satyr, Marsyas, stg. l., holding wine-skin; on r., column; on l., L . CENSOR.
S. 737. *B*. 24.. .. .. 8·50

Very Fine

235 *P. Crepusius* (82-81 B.C.) Laur. hd. of Apollo r., sceptre and letter behind, symbol below chin. ℞. Horseman galloping r., brandishing spear; on l., numeral; in ex., P . CREPVSI. *S.* 738. *B.* 1 .. .. £6·50

236 *C. Mamilius Limetanus* (82-81 B.C.) Bust of Mercury r., caduceus behind, letter above. ℞. Ulysses walking r., his dog before him; on l., C . MAMIL.; on r., LIMETAN. *S.* 741. *B.* 6 .. .. 9·00

237 *Q. Antonius Balbus* (81 B.C.) Laur. hd. of Jupiter r., S . C. behind. ℞. Victory in quadriga r., letter below horses; in ex., Q . ANTO . BALB./PR. *S.* 742. *B.* 1 .. .. 6·00

238 *C. Marius C.f. Capito* (79 B.C.) Bust of Ceres r., CAPIT. and numeral behind, symbol below chin. ℞. Ploughman with yoke of oxen l., numeral above; in ex., C . MARI . C . F./S . C. *S.* 744b. *B.* 9. **Plate 3** 8·00

239 *A. Postumius A.f.S.n. Albinus* (79 B.C.) Bust of Diana r., bucranium above. ℞. Rock surmounted by togate figure stg. l., about to sacrifice ox stg. r.; around, A . POST . A . F . S . N . ALBIN. *S.* 745. *B.* 7 .. .. 9·00

240 — Veiled hd. of Hispania r., HISPAN. behind. ℞. Togate figure stg. l. between Roman eagle and fasces; A . POST . A . F . S . N . ALBIN. in field and ex. *S* 746. *B.* 8 .. .. 10·00

241 *Q. Caecilius Metellus Pius* (77 B.C.) Diad. hd. of Pietas r., stork before. ℞. Elephant walking l., Q.C.M.P.I. in ex. *S.* 750. *B.* 43. **Plate 3** .. 10·50

242 *Cn. Cornelius Lentulus Marcellinus* (76-74 B.C.) Diad. bust of the Genius of the Roman People r., G . P . R. above. ℞. Globe between sceptre and rudder; in field, EX S . C.; below, CN . LEN . Q. *S.* 752. *B.* 54 .. 9·00

236   244

244 *L. Cornelius Sulla and L. Manlius* (82-81 B.C.) Hd. of Roma r., L . MANLI. before, PRO . Q. behind. ℞. Sulla in quadriga r., crowned by Victory flying above; in ex., L . SVLLA IM. *S.* 757. *B.* (*Manlia*) 4 .. 8·50

245 — *N* aureus. Similar. *S.* 756 .. .. 350·00

246 *L. Cornelius Sulla* (82-81 B.C.) Diad. hd. of Venus r., Cupid before, L . SVLLA below. ℞. Jug and lituus between two trophies, IMPER. above, ITERVM below. *S.* 761. *B.* 29. **Plate 3** .. .. 10·50

78-55 B.C.

247 *C. Naevius Balbus* (78-77 B.C.) Diad. hd. of Juno r., S . C. behind. ℞. Victory in triga r., numeral above, C . NÆ . BALB. in ex. *S.* 769. *B.* 6 6·00

248 *L. Procilius* (78-77 B.C.) Hd. of Juno Sospita r., S.C. behind. ℞. Juno Sospita in biga r., L . PROCILI . F. in ex. *S.* 772. *B.* 2 .. .. .. 8·00

249 251

249 *M. Volteius M.f.* (76 B.C.) Laur. hd. of Jupiter r. ℞. Tetrastyle temple of Jupiter Capitolinus, M . VOLTEI . M . F. in ex. *S.* 774. *B.* 1 £10·00

250 *L. Rutilius Flaccus* (75 B.C.) Hd. of Roma r., FLAC. behind. ℞. Victory in biga r., L . RVTILI. in ex. *S.* 780. *B.* 1 .. .. 6·50

251 *L. Lucretius Trio* (74 B.C.) Laur. hd. of Neptune r., trident and numeral behind. ℞. Winged Genius on dolphin r., L . LVCRETI./TRIO below. *S.* 784. *B.* 3 .. .. 9·00

252 *C. Postumius* (74-73 B.C.) Bust of Diana r. ℞. Hound running r., spear below; in ex., C . POSTVMI./TA. *S.* 785. *B.* 9 .. .. .. 8·00

253 *L. Farsuleius Mensor* (73 B.C.) Diad. bust of Liberty r., S . C. and cap behind, MENSOR before. ℞. Roma in biga r., helping citizen to mount into the chariot; below horses, numeral; in ex., L . FARSVLEI. *S.* 789. *B.* 2. **Plate 4** .. .. 9·00

254 *Q. Fufius Calenus* and *Mucius Cordus* (69 B.C.) Jugate hds. of Honos and Virtus r., KALENI below; on l., HO.; on r., VIRT. ℞. Roma and Italia clasping r. hands; on l., ITAL.; on r., RO.; in ex., CORDI. *S.* 797. *B.* 1 9·00

255 *M. Plaetorius M.f. Cestianus* (68-66 B.C.) Helmeted bust of Vacuna r., CESTIANVS behind, S . C. before, cornucopiae below chin. ℞. M . PLAETORIVS M . F . AED . CVR. around eagle stg. r. on thunderbolt, hd. turned. *S.* 809. *B.* 4. **Plate 4** .. .. 8·50

256 *Q. Pomponius Musa* (68-66 B.C.) Laur. hd. of Apollo r., lyre-key behind. ℞. Calliope stg. r., playing lyre set on column; on r., Q . POMPONI.; on l., MVSA. *S.* 811. *B.* 9 .. .. 20·00

257 *M. Aemilius Lepidus* (66 B.C.) Turreted hd. of Alexandria r., ALEXANDREA below. ℞. TVTOR REG . S . C . PONTIF . MAX. M. Lepidus stg. l., crowning the young Ptolemy V, M . LEPIDVS in ex. *S.* 831. *B.* 23. **Plate 4** 50·00

258 — Veiled hd. of the vestal virgin, Aemilia, r., wreath behind, simpulum below chin. ℞. AIMILIA REF . S . C. View of the Basilica Aemilia, M . LEPIDVS in ex. *S.* 834. *B.* 25 .. .. 60·00

259 *C. Calpurnius Piso L.f. Frugi* (64 B.C.) Laur. hd. of Apollo r., symbol behind. ℞. Horseman galloping r., holding palm, letter above, C . PISO L . F . FRVG. below. *S.* 840a. *Seaby 24g* .. .. 6·00

260   264

Very Fine

260 *Faustus Cornelius Sulla* (63-62 B.C.) Diad. bust of Diana r., crescent
above, lituus behind, FAVSTVS before. ℞. Sulla seated l. between
Bocchus kneeling r. and Jugurtha kneeling l.; FELIX behind Sulla. *S.* 879.
B. 59 ..   .. £22·50

261 *C. Coelius Caldus* (62 B.C.) Bare hd. of the consul C. Coelius Caldus r.,
C . COEL . CALDVS before, COS. below, tablet behind. ℞. Rad. hd. of Sol
r., CALDVS III . VIR before, oval shield behind, round shield below chin.
S. 891. *B.* 4 ..   .. 20·00

262 *C. Hosidius C.f. Geta* (60 B.C.) Diad. bust of Diana r., GETA before, III .
VIR behind. ℞. The Calydonian boar r., pierced by spear and attacked
by dog; in ex., C . HOSIDI C . F. *S.* 903. *B.* 1 ..   .. 8·00

263 *Q. Caepio Brutus* (60 B.C.) Bare hd. of L. Junius Brutus the elder r.,
BRVTVS behind. ℞. Bare hd. of C. Servilius Ahala r., AHALA behind.
S. 907. *B.* 30   ..   .. 20·00

264 — Hd. of Liberty r., LIBERTAS behind. ℞. The consul L. Junius Brutus
walking l. between two lictors preceded by an accensus; in ex., BRVTVS.
S. 906. *B.* 31   ..   .. 15·00

265 *Q. Pompeius Rufus* (59 B.C.) Bare hd. of the consul Q. Pompeius Rufus
r., Q . POM . RVFI before, RVFVS COS. behind. ℞. Bare hd. of Sulla r.,
SVLLA COS. before. *S.* 908. *B.* 4 ..   .. 30·00

266 *M. Aemilius Scaurus* amd *P. Plautius Hypsaeus* (58 B.C.) King Aretas
kneeling r. beside camel; above, M . SCAVR./AED . CVR.; in field, EX S . C.;
in ex., REX ARETAS. ℞. Jupiter in quadriga l., P . HYPSAE/AED . CVR.
above, C . HYPSAE COS./PREIVE. in ex.; on r., CAPTV. *S.* 913. *B.* 8 .. 9·00

267 *Q. Cassius* (57 B.C.) Hd. of Liberty r., Q . CASSIVS before, LIBERT. behind.
℞. Temple of Vesta between voting urn and tablet. *S.* 918. *B.* 8. **Plate 4** 10·00

268 *L. Marcius Philippus* (56 B.C.) Diad. hd. of Ancus Marcius r., lituus behind, ANCVS below. ℞. Equestrian statue of Q. Marcius Rex r., on
arcade of five arches; on l., PHILIPPVS; between arches, AQVA MAR. *S.* 919.
B. 28 ..   .. 8·50

269 *Mn. Acilius* (55 B.C.) Laur. hd. of Salus r., SALVTIS behind. ℞. MN .
ACILIVS III . VIR VALETV. Valetudo (Salus) stg. l., leaning on column and
holding serpent. *S.* 922. *B.* 8 ..   .. 8·00

268   270

270 *Paullus Aemilius Lepidus* (55 B.C.) PAVLLVS LEPIDVS CONCORDIA. Veiled hd. of Concord r. ℞. Trophy between L. Aemilius Paullus stg. l. and Perseus of Macedon and his two sons stg. r.; above, TER.; in ex., PAVLLVS. *S.* 926. *B.* 10 .. .. £10·50

271 *L. Scribonius Libo* (55 B.C.) Diad. hd. of Bonus Eventus r., BON . EVENT. before, LIBO behind. ℞. Well-head ornamented with two lyres, festoon and hammer; above, PVTEAL; in ex., SCRIBON. *S.* 928. *B.* 8. **Plate 4** .. .. 8·00

54-44 B.C.

For other coins of this period, see the Imperatorial list.

272 *A. Plautius* (54 B.C.) Turreted hd. of Cybele r., A . PLAVTIVS before, AED . CVR . S . C. behind. ℞. Bacchius kneeling r. beside camel, BACCHIVS in ex.; on r., IVDAEVS. *S.* 932. *B.* 13 .. .. 12·50

273   278

273 *Cn. Plancius* (54 B.C.) Hd. of Diana Planciana r., wearing petasus, CN . PLANCIVS before, AED . CVR . S . C. behind. ℞. Cretan goat stg. r., bow and quiver behind. *S.* 933. *B.* 1 .. .. 9·00

274 *L. Cassius Longinus* (52-50 B.C.) Veiled hd. of Vesta l., cup behind, letter below chin. ℞. Togate figure stg. l., dropping tablet into cista; on r., LONGIN . III . V. *S.* 935. *B.* 10 .. .. 10·50

275 *Q. Sicinius* and *C. Coponius* (49-48 B.C.) Diad. hd. of Apollo r., Q . SICINIVS before, III . VIR behind, star below. ℞. C . COPONIVS PR . S . C. Club of Hercules with lion's scalp between bow and arrow. *S.* 939. *B.* 1 9·00

276 *Decimus Postumius Albinus Bruti f.* (49-48 B.C.) A . POSTVMIVS COS. Bare hd. of the consul A. Postumius Albinus r. ℞. ALBINV./BRVTI F. in corn-wreath. *S.* 943a. *B.* 14 .. .. 15·00

277 *C. Vibius C.f. C.n. Pansa* (48 B.C.) Mask of Pan r., PANSA below. ℞. Jupiter Axurus seated l., holding patera and sceptre; on l., IOVIS AXVR.; on r., C . VIBIVS C.F.C.N. *S.* 947. *B.* 18 .. .. 12·50

278 *L. Hostilius Saserna* (48 B.C.) Hd. of Vercingetorix r., Gaulish shield behind. ℞. Naked warrior in biga r., L . HOSTILIVS above, SASERN. below. *S.* 952. *B.* 2 .. .. 50·00

279 *L. Hostilius Saserna* (48 B.C.) Hd. of Gallia r., Gaulish trumpet behind. ℞. Diana stg. facing, holding spear, stag at feet; on r., L . HOSTILIVS; on l., SASERNA. *S.* 953. *B.* 4. **Plate 4** .. .. 17·50

280 *L. Plautius Plancus* (47 B.C.) Mask of Medusa facing, L . PLAVTIVS below. ℞. Aurora flying r., leading the four horses of the Sun, PLANCVS below. *S.* 959b. *B.* 14. **Plate 4** .. .. 17·50

281   283

Very Fine

281   *L. Papius Celsus* (46 B.C.)   Hd. of Juno Sospita r.   ℞.   She-wolf stg. r.,
      lighting fire; on r., eagle fanning flames; above, CELSVS III . VIR; in ex.,
      L . PAPIVS.   *S.* 964.   *B.* 2 ..   ..   £10·50
282   *Mn. Cordius Rufus* (46 B.C.)   Jugate hds. of the Dioscuri r., RVFVS III . VIR
      behind and below.   ℞.   Venus Verticordia stg. l., holding scales and
      sceptre, Cupid on shoulder; on r., M̂N . CORDIVS.   *S.* 976.   *B.* 2.
      Plate 4   ..   ..   9·00
283   — Corinthian helmet r., surmounted by owl; on l., RVFVS.   ℞.   MN .
      CORDIVS around aegis with hd. of Medusa in centre.   *S.* 978.   *B.* 4   ..   15·00

                284   286

284   *T. Carisius* (45 B.C.)   Hd. of Juno Moneta r., MONETA behind.   ℞.
      Cap of Vulcan over anvil between tongs and hammer; above, T . CARISIVS.
      S. 982.   *B.* 1 ..   ..   12·50
285   — Hd. of Aphrodisian Sibyl r.   ℞.   Sphinx seated r., T . CARISIVS
      before, III . VIR. in ex.   *S.* 983.   *B.* 10   **Plate 4**   ..   ..   12·50
286   *C. Considius Paetus* (45 B.C.)   Laur. hd. of Apollo r., A behind.   ℞.
      Curule chair, C . CONSIDI above, PAETI in ex.   *S.* 991.   *B.* 2   ..   ..   9·00
287   *Q. Caecilius Metellus Pius Scipio* (47-46 B.C.)   Q . METEL . PIVS.   Laur.
      hd. of Jupiter r.   ℞.   Elephant walking r., SCIPIO above, IMP. in ex.
      S. 1046.   *B.* 47   ..   ..   12·50
288   *M. Porcius Cato* (47-46 B.C.)   M . CATO PRO PR.   Bust of Liberty r., R̂OMA
      behind.   ℞.   Victory seated r., holding wreath and palm, VICTRIX in ex.
      S. 1053a.   *Seaby* 10a..   ..   ..   8·00

                287   289

289   — **Æ quinarius.**   M . CATO PRO PR.   Young male hd. r.   ℞.   As pre-
      vious, but patera instead of wreath.   *S.* 1054.   *B.* 11   ..   ..   ..   8·00

44-28 B.C. Very Fine

Most of the coins of this period are to be found in the Imperatorial list.

290   *L. Mussidius Longus* (42 B.C.)   Veiled hd. of Concord r., CONCORDIA behind.   ℞.   L. MVSSIDIVS LONGVS.   Clasped hands holding caduceus. S. 1092.   B. 5 ..   ..   £12·50

291   — Rad. bust of Sol facing.   ℞. — Two statues of Venus Cloacina on platform inscribed CLOACIN.   S. 1094.   B. 7   ..   ..   ..   17·50

292   *L. Livineius Regulus* (42 B.C.)   Bare hd. of the praetor L. Regulus r.   ℞. Curule chair between six fasces, L . LIVINEIVS above, REGVLVS in ex. S. 1110.   B. 11   ..   ..   15·00

293   — *Obv.* Similar.   ℞.   Modius between two ears of corn, L . LIVINEIVS above, REGVLVS in ex.   S. 1111.   B. 13.   **Plate 4**   ..   ..   17·50

291   294

294   *P. Clodius* (41 B.C.)   Laur. hd. of Apollo r., lyre behind.   ℞.   Diana Lucifera stg. facing, holding two long torches; on r., P . CLODIVS; on l., M . F.   S. 1117.   B. 15   ..   ..   ..   8·00

295   *C. Clodius C.f. Vestalis* (39 B.C.)   Bust of Flora r., C . CLODIVS before, C . F. behind.   ℞.   Vestal virgin, Claudia Quinta, seated l., holding bowl; on r., VESTALIS.   S. 1135.   B. 13.   **Plate 4**   ..   ..   11·00

296   *C. Vibius Varus* (39 B.C.)   Hd. of Bacchus r.   ℞.   Panther springing l. towards altar; in ex., C . VIBIVS; on r., VARVS.   S. 1138.   B. 24   ..   10·50

296A   — *A aureus.*   Laur. hd. of Apollo r.   ℞.   Venus stg. l. beside column, holding mirror; on l., C . VIBIVS; on r., VARVS.   S. 1137 ..   ..   300·00

296   297

297   *P. Accoleius Lariscolus* (37 B.C.)   P . ACCOLEIVS LARISCOLVS.   Bust of Acca Larentia r.   ℞.   The three Nymphae Querquetulanae stg. facing. S. 1148.   B. 1 ..   ..   15·00

298   *Petillius Capitolinus* (37 B.C.)   PETILLIVS CAPITOLINVS.   Eagle stg. r. on thunderbolt.   ℞.   Front view of hexastyle temple.   S. 1150.   B. 2. **Plate 4**   ..   ..   10·50

For full details of all silver coins of these periods, and illustrations of most of them see "Roman Silver Coins" by H. A. Seaby.

Vol. 1, the Republic to Augustus, £2·00.

ROMAN IMPERATORIAL COINS

References: C. = Cohen, *Médailles Impériales.*

S. = Sydenham, *The Coinage of the Roman Republic.*

POMPEY THE GREAT

300

(Cnaeus Pompeius Magnus). Born 106 B.C., *and became one of Rome's most successful generals. It was a campaign in Africa in* 81 B.C. *that earned him the surname of Magnus and ten years later he pacified Spain. In* 67 B.C. *he cleared the Mediterranean of pirates, and in* 60 B.C. *joined with Caesar and Crassus to form the first triumvirate. Opposed Caesar in the Civil War, and was defeated by him at Pharsalus: subsequently fled to Egypt, and was murdered on landing there in* 48 B.C.

Fine

299 **N aureus.** MAGNVS. Hd. of Africa r., wearing elephant's skin; all within wreath. ℞. PRO COS. Pompey in quadriga r. *C.* 19. *S.* 1028 *Extr. rare*

300 **Æ denarius.** MAG . PIVS IMP . ITER. Bare hd. of Pompey r; behind, capis; before, lituus. ℞. PRÆF. above, CLAS . ET ORÆ/MARIT . EX S . C. in ex. Neptune stg. l. between the brothers Anapias and Amphinomus carrying their parents on their shoulders. *C.* 17. *S.* 1344 .. .. £30·00

301 NEPTVNI behind similar hd., dolphin below, trident before. ℞. Q . NASIDIVS. Galley r. *C.* 20. *S.* 1350 .. .. 45·00

302 **Æ as.** MAGN. Janiform hd. of Pompey. ℞. PIVS IMP. Prow r. *C.* 16. *S.* 1044a .. .. *Fair* £12·50

JULIUS CAESAR

304A

(Caius Julius Caesar). Born 100 B.C., *and as a young man was opposed to the powerful dictator Sulla. He soon became a prominent figure amongst the aristocracy of Rome and in* 59 B.C. *he was elected consul after having formed the first triumvirate with Pompey and Crassus. The years* 58-50 B.C. *were spent in almost continuous campaigning in Gaul and*

it was during this period that Caesar made his two expeditions to Britain (55 and 54 B.C.). He defeated Pompey at Pharsalus in 48 B.C. and spent the next two years defeating the remnants of the Pompeian party. He then returned to Rome undisputed master of the Roman world, but after only a short period of supreme power a conspiracy against his life was formed and he was assassinated on the Ides (15th) of March, 44 B.C.

Fine

303 **N aureus.** C . CAESAR COS . TER. Veiled hd. of Pietas r. R . A . HIRTIVS
PR. Lituus, vase and axe. *C.* 2. *S.* 1017 .. .. £75·00

304 **R denarius.** COS . TERT . DICT . ITER. Hd. of Ceres r. R . AVGVR
PONT . MAX. Sacrificial implements; in field, D or M. *C.* 4. *S.* 1023-4 12·50

304A CAESAR PARENS PATRIAE. Laur. and veiled hd. of Caesar r. R . C .
COSSVTIVS MARIDIANVS in form of cross, A.A.A.F.F. in angles. *C.* 8.
S. 1069 .. .. 65·00

305 *Obv.* No legend. Diad. hd. of Venus r. R . CAESAR. Aeneas advancing l., carrying Anchises and palladium. *C.* 12. *S.* 1013.. .. .. 10·00

306 *Obv.* Similar, but with Cupid behind hd. of Venus. R . CAESAR.
Two captives seated at foot of trophy. *C.* 13. *S.* 1014 .. .. .. 12·50

307 CAESAR DICT . PERPETVO. Laur. and veiled hd. of Caesar r. R . P .
SEPVLLIVS MACER. Venus stg. l., holding Victory and sceptre. *C.* 39.
S. 1074 .. .. 35·00

308 *Obv.* No legend. Laur. hd. of Caesar r. R . TI . SEMPRONIVS GRACCVS
Q . DESIG. Standard, legionary-eagle, plough and sceptre; in field, S . C.
C. 48. *S.* 1128 .. .. 45·00

309 CAESAR. Elephant walking r., trampling on serpent. R . No legend.
Sacrificial implements. *C.* 49. *S.* 1006. **Plate 5** .. .. .. 8·00

310 **Æ dupondius** (?). CAESAR DIC . TER. Winged bust of Victory r. R .
C . CLOVI . PRAEF. Minerva advancing l., holding trophy, spears and shield.
C. 7. *S.* 1025 .. .. 15·00

311 *J. Caesar and M. Antony,* **R denarius.** CAESAR DIC. Laur. hd. of
Caesar r. R . M . ANTON . IMP. Bare hd. of Antony r. *C.* 2. *S.* 1165 50·00

306   313

313 *J. Caesar and Augustus,* **R denarius.** DIVOS IVLIVS DIVI F. Their hds.
face to face. R . M . AGRIPPA COS./DESIG. in two lines across field. *C.* 5.
S. 1330 .. .. 125·00

314 — **Æ sestertius** (?). DIVOS IVLIVS. Laur. hd. of Caesar r. R .
CAESAR DIVI F. Bare hd. of Augustus r. *C.* 3. *S.* 1335 *Fair* £12·50
See also no. 421.

BRUTUS

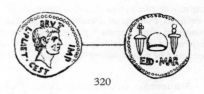

320

(Marcus Junius Brutus). Born 85 B.C., and supported Pompey in the Civil War. After Pharsalus he was pardoned by Caesar, but despite this indulgence he took part in the plot against Caesar's life and after the assassination he withdrew to Macedonia. He joined forces with Cassius but they were defeated by Antony and Octavian at Philippi and Brutus took his own life (42 B.C.).

Fine

315 **N aureus.** M . SERVILIVS LEG. Laur. hd. of Liberty r. R. Q . CAEPIO
BRVTVS IMP. Trophy. *C.* 9. *S.* 1314 .. ..£300·00

316 BRVTVS IMP. Bare hd. of Brutus r.; all within wreath. R. CASCA LONGVS.
Trophy with two prows and arms at base. *C.* 14. *S.* 1297a *Illustrated
on p.* 11 .. .. *Extr. rare*

317 **R denarius.** CASCA LONGVS. Laur. hd. of Neptune r. R. BRVTVS
IMP. Victory walking r. on broken sceptre. *C.* 3. *S.* 1298 .. 30·00

318 LEIBERTAS. Bare hd. of Liberty r. R. CAEPIO BRVTVS PRO COS. Lyre
between plectrum and branch. *C.* 5. *S.* 1287 .. .. 25·00

319 BRVTVS. Axe, simpulum and knife. R. LENTVLVS SPINT. Jug and
lituus. *C.* 6. *S.* 1310 .. .. 25·00

320 BRVT . IMP . L . PLAET . CEST. Bare hd. of Brutus r. R. EID . MAR. Cap
of Liberty between two daggers. *C.* 15. *S.* 1301 .. .. .. 500·00

321 **R quinarius.** L . SESTI PRO Q. Quaestorial chair, staff and modius. R . Q .
CAEPIO BRVTVS PRO COS. Tripod between simpulum and apex. *C.* 13.
S. 1292 .. .. 25·00
See also nos. 263 *and* 264.

CASSIUS

(C. Cassius Longinus). One of the assassins of Julius Caesar, he withdrew to Syria after the dictator's death and later joined forces with Brutus. He committed suicide during the battle of Philippi (42 B.C.)

322 **N aureus.** C . CASSI . IMP . LEIBERTAS. Diad. hd. of Liberty r. R.
LENTVLVS SPINT. Jug and lituus. *C.* 3. *S.* 1306 .. .. .. 300·00

323 **R denarius.** Similar. *C.* 4. *S.* 1307 .. .. 20·00

AHENOBARBUS

(Cn. Domitius Ahenobarbus). A member of the Pompeian party, he was pardoned by Caesar, but after the latter's death he followed Brutus to Macedonia. He was placed in command of a fleet and won a decisive victory on the day of the first battle of Philippi, for which he was saluted Imperator. After the deaths of Brutus and Cassius he became a pirate, but in 40 B.C. he was reconciled to M. Antony, who made him governor of Bithynia. He deserted to Octavian shortly before the battle of Actium and died soon afterwards.

324 **N aureus.** AHENOBAR. Bare hd. of Cn. Domitius Ahenobarbus r. ℞. CN . DOMITIVS L . F . IMP. View of tetrastyle temple, showing front and l. hand side wall; above, NEPT. *C.* 1. *S.* 1176 .. .. .. *Extr. rare*

Fine

325 **℞ denarius.** — Bare hd. of L. Domitius Ahenobarbus r. ℞. CN . DOMITIVS IMP. Prow r., surmounted by trophy. *C.* —. *S.* 1177 .. £45·00
See also no. 340.

LABIENUS

Q. Labienus joined Brutus and was sent into Parthia to seek the help of Orodes. In company with Pacorus, the son of Orodes, he overran Syria and Palestine but was eventually defeated by P. Ventidius, the legate of Antony.

326 **N aureus.** Q . LABIENVS PARTHICVS IMP. Bare hd. of Labienus r. ℞. No legend. Horse stg. r., with bridle and saddle. *C.* 1. *S.* 1356 *Extr. rare*
327 **℞ denarius.** Similar. *C.* 2. *S.* 1357 .. .. 650·00

SEXTUS POMPEY

330

Sextus Pompeius Magnus was the younger son of Pompey the Great by his third wife Mucia. He fought along with his brother against Caesar at Munda, and managed to escape with his life. After Caesar's death he gathered a fleet, became master of the Mediterranean, and seized Sicily. He was eventually defeated by the fleet of Octavian and fled from Sicily to Asia, where he was taken prisoner and put to death (35 B.C.)

328 **℞ denarius.** MAG . PIVS IMP . ITER. Hd. of Neptune r. ℞. PRÆF. CLAS . ET ORÆ MARIT . EX S . C. Naval trophy. *C.* 1. *S.* 1347.. .. 25·00
329 MAG . PIVS IMP . ITER. The Pharos of Messana with galley in front. ℞. PRÆF . CLAS . ET ORÆ MARIT . EX S . C. The monster Scylla. *C.* 2. *S.* 1348 .. .. 25·00
330 *Sextus Pompey, Pompey and Cnaeus Pompey,* **N aureus.** — Bare hd. of Sextus Pompey r.; all within wreath. ℞. — Bare heads of Pompey and Cnaeus Pompey face to face. *C.* 1. *S.* 1346 .. .. .. 500·00

LEPIDUS

331

(*M. Aemilius Lepidus*). *Junior partner in the Second Triumvirate with Octavian and Antony, having been Caesar's colleague in the consulship in* 46 B.C. *After Philippi he was given the governorship of Africa, but later, after an attempt to acquire Sicily for himself, he was deprived of all his powers and offices except that of Pontifex Maximus which he held until his death in* 13 B.C.

Fine

331   *N* **aureus.**   M . LEPIDVS III . VIR R . P . C.   Bare hd. of Lepidus l.   ℞.
L . MVSSIDIVS T . F . LONGVS IIII . VIR A . P . F.   Mars stg. r., holding
spear and parazonium.   *C.* 2.   *S.* 1099   ..   ..   *Extr. rare*

332   *Lepidus and M. Antony,* *N* **aureus.** — Bare hd. of Lepidus r.   ℞.
M . ANTONIVS III . VIR R . P . C.   Bare hd. of M. Antony r.   *C.* 1.   *S.* 1161

Extr. rare

333   — **Æ denarius.**   M . LEPID . IMP. Simpulum, sprinkler, axe and apex.
℞.   M . ANTON . IMP.   Lituus, jug and raven.   *C.* 2.   *S.* 1156..   .. £45·00

334   — **Æ quinarius.**   Similar, but with legends LEP . IMP. and M . ANT . IMP.
C. 3.   *S.* 1158*a*   ..   ..   12·50

335   *Lepidus and Augustus,* *N* **aureus.**   LEPIDVS PONT . MAX . III . V . R . P . C.
Bare hd. of Lepidus r.   ℞.   CAESAR IMP . III . VIR R . P . C.   Bare hd.
of Augustus r.   *C.* 1.   *S.* 1323 *note*   ..   ..   *Unique*

336   — **Æ denarius.**   Similar.   *C.* 2.   *S.* 1323   ..   ..   75·00
See also nos. 257 *and* 258.

MARK ANTONY

339

Marcus Antonius was born in 83 B.C. *and was already a cavalry commander at the age of* 22. *He joined Julius Caesar in Gaul and was appointed tribune of the people and augur in* 49 B.C. *and consul in* 48 B.C. *In* 43 B.C. *he formed the Second Triumvirate with Octavian and Lepidus. After the battle of Philippi he went to Asia, his province, where he met Cleopatra and was immediately captivated by her. Ultimately he quarrelled with Octavian who defeated him at the battle of Actium. He fled to Egypt with Cleopatra and committed suicide at Alexandria in* 30 B.C.

337   *N* **aureus.**   ANT . AVG . IMP . III . V . R . P . C.   Bare hd. of Antony r.
℞.   PIETAS COS.   Pietas stg. l., holding rudder and cornucopiae, stork
at feet.   *C.* 67.   *S.* 1173   ..   ..   400·00

338 **Æ denarius.** M . ANTO . COS . III . IMP . IIII. Hd. of Jupiter Ammon r. R̶. ANTONIO AVG . SCARPVS IMP. Victory advancing r. *C.* 1. *S.* 1280 £30·00

339 ANTON . AVG . IMP . III . COS . DES . III . III . V . R . P . C. Bare hd. of Antony r. R̶. ANTONIVS/AVG . IMP . III . in two lines across field. *C.* 2. *S.* 1209 .. .. 45·00

339A ANT . AVG . III . VIR . R . P . C. Galley r. R̶. CHORTIS SPECVLATORVM. Three standards. *C.* 6. *S.* 1214 .. 30·00

340 ANT . IMP . III . VIR R . P . C. Bare hd. of Antony r. R̶. CN . DOMIT . AHENOBARBVS IMP. Prow r.; above, star. *C.* 10. *S.* 1179 .. .. 45·00

341   342

341 M . ANTONI IMP. — R̶. III . VIR R . P . C. Hd. of Sol facing in temple of two columns. *C.* 12. *S.* 1168 .. .. 25·00

342 M . ANTONIVS M . F . M . N . AVGVR IMP . TERT. Antony as priest stg. r., holding lituus. R̶. III . VIR R . P . C. COS . DESIG . ITER . ET TER. Rad. hd. of Sol r. *C.* 13. *S.* 1199 .. .. 15·00

343 ANT . AVG . III . VIR R . P . C. Galley r. R̶. LEG . II. Legionary eagle between two standards. *C.* 27. *S.* 1216 .. .. 7·50

344 Similar, but LEG . VI. *C.* 33. *S.* 1223. **Plate 5** .. .. .. 7·50

345 Similar, but LEG . XII . ANTIQVAE. *C.* 40. *S.* 1231 .. .. .. 20·00

346 Similar, but LEG . XXI. *C.* 58. *S.* 1244 .. .. 7·50
      Other legionary denarii were struck from LEG . PRI . to LEG . XXIII.

347 *Obv.* As 339. R̶. M . SILANVS AVG./Q . PRO COS. in two lines across field. *C.* 71. *S.* 1208 .. .. 45·00

348 **Æ quinarius.** III . VIR R . P . C. Veiled and diad. hd. of Concord r. R̶. M . ANTON . C . CAESAR. Two clasped hands holding caduceus. *C.* 67. *S.* 1195 .. .. 10·00

349 M . ANT . IMP. Lituus, jug and raven. R̶. No legend. Victory stg. r., crowning trophy. *C.* 82. *S.* 1159 .. .. 10·00

350 *Restitution by M. Aurelius and L. Verus,* **Æ denarius.** ANTONIVS AVGVR III . VIR R . P . C. Galley l. R̶. ANTONINVS ET VERVS AVG . REST. Legionary eagle between two standards; in lower field, LEG . VI. *C.* 83 .. .. 15·00

351 *M. Antony and Augustus,* **Æ aureus.** M . ANT . IMP . AVG . III . VIR R . P . C . M . BARBAT . Q . P. Bare hd. of Antony r. R̶. CAESAR IMP . PONT . III . VIR R . P . C. Bare hd. of Augustus r. *C.* 7. *S.* 1180 .. 300·00

352 — **Æ denarius.** Similar. *C.* 8. *S.* 1181 .. .. .. 25·00

353 *M. Antony, Augustus and Octavia,* **Æ tripondius.** M . ANT . IMP . COS . DESIG . ITER . ET TERT . III . VIR R . P . C. Jugate hds. of Antony and Augustus r., facing hd. of Octavia l. R̶. M . OPPIVS CAPITO PRO PR . PRAEF . CLAS . F . C. Galley r. *C.* 1 .. .. .. *Fair* £35·00

FULVIA

355

Fine

First wife of M. Antony whom she married in 44 B.C. She died at Sicyon in 40 B.C.

354 **Æ quinarius.** III . VIR R . P . C. Hd. of Victory r., with features
resembling Fulvia. ℞. ANTONI IMP . A . XLI. Lion walking r. *C.* 3.
S. 1163 .. .. £15·00

355 Similar, but with no *obv.* legend and with *rev.* legend LVGVDVNI A . XL.
C. 4. *S.* 1160.. .. .. 20·00

The numerals on the rev. *refer to Antony's age.*

MARK ANTONY JUNIOR

*The son of M. Antony and Fulvia. He was executed at Alexandria after his father's
death by the orders of Octavian.*

356 *M. Antony and M. Antony Junior,* *N* **aureus.** ANTON . AVG . IMP . III .
COS . DES . III . III . V . R . P . C. Bare hd. of M. Antony r. ℞. M .
ANTONIVS M . F . F. Bare hd. of M. Antony Junior r. *C.* 1. *S.* 1207 *Extr. rare*

OCTAVIA

357

*Sister of Octavian and the second wife of M. Antony whom she married in 40 B.C. She
was repudiated in 32 B.C. by Antony who had left her for Cleopatra. She died in 11 B.C.*

357 *M. Antony and Octavia,* *N* **aureus.** M . ANTONIVS M . F . M . N . AVGVR
IMP . TER. Bare hd. of M. Antony r. ℞. COS . DESIGN . ITER . ET TER .
III . VIR R . P . C. Hd. of Octavia r. *C.* 1. *S.* 1200 .. .. *Extr. rare*

358 — **Æ cistophorus.** M . ANTONIVS IMP . COS . DESIG . ITER . ET TERT.
Hd. of M. Antony r., bound with ivy; all within wreath. ℞. III . VIR
R . P . C. Hd. of Octavia r. on cista mystica between two interlaced
serpents. *C.* 2. *S.* 1197 .. .. 50·00

359 M. *Antony and Octavia*, **Æ cistophorus.** *Obv.* Legend as previous. Jugate hds. of Antony and Octavia r. Ŗ. — Bacchus stg. l. on cista mystica between two interlaced serpents. *C.* 3. *S.* 1198 .. .. £65·00

Fair

360 — **Æ sestertius.** M . ANT . IMP . TER . COS . DES . ITER . ET TER . III . VIR R . P . C. Hds. of Antony and Octavia face to face. Ŗ. L . ATRATINVS AVGVR PRAEF . CLASS . F . C. Man and woman in quadriga of hippocamps r. *C.* 4. .. .. 30·00

361 — **Æ dupondius.** C . FONTEIVS CAPITO PRO PR. Jugate hds. of Antony and Octavia r. Ŗ. M . ANT . IMP . COS . DESIG . ITER . ET TER . III . VIR R . P . C. Galley r. *C.* 10 .. .. 25·00

362 — **Æ as.** M . ANT . IMP . TER . COS . DESIG . ITER . ET TER . III . VIR R . P . C. Similar. Ŗ. M . OPPIVS CAPITO PRO PR . PRAEF . CLASS . F . C. Galley r. *C.* 11 .. .. 15·00
See also no. 353.

Fine

CLEOPATRA

Eldest daughter of Ptolemy Auletes, king of Egypt, whom she succeeded as joint ruler with her brothers Ptolemy XIII and XIV: the former died and the latter was afterwards driven from the throne and subsequently put to death. Cleopatra is credited with having had as her lovers both Caesar and Antony: the association with the latter is certain. After the battle of Actium she fled to Alexandria where, after Antony's death, she ended her own life in 30 B.C., being then in her thirty-ninth year.

363 M. *Antony and Cleopatra*, **Æ denarius.** ANTONI ARMENIA DEVICTA. Bare hd. of Antony r. Ŗ. CLEOPATRAE REGINAE REGVM FILIORVM REGVM. Diad. and dr. bust of Cleopatra r. *C.* 1. *S.* 1210 .. .. .. 150·00

82

CAIUS ANTONIUS

Brother of Mark Antony who gave him the government of Macedonia after the death of Julius Caesar. In 43 B.C. he fell into the hands of Brutus who put him to death the following year in revenge for the execution of Cicero.

Fine

364 Æ**R denarius.** C . ANTONIVS M . F . PRO COS. Bust of the Genius of Macedonia r., wearing chlamys and cap. R. PONTIFEX. Two simpula and axe. *C.* 1. *S.* 1286 .. .. £250·00

LUCIUS ANTONIUS

Youngest brother of Mark Antony, was consul in 41 B.C., when he engaged in war against Octavian at the instigation of Fulvia, his brother's wife. After an unsuccessful defence of the town of Perusia, his life was spared, and he was later appointed by Octavian to command in Iberia.

365 *M. Antony and L. Antony*, ў **aureus.** M . ANT . IMP . AVG . III . VIR R .

P . C . M . NERVA PROQ . P. Bare hd. of M. Antony r., R. L . ANTONIVS COS. Bare hd. of L. Antony r. *C.* 1. *S.* 1184 .. .. .. *Extr. rare*

366 — Æ**R denarius.** Similar. *C.* 2. *S.* 1185 .. .. 65·00

Strictly speaking, the earliest issues of Augustus (43-27 B.C.) should be included in this section. To avoid confusion, however, it has been thought best to list all the coins of the first Roman emperor together under the Imperial section.

For full details of **all** the silver coins of the period see:

ROMAN SILVER COINS, *by H. A. Seaby.*

Vol. I, The Republic to Augustus, £2·00.

ROMAN IMPERIAL COINAGE

References: C.   = Cohen, *Médailles Impériales.*

   R.I.C.   = Mattingly and Sydenham, and others, *Roman Imperial Coinage.*

   B.M.C.   = *British Museum Catalogue of Coins of The Roman Empire.*

   B.M.C.G.= *British Museum Catalogues of Greek Coins* (for local coins).

AUGUSTUS

27 B.C. – A.D. 14

384

Caius Octavius Thurinus was born in Rome in 63 B.C. *and was the great-nephew of Julius Caesar who adopted him as his heir shorty before his death. In 43* B.C. *Caius Julius Caesar Octavianus, as he was now called, formed the second triumvirate with the other Caesarian leaders, M. Antony and Lepidus. The Republican leaders, Brutus and Cassius, were defeated at Philippi (42* B.C.*) and the victorious triumvirs divided the Roman world amongst themselves. Lepidus had little ability and soon disappeared from the political scene. Relations between Octavian and Antony were always strained and at length they declared war. Antony was defeated at the battle of Actium (31* B.C.*) and his suicide the following year left Octavian master of the Roman world at the age of thirty-three.*

   The next few years he spent in completely reorganizing the Constitution, and in 27 B.C. *he was given the name " Augustus " by which he is best known to history. His long reign was a period of peace and recovery for a world which had been torn by internal wars for so many years. Public works were undertaken on a large scale and he could justly claim that he had "found Rome of brick and left it marble". He died in* A.D. *14 at the age of seventy-seven and was succeeded by his step-son, Tiberius.*

   Mints (from 27 B.C.):—Rome, Emerita, Caesaraugusta (?), Colonia Patricia (?), Lugdunum, Ephesus, Pergamum (?).

                                                        Fine

367 **Aʹ aureus.** AVGVSTVS DIVI F. Laur. hd., r. ℞. C . CAES . AVGVS . F. Caius Caesar galloping r.; in background, legionary eagle between two standards. *C.* 39. *R.I.C.* 348. *B.M.C.* 498   ..   ..£120·00

368 CAESAR AVGVSTVS DIVI F. PATER PATRIAE. Laur. hd., r. ℞. C . L . CAESARES AVGVSTI F . COS . DESIG . PRINC . IVVENT. Caius and Lucius Caesars stg. facing, shields and spears between them. *C.* 42. *R.I.C.* 350. *B.M.C.* 513   ..   ..   95·00

369 **Aʹ quinarius.** AVGVSTVS DIVI F. Laur. hd., r. ℞. TR . POT . XVI. Victory seated r. on globe, holding wreath. *C.* 313. *R.I.C.* 345. *B.M.C* 496   ..   ..   175·00

Titles and Powers, 27 B.C. – A.D. 14

B.C.	Tribunician Power	Imperatorial Acclamation	Consulship	Other Titles
27			COS.VII.	AVGVSTVS.
26			COS.VIII.	
25		IMP.VIII.	COS.VIIII.	
24			COS.X.	
23	TR.P.		COS.XI.	
22	TR.P. – TR.P.II			
21	TR.P.II – III.			
20	TR.P.III – IIII.	IMP.VIIII.		
19	TR.P.IIII. – V.			
18	TR.P.V. – VI.			
17	TR.P.VI. – VII.			
16	TR.P.VII. – VIII.			
15	TR.P.VIII. – VIIII.	IMP.X.		
14	TR.P.VIIII. – X.			
13	TR.P.X. – XI.			
12	TR.P.XI. – XII.	IMP.XI.		P.M.
11	TR.P.XII. – XIII.	IMP.XII.		
10	TR.P.XIII. – XIIII.			
9	TR.P.XIIII. – XV.	IMP.XIII.		
8	TR.P.XV. – XVI.	IMP.XIIII.		
7	TR.P.XVI. – XVII.			
6	TR.P.XVII. – XVIII.			
5	TR.P.XVIII. – XVIIII.		COS.XII.	
4	TR.P.XVIIII. – XX.			
3	TR.P.XX – XXI.			
2	TR.P.XXI – XXII.		COS.XIII.	P.P.
1	TR.P.XXII. – XXIII.			
A.D.				
1	TR.P.XXIII. – XXIIII.	IMP.XV.		
2	TR.P.XXIIII. – XXV.			
3	TR.P.XXV. – XXVI.			
4	TR.P.XXVI. – XXVII.	IMP.XVI.(?)		
5	TR.P.XXVII. – XXVIII.	IMP.XVII.		
6	TR.P.XXVIII. – XXVIIII.			
7	TR.P.XXVIIII. – XXX.	IMP.XVIII.(?)		
8	TR.P.XXX – XXXI.	IMP.XVIIII.		
9	TR.P.XXXI. – XXXII.			
10	TR.P.XXXII. – XXXIII.			
11	TR.P.XXXIII. – XXXIIII.	IMP.XX.		
12	TR.P.XXXIIII. – XXXV.	IMP.XXI.		
13	TR.P.XXXV. – XXXVI.			
14	TR.P.XXXVI. – XXXVII.			

Augustus received the tribunician power on June 27th, 23 B.C., and it was subsequently renewed each year on that date.

		Fine
370	Æ **cistophorus**. IMP . CAESAR. Bare hd., r. ℞. AVGVSTVS. Sphinx r. C. 31. R.I.C. 14. B.M.C. 701	£75·00
371	Similar. ℞. AVGVSTVS. Six ears of corn. C. 32. R.I.C. 13. B.M.C. 697	37·50
372	IMP . CAESAR DIVI F . COS . VI . LIBERTATIS P . R . VINDEX. Laur. hd., r. ℞. PAX. Pax stg. l., holding caduceus; on r., cista mystica: all within wreath. C. 218. R.I.C. 10. B.M.C. 691	50·00

The following coins, nos. 373-400, are all denarii, and all have as obverse type the hd. of Augustus either bare or laur., unless otherwise stated.   There are many varieties of obverse legend but the following are the commonest forms:—

    A. AVGVSTVS.
    B. AVGVSTVS DIVI F.
    C. CAESAR AVGVSTVS.
    D. CAESAR AVGVSTVS DIVI F . PATER PATRIAE.

N *indicates that there is no obverse legend.*

Fine

373 **Æ denarius.** CAESAR COS . VI . ℞. AEGYPTO CAPTA. Crocodile r.
    C. 2. R.I.C. 19. B.M.C. 650 .. .. £50·00

374 N. ℞. AVGVSTVS. Capricorn l., bearing cornucopiae on back and
    holding globe and rudder. C. 25. R.I.C. 267. B.M.C. 345 .. .. 25·00

375 Similar to 367. C. 40. R.I.C. 348. B.M.C. 500 .. .. .. 25·00

376 Similar to 368. C. 43. R.I.C. 350. B.M.C. 519 .. .. .. 10·00

377   380

377 IMP. Helmeted hd. of Mars r. ℞. CAESAR on circular shield behind
    which are two spears. C. 44. R.I.C. 8. B.M.C. 644 .. .. .. 25·00

378 N. ℞. CAESAR AVGVSTVS S. P. Q. R. Circular shield, inscribed CL . V.,
    between two laurel-branches. C. 51. R.I.C. 270. B.M.C. 354.. .. 27·50

379 N. Bust of Victory r. ℞. CAESAR DIVI F. Augustus as Neptune stg. l.,
    holding acrostolium and sceptre. C. 60. R.I.C. 1. B.M.C. 615 .. 22·50

380 N. ℞. CAESAR DIVI F. Mercury seated r. on rock, playing lyre. C. 61.
    R.I.C. 25. B.M.C. 596 .. .. 25·00

381 S . P . Q . R . IMP . CAESARI AVG . COS . XI . TR . POT . VI. ℞. CIVIB . ET
    SIGN . MILIT. A PART . RECVP. Triumphal arch surmounted by Augustus
    in quadriga between two Parthians. C. 83. R.I.C. 311. B.M.C. 427
    note .. .. 50·00

382 IMP . CAESAR DIVI F . III . VIR ITER . R . P . C. ℞. COS . ITER . ET TER .
    DESIG. Statue of J. Caesar in tetrastyle temple inscribed DIVO IVL. C. 90.
    R.I.C., p. 42 .. .. 27·50

383 — ℞. — Sacrificial implements. C. 91. R.I.C., p. 42 .. .. 25·00

384 C. ℞. DIVVS IVLIVS. Comet. C. 98. R.I.C. 271. B.M.C. 323 .. 25·00

385 N. Laur. hd. of Apollo r. ℞. IMP . CAESAR. Augustus, as pontifex,
    ploughing r. C. 117. R.I.C. 6. B.M.C. 638 .. .. .. 20·00

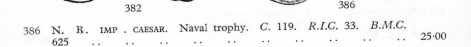

382   386

386 N. ℞. IMP . CAESAR. Naval trophy. C. 119. R.I.C. 33. B.M.C.
    625 .. .. 25·00

Fine

387   **Ʀ denarius.**   N.   Ʀ.   Temple surrounded by balustrade and inscribed IMP . CAESAR.*C.* 122.   *R.I.C.* 35.   *B.M.C.* 631   ..   ..   £27·50

388   N.   Ʀ.   IMP . CAESAR.   Statue of Augustus on rostral column.   *C.* 124. *R.I.C.* 38.   *B.M.C.* 633   ..   ..   25·00

389   B.   Ʀ.   IMP . X.   Bull butting l.   *C.* 141.   *R.I.C.* 327.   *B.M.C.* 458 ..   25·00

390   B.   Ʀ.   IMP . X . ACT.   Apollo stg. l., holding lyre and plectrum.   *C.* 144.   *R.I.C.* 328.   *B.M.C.* 461   ..   ..   27·50

391   CAESARI AVGVSTO.   Ʀ.   MAR . VLT.   Legionary eagle between two standards within circular hexastyle temple.   *C.* 190.   *R.I.C.* 287.   *B.M.C.* 373   ..   ..   27·50

392   C.   Ʀ.   OB   CIVIS   SERVATOS.   Oak-wreath.   *C.* 210.   *R.I.C.* 289. *B.M.C.* 376   ..   ..   22·50

393   D.   Ʀ.   PONTIF . MAXIM.   Livia seated r.   *C.* 223.   *R.I.C.* 352. *B.M.C.* 545   ..   ..   45·00

394   A.   Ʀ.   SIGNIS / PARTHICIS / RECEPTIS in three lines across field.   *C.* 257. *R.I.C.* 48.   *B.M.C.* 681   ..   ..   100·00

395   D.   Ʀ.   TI . CAESAR AVG . F . TR . POT . XV.   Tiberius in quadriga r. *C.* 300.   *R.I.C.* 355.   *B.M.C.* 509 ..   ..   35·00

396   C.   Ʀ.   C . ANTISTIVS REGINVS III . VIR.   Sacrificial implements.   *C.* 347. *R.I.C.* 179.   *B.M.C.* 119   ..   ..   35·00

397   A.   Ʀ.   L . CANINIVS GALLVS III . VIR.   Barbarian kneeling r., presenting standard.   *C.* 383.   *R.I.C.* 175.   *B.M.C.* 127   ..   ..   ..   35·00

398   IMP . CAESAR AVGVST.   Ʀ.   P . CARISIVS LEG . PRO PR.   View of the city of Emerita with gateway, inscribed EMERITA, in foreground.   *C.* 397. *R.I.C.* 229.   *B.M.C.* 289   ..   ..   40·00

399   S . C . OB R . P . CVM SALVT . IMP . CAESAR . AVG . CONS. around oak-wreath within which is hd. of Augustus facing.   Ʀ.   L . MESCINIVS RVFVS III . VIR.   Mars stg. l., on pedestal inscribed S . P . Q . R . V . S . PRO S . ET RED . AVG.   *C.* 465.   *R.I.C.* 159.   *B.M.C.* 90   ..   ..   ..   200·00

400   C.   Ʀ.   P . PETRON . TVRPILIAN . III . VIR.   Pegasus r.   *C.* 491.   *R.I.C.* 111.   *B.M.C.* 23.   **Plate 5** ..   ..   50·00

401   **Ʀ quinarius.**   CAESAR IMP . VII.   Bare hd., r.   Ʀ.   ASIA RECEPTA. Victory stg. l. on cista mystica.   *C.* 14.   *R.I.C.* 18.   *B.M.C.* 647   ..   10·50

402   AVGVST.   Bare hd., l.   Ʀ.   P . CARISI . LEG.   Victory stg. r., crowning trophy.   *C.* 387.   *R.I.C.* 221.   *B.M.C.* 295   ..   ..   ..   15·00

401   403

403   **Æ sestertius.**   CAESAR AVGVSTVS DIVI F . PATER PATRIAE.   Laur. hd., r. Ʀ.   ROM . ET AVG.   The Altar of Lugdunum.   *C.* 236.   *R.I.C.* 361. *B.M.C.* 565   ..   ..   100·00

Fine

404 **Æ sestertius.** OB / CIVIS / SERVATOS. Oak-wreath between two laurel-branches. ℞. Q . AELIVS L . F . LAMIA III . VIR A.A.A.F.F. around large S . C. *C.* 341. *R.I.C.* 93. *B.M.C.* 175 .. .. £17·50

405 — ℞. CN . PISO CN . F . III . VIR A.A.A.F.F. around large S . C. *C.* 377. *R.I.C.* 70. *B.M.C.* 134 .. .. 17·50

406 **Æ dupondius.** AVGVSTVS / TRIBVNIC. / POTEST. within oak-wreath. ℞. C . ASINIVS GALLVS III . VIR A.A.A.F.F. around large S . C. *C.* 368. *R.I.C.* 77. *B.M.C.* 158 .. .. 9·00

407 — ℞. C . CASSIVS CELER III . VIR A.A.A.F.F. around large S . C. *C.* 408. *R.I.C.* 80. *B.M.C.* 166 .. .. 9·00

408 (*Triumphal Coinage*) CAESAR AVGVST . PONT . MAX . TRIBVNIC . POT. Laur. hd. l., with Victory stg. l. behind. ℞. M . SALVIVS OTHO III . VIR A.A.A.F.F. around large S . C. *C.* 518. *R.I.C.* 191. *B.M.C.* 224 .. .. 120·00

409 **Æ as.** IMP . CAESAR DIVI F . AVGVSTVS IMP . XX. Bare hd., l. ℞. PONTIF . MAXIM . TRIBVN . POT . XXXIIII. around large S . C. *C.* 226. *R.I.C.* 219. *B.M.C.* 275 .. .. 9·00

410 CAESAR PONT . MAX. Laur. hd., r. ℞. As 403. *C.* 240. *R.I.C.* 360. *B.M.C.* 549 .. .. 8·00

411 CAESAR AVGV. TRIBVN . POTES. Bare hd., l. ℞. P . CARISIVS / LEG. / AVGVSTI in three lines across field. *C.* 392. *R.I.C.* 236. *B.M.C.* 298 *note* .. .. 15·00

412 CAESAR AVGVST . PONT . MAX . TRIBVNIC . POT. Bare hd., r. ℞. P . LVRIVS AGRIPPA III . VIR A.A.A.F.F. around large S . C. *C.* 445. *R.I.C.* 186. *B.M.C.* 209 .. .. 10·00

413 — ℞. M . MAECILIVS TVLLVS III . VIR A.A.A.F.F. around large S . C. *C.* 448. *R.I.C.* 192. *B.M.C.* 220 .. .. 10·00

414 **Æ semis.** As 403. *C.* 438. *R.I.C.* 363. *B.M.C.* 568.. .. .. 12·00

415 **Æ quadrans.** IMP . CAESAR. Laur. hd., r. ℞. AVGVSTVS. Eagle stg. facing, hd. l. *C.* 29. *R.I.C.* 357. *B.M.C.* 561 .. .. .. 10·00

416 LAMIA SILIVS ANNIVS. Lituus and simpulum. ℞. III . VIR A.A.A.F.F. around large S . C. *C.* 339. *R.I.C.* 181. *B.M.C.* 201 .. .. .. 3·75

417 — Cornucopiae between S. and C. ℞. III . VIR A.A.A.F.F. around anvil. *C.* 340. *R.I.C.* 182. *B.M.C.* 202 .. .. 3·75

418 GALVS MESSALLA III . VIR. Anvil. ℞. APRONIVS SISENNA A.A.A.F.F. around large S . C. *C.* 370. *R.I.C.* 211. *B.M.C.* 246 .. .. .. 3·75

419 P . BETILIENVS BASSVS around large S . C. ℞. III . VIR A.A.A.F.F. Anvil. *C.* 376. *R.I.C.* 215. *B.M.C.* 265 .. .. 3·75

420 PVLCHER TAVRVS REGVLVS. Clasped hands holding caduceus. ℞. III . VIR A.A.A.F.F. around large S . C. *C.* 413. *R.I.C.* 183. *B.M.C.* 204 3·75

421 *Augustus and J. Caesar,* **Æ denarius.** AVGVSTVS DIVI F. Bare hd., r. ℞. M . SANQVINIVS III . VIR. Laur. hd. of J. Caesar r., surmounted by comet. *C.* 1. *R.I.C.* 142. *B.M.C.* 71 .. .. 100·00

421A *Augustus and Tiberius,* **Ν aureus.** CAESAR AVGVSTVS DIVI F . PATER PATRIAE. Laur. hd., r. ℞. TI . CAESAR AVG . F . TR . POT . XV. Bare hd. of Tiberius r. *C.* 1. *R.I.C.* 356. *B.M.C.* 506 .. .. 250·00

421B — **Æ denarius.** As last. *C.* 2. *R.I.C.* 356. *B.M.C.* 507 .. .. 75·00

Commemorative Coins struck after his death   **Fine**

422 *Struck by Tiberius,* **Æ sestertius.** DIVO AVGVSTO S . P . Q . R . OB CIVES
SER. Oak-wreath supported by two capricorns. ℞. TI . CAESAR DIVI
AVG . F . AVGVST . P . M . TR . POT . XXXVII. around large S . C. *C.* 303.
R.I.C. (Tib.) 41. *B.M.C.* 109 .. .. £35·00

423 — DIVO AVGVSTO S . P . Q . R. Augustus seated on l. on car drawn by
four elephants. ℞. As previous, but legend ends TR . POT . XXXIIX.
C. 308. *R.I.C. (Tib.)* 42. *B.M.C.* 125 .. .. 40·00

424 **Æ as.** DIVVS AVGVSTVS PATER. Rad. hd., l. ℞. PROVIDENT . S . C.
Large altar. *C.* 228. *R.I.C. (Div. Aug.)* 6. *B.M.C.* 146 .. .. 7·50

425 — — ℞ S . C. Livia seated r. *C.* 244. *R.I.C. (Div. Aug.)* 2.
B.M.C. 151 .. .. 10·00

426 — — ℞. S . C. Eagle facing on globe, hd. r. *C.* 247. *R.I.C. (Div.
Aug.)* 3. *B.M.C.* 155 .. .. 9·00

427 — — ℞. S . C. Winged thunderbolt. *C.* 249. *R.I.C. (Div. Aug.)* 1.
B.M.C. 157 .. .. 9·00

428 *Struck by Caligula,* **Æ dupondius.** DIVVS AVGVSTVS S . C. Rad. hd., l.
℞. CONSENSV SENAT . ET EQ . ORDIN . P . Q . R. Augustus seated l.
C. 87. *R.I.C. (Div. Aug.)* 8. *B.M.C. (Cal.)* 88 .. .. 14·00

429 *Restitution by Titus,* **Æ sestertius.** DIVVS AVGVSTVS PATER. Augustus
seated l. beside altar. ℞. IMP . T . CAES . DIVI VESP . F . AVG. P.M. TR.P.P.P.
COS . VIII. around large S . C. *C.* 549. *R.I.C. (Tit.)* 185. *B.M.C.* 261 *note* .. 50·00

430 **Æ as.** DIVVS AVGVSTVS PATER. Rad. hd., r. ℞. IMP . T . VESP . AVG .
REST . S . C. As 426. *C.* 550. *R.I.C. (Tit.)* 199. *B.M.C., p.* 284* .. 14·00

431 *Restitution by Domitian,* **Æ as.** *Obv.* Similar, but hd. l. ℞. IMP .
D . CAES . AVG . RESTITVIT S . C. As 426. *C.* 562. *R.I.C. (Dom.)* 456.
B.M.C. 506 .. .. 18·00

432 *Restitution by Nerva,* **Æ sestertius.** DIVVS AVGVSTVS. Laur. hd., r.
℞. IMP . NERVA CAESAR AVGVSTVS REST. around large S . C. *C.* 570.
R.I.C. (Ner.) 136. *B.M.C.* 149 .. .. 75·00

433 **Æ as.** DIVVS AVGVSTVS. Bare hd., r. ℞. IMP . NERVA CAES . AVG .
REST . S . C. Winged thunderbolt. *C.* 567. *R.I.C. (Ner.)* 130. *B.M.C.*
161 .. .. 20·00

434 *Struck by Trajan Decius,* **Æ antoninianus.** DIVO AVGVSTO. Rad. hd., r.
℞. CONSECRATIO. Large altar. *C.* 578. *R.I.C. (Dec.)* 78 .. .. 12·50

Colonial and Provincial Coinage   Fair

435 *Spain, Celsa*, Æ 28. Hd. r. within laurel-wreath.   R. Bull stg. r. .. £2·25
436 — *Ilici*, Æ 21. Laur. hd., r.   R. Tetrastyle temple inscribed IVNONI .. 3·00
437 — *Corduba (Colonia Patricia)*, Æ 24. Hd. l. R. COLONIA PATRICIA
in wreath ..   .. 2·25
438 — *Julia Traducta*, Æ 24. Hd. l.   R. IVLIA TRAD. in wreath ..   .. 2·50
439 — *Osset*, Æ 24. Bare hd., r.   R. Male figure stg. l., holding bunch
of grapes ..   .. 2·50
440 *Achaia, Patrae*, Æ 27. DIVVS AVGVSTVS PATER. Rad. hd., l. R. Colonist
ploughing r.   *B.M.C.* G.19 ..   .. 3·50
441 *Ionia, Smyrna*, Æ 18. Bare hd., r.   R. Aphrodite stg. l. *B.M.C.*
G.248 ..   .. 2·50
442 *Caria, Aphrodisias*, Æ 15. Laur. hd., r.   R. Double-axe. *B.M.C.*
G.90 ..   .. 2·00
443 *Cyprus*, Æ 17. Bare hd., r.   R. Temple of Aphrodite at Paphos.
B.M.C. G.2 ..   .. 2·50
444 *Syria, Antioch*, Æ 27. Laur. hd., r.   R. s . c. in wreath. *B.M.C.*
G.126 ..   .. 2·25
445 *Byzacene, Thaena*, Æ 30. Bare hd., r.   R. Dr. bust of Astarte r. .. 5·00

LIVIA

447

*Wife of Tiberius Claudius Nero and afterwards of Augustus, who compelled her husband
to divorce her in* 38 B.C. *Mother of Tiberius and Nero Claudius Drusus by her first husband:
died in* A.D. 29 *at the age of* 85.

Fine

446 **Æ sestertius.** S . P . Q . R . IVLIAE AVGVST. Carpentum drawn r. by
two mules.   R. TI . CAESAR DIVI AVG . F . AVGVST . P . M . TR . POT . XXIIII.
around large S . C. *C.* 6. *R.I.C.* (*Tib.*) 21. *B.M.C.* 76.. ..   .. 60·00
447 **Æ dupondius.** PIETAS. Diad. and veiled bust, r.   R. DRVSVS CAESAR
TI . AVGVSTI F . TR . POT . ITER. around large S . C. *C.* 1. *R.I.C.* (*Tib.*) 24.
B.M.C. 98 ..   .. 30·00
448 IVSTITIA. Diad. bust, r.   R. TI . CAESAR DIVI AVG . F . AVG . P . M . TR .
POT . XXIIII. around large S . C. *C.* 4. *R.I.C.* (*Tib.*) 22. *B.M.C.* 79 .. 30·00
449 SALVS AVGVSTA. Bust r.   R. As previous. *C.* 5. *R.I.C.* (*Tib.*) 23.
B.M.C. 81 ..   .. 30·00
450 *Spain, Turiaso*, Æ 28. Hd. r.   R. Augustus on horseback l. ..   .. 15·00
451 *Augustus and Livia: Spain, Romula*, Æ 31. Rad. hd. of Augustus r.,
star above, thunderbolt before.   R. Hd. of Livia l. on globe, star above. 20·00

AGRIPPA

456

(Marcus Vipsanius Agrippa).   Born 63 B.C. and a close friend of Augustus from boyhood. A renowned commander by both land and sea, he was destined by Augustus to succeed him, but he pre-deceased the emperor in 12 B.C.   It has been written of Agrippa that "he is the supreme example in history of a man of the first order whom loyalty constrained to take the second place".

Fine

452   *Augustus and Agrippa, Ɲ* **aureus.** CAESAR AVGVSTVS. Bare hd. of Augustus r.   R.   M . AGRIPPA PLATORINVS III . VIR.   Hd. of Agrippa r., wearing combined mural and rostral crown.   *C.* 2.   *R.I.C.* (*Aug.*) 170. *B.M.C.* 110 .. .. *Extr. rare*

453   — **Ɍ denarius.** *Obv.* Similar. R. — Bare hd. of Agrippa r. *C.* 3.   *R.I.C.* (*Aug.*) 169.   *B.M.C.* 112 .. ..£150·00

454   — **Æ 25** *of Nemausus.* IMP . DIVI F. Their hds. back to back. R. COL . NEM.   Crocodile r., chained to palm.   *C.* 7.   *R.I.C., p.* 44.. .. 10·00

455   — — Similar, but with *obv.* legend IMP . DIVI F . P . P.   *C.* 8.   *R.I.C.*, *p.* 44 .. .. 10·00

456   *Struck by Tiberius,* **Æ as.** M . AGRIPPA L . F . COS . III. Hd. l., wearing rostral crown.   R.   S . C.   Neptune stg. l., holding dolphin and trident. *C.* 3.   *R.I.C.* (*Tib.*) 32.   *B.M.C.* 161 .. .. 12·50

457   *Restitution by Titus,* **Æ as.** Similar, but with *rev.* legend IMP . T . VESP . AVG . REST . S . C.   *C.* 6.   *R.I.C.* (*Tit.*) 209.   *B.M.C.* 281 .. .. .. 30·00

458   *Restitution by Domitian,* **Æ as.** Similar, but with *rev.* legend IMP . D . AVG . REST . S . C.   *C.* 7.   *R.I.C.* (*Dom.*) 457.   *B.M.C.* 510 .. .. 35·00

JULIA

Born in 39 B.C., she was the daughter of Augustus and Scribonia.   She first married her cousin Marcellus in 25 B.C., and on his death took Agrippa as her husband.   In 11 B.C. she was married a third time, to the future emperor Tiberius, but in 2 B.C. she was banished by Augustus to the island of Pandataria, off the Campanian coast.   She spent the remainder of her life in exile and died a few weeks after her father in A.D. 14.

459   *Augustus and Julia,* **Ɍ denarius.** AVGVSTVS. Bare hd. of Augustus r. R.   C . MARIVS TRO . III . VIR.   Bust of Julia r.   *C.* 1.   *R.I.C.* (*Aug.*) 167. *B.M.C.* 104 .. .. 225·00

CAIUS and LUCIUS CAESARS

Caius and Lucius were the sons of Agrippa and Julia and were destined by Augustus to succeed him, but they died in A.D. 4 *and* A.D. 2 *respectively.*

Fine

460 *Caius alone,* **Æ denarius.** CAESAR. Bare hd. of Caius r.; all within wreath. ℞. AVGVST. divided by candelabrum; all within wreath. *C.* 2. *R.I.C.* (*Aug.*) 372. *B.M.C.* 684 .. ..£125·00

461 *Augustus, Julia, Caius and Lucius,* **Æ denarius.** AVGVSTVS. Bare hd. of Augustus r. ℞. C . MARIVS TRO III . VIR. Hds. of Lucius, Julia and Caius r. *C.* 1. *R.I.C.* (*Aug.*) 166. *B.M.C.* 106 .. .. .. 450·00

The brothers are also depicted on certain reverses of Augustus (*see Nos.* 367, 368, 375 *and* 376).

For full details of **all** the silver coins of the above period see:

ROMAN SILVER COINS, *by H. A. Seaby.*

Vol. I, The Republic to Augustus, £2·00

TIBERIUS
A.D. 14-37

472

(*Tiberius Claudius Nero*). *Born in* 42 B.C., *Tiberius was the elder son of Ti. Claudius Nero and Livia. After the death of Agrippa, Augustus became increasingly dependent on his step-son in military matters, and Tiberius spent much time campaigning on the frontiers of the Empire. His marriage with Augustus' daughter, Julia, was not a happy one however, and in* 6 B.C. *he retired to the island of Rhodes where he spent the next eight years. Augustus never had any affection for his step-son and it was only after the deaths of his two grandsons, Caius and Lucius, that he grudgingly recognized Tiberius as the probable heir to the throne.*

He succeeded Augustus in A.D. 14 *and proved himself a very able administrator. The empire in general prospered under his rule, but there was much tragedy within the emperor's family and treason trials became increasingly frequent.   In* A.D. 26 *Tiberius retired to Capreae and never again returned to Rome.   He died at Misenum on March 16th,* A.D. 37, *at the age of* 78.

The Ministry and Crucifixion of Jesus Christ occurred in this reign.

Titles and Powers, A.D. 4-37.

A.D.	Tribunician Power	Imperatorial Acclamation	Consulship	Other Titles
4	TR.P.VI.			
5	TR.P.VI. − VII.	IMP.III.		
6	TR.P.VII. − VIII.			
7	TR.P.VIII. − VIIII.	IMP.IIII. (?)		
8	TR.P.VIIII. − X.	IMP.V.		
9	TR.P.X. − XI.			
10	TR.P.XI. − XII.			
11	TR.P.XII. − XIII.	IMP.VI.		
12	TR.P.XIII. − XIIII.	IMP.VII.		
13	TR.P.XIIII. − XV.			
14	TR.P.XV. − XVI.			
15	TR.P.XVI. − XVII.			AVGVSTVS. P.M.
16	TR.P.XVII. − XVIII.			
17	TR.P.XVIII. − XVIIII.			
18	TR.P.XVIIII. − XX.	IMP.VIII.	COS.III.	
19	TR.P.XX. − XXI.			
20	TR.P.XXI. − XXII.			
21	TR.P.XXII. − XXIII.		COS.IIII.	
22	TR.P.XXIII. − XXIIII.			
23	TR.P.XXIIII. − XXV.			
24	TR.P.XXV. − XXVI.			
25	TR.P.XXVI. − XXVII.			
26	TR.P.XXVII. − XXVIII.			
27	TR.P.XXVIII. − XXVIIII.			
28	TR.P.XXVIIII. - XXX.			
29	TR.P.XXX. − XXXI.			
30	TR.P.XXXI. − XXXII.			
31	TR.P.XXXII. − XXXIII.		COS.V.	
32	TR.P.XXXIII. − XXXIIII.			
33	TR.P.XXXIIII. − XXXV.			
34	TR.P.XXXV. − XXXVI.			
35	TR.P.XXXVI. − XXXVII.			
36	TR.P.XXXVII. − XXXVIII.			
37	TR.P.XXXVIII.			

Tiberius first received the tribunician power in 6 B.C. when it was granted to him for a period of five years.   Soon after this he retired to Rhodes and he was still there when his term of tribunician power expired in 1 B.C.   It was then allowed to lapse for four years, but after the deaths of Augustus' grandsons, Caius and Lucius, Tiberius was reinvested with the power on June 27th, A.D. 4, and it was subsequently renewed each year on that date.

His first two consulships were in 13 B.C. and 7 B.C.

Mints:—Rome, Lugdunum, Caesarea, Samosata (?).

Struck under Augustus

Fine

462 **Æ as.** TI . CAESAR AVGVST . F . IMPERAT . V. Bare hd., r. ℞ . PONTIFEX
TRIBVN. POTESTATE XII. around large S . C. *C.* 27. *R.I.C.* (*Aug.*) 220.
B.M.C. 271 .. .. £15·00

463 TI . CAESAR AVGVST . F . IMPERAT . VII. Laur. hd., r. ℞ . ROM . ET AVG.
The Altar of Lugdunum. *C.* 37. *R.I.C.* (*Aug.*) 370. *B.M.C.* 585 .. 10·00

464 **Æ semis.** Similar. *C.* 38. *R.I.C.* (*Aug.*) 371. *B.M.C.* 588 .. .. 10·00
See also nos. 395, 421A *and* 421B.

As Augustus (i.e. Emperor)

465 ***N* aureus.** TI . CAESAR DIVI AVG . F . AVGVSTVS. Laur. hd., r. ℞ .
PONTIF . MAXIM. Livia seated r. *C.* 15. *R.I.C.* 3. *B.M.C.* 30. **Plate
5** .. .. 75·00

466 ***N* quinarius.** TI . DIVI F . AVGVSTVS. Laur. hd., r. ℞ . TR . POT .
XXXII. Victory seated r. on globe. *C.* 59. *R.I.C.* 4. *B.M.C.* 23.
Illustrated on p. 11 .. .. 150·00

467 **Æ denarius.** As 465. *C.* 16. *R.I.C.* 3. *B.M.C.* 34 .. .. .. 20·00

468 *Obv.* As 465. ℞ . TR . POT . XVII . IMP . VII. Tiberius in quadriga r.
C. 48. *R.I.C.* 2. *B.M.C.* 7.. .. .. 37·50

469 **Æ sestertius.** CIVITATIBVS ASIAE RESTITVTIS. Tiberius seated l., holding
patera and sceptre. ℞ . TI . CAESAR DIVI AVG . F . AVGVST . P . M . TR . POT.
XXIIII around large S . C. *C.* 3. *R.I.C.* 19. *B.M.C.* 70.. .. .. 50·00

470 No *obv.* legend. Empty triumphal car drawn r. by four horses. ℞ . As
previous, but legend ends TR . POT . XXXVI. *C.* 65. *R.I.C.* 37. *B.M.C.*
103 .. .. 50·00

471 No *obv.* legend. Front view of hexastyle temple. ℞ . As previous, but
legend ends TR . POT . XXXIIX. *C.* 70. *R.I.C.* 38. *B.M.C.* 132 .. .. 50·00

472 **Æ dupondius.** TI . CAESAR DIVI AVG . F . AVGVST . IMP . VIII. Laur. hd.,
l. ℞ . MODERATIONI S . C. Facing bust of Moderation on shield encircled by laurel-wreath. *C.* 5. *R.I.C.* 31. *B.M.C.* 90 .. .. .. 45·00

473 **Æ as.** *Obv.* Similar. ℞ . PONTIF . MAX . TRIBVN . POTEST . XXXVII . S .
C. Rudder and globe. *C.* 13. *R.I.C.* 39. *B.M.C.* 117 .. .. 12·50

474 *Obv.* Similar, but IMP . VII. and bare hd. l. ℞ . PONTIF . MAXIM .
TRIBVN . POTEST . XVII . S . C. Livia seated r. *C.* 18. *R.I.C.* 16. *B.M.C.*
68 .. .. 15·00

475 *Obv.* As 472. ℞ . PONTIF . MAXIM . TRIBVN . POTEST . XXXVII . S . C.
Winged caduceus. *C.* 22. *R.I.C.* 40. *B.M.C.* 120 .. .. .. 12·50

Commemorative Coins struck after his death.

476 *Restitution by Titus,* **Æ sestertius.** *Obv.* As 469, but RESTITVT. ℞ .
IMP . T . CAES . DIVI VESP . F . AVG . P . M . TR . P . P . P . COS . VIII . REST.
around large S . C. *C.* 71. *R.I.C.* (*Tit.*) 210. *B.M.C.* 282 .. .. 60·00

477 **Æ as.** TI . CAESAR DIVI AVG . F . AVGVST . IMP . VIII. Bare hd., r. ℞ .
IMP . T . CAES . DIVI VESP . F . AVG . RESTITVIT around large S . C. *C.* 74.
R.I.C. (*Tit.*) 214. *B.M.C., p.* 286* .. .. 20·00

478 *Restitution by Domitian,* **Æ as.** *Obv.* Similar, but laur. hd., l. ℞ .
IMP . D . CAES . DIVI VESP . F . AVG . REST. around large S . C. *C.* 76. *R.I.C.*
(*Dom.*) 458. *B.M.C.* 509 .. .. 25·00

Colonial and Provincial Coinage.   Fair

479 *Spain, Dertosa,* Æ **24.** Laur. hd., r. ℞. Ship sailing l. .. .. £3·50

480 — *Calagurris Julia,* Æ **28.** Laur. hd., r. ℞. Bull stg. r. .. .. 2·25

481 — *Caesaraugusta,* Æ **28.** Laur. hd., r. ℞. Priest ploughing l. .. 2·50

482 *Syria, Antioch,* Æ **26.** Laur. hd., r. ℞. Greek inscription in wreath.
     B.M.C.G. 150 .. .. 2·25

483 *Zeugitana, Utica,* Æ **30.** Bare hd., l. ℞. Livia seated r. .. .. 5·00

484 *Tiberius and Livia: Byzacene, Thapsus,* Æ **28.** Bare hd., r. ℞. Veiled
     hd. of Livia l. .. .. 10·00

485 *Tiberius, Drusus and Germanicus: Spain, Hispalis,* Æ **28.** Laur. hd. r.
     ℞. Hds. of Drusus and Germanicus face to face. .. .. .. 7·50

486 *Tiberius, Nero and Drusus: Spain, Carthago Nova,* Æ **27.** Bare hd., l.
     ℞. Hds. of Nero and Drusus face to face. .. .. .. 7·50

DRUSUS

488

The son of Tiberius by his first wife, Vipsania, Drusus was born c. 14 B.C. *After the
death of Germanicus he became the heir to the throne and in* A.D. 22 *he was granted the
Tribunician Power.   The following year, however, he fell a victim to the praetorian prefect,
Sejanus, who induced his wife, Livilla, to poison him.*

                                                                          Fine
487 Æ **sestertius.** No *obv.* legend. Two crossed cornuacopiae, surmounted
     by the hds. of Drusus' children, with winged caduceus between. ℞.
     DRVSVS CAESAR TI . AVG . F . DIVI AVG . N . PONT . TR . POT . II. around large
     s . c. *C.* 1. *R.I.C.* (*Tib.*) 28. *B.M.C.* 95 .. .. 55·00

488 Æ **as.** DRVSVS CAESAR TI . AVG . F . DIVI AVG . N. Bare hd., l. ℞.
     PONTIF . TRIBVN . POTEST . ITER. around large s . c. *C.* 2. *R.I.C.* (*Tib.*) 26.
     B.M.C. 99 .. .. 12·50

489 *Restitution by Titus,* Æ **as.** *Obv.* Similar. ℞. IMP . T . CAES . DIVI
     VESP . F . AVG . REST. around large s. c. *C.* 6. *R.I.C.* (*Tit.*) 216. *B.M.C.*
     286 .. .. 25·00

490 *Tiberius and Drusus,* Æ **drachm** *of Caesarea.* TI . CAES . AVG . P . M . TR̂ .
     P . XXXV. Laur. hd. of Tiberius r. ℞. DRVSVS CAES . TI . AVG . COS .
     III . TR̂ . P. Bare hd. of Drusus l. *C.* 2. *R.I.C.* (*Tib*) 7. *B.M.C.* 171 100·00

NERO CLAUDIUS DRUSUS

491

Born in 38 B.C., he was the younger son of Tiberius Claudius Nero and Livia, and the brother of Tiberius. He married Antonia, the daughter of Mark Antony, and was the father of Germanicus and the future emperor Claudius. After campaigning very successfully in Germany he was killed by a fall from a horse in summer camp in 9 B.C.

All the coins bearing his name and portrait were struck under his son, the emperor Claudius (A.D. 41-54).

Fine

491 **A′ aureus.** NERO CLAVDIVS DRVSVS GERMANICVS IMP. Laur. hd., l.
R. DE GERM. Triumphal arch surmounted by equestrian statue r.
C. 1 *R.I.C. (Claud.)* 75. *B.M.C.* 95 ..   .. £175·00

492 **Æ denarius.** *Obv.* Similar. R. DE GERMANIS. Standard, two
shields, four spears and two trumpets. *C.* 6. *R.I.C. (Claud.)* 77.
B.M.C. 107 ..   ..   75·00

493 **Æ sestertius.** *Obv.* Similar, but hd. bare. R. TI . CLAVDIVS CAESAR
AVG . P . M . TR . P . IMP . P . P . S . C. Claudius seated l. amidst arms.
C. 8. *R.I.C. (Claud.)* 78. *B.M.C.* 157 ..   ..   ..   35·00

See also no. 534.

ANTONIA

496

Younger daughter of Mark Antony and Octavia, she was born about 36 B.C. She married Nero Claudius Drusus about 16 B.C. and lived long enough to see her grandson, Caligula, ascend the throne in A.D. 37. Caligula at first conferred honours upon her, but she soon fell out of favour, and her subsequent death was probably due to poison administered by the orders of the emperor.

All the coins bearing her name and portrait were struck under her son, the emperor Claudius (A.D. 41-54).

494 **A′ aureus.** ANTONIA AVGVSTA. Dr. bust r., wearing wreath of corn-ears.
R. CONSTANTIAE AVGVSTI. Ceres stg. facing, holding torch and cornucopiae. *C.* 1. *R.I.C. (Claud.)* 80. *B.M.C.* 109 ..   ..   ..   200·00

Fine

495 **Æ denarius.** *Obv.* Similar. ℞. SACERDOS DIVI AVGVSTI. Two lighted torches, joined by garland. *C.* 5. *R.I.C. (Claud.)* 81. *B.M.C.* 114 .. ..£100·00

496 **Æ dupondius.** ANTONIA AVGVSTA. Dr. bust, r. ℞. TI . CLAVDIVS CAESAR AVG . P . M . TR . P . IMP . P . P . S . C. Claudius stg. l., holding simpulum. *C.* 6. *R.I.C. (Claud.)* 82. *B.M.C.* 166 .. .. .. 20·00

See also no. 552.

GERMANICUS

500

The elder son of Nero Claudius Drusus and Antonia, Germanicus was born in 15 B.C. He was adopted by Tiberius in A.D. 4 and during the early years of Tiberius' reign he campaigned with considerable success in Germany. He was recalled to Rome in A.D. 17 and granted a splendid triumph, after which he was despatched to the East where he died mysteriously at Antioch in A.D. 19. He married Agrippina Senior, the daughter of Agrippa and Julia, and had nine children, one of whom was the future emperor Caligula.

All the coins bearing his name and portrait were struck about twenty years and more after his death.

497 *Struck by Caligula,* N **aureus.** C . CAESAR AVG . GERM . P . M . TR . POT. Laur. hd. of Caligula r. ℞. GERMANICVS CAES . P . C . CAES . AVG . GERM. Bare hd. of Germanicus r. *C.* 1. *R.I.C. (Cal.)* 20. *B.M.C.* 18 .. 200·00

498 — **Æ denarius.** C . CAESAR AVG . PON . M . TR . POT . III . COS . III. Laur. hd. of Caligula r. ℞. As previous. *C.* 5. *R.I.C. (Cal.)* 22. *B.M.C.* 28 .. .. 75·00

499 — **Æ dupondius.** GERMANICVS CAESAR. Germanicus in quadriga r. ℞. SIGNIS RECEPT . DEVICTIS GERM . S . C. Germanicus stg. l., holding sceptre. *C.* 7. *R.I.C. (Cal.), p.* 119. *B.M.C.* 93 .. .. .. 20·00

500 — **Æ as.** GERMANICVS CAESAR TI . AVG . F . DIVI AVG . N. Bare hd., l. ℞. C . CAESAR DIVI AVG . PRON . AVG . P . M . TR . P . III . P . P. around large S . C. *C.* 4. *R.I.C. (Cal.)* 47. *B.M.C.* 74 .. .. .. 12·50

501 *Struck by Claudius,* **Æ as.** *Obv.* Similar, but hd. r. ℞. TI . CLAVDIVS CAESAR AVG . GERM . P . M . TR . P . IMP . P . P. around large S . C. *C.* 9. *R.I.C. (Claud.)* 84. *B.M.C.* 215 .. .. 12·50

502 *Restitution by Titus,* **Æ as.** *Obv.* Similar. ℞. IMP . T . CAES . DIVI VESP . F . AVG . REST. around large S . C. *C.* 12. *R.I.C. (Tit)* 226. *B.M.C.* 293 .. .. 5·00

AGRIPPINA SENIOR

505

Born in 15 B.C., *she was the daughter of Agrippa and Julia. She married Germanicus about* A.D. *5 and accompanied him on all his campaigns. In* A.D. *29 Tiberius banished her to the island of Pandataria where she died of starvation in* A.D. *33.*

All the coins bearing her name and portrait were struck after her death.

Fine

503 *Struck by Caligula,* N *aureus.* C . CAESAR AVG . GERM . P . M . TR . POT. Laur. hd. of Caligula r. ℞. AGRIPPINA MAT . C . CAES . AVG . GERM. Dr. bust of Agrippina r. *C.* 1. *R.I.C. (Cal.)* 16. *B.M.C.* 14 .. ..£200·00

504 — ℞ **denarius.** C . CAESAR AVG . PON . M . TR . POT . IIII . COS . IIII. Laur. hd. of Caligula r. ℞. As previous. *C.* 7. *R.I.C. (Cal.)* 19. *B.M.C., p.* 150 *note* .. .. 75·00

505 — Æ **sestertius.** AGRIPPINA M . F . MAT . C . CAESARIS AVGVSTI. Dr. bust, r. ℞. S . P . Q . R . MEMORIAE AGRIPPINAE. Carpentum drawn l. by two mules. *C.* 1. *R.I.C. (Cal.)* 42. *B.M.C.* 81 .. .. .. 50·00

506 *Struck by Claudius,* Æ **sestertius.** AGRIPPINA M . F . GERMANICI CAESARIS. Dr. bust, r. ℞. TI . CLAVDIVS CAESAR AVG . GERM . P . M . TR . P . IMP . P . P. around large S . C. *C.* 3. *R.I.C. (Claud.)* 85. *B.M.C.* 219 .. 45·00

NERO and DRUSUS CAESARS

Sons of Germanicus and Agrippina Senior, died A.D. *31 and 33 respectively. Their coins were struck later by their brother, the emperor Caligula* (A.D. 37-41).

507 Æ **dupondius.** NERO ET DRVSVS CAESARES. Nero and Drusus galloping r. ℞. C . CAESAR AVG . GERMANICVS PON . M . TR . POT. around large S . C. *C.* 1. *R.I.C. (Cal.)* 43. *B.M.C.* 44 .. .. 25·00

CALIGULA

A.D. 37-41

513

Caius Caesar was the youngest son of Germanicus and Agrippina Senior, and was born at Antium in A.D. 12.   His nickname, Caligula, was bestowed on him by the soldiers when he was only a few years old: he used to wear the miniature uniform of a private soldier, including the half-boot (caliga).   He was named by Tiberius as his heir and succeeded that emperor in A.D. 37.   In his early months, when he was probably under the influence of his grandmother Antonia, he showed promise of becoming a good emperor, but later in the year he became seriously ill and possibly somewhat insane.   From then on, his reign was noted for his personal depravity and public oppression, and he was eventually murdered by a group of Praetorians on January 24th, A.D. 41.

Titles and Powers, A.D. 37-41.

A.D.	Tribunician Power	Imperatorial Acclamation	Consulship	Other Titles
37	TR.P.		COS.	AVGVSTVS. P.M.
38	TR.P. – TR.P.II.			P.P.
39	TR.P.II. – III.		COS.II.	
40	TR.P.III. – IIII.		COS.III.	
41	TR.P.IIII.		COS.IIII.	

Caligula received the tribunician power on March 18th, A.D. 37, and it was subsequently renewed each year on that date.

Mints:—Rome, Lugdunum (?), Caesarea.

Fine

508 *N* **aureus.**   C . CAESAR AVG . GERM . P . M . TR . POT.   Laur. hd., r.   ℞. S . P . Q . R ./ P . P . / OB C . S. in oak-wreath.   C. 18.   R.I.C. 4.   B.M.C., p. 148 *note*   ..   ..£225·00

509 *N* **quinarius.**   C . CAESAR AVG . GERMANICVS.   Laur. hd., r.   ℞.   P . M . TR . POT . IIII.   Victory seated r. on globe.   C. 16.   R.I.C. 3.   B.M.C. 31   300·00

510 Æ **denarius.**   C . CAESAR AVG . PON . M . TR . POT . III . COS . III.   Laur. hd., r.   ℞.   As 508.   C. 21.   R.I.C. 5.   B.M.C. 29, *note*   ..   ..   ..   90·00

511 Æ **drachm** *of Caesarea.*   *Obv.*   As 509, but hd. bare.   ℞.   IMPERATOR PONT . MAX . AVG . TR . POT.   Lituus and simpulum.   C. 12.   R.I.C. 8. B.M.C. 102   ..   ..   75·00

512 Æ **sestertius.**   C . CAESAR AVG . GERMANICVS PON . M . TR . POT.   Laur. hd., l.   ℞.   ADLOCVT . COH.   Caligula stg. l. on platform, haranguing five soldiers.   C. 1.   R.I.C. 23.   B.M.C. 33   ..   ..   ..   75·00

513 *Obv.*   Similar.   ℞.   AGRIPPINA DRVSILLA IVLIA S . C.   The three sisters of Caligula stg. facing.   C. 4.   R.I.C. 26.   B.M.C. 36   ..   ..   ..   100·00

514 C . CAESAR DIVI AVG . PRON . AVG . P . M . TR . P . IIII . P . P.   Pietas seated l., PIETAS in ex.   ℞.   DIVO AVG . S . C.   Caligula stg. l., sacrificing in front of hexastyle temple.   C. 11.   R.I.C. 37.   B.M.C. 69   ..   ..   50·00

515 *Obv.*   Legend as previous.   Laur. hd., l.   ℞.   S . P . Q . R ./ P . P . / OB CIVES / SERVATOS in oak-wreath.   C. 26.   R.I.C. 29.   B.M.C., p 157 *note*   65·00

Fine

516 **Æ as.** *Obv.* As 512, but hd. bare. ℞. VESTA S . C. Vesta seated l.
C. 27. *R.I.C.* 30. *B.M.C.* 46. **Plate 5** .. .. £12·50

517 **Æ quadrans.** C . CAESAR DIVI AVG . PRON . AVG . S . C. Cap of Liberty.
℞. COS . TERT . PON . M . TR . P . III . P . P. around R . C . C. C. 6.
R.I.C. 39. *B.M.C.* 61 .. .. 3·75

518 *Caligula and Augustus,* **N aureus.** C . CAESAR AVG . PON . M . TR . POT .
III . COS . III. Laur. hd., r. ℞. DIVVS AVG . PATER PATRIAE. Rad. hd.
of Augustus r. C. 6. *R.I.C.* 14. *B.M.C.* 24 .. .. .. 200·00

519 **— R denarius.** *Obv.* As 508, but hd. bare. ℞. As previous. C. 3.
R.I.C. 12. *B.M.C.* 10 .. .. 75·00

Colonial and Provincial Coinage.

Fair

520 *Spain, Segobriga,* **Æ 30.** Laur. hd., l. ℞. SEGO / BRIGA in wreath .. 5·00
521 *Corinth,* **Æ 20.** Bare hd., r. ℞. Pegasus flying r. *B.M.C. G.* 531 .. 3·50
522 *Crete,* **R drachm.** Bare hd., l. ℞. Rad. hd. of Augustus r. *B.M.C.*
G. 3 .. .. 30·00
523 *Phrygia, Aezanis,* **Æ 20.** Laur. hd., r. ℞. Zeus stg. l., holding eagle
and sceptre. *B.M.C. G.* 58 .. .. 3·00

CAESONIA

Fourth wife of Caligula, murdered with her daughter at the same time as her husband.

524 *Caligula and Caesonia: Spain, Carthago Nova,* **Æ 28.** C . CAESAR AVG .
GERMANIC . IMP . P . M . TR . P . COS. Laur. hd. of Caligula r. ℞. CN .
ATEL . FLAC . CN . POM . FLAC . II . VIR Q . V . I . N . C. Bust of Caesonia r.,
dividing SAL . / AVG. .. .. 30·00

CLAUDIUS
A.D. 41-54

537

(Tiberius Claudius Drusus). The younger son of Nero Claudius Drusus and Antonia, Claudius was born at Lugdunum in 10 B.C. A childhood attack of infantile paralysis had left him with a grotesque appearance and it was also generally assumed that he was weak-

minded.   He thus took little part in public life, devoting himself to antiquarian studies, until, on the death of his nephew Caligula, he was proclaimed emperor by the Praetorian Guard. It soon became clear that he was by no means as weak-minded as people had thought, and in fact he proved himself a very capable administrator.   In A.D. 43 he personally took part in the invasion of Britain, thus beginning the Roman occupation of our island which was to last until the fifth century.   He married his niece, Agrippina Junior, in A.D. 49 and in the following year he adopted her son, Nero, who then became the heir to the throne.   He died on October 13th, A.D. 54, possibly as the result of poison administered on the orders of Agrippina.

Titles and Powers, A.D. 41-54.

A.D.	Tribunician Power	Imperatorial Acclamation	Consulship	Other Titles
41	TR.P.	IMP. – IMP.IV.		AVGVSTVS. P.M.
42	TR.P. – TR.P.II.		COS.II.	P.P.
43	TR.P.II. – III.		COS.III.	
44	TR.P.III. – IIII.	IMP.V. – VII.		
45	TR.P.III. – V.	IMP.VIII.		
46	TR.P.V. – VI.	IMP.VIII. – XI.		BRITANNICVS.
47	TR.P.VI. – VII.	IMP.XII. – XIII.	COS.IIII.	CENSOR.
48	TR.P.VII. – VIII.	IMP.XIV. – XV.		CENSOR.
49	TR.P.VIII. – VIIII.	IMP.XVI.		
50	TR.P.VIIII. – X.	IMP.XVII. – XX.		
51	TR.P.X. – XI.	IMP.XXI. – XXIII.	COS.V.	
52	TR.P.XI. – XII.	IMP.XXIIII. – XXVI.		
53	TR.P.XII. – XIII.	IMP.XXVII.		
54	TR.P.XIII. – XIIII.			

Claudius received the tribunician power on January 25th, A.D. 41, and it was subsequently renewed each year on that date.

His first consulship was in A.D. 37.

Mints:—Rome, Lugdunum (?), Ephesus, Caesarea.

Fine

525 *N* **aureus.** TI . CLAVD . CAESAR AVG . P . M . TR . P . VI . IMP . XI. Laur. hd., r. ℞. DE BRITANN. on triumphal arch. *C.* 17. *R.I.C.* 9. *B.M.C.* 32 ..   ..£200·00

526 TI . CLAVD . CAESAR AVG . GERM . P . M . TR . P. Laur. hd., r. ℞. EX S . C. / OB CIVES / SERVATOS in oak-wreath. *C.* 34. *R.I.C.* 20. *B.M.C.* 16 ..   ..   100·00

527 *N* **quinarius.** *Obv.* Similar. ℞. VICTORIA AVGVST. Victory seated r. on globe. *C.* 101. *R.I.C.* 50. *B.M.C., p.* 167 *note* ..   ..   ..   250·00

528 *Æ* **cistophorus** *of Ephesus.* TI . CLAVD . CAES . AVG. Bare hd., l. ℞. COM . ASI. Claudius and Fortune stg. within distyle temple inscribed ROM . ET AVG. *C.* 3. *R.I.C.* 52. *B.M.C.* 228 ..   ..   75·00

529 *Æ* **didrachm** *of Caesarea.* *Obv.* As 526, but hd. l. ℞. DE BRITANNIS. Claudius in quadriga r. *C.* 15. *R.I.C.* 56. *B.M.C.* 237   ..   ..   100·00

530 *Æ* **denarius.** As 525. *C.* 18. *R.I.C.* 9. *B.M.C.* 35 ..   ..   ..   100·00

531 TI . CLAVD . CAESAR AVG . P . M . TR . P . IIII. Laur. hd., r. ℞. PACI AVGVSTAE. Nemesis advancing r., preceded by serpent. *C.* 56. *R.I.C.* 29. *B.M.C.* 27 ..   ..   35·00

532 *Obv.* As 525. ℞. S . P . Q . R . / P . P . / OB C . S. in oak-wreath. *C.* 87. *R.I.C.* 41. *B.M.C.* 45 ..   ..   35·00

Fine

533 **Æ sestertius.** TI . CLAVDIVS CAESAR AVG . P . M . TR . P . IMP. Laur. hd.,
r. R. EX S . C . / OB / CIVES / SERVATOS in oak-wreath. C. 39. R.I.C.
60. B.M.C. 115 ..   ..   £25·00

534 *Obv.* Similar, but legend ends IMP . P . P. R. NERO CLAVDIVS DRVSVS
GERMAN . IMP . S . C. Triumphal arch surmounted by equestrian statue r.
between two trophies. C. 48. R.I.C. 62. B.M.C. 121 ..   35·00

535 *Obv.* Similar. R. SPES AVGVSTA S . C. Spes advancing l. C. 85.
R.I.C. 64. B.M.C. 124 ..   ..   22·50

536 **Æ dupondius.** *Obv.* As 533, but bare hd., l. R. CERES AVGVSTA
S . C. Ceres seated l. C. 1. R.I.C. 67. B.M.C. 136 ..   ..   12·00

537 **Æ as.** *Obv.* Similar. R. CONSTANTIAE AVGVSTI S . C. Constantia
stg. l., holding spear. C. 14. R.I.C. 68. B.M.C. 140 ..   ..   9·00

538 *Obv.* Similar. R. LIBERTAS AVGVSTA S . C. Liberty stg. r. C. 47.
R.I.C. 69. B.M.C. 145. **Plate 5** ..   ..   9·00

539 *Obv.* Similar. R. S . C. Minerva advancing r., brandishing javelin
and holding shield. C. 84. R.I.C. 66. B.M.C. 149 ..   ..   9·00

540 **Æ quadrans.** TI . CLAVDIVS CAESAR AVG. Modius. R. PON . M .
TR . P . IMP . COS . DES . IT. around large S . C. C. 70. R.I.C. 72. B.M.C.
179 ..   ..   3·25

541 — Hand holding scales; in field, P . N . R. R. PON . M . TR . P . IMP . P .
P . COS . II. around large S . C. C. 73. R.I.C. 72. B.M.C. 181 ..   3·25

Commemorative Coins struck after his death.

542 *Struck by Nero,* **N aureus.** DIVVS CLAVDIVS AVGVSTVS. Laur. hd., l. R.
EX S . C. Carpentum drawn r. by four horses. C. 31. R.I.C. (*Nero*) 1.
B.M.C. 4   ..   ..   150·00

543 — **R denarius.** Similar. C. 32. R.I.C. (*Nero*) 1. B.M.C. 6   50·00

544 *Restitution by Titus,* **Æ sestertius.** TI . CLAVDIVS CAESAR AVG . P . M .
TR . P . IMP . P . P. Laur. hd., r. R. IMP . T . VESP . AVG . REST . S . C.
Spes advancing l. C. 103. R.I.C. (*Tit.*) 234. B.M.C. 297 ..   45·00

545 — **Æ dupondius.** *Obv.* Similar, but hd. bare. R. — Ceres seated
l. C. 102. R.I.C. (*Tit.*) 236. B.M.C., *p.* 290* ..   ..   25·00

546 **Æ as.** *Obv.* Similar. R. — As 539. C. 105. R.I.C. (*Tit.*) 241.
B.M.C. 300   ..   ..   20·00

547 *Restitution by Domitian,* **Æ sestertius.** *Obv.* As 544, but hd. l.
R. IMP . D . CAES . AVG . REST . S . C. Spes advancing l. C. 108.
R.I.C. (*Dom.*) 461. B.M.C., *p.* 417* ..   ..   ..   60·00

548 — **Æ as.** *Obv.* As 544, but bare hd., l. R. IMP . D . AVG . REST .
S . C. As 539. C. —. R.I.C. (*Dom.*) 462. B.M.C. 512 ..   27·50

Colonial and Provincial Coinages

Fair

549 *Achaia, Patrae,* **Æ 26.** Bare hd., l. R. Legionary eagle between
two standards. B.M.C. G.21   ..   ..   2·25

550 *Ionia, Miletus,* **Æ 20.** Laur. hd., l. R. Cultus-statue of Apollo r.
B.M.C. G.146 ..   ..   2·25

551 *Phrygia, Cadi,* **Æ 18.** Laur. hd., r. R. Zeus stg. l., holding eagle
and sceptre. B.M.C. G.16 ..   ..   2·00

552 *Egypt, Alexandria,* **billon tetradrachm.** Laur. hd., r. R. Bust of
Antonia r. B.M.C. G.65 ..   ..   *Fine* £10·00

553 — — — R. Messalina, as Demeter, stg. l. B.M.C. G.70
Fine £7·50

554 — **Æ 20.** — R. Ears of corn, bound together. B.M.C. G.101 ..   1·75

MESSALINA

Valeria Messalina was the third wife of Claudius, whom she married some time before his accession, and the mother of Octavia and Britannicus. She was put to death for her part in a conspiracy against Claudius in A.D. 48.

                                                                                    Fine

555   Æ **didrachm** *of Caesarea.* MESSALLINA AVGVSTI. Dr. bust, r.   Ŗ.
BRITANNICVS OCTAVIA ANTONIA. Britannicus stg. l. between Octavia
and Antonia. *Sydenham* 63.   *R.I.C.* 59.   *B.M.C.* 242 ..   ..   *Very rare*
See also no. 553.

BRITANNICUS

(Ti. Claudius Britannicus).   The son of Claudius and Messalina, he was born in A.D. 42. *Although originally named Germanicus, this was changed to Britannicus in celebration of his father's British conquest.   He was poisoned on the orders of Nero in* A.D. 55.

556   Æ **sestertius.** TI . CLAVDIVS CAESAR AVG . F . BRITANNICVS. Bare-
headed and dr. bust, l.   Ŗ.   s . c.   Mars advancing l., holding spear
and shield.   *C.* 2.   *R.I.C.* 88.   *B.M.C.* 226   ..   ..   ..   *Extr. rare*
See also no. 555.

AGRIPPINA JUNIOR

Born in A.D. 16, *she was the eldest daughter of Germanicus and Agrippina Senior. She was first married to Cn. Domitius Ahenobarbus, by whom she had a son, the future emperor Nero.   In* A.D. 39 *she was banished by her brother, the emperor Caligula, but was recalled by her uncle Claudius, who married her in* A.D. 49.   *She was believed to have poisoned her husband in* A.D. 54 *to make room for Nero, but she soon fell out of favour with her son who arranged for her murder in* A.D. 59.

557   Æ **sestertius.** AGRIPPINA AVG . GERMANICI F . CAESARIS AVG.   Dr.
bust, r.   Ŗ.   No legend.   Carpentum drawn l. by two mules.   *C.*—.
R.I.C. (*Clau.*) 89.   *B.M.C., p.* 195 ..   ..   *Very rare*
558   *Egypt, Alexandria,* Æ **25.**   Bust r., crowned with corn.   Ŗ.   Bust of
Euthenia r., crowned with corn.   *B.M.C.* G.108 ..   ..   *Fair* £5·00

Fine

559 *Claudius and Agrippina,* Æ **aureus.** TI . CLAVD . CAESAR AVG . GERM .
P . M . TRIB . POT . P . P.   Laur. hd. of Claudius r.   ℞.   AGRIPPINAE
AVGVSTAE.   Dr. bust of Agrippina r., crowned with corn.   *C.*3.   *R.I.C.*
(*Clau.*) 92.   *B.M.C.* 72   ..   ..£150·00

560 — Æ **cistophorus** *of Ephesus.* TI . CLAVD . CAES . AVG . AGRIPP . AVGVSTA.
Their conjoined busts l.   ℞.   DIANA EPHESIA.   Diana of Ephesus facing.
C. 1.   *R.I.C.* 54.   *B.M.C.* 231   ..   ..   100·00

561 — Æ **denarius.**   As 559.   *C.* 4.   *R.I.C.* 92.   *B.M.C.* 75   ..   ..   65·00

562 *Nero and Agrippina,* Æ **aureus.** NERO CLAVD . DIVI F . CAES . AVG .
GERM . IMP . TR . P . COS.   Their conjoined busts, r.   ℞.   AGRIPP . AVG .
DIVI CLAVD . NERONIS CAES . MATER EX S . C.   Claudius and Augustus in
quadriga of elephants l.   *C.* 3.   *R.I.C.* 10.   *B.M.C.* 7 ..   ..   ..   150·00

563 — Æ **didrachm** *of Caesarea.* NERO CLAVD . DIVI CLAVD . F . CAESAR
AVG . GERMANI.   Laur. hd. of Nero r.   ℞.   AGRIPPINA AVGVSTA MATER
AVGVSTI.   Diad. and veiled bust of Agrippina r.   *C.* 2.   *R.I.C.* 12.
B.M.C. 423   ..   ..   65·00

564 — Æ **denarius.** AGRIPP . AVG . DIVI CLAVD . NERONIS CAES . MATER.
Bare hd. of Nero r., facing dr. bust of Agrippina l.   ℞.   NERONI CLAVD .
DIVI F . CAES . AVG . GERM . IMP . TR . P . around oak-wreath within which
is EX S . C.   *C.* 7.   *R.I.C.* 9.   *B.M.C.* 3 ..   ..   75·00
See also no. 604.

NERO
A.D. 54-68

579

The son of *Cn. Domitius Ahenobarbus and Agrippina Junior, Nero was born at Antium
in* A.D. 37.   *Originally named L. Domitius Ahenobarbus, this was changed to Nero Claudius
Caesar Drusus Germanicus after his adoption by Claudius in* A.D. 50.   *He succeeded to the
throne in* A.D. 54 *and at first the government was in the capable hands of Seneca and Burrus.
The young emperor soon decided to free himself from all restraints, however, and after the
death of Burrus* (A.D. 62) *and the retirement of Seneca, Nero's conduct became unbridled.
He was very enthusiastic about art and sport but his extravagances and vanity made him most
unpopular and it was rumoured that he had started the great fire which destroyed half of*

Rome in A.D. 64. *At last, in* A.D. 68, *revolt broke out in Gaul, Spain and Africa, the Praetorians at Rome deserted him and Nero fled and committed suicide.*

Titles and Powers, A.D. 50-68.

A.D.	Tribunician Power	Imperatorial Acclamation	Consulship	Other Titles
50				CAESAR
51				
52				
53				
54	TR.P.			
55	TR.P. – TR.P.II.		COS.	AVGVSTVS. P.M.P.P.
56	TR.P.II. – III.			
57	TR.P.III. – IIII.	IMP.III.	COS.II.	
58	TR.P.IIII. – V.	IMP.IIII. – V.	COS.III.	
59	TR.P.V. – VI.	IMP.VI.		
60	TR.P.VI. – VII.	IMP.VII.	COS.IIII.	
61	TR.P.VII. – VIII.	IMP.VIII. – VIIII.		
62	TR.P.VIII. – VIIII.			
63	TR.P.VIIII. – X.			
64	TR.P.X. – XI.			
65	TR.P.XI. – XII.			
66	TR.P.XII. – XIII.	IMP.XI.		
67	TR.P.XIII. – XIIII.	IMP.XII.		
68	TR.P.XIIII.		COS.V.	

Nero received the tribunician power on December 9th, A.D. 54, and it was subsequently renewed each year on that date.

Mints: Rome, Lugdunum, Caesarea.

Struck under Claudius

Fine

565 **N aureus.** NERO CLAVD . CAES . DRVSVS GERM . PRINC . IVVENT. Bareheaded and dr. bust, l. ℞. SACERD . COOPT . IN OMN . CONL . SVPRA NVM . EX S . C. Simpulum, lituus, tripod and patera. *C.* 311. *R.I.C.* 98. *B.M.C.* 84 .. ..£120·00

566 **Æ didrachm** *of Caesarea.* NERONI CLAVD . CAES . DRVSO GERM. Similar. ℞. COS . DES . PRINC . IVVENT . on shield surrounded by laurel-wreath. *C.* 82. *R.I.C.* 59a. *B.M.C.* 236 .. .. 110·00

567 **Æ denarius.** NERONI CLAVDIO DRVSO GERM . COS . DESIGN. Similar, but bust r. ℞. EQVESTER ORDO PRINCIPI IVVENT . on shield behind which is spear. *C.* 97. *R.I.C.* 95. *B.M.C.* 93 .. .. 45·00

As Augustus   Fine

568 **A aureus.** NERO CAESAR AVGVSTVS. Laur. hd., r. ℞. AVGVSTVS
AVGVSTA. Nero and his wife Messalina stg. l., side by side. *C.* 42.
R.I.C. 41. *B.M.C.* 52 .. .. £90·00

568A NERO CAESAR. Laur. hd., r. ℞. AVGVSTVS GERMANICVS. Nero radiate
stg. facing, holding branch and Victory. *C.* 44. *R.I.C.* 42. *B.M.C.* 56.
Plate 5.. .. .. 90·00

569 IMP . NERO CAESAR AVG . P . P. Laur. hd., r. ℞. SALVS. Salus seated
l., holding patera. *C.* 315. *R.I.C.* 54. *B.M.C.* 98 *note* .. .. 75·00

570 **A quinarius.** NERO CL . DIVI F . CAES . AVG . P . M . TR . P . II. Bare hd.,
r. ℞. VICT . AVG. Victory flying l., holding shield. *C.* 336. *R.I.C.*
17. *B.M.C.* 11 .. .. *Extr. rare*

571 **Æ didrachm** *of Caesarea.* NERO CLAVD . DIVI CLAVD . F . CAESAR AVG .
GERMANI. Laur. hd., r. ℞. ARMENIAC. Victory advancing r. *R.I.C.*
37. *B.M.C.* 405 .. .. 90·00

572 **Æ denarius.** NERO CAESAR. Laur. hd., r. ℞. AVGVSTVS GERMANICVS.
Nero radiate stg. facing, holding branch and Victory. *C.* 45. *R.I.C.* 42.
B.M.C. 60 .. .. 25·00

573 *Obv.* As 568. ℞. IVPPITER CVSTOS. Jupiter seated l. *C.* 119.
R.I.C. 45. *B.M.C.* 74 .. .. 18·00

574 NERO CAESAR AVG . IMP. Bare hd., r. ℞. PONTIF . MAX . TR . P . IIII .
P . P . around oak-wreath within which is EX S . C. *C.* 209. *R.I.C.* 21.
B.M.C. 16 .. .. 35·00

575 As 569. *C.* 316. *R.I.C.* 54. *B.M.C.* 98 .. .. 18·00

576 *Obv.* As 568. ℞. VESTA. Vesta seated in circular hexastyle temple.
C. 335. *R.I.C.* 58. *B.M.C.* 104 .. .. 30·00

577 **Æ hemidrachm** *of Caesarea. Obv.* As 571. ℞. No legend.
Victory seated r. on globe. *C.* 352. *R.I.C.* 40. *B.M.C.* 409 .. .. 10·00

578 **Æ sestertius.** IMP . NERO CAESAR AVG . P . MAX . TR . POT . P . P. Laur.
hd., l. ℞. ANNONA AVGVSTI CERES S . C. Ceres seated l., facing
Abundance stg. r.; in background, ship. *C.* 20. *R.I.C.* 80. *B.M.C.*,
p. 260 *note* .. .. 30·00

579 NERO CLAVD . CAESAR AVG . GER . P . M . TR . P . IMP . P . P. Laur. bust, r.
℞. AVGVSTI POR . OST . S . C. Bird's eye view of the harbour of Ostia,
showing pier, breakwaters, lighthouse and thirteen ships; in foreground,
the Tiber reclining l. *C.* 39. *R.I.C.* 95. *B.M.C.*, *p.* 223 *note.*
Illustrated on p. 103 .. .. 150·00

580 NERO CLAVDIVS CAESAR AVG . GERM . P . M . TR . P . IMP . P . P. Laur. bust, l.
℞. DECVRSIO S . C. Nero galloping r., accompanied by soldier galloping
beside him. *C.* 85. *R.I.C.* 133. *B.M.C.* 147 .. .. .. 37·50

581 IMP . NERO CAESAR AVG . PONT . MAX . TR . POT . P . P. Laur. hd., r. ℞.
PACE P . R . TERRA MARIQ . PARTA IANVM CLVSIT . S . C. Temple of Janus
with closed doors. *C.* 158. *R.I.C.* 187. *B.M.C.* 321 .. .. .. 37·50

582 *Obv.* As 579. ℞. ROMA S . C. Roma seated l., holding Victory and
parazonium. *C.* 261. *R.I.C.* 207. *B.M.C.* 324 .. .. .. 25·00

583 Similar. ℞. S . C. Triumphal arch. *C.* 308. *R.I.C.* 148. *B.M.C.*
183 .. .. 35·00

584 **Æ dupondius.** NERO CLAVD . CAESAR AVG . GERM . P . M . TR . P . IMP .
P . P. Rad. hd., r. ℞. SECVRITAS AVGVSTI S . C. Security seated r.,
altar at feet; in ex., II. *C.* 326. *R.I.C.* 294. *B.M.C.*, *p.* 241 *note* .. 7·50

585 IMP . NERO CAESAR AVG . P . MAX . TR . P . P . P. Laur. hd., r. ℞. VICTORIA
AVGVSTI S . C. Victory advancing l. *C.* 343. *R.I.C.* 304. *B.M.C.* 353 7·50

Fine

586 **Æ as.** (*orichalcum*) NERO CLAVD . CAESAR AVG . GERMANI. Rad. hd., r.
℞. PONTIF . MAX . TR . P . IMP . P . P . S . C. Nero, as Apollo, advancing
r., playing lyre; in ex., I. *C.* 203. *R.I.C.* 368. *B.M.C.* 254 .. .. £8·00

587 *Obv.* Legend as 579. Laur. hd., r. ℞. GENIO AVGVSTI S . C. Genius
stg. l., altar at feet; in ex., I. *C.* 107. *R.I.C.* 344. *B.M.C.* 252 .. .. 8·00

588 **Æ as.** (*copper*) IMP . NERO CAESAR AVG . P . M . TR . POT . P . P. Bare hd.,
r. ℞. ARA PACIS S . C. The Altar of Peace. *C.* 29. *R.I.C.* 316.
B.M.C. 364 .. .. 10·00

589 NERO CAESAR AVG . GERM . IMP. Laur. hd., r. ℞. PACE P . R . VBIQ .
PARTA IANVM CLVSIT S . C. Temple of Janus with closed doors. *C.* 171.
R.I.C. 198. *B.M.C.* 227 .. .. 8·00

590 *Obv.* As 585, but hd. bare. ℞. S . C. Victory flying l., holding shield
inscribed S . P . Q . R. *C.* 302. *R.I.C.* 329. *B.M.C.* 381 .. .. 6·00

591 **Æ semis.** (*orichalcum*) NERO CAES . AVG . IMP. Laur. hd., r. ℞.
CERTA . QVINQ . ROM . CON . S . C. Table surmounted by vase and wreath;
in field, S. *C.* 62. *R.I.C.* 405. *B.M.C.* 275. *Illustrated on p.* 11 .. 5·00

592 **Æ semis.** (*copper*) NERO CLAVDIVS CAESAR AVG . GERMANIC. Laur. hd., r.
℞. PON . MAX . TR . P . IMP . P . P. Roma seated l., holding wreath and
parazonium. *R.I.C.* 250. *B.M.C., p.* 254 *note* .. .. 7·50

593 **Æ quadrans.** (*orichalcum*) NERO CLAV . CAE . AVG . GER. Owl stg. on
altar. ℞. P . M . TR . P . IMP . P . P . S . C. Laurel-branch. *C.* 185.
R.I.C. 414. *B.M.C.* 288 .. .. 3·75

594 **Æ quadrans.** (*copper*) — Column surmounted by helmet, shield to r.,
spear behind. ℞. As previous. *C.* 182. *R.I.C.* 428. *B.M.C.* 294 .. 4·25

Colonial and Provincial Coinage

Fair

595 *Euboea, Chalcis,* **Æ 20.** Laur. hd., r. ℞. Hd. of Hera r., on capital
of Ionic column. *B.M.C. G.*108 .. .. 2·50

596 *Corinth,* **Æ 19.** Bare hd., r. ℞. ISTHMIA in wreath. *B.M.C. G.*565 .. 2·50

597 *Ionia, Smyrna,* **Æ 18.** Laur. hd., r. ℞. Zeus seated l. *B.M.C. G.*285 2·00

598 *Lydia, Maeonia,* **Æ 18.** Laur. hd., r. ℞. Hestia stg. r. *B.M.C. G.*32 2·50

599 *Phrygia, Prymnessus,* **Æ 21.** Laur. hd., r. ℞. Dikaiosyne stg. l.
*B.M.C. G.*24 .. .. 2·50

Fine

600	*Syria, Antioch*, **Æ tetradrachm.** Laur. hd., r. ℞. Eagle stg. l. on thunderbolt. *B.M.C. G.*190..	£7·50

601 — **Æ 21.** Bare hd., r. ℞. s . c . in wreath. *B.M.C. G.*182 ..   5·00

602 *Egypt, Alexandria*, **billon tetradrachm.** Rad. bust, l. ℞. Rad. hd. of Augustus r. *B.M.C. G.*112 ..   4·00

603 — Similar. ℞. Laur. hd. of Tiberius r. *B.M.C. G.*114 ..   4·00

604 — Laur. hd., r. ℞. Bust of Agrippina Junior r. *B.M.C. G.*116 ..   6·00

605 — Similar. ℞. Bust of Octavia r. *B.M.C. G.*119 ..   7·50

606 — Rad. bust, l. ℞. Laur. bust of Zeus Olympius r. *B.M.C. G.*127 ..   2·50

607 — Similar. ℞. Laur. bust of Apollo r. *B.M.C. G.*144 ..   2·50

608 — Laur. hd., r. ℞. Eirene stg. r., holding caduceus and helmet. *B.M.C. G.*148 ..   3·00

609 — Rad. bust, r. ℞. Eagle stg. l. on thunderbolt. *B.M.C. G.*166 ..   2·50

610 — Laur. hd., r. ℞. Serpent Agathodaemon r. *B.M.C. G.*171 ..   4·00

611 — Rad. bust, l. ℞. Galley sailing r. *B.M.C. G.*176 ..   5·00

OCTAVIA

The daughter of Claudius and Messalina, Octavia was born about A.D. 40. *She married Nero in* A.D. 53 *as his first wife, but in* A.D. 62 *he divorced her and later in the same year she was murdered.*

612 *Corinth*, **Æ 20.** OCTAVIAE NERONIS AVG. Dr. bust, r. ℞. GEN . COL . COR . Q . FVL . FLACCO II . VIR. Female stg. l., holding patera and cornucopiae. *C.* 1 ..   *Fair* £35·00

See also nos 555 and 605.

POPPAEA

Poppaea Sabina was married to Nero in A.D. 62 *as his second wife. She herself had been married twice before, firstly to Rufus Crispinus and then to the future emperor Otho. She died from the effects of an accidental kick by Nero in* A.D. 65.

613 *Egypt, Alexandria*, **billon tetradrachm.** Rad. hd. of Nero r. ℞. Bust of Poppaea r. *B.M.C. G.*122 ..   7·50

CLAUDIA

The daughter of Nero and Poppaea, she was born at Antium in A.D. *63 but died later the same year at the age of only four months.*

614 *Colonial,* Æ **20.** DIVA CLAVD . NER . F. Female stg. in circular hexastyle
temple. ℞. DIVA POPPAEA AVG. Female seated in distyle temple.
C. 1 .. .. *Fair* £30·00

CLODIUS MACER
A.D. 68

616

(Lucius Clodius Macer). Governor of Africa under Nero, he refused to acknowledge Galba and threatened the Roman corn supply from Africa. He raised a new legion which he named Legio I Macriana Liberatrix, but he was soon reduced and executed by Galba's orders.

615 **Æ denarius.** L . CLODI MACRI S . C. Lion's hd. r. ℞. LIB . LEG .
III . AVG. Legionary eagle between two standards. *C.* 5. *R.I.C.* 7.
B.M.C. 3 .. .. *Fine* 650·00
616 L . CLODIVS MACER S . C. Bare hd., r. ℞. PROPRAE . AFRICAE. Galley r.
C. 13. *R.I.C.* 11. *B.M.C.* 1 .. .. *Extr. rare*

GALBA
A.D. 68-69

617

(Servius Sulpicius Galba). Born in 3 B.C., *he held various important posts and was an administrator with a brilliant record when he was appointed governor of Hispania Tarraconensis in* A.D. *60. During the period of disturbances preceding the death of Nero he was proclaimed emperor by his troops, and the Senate having declared in his favour he proceeded to Rome. However, his strict discipline and rigid economy made him very unpopular with the army and on January 2nd,* A.D. *69, the legions of Lower Germany proclaimed their commander Vitellius emperor. In Rome, Otho organized a conspiracy and Galba was assassinated in the Forum on January 15th.*

Mints: Rome; Tarraco; Narbo(?); Vienna(?); Lugdunum; Carthage(?). *The coins of Lugdunum are probably all posthumous and struck under Vespasian, A.D. 70-71.*

Fine

617 **N aureus.** IMP . SER . GALBA AVG. Bare hd., r. ℞. S . P . Q . R . / OB C . S . in oak-wreath. *C.* 286. *R.I.C.* 19. *B.M.C.* 29 .. .. ..£125·00

618 **Æ denarius.** SER . GALBA IMPERATOR. Laur. hd., r. ℞. CONCORDIA PROVINCIARVM. Concord stg. l., holding olive-branch and cornucopiae. *C.* 34. *R.I.C.* 118. *B.M.C.* 217 .. .. 32·50

619 IMP . SER . GALBA CAESAR AVG. Laur. hd., r. ℞. DIVA AVGVSTA. Livia stg. l., holding patera and sceptre. *C.* 55. *R.I.C.* 4. *B.M.C.* 8 .. .. 20·00

620 GALBA IMP. Laur. hd., r. ℞. ROMA RENASCENS. Roma advancing r., holding Victory and spear. *C.* 209. *R.I.C.* 90. *B.M.C.* 183 .. .. 27·50

621 As 617. *C.* 287. *R.I.C.* 20 var. *B.M.C.* 34 .. .. .. 20·00

622 SER . GALBA IMP. Galba galloping r. ℞. TRES GALLIAE beneath busts of the three Gauls (Aquitania, Narbonensis and Lugdunensis) r. *C.* 307. *R.I.C.* 110. *B.M.C.* 211 .. .. 300·00

623 **Æ quinarius.** SER . GALBA IMP . CAESAR AVG . P . M . TR . P. Laur. hd., r. ℞. VICTORIA GALBAE AVG. Victory stg. r. on globe. *C.* 317. *R.I.C.* 124. *B.M.C.* 244 .. .. 65·00

624 **Æ sestertius.** SER . SVLPI . GALBA IMP . CAESAR AVG . P . M . TR . P. Laur. and dr. bust, r. ℞. HONOS ET VIRTVS S . C. Honos stg. r., facing Virtus stg. l. *C.* 91. *R.I.C.* 152. *B.M.C.*, *p.* 357 *note* .. .. 80·00

625 SER . GALBA IMP . CAESAR AVG . TR . P. Laur. hd., r. .℞ LIBERTAS PVBLICA S . C. Liberty stg. l. *C.* 108. *R.I.C.* 35. *B.M.C.* 68 .. .. 40·00

626 IMP . SER . SVLPIC . GALBA CAESAR AVG. Laur. and dr. bust, r. ℞. ROMA S . C. Roma seated l. on cuirass. *C.* 174. *R.I.C.* 43. *B.M.C.*, *p.* 323 *note* .. .. 45·00

627 SER GALBA IMP . CAES . AVG. Similar. ℞. S . P . Q . R . / OB / CIV . SER . in oak-wreath. *C.* 289. *R.I.C.* 50. *B.M.C.* 109 .. .. .. 40·00

628 **Æ dupondius.** *Obv.* As 625. ℞. PAX AVGVST . S . C. Pax stg. l. *C.* 150. *R.I.C.* 63. *B.M.C.*, *p.* 330 *note* .. .. 20·00

629 **Æ as.** IMP . SER . SVLP . GALBA CAES . AVG . TR . P. Laur. hd., r. ℞. As 625. *C.* 129. *R.I.C.* 60. *B.M.C.* 144. **Plate 5** .. .. 17·50

630 IMP . SER . GALBA AVG . TR . P. Bare hd., r. ℞. S . C. Legionary eagle between two standards. *C.* 275. *R.I.C.* 67. *B.M.C.*, *p.* 334 *note* 20·00

631 IMP . SER . GALBA . CAES . AVG . TR . P. Bare hd., r. ℞. VESTA S . C. Vesta seated l. *C.* 309. *R.I.C.* 72. *B.M.C.*, *p.* 335 *note* .. .. 17·50

Colonial and Provincial Coinage

Fair

632 *Corinth,* Æ **20.** Bare hd., r. ℞. Nike advancing l. *B.M.C.* G.579 .. 5·00

633 *Achaia, Patrae,* Æ **25.** Bare hd., l. ℞. Legionary eagle between two standards. *B.M.C.* G.24 .. .. 6·00

634 *Egypt, Alexandria,* **billon tetradrachm.** Laur. hd., r. ℞. Eleutheria stg. l., leaning on column. *B.M.C.* G.192.. .. .. .. 4·00

635 — Similar. ℞. Helmeted bust of Roma r. *B.M.C.* G.197 .. .. 4·00

636 — Similar. ℞. Bust of Alexandria r., wearing elephant's skin headdress. *B.M.C.* G.199 .. .. 4·00

637 Æ **24.** Similar. ℞. Bust of Isis r. *B.M.C.* G.202 .. .. ..7·50

CIVIL WARS

A.D. 68-69

During the wars of this period a number of coins were struck without the portrait or title of an emperor. Cohen gives them as a supplement to Galba; B.M.C. and R.I.C. give them a special chapter (before Galba) and add some of those that Cohen gives to Augustus (as they bear his name).

Mints: Spain (probably Tarraco and one other); Gaul (probably Vienna); Upper Germany (mint uncertain); Africa (probably Carthage).

                                                       Fine

638   **Æ aureus.** GENIVS P . R. Hd. of the Genius of the Roman People r. ℞. MARS VLTOR. Mars advancing r. *C.* 379. *R.I.C.* 10. *B.M.C.* 21

                                                         Very rare

639   **Æ denarius.** FIDES PRAETORIANORVM. Clasped hands. ℞. FIDES EXERCITVVM. Clasped hands. *C.* 363. *R.I.C.* 5. *B.M.C.* 65 ..   .. £65·00

640   ROMA RESTITVTA. Helmeted bust of Roma r. ℞. IVPPITER LIBERATOR. Jupiter seated l. *C.* 374. *R.I.C.* 8. *B.M.C.* 19 ..   .. 75·00

641   AVGVSTVS DIVI F. Laur. hd. of Augustus l. ℞. SENAT . P . Q . R. Victory flying l., holding shield. *C. Augustus* 253. *R.I.C.* 21. *B.M.C.* 57   ..   .. 100·00

OTHO

A.D. 69

645

(M. Salvius Otho). Born in A.D. *32, he was a close friend of Nero who appointed him governor of Lusitania. He supported Galba in his revolt in the hope of being adopted by him and succeeding to the Empire. Galba, however, adopted L. Calpurnius Piso, whereupon Otho conspired against him, was himself proclaimed emperor and had Galba and Piso put to death. Defeated in battle by the army of Vitellius, who had been proclaimed emperor by the legions of Lower Germany, Otho committed suicide on April 17th.*

Mint: Rome.

642   **Æ aureus.** IMP . OTHO CAESAR AVG . TR . P. Bare hd., r. ℞. SECVRITAS P . R. Security stg. l., holding wreath and sceptre. *C.* 14. *R.I.C.* 11. *B.M.C., p.* 366 *note* ..   .. 225·00

643   **Æ denarius.** IMP . M . OTHO CAESAR AVG . TR . P. Bare hd., r. ℞. PAX ORBIS TERRARVM. Pax stg. l. *C.* 3. *R.I.C.* 3. *B.M.C.* 3 ..   .. 40·00

644   As 642. *C.* 15. *R.I.C.* 12. *B.M.C.* 19 ..   .. 35·00

645   *Obv.* As 643. ℞. VICTORIA OTHONIS. Victory advancing l. *C.* 24. *R.I.C.* 16. *B.M.C.* 24   ..   .. 45·00

Colonial and Provincial Coinage

646   *Syria, Antioch,* **Æ tetradrachm.** Laur. hd., r. ℞. Eagle stg. l. on laurel branch. *B.M.C.* G.214   ..   .. 45·00

647   — **Æ 23.** Laur. hd., r. ℞. S . C . in wreath. *B.M.C.* G.207   .. 20·00

648 *Egypt, Alexandria,* **billon tetradrachm.** Laur. hd., r. ℞. Veiled
bust of Eirene r. *B.M.C. G.*206 ..   ..   £12·50

649 — — Similar. ℞. Kratesis stg. l., holding Nike and trophy. *B.M.C.*
*G.*210 ..   ..   12·50

650 — **Æ 21.** Similar. ℞. Canopus of Osiris r. *B.M.C. G.*216   ..   20·00

VITELLIUS
A.D. 69

659

(*Aulus Vitellius*).   *Born in* A.D. 14, *Vitellius was a close friend of all the emperors from
Tiberius to Nero and held several important posts, including the proconsulship of Africa.
Given the command of the Legions in Lower Germany by Galba, he was proclaimed emperor
by his troops on January 2nd,* A.D. 69, *and his generals defeated the army of Otho in North
Italy.   Vitellius, however, was a voracious glutton and gave more attention to the pleasures
of the table than to the business of government.   Vespasian having been proclaimed emperor
at Alexandria on July 1st, the Danubian legions declared for him and invaded Italy.   The
troops despatched against them were defeated, and Vitellius was later seized in his palace
and murdered.   His body was dragged through the streets of Rome and thrown into the Tiber.*

Mints: Rome; Tarraco; Lugdunum.

651 **N aureus.** A . VITELLIVS IMP . GERMAN. Laur. hd., l. ℞. CONSENSVS
EXERCITVVM. Mars advancing l., holding spear and legionary eagle.
C. 33. *R.I.C.* 4. *B.M.C.* 82   ..   ..   200·00

652 **R denarius.** A . VITELLIVS GERMANICVS IMP. Bare hd., r. ℞. CON-
CORDIA P . R. Concord seated l. *C.* 21. *R.I.C.* 2. *B.M.C.* 1 ..   ..   25·00

653 A . VITELLIVS GERMAN . IMP . TR . P. Laur. hd., r. ℞. S . P . Q . R . / OB /
C . S. in oak-wreath. *C.* 86. *R.I.C.* 22. *B.M.C.* 15   ..   ..   25·00

654 A . VITELLIVS GERM . IMP . AVG . TR . P. Laur. hd., r. ℞. XV . VIR SACR .
FAC. Tripod with dolphin above and raven beneath. *C.* 111. *R.I.C.* 24.
B.M.C. 39   ..   ..   20·00

655 *Obv.* As 652. ℞. No legend. Victory seated l., holding patera and
palm. *C.* 121. *R.I.C.* 26. *B.M.C.* 4   ..   ..   30·00

656 **Æ sestertius.** A . VITELLIVS GERMANICVS IMP . AVG . P . M . TR . P. Laur.
and dr. bust, r. ℞. PAX AVGVSTI S . C. Pax stg. l. *C.* 67. *R.I.C.* 8.
B.M.C., p. 377, †   ..   ..   120·00

657 **Æ dupondius.** A . VITELLIVS GERMA . IMP . AVG . P . M . TR . P. Similar.
℞. CONCORDIA AVGVSTI S . C. Concord seated l. *C.* 15. *R.I.C.* 20.
B.M.C. 65   ..   ..   45·00

658 **Æ as.** A . VITELLIVS GERMAN . IMP . AVG . P . M . TR . P. Laur. hd., r.
℞. CERES AVG . S . C. Ceres seated l., holding corn-ears and torch.
C. 5. *R.I.C.* 19. *B.M.C.* 71   ..   ..   40·00

659 *Obv.* As 651. ℞. FIDES EXERCITVVM S . C. Clasped hands. *C.* 34.
R.I.C. 4. *B.M.C.* 103   ..   ..   35·00

660 *Egypt, Alexandria,* **billon tetradrachm.** Laur. hd., r. ℞. Nike
advancing l. *B.M.C. G.*218   ..   ..   17·50

661 — **Æ 26.** Laur. hd., r. ℞. Bust of Serapis r. *B.M.C. G.*219   ..   20·00

LUCIUS VITELLIUS

663

The father of the Emperor, he had a distinguished career during which he was three times consul, governor of Syria and head of the government during Claudius' absence on the British expedition.   He died of paralysis in A.D. 52.

Fine

662   **Aʹ aureus.**   A . VITELLIVS GERMAN . IMP . TR . P.   Laur. hd. of Vitellius r.
      ℞.   L . VITELLIVS COS . III . CENSOR.   Laur. and dr. bust of L. Vitellius r.,
      eagle-tipped sceptre before.   *C.* 3.   *R.I.C.* 6.   *B.M.C.* 10   ..   ..£400·00

663   **Æ denarius.**   A . VITELLIVS GERM . IMP . AVG . TR . P.   Similar.   ℞.
      As previous.   *C.* 2.   *R.I.C.* 7.   *B.M.C.* 26   ..   ..   ..   145·00

VITELLIUS AND HIS CHILDREN

664

664   **Aʹ aureus.**   A . VITELLIVS GERM . IMP . AVG . TR . P.   Laur. hd., r.   ℞.
      LIBERI IMP . GERM . AVG.   Dr. busts of his son and daughter face to face.
      C. 3.   *R.I.C.* 15.   *B.M.C.* 27   ..   ..   300·00

665   **Æ denarius.**   *Obv.* Similar.   ℞.   LIBERI IMP . GERMAN.   As previous.
      C. 2.   *R.I.C.* 14.   *B.M.C.* 29   ..   ..   100·00

VESPASIAN
A.D. 69-79

684A

T. Flavius Vespasianus was born at Falacrina in A.D. 9, *the son of Flavius Sabinus, a tax-gatherer, and Vespasia Polla.   Despite his humble origin, his military skill carried him to a series of important posts, and he commanded part of the forces which invaded Britain under Claudius. In* A.D. *67 Nero appointed him to quell the Jewish rebellion and he prosecuted the war successfully during the troubled period following Nero's death. On July 1st,* A.D. *69, the legions at Alexandria proclaimed him emperor and the Danubian legions followed suit and invaded Italy, defeating the forces of Vitellius at the Battle of Cremona. Vespasian reached Rome in* A.D. *70 and quickly set about repairing the damage caused by the civil wars. He proved to be a just and industrious ruler and the condition of the State soon improved. He died at Reate on June 24th,* A.D. *79, and was deified by the Senate.*

Titles and Powers, A.D. 69-79.

A.D.	Tribunician Power	Imperatorial Acclamation	Consulship	Other Titles
69	TR.P.	IMP. IMP.II.		AVGVSTVS.
70	TR.P. – TR.P.II.	IMP.III. IMP.IIII. IMP.V.	COS.II.	P.M. P.P.
71	TR.P.II – III.	IMP.VI. IMP.VII. IMP.VIII.	COS.III.	
72	TR.P.III. – IIII.	IMP.VIII.	COS.IIII.	
73	TR.P.IIII. – V.	IMP.X.		CENSOR.
74	TR.P.V. – VI.	IMP.XI. IMP.XII.	COS.V.	
75	TR.P.VI. – VII.	IMP.XIII. IMP.XIIII.	COS.VI.	
76	TR.P.VII. – VIII.	IMP.XV. – XVIII.	COS.VII.	
77	TR.P.VIII. – VIIII.		COS.VIII.	
78	TR.P.VIIII. – X.	IMP.XVIIII.		
79	TR.P.X.	IMP.XX.	COS.VIIII.	

Vespasian received the tribunician power on July 1st, A.D. 69, and it was subsequently renewed each year on that date.

His first consulship was in A.D. 51.

Mints: Rome; Tarraco; Lugdunum; Poetovio (?); Byzantium; Philippi (?); Ephesus; mint in Lycia (?); Antioch; Samosata (?); Tyre (?); mint in Judaea (?); Alexandria.

The following are the commonest forms of obverse legend:

A. IMP . CAES . VESP . AVG . P . M . COS . IIII.

B. IMP . CAES . VESPASIAN . AVG . COS . III.

C. IMP . CAES . VESPASIAN . AVG . P . M . TR . P . P . P . COS . III.

D. IMP . CAESAR VESPASIANVS AVG.

Other obverse legends are given in full.

The obverse type is laur. hd. of Vespasian r., unless otherwise stated.

Fine

666 **N aureus.** A. ℞. VIC . AVG. Victory stg. r. on globe. *C.* 586.
R.I.C. 51. *B.M.C.* 72 .. ..£100·00

667 **N quinarius.** D. ℞. VICTORIA AVGVST. Victory seated l. *C.* 593.
R.I.C. 125. *B.M.C.* 283 .. .. 175·00

668 **Æ cistophorus.** IMP . VESP . CAES . AVG . PONT . MAX . TRIB . POT . COS .
II . P . P. (or COS . IIII.) ℞. COM . ASI. Vespasian and woman stg. within
temple inscribed ROM . ET AVG. *C.* —. *R.I.C.* —. *B.M.C.* 449 .. .. *Unique*

Fine

669 **Æ denarius.** CAESAR VESPASIANVS AVG. Laur. hd., l. ℞. ANNONA
AVG. Annona seated l. *C.* 30. *R.I.C.* 131*b*. *B.M.C.* 298 .. .. £4·50
670 A. ℞. AVGVR TRI . POT. Sacrificial implements. *C.* 45. *R.I.C.* 42.
B.M.C. 64 .. .. 4·00
671 IMP . CAESAR VESPAS . AVG . COS . III . TR . P . P . P. ℞. CONCORDIA AVG.
Ceres seated l., holding corn-ears and cornucopiae; in ex., EPHE . (Ephesus).
C. 67. *R.I.C.* 329. *B.M.C.* 453 .. .. 12·50
672 D. ℞. COS . ITER . TR . POT. Pax seated l., holding branch and
caduceus. *C.* —. *R.I.C.* 10. *B.M.C.* 26 .. .. .. 4·00
673 D. ℞. COS . VIII. Pair of oxen under yoke l. *C.* —. *R.I.C.* 107.
B.M.C. 206 .. .. 6·00
674 D. ℞. — Prow r., star above. *C.* 136. *R.I.C.* 108. *B.M.C.* 210 7·50
675 *Obv.* As 669. ℞. IMP . XIX. Modius. *C.* 215. *R.I.C.* 110.
B.M.C. 218 .. .. 6·00
676 D. ℞. IOVIS CVSTOS. Jupiter stg. facing, altar at feet. *C.* 222.
R.I.C. 124*a*. *B.M.C.* 276 .. .. 4·00
677 D. ℞. IVDAEA. Judaea seated r. at foot of trophy. *C.* 226. *R.I.C.*
266. *B.M.C.* 370 .. .. 30·00
678 D. ℞. PON . MAX . TR . P . COS . V. Winged caduceus. *C.* 362.
R.I.C. 75. *B.M.C.* 138 .. .. 4·00
679 D. ℞. — Vespasian seated r., holding branch and sceptre. *C.* 364.
R.I.C. 77. *B.M.C.* 136 .. .. 4·00
680 D. ℞. PON . MAX . TR . P . COS . VI. Pax seated l., holding branch.
C. 366. *R.I.C.* 90. *B.M.C.* 161 .. .. 4·00
681 D. ℞. TITVS ET DOMITIAN . CAES . PRIN . IV. Titus and Domitian
seated l. on curule chair. *C.* 541. *R.I.C.* 23. *B.M.C.,* *p.* 8 *note* .. 12·50
682 D. Laur. hd., l. ℞. TR . POT . X . COS . VIIII. Capricorn l., globe
below. *C.* 556. *R.I.C.* 117. *B.M.C.* 252 .. .. .. 6·50
683 A. ℞. VESTA. Vesta stg. l., holding simpulum and sceptre. *C.* 574.
R.I.C. 50. *B.M.C.* 71 .. .. 6·00

684 **Æ quinarius.** IMP . CAES . VESP . AVG . P . M . COS . V . CENS. ℞. VICTORIA
AVGVSTI. Victory advancing r. *C.* 613. *R.I.C.* 78. *B.M.C.* 142 .. 25·00

684A **Æ sestertius.** C. ℞. CAES . AVG . F . DES . IMP . AVG . F . COS . DES .
ITER . S . C. Titus and Domitian stg. facing each other. *C.* 48. *R.I.C.*
413 *note.* *B.M.C.* 528 *note.* *Illust. on p.* 112 .. .. .. 40·00
685 C. ℞. FORTVNAE REDVCI S . C. Fortune stg. l., holding branch, rudder
and cornucopiae. *C.* 188. *R.I.C.* 422. *B.M.C.* 529 .. .. 15·00
686 C. ℞. IVDAEA CAPTA S . C. Palm-tree to l. of which stands Jew and to
r. of which sits Jewess in attitude of mourning. *C.* 232. *R.I.C.* 424.
B.M.C. 533 *note* .. .. 75·00
687 C. (but CAESAR VESPAS). ℞. PAX AVGVSTI S . C. Pax stg. l. *C.* 326.
R.I.C. 437. *B.M.C.* 555 .. .. 15·00
688 C. ℞. ROMA S . C. Roma stg. l., holding Victory and spear. *C.* 419.
R.I.C. 443. *B.M.C.* 560 .. .. 15·00
689 C. ℞. ROMA RESVRGES S . C. Vespasian stg. l., raising kneeling figure
of Roma who is presented by Minerva. *C.* 425. *R.I.C.* 445. *B.M.C.*
566 .. .. 50·00
690 C. (but VESPAS). ℞. S . C. Mars advancing r., holding spear and
trophy. *C.* 440. *R.I.C.* 447. *B.M.C.* 568 .. .. .. 15·00
691 IMP . CAES . VESPASIAN . AVG . P . M . TR . P . P . P . COS . V . CENS. ℞. S .
C. Spes advancing l. *C.* 451. *R.I.C.* 749. *B.M.C.,* *p.* 206 *note* .. 17·50
692 C. ℞. S . P . Q . R . OB CIVES SERVATOS in oak-wreath. *C.* 529. *R.I.C.*
458. *B.M.C.* 573 *note* .. .. 17·50

Fine

693 **Æ sestertius.** IMP . CAESAR VESPASIANVS AVG . P . M . T . P . P . P . COS . III.
Ŗ. VICTORIA AVGVSTI S . C. Victory stg. r., inscribing OB CIV . SER . on
shield attached to palm-tree. *C.* 622. *R.I.C.* 466. *B.M.C.* 578 .. £25·00

694 **Æ dupondius.** B. Rad. hd., r. Ŗ. CONCORDIA AVGVSTI S . C. Concord seated l., altar at feet. *C.* 71. *R.I.C.* 471. *B.M.C.* 588 .. .. 5·00

695 IMP . CAES . VESP . AVG . P . M . T . P . COS . IIII . CENS. Rad. hd., l. Ŗ.
FELICITAS PVBLICA S . C. Felicity stg. l. *C.* 151. *R.I.C.* 539*b*. *B.M.C.*
661 .. .. 5·00

696 B. (but COS . VIII . P . P). Rad. hd., r. Ŗ. FIDES PVBLICA S . C. Fides
stg. l. *C.* 168. *R.I.C.* 753*a*. *B.M.C.* 831 .. .. .. 5·00

697 B. (but COS . VIII . P . P). Ŗ. FORTVNAE REDVCI S. C. Fortune stg. l.
C. 181. *R.I.C.* 754*b*. *B.M.C.* 833.. .. .. 5·00

698 D. Laur. hd., l. Ŗ. PON . MAX . TR . POT . P . P . COS . V . CENS. Winged caduceus between two cornuacopiae. *C.* 378. *R.I.C.* 798*c*. *B.M.C.*
888 *note* .. .. 6·00

699 B. Rad. hd., r. Ŗ. ROMA S . C. Roma seated l., holding wreath and
parazonium. *C.* 411. *R.I.C.* 476. *B.M.C.* 591 .. .. .. 6·00

700 B. (but CAESAR). Rad. hd., r. Ŗ. SECVRITAS AVGVSTI S . C. Security
seated r., altar at feet. *C.* 507. *R.I.C.* 479. *B.M.C.* 808 .. .. 5·00

701 **Æ as.** IMP . CAESAR VESP . AVG . COS . V . CENS. Ŗ. AEQVITAS AVGVST .
S . C. Equity stg. l. *C.* 2. *R.I.C.* 557*a*. *B.M.C.* 700 .. .. 5·00

702 B. Ŗ. IVDEA CAPTA S . C. Judaea seated r. at foot of palm-tree. *C.* 244.
R.I.C. 489. *B.M.C.* 604 .. .. 35·00

703 B. (but COS . VIII . P . P .). Ŗ. PROVIDENT . S . C. Large altar. *C.* 400.
R.I.C. 763. *B.M.C.* 846 .. .. 6·00

704 B. (but COS . IIII.). Ŗ. S . C. Eagle stg. facing on globe. *C.* 481. *R.I.C.*
747. *B.M.C.* 822 .. .. 6·00

705 B. Ŗ. VICTORIA NAVALIS S . C. Victory stg. r. on prow. *C.* 632.
R.I.C. 503. *B.M.C.* 616 .. .. 7·00

706 **Æ semis.** IMP . VESP . AVG. Laur. hd., l. Ŗ. P . M . TR . POT . P . P.
Winged caduceus. *C.* 349. *R.I.C.* 794. *B.M.C.* 880 .. .. 6·00

707 **Æ quadrans.** IMP . VESPASIAN . AVG. Trophy. Ŗ. P . M . TR . P . P .
P . COS . III . S . C. Standard. *C.* 344. *R.I.C.* 507. *B.M.C., p.* 134* .. 6·00

708 *Vespasian, Titus and Domitian, N* **aureus.** D. Ŗ. CAESAR . AVG . F .
COS . CAESAR . AVG . F . PR. Bare hds. of Titus and Domitian face to face.
C. 4. *R.I.C.* 2. *B.M.C.* 1 .. .. 400·00

708A — **Æ denarius.** Similar. *C.* 5. *R.I.C.* 2. *B.M.C.* 2 .. .. 35·00

Commemorative Coins struck after his death

709 *Struck by Titus, N* **aureus.** DIVVS AVGVSTVS VESPASIANVS. Laur. hd., r.
Ŗ. EX S . C. Shield on column surmounted by vase; laurel-branch each
side. *C.* 148. *R.I.C.* (*Tit.*) 62. *B.M.C.* 123 .. .. .. 125·00

710 — **Æ denarius.** *Obv.* Similar. Ŗ. — Victory stg. l., placing shield
on trophy; captive (Jewess) sits l. below. *C.* 144. *R.I.C.* (*Tit.*) 59*a*. *B.M.C.*
112. **Plate 5** .. .. 7·50

711 — — *Obv.* Similar. Ŗ. S . C. on shield supported by two capricorns
back to back. *C.* 497. *R.I.C.* (*Tit.*) 63. *B.M.C.* 129 .. .. 6·50

712 — **Æ sestertius.** DIVO AVG . VESP . S . P . Q . R. Vespasian seated r. on
quadriga of elephants. Ŗ. IMP . T . CAES . DIVI VESP . F . AVG . P . M . TR .
P . P . P . COS . VIII . around large S . C. *C.* 205. *R.I.C.* (*Tit.*) 143.
B.M.C. 221 .. .. 45·00

Fine

713 — **Æ dupondius.** *Obv.* As 709, but hd. rad. ℞. CONCORD . AVGVST
s . c. Concord seated l. *C.* 63. *R.I.C.* (*Tit.*) 149. *B.M.C.* 251 .. £10·00
714 *Struck by Trajan Decius,* **Æ antoninianus.** DIVO VESPASIANO. Rad. hd.,
r. ℞. CONSECRATIO. Large altar. *C.* 652. *R.I.C.* (*Dec.*) 80.. .. 8·00

Colonial and Provincial Coinage

715 *Macedon, Thessalonica,* **Æ 23.** Laur. bust, l. ℞. ΘΕΣΣΑΛΟΝΙΚΕΩΝ in
wreath. *B.M.C. G.*— .. .. 5·00
716 *Cyprus,* **Æ 27.** Laur. hd., r. ℞. Zeus Salaminios stg. facing. *B.M.C.
G.*22 .. .. 7·50
717 *Cappadocia, Caesarea,* **Æ didrachm.** Laur. hd., r. ℞. Nike stg. r.
*B.M.C. G.*16 .. .. 12·00
718 *Syria, Antioch,* **Æ tetradrachm.** Laur. hd., r. ℞. Eagle stg. l. on
club. *B.M.C. G.*230 .. .. 10·00
719 — **Æ 27.** Laur. hd., l. ℞. s . c. in wreath. *B.M.C. G.*216 .. 3·50
720 *Egypt, Alexandria,* **billon tetradrachm.** Laur. hd., r. ℞. Laur. hd.
of Titus r. *B.M.C. G.*223 .. .. 15·00
721 — Similar. ℞. Eirene stg. l. *B.M.C. G.*229 .. .. .. 6·00
722 — Similar. ℞. Nike advancing l. *B.M.C. G.*236 .. .. 6·00
723 — Similar. ℞. Roma stg. l., holding spear and shield. *B.M.C. G.*240 6·00
724 — Similar. ℞. Alexandria stg. l., holding wreath and sceptre.
*B.M.C. G.*244 .. .. 6·00
725 **Æ 25.** Similar. ℞. Bust of Serapis r. *B.M.C. G.*255 .. .. 3·50
726 — Similar. ℞. Bust of Isis r. *B.M.C. G.* 264 .. .. .. 3·50

DOMITILLA

728

(*Flavia Domitilla*). *First wife of Vespasian and mother of Titus, Domitian and
Domitilla the Younger: died before her husband became emperor.*

727 **Æ denarius.** DIVA DOMITILLA AVGVSTA. Dr. bust, r. ℞. CONCORDIA
AVGVST. Peacock stg. r. *C.* 2. *R.I.C.* (*Tit.*) 70. *B.M.C.* 136 .. 200·00
728 *Vespasian and Domitilla,* **N aureus.** DIVVS AVGVSTVS VESPASIANVS. His
rad. hd. r. ℞. As *obv.* of previous. *C.* 1. *R.I.C.* (*Tit.*) 69. *B.M.C.*
(*Dom.*) 68 .. .. *Very rare*

DOMITILLA THE YOUNGER
Daughter of Vespasian and Flavia Domitilla

729 **Æ sestertius.** MEMORIAE DOMITILLAE s . p . q . r. Carpentum drawn r.
by two mules. ℞. IMP . T . CAES . DIVI VESP . F . AVG . P . M . TR . P . P . P .
COS . VIII . around large s . c. *C.* 1. *R.I.C.* (*Tit.*) 153. *B.M.C.* 226 .. 75·00
*Although Cohen gives this to Domitilla the Younger, Mattingly and Syden-
ham think it may be of her mother.*

TITUS
A.D. 79-81

736A

(*Titus Flavius Vespasianus*).   Born in A.D. 41, *Titus was the elder son of Vespasian and Flavia Domitilla and was educated with Britannicus, the ill-fated son of Claudius. He later served in Germany and Britain and commanded a legion in his father's Jewish campaign.   When Vespasian left to assume the purple, Titus remained to carry on the war and captured Jerusalem in A.D. 70.   On his return to Rome, Vespasian made him his colleague in the government and his succession in A.D. 79 was thus smooth.   He proved himself a most benevolent emperor and his premature death in A.D. 81 caused great sorrow.*

Titles and Powers, A.D. 69-81.

A.D.	Tribunician Power	Imperatorial Acclamation	Consulship	Other Titles
69				CAESAR.
70			COS.	
71	TR.P.	IMP. IMP.II.		
72	TR.P. – TR.P.II	IMP.III.	COS.II.	
73	TR.P.II. – III.	IMP.IIII.		CENSOR.
74	TR.P.III. – IIII.	IMP.V. IMP.VI.	COS.III.	
75	TR.P.IIII. – V.	IMP.VII. IMP.VIII.	COS.IIII.	
76	TR.P.V. – VI.	IMP.VIIII. – XII.	COS.V.	
77	TR.P.VI. – VII.		COS.VI.	
78	TR.P.VII. – VIII.	IMP.XIII.		
79	TR.P.VIII. – VIIII.	IMP.XIIII. IMP.XV.	COS.VII.	AVGVSTVS. P.M. P.P.
80	TR.P.VIIII. – X.		COS.VIII.	
81	TR.P.X. – XI.	IMP.XVI. IMP.XVII.		

Titus received the tribunician power on July 1st, A.D. 71, and it was subsequently renewed each year on that date.

Mints: Rome; Lugdunum; Ephesus (?).

Unless otherwise stated the obverse type is laur. hd. of Titus r.

As Caesar

A.D. 69-79, *under Vespasian*

All *R.I.C.* and *B.M.C.* references are to the coinage of Vespasian.   **Fine**

730   **N aureus.   T . CAESAR IMP . VESPASIAN.   R.   PAX AVGVST.   Pax seated l.
C. 134.   R.I.C. 212.   B.M.C. 310 ..   ..£100·00

731   **AR denarius.   T . CAESAR VESPASIANVS.   R.   ANNONA AVG.   Annona
seated l.   C. 17.   R.I.C. 218.   B.M.C. 319   ..   ..   5·00

732   *Obv.* As 730.   R.   PONTIF . TR . P . COS . III.   Winged caduceus.
C. 160.   R.I.C. 173A.   B.M.C. 151   ..   ..   5·00

Fine

733 **Æ quinarius.** *Obv.* As 730. ℞. VICTORIA AVGVSTI. Victory advancing r. *C.* 373. *R.I.C.* 216. *B.M.C.* 313 .. .. £22·00

734 **Æ sestertius.** T . CAES . VESPASIAN . IMP . PON . TR . POT . COS . III . CENS. ℞. S . C. Spes advancing l. *C.* 210. *R.I.C.* 664. *B.M.C., p.* 162, ‡.. 25·00

735 **Æ dupondius.** T . CAESAR IMP . COS . IIII. Rad. hd., r. ℞. FELICITAS PVBLICA S . C. Felicity stg. l. *C.* 83. *R.I.C.* 671. *B.M.C., p.* 166, †.. 5·00

736 T . CAES . IMP . AVG . F . TR . P . COS . VI . CENSOR. Laur. hd., l. ℞. ROMA S . C. Roma seated l. *C.* 187. *R.I.C.* 781*b*. *B.M.C., p.* 213, * *note* .. 5·50

736A T . CAES . VESPASIAN . IMP . P . TR . P . COS . II. Rad. hd., r. ℞. ROMA VICTRIX S . C. Similar. *C.* 192. *R.I.C.* 617. *B.M.C.* 641. *Illustrated on p.* 117 .. .. 6·00

737 **Æ as.** T . CAES . VESPASIAN . IMP . P . TR . P . COS . II. ℞. AEQVITAS AVGVSTI S . C. Equity stg. l. *C.* 6. *R.I.C.* 618. *B.M.C.* 825D *note* .. 5·00

738 *Obv.* As 736, but hd. r. ℞. IVDAEA CAPTA S . C. Judaea seated r. at foot of palm-tree. *C.* 118. *R.I.C.* 784. *B.M.C.* 862 .. .. .. 35·00

739 T . CAESAR IMP . COS . III . CENS. Laur. hd., l. ℞. PAX AVGVST . S . C. Pax stg. l., leaning on column. *C.* 144. *R.I.C.* 668*b*. *B.M.C.* 710 *note* 5·00

740 T . CAES . IMP . PON . TR . P . COS . II . CENS. ℞. PROVIDENT . S . C. Large altar. *C.* 174. *R.I.C.* 655. *B.M.C., p.* 155, † .. .. .. 6·00

741 **Æ semis.** T . CAES . IMP. ℞. VESP . PON . TR . P. Winged caduceus. *C.* 339. *R.I.C.* 808. *B.M.C.* 882 *note* .. .. 6·50

As Augustus

The following are the commonest forms of obverse legend:

A. IMP . T . CAES . VESP . AVG . P . M . TR . P . COS . VIII.

B. IMP . T . CAES . VESP . AVG . P . M . TR . P . P . P . COS . VIII.

C. IMP . TITVS CAES . VESPASIAN . AVG . P . M.

742 **Æ aureus.** C. ℞. TR . P . VIIII . IMP . XV . COS . VII . P . P . Radiate figure stg. facing on rostral column holding spear. *C.* 288. *R.I.C.* 16*a*. *B.M.C.* 27 *note* .. .. 100·00

743 **Æ cistophorus.** C. ℞. No legend. Legionary eagle between two standards. *C.* 398. *R.I.C.* 74. *B.M.C.* 149 .. .. 100·00

744 **Æ denarius.** C. ℞. TR . P . VIIII . IMP . XIIII . COS . VII . P . P. Jewish captive kneeling r. in front of trophy. *Cf. C.* 274. *R.I.C.* 5. *B.M.C.* 15 .. .. 8·00

745 C. Laur. hd., l. ℞. TR . P . IX . IMP . XV . COS . VIII . P . P. Dolphin entwined around anchor. *C.* 310. *R.I.C.* 26*b*. *B.M.C.* 72 *note* .. 6·50

746 C. ℞. — Throne. *C.* 313. *R.I.C.* 24*a*. *B.M.C.* 61. **Plate 5** .. 5·00

747 C. ℞. — Wreath on curule chair. *C.* 318. *R.I.C.* 25*a*. *B.M.C.* 66.. 5·00

748 **Æ quinarius.** IMP . T . CAESAR VESPASIANVS AVG. ℞. VICTORIA AVGVSTI. Victory seated l. *C.* 376. *R.I.C.* 29*a*. *B.M.C., p.* 241, *.. 22·00

749 **Æ sestertius.** B. ℞. ANNONA AVG. Annona stg. l., modius at feet; in background, ship's stern. *C.* 14. *R.I.C.* 86. *B.M.C.* 152 .. .. 20·00

750 B. Laur. hd., l. ℞. FELICIT . PVBLIC . S . C. Felicity stg. l. *C.* 74. *R.I.C.* 89. *B.M.C.* 158 .. .. 20·00

751 B. Laur. hd., l. ℞. PAX AVGVST . S . C. Pax stg. l. *C.* 140. *R.I.C.* 94. *B.M.C.* 171 .. .. 20·00

752 B. ℞. S . C. Spes advancing l. *C.* 221. *R.I.C.* 100. *B.M.C.* 186 20·00

Fine

753 **Æ sestertius.** B. Titus seated l. on curule chair amidst arms. R. View of the Coliseum, showing part of interior with rows of spectators. *C.* 400. *R.I.C.* 110. *B.M.C.* 190 .. ..£225·00

754 **Æ dupondius.** A. Rad. hd., r. R. CERES AVGVST . S . C. Ceres stg. l. *C.* 34. *R.I.C.* 111*a*. *B.M.C.* 191A .. .. 6·00

755 A. Rad. hd., l. R. CONCORDIA AVGVST . S . C. Concord seated l. *C.* 43. *R.I.C.* 112*b*. *B.M.C.* 194 *note* .. .. 6·00

756 A. Rad. hd., l. R. SALVS AVG . S . C. Salus seated l., holding patera. *C.* 195. *R.I.C.* 116*b*. *B.M.C.* 197 .. .. 6·00

757 **Æ as.** A. R. AEQVITAS AVGVST . S . C. Equity stg. l. *C.* 4. *R.I.C.* 121*a*. *B.M.C.* 203 .. .. 6·00

758 A. R. GENI . P . R . S . C. Genius stg. l., altar at feet. *C.* 96. *R.I.C.* 126. *B.M.C.* 209 .. .. 7·00

759 A. R. S . C. Spes advancing l. *C.* 219. *R.I.C.* 130. *B.M.C.* 216.. 6·00

760 A. R. VICTORIA AVGVST . S . C. Victory stg. r., on prow. *C.* 368. *R.I.C.* 133. *B.M.C.* 217 .. .. 7·50

762 **Æ quadrans.** IMP . T . VESP . AVG . COS . VIII. Modius. R. S . C . in laurel-wreath. *C.* 252. *R.I.C.* 136. *B.M.C.* 220 .. .. .. 6·00

Colonial and Provincial Coinage

763 *Decapolis, Gadara*, **Æ 19.** Laur. hd., r. R. Two cornuacopiae crossed. *B.M.C.* G.3 .. .. 12·50

764 *Egypt, Alexandria*, **billon tetradrachm.** Laur. hd., r. R. Homonoia seated l., holding olive-branch. *B.M.C.* G.278 .. .. 6·00

765 — Similar. R. Bust of Serapis r. *B.M.C.* G.281 .. .. .. 7·50

JULIA TITI

770

Daughter of Titus and Marcia Furnilla. Her uncle Domitian fell in love with her and she lived with him for some time as his wife.

766 **N aureus.** IVLIA AVGVSTA. Dr. bust, r. R. DIVI TITI FILIA. Peacock stg. facing, tail in splendour. *C.* 6. *R.I.C.* (*Dom.*) 218. *B.M.C.* 250.. 450·00

767 **Æ cistophorus.** IVLIA AVGVSTA DIVI TITI F. Dr. bust, r. Ṛ. VESTA. Vesta seated l., holding palladium and sceptre. *C.* 15. *R.I.C.* (*Dom.*) 231. *B.M.C.* 258 ..   .. £180·00

768 **Æ denarius.** IVLIA AVGVSTA TITI AVGVSTI F. Diad. and dr. bust, r. Ṛ. VENVS AVGVST. Venus stg. r., leaning on column, holding helmet and sceptre. *C.* 14. *R.I.C.* (*Tit.*) 56. *B.M.C.* 141 ..   ..   ..   65·00

769 **Æ sestertius.** DIVAE IVLIAE AVG . DIVI TITI F . S . P . Q . R. Carpentum drawn r. by two mules. Ṛ. IMP . CAES . DOMIT . AVG . GERM . COS . XVI . CENS . PER . P . P . around large S . C. *C.* 10. *R.I.C.* (*Dom.*) 411. *B.M.C.* 472 ..   ..   50·00

770 **Æ dupondius.** IVLIA IMP . T . AVG . F . AVGVSTA. Dr. bust r. Ṛ. VESTA S . C. As 767. *C.* 18. *R.I.C.* (*Tit.*) 180. *B.M.C.* 256. *Illustrated on p.* 119 ..   ..   35·00

DOMITIAN
A.D. 81-96

801

T. *Flavius Domitianus was the younger son of Vespasian and Flavia Domitilla and was born in Rome in* A.D. 51. *During the reigns of his father and brother Domitian was kept very much in the background, but on the death of Titus his succession was not disputed. At first he showed great promise, but he was very unpopular with the senatorial nobility and this resulted in numerous plots and conspiracies. Domitian, who was suspicious by nature, reacted violently, and the last years of his reign were ones of terror and oppression. He was eventually murdered on September 18th,* A.D. 96, *as the result of a palace plot involving his wife, Domitia, his chamberlain and the Praetorian Prefect.*

Unless otherwise stated the obverse type is laur. hd. of Domitian r.

> **We have now generally changed the condition of the gold and silver to Very Fine.**

Mints: Rome; Lugdunum; Ephesus (?).

As Caesar
A.D. 69-79, *under Vespasian*

All *R.I.C.* and *B.M.C.* references are to the coinage of Vespasian

Very Fine

771 **Ạ́ aureus.** CAESAR AVG . F . DOMITIANVS. Ṛ. COS . IIII. Cornucopiae. *C.* 46. *R.I.C.* 237. *B.M.C.* 196 ..   ..   200·00

772 **Æ denarius.** *Obv.* Similar. Ṛ — Pegasus walking r. *C.* 47. *R.I.C.* 238. *B.M.C.* 193 ..   ..   11·00

773 *Obv.* Similar. Ṛ. COS . V. Wolf and twins, boat in exergue. *C.* 51. *R.I.C.* 241. *B.M.C.* 240 ..   ..   12·50

774 CAESAR AVG . F . DOMITIANVS COS . VI. Ṛ. PRINCEPS IVVENTVTIS. Clasped hands holding legionary eagle on prow. *C.* 393. *R.I.C.* 246. *B.M.C.* 269 ..   ..   11·00

775 **Æ quinarius.** CAES . AVG . F . DOMIT . COS . II. Ṛ. VICTORIA AVGVSTI. Victory advancing r. *Cf. C.* 632. *R.I.C.* 231. *B.M.C.,* p. 23, †..   ..   35·00

Titles and Powers, A.D. 69-96

A.D.	Tribunician Power	Imperatorial Acclamation	Consulship	Other Titles
69				CAESAR.
70				PRAETOR.
71			COS.	
72				
73			COS.II.	
74			COS.III.	
75				
76			COS.IIII.	
77			COS.V.	
78				
79			COS.VI.	
80			COS.VII.	
81	TR.P.	IMP.		AVGVSTVS. P.M. P.P.
82	TR.P. – TR.P.II.	IMP.II.	COS.VIII.	
83	TR.P.II. – III.	IMP.III. IMP.IIII.	COS.VIIII.	GERM.
84	TR.P.III. – IIII.	IMP.V.IMP. VI. IMP.VII.	COS.X.	
85	TR.P.IIII. – V.	IMP.VIII – XI.	COS.XI.	CENSOR, later PERPETVVS.
86	TR.P.V. – VI.	IMP.XII. – XIIII.	COS.XII.	
87	TR.P.VI. – VII.		COS.XIII.	
88	TR.P.VII. – VIII.	IMP.XV.	COS.XIIII.	
89	TR.P.VIII. – VIIII.	IMPXVI. – XXI.		
90	TR.P.VIIII. – X.		COS.XV.	
91	TR.P.X. – XI.			
92	TR.P.XI. – XII.	IMP.XXII.	COS.XVI.	
93	TR.P.XII. – XIII.			
94	TR.P.XIII. – XIIII.			
95	TR.P.XIIII. – XV.		COS.XVII.	
96	TR.P.XV. – XVI.			

Domitian received the tribunician power on September 13th, A.D. 81, and it was subsequently renewed each year on that date.

Fine

776 **Æ sestertius.** CAESAR AVG . F . DOMITIANVS COS . IIII. ℞. s . c. Spes advancing l. *C.* 450. *R.I.C.* 714. *B.M.C.* 729 .. .. £25·00

777 **Æ dupondius.** — Laur. and dr. bust r., ℞. FELICITAS PVBLICA S . C. Felicity stg. l. *C.* 102. *R.I.C.* 715. *B.M.C., p.* 171, ‡.. .. .. 5·00

778 **Æ as.** CAESAR AVG . F . DOMITIAN . COS . V. ℞. As 776. *C.* 453. *R.I.C.* 723. *B.M.C., p.* 177, ‡ .. .. 5·00

779 CAESAR AVG . F . DOMITIAN . COS . II. Laur. hd., l. ℞. VICTORIA AVGVST S . C. Victory stg. r. on prow. *C.* 629. *R.I.C.* 706. *B.M.C.* 693 6·00

A.D. 79-81, *under Titus*

All *R.I.C.* and *B.M.C.* references are to the coinage of Titus **Very Fine**

780 **N aureus.** CAESAR AVG . F . DOMITIANVS COS . VII. ℞. PRINCEPS IVVENTVTIS. Garlanded and lighted altar. *C.* 396. *R.I.C.* 46. *B.M.C., p.* 238, † *note* .. .. 225·00

781 **Æ denarius.** CAESAR DIVI F . DOMITIANVS COS . VII. ℞. — Goat stg. l. within laurel-wreath. *C.* 390. *R.I.C.* 49. *B.M.C.* 88 .. .. 15·00

782 *Obv.* Similar. ℞. As 780. *C.*—. *R.I.C.* 50. *B.M.C.* 92 .. 11·00

783 *Obv.* Similar. ℞. PRINCEPS IVVENTVTIS. Helmet on throne. *C.*—. *R.I.C.* 51. *B.M.C.* 98 .. .. 12·50

784 **Æ quinarius.** *Obv.* Similar. ℞. VICTORIA AVGVST. Victory seated l. *C.* 624. *R.I.C.* 53. *B.M.C.* 104A .. .. 35·00

Fine

785 **Æ sestertius.** CAES . DIVI AVG . VESP . F . DOMITIANVS COS . VII. ℞.
s . c. Minerva advancing r., brandishing javelin. *C.* 439. *R.I.C.* 157c.
B.M.C. 231   ..   .. £20·00

786 **Æ dupondius.** *Obv.* Similar. ℞. CERES AVGVST . s . c. Ceres
stg. l. *C.* 32. *R.I.C.* 165a. *B.M.C.* 237   ..   ..   ..   6·00

787 CAES . DIVI VESP . F . DOMITIAN . COS . VII. ℞. CONCORDIA AVG . s . c.
Concord seated l. *C.* 39. *R.I.C.* 166a. *B.M.C.* 239 ..   ..   ..   6·00

788 **Æ as.** *Obv.* Similar, but hd. l. ℞. s . c. Minerva stg. l., shield
at feet. *C.* 443. *R.I.C.* 169b. *B.M.C.* 246 *note*   ..   ..   5·50

789 *Obv.* As 785, but DOMITIAN. ℞. As 776. *C.* 459. *R.I.C.* 168b.
B.M.C. 248   ..   ..   5·50

As Augustus

The following are the commonest forms of obverse legend:

A. IMP . CAES . DOMIT . AVG . GERM . P . M . TR . P . IIII . (—XVI).
B. IMP . CAES . DOMIT . AVG . GERM . COS . XI . CENS . POT . P . P.
C. IMP . CAES . DOMIT . AVG . GERM . COS . XI . (—XVII) CENS . PER . P . P.
D. IMP . CAES . DOMITIAN . AVG . GERM . COS . X . (or XI).
E. IMP . CAES . DOMITIANVS AVG . P . M.

Very Fine

790 **N aureus.** DOMITIANVS AVGVSTVS. ℞. GERMANICVS COS . XV. Minerva
stg. l., shield at feet. *C.* 151. *R.I.C.* 162. *B.M.C.* 171   ..   .. 200·00

791 A. (TR . P . V). ℞. IMP . XI . COS . XII . CENS . P . P . P. Minerva
stg. l., holding spear. *C.* 191. *R.I.C.* 76. *B.M.C.*, *p.* 318, * *note*   .. 175·00

792 **N quinarius.** A. (TR . P . VII). ℞. IMP . XIIII . COS . XIIII . CENS .
P . P . P. Victory advancing r. *C.* 238. *R.I.C.* 112. *B.M.C.* 126 *Very rare*

793 **Æ cistophorus.** IMP . CAES . DOMITIAN . AVG . P . M . COS . VIII. ℞.
No legend. Legionary eagle between two standards. *C.* 667. *R.I.C.*
226. *B.M.C.* 252   ..   .. 75·00

794 **Æ denarius.** A. (TR . P . V). ℞. IMP . XI . COS . XII . CENS . P . P . P.
Minerva stg. l., shield at feet. *C.* 193. *R.I.C.* 75. *B.M.C.* 90 ..   ..   6·00

795 A. (TR . P . VIII). ℞. IMP . XVII . COS . XIIII . CENS . P . P . P. Minerva
stg. l., holding spear. *C.* 244. *R.I.C.* 134. *B.M.C.* 150   ..   6·00

796 A. (TR . P . XI). ℞. IMP . XXI . COS . XV . CENS . P . P . P. Minerva
stg. r. on prow, brandishing javelin, owl at feet. *C.* 270. *R.I.C.* 157.
B.M.C. 183   ..   ..   6·00

797 A. (TR . P . XII). ℞. IMP . XXII . COS . XVI . CENS . P . P . P. Minerva
advancing r., brandishing javelin. *C.* 280. *R.I.C.* 171. *B.M.C.* 200.
Plate 5..   ..   ..   6·00

798 E. ℞. TR . P . COS . VII . DES . VIII . P . P. Dolphin entwined around
anchor. *C.* 568. *R.I.C.* 20. *B.M.C.* 20 ..   ..   10·00

799 E. ℞. — Garlanded and lighted altar. *C.* 577. *R.I.C.* 19. *B.M.C.*
23   ..   ..   10·00

800 **Æ quinarius.** E. ℞. VICTORIA AVGVST. Victory advancing r.
C. 621. *R.I.C.* 42. *B.M.C.* 55   ..   .. 25·00

Fine

801 **Æ sestertius.** B. ℞. GERMANIA CAPTA s . c. Trophy between
German woman seated l. and German captive stg. r. *C.* 136. *R.I.C.*
278a. *B.M.C.* 325. *Illustrated on p.* 120 ..   ..   60·00

802 C. (COS . XV). ℞. IOVI VICTORI s . c. Jupiter seated l. *C.* 314.
R.I.C. 388. *B.M.C.* 439   ..   .. 17·50

Fine

803 **Æ sestertius.** IMP . DOMITIAN . CAES . DIVI VESP . F . AVG . P . M . TR . P .
P . P . COS . VIII. ℞. S . C. Mars advancing r., carrying spear and
trophy. *C.* 423. *R.I.C.* 449. *B.M.C.* 517 .. .. £20·00

804 D. (COS . XI). ℞. S . C. Domitian stg. l., sacrificing over altar in
front of shrine of Minerva. *C.* 491. *R.I.C.* 256. *B.M.C.* 296 .. 35·00

805 B. ℞. S . C. Domitian stg. l., the Rhine reclining r. at feet. *C.* 504.
R.I.C. 286. *B.M.C.* 334 .. .. 50·00

806 IMP . CAES . DIVI VESP . F . DOMITIAN . AVG . P . M. Laur. hd., l. ℞.
TR . P . COS . VII . DES . VIII . P . P . S . C. Minerva stg. l., holding spear.
C. 556. *R.I.C.* 233b. *B.M.C.* 264 .. .. 20·00

807 **Æ dupondius.** C. (COS . XIIII). Rad. hd., r. ℞. FIDEI PVBLICAE
S . C. Fides stg. r. *C.* 116. *R.I.C.* 366. *B.M.C., p.* 390, * .. .. 5·00

808 D. (COS . XI). Rad. hd., r. ℞. S . C. Two German shields crossed
over vexillum, trumpets and spears. *C.* 537. *R.I.C.* 267. *B.M.C.* 311 10·00

809 C. (COS . XVI). Rad. hd., r. ℞. VIRTVTI AVGVSTI S . C. Virtus stg.
r., holding parazonium and spear. *C.* 659. *R.I.C.* 406. *B.M.C.* 468 .. 4·50

810 **Æ as.** IMP . CAES . DOMIT . AVG . GERM . P . M . TR . P . VIII . CENS . PER .
P . P. ℞. COS . XIIII . LVD . SAEC . FEC . S . C. Domitian stg. l., accom-
panied by harpist and flute-player, sacrificing over altar in front of temple.
C. 85. *R.I.C.* 385a. *B.M.C.* 434 .. .. 9·00

811 C. (COS . XIIII). ℞. FORTVNAE AVGVSTI S . C. Fortune stg. l. *C.* 128.
R.I.C. 371. *B.M.C.* 416. **Plate 5** .. .. 4·50

812 B. ℞. IOVI CONSERVAT . S . C. Jupiter stg. l., holding thunderbolt
and sceptre. *C.* 303. *R.I.C.* 300. *B.M.C.* 354 .. .. .. 7·50

813 C. (COS . XIII). ℞. MONETA AVGVSTI S . C. Moneta stg. l. *C.* 329.
R.I.C. 354b. *B.M.C.* 402 .. .. 4·50

814 D. (COS . X). ℞. SALVTI AVGVST . S . C. Large altar. *C.* 414.
R.I.C. 250a. *B.M.C.* 291 .. .. 6·00

815 *Obv.* As 806, but hd. r. ℞. TR . P . COS . VIII . DES . VIIII . P . P . S . C.
Minerva advancing r., brandishing javelin. *C.* 587. *R.I.C.* 242a.
B.M.C. 281 .. .. 5·00

816 **Æ semis.** IMP . DOMIT . AVG . GERM . COS . XI. Laur. and dr. bust of
Apollo r. ℞. S . C. Lyre. *C.* 541. *R.I.C.* 273. *B.M.C.* 318 .. 5·00

817 IMP . DOMITIANVS AVG. ℞. S . C. Cornucopiae. *C.* 543. *R.I.C.* 425.
B.M.C. 481 .. .. 6·00

818 **Æ quadrans.** IMP . DOMIT . AVG . GERM. Helmeted and dr. bust of
Minerva r. ℞. S . C. Olive-branch. *C.* 544. *R.I.C.* 428. *B.M.C.*
488 .. .. 4·50

819 — Trophy. ℞. As previous. *C.* 545. *R.I.C.* 433. *B.M.C.* 494 .. 4·50

820 — around large S . C. ℞. No legend. Rhinoceros l. *C.* 674.
R.I.C. 435. *B.M.C.* 498 .. .. 5·00

Colonial and Provincial Coinage

Fair

821   *Macedon*, Æ **24.** Laur. hd., r. ℞. Macedonian shield. *B.M.C. G.*—   £2·25
822   *Pamphylia, Perga*, Æ **19.** Laur. hd., r. ℞. Artemis advancing r. *B.M.C. G.*23 ..   ..   1·75
823   *Syria, Antioch*, Æ **24.** Laur. hd., l. ℞. s . c. in wreath. *B.M.C. G.* 242 ..   ..   2·00
824   *Egypt, Alexandria*, **billon tetradrachm.** Laur. hd., r. ℞. Bust of Nilus r. *B.M.C. G.*285   ..   ..   5·00
825   — Æ **33.** Similar. ℞. Domitian in biga of Centaurs r. *B.M.C. G.*338 ..   ..   6·00
826   — Æ **24.** Similar. ℞. Bust of Serapis r. *B.M.C. G.*300 ..   ..   2·50
827   — Æ **18.** Similar. ℞. Hawk stg. r. *B.M.C. G.*332   ..   ..   2·00

DOMITIA

832

Domitia Longina, *the daughter of Cn. Domitius Corbulo, was married to Domitian in* A.D. 82. *She was implicated in her husband's assassination in* A.D. 96 *after which she retired into private life, and survived until* A.D. 150 *when she died at a very advanced age.*

All *R.I.C.* and *B.M.C.* references are to the coinage of Domitian. **Very Fine**

828   **N aureus.** DOMITIA AVGVSTA IMP . DOMIT. Dr. bust, r. ℞. CONCORDIA AVGVST. Peacock stg. r. *C.* 1. *R.I.C.* 212. *B.M.C.* 60   ..   ..   450·00
829   **Æ cistophorus.** DOMITIA AVGVSTA. Dr. bust, r. ℞. VENVS AVG. Venus stg. r., leaning on column. *C.* 19. *R.I.C.* 230. *B.M.C.* 256 ..   225·00
830   **Æ denarius.** As 828. *C.* 2. *R.I.C.* 212. *B.M.C.* 61 ..   ..   175·00
831   *Obv.* As 828. ℞. DIVVS CAESAR IMP . DOMITIANI F. Baby boy seated l. on globe amidst seven stars. *C.* 11. *R.I.C.* 213. *B.M.C.* 63 ..   ..   250·00

Fine

832   **Æ sestertius.** DOMITIAE AVG . IMP . CAES . DIVI F. DOMITIAN . AVG. Dr. bust, r. ℞. DIVI CAESAR . MATRI S . C. Domitia seated l., extending r. hand to child stg. before her. *C.* 6. *R.I.C.* 440*a*. *B.M.C.* 501 *note*

Very rare

833   **Æ dupondius.** *Obv.* Similar, but DOMITIA. ℞. DIVI CAESARIS MATER S . C. Domitia stg. l., holding patera and sceptre, altar at feet. *C.* 9. *R.I.C.* 442. *B.M.C.* 503 ..   ..   200·00
834   **Æ as.** *Obv.* Similar. ℞. DIVI CAES . MATER S . C. Ceres stg. l., holding corn-ears and sceptre. *C.* 5. *R.I.C.* 443. *B.M.C., p.* 414, * ..   200·00
834A   *Domitia and Domitian*, **Æ cistophorus.** *Obv.* As 829. ℞. As *obv.* of 793. *C.* 2. *R.I.C.* 228. *B.M.C.* 255 ..   .. *Very Fine* £180·00

ANONYMOUS QUADRANTES

The following pieces, Nos. 835-845, bear no obv. legend or emperor's name, but are attributed by Mattingly (R.I.C., Vol. II, pp. 214-5) to the period Domitian-Antoninus Pius: the Cohen references are to Vol. VIII, pp. 267-271.

		Fine
835	Rhinoceros l. ℞. s . c. Olive-branch. *C.* 2. *R.I.C.* 36	£5·00
836	Similar. ℞. s . c. Owl. *C.* 3. *R.I.C.* 37	4·50
837	Helmeted and dr. bust of Minerva r. ℞. s . c. Owl. *C.* 7. *R.I.C.* 7	3·75
838	Laur. hd. of Jupiter r. ℞. s . c. Eagle. *C.* 14. *R.I.C.* 1 and 2 ..	4·25
839	Diad. and dr. bust of Neptune l., trident behind. ℞. s . c. Dolphin. *C.* 18. *R.I.C.* 15	6·00
840	Hd. of Tiber r., crowned with reeds. ℞. s . c. Wolf and twins. *C.* 22. *R.I.C.* 17	7·50
841	Helmeted and cuir. bust of Mars r. ℞. s . c. Cuirass. *C.* 27. *R.I.C.* 19	3·75
842	Helmeted hd. of Mars r. ℞. s . c. Trophy. *C.* 32. *R.I.C.* 21 ..	3·75
843	Dr. bust of Mercury r., wearing winged petasus. ℞. s . c. Winged caduceus. *C.* 34. *R.I.C.* 31	4·25
844	Griffin l., touching wheel with paw. ℞. s . c. Tripod. *C.* 38. *R.I.C.* 28	5·50
845	Laur. and dr. bust of Apollo r. ℞. s . c. Tripod. *C.* 40. *R.I.C.* 26	5·00

NERVA

A.D. 96-98

863

(M. Cocceius Nerva) Born in A.D. 32, he became a distinguished lawyer and was consul with Vespasian in 71 and with Domitian in 90. On the assassination of the latter he was proclaimed emperor and during his short reign he did much to improve the condition of the state. However, he lacked the capacity to command and he only had the half-hearted support of the army. This led him to adopt Trajan, who was very popular with the army, and on the death of Nerva on Jan. 25th, A.D. 98, Trajan succeeded to the empire.

Titles and Powers, A.D. 96-98

A.D.	Tribunician Power	Imperatorial Acclamation	Consulship	Other Titles
96	TR.P.	IMP.		AVGVSTVS. P.M. P.P.
97	TR.P. – TR.P.II.	IMP.II.	COS.III.	GERM.
98	TR.P.II.		COS.IIII.	

Nerva received the tribunician power on September 18th, A.D. 96, and it was renewed on the same date in the following year.

His first two consulships were in A.D. 71 and A.D. 90.

Mints: Rome; Asia Minor.

The following are the commonest forms of obverse legend:

A. IMP . NERVA CAES . AVG . P . M . TR . P . COS . II . P . P.

B. IMP . NERVA CAES . AVG . P . M . TR . P . COS . III . P . P.

The obverse type is laur. hd. of Nerva r., unless otherwise stated.

Very Fine

846 **N aureus.** B. R. CONCORDIA EXERCITVVM. Clasped hands holding
    legionary eagle set on prow. *C.* 28. *R.I.C.* 15. *B.M.C.* 27 .. .. £250·00

847 **N quinarius.** B. R. VICTORIA AVGVST. Victory seated l. *C.* 148.
    R.I.C. 22. *B.M.C.* 51 .. .. 400·00

848 **R cistophorus.** IMP . NERVA CAES . AVG . P . M . TR . POT . P . P. R.
    COS. III. Six corn-ears bound together. *C.* 45. *R.I.C.* 120. *B.M.C.* 81 120·00

849 **R denarius.** B. (but TR . P . II.) R. AEQVITAS AVGVST. Equity stg.
    l. *C.* 9. *R.I.C.* 25. *B.M.C.* 52 .. .. 10·00

850 A. R. CONCORDIA EXERCITVVM. Clasped hands. *C.* 16. *R.I.C.* 2.
    B.M.C. 6 .. .. 10·00

851 As 846. *C.* 29. *R.I.C.* 15. *B.M.C.* 29 .. .. 10·00

852 IMP . NERVA CAES . AVG . P . M . TR . POT. R. COS . III . PATER PATRIAE.
    Sacrificial implements. *C.* 48. *R.I.C.* 24. *B.M.C.* 33 .. .. 12·00

853 B. R. FORTVNA AVGVST. Fortune stg. l. *C.* 66. *R.I.C.* 16. *B.M.C.*
    37 .. .. 10·00

854 A. R. LIBERTAS PVBLICA. Liberty stg. l. *C.* 106. *R.I.C.* 7. *B.M.C.*
    17 .. .. 10·00

855 B. R. SALVS PVBLICA. Salus seated l., holding corn-ears. *C.* 134.
    R.I.C. 20. *B.M.C.* 48 .. .. 10·00

856 **R quinarius.** IMP . NERVA CAES . AVG . GERM . P . M . TR . P . II. R.
    IMP . II . COS . IIII . P . P. Victory advancing r. *C.* 93. *R.I.C.* 45.
    B.M.C. 68 .. .. 75·00

Fine

857 **Æ sestertius.** B. R. CONCORDIA EXERCITVVM S . C. As 846. *C.* 30.
    R.I.C. 80. *B.M.C.* 102 .. .. 30·00

858 B. R. FISCI IVDAICI CALVMNIA SVBLATA S . C. Palm-tree. *C.* 57.
    R.I.C. 82. *B.M.C.* 105 .. .. 125·00

859 IMP . NERVA CAES . AVG . P . M . TR . P . COS . II . DESIGN . III . P . P. R.
    LIBERTAS PVBLICA S . C. Liberty stg. l. *C.* 110. *R.I.C.* 76. *B.M.C.*,
    p. 18, * .. .. 25·00

Fine

860 **Æ sestertius.** B. R. PAX AVG . S . C. Pax seated l. C. 123. R.I.C.
88. B.M.C. 113 .. .. £25·00

861 B. R. PLEBEI VRBANAE FRVMENTO CONSTITVTO S . C. Modius containing six corn-ears and poppy. C. 127. R.I.C. 89. B.M.C. 115.. .. 90·00

862 B. (but TR . P . II). R. VEHICVLATIONE ITALIAE REMISSA S . C. Two
mules grazing back to back; in background, cart with shafts pointing
upwards. C. 144. R.I.C. 104. B.M.C., p. 25, ‡ .. .. .. 90·00

863 **Æ dupondius.** A. Rad. hd., r. R. FORTVNA AVGVST . S . C. Fortune
stg. l. C. 62. R.I.C. 61. B.M.C. 93. Illustrated on p. 125 .. .. 10·00

864 **Æ as.** B. R. AEQVITAS AVGVST . S . C. Equity stg. l. C. 7. R.I.C.
77. B.M.C. 127 .. .. 9·00

865 A. R. CONCORDIA EXERCITVVM S . C. Clasped hands. C. 17. R.I.C.
53. B.M.C. 95 .. .. 9·00

866 B. R. As 859. C. 115. R.I.C. 86. B.M.C. 131 .. .. .. 9·00

867 **Æ quadrans.** IMP . NERVA CAES . AVG. Modius. R. s . c. Winged
caduceus. C. 137. R.I.C. 111. B.M.C. 147 note .. .. .. 6·00

Colonial and Provincial Coinage

868 *Cappadocia, Caesarea,* **Æ didrachm.** Laur. hd., r. R. Clasped
hands holding standard on prow. B.M.C. G.44 .. .. 10·00

869 *Syria, Antioch,* **Æ 22.** Laur. hd., r. R. s . c. in wreath. B.M.C.
G.262 .. .. 5·00

870 *Egypt, Alexandria,* **billon tetradrachm.** Laur. hd., r. R. Tyche
stg. l. B.M.C. G.350 .. .. 5·00

871 — — Similar. R. Bust of Serapis r. B.M.C. G.351.. .. .. 5·00

TRAJAN
A.D. 98-117

913A

Marcus Ulpius Trajanus was born at Italica in Spain about A.D. 52. *He held several important military posts and was eventually appointed governor of Upper Germany by Nerva who later adopted him as the heir to the throne. On his succession, Trajan decided that the time was ripe for territorial expansion and he successfully undertook the conquest of Dacia which then became a Roman province. The famous column which was erected to commemorate Trajan's Dacian Wars still stands in Rome. He also carried out a spectacular building programme in Rome and he constructed or repaired many roads, bridges and aqueducts throughout the Empire. In the latter part of his reign, Trajan turned his attention to the Eastern frontier and in* A.D. 113 *he set out to annex both Armenia and Mesopotamia. He achieved considerable success in his Eastern campaigns and four new provinces were added to the Empire. At this point, however, revolts broke out in a number of provinces and Trajan was obliged to withdraw to Antioch. He determined to return to Rome to direct operations, but he died on the journey at Selinus in Cilicia (August,* A.D. 117).

Mints: Rome; Asia Minor.

Titles and Powers, A.D. 97-117

A.D.	Tribunician Power	Imperatorial Acclamation	Consulship	Other Titles
97	TR.P.			CAESAR. GERM.
98	TR.P. (later TR.P.II) – TR.P.III.	IMP.	COS.II.	AVGVSTVS. P.M. P.P.
99	TR.P.III. – IIII.			
100	TR.P.IIII. – V.		COS.III.	
101	TR.P.V – VI	IMP.II.	COS.IIII.	
102	TR.P.VI. – VII.	IMP.III. IMP.IIII.		DACICVS.
103	TR.P.VII. – VIII.		COS.V.	OPTIMVS PRINCEPS.
104	TR.P.VIII. – VIIII.	IMP.V.		
105	TR.P.VIIII. – X.			
106	TR.P.X. – XI.	IMP.VI.		
107	TR.P.XI. – XII.			
108	TR.P.XII. – XIII.			
109	TR.P.XIII. – XIIII.			
110	TR.P.XIIII. – XV.			
111	TR.P.XV. – XVI.			
112	TR.P.XVI. – XVII.		COS.VI.	
113	TR.P.XVII. – XVIII.			
114	TR.P.XVIII. – XVIIII.	IMP.VII		OPTIMVS.
115	TR.P.XVIIII. – XX.	IMP.VIII. – XIII.		PARTHICVS.
116	TR.P.XX. – XXI.			
117	TR.P.XXI.			

Trajan received the tribunician power late in A.D. 97. For a short period after his accession, he remained TR.P., but soon afterwards he apparently decided to continue the dating of Nerva (TR.P.II.) and became TR.P.III. on September 18th, A.D. 98. He subsequently renewed his tribunician power each year on that date.

His first consulship was in A.D. 91.

The following are the commonest forms of obverse legend:

A. IMP . CAES . NER . TRAIANO OPTIMO AVG . GER . DAC.
B. IMP . CAES . NER . TRAIANO OPTIMO AVG . GER . DAC . PARTHICO P . M . TR . P .
    COS . VI . P . P.
C. IMP . CAES . NERVA TRAIAN . AVG . GERM . P . M.
D. IMP . CAES . NERVAE TRAIANO AVG . GER . DAC . P . M . TR . P . COS . V . P . P.
E. IMP . TRAIANO AVG . GER . DAC . P . M . TR . P.
F. IMP . TRAIANO AVG . GER . DAC . P . M . TR . P . COS . VI . P . P.

Unless otherwise stated the obverse type is laur. hd. r., or laur. and dr., or dr. and cuir., bust r.

Very Fine

872 **N aureus.** A. R. P . M . TR . P . COS . VI . P . P . S . P . Q . R. Genius
     stg. l., holding patera and corn-ears. C. 275. R.I.C. 347. B.M.C. 545 £145·00

873 **N quinarius.** C. (but without P . M.). R. PONT . MAX . TR . POT .
     COS . II. Victory seated l., holding patera and wreath. C. 296. R.I.C.
     23. B.M.C., p. 34, * note ..   .. 300·00

874 **R cistophorus.** IMP . NERVA CAES . TRAIAN . AVG . GERM . P . M . TR .
     P . P . P. R. COS . II. Six corn-ears bound together. C. 50. R.I.C.
     715. B.M.C. 707 ..   .. 75·00

875 **R denarius.** F. R. ALIM . ITAL. (in ex.) S . P . Q . R. OPTIMO PRINCIPI.
     Abundance stg. l., child at feet. C. 9. R.I.C. 243. B.M.C. 468..   .. 10·00

876 E. R. COS . V . P . P . S . P . Q . R . OPTIMO PRINC. Roma seated l.
     C. 69. R.I.C. 116. B.M.C. 276 ..   .. 5·00

877 E. R. — Spes advancing l. C. 84. R.I.C. 127. B.M.C. 319   .. 5·00

878 E. R. — Equity stg. l. C. 85. R.I.C. 118. B.M.C. 281 ..   .. 5·00

Very Fine

879 **Æ denarius.** E. ℞. — Arabia stg. l., camel at feet. *C.* 89. *R.I.C.*
142. *B.M.C.* 297 .. .. £7·50

880 E. ℞. — Trophy. *C.* 100. *R.I.C.* 147*b*. *B.M.C.* 359 .. .. 6·50

881 E. ℞. — DAC . CAP. (in ex.). Dacian captive seated r. on pile of arms.
C. 118. *R.I.C.* 96. *B.M.C.* 385 .. .. 9·00

882 E. ℞. — DANVVIVS. (in ex.). The Danube reclining l. on rocks.
C. 136. *R.I.C.* 100. *B.M.C.* 395 .. .. 12·00

883 F. (but TRAIANVS.). ℞. DIVVS PATER TRAIAN. Trajan's father seated l.,
holding patera and sceptre. *C.* 140. *R.I.C.* 252. *B.M.C.* 500.. .. 20·00

884 A. ℞. FORT . RED. (in ex.) P . M . TR . P . COS . VI . P . P . S . P . Q . R.
Fortune seated l. *C.* 154. *R.I.C.* 318. *B.M.C.* 578. **Plate 5** .. .. 5·00

885 A. (but TRAIAN . OPTIM. and GERM.). ℞. PARTHICO P . M . TR . P . COS .
VI . P . P . S . P . Q . R. Rad. and dr. bust of Sol. r. *C.* 188. *R.I.C.* 326.
B.M.C. 624 .. .. 17·50

886 C. (but without P . M.). ℞. P . M . TR . P . COS . II . P . P. Victory
seated l. *C.* 213. *R.I.C.* 10. *B.M.C.* 41.. .. .. 5·00

887 A. ℞. P . M . TR . P . COS . VI . P . P . S . P . Q . R. Mars advancing r.
C. 270. *R.I.C.* 337. *B.M.C.* 536 .. .. 5·00

888 A. ℞. — Virtus stg. r., holding spear and parazonium. *C.* 274.
R.I.C. 355. *B.M.C.* 559 .. .. 5·00

889 F. (but COS . V.). ℞. S . P . Q . R . OPTIMO PRINCIPI. Genius stg. l.,
altar at feet. *C.* 394. *R.I.C.* 184. *B.M.C.* 206 .. .. 5·00

890 — ℞. — Trajan stg. facing, crowned by Victory who stands l. beside
him. *C.* 514. *R.I.C.* 212. *B.M.C.* 236 .. .. 10·00

891 F. ℞. — Trajan's Column with two eagles at base. *C.* 558. *R.I.C.*
292. *B.M.C.* 452 .. .. 15·00

892 F. ℞. — Legionary eagle between two standards. *C.* 577. *R.I.C.*
294. *B.M.C.* 458 .. .. 6·50

893 E. ℞. VESTA (in ex.) COS . V . P . P . S . P . Q . R . OPTIMO PRINC. Vesta
seated l. *C.* 644. *R.I.C.* 108. *B.M.C.* 405 .. .. 5·00

894 F. ℞. VIA TRAIANA (in ex.) S . P . Q . R . OPTIMO PRINCIPI. Via Traiana
reclining l., holding wheel. *C.* 648. *R.I.C.* 266. *B.M.C.* 487.. .. 12·00

895 **Æ quinarius.** A. ℞. P . M . TR . P . COS . VI . P . P . S . P . Q . R.
Victory advancing r. *C.* 282. *R.I.C.* 351. *B.M.C.* 557.. .. .. 32·50

Fine

896 **Æ sestertius.** D. ℞. AQVA TRAIANA (in ex.) S . P . Q . R . OPTIMO
PRINCIPI S . C. River god reclining l. under arched grotto supported by
two columns. *C.* 20. *R.I.C.* 463. *B.M.C.* 873 .. .. 25·00

897 D. ℞. ARAB . ADQVIS. (in ex.) S . P . Q . R . OPTIMO PRINCIPI S . C.
As 879. *C.* 32. *R.I.C.* 466. *B.M.C.* 877 .. .. 18·00

898 B. ℞. ARMENIA ET MESOPOTAMIA IN POTESTATEM P . R . REDACTAE S . C.
Trajan stg. r., reclining figures of Armenia, Euphrates and Tigris at feet.
C. 39. *R.I.C.* 642. *B.M.C.* 1035 .. .. 50·00

Fine

899 **Æ sestertius.** D. (but COS . VI.). R. DACIA AVGVST . PROVINCIA S . C. Dacia seated l. on rock, holding legionary eagle. *C.* 125. *R.I.C.* 622. *B.M.C.* 960 .. .. £35·00

900 — R. FELICITAS AVGVST . S . C. Felicity stg. l. *C.* 143. *R.I.C.* 624. *B.M.C.* 964 *note* .. .. 10·00

901 B. (but without PARTHICO.). R. FORT . RED. (in ex.) SENATVS POPVLVSQVE ROMANVS S . C. Fortune seated l. *C.* 158. *R.I.C.* 652. *B.M.C.* 1026.. 12·00

902 B. R. PROVIDENTIA AVGVSTI S . P . Q . R . S . C. Providence stg. l., leaning on column, globe at feet. *C.* 320. *R.I.C.* 663. *B.M.C.* 1041.. 10·00

903 B. R. REX PARTHIS DATVS S . C. Trajan seated l. on platform, presenting King Parthamaspates to Parthia kneeling r. *C.* 328. *R.I.C.* 667. *B.M.C.* 1045 .. .. 45·00

904 D. R. S . P . Q . R . OPTIMO PRINCIPI S . C. Ceres stg. l., modius at feet. *C.* 369. *R.I.C.* 479. *B.M.C.* 771 *note* .. .. 10·00

905 D. R. — Pax stg. l., r. foot on Dacian captive. *C.* 407. *R.I.C.* 503. *B.M.C.* 800 .. .. 12·00

906 D. R. — Victory stg. r., inscribing VIC . DAC. on shield attached to palm-tree. *C.* 454. *R.I.C.* 528. *B.M.C.* 812 .. .. .. 14·00

907 D. R. — Spes advancing l. *C.* 459. *R.I.C.* 519. *B.M.C.* 810 .. 10·00

908 D. R. — Fortune stg. l. *C.* 477. *R.I.C.* 500. *B.M.C.* 797.. .. 10·00

909 D. R. — Trajan galloping r., thrusting spear at Dacian beneath horse. *C.* 504. *R.I.C.* 536. *B.M.C.* 834 .. .. 14·00

910 D. R. — Single-span bridge with tower at each end and boat beneath (the "Danube Bridge"). *C.* 542. *R.I.C.* 569. *B.M.C.* 847 .. .. 40·00

911 C. R. TR . P . COS . II . P . P . S . C. Pax seated l. *C.* 590. *R.I.C.* 383. *B.M.C.* 713 *note* .. .. 14·00

912 **Æ dupondius.** D. Rad. hd., r. R. As 897. *C.* 36. *R.I.C.* 467. *B.M.C.* 919 *note* .. .. 9·00

913 B. Rad. and dr. bust, r. R. SENATVS POPVLVSQVE ROMANVS S . C. Trajan advancing r., hd. turned, between two trophies. *C.* 356. *R.I.C.* 676. *B.M.C.* 1052 .. .. 9·00

913A B. (but without PARTHICO.). Similar. R. — Trajan's Column with two eagles at base. *C.* 360. *R.I.C.* 679. *B.M.C.*, *p.* 219 ‡. *Illustrated on p.* 127 .. .. 12·00

914 D. Similar. R. S . P . Q . R . OPTIMO PRINCIPI S . C. Equity stg. l. *C.* 465. *R.I.C.* 498. *B.M.C.* 884 .. .. 5·00

915 D. Similar. R. — Salus seated l., feeding serpent arising from altar. *C.* 487. *R.I.C.* 516. *B.M.C.* 893 .. .. 5·00

916 IMP . CAES . NERVA TRAIAN . AVG . GERM . DACICVS P . M. Rad. hd., r. R. TR . P . VII . IMP . IIII . COS . V . P . P . S . C. Abundance seated l. on chair formed by two cornuacopiae. *C.* 603. *R.I.C.* 454. *B.M.C.* 762 .. 5·50

917 C. Similar. R. TR . POT . COS . IIII . P . P . S . C. As previous. *C.* 639. *R.I.C.* 428. *B.M.C.* 749 .. .. 5·00

918 **Æ as.** D. R. S . P . Q . R . OPTIMO PRINCIPI S . C. As 909. *C.* 505. *R.I.C.* 536. *B.M.C.* 942 .. .. 7·50

919 D. R. — Dacia seated l. on pile of arms; to l., trophy. *C.* 532. *R.I.C.* 561. *B.M.C.* 928 .. .. 7·50

920 D. R. — As 892. *C.* 579. *R.I.C.* 588. *B.M.C.* 946A .. .. 7·50

921 D. R. — in oak-wreath. *C.* 583. *R.I.C.* 476. *B.M.C.* 959 .. 8·00

922 C. R. TR . POT . COS . III . P . P . S . C. Victory advancing l., holding shield inscribed S . P . Q . R. *C.* 628. *R.I.C.* 417. *B.M.C.* 740.. .. 4·50

923 **Æ as.** (*orichalcum*) IMP . CAES . NER . TRAIANO OPTIMO AVG . GERM. Rad. and dr. bust, r. R. DAC . PARTHICO . P . M . TR . POT . XX . COS . VI . P . P. around oak-wreath within which is S . C. *C.* 122. *R.I.C.* 644. *B.M.C.* 1090 .. .. 8·00

Fine

924 **Æ semis.** Similar. *C.* 123. *R.I.C.* 645. *B.M.C.* 1103 .. .. £6·00
925 IMP . CAES . NER . TRAIAN . AVG. ℞ . s . c. Gaming table surmounted
by vase and wreath. *C.* 349. *R.I.C.* 685. *B.M.C.* 1068 *note* .. .. 6·00
926 **Æ quadrans.** IMP . CAES . TRAIAN . AVG . GERM. Bust of Hercules r.
℞. s . c. Boar r. *C.* 341. *R.I.C.* 702. *B.M.C.* 1062.. .. .. 4·50
927 — — ℞. s . c. Club. *C.* 344. *R.I.C.* 699. *B.M.C.* 1071.. .. 4·50

Commemorative Coins struck after his death

928 *Struck by Hadrian,* **N aureus.** DIVO TRAIANO PARTH . AVG . PATRI.
Laur., dr. and cuir. bust, r. ℞. No legend. Phoenix stg. r. on laurel-
branch. *C.* 659. *R.I.C.* (*Had.*) 28. *B.M.C.* 49 .. .. .. 250·00
929 *Struck by Trajan Decius,* **Æ antoninianus.** DIVO TRAIANO. Rad. hd., r.
℞. CONSECRATIO. Eagle stg. facing, hd. l. *C.* 666. *R.I.C.* (*Dec.*) 85a 9·00

Colonial and Provincial Coinage

930 *Cos,* Æ **17.** Laur. bust, r. ℞. Club. *B.M.C.* G.240.. .. .. 3·50
931 *Lydia, Nacrasa,* Æ **17.** Laur. hd., r. ℞. Statue of Artemis in shrine.
B.M.C. G.16 .. .. 3·50
932 *Pamphylia, Magydus,* **Æ 20.** Laur. hd., r. ℞. Athena stg. l. *B.M.C.*
G.2 .. .. 3·50
933 *Cappadocia, Caesarea,* **Æ tridrachm.** Laur. bust, r. ℞. Arabia stg. l.,
camel at feet. *B.M.C.* G.59 .. .. 20·00
934 — **Æ didrachm.** Similar. ℞. Clasped hands holding standard.
B.M.C. G. 53 .. .. 7·50
935 — — Similar. ℞. Apollo stg. l. *B.M.C.* G.68 .. .. 10·00
936 — **Æ drachm.** Laur. hd., r. ℞. Hd. of Zeus Ammon r. *B.M.C.*
G.54 .. .. 6·50
937 — **Æ hemidrachm.** Similar. *B.M.C.* G.56 .. .. .. 6·00
938 — **Æ 20.** Laur. hd., r. ℞. Inscription in wreath. *B.M.C.* G.106.. 2·50
939 *Chalcidice, Chalcis ad Belum,* Æ **24.** Laur. bust, r. ℞. Inscription in
wreath. *B.M.C.* G.1 .. .. 7·50
940 *Syria, Antioch,* **billon tetradrachm.** Laur. hd., r. ℞. Eagle stg.
facing on thunderbolt, hd. l. *B.M.C.* G.288 .. .. 10·00
941 — **Æ 28.** Similar. ℞. s . c. in wreath. *B.M.C.* G.278 .. .. 3·00
942 *Syria, Laodicea ad Mare,* Æ **25.** Laur. hd., r. ℞. Veiled and turreted
bust of the Tyche of Laodicea r. *B.M.C.* G.41 .. .. 4·50
943 *Phoenicia, Tyre,* **Æ tetradrachm.** Laur. hd. r., eagle and club below.
℞. Laur. hd. of Melqarth r. *B.M.C.* G.14 .. .. .. 12·50
944 *Galilaea, Tiberias,* **Æ 19.** Laur. bust, r. ℞. Palm-branch between
crossed cornuacopiae. *B.M.C.* G.17 .. .. 15·00
945 *Egypt, Alexandria,* **billon tetradrachm.** Rad. hd., r. ℞. Bust of
Zeus r. *B.M.C.* G.356 .. .. 3·00
946 — — Similar. ℞. Dikaiosyne stg. l., holding scales and cornucopiae.
B.M.C. G.360 .. .. 3·00
947 — — Laur. hd., r. ℞. Canopus of Osiris r. *B.M.C.* G.373 .. 4·00
948 — — Similar. ℞. Bust of Nilus r. *B.M.C.* G.378 .. .. 3·00
949 — — Similar. ℞. Agathodaemon serpent r. *B.M.C.* G.390 .. 4·00
950 — **Æ 35.** Laur. bust, r. ℞. Zeus enthroned l., eagle at feet. *B.M.C.*
G.399 .. .. 6·00
951 — — Laur. hd., r. ℞. Triumphal arch sumounted by emperor in
chariot flanked by trophies. *B.M.C.* G.545 .. .. .. 10·00

Fine

952   *Egypt, Alexandria,* **Æ 32.**   Laur. and cuir. bust, r.   R .   Modius in car
drawn r. by two winged serpents.   *B.M.C. G.*554   ..   ..   .. £10·00

953   — **Æ 23.**   Laur. hd., r.   R .   As 949.   *B.M.C. G.*501 ..   ..   ..   5·00

954   — **Æ 14.**   Similar.   R .   Elephant r.   *B.M.C. G.*493 ..   ..   ..   3·00

The Restored Coins of Trajan

In this interesting series, issued circa A.D. 107, there are restorations of many of the
Republican denarii as well as aurei of the Emperors Augustus, Tiberius, Claudius, Galba,
Vespasian, Titus and Nerva.

    For a full list of the denarii, see "Roman Silver Coins", Vol. II.

Very Fine

955   *N* **aureus** *of Titus.*   DIVVS TITVS.   Laur. hd., l.   R .   IMP . CAES . TRAIAN .
AVG . GER . DAC . P . P . REST.   Thunderbolt on throne.   *C.* (*Titus*) 403.
R.I.C. (*Traj.*) 833.   *B.M.C.* 705   ..   .. 750·00

956   **Æ denarius.**   BON . EVENT . LIBO.   Hd. of Bonus Eventus r.   R .   —
Well-head ornamented with lyres and garland; above, PVTEAL; below,
SCRIBON.   *R.I.C.* 787.   *B.M.C.* 686   ..   .. 275·00
*The prototype of this coin was issued by L. Scribonius Libo in 55 B.C.
(Babelon 8).*

957   — *of J. Caesar.*   Diad. hd. of Venus r.   R .   — Aeneas advancing l.,
carrying Anchises and palladium; to r., CAESAR.   *R.I.C.* 801.   *B.M.C.*
p. 141, 31   ..   .. 250·00
The prototype of this coin was issued circa 48 B.C. (Cohen 12).

PLOTINA

960

    *Pompeia Plotina was the wife of Trajan, whom she married long before his elevation to
the throne, and she was famed for her simplicity, dignity and virtue.   She bore no children,
but Hadrian was a favourite of hers and she was largely responsible for his succession in
A.D. 117.   She died during Hadrian's reign in A.D. 129, and was consecrated.*

    R.I.C. and *B.M.C.* references are to the coinage of Trajan.

Very Fine

958 **N aureus.** PLOTINA AVG . IMP . TRAIANI. Diad. and dr. bust, r. R. CAES . AVG . GERMA . DAC . COS . VI . P . P. Vesta seated l. *C.* 2. *R.I.C.* 730. *B.M.C.* 525 .. ..£750·00

959 **R denarius.** Similar. *C.* 3. *R.I.C.* 730. *B.M.C.* 526 .. .. 250·00

960 **Æ sestertius.** *Obv.* Similar. R. FIDES AVGVST . S . C. Fides stg. r., holding corn-ears and basket of fruit. *C.* 12. *R.I.C.* 740. *B.M.C.* 1080. *Illustrated on p.* 132 .. .. *Fine* £225·00

TRAJAN PATER
Father of Trajan, died A.D. 100

961 **N aureus.** IMP . TRAIANVS AVG . GER . DAC . P . M . TR . P . COS . VI . P . P. Laur., dr. and cuir. bust of Trajan r. R. DIVVS PATER TRAIAN. Bareheaded and dr. bust of Trajan Pater r. *C.* 1. *R.I.C.* (*Traj.*) 762. *B.M.C.* 505 .. .. 550·00
See also no. 883.

MARCIANA
Sister of Trajan, died A.D. 114

966

R.I.C. and *B.M.C.* references are to the coinage of Trajan.

962 **R denarius.** MARCIANA AVG . SOROR IMP . TRAIANI. Diad. and dr. bust, r. R. CAES . AVG . GERMA . DAC . COS . VI . P . P. Matidia seated l. between two children; in ex., MATIDIA AVG . F. *C.* 2. *R.I.C.* 742. *B.M.C.* 531 .. .. 275·00

Commemorative Coins struck after her death

963 **N aureus.** DIVA AVGVSTA MARCIANA. Diad. and dr. bust, r. R. CONSECRATIO. Eagle stg. l. on sceptre, hd. turned. *C.* 3. *R.I.C.* 743. *B.M.C.* 647 .. .. 750·00

964 **N quinarius.** Similar. *C.* 5. *R.I.C.* 744. *B.M.C.* 647 *note* .. .. 1200·00

965 **R denarius.** Similar. *C.* 4. *R.I.C.* 743. *B.M.C.* 650 .. .. 225·00

966 **Æ sestertius.** *Obv.* Similar. R. EX SENATVS CONSVLTO S . C. Marciana seated on car drawn l. by two elephants. *C.* 13. *R.I.C.* 750. *B.M.C.* 1086 .. .. *Fine* £275·00

MATIDIA
Daughter of Marciana and
mother-in-law of Hadrian

969

Very Fine

967 **N aureus.** MATIDIA AVG . DIVAE MARCIANAE F. Diad. and dr. bust, r.
R. PIETAS AVGVST. Matidia stg. l. between two children. *C.* 9.
R.I.C. (*Traj.*) 759. *B.M.C.* 659 .. ..£750·00

968 **R denarius.** Similar. *C.* 10. *R.I.C.* 759. *B.M.C.* 660 .. .. 275·00

969 **Æ sestertius.** Similar, but with s . c. on *rev. C.* 11. *R.I.C.* 761.
B.M.C. 1088 .. .. *Fine* £275·00

Commemorative Coins struck after her death

970 **N aureus.** DIVA AVGVSTA MATIDIA. Diad. and dr. bust, r. R. CON-
SECRATIO. Eagle stg. facing on sceptre, hd. r. *C.* 3. *R.I.C.* 753.
B.M.C. (*Had.*) 328 *note* .. .. 750·00

971 **R denarius.** *Obv.* Similar. R. — Eagle stg. l. on sceptre. *C.* 6.
R.I.C. 756. *B.M.C.* (*Had.*) 330 .. .. 275·00

HADRIAN
A.D. 117-138

1022

    P. Aelius Hadrianus was born at Italica in A.D. 76 *and, having lost his father at the age of ten, was placed under the care of guardians, one of whom was the future emperor Trajan. He soon embarked upon a military career and in* A.D. 100 *he married Trajan's grand-neice, Sabina. He was appointed governor of Syria during Trajan's Parthian war and was adopted by the emperor shortly before the latter's death. Much of Hadrian's reign was spent in visiting the provinces of his vast empire, and he greatly improved the defences of the frontiers. He is best known in this county as the builder of the great wall from the Tyne to the Solway: much of this immense work is still to be seen. There is little doubt that he was one of the most capable emperors who ever occupied the throne and he devoted his whole life to the improvement of the state. His rule was firm and humane and he was also a patron of the arts. He died at Baiae on July 10th,* A.D. 138, *after a long illness.*

Titles and Powers, A.D. 117-138

A.D.	Tribunician Power	Imperatorial Acclamation	Consulship	Other Titles
117	TR.P.	IMP.	COS.	AVGVSTVS. P.M.
118	TR.P. − TR.P.II.		COS.II.	
119	TR.P.II. − III.		COS.III.	
120	TR.P.III. − IIII.			
121	TR.P.IIII. − V.			
122	TR.P.V. − VI.			
123	TR.P.VI. − VII.			
124	TR.P.VII. − VIII.			
125	TR.P.VIII. − VIIII.			
126	TR.P.VIIII. − X.			
127	TR.P.X. − XI.			
128	TR.P.XI. − XII.			P.P.
129	TR.P.XII. − XIII.			
130	TR.P.XIII. − XIIII.			
131	TR.P.XIIII. − XV.			
132	TR.P.XV. − XVI.			
133	TR.P.XVI. − XVII.			
134	TR.P.XVII. − XVIII.			
135	TR.P.XVIII. − XVIIII.	IMP.II.		
136	TR.P.XVIIII. − XX.			
137	TR.P.XX. − XXI.			
138	TR.P.XXI. (−XXII ?)			

The exact date of renewal for Hadrian's tribunician power is not known, but it was probably some time in August.

Mints: Rome; Asia Minor (probably Ephesus, Sardes, Smyrna and other mints).

The following are the commonest forms of obverse legend:

A. HADRIANVS AVGVSTVS.
B. HADRIANVS AVGVSTVS P . P.
C. HADRIANVS AVG . COS . III . P . P.
D. IMP . CAESAR TRAIAN . HADRIANVS AVG.
E. IMP . CAESAR TRAIANVS HADRIANVS AVG.
F. IMP . CAESAR TRAIANVS HADRIANVS AVG . P . M . TR . P . COS . III.

Unless otherwise stated the obverse type is laur. hd. r., or laur. bust r., dr. or dr. and cuir.

Very Fine

972 **N aureus.** A. R. COS . III. Hadrian on horseback r., raising
r. hand. *C.* 406. *R.I.C.* 186. *B.M.C.* 430 .. ..£145·00

973 **N quinarius.** D. R. P . M . TR . P . COS . III. Victory advancing r.
C. 1124. *R.I.C.* 103. *B.M.C.* 221 .. .. 300·00

974 **R cistophorus.** B. Bare hd., r. R. COS . III. Jupiter stg. l.,
holding eagle and sceptre. *C.* 275. *R.I.C.* 497. *B.M.C.* 1066 .. 100·00

975 B. Bare hd., r. R. DIANA EPHESIA. Cultus-statue of Diana of
Ephesus facing between two stags. *C.* 534. *R.I.C.* 525. *B.M.C.*
1085 *note* .. .. 100·00

976 **R denarius.** IMP . CAES . TRAIAN . HADRIANO OPT . AVG . GER . DAC.
R. ADOPTIO (in ex.) PARTHIC . DIVI TRAIAN . AVG . F . P . M . TR . P .
COS . P . P. Trajan and Hadrian clasping r. hands. *C.* 4. *R.I.C.* 3c.
B.M.C. 6 .. .. 12·50

977 C. R. AEGYPTOS. Egypt reclining l., holding sistrum, ibis at feet.
C. 100. *R.I.C.* 297. *B.M.C.* 801 .. .. 9·00

978　**Æ denarius.** C. Bare hd., r. Ṟ. AFRICA. Africa reclining l., holding scorpion and cornucopiae, basket of fruit at feet. *C.* 140. *R.I.C.* 299. *B.M.C.* 813　..　　..　　..　　..　　..　　..　　£10·00

979　C. Bare hd., r. Ṟ. ANNONA AVG. Modius. *C.* 172. *R.I.C.* 230. *B.M.C.* 595　..　　..　　..　　..　　..　　..　　..　　..　　6·50

980　C. Ṟ. ASIA. Asia stg. l., r. foot on prow, holding hook and rudder. *C.* 189. *R.I.C.* 301. *B.M.C.* 834　..　　..　　..　　..　　12·00

981　A. Ṟ. COS . III. Diana stg. r., holding bow and arrow. *C.* 315. *R.I.C.* 147. *B.M.C.* 334　..　　..　　..　　..　　..　　5·50

982　A. Ṟ. — Hercules seated r. on cuirass, holding club and distaff. *C.* 331. *R.I.C.* 149. *B.M.C.* 340 *note*　..　　..　　..　　..　　5·50

983　A. Ṟ. — Crescent and seven stars. *C.* 465. *R.I.C.* 202. *B.M.C.* 463 *note*　..　　..　　..　　..　　..　　..　　..　　6·50

984　C. Ṟ. FELICITATI AVGVSTI. Galley l. *C.* 712. *R.I.C.* 240. *B.M.C.* 621　..　　..　　..　　..　　..　　..　　..　　..　　9·00

985　C. Bare-headed and dr. bust, r. Ṟ. FIDES PVBLICA. Fides stg. r. *C.* 716. *R.I.C.* 241A. *B.M.C.* 627　..　　..　　..　　..　　5·00

986　C. Ṟ. FORTVNA AVG. Fortune stg. l. *C.* 765. *R.I.C.* 244. *B.M.C.* 640　..　　..　　..　　..　　..　　..　　..　　..　　5·00

987　C. Bare hd., r. Ṟ. GERMANIA. Germania stg. l., holding spear and leaning on shield. *C.* 802. *R.I.C.* 303. *B.M.C.* 840　..　　..　　14·00

988　C. Ṟ. HISPANIA. Hispania reclining l., holding olive-branch, rabbit at feet. *C.* 830. *R.I.C.* 305. *B.M.C.* 848 *note*..　　..　　..　　..　　8·50

989　C. Bare hd., r. Ṟ. ITALIA. Italia stg. l., holding sceptre and cornucopiae. *C.* 867. *R.I.C.* 307. *B.M.C.* 850　..　　..　　..　　10·00

990　D. Ṟ. LIBERAL . AVG . III. (in ex.) P . M . TR . P . COS . III. Hadrian seated l. on platform, distributing money to citizen. *C.* 909. *R.I.C.* 129. *B.M.C.* 293　..　　..　　..　　..　　..　　..　　12·50

991　C. Bare hd., r. Ṟ. MONETA AVG. Moneta stg. l. *C.* 963. *R.I.C.* 256. *B.M.C.* 677　..　　..　　..　　..　　..　　..　　..　　5·00

992　C. Ṟ. NILVS. Nilus reclining r., holding reed and cornucopiae; at feet, hippopotamus; beneath, crocodile. *C.* 991. *R.I.C.* 310. *B.M.C.* 862　..　　..　　..　　..　　..　　..　　..　　..　　10·00

993　D. Ṟ. P . M . TR . P . COS . III. Eternity stg. l., holding heads of Sun and Moon. *C.* 1114. *R.I.C.* 81. *B.M.C.* 162　..　　..　　6·00

994　D. Ṟ. — Victory flying r., holding trophy. *C.* 1131. *R.I.C.* 101. *B.M.C.* 212　..　　..　　..　　..　　..　　..　　..　　5·00

995　D. Ṟ. — Salus seated l., feeding serpent arising from altar. *C.* 1151. *R.I.C.* 98. *B.M.C.* 207　..　　..　　..　　..　　..　　..　　5·00

995A　D. Ṟ. — Hadrian stg. l., holding rudder on globe and spear. *C.* 1162. *R.I.C.* 110. *B.M.C.* 237. **Plate 5**　..　　..　　..　　6·00

996　C. Ṟ. RESTITVTORI GALLIAE. Hadrian stg. r., raising kneeling Gallia. *C.* 1247. *R.I.C.* 324. *B.M.C.* 878　..　　..　　..　　..　　10·00

997　C. Ṟ. ROMVLO CONDITORI. Romulus advancing r., carrying spear and trophy. *C.* 1316. *R.I.C.* 266. *B.M.C.* 710　..　　..　　..　　6·50

998　C. Bare hd., r. Ṟ. VOTA PVBLICA. Hadrian stg. l., sacrificing over tripod-altar. *C.* 1481. *R.I.C.* 290. *B.M.C.* 777　..　　..　　..　　6·00

999　**Æ quinarius.** D. Ṟ. P . M . TR . P . COS . III. Victory advancing r. *C.* 1125. *R.I.C.* 103. *B.M.C.* 227　..　　..　　..　　..　　20·00

Fine

1000 **Æ sestertius.** C. Bare hd., r. ℞. AEQVITAS AVG . S . C. Equity
stg. l. *C.* 123. *R.I.C.* 743. *B.M.C.* 1482 *note* .. .. .. £10·00
1001 C. Bare-headed and dr. bust, r. ℞. AFRICA S . C. As 978. *C.* 142.
R.I.C. 840. *B.M.C.* 1707 .. .. 25·00
1002 C. ℞. ALEXANDRIA S . C. Alexandria reclining l., holding corn-ears
and vine-branch. *C.* 158. *R.I.C.* 843. *B.M.C.* 1716 .. .. .. 25·00
1003 F. ℞. ANN . DCCCLXXIIII . NAT . VRB . P . CIR . CON . S . C. Young
male reclining l., hd. turned, holding wheel in r. hand and three obelisks
in l. *C.* 164. *R.I.C.* 609. *B.M.C.* 1242 .. .. .. *Very rare*
1004 F. ℞. CONCORDIA EXERCITVVM S . C. Concord stg. l., holding legionary eagle and standard. *C.* 268. *R.I.C.* 581c. *B.M.C.* 1182 .. 12·00
1005 A. ℞. COS . III . S . C. Neptune stg. l., holding acrostolium and
trident. *C.* 312. *R.I.C.* 635. *B.M.C.* 1291 .. .. 10·00
1006 A. ℞. — Roma seated l., holding Victory and cornucopiae. *C.* 343.
R.I.C. 636. *B.M.C.* 1297 .. .. 10·00
1007 A. ℞. — Equity stg. l. *C.* 385. *R.I.C.* 637. *B.M.C.* 1306 .. 10·00
1008 A. ℞. COS . III . P . P . CLEMENTIA AVG . S . C. Clemency stg. l.,
holding patera and sceptre. *C.* 515. *R.I.C.* 701. *B.M.C.* 1383 *note.*
Plate 6 .. .. 10·00

1009 C. Bare-headed and dr. bust, r. ℞. DISCIPLINA AVG . S . C. Hadrian
advancing r., followed by an accensus and three soldiers. *C.* 541.
R.I.C. 746. *B.M.C.* 1484 .. .. 50·00
1010 A. ℞. EXPED . AVG . COS . III . S . C. Hadrian galloping l., raising r.
hand. *C.* 590. *R.I.C.* 645. *B.M.C.* 1313 .. .. .. 20·00
1011 C. ℞. FELICITAS AVG . S . C. Felicity stg. l., wheel at feet. *C.* 609.
R.I.C. 749. *B.M.C.* 1492 .. .. 10·00
1012 C. Bare-headed and dr. bust, r. ℞. — Hadrian and Felicity clasping
r. hands. *C.* 633. *R.I.C.* 754. *B.M.C.* 1501 .. .. .. 12·00
1013 A. ℞. FELICITATI AVG . COS . III . P . P . S . C. Galley l. *C.* 657.
R.I.C. 706. *B.M.C.* 1396 .. .. 20·00
1014 A. Laur. hd., l. ℞. As previous. *C.* 661. *R.I.C.* 706. *B.M.C.*
1394 *note* .. .. 25·00
1015 E. ℞. FORT . RED . S . C. (in ex.) PONT . MAX . TR . POT . COS . II.
Fortune seated l. *C.* 756. *R.I.C.* 551a. *B.M.C.* 1130 .. .. 12·00
1016 B. ℞. HILARITAS P . R . COS . III . S . C. Hilaritas stg. l. between two
children. *C.* 819. *R.I.C.* 970. *B.M.C.* 1372 .. .. .. 12·00
1017 F. ℞. LIBERTAS PVBLICA S . C. Liberty seated l., holding laurel-
branch and sceptre. *C.* 948. *R.I.C.* 583a. *B.M.C.* 1192 .. .. 10·00
1018 C. ℞. MAVRETANIA S . C. Mauretania stg. l., holding horse by bridle.
C. 957. *R.I.C.* 859. *B.M.C.* 1763 .. .. 35·00
1019 E. ℞. PONT . MAX . TR . POT . COS . III . S . C. Felicity stg. l. *C.* 1192.
R.I.C. 563a. *B.M.C.* 1152 .. .. 10·00

Fine

1020 **Æ sestertius.** F. ℞. RELIQVA VETERA HS . NOVIES MILL . ABOLITA S .
C. Lictor stg. l., applying torch to heap of papers. *C.* 1210. *R.I.C.*
590a. *B.M.C.* 1206 *note* .. .. £50·00

1021 C. Bare-headed and dr. bust, r. ℞. RESTITVTORI HISPANIAE S . C.
Hadrian stg. l., raising kneeling Hispania. *C.* 1263. *R.I.C.* 954.
B.M.C. 1816 *note* .. .. 25·00

1022 F. ℞. RESTITVTORI ORBIS TERRARVM S . C. Hadrian stg. l., raising
turreted female figure. *C.* 1285. *R.I.C.* 594a. *B.M.C.* 1211. *Illustrated on p.* 134 .. .. 20·00

1023 C. ℞. SALVS AVG . S . C. Salus stg. l., feeding serpent arising from
altar. *C.* 1333. *R.I.C.* 786. *B.M.C.* 1558 .. .. .. 10·00

1024 C. ℞. S . C. Diana stg. l., holding bow and arrow. *C.* 1364. *R.I.C.*
777. *B.M.C.* 1546 *note* .. .. 10·00

1025 D. ℞. VIRT . AVG. (across field) P . M . TR . P . COS . III . S . C. Virtus
stg. l., holding parazonium and spear. *C.* 1465. *R.I.C.* 614a. *B.M.C.*
1263 *note* .. .. 12·00

1026 **Æ dupondius.** C. ℞. AEGYPTOS S . C. Similar to 977. *C.* 111.
R.I.C. 839. *B.M.C.* 1703 .. .. 9·00

1027 A. Rad. hd., r. ℞. COS . III . S . C. Salus stg. r., feeding serpent
held in arms. *C.* 370. *R.I.C.* 657. *B.M.C.* 1325 *note* .. .. 4·50

1028 A. Similar. ℞. — Pegasus r. *C.* 436 *var.* *R.I.C.* 658. *B.M.C.*
1330 .. .. 8·00

1029 B. Similar. ℞. As 1016. *C.* 820. *R.I.C.* 974. *B.M.C.* 1375 .. 5·00

1030 F. Rad. and dr. bust, r. ℞. PROVIDENTIA DEORVM S . C. Hadrian
stg. l., receiving sceptre from eagle flying r. *C.* 1208. *R.I.C.* 602a.
B.M.C. 1236 .. .. 10·00

1031 F. Similar. ℞. VIRTVTI AVGVSTI S . C. Virtus stg. r. *Cf. C.* 1470.
R.I.C. 605. *B.M.C.* 1239 .. .. 5·00

1032 **Æ as.** C. ℞. ADVENTVI AVG . GALLIAE S . C. Hadrian and Gallia stg.
facing each other; between them, altar. *C.* 33. *R.I.C.* 885. *B.M.C.*
1644 .. .. 9·00

1033 C. ℞. ANNONA AVG . S . C. Modius. *C.* 174. *R.I.C.* 798. *B.M.C.*
1582 .. .. 5·50

1034 E. ℞. BRITANNIA (in ex.) PONT . MAX . TR . POT . COS . III . S . C.
Britannia seated facing, holding spear, shield at side. *C.* 197. *R.I.C.*
577a. *B.M.C.* 1174 .. .. 45·00

1035 C. ℞. CAPPADOCIA S . C. Cappadocia stg. l., holding model of Mount
Argaeus and standard. *C.* 207. *R.I.C.* 848. *B.M.C.* 1733 .. .. 14·00

1036 A. ℞. CLEMENTIA AVG . COS . III . P . P . S . C. As 1008. *C.* 225.
R.I.C. 714. *B.M.C.* 1438. **Plate 6** .. .. 5·00

1037 A. ℞. COS . III . S . C. Janus stg. facing, holding sceptre. *C.* 281.
R.I.C. 662. *B.M.C.* 1335 .. .. 6·50

1038 A. ℞. — Galley r. *C.* 446. *R.I.C.* 673. *B.M.C.* 1342 .. .. 7·50

1039 A. Bare-headed and dr. bust, r. ℞. COS . III . P . P . S . C. Hadrian
galloping r., holding spear. *C.* 494. *R.I.C.* 717. *B.M.C.* 1450 .. 9·00

Fine

1040 **Æ as.** C. R. DACIA s . c. Dacia seated l. on rock, holding legionary
eagle and curved sword. *C.* 527. *R.I.C.* 850. *B.M.C.* 1741 *note* .. £14·00

1041 E. R. PIE . AVG. (across field) PONT . MAX . TR . POT . COS . III . S . C.
Pietas stg. l. before altar, raising both hands. *C.* 1022. *R.I.C.* 579a.
B.M.C. 1176 ..   ..   5·00

1042 D. R. P . M . TR . P . COS . III . S . C. Pax stg. l. *C.* 1142. *R.I.C.*
616b. *B.M.C.* 1267 *note*   ..   ..   5·00

1043 C. R. SALVS AVG . S . C. Salus stg. r., feeding serpent arising from
altar. *C.* 1338. *R.I.C.* 832. *B.M.C.* 1621   ..   ..   ..   4·50

1044 C. R. s . c. in laurel-wreath. *C.* 1394. *R.I.C.* 831. *B.M.C.* 1618   6·00

1045 **Æ as.** (*orichalcum*) A. R. COS . III . S . C. Lyre. *C.* 442. *R.I.C.* 684.
B.M.C. 1354 ..   ..   9·00

1046 **Æ semis.** A. R. — Roma seated l. on cuirass. *C.* 347. *R.I.C.*
685. *B.M.C.* 1356 ..   ..   6·00

1047 **Æ quadrans.** B. R. — Legionary eagle between two standards.
C. 450. *R.I.C.* 977. *B.M.C.*, *p.* 448, * ..   ..   9·00

1048 A. R. COS . III . P . P . S . C. Eagle stg. on thunderbolt, hd. l. *C.* 505.
R.I.C. 732. *B.M.C.* 1474 *note*   ..   ..   6·00

1049 **Æ uncia.** No *obv.* legend. R. s . c. in laurel-wreath. *C.* 1396.
R.I.C. 629b. *B.M.C.* 1833   ..   ..   10·00

Commemorative Coins struck after his death   Very Fine

1050 *Struck by Antoninus Pius,* N *aureus.* DIVVS HADRIANVS AVG. Laur. hd.
r. R. CONSECRATIO. Hadrian seated on eagle flying r. *C.* 270.
R.I.C. (*Had.*) 389A. *B.M.C.* (*Ant.*) 32 ..   .. 550·00

1051 — **Æ denarius.** — Bare hd. r. R. — Eagle stg. facing on globe,
hd. l. *C.* 271. *R.I.C.* (*Had.*) 389B. *B.M.C.* (*Ant.*) 33   60·00

1052 *Struck by Trajan Decius,* **Æ antoninianus.** DIVO HADRIANO. Rad.
hd., r. R. CONSECRATIO. Eagle stg. facing, hd. l. *C.* 1509. *R.I.C.*
(*Dec.*) 87   ..   ..   55·00

Colonial and Provincial Coinage   Fine

1053 *Crete,* **Æ 15.** Laur. bust, r. R. Altar. *B.M.C. G.*33   ..   ..   3·50
1054 *Bithynia,* **Æ 33.** Laur. hd., r. R. Octastyle temple. *B.M.C. G.*12..   10·00
1055 *Lydia, Sardes,* **Æ 23.** Laur. bust, r. R. Temple of Aphrodite
Paphia. *B.M.C. G.*134   ..   ..   6·00
1056 *Cappadocia, Caesarea,* **Æ hemidrachm.** Laur. bust, r. R. Nike r.,
holding wreath and palm. *B.M.C. G.*140   ..   ..   ..   4·50
1057 *Commagene, Samosata,* **Æ 17.** Laur. bust, r. R. Greek inscription
in four lines within wreath. *B.M.C. G.*20   ..   ..   ..   3·00
1058 *Egypt, Alexandria,* **billon tetradrachm.** Laur. bust, r. R. Diad.
bust of Sabina r. *B.M.C. G.* 566   ..   ..   10·00
1059 — — Similar. R. Hd. of Zeus Ammon r. *B.M.C. G.*573   ..   2·25
1060 — — Laur. hd., l. R. Demeter stg. l., holding corn-ears and torch.
*B.M.C. G.*580   ..   ..   2·25
1061 — — Laur. bust, r. R. Rad. bust of Helios r. *B.M.C. G.*584   ..   2·25
1062 — — Similar. R. Athena stg. l., holding Nike and leaning on shield.
*B.M.C. G.*587   ..   ..   2·25
1063 — — Similar. R. Dikaiosyne stg. l. *B.M.C. G.*590   ..   ..   2·25
1064 — — Laur. hd., r. R. Pronoia stg. l., holding phoenix and sceptre.
*B.M.C. G.*598   ..   ..   2·50

Fine

1065	*Egypt, Alexandria*, **billon tetradrachm.** Similar. ℞. Tyche stg. l. B.M.C. G.601	£2·25
1066	— — Laur. hd., l. ℞. Bust of Serapis r. B.M.C. G.609	2·50
1067	— — Laur. bust, r. ℞. Serapis seated l., Kerberos at feet. B.M.C. G.620	2·50
1068	— — Similar. ℞. Canopus of Osiris r. B.M.C. G.630	3·25
1069	— — Similar. ℞. Bust of Nilus r. B.M.C. G.641	2·50
1070	— — Laur. hd., r. ℞. Nilus seated l., holding reed and cornucopiae. B.M.C. G.651	2·50
1071	— — Similar. ℞. Eagle stg. r. B.M.C. G.657	2·25
1072	— — Similar. ℞. Serpent Agathodaimon erect r. B.M.C. G.665	3·50
1073	— — Laur. bust, r. ℞. Hadrian stg. l., receiving ears of corn from Alexandria stg. r. B.M.C. G.669	3·25
1074	— Æ 34. Laur. hd., l. ℞. Zeus reclining l. B.M.C. G.675	6·00
1075	— — Laur. hd., r. ℞. Hadrian in quadriga of elephants r. B.M.C. G.860	7·50
1076	— Æ 33. Laur. hd., l. ℞. Tyche reclining l. on couch. B.M.C. G.730	6·00
1077	— Æ 32. Laur. bust, r. ℞. Isis Pharia stg. r., holding inflated sail. B.M.C. G.754	7·00
1078	— Æ 24. Laur. hd., r. ℞. Bull r. B.M.C. G.814	4·00
1079	— Æ 20. Similar. ℞. Modius between two torches. B.M.C. G.903	3·00
1080	— Æ 18. Similar. ℞. Dolphin entwined around anchor. B.M.C. G.817 *var.*	3·50
1081	— Æ 14. Similar. ℞. Rhinoceros r. B.M.C. G.835	2·50
1082	— — Similar. ℞. Head-dress of Isis. B.M.C. G.901	1·75

SABINA

1093A

The daughter of Matidia and grandniece of Trajan, Sabina married Hadrian in A.D. 100. *She accompanied her husband on most of her journeys, but their marriage was very unhappy. She died in* A.D. 137 *and was consecrated by Hadrian.*

The coins of Sabina have the following obverse legends:

A. SABINA AVGVSTA.
B. SABINA AVGVSTA HADRIANI AVG . P . P.

Her bust is usually depicted diademed and draped and there are a large number of varieties in the arrangement of the hair, though no attempt is made here to differentiate between them. Unless otherwise stated, the bust is to right.

All *R.I.C.* and *B.M.C.* references are to the coinage of Hadrian. **Very Fine**

1083 **N aureus.** A. ℞. VESTA. Vesta seated l., holding palladium and sceptre. *C.* 78. *R.I.C.* 397*a.* *B.M.C.* 950 .. ..£300·00

1084 **N quinarius.** B. ℞. CONCORDIA AVG. Concord stg. l. *C.* 2. *R.I.C.* 400. *B.M.C.* 907 .. .. 550·00

1085 **R cistophorus.** B. ℞. COS . III. Cybele enthroned l., lion at feet. *C.* 35. *R.I.C.* 533. *B.M.C.* 1095.. .. .. 250·00

1086 **R denarius.** B. ℞. CONCORDIA AVG. Concord seated l. *C.* 12. *R.I.C.* 398. *B.M.C.* 895 .. .. 10·00

1087 A. ℞. IVNONI REGINAE. Juno stg. l., holding patera and sceptre. *C.* 43. *R.I.C.* 395*a.* *B.M.C.* 940.. .. .. 10·00

1088 B. ℞. PVDICITIA. Pudicitia seated l. *C.* 57. *R.I.C.* 406. *B.M.C.* 911 *note* .. .. 12·00

1089 A. ℞. VENERI GENETRICI. Venus stg. r., holding apple. *C.* 73. *R.I.C.* 396. *B.M.C.* 944 .. .. 12·00

1090 B. ℞. As 1083. *C.* 81. *R.I.C.* 410. *B.M.C.* 915 .. .. 12·00

1091 **R quinarius.** B. ℞. As 1087, but cornucopiae instead of sceptre. *C.* 45. *R.I.C.* 404. *B.M.C.* 910 .. .. 120·00

Fine

1092 **Æ sestertius.** B. ℞. CONCORDIA AVG . S . C. Concord stg. l. *C.* 6. *R.I.C.* 1026. *B.M.C.* 1861.. .. .. .. 20·00

1093 B. ℞. PIETAS S . C. Pietas seated l. *C.* 48. *R.I.C.* 1029. *B.M.C.* 1870 .. .. 22·50

1093A B. ℞. S . C. Vesta seated l., holding palladium and sceptre. *C.* 65. *R.I.C.* 1020. *B.M.C.* 1882. *Illustrated on p.* 140 .. .. .. 22·50

1094 B. ℞. S . C. Ceres seated l. on basket, holding corn-ears and torch. *C.* 69. *R.I.C.* 1019. *B.M.C.* 1879 .. .. 22·50

1095 B. ℞. VENERI GENETRICI S . C. As 1089. *C.* 74. *R.I.C.* 1035. *B.M.C.* 1883 .. .. 20·00

1096 **Æ dupondius.** B. Bust l. ℞. CONCORDIA AVG . S . C. Concord seated l. *C.* 19. *R.I.C.* 1037. *B.M.C.* 1893 *note* .. .. 14·00

1097 B. ℞. S . C. As 1083. *C.* 66. *R.I.C.* 1024. *B.M.C.* 1902 .. 10·50

1098 B. ℞. As 1094. *C.* 70. *R.I.C.* 1023. *B.M.C.* 1900 .. .. 10·50

1099 **Æ as.** A. Bust l. ℞. As 1092. *C.* 4. *R.I.C.* 1047. *B.M.C.* 1887 *note* .. .. 14·00

1100 B. ℞. As 1093. *C.* 49. *R.I.C.* 1039. *B.M.C.* 1896 .. .. 10·50

See also no. 1058

Commemorative Coins struck after her death **Very Fine**

1101 **N aureus.** DIVA AVG . SABINA. Veiled, diad. and dr. bust, r. ℞. CONSECRATIO. Sabina seated on eagle flying r. *C.* 27. *R.I.C.* 418*a.* *B.M.C.* 956 .. .. 600·00

1102 **R denarius.** *Obv.* Similar. ℞. — Eagle stg. facing on sceptre, hd. l. *C.* 31. *R.I.C.* 420*a.* *B.M.C.* 959 .. .. 35·00

1103 *Obv.* Similar, but wreath of corn-ears instead of diadem. ℞. PIETATI AVG. Large altar. *C.* 56. *R.I.C.* 422*a.* *B.M.C.* 960 .. .. 45·00

1104 **Æ sestertius.** DIVA AVGVSTA SABINA. As previous. ℞. CONSECRATIO S . C. As 1102. *C.* 33. *R.I.C.* 1052. *B.M.C.* 1906 .. *Fine* £85·00

142

ANTINOÜS
Favourite of Hadrian

1105   *Egypt, Alexandria*, Æ **34.** ANTINOOV HPWOC. Bare-headed bust of
Antinoüs l. ℞. L KA. Antinoüs as Hermes on horseback r., holding
caduceus. *B.M.C. G.*925 ..   ..£100·00

AELIUS
Caesar, A.D. 136-138

1117

  L. Ceionius Commodus was adopted by Hadrian as his heir in A.D. 136 *and renamed
L. Aelius Verus Caesar. He was appointed governor of Pannonia but he predeceased the
emperor, dying of tuberculosis on January* 1*st,* A.D. 138.

  The coins of Aelius have the following obverse legends:

    A.   L . AELIVS CAESAR.
    B.   L . AELIVS CAESAR TR . P . COS . II.

  Unless otherwise stated, the obverse type is bare hd. r., or bare-headed and dr. bust r.

  All *R.I.C.* and *B.M.C.* references are to the coinage of Hadrian   **Very Fine**

1106 **N aureus.** A.   ℞.   PIETAS (in ex.) TRIB . POT . COS . II. Pietas stg. r.,
altar at feet. *C.* 41. *R.I.C.* 444. *B.M.C.* 1003 *note* ..   ..   .. 300·00
1107 **N quinarius.** A.   ℞.   TR . POT . COS . II. Felicity stg. l. *C.* 51.
R.I.C. 430. *B.M.C.* 968 ..   .. 500·00
1108 **R denarius.** A.   Bare hd., l.   ℞.   CONCORD (in ex.) TR . POT .
COS . II. Concord seated l. *C.* 5. *R.I.C.* 436. *B.M.C.* 984 ..   20·00
1109 B.   ℞.   CONCORDIA. Concord stg. l., leaning on column. *C.* 14.
R.I.C. 428. *B.M.C.* 965 ..   .. 17·50
1110 As 1107. *C.* 50. *R.I.C.* 430. *B.M.C.* 969 ..   .. 15·00
1111 A.   ℞.   TR . POT . COS . II. Pietas stg. l., altar at feet. *C.* 53. *R.I.C.*
432. *B.M.C.* 972 ..   .. 15·00
1112 **R quinarius.** As 1107. *R.I.C.* 430. *B.M.C.* 968 *note*   ..   .. 200·00

1113 **Æ sestertius.** A.   ℞.   As 1108, but with S . C. added. *C.* 6.   **Fine**
R.I.C. 1057. *B.M.C.* 1918 *note* ..   .. 25·00
1114 A.   ℞.   PANNONIA (across field) TR . POT . COS . II . S . C. Pannonia stg.
facing, hd. l., holding standard. *C.* 24. *R.I.C.* 1059. *B.M.C.* 1919.. 30·00
1115 A.   ℞.   TR . POT . COS . II . S . C. Spes advancing l. *C.* 56. *R.I.C.*
1055. *B.M.C.* 1914   ..   .. 25·00
1116 **Æ dupondius.** Similar. *C.* 57. *R.I.C.* 1067. *B.M.C.* 1931   .. 12·00
1117 **Æ as.** As 1114. *C.* 25. *R.I.C.* 1071. *B.M.C.* 1936. *Illustrated above* 14·00
1118 A.   ℞.   TR . POT . COS . II . S . C. Fortuna-Spes stg. facing, hd. l.,
holding flower, cornucopiae and rudder. *C.* 64. *R.I.C.* 1065. *B.M.C.*
1927 ..   .. 12·00

Colonial and Provincial Coinage

1119 *Egypt, Alexandria*, **billon tetradrachm.** Bare hd., r.   ℞.   Homonoia
stg. l., holding patera and cornucopiae, altar at feet. *B.M.C. G.*921 .. 10·00
1120 — Æ **33.** Bare-headed and dr. bust, r.   ℞.   Homonoia seated l.,
holding patera. *B.M.C. G.*923 ..   .. 12·50

ANTONINUS PIUS
A.D. 138-161

1156

Titus Aurelius Fulvus Boionius Arrius Antoninus was born at Lanuvium in A.D. 86. *He adopted a senatorial career and was consul in 120, later distinguishing himself as proconsul in Asia. He was adopted by Hadrian as his heir on February 25th, 138, and during the emperor's last months, Antoninus was virtually ruler, and his succession on July 10th was smooth. The history of his reign is almost a blank in the records, owing to the tranquillity and prosperity which the Roman world enjoyed under his patient, judicious and impartial rule. He died at Lorium on March 7th,* A.D. 161, *and was succeeded by Marcus Aurelius who had been selected by Hadrian as the eventual heir to the throne.*

It is worthy of mention that the series of commemorative coins struck after his death was the largest since that of Augustus.

Titles and Powers, A.D. 138-161

A.D.	Tribunician Power	Imperatorial Acclamation	Consulship	Other Titles
138	TR.P.		COS.DES.II.	CAESAR. later,
		IMP.		AVGVSTVS. P.M. PIVS.
139	TR.P. − TR.P.II		COS.II., DES.III.	P.P.
140	TR.P.II. − III.		COS.III.	
141	TR.P.III. − IIII.			
142	TR.P.IIII. − V.			
143	TR.P.V. − VI.	IMP.II.		
144	TR.P.VI. − VII.		COS.DES.IIII.	
145	TR.P.VII. − VIII.		COS.IIII.	
146	TR.P.VIII. − VIIII.			
147	TR.P.VIIII. − X. − XI.			
148	TR.P.XI. − XII.			
149	TR.P.XII. − XIII.			
150	TR.P.XIII. − XIIII.			
151	TR.P.XIIII − XV.			
152	TR.P.XV. − XVI.			
153	TR.P.XVI. − XVII.			
154	TR.P.XVII. − XVIII.			
155	TR.P.XVIII. − XVIIII.			
156	TR.P.XVIIII. − XX.			
157	TR.P.XX. − XXI.			
158	TR.P.XXI. − XXII.			
159	TR.P.XXII. − XXIII.			
160	TR.P.XXIII. − XXIIII.			
161	TR.P.XXIIII.			

Antoninus received the tribunician power on February 25th, A.D. 138, and it was subsequently renewed each year on that date until A.D. 147. In this year he renewed the power on February 25th, as usual, but again renewed it on December 10th which now became the normal date for the advancement of the tribunician power.

His first consulship was in A.D. 120.

Mint: Rome.

As Caesar

February 25th–July 10th, A.D. 138, under Hadrian   **Very Fine**

1121 **N aureus.** IMP . T . AEL . CAES . ANTONINVS. Bare hd., r. R . CONCORD. (in ex.) TRIB . POT . COS. Concord seated l. *C.* 130. *R.I.C.* (*Had.*) 453*b*. *B.M.C.*, *p.* 371, * .. ..£200·00

1122 **N quinarius.** *Obv.* Similar. R . TRIB . POT . COS. Felicity stg. l. *C.* 1059. *R.I.C.* 451. *B.M.C.* 1012 .. .. 300·00

1123 **R denarius.** *Obv.* Similar. R . — Pietas stg. l., altar at feet. *C.* 1062. *R.I.C.* 452*a*. *B.M.C.* 1013 .. .. 10·00

Fine

1124 **Æ sestertius.** IMP . T . AELIVS CAESAR ANTONINVS. Bare hd., r. R . PIETAS (in ex.) TRIB . POT . COS . S . C. Pietas stg. r., altar at feet. *C.* 602. *R.I.C.* 1082. *B.M.C.* 1942 .. .. 17·50

1125 **Æ as.** IMP . T . AEL . CAESAR HADR . ANTONINVS. Bare-headed and dr. bust, r. R . TRIB . POT . COS . S . C. Clasped hands holding caduceus and corn-ears. *C.* 1067. *R.I.C.* 1088*b*. *B.M.C.* 1948 *note* .. .. 12·00

As Augustus

The following are the commonest forms of obverse legend:

A. ANTONINVS AVG . PIVS P . P.
B. ANTONINVS AVG . PIVS P . P . IMP . II.
C. ANTONINVS AVG . PIVS P . P . TR . P.
D. ANTONINVS AVG . PIVS P . P . TR . P . XI . (-XXIIII).
E. ANTONINVS AVG . PIVS P . P . TR . P . COS . III.
F. IMP . CAES . T . AEL . HADR . ANTONINVS AVG . PIVS P . P.

The obverse type is laur. hd. of Antoninus r., unless otherwise stated.   **Very Fine**

1126 **N aureus.** D. (TR . P . XVI.) R . COS . IIII. Antoninus stg. l., holding globe. *C.* 309. *R.I.C.* 226*c*. *B.M.C.* 796 .. .. .. 125·00

1127 B. R . TR . POT . XX . COS . IIII. Victory advancing l. *C.* 1013. *R.I.C.* 266*a*. *B.M.C.* 887 .. .. 125·00

1128 **N quinarius.** A. R . TR . P . COS . III. Victory flying l., placing diadem on two shields set on altar. *C.* 837. *R.I.C.* 83. *B.M.C.* 231 250·00

1129 **R denarius.** E. R . AEQVITAS AVG. Equity stg. l. *C.* 14. *R.I.C.* 61. *B.M.C.* 173 .. .. 5·00

1130 E. Bare hd., r. R . APOLLINI AVGVSTO. Apollo stg. l., holding patera and lyre. *C.* 59. *R.I.C.* 63B. *B.M.C.* 186 .. .. .. 8·00

1131 IMP . T . AEL . CAES . HADRI . ANTONINVS. Bare hd., r. R . AVG . PIVS P . M . TR . P . COS . DES . II. Felicity stg. l. *C.* 77. *R.I.C.* 11. *B.M.C.* 17 .. .. 7·50

1132 *Obv.* Similar, but HADR. R . AVG . PIVS . P . M . TR . P . COS . II. Sacrificial implements. *C.* 93. *R.I.C.* 28. *B.M.C.* 69 .. .. 8·00

1133 E. R . CLEMENTIA AVG. Clemency stg. l., holding patera and sceptre. *C.* 124. *R.I.C.* 64. *B.M.C.* 194 .. .. 6·00

Very Fine

1134 **Æ denarius.** D. (TR . P . XVII.) R. COS . IIII. Vesta stg. l., holding
simpulum and palladium. *C.* 198. *R.I.C.* 229a. *B.M.C.* 806 .. £5·00

1135 D. (TR . P . XII.) R. — Equity stg. l. *C.* 240. *R.I.C.* 177. *B.M.C.*
654 .. .. 5·00

1136 — R. — Annona stg. l., modius at feet, holding corn-ears and anchor.
C. 284. *R.I.C.* 175. *B.M.C.* 657.. .. .. 5·00

1137 A. R. — Clasped hands holding caduceus and corn-ears. *C.* 344.
R.I.C. 136. *B.M.C.* 530 .. .. 6·00

1138 E. R. ITALIA. Italy seated l. on globe, holding cornucopiae and
sceptre. *C.* 463. *R.I.C.* 73. *B.M.C.* 214 .. .. .. 12·00

1139 A. R. LIB . IIII. (across field) TR . POT . COS . IIII. Liberalitas stg. l.
C. 491. *R.I.C.* 155. *B.M.C.* 571.. .. .. 7·50

1140 F. R. PAX (in ex.) TR . POT . XIIII . COS . IIII. Pax stg. l. *C.* 582.
R.I.C. 200c. *B.M.C.* 729 .. .. 5·00

1141 D. (TR . P . XXIII.) R. SALVTI AVG . COS . IIII. Salus stg. l., feeding
serpent arising from altar. *C.* 741. *R.I.C.* 305. *B.M.C.* 988.. .. 5·00

1142 D. (TR . P . XXII) R. TEMPLVM DIV . AVG . REST . COS . IIII. Octastyle
temple with seated figures of Augustus and Livia within. *C.* 804.
R.I.C. 290a *B.M.C.* 939 .. .. 12·00

1143 F. R. TRANQ. (in ex.) TR . POT . XIIII . COS . IIII. Tranquillity stg. r.,
holding rudder and corn-ears. *C.* 825. *R.I.C.* 202 *B.M.C.* 736 .. 12·50

1144 A. R. TR . POT . COS . II. Liberty stg. l. *C.* 861. *R.I.C.* 50.
B.M.C. 104 .. .. 5·50

1145 A. Bare hd., r. R. TR . POT . COS . III. She-wolf stg. r. in grotto,
suckling Romulus and Remus. *C.* 914. *R.I.C.* 95. *B.M.C.* 243 *note* 15·00

1146 F. R. TR . POT . XV . COS . IIII. Annona stg. l., holding corn-ears
and resting l. hand on modius set on prow. *C.* 961. *R.I.C.* 210.
B.M.C. 741 .. .. 5·00

1147 B. R. TR . POT . XIX . COS . IIII. Salus seated l., feeding serpent
arising from altar. *C.* 982. *R.I.C.* 254. *B.M.C.* 859 .. .. .. 5·00

1148 A. R. VOTA SVSCEP . DECENN . III . COS . IIII. Antoninus stg. l.,
sacrificing over tripod-altar. *C.* 1117. *R.I.C.* 293 *note*. *B.M.C.* 582 9·00

1149 E. R. No legend. Antoninus stg. r., holding parazonium and spear.
C. 1176. *R.I.C.* 105b(b). *B.M.C.* 261 *note* .. .. .. 15·00

1150 **Æ quinarius.** B. Bare-headed, dr. and cuir. bust, r. R. TR .
POT . XX . COS . IIII. Victory advancing l. *C.*—. *R.I.C.* 266c .. .. 150·00

Fine

1151 **Æ sestertius.** E. R. ANNONA AVG . S . C. Annona stg. r. between
modius and boat, holding corn-ears and cornucopiae. *C.* 34. *R.I.C.*
597. *B.M.C.* 1226 .. .. 8·00

1152 F. Laur. and dr. bust, r. R. ANNONA AVG. (in ex.) TR . POT . XIIII .
COS . IIII . S . C. Annona seated l., modius at feet. *C.* 47. *R.I.C.* 871a.
B.M.C. 1866 *note* .. .. 8·00

1153 E. R. As 1130, but with S . C. added. *C.* 62. *R.I.C.* 598. *B.M.C.*
1229 .. .. 12·00

Fine

1154 **Æ sestertius.** E. ℞. BRITAN. (across field) IMPERATOR II . S . C.
Victory stg. l. on globe. *C.* 114. *R.I.C.* 719. *B.M.C.* 1613 ..   .. £45·00

1155 E. ℞. BRITANNIA S . C. Britannia seated l. on rock, holding standard
and spear and resting l. arm on shield. *C.* 116. *R.I.C.* 742. *B.M.C.*
1639. **Plate 6**   .. .. 75·00

1156 E. ℞. CONCORDIAE S . C. Antoninus and Faustina Senior clasping
r. hands; between them, smaller figures of M. Aurelius and Faustina
Junior stg. either side of altar, clasping r. hands. *C.* 146. *R.I.C.* 601.
B.M.C. 1236. *Illustrated on p.* 143   .. .. .. 75·00

1157 C. ℞. COS . IIII . S . C. Antoninus in quadriga r. *C.* 319. *R.I.C.*
766. *B.M.C.* 1668 ..   .. 18·00

1158 A. ℞. FELICITAS AVG . COS . II . S . C. Felicity stg. l. *C.* 368.
R.I.C. 535. *B.M.C.* 1140 ..   .. 8·00

1159 E. ℞. GENIO SENATVS S . C. Genius of the Senate stg. l., holding
branch and sceptre. *C.* 400. *R.I.C.* 605. *B.M.C.* 1241   .. .. 10·50

1160 E. ℞. IMPERATOR II . S . C. Fides stg. r. *C.* 426. *R.I.C.* 716a.
B.M.C. 1608 ..   .. 9·00

1161 D. (TR . P . XVI). ℞. INDVLGENTIA AVG . COS . IIII . S . C. Indulgence
seated l., holding sceptre. *C.* 452. *R.I.C.* 904. *B.M.C.* 1920 ..   .. 9·00

1162 E. ℞. As 1138, but with S . C. added. *C.* 464. *R.I.C.* 746a.
B.M.C. 1641 ..   .. 20·00

1163 D. (TR . P . XVII). ℞. LIBERTAS COS . IIII . S . C. Liberty stg. r.
C. 535. *R.I.C.* 916a. *B.M.C.* 1944   .. .. 8·00

1164 E. Laur. and dr. bust, r. ℞. OPI AVG . S . C. Ops seated l., holding
sceptre. *C.* 569. *R.I.C.* 612. *B.M.C.* 1258   .. .. .. 14·00

1165 A. ℞. PAX AVG . COS . IIII . S . C. Pax stg. l., applying torch to pile
of arms and holding cornucopiae. *C.* 594. *R.I.C.* 777. *B.M.C.* 1698 12·00

1166 D. (TR . P . XXIII). Laur. and dr. bust, r. ℞. PIETATI AVG . COS .
IIII . S . C. Pietas stg. l. between two children, holding two more in her
arms. *C.* 626. *R.I.C.* 1032. *B.M.C.* 2088 *note*   .. .. 10·00

1167 E. ℞. PROVIDENTIAE DEORVM S . C. Winged thunderbolt. *C.* 682.
R.I.C. 618. *B.M.C.* 1266 ..   .. 12·00

1168 E. ℞. REX ARMENIIS DATVS S . C. Antoninus stg. l., crowning the
king of Armenia who stands l. before him. *C.* 686. *R.I.C.* 619.
B.M.C. 1272 ..   .. 50·00

1169 E. ℞. ROMAE AETERNAE S . C. Decastyle temple. *C.* 699. *R.I.C.*
622. *B.M.C.* 1279   .. .. 18·00

1170 D. (TR . P . XV). ℞. SALVS AVG . COS . IIII . S . C. Salus stg. l., feeding
serpent arising from altar. *C.* 728. *R.I.C.* 886. *B.M.C.* 1901 ..   .. 8·00

Fine

1171 **Æ sestertius.** A. ℞. SYRIA COS . II . S . C. Syria stg. l., holding wreath (?) and cornucopiae, the Orontes swimming at feet. *C.* 796. *R.I.C.* 590. *B.M.C.* 1199 note .. .. £35·00

1172 E. ℞. TIBERIS S . C. The Tiber reclining l., resting r. hand on boat and holding reed in l. *C.* 820. *R.I.C.* 643. *B.M.C.* 1313 note 25·00

1173 A. ℞. TR . POT . COS . II . S . C. Pax stg. l. *C.* 856. *R.I.C.* 547. *B.M.C.* 1147 .. .. 9·00

1174 A. ℞. TR . POT . COS . III . S . C. She-wolf stg. r., suckling Romulus and Remus. *C.* 917. *R.I.C.* 648. *B.M.C.* 1318 .. .. .. 18·00

1175 F. ℞. TR . POT . XV . COS . IIII . S . C. Fortune stg. r. *C.* 958. *R.I.C.* 888. *B.M.C.* 1885 .. .. 8·00

1176 F. ℞. — Antoninus seated l., crowned by Victory flying behind him. *C.* 969. *R.I.C.* 889. *B.M.C.* 1887 .. .. 18·00

1177 B. ℞. TR . POT . XIX . COS . IIII . S . C. Concord stg. l., holding standard in each hand. *C.* 988. *R.I.C.* 943a. *B.M.C.* 1995 .. 9·00

1178 B. ℞. TR . POT . XX . COS . IIII . S . C. Security seated l., on chair composed of two cornuacopiae, holding sceptre. *C.* 1008. *R.I.C.* 967. *B.M.C.* 2016 .. .. 8·00

1179 D. (TR . P . XXII). Laur. and dr. bust, r. ℞. VOTA SOL . DECENN . II . COS . IIII . S . C. Similar to 1148. *C.* 1112. *R.I.C.* 1009. *B.M.C.* 2067 note .. .. 15·00

1180 **Æ dupondius.** F. Rad. hd., r. ℞. ANNONA AVG (in ex.) TR . POT . XV . COS . IIII . S . C. As 1152. *C.* 51. *R.I.C.* 898. *B.M.C.* 1896 .. 4·50

1181 D. (TR . P . XII). Rad. hd., r. ℞. COS . IIII . S . C. Equity stg. l. *C.* 233. *R.I.C.* 858. *B.M.C.* 1831 4·50

1182 B. Rad. hd., r. ℞. LIB . VIII. (across field) P . M . TR . POT . XXI . COS . IIII . S . C. Liberalitas stg. l. *C.* 529. *R.I.C.* 991. *B.M.C.*, p. 346, ‡ 6·00

1183 D. (TR . P . XIX). Rad. hd., r. ℞. LIBERTAS COS . IIII . S . C. Liberty stg. l. *C.* 545. *R.I.C.* 950. *B.M.C.*, p. 334, † .. .. 4·50

1184 E. (but COS . IIII). Rad. hd., r. ℞. S . C. Security seated l., holding sceptre. *C.* 758. *R.I.C.* 808. *B.M.C.* 1742 .. .. 5·00

1185 B. Rad. hd., r. ℞. TR . POT . XIX . COS . IIII . S . C. Providence stg. l., globe at feet. *C.* 978. *R.I.C.* 953. *B.M.C.*, p. 336, ‡ 4·50

1186 — ℞. TR . POT . XX . COS . IIII . S . C. Annona stg. r., l. foot on prow, holding rudder and modius. *C.* 1019. *R.I.C.* 969. *B.M.C.* 2022 .. 4·50

1187 **Æ as.** E. ℞. ANCILIA (in ex.) IMPERATOR II . S . C. Two oval shields with rounded projections. *C.* 30. *R.I.C.* 736a. *B.M.C.* 1629 12·50

1188 D. (TR . P . XVIII). ℞. BRITANNIA COS . IIII . S . C. Britannia seated l. on rock. *C.* 117. *R.I.C.* 934. *B.M.C.* 1971 .. .. .. 20·00

1189 F. ℞. IVSTITIA (in ex.) TR . POT . XIIII . COS . IIII . S . C. Justice seated l., holding patera and sceptre. *C.* 474. *R.I.C.* 881. *B.M.C.* 1879 .. 5·00

1190 D. (TR . P . XII). ℞. MVNIFICENTIA AVG . COS . IIII . S . C. Elephant walking r. *C.* 565. *R.I.C.* 862a. *B.M.C.* 1840 .. .. 12·50

1191 As 1170. *C.* 729. *R.I.C.* 900a. *B.M.C.* 1904 .. .. 4·50

1192 E. (but COS . IIII). ℞. S . P . Q . R . OPTIMO PRINCIPI S . C. in oak-wreath. *C.* 791. *R.I.C.* 827a. *B.M.C.* 1762 .. .. .. 10·50

1193 A. ℞. TR . POT . COS . III . S . C. Mars descending r. through air to Rhea Silvia reclining l. asleep on ground. *C.* 885. *R.I.C.* 694a. *B.M.C.* 1370 .. .. 17·50

1194 A. ℞. — Fortune stg. l. *C.* 899. *R.I.C.* 700a. *B.M.C.* 1376 .. 4·50

1195 A. ℞. — Sacrificial implements. *C.* 922. *R.I.C.* 704a. *B.M.C.* 1379 .. .. 5·50

Fine

1196 **Æ as.** A. R. TR . POT . XXIIII . COS . IIII . S . C. Eternity stg. l., holding caduceus and globe surmounted by phoenix. *C.* 1054. *R.I.C.* 1051. *B.M.C.* 2115 .. .. £5·00

1197 **Æ quadrans.** A. R. COS . III . S . C. Winged caduceus. *C.* 182. *R.I.C.* 712. *B.M.C., p.* 224, § .. .. 6·00

1198 IMP . II. Eagle stg. facing, hd. l. R. COS . IIII . S . C. Legionary eagle between two standards. *C.* 346. *R.I.C.* 838. *B.M.C.* 1772 .. 7·50

Commemorative Coins struck after his death Very Fine

1199 *Struck by M. Aurelius and L. Verus, Æ* **aureus.** DIVVS ANTONINVS. Bare hd., r. R. CONSECRATIO. Funeral pyre surmounted by Antoninus in quadriga. *C.* 163. *R.I.C.* (*Aur.*) 435. *B.M.C.* 55 .. .. 150·00

1200 — **Æ denarius.** Similar. R. — Eagle stg. r., hd. turned. *C.* 154. *R.I.C.* 429. *B.M.C.* 41 .. .. 7·00

1201 — — Similar. R. — Eagle stg. r. on altar, hd. turned. *C.* 155. *R.I.C.* 431. *B.M.C.* 48. **Plate 6** .. .. 7·00

1202 — — Similar. R. — As 1199. *C.* 164. *R.I.C.* 436. *B.M.C.* 57 7·50

1203 — — Similar. R. DIVO PIO. Column surmounted by statue of Antoninus. *C.* 353. *R.I.C.* 440. *B.M.C.* 69 .. .. 8·50

1204 — — Similar. R. — Large altar. *C.* 357. *R.I.C.* 441. *B.M.C.* 71 7·50

Fine

1205 — **Æ sestertius.** Similar. R. CONSECRATIO S . C. As 1199. *C.* 165. *R.I.C.* 1266. *B.M.C.* 874 .. .. 12·00

1206 — — Similar. R. DIVO PIO S . C. As 1203. *C.* 354. *R.I.C.* 1269. *B.M.C.* 881 .. .. 14·00

1207 — — Similar. R. — Large altar. *C.* 358. *R.I.C.* 1272. *B.M.C.* 886 .. .. 14·00

1208 — **Æ as.** Similar. R. — As 1203. *C.* 355. *R.I.C.* 1270. *B.M.C.* 893 .. .. 10·00

Very Fine

1209 *Struck by Trajan Decius, Æ* **antoninianus.** DIVO PIO. Rad. hd., r. R. CONSECRATIO. Eagle stg. r., hd. turned. *C.* 1188. *R.I.C.* (*Dec.*) 89 .. .. 15·00

1210 — — Similar. R. — Large altar. *C.* 1189. *R.I.C.* (*Dec.*) 90 .. 15·00

Colonial and Provincial Coinage Fair

1211 *Phrygia, Eumeneia, Æ* **25.** Laur. bust, r. R. Nike advancing l., leading bull. *B.M.C.* G.56.. .. .. 2·25

1212 *Cappadocia, Caesarea, Æ* **didrachm.** Laur. hd., r. R. Mount Argaeus, surmounted by figure holding globe and sceptre. *B.M.C.* G.— .. .. *Very fine* £12·00

1213 *Commagene, Samosata, Æ* **24.** Laur. bust, r. R. Tyche of Samosata seated l. *B.M.C.* G.26 .. .. 2·00

1214 *Cyrrhestica, Beroea, Æ* **26.** Laur. hd., r. R. BEPOIAIWN in wreath. *B.M.C.* G.12 .. .. 2·00

		Fair
1215	*Syria, Antioch,* Æ **22.** Laur. hd., l. R. s.c. in wreath. *B.M.C.* G.323 ..	£1·50
1216	— *Laodiceia ad Mare,* Æ **24.** Laur. hd., r. R. Bust of Tyche r. *B.M.C. G.*60 ..	2·00
1217	*Arabia Petraea, Petra,* Æ **15.** Laur. hd., r. R. ΠΕΤΡΑ / ΜΗΤΡΟ / ΠΟΛΙϹ in wreath. *B.M.C. G.*—	3·25

Very Fine

1218	*Egypt, Alexandria,* **billon tetradrachm.** Laur. hd., r. R. Poseidon stg. r., holding trident and dolphin. *B.M.C. G.*932	5·00
1219	— — Similar. R. Athena Stathmia stg. l., holding scales and cornucopiae. *B.M.C. G.*943	5·00
1220	— — Bare hd., r. R. Dikaiosyne seated l. *B.M.C. G.*951 ..	4·50
1221	— — Bare hd., l. R. Eirene stg. l. *B.M.C. G.*958 ..	4·50
1222	— — Laur. hd., r. R. Bust of Serapis r. *B.M.C. G.*978 ..	5·50
1223	— — Bare-headed, dr. and cuir. bust, r. R. Canopus of Osiris r. *B.M.C. G.*992	6·00
1224	— — Laur. hd., r. R. Phoenix stg. r. *B.M.C. G.*1004	7·00

		Fair
1225	*Egypt, Alexandria,* Æ **34.** Laur., dr. and cuir. bust, r. R. Bust of Selene r. on crescent, crab beneath. *B.M.C. G.*1082	3·75
1226	— — Laur. hd., r. R. Isis seated r., suckling Harpokrates. *B.M.C. G.*1123	3·00
1227	— Æ **32.** Laur., dr. and cuir. bust, r. R. Serapis seated l. within distyle shrine. *B.M.C. G.*1193.	3·00
1228	— Æ **26.** Laur. hd., r. R. Tyche stg. l. *B.M.C. G.*1075 ..	1·75
1229	— Æ **23.** Similar. R. Elpis stg. l. *B.M.C. G.*1066	1·50
1230	— Æ **14.** Laur. bust, r. R. Centaur advancing r. *B.M.C. G.*1043	2·00

N.B.—*There are many coins, not of Antoninus Pius, on which the predominant word in the obverse legend is* ANTONINVS. *These are pieces of M. Aurelius, Caracalla or Elagabalus, and can be distinguished by the rest of the legend and the portrait.*

Antoninus Pius and M. Aurelius

Very Fine

All *R.I.C.* and *B.M.C.* references are to the coinage of Antoninus Pius.

1231	*N* **aureus.** ANTONINVS AVG . PIVS P . P . TR . P . COS . III. Laur. hd. of Antoninus r. R. AVRELIVS CAESAR AVG . PII F . COS. Bare-headed, dr. and cuir. bust of Aurelius r. *C.* 19. *R.I.C.* 417*d*. *B.M.C.* 153	175·00
1232	Æ **denarius.** ANTONINVS AVG . PIVS P . P. Bare hd., r. R. AVRELIVS CAES . AVG . PII F . COS . DES. Bare hd., r. *C.* 2. *R.I.C.* 411*a*. *B.M.C.* 125 ..	12·50
1233	*Obv.* As 1231. R. AVRELIVS CAESAR AVG . PII F . COS. Bare hd., r. *C.* 15. *R.I.C.* 417*a*. *B.M.C.* 155..	12·50

Fine

1234	Æ **sestertius.** *Obv.* Similar. R. AVRELIVS CAESAR AVG . PII F . COS . S . C. Bare-headed and dr. bust, r. *C.* 34. *R.I.C.* 1212. *B.M.C.* 1209	20·00
1235	Æ **dupondius.** Similar, but hd. of Antoninus rad. *C.* 36. *R.I.C.* 1221*a*. *B.M.C.* 1219 *note* ..	12·50
1236	Æ **as.** Similar, but hd. of Antoninus laur. *C.* 35. *R.I.C.* 1223. *B.M.C.* 1222 ..	12·50
1237	*Cyprus,* Æ **32.** Laur. hd. of Antoninus r. R. Bare-headed and dr. bust of Aurelius r. *B.M.C. G.*42 ..	8·00

150

FAUSTINA SENIOR

1257

Wife of Antoninus Pius, whom she married before his accession, and mother of Faustina Junior. She died in A.D. 141 and was consecrated by Antoninus who also issued a very extensive commemorative coinage in her honour.

The following are the commonest forms of obverse legend:

A. FAVSTINA AVG. ANTONINI AVG . PII P . P.
B. DIVA FAVSTINA.
C. DIVA AVGVSTA FAVSTINA.

The obverse type is draped bust of Faustina r., unless otherwise stated.
All *R.I.C.* and *B.M.C.* references are to the coinage of Antoninus Pius.

Very Fine

1238 *N* **aureus.** A. (but without PII.). R. CONCORDIA AVG. Concord seated l. *C.* 145. *R.I.C.* 327. *B.M.C.* 41 *note..* .. .. ..£175·00

1239 **R denarius.** Similar. *C.* 146. *R.I.C.* 327. *B.M.C.* 41 .. .. 10·00

1240 FAVSTINA AVGVSTA. R. CONCORDIA AVG. Concord stg l. *C.* 151. *R.I.C.* 335. *B.M.C.* 133 .. .. 10·00

1241 — R. IVNONI REGINAE. Juno stg. l., peacock at feet. *C.* 215. *R.I.C.* 338. *B.M.C.* 136 .. .. 10·00

1242 **R quinarius.** — R. — Throne, against which rests sceptre and beneath which stands peacock. *C.—.* *R.I.C.* 339c. *B.M.C.* 144 *Very rare*

Fine

1243 **Æ sestertius.** A. R. VENERI AVGVSTAE S . C. Venus stg. r., holding apple. *C.* 282. *R.I.C.* 1081. *B.M.C.* 1120 .. .. .. 17·50

1244 **Æ as.** A. R. IVNONI REGINAE S . C. As 1241. *C.* 217. *R.I.C.* 1090. *B.M.C.* 1128.. .. .. 8·50

Commemorative Coins struck after her death

All struck under Antoninus Pius **Very Fine**

1245 *N* **aureus.** B. R. AVGVSTA. Ceres stg. l., holding torch and sceptre. *C.* 95. *R.I.C.* 356. *B.M.C.* 395 .. .. 140·00

1246 *N* **quinarius.** B. R. AETERNITAS. Juno (?) stg. l., holding sceptre. *C.* 25. *R.I.C.* 344. *B.M.C.* 344 .. .. 300·00

1247 **R denarius.** B. R. AED . DIV . FAVSTINAE. Hexastyle temple with seated figure of Faustina within. *C.* 1. *R.I.C.* 343. *B.M.C.* 339 .. 12·50

1248 B. R. AETERNITAS. As 1246. *C.* 26. *R.I.C.* 344. *B.M.C.* 345 .. 6·50

1249 B. R. — Eternity stg. l., with veil blown out around head, holding globe. *C.* 32. *R.I.C.* 351. *B.M.C.* 373.. .. .. 6·50

1250 B. R. AVGVSTA. Ceres stg. r., holding sceptre and corn-ears. *C.* 93. *R.I.C.* 358. *B.M.C.* 389. **Plate 6** .. .. .. 6·00

1251 B. R. — Vesta stg. l., holding simpulum and palladium. *C.* 108. *R.I.C.* 368. *B.M.C.* 435 .. .. 6·50

Very Fine

1252 **Æ denarius.** B. R. — Throne, against which rests sceptre. *C.* 131. *R.I.C.* 377. *B.M.C.* 454 .. .. £8·00

1253 B. R. CERES. Ceres stg. l., holding corn-ears and torch. *C.* 136. *R.I.C.* 378. *B.M.C.* 461 .. 6·00

1254 C. (but AVG). R. CONCORDIAE. Antoninus and Faustina clasping r. hands. *C.* 159. *R.I.C.* 381*b*. *B.M.C.* 298 .. .. .. 12·50

1255 B. Veiled and dr. bust, r. R. CONSECRATIO. Peacock walking r., hd. turned. *C.* 176. *R.I.C.* 384. *B.M.C.* 476 .. .. .. 12·00

1256 C. (but AVG). R. PIETAS AVG. Pietas stg. l., altar at feet. *C.* 234. *R.I.C.* 394*a*. *B.M.C.* 311 .. 6·50

1257 — R. PVELLAE FAVSTINIANAE. Antoninus seated l. on platform accompanied by woman, both leaning forward to receive little girl held by man stg. r. at foot of platform; in foreground, man running l., pushing a little girl before him. *C.* 262. *R.I.C.* 399*a*. *B.M.C.* 325. *Illustrated on p.* 150 .. .. 75·00

1258 **Æ quinarius.** C. (but AVG). Veiled and dr. bust, r. R. No legend. As 1252. *C.*—. *R.I.C.*—. *B.M.C., p.* 50, * *note* .. *Very rare*

Fine

1259 **Æ sestertius.** B. R. AETERNITAS S . C. Eternity stg. l., holding phoenix. *C.* 12. *R.I.C.* 1105. *B.M.C.* 1490 .. .. .. 9·00

1260 B. R. — Eternity seated l., holding phoenix and sceptre. *C.* 15. *R.I.C.* 1103A. *B.M.C.* 1482 .. 9·00

1261 B. R. AVGVSTA S . C. As 1253. *C.* 88. *R.I.C.* 1118. *B.M.C.* 1514 8·00

1262 B. R. — Ceres stg. l., holding two torches. *C.* 91. *R.I.C.* 1120. *B.M.C.* 1516 .. .. 8·00

1263 B R — As 1256. *C.* 125. *R.I.C.* 1127. *B.M.C.* 1523 .. 9·00

1264 B. R. CERES S . C. As 1253. *C.* 137. *R.I.C.* 1128. *B.M.C.* 1526.. 9·00

1265 B. R. IVNO S . C. Juno stg. l., holding patera and sceptre. *C.* 210. *R.I.C.* 1143. *B.M.C.* 1531 .. .. .. 9·00

1266 C. R. PIETAS AVG . S . C. As 1256. *C.* 240. *R.I.C.* 1146A. *B.M.C.* 1445 .. .. 9·00

1267 **Æ dupondius.** B. R. AETERNITAS S . C. As 1246. *C.* 29. *R.I.C.* 1155. *B.M.C.* 1540.. .. .. 5·00

1268 B. R. — Eternity stg. l., holding globe. *C.* 42. *R.I.C.* 1164. *B.M.C.* 1559 .. 5·00

1269 B. R. AVGVSTA S . C. Vesta stg. l., holding patera and palladium, altar at feet. *C.* 118. *R.I.C.* 1180. *B.M.C.* 1583 .. .. 5·50

1270 **Æ as.** B. R. AETERNITAS S . C. Eternity seated l. on globe, holding sceptre. *C.* 22. *R.I.C.* 1159. *B.M.C.* 1551 .. .. .. 5·00

1271 B. R. AVGVSTA S . C. Ceres stg. r., holding torch and corn-ears. *C.* 86. *R.I.C.* 1172. *B.M.C.* 1565 .. .. 5·00

1272 As 1265. *C.* 211. *R.I.C.* 1190. *B.M.C.* 1596 .. 5·50

1273 C. R. PIET . AVG . S . C. Large altar. *C.* 256. *R.I.C.* 1191A. *B.M.C.* 1466 .. .. 8·00

1274 C. R. S . C. Crescent and seven stars. *C.* 275. *R.I.C.* 1199. *B.M.C.* 1476 .. .. 8·00

152

GALERIUS ANTONINUS

Son of Antoninus and Faustina, died very young.

Fine

1275 Æ **33** *of uncertain Greek city.* ΘΕΑ ΦΑΥCΤΕΙΝΑ. Veiled and dr. bust of
Faustina r. ℞. M . ΓΑΛΕΡΙΟC ΑΝΤΩΝΙΝΟC ΑΥΤΟΚΡΑΤΟΡΟC ΑΝΤΩΝΙΝΟΥ
ΥΙΟC. Bare-headed and dr. bust of Galerius Antoninus r. *C.* 1.
£125·00

MARCUS AURELIUS
A.D. 161-180

1335

    Marcus Annius Verus was born at Rome in A.D. 121, *the son of Annius Verus and
Domitia Lucilla. Hadrian recognized the fine qualities of the youth and he was betrothed
to the daughter of Aelius Caesar. After the death of Aelius, he was adopted by Antoninus
and took the names of M. Aelius Aurelius Verus. In* A.D. 139 *he was given the title of
Caesar and in* 145 *he married Faustina Junior, the daughter of Antoninus. The tribunician
power was conferred on him in* 147 *and his succession to the throne on March 7th,* A.D. 161,
*was smooth. He immediately admitted L. Verus as his partner in the administration, and
betrothed him to his daughter Lucilla. The reign of Aurelius was disturbed by many frontier
wars, and the legions returning from the Parthian War in* A.D. 166 *brought with them a
plague which spread throughout the empire and left many districts almost depopulated.
Aurelius spent much of the latter part of his reign campaigning on the Danube frontier, and
it was during these wars that he wrote his celebrated "Meditations". He died on March 17th,*
A.D. 180, *and was immediately deified. It has been written of Aurelius that "in the evening
of Rome's greatness her ruler fittingly personified the virtues that had been her glory".
He was a careful, generous and conscientious ruler and is best remembered for his devotion
to Stoic philosophy.*

Titles and Powers, A.D. 139-180

A.D.	Tribunician Power	Imperatorial Acclamation	Consulship	Other Titles
139			COS.DES.	CAESAR.
140			COS.	
141				
142				
143				
144			COS.DES.II.	
145			COS.II.	
146				
147	TR.P. – TR.P.II.			
148	TR.P.II. – III.			
149	TR.P.III. – IIII.			
150	TR.P.IIII. – V.			
151	TR.P.V. – VI.			
152	TR.P.VI. – VII.			
153	TR.P.VII. – VIII.			
154	TR.P.VIII. – VIIII.			
155	TR.P.VIIII. – X.			
156	TR.P.X. – XI.			
157	TR.P.XI. – XII.			
158	TR.P.XII. – XIII.			
159	TR.P.XIII. – XIIII.			
160	TR.P.XIIII. – XV.			
161	TR.P.XV. – XVI.	IMP.	COS.III.	AVGVSTVS. P.M.
162	TR.P.XVI. – XVII.			
163	TR.P.XVII. – XVIII.	IMP.II.		
164	TR.P.XVIII. – XVIIII.			ARMENIACVS.
165	TR.P.XVIIII. – XX.	IMP.III.		
166	TR.P.XX. – XXI.	IMP.IIII.		PARTH.MAX.MEDICVS. P.P.
167	TR.P.XXI. – XXII.			
168	TR.P.XXII. – XXIII.	IMP.V.		
169	TR.P.XXIII. – XXIIII.			
170	TR.P.XXIIII. – XXV.			
171	TR.P.XXV. – XXVI.	IMP.VI.		
172	TR.P.XXVI. – XXVII.			
173	TR.P.XXVII. – XXVIII.			
174	TR.P.XXVIII. – XXVIIII.	IMP.VII.		
175	TR.P.XXVIIII. – XXX.	IMP.VIII.		GERM. SARM.
176	TR.P.XXX. – XXXI.			
177	TR.P.XXXI. – XXXII.	IMP.VIIII.		
178	TR.P.XXXII. – XXXIII.			
179	TR.P.XXXIII. – XXXIIII.	IMP.X.		
180	TR.P.XXXIIII.			

Aurelius became TR.P.II. on December 10th, A.D. 147, and his tribunician power was subsequently renewed each year on that date.

Mint: Rome.

As Caesar

A.D. 139-161, *under Antoninus Pius*

The following are the commonest forms of obverse legend:

A.   AVRELIVS CAESAR AVG . PII F.
B.   AVRELIVS CAESAR AVG . PII F . COS.
C.   AVRELIVS CAESAR AVG . PII FIL.
D.   AVRELIVS CAES . ANTON . AVG . PII F.
E.   AVRELIVS CAESAR ANTONINI AVG . PII FIL.

Unless otherwise stated the obverse type is bare hd., r., or bare-headed, dr. and/or cuir. bust r.

All *R.I.C.* and *B.M.C.* references are to the coinage of Antoninus Pius.

Very Fine

1276   **N aureus.** A. ℞. TR . POT . II . COS . II. Fides stg. r. *C.* 610. *R.I.C.* 440*b*. *B.M.C.* 641 ..   ..£140·00

1277   **N quinarius.** C. ℞. TR . POT . VII . COS . II. Roma stg. l., holding Victory and parazonium. *C.* 658. *R.I.C.* 457*a*. *B.M.C.* 803..   .. 275·00

1278   **Æ denarius.** E. ℞. CLEM. (in ex.) TR . POT . III . COS . II. Clemency stg. l., holding patera. *C.* 19. *R.I.C.* 448*b*. *B.M.C.* 703   ..   ..   6·50

1279   A.   ℞. COS . II. Honos stg. l., holding olive-branch and cornucopiae. *C.* 110. *R.I.C.* 429*a*. *B.M.C.* 594   ..   ..   ..   6·50

1280   B.   ℞. HONOS. As previous. *C.* 236. *R.I.C.* 422. *B.M.C.* 264 ..   6·50

1281   B.   ℞. IVVENTAS. Juventas stg. l., dropping incense on candelabrum and holding patera. *C.* 389. *R.I.C.* 423*a*. *B.M.C.* 270   ..   .. 10·00

1282   A.   ℞. TR . POT . II . COS . II. Minerva stg. r., holding spear and leaning on shield. *C.* 608. *R.I.C.* 438*b*. *B.M.C.* 636 ..   ..   ..   6·50

1283   C.   ℞. TR . POT . VI . COS . II. Genius stg. l., holding patera and legionary eagle, altar at feet. *C.* 645. *R.I.C.* 453*a*. *B.M.C.* 775   ..   6·50

1284   C.   ℞. TR . POT . VIII . COS . II. Minerva stg. l., holding owl and leaning on shield. *C.* 663. *R.I.C.* 459. *B.M.C.* 822   ..   ..   6·50

1285   D.   ℞. TR . POT . X . COS . II. Equity stg. l. *C.* 702. *R.I.C.* 466*a*. *B.M.C.* 869   ..   ..   6·50

1286   A. (but CAES.) ℞. VIRTVS COS . II. Virtus stg. r. *C.* 1006. *R.I.C.* 433. *B.M.C.* 610 ..   ..   6·50

Fine

1287   **Æ sestertius.** A. ℞. CLEM. (in ex.) TR . POT . III . COS . II . S . C. Clemency stg. l., holding patera in each hand. *C.* 20. *R.I.C.* 1278. *B.M.C., p.* 303, *   ..   ..   9·00

1288   E. ℞. HONOS (across field) TR . POT . VI . COS . II . S . C. As 1279. *C.* 244. *R.I.C.* 1303. *B.M.C.* 1914   ..   ..   10·00

1289   B. ℞. IVVENTAS S . C. As 1281. *C.* 390. *R.I.C.* 1232*b*. *B.M.C.* 1399   ..   ..   10·00

1290   B. (but COS . II.) ℞. S . C. Minerva advancing r., brandishing javelin. *C.* 576. *R.I.C.* 1243*a*. *B.M.C.* 1776   ..   ..   ..   9·00

1291   C. ℞. TR . POT . VIIII . COS . II . S . C. As 1284. *C.* 678. *R.I.C.* 1321. *B.M.C.* 1982 ..   ..   8·00

1292   D. ℞. TR . POT . X . COS . II . S . C. Fortune stg. l. *C.* 693. *R.I.C.* 1328. *B.M.C.* 2008 *note*   ..   ..   8·00

1293   A. ℞. TR . POT . XIII . COS . II . S . C. Virtus stg. r. *C.* 748. *R.I.C.* 1349B(*b*). *B.M.C.* 2086   ..   ..   8·00

1294   E. ℞. TR . POT . XIIII . COS . II . S . C. Mars advancing r., carrying spear and trophy. *C.* 755. *R.I.C.* 1352c. *B.M.C.* 2103 *note* ..   ..   8·00

Fine

1295 **Æ dupondius.** B. ℞. IVVENTAS S . C. As 1281. *C.* 393. *R.I.C.* 1238. *B.M.C.* 1407 .. .. £6·00

1296 A. ℞. TR . POT . COS . II . S . C. As 1282. *C.* 597. *R.I.C.* 1266. *B.M.C.*, *p.* 293, ‡ .. .. 5·00

1297 **Æ as.** A. ℞. HONOS (across field) TR . POT . II . COS . II . S . C. Honos stg. r., holding sceptre and cornucopiae. *C.* 239. *R.I.C.* 1271a. *B.M.C.* 1819 .. .. 5·50

1298 A. ℞. IVVENTVS in three lines within oak-wreath, COS . II . S . C. around. *C.* 398. *R.I.C.* 1261. *B.M.C.* 1796 *note* .. .. 12·50

1299 B. ℞. PIETAS AVG . S . C. Sacrificial implements. *C.* 455. *R.I.C.* 1240a. *B.M.C.* 1411. **Plate 6** .. .. 6·00

1300 C. ℞. TR . POT . VI . COS . II . S . C. Minerva stg. l., holding Victory and leaning on shield. *C.* 639. *R.I.C.* 1305b. *B.M.C.* 1918 *note* .. 5·00

1301 A. ℞. As 1294. *C.* 759. *R.I.C.* 1354A(a). *B.M.C.* 2105 *note* .. 5·00

1302 A. ℞. TR . POT . XV . COS . III . S . C. Pietas stg. l. between two children, holding two more in her arms. *C.* 776. *R.I.C.* 1361a. *B.M.C.*, *p.* 365, * .. .. 5·50

1303 B. (but COS . II.) ℞. VOTA PVBLICA S . C. Concord stg. facing between Aurelius and Faustina Junior clasping r. hands. *C.* 1023. *R.I.C.* 1269. *B.M.C.* 1801 .. .. 12·50

As Augustus

The following are the commonest forms of obverse legend:

A. M . ANTONINVS AVG . ARMENIACVS.
B. M . ANTONINVS AVG . GERM . SARM.
C. M . ANTONINVS AVG . TR . P . XXIII . (-XXIX).
D. M . AVREL . ANTONINVS AVG.
E. M . AVREL . ANTONINVS AVG . ARM . PARTH . MAX.
F. M . AVREL . ANTONINVS AVG . ARMENIACVS P . M.
G. IMP . M . ANTONINVS AVG.
H. IMP . M . AVREL . ANTONINVS AVG.
I. IMP . CAES . M . AVREL . ANTONINVS AVG . P . M.

Unless otherwise stated the obverse type is laur. hd. r., or laur., dr. and/or cuir. bust r.

Very Fine

1304 **N aureus.** C. (TR . P . XXIII.) ℞. FELICITAS AVG . COS . III. Felicity stg. l. *C.* 177. *R.I.C.* 199. *B.M.C.* 489 .. .. .. 125·00

1305 E. (but without AVREL.) ℞. TR . P . XX . IMP . IIII . COS . III. Victory stg. r., attaching shield, inscribed VIC . PAR., to palm tree. *C.* 877. *R.I.C.* 160. *B.M.C.* 405 .. .. 140·00

1306 **N quinarius.** G. (but without IMP.) ℞. TR . P . XXIIII . COS . III. As 1294. *C.* 910. *R.I.C.* 223. *B.M.C.* 529 .. .. .. 250·00

Very Fine

1307 **Æ denarius.** A. (but without M.) ℞. ARMEN. (in ex.) P . M . TR . P .
XIX . IMP . II . COS . III. Armenia seated l. on ground in attitude of
mourning. *C.* 9. *R.I.C.* 122. *B.M.C.* 366 .. .. £10·00

1308 H. Bare hd., r. ℞. CONCORD . AVG . TR . P . XV . COS . III. Concord
seated l. *C.* 30. *R.I.C.* 2. *B.M.C.* 1 .. .. 5·00

1309 C. (TR . P . XXV.) ℞. COS . III. Jupiter seated l. *C.* 113. *R.I.C.*
227. *B.M.C.* 534 .. .. 5·00

1310 — ℞. — Roma seated l. on cuirass. *C.* 133. *R.I.C.* 233. *B.M.C.*
537 .. .. 5·00

1311 C. (TR . P . XXIIII.) ℞. FORT . RED . COS . III. Fortune seated l.
C. 205. *R.I.C.* 220. *B.M.C.* 521.. .. .. 5·00

1312 C. (TR . P . XXVI.) ℞. IMP . VI . COS . III. Victory seated l. *C.* 277.
R.I.C. 258. *B.M.C* 565 .. .. 5·00

1313 C. (TR . P . XXVII.) ℞. — German seated l. at foot of trophy. *C.*
300. *R.I.C.* 280. *B.M.C.* 581 .. .. 10·00

1314 A. ℞. PAX AVG . TR . P . XX . COS . III. Pax stg. l. *C.* 437. *R.I.C.* 146.
B.M.C. 395 .. .. 5·00

1315 A. (but without M.) Bare hd., r. ℞. P . M . TR . P . XVIII . IMP . II .
COS . III. Mars stg. r., holding spear and leaning on shield. *C.* 468.
R.I.C. 91. *B.M.C.* 261 .. .. 5·00

1316 G. (but with TR . P . XXV. added). ℞. PRIMI DECENNALES COS . III. in
four lines within oak-wreath. *C.* 493. *R.I.C.* 245. *B.M.C.* 549 .. 15·00

1317 G. ℞. PROV . DEOR . TR . P . XVII . COS . III. Providence stg. l.
C. 525. *R.I.C.* 73. *B.M.C.* 221 .. .. 5·00

1318 C. (TR . P . XXIIII.) ℞. SALVTI AVG . COS . III. Salus stg. l., feeding
serpent arising from altar. *C.* 546. *R.I.C.* 222. *B.M.C.* 525 .. 5·00

1318A B. ℞. TR . P . XXIX . IMP . VIII . COS . III. Victory seated l. *C.* 923.
R.I.C. 333. *B.M.C.* 632. **Plate 6** .. .. 5·50

1319 B. ℞. TR . P . XXX . IMP . VIII . COS . III . P . P. Roma stg. l. *C.* 935.
R.I.C. 354. *B.M.C.* 680 .. .. 5·50

1320 B. ℞. TR . P . XXXI . IMP . VIII . COS . III . P . P. Victory advancing l.
C. 949. *R.I.C.* 378. *B.M.C.* 735 .. .. 5·50

1321 D. ℞. TR . P . XXXIIII . IMP . X . COS . III . P . P. Fortune seated l.
C. 972. *R.I.C.* 409. *B.M.C.* 805 *note* .. .. 7·00

1322 *Obv.* As 1316. ℞. VOTA SVSCEP . DECENN . II . COS . III. Aurelius stg.
l., sacrificing over tripod-altar. *C.* 1036. *R.I.C.* 251. *B.M.C.* 553 .. 8·00

1323 **Æ quinarius.** M . ANTONINVS AVG. ℞. TR . P . XXX . IMP . VIII .
COS . III. As 1294. *C.* 928. *R.I.C.* 351. *B.M.C.* 668 .. .. 75·00

Fine

1324 **Æ sestertius.** B. (but SARMATICVS.) ℞. CLEMENTIA AVG . TR . P .
XXX . IMP . VIII . COS . III . S . C. Clemency stg. l. *C.* 28. *R.I.C.* 1158.
B.M.C. 1537 .. .. 6·00

1325 I. ℞. CONCORD . AVGVSTOR . TR . P . XVI . COS . III . S . C. M. Aurelius
and L. Verus clasping r. hands. *C.* 54. *R.I.C.* 826. *B.M.C.* 1009 .. 8·00

Fine

1326 **Æ sestertius.** B. (but with TR . P . XXXI. added.) R. DE GERMANIS (in ex.) IMP . VIII . COS . III . P . P . S . C. Pile of arms. *C.* 163. *R.I.C.* 1184. *B.M.C.* 1596 .. .. £12·50

1327 — R. DE SARMATIS (in ex.) IMP . VIII . COS . III . P . P . S . C. Pile of arms. *C.* 174. *R.I.C.* 1190. *B.M.C.* 1601 .. .. 12·50

1328 D. (but with TR . P . XXXIII. added.) R. FELICITAS AVG . IMP . VIIII . COS . III . P . P . S . C. Felicity stg. l. *C.* 185. *R.I.C.* 1237. *B.M.C.*, *p.* 677, † .. .. 6·00

1329 C. (TR . P . XXVII.) R. GERMANICO AVG . IMP . VI . COS . III . S . C. Trophy between German captive stg. r. and German woman seated l *C.* 227. *R.I.C.* 1058. *B.M.C.* 1433 .. .. 17·50

1330 — R. IMP . VI . COS . III . S . C. Jupiter seated l., holding Victory and sceptre. *C.* 248. *R.I.C.* 1064. *B.M.C.* 1437 .. .. .. 6·00

1331 C. (TR . P . XXVI.) R. — Roma seated l., holding Victory and spear. *C.* 281. *R.I.C.* 1033. *B.M.C.* 1416 .. .. 6·00

1332 B. (but with TR . P . XXX . P . P. added.) R. IMP . VIII . COS . III . PAX AETERNA AVG . S . C. Pax stg. l., setting fire to pile of arms. *C.* 360. *R.I.C.* 1163. *B.M.C.* 1549 .. .. 7·00

1333 M . ANTONINVS AVG . GERM . TR . P . XXIX. R. LIBERALITAS AVG . VI . IMP . VII . COS . III . S . C. Liberalitas stg. l. *C.* 419. *R.I.C.* 1147. *B.M.C.* 1507 .. .. 7·00

1334 *Obv.* As 1316. R. PRIMI DECENNALES COS . III . S . C. in five lines within oak-wreath. *C.* 497. *R.I.C.* 1006. *B.M.C.* 1398 .. .. 12·00

1335 C. (TR . P . XXVII.) R. RELIG . AVG. (in ex.) IMP . VI . COS . III . S . C. Tetrastyle temple with Mercury stg. l. on pedestal within. *C.* 535. *R.I.C.* 1075. *B.M.C.* 1441 *note.* *Illust. on p.* 152 .. .. 17·50

1336 — R. RESTITVTORI ITALIAE IMP . VI . COS . III . S . C. Aurelius stg. l., raising kneeling figure of Italy. *C.* 538. *R.I.C.* 1077. *B.M.C.* 1449 12·50

1337 I. R. SALVTI AVGVSTOR . TR . P . XVII . COS . III . S . C. As 1318. *C.* 564. *R.I.C.* 843. *B.M.C.* 1038 .. .. 6·00

1338 F. R. TR . POT . XIX . IMP . II . COS . III . S . C. Felicity stg. l. *C.* 798. *R.I.C.* 901. *B.M.C.* 1233 .. .. 6·00

1339 F. R. — Aurelius stg. l. with two standards either side of him. *C.* 804. *R.I.C.* 908. *B.M.C.* 1239 .. .. 7·50

1340 F. R. TR . POT . XX . IMP . III . COS . III . S . C. Providence stg. l., globe at feet. *C.* 805. *R.I.C.* 923. *B.M.C.* 1279 .. .. 6·00

1341 E. R. TR . POT . XX . IMP . III . COS . III . S . C. Victory, as 1305. *C.* 810. *R.I.C.* 934. *B.M.C.* 1290 .. .. 7·50

1342 E. (but without AVREL.) R. TR . POT . XXII . IMP . V . COS . III . S . C. Equity seated l. *C.* 820. *R.I.C.* 960. *B.M.C.* 1333 .. .. 6·00

1343 D. (but with TR . P . XXXIIII. added.) R. VIRTVS AVG . IMP . X . COS . III . P . P . S . C. Virtus seated r. *C.* 1004. *R.I.C.* 1249. *B.M.C.* 1711 7·50

1344 *Obv.* As 1316. R. VOTA SOLVTA DECENNALIVM COS . III . S . C. As 1322. *C.* 1034. *R.I.C.* 1016. *B.M.C.* 1401 .. .. 12·00

1345 **Æ dupondius.** C. (TR . P . XXVII.) Rad. hd., r. R. As 1330. *C.* 249. *R.I.C.* 1065. *B.M.C.* 1458 .. .. 4·00

1346 C. (TR . P . XXVI.) Rad. and cuir. bust, r. R. IMP . VI . COS . III . S . C. Roma seated l. on cuirass. *C.* 286. *R.I.C.* 1040. *B.M.C.* 1429 *note* 4·50

1347 C. (TR . P . XXVIII.) Rad. hd., r. R. IMP . VII . COS . III . S . C. Victory seated l. *C.* 330. *R.I.C.* 1114. *B.M.C.*, *p.* 636, § .. 4·00

1348 B. (but with TR . P . XXXI. added.) Rad. hd., r. R. IMP . VIIII . COS . III . P . P . S . C. Winged thunderbolt. *C.* 378. *R.I.C.* 1219. *B.M.C.* 1640 .. .. 5·00

Fine

1349 **Æ dupondius.** C. (TR . P . XXIIII.) Rad. hd., r. ℞. SALVTI AVG .
COS . III . S . C. As 1318. C. 549. R.I.C. 982. B.M.C. 1380 .. £4·00
1350 F. Rad. hd., r. ℞. TR . P . XVIII . IMP . II . COS . III . S . C. As 1315.
C. 839. R.I.C. 864. B.M.C. 1097 .. .. 4·00
1351 D. (but with P . M. added.) Rad. hd., r. ℞. — Minerva stg. l.,
holding olive-branch and leaning on shield. C. 843. R.I.C. 873.
B.M.C., p. 558, ‡ .. .. 4·00
1352 **Æ as.** I. ℞. CONCORD . AVGVSTOR . TR . P . XV . COS . III . S . C. As
1325. C. 46. R.I.C. 801. B.M.C. 854 note .. .. .. 5·00
1353 C. (TR . P . XXV.) ℞. COS . III . S . C. Minerva stg. r., brandishing
javelin. C. 125. R.I.C. 991. B.M.C. 1393 .. .. .. 4·00
1354 C. (TR . P . XXIX.) ℞. IMP . VII . COS . III . S . C. The Tiber
reclining l., resting r. hand on boat. C. 348. R.I.C. 1142. B.M.C.
1498 .. .. 8·00

1355 B. (but with TR . P . XXXI . added.) ℞. IMP . VIII . COS . III . P . P .
PAX AETERNA AVG . S . C. As 1332. C. 363. R.I.C. 1202. B.M.C. 1631 4·50
1356 C. (TR . P . XXVIII.) ℞. MARTI VICTORI IMP . VI . COS . III . S . C.
Mars stg. r., leaning on shield set on captive and holding spear. C. 432.
R.I.C. 1106. B.M.C. 1478 .. .. 4·00
1357 As 1337. C. 565. R.I.C. 850. B.M.C. 1046 .. .. 4·00
1358 M . ANTONINVS AVG . P . M. ℞. TR . P . XVIII . IMP . II . COS . III . S . C.
Victory advancing l. C. 864. R.I.C. 884. B.M.C. 1087 .. .. 4·00
1359 D. ℞. TR . P . XXXIIII . IMP . X . COS . III . P . P . S . C. She-wolf stg. r.
in grotto, suckling Romulus and Remus. C. 976. R.I.C. 1247. B.M.C.
1715 .. .. 9·00

Commemorative Coins struck after his death   Very Fine

1361 *Struck by Commodus,* N **aureus.** DIVVS M . ANTONINVS PIVS. Bare hd.,
r. ℞. CONSECRATIO. Funeral pyre surmounted by Aurelius in
quadriga. C. 96. R.I.C. (Com.) 275. B.M.C. 25 .. .. .. 225·00
1362 — **Æ denarius.** Similar. ℞. — Eagle stg. r. on altar, hd. turned.
C. 84. R.I.C. 272. B.M.C. 17 .. .. 10·00
1363 — — Similar. ℞. — As 1361. C. 97. R.I.C. 275. B.M.C. 27 10·00

Fine

1364 *Struck by Commodus,* **Æ sestertius.** Similar. ℞. CONSECRATIO S . C.
Eagle stg. r. on globe, hd. turned. C. 89. R.I.C. 654. B.M.C. 385 .. 12·00
1365 — — Similar. ℞. — Aurelius seated on eagle flying r. C. 94.
R.I.C. 660. B.M.C. 394 .. .. 12·00
1366 — — Similar. ℞. — As 1361. C 98. R.I.C. 662. B.M.C. 399 .. 12·00
1367 — **Æ as.** Similar. ℞. — As 1364. C. 90. R.I.C. 663. B.M.C.
403 .. .. 9·00

Very Fine

1368 *Struck by Trajan Decius,* **R antoninianus.** DIVO MARCO ANTONINO.
       Rad. hd., r. R. CONSECRATIO. Eagle stg. r., hd. turned. *C.* 1057.
       R.I.C. (Dec.) 91*b* ..   .. £17·50
1369 — — DIVO MARCO. Rad. hd., r. R. — Large altar. *C.* 1059.
       R.I.C. (Dec.) 92*b* ..   .. 17·50

Colonial and Provincial Coinage

Fair

1370 *Zacynthus,* Æ **19.** Laur. hd., r. R. Pan stg. r., holding bunch of
       grapes and young Dionysos. *B.M.C. G.*93 ..   .. 2·50
1371 *Cappadocia, Caesarea,* **R didrachm.** Laur. bust, r. R. Mount
       Argaeus, surmounted by small figure holding globe and sceptre.
       B.M.C. G. 69... ..   .. *Very fine* £12·00
1372 *Commagene, Antiochia ad Euphratem,* Æ **21.** Laur. and cuir. bust, r.
       R. Bust of Athena r. *B.M.C. G.*1 ..   .. 5·00
1373 *Decapolis, Antiochia ad Hippum,* Æ **25.** Laur. and dr. bust, r. R.
       Tyche of the City l., leading horse by bridle. *B.M.C. G.*1 ..   .. 6·50

Very Fine

1374 *Egypt, Alexandria,* **billon tetradrachm.** Bare-headed, dr. and cuir.
       bust, r. R. Dikaiosyne seated l. *B.M.C. G.*223. (*As Caesar*) .. 7·50
1375 — — Laur. hd., r. R. Tyche seated l. *B.M.C. G.*1270 ..   .. 7·00
1376 — — Similar. R. Two captives seated at foot of trophy. *B.M.C.*
       G.1281 ..   .. 10·00
1377 — Æ **34.** Laur., dr. and cuir. bust, r. R. Homonoia stg. l. *B.M.C.*
       G.1292 ..   .. *Fair* £3·50

FAUSTINA JUNIOR

1409

*Annia Galeria Faustina was the younger daughter of Antoninus Pius and Faustina
Senior, and was married to M. Aurelius in* A.D. *145. She was given the title of Augusta on
the birth of her first child in* A.D. *146, and she subsequently bore many children, one of whom
was the future emperor Commodus. She accompanied her husband on his journey to the East
in* A.D. *175 and died at Halala, a village at the foot of the Taurus Mountains.*

Struck under Antoninus Pius

The following are the commonest forms of obverse legend:

   A. FAVSTINA AVG . PII AVG . FIL.
   B. FAVSTINAE AVG . PII AVG . FIL.

The normal obverse type is dr. bust of Faustina r.

All *R.I.C.* and *B.M.C.* references are to the coinage of Antoninus Pius.

Very Fine

1378 **N aureus.** B. R. IVNONI LVCINAE. Juno stg. l. *C.* 131. *R.I.C.*
      505*a.* *B.M.C.* 1045 .. ..£160·00

1379 **N quinarius.** FAVSTINA AVGVSTA. R. AVGVSTI PII FIL. Diana stg. l.,
      holding arrow and bow. *C.* 20. *R.I.C.* 494*a.* *B.M.C.* 1098 .. .. 300·00

1380 **R denarius.** — R. — Concord stg. l. *C.* 21. *R.I.C.* 496. *B.M.C.*
      1103 .. .. 6·50

1381 A. R. CONCORDIA. Concord seated l., holding flower. *C.* 54.
      R.I.C. 502*a.* *B.M.C.* 1086.. .. .. 7·00

1382 B. R. LAETITIAE PVBLICAE. Laetitia stg. l. *C.* 155. *R.I.C.* 506*a.*
      B.M.C. 1048 .. .. 6·50

1383 FAVSTINA AVGVSTA AVG . PII F. R. PVDICITIA. Pudicitia stg. l., altar
      at feet. *C.* 184. *R.I.C.* 508*a.* *B.M.C.* 1092 .. .. .. 6·50

1384 B. R. VENVS. Venus stg. l., holding apple and rudder around which
      is entwined dolphin. *C.* 266. *R.I.C.* 517*a.* *R.M.C.* 1075 .. .. 7·50

Fine

1385 **Æ sestertius.** A. R. CONCORDIA S . C. Concord stg. l. *C.* 47.
      R.I.C. 1373. *B.M.C.* 2173 *note* .. .. 8·00

1386 A. R. S . C. Diana stg. l., holding arrow and leaning on bow.
      C. 206. *R.I.C.* 1383. *B.M.C.* 2180 .. .. 8·00

1387 B. R. VENERI GENETRICI S . C. Venus stg. l., holding apple and child.
      C. 237. *R.I.C.* 1386. *B.M.C.* 2146 .. .. 8·00

1388 **Æ dupondius.** B. R. PVDICITIA S . C. Pudicitia stg. l. *Cf. C.* 179.
      R.I.C. 1403. *B.M.C.* 2157 .. .. 5·00

1389 **Æ as.** A. R. IVNO S . C. Juno stg. l. *C.* 124. *R.I.C.* 1398.
      B.M.C. 2188 .. .. 5·00

1389A A. R. PIETAS S . C. Pietas stg. l., child at feet. *C.* 173. *R.I.C.*
       1402. *B.M.C.* 2189 .. .. 5·00

1390 FAVSTINA AVG . ANTONINI AVG . PII FIL. R. VENVS S . C. Venus stg. r.,
      holding apple. *C.* 257. *R.I.C.* 1410*c.* *B.M.C.* 2169 .. .. .. 5·00

Struck under Marcus Aurelius

All *R.I.C.* and *B.M.C.* references are to the coinage of M. Aurelius.

All have obverse legend FAVSTINA AVGVSTA *and obverse type dr. bust r., or diad. and dr.*
bust r. Reverses are as follows:

Very Fine

1391 **N aureus.** SALVTI AVGVSTAE. Salus seated l., feeding serpent arising
      from altar. *C.* 198. *R.I.C.* 716. *B.M.C.* 151. **Plate 6** .. .. 145·00

1392 **N quinarius.** VENVS. Venus stg. l., holding apple and sceptre.
      R.I.C. 725. *B.M.C.* 164 .. .. 300·00

Very Fine

1393 **Æ denarius.** DIANA LVCIF. Diana stg. l., holding torch. *C.* 85.
      R.I.C. 674. *B.M.C.* 87 .. .. £6·00
1394 FECVND . AVGVSTAE. Fecunditas stg. l. between two children, holding
      two more in her arms. *C.* 95. *R.I.C.* 676. *B.M.C.* 89.. .. .. 6·00
1395 FECVNDITAS. Fecunditas stg. r., holding sceptre and child. *C.* 99.
      R.I.C. 677. *B.M.C.* 91 .. .. 6·00
1396 FORTVNAE MVLIEBRI. Fortune seated l. *C.* 107. *R.I.C.* 683. *B.M.C.*
      96 .. .. 15·00
1397 HILARITAS. Hilaritas stg. l. *C.* 111. *R.I.C.* 686. *B.M.C.* 100 .. 6·00
1398 IVNO. Juno stg. l., peacock at feet. *C.* 120. *R.I.C.* 688. *B.M.C.* 104 6·00
1399 LAETITIA. Laetitia stg. l. *C.* 147. *R.I.C.* 700. *B.M.C.* 129 *note* .. 6·00
1400 SAECVLI FELICIT. Two children seated on throne. *C.* 190. *R.I.C.* 710.
      B.M.C. 136 .. .. 7·50
1401 SALVS. As 1391. *C.* 195. *R.I.C.* 714. *B.M.C.* 148 .. .. .. 6·00
1402 VESTA. Vesta seated l. *C.* 286. *R.I.C.* 737. *B.M.C.* 175 .. .. 6·50

1403 **Æ sestertius.** DIANA LVCIFERA S . C. Diana stg. r., holding torch.   **Fine**
      C. 91. *R.I.C.* 1631. *B.M.C.* 901.. .. .. 6·50
1404 FECVND . AVGVSTAE S . C. As 1394. *C.* 96. *R.I.C.* 1635. *B.M.C.* 902 6·50
1405 HILARITAS S . C. Hilaritas stg. l. *C.* 112. *R.I.C.* 1642. *B.M.C.* 911.. 6·50
1406 IVNO S . C. As 1398. *C.* 121. *R.I.C.* 1645. *B.M.C.* 914 .. .. 6·50
1407 IVNONI LVCINAE S . C. Juno stg. l. between two children, holding a third
      child in her arms. *C.* 136. *R.I.C.* 1649. *B.M.C.* 918 .. .. 7·50
1408 IVNONI REGINAE S . C. As 1398. *C.* 142. *R.I.C.* 1651. *B.M.C.* 919 .. 6·50
1409 MATRI MAGNAE S . C. Cybele seated r. on throne flanked by two lions,
      holding drum. *C.* 169. *R.I.C.* 1663. *B.M.C.* 932. *Illustrated on*
      p. 159 .. .. 10·00
1410 SAECVLI FELICIT . S . C. As 1400. *C.* 193. *R.I.C.* 1665. *B.M.C.* 936 8·50
1411 SALVTI AVGVSTAE S . C. As 1391. *C.* 200. *R.I.C.* 1668. *B.M.C.* 945 6·50
1412 VENVS FELIX S . C. Venus seated l., holding Victory and sceptre. *C.* 275.
      R.I.C. 1686. *B.M.C.* 957 .. .. 6·50
1413 VENVS VICTRIX S . C. Venus stg. l., holding Victory and leaning on shield.
      C. 283. *R.I.C.* 1688. *B.M.C.* 960 .. .. 6·50

1414 **Æ dupondius.** IVNO S . C. As 1398. *C.* 123. *R.I.C.* 1647. *B.M.C.*
      983 .. .. 4·00
1415 LAETITIA S . C. Laetitia stg. l. *C.* 151. *R.I.C.* 1655. *B.M.C.* 988 .. 4·00
1416 SAECVLI FELICIT . S . C. As 1400. *C.* 194. *R.I.C.* 1666. *B.M.C.* 991.. 5·50
1417 TEMPOR . FELIC . S . C. Faustina stg. l. amidst four children, holding two
      more in her arms. *C.* 223. *R.I.C.* 1675. *B.M.C.* 996. **Plate 6** .. 5·50
1418 **Æ as.** DIANA LVCIF . S . C. As 1393. *C.* 86. *R.I.C.* 1629. *B.M.C.*
      972 .. .. 4·00
1419 FECVNDITAS S . C. As 1395. *C.* 101. *R.I.C.* 1639. *B.M.C.* 980 .. 4·00
1420 SALVTI AVGVSTAE S . C. As 1391. *C.* 201. *R.I.C.* 1671. *B.M.C.* 995 4·00

1421 VENERI VICTRICI S . C. Venus stg. r., grasping r. arm of Mars who stands
      facing, hd. l., holding shield. *C.* 241. *R.I.C.* 1680. *B.M.C.* 999 .. 15·00

Fine

1422 **Æ as.** As 1412. *C.* 276. *R.I.C.* 1687. *B.M.C.* 1002   ..   .. £4·50

Commemorative Coins struck after her death

Unless otherwise stated, the obverse legend is DIVA FAVSTINA PIA *and the obverse type, dr. bust of Faustina r.*

All *R.I.C.* and *B.M.C.* references are to the coinage of M. Aurelius.

Very Fine

1423 **N aureus.** DIVAE FAVSTINAE PIAE. Veiled, diad. and dr. bust, r. R.
MATRI CASTRORVM. Faustina seated l., holding phoenix on globe and
sceptre; to l., three standards. *C.* 159. *R.I.C.* 751. *B.M.C.* 704 .. 300·00

1424 **R denarius.** R. AETERNITAS. Eternity stg. facing, hd. l., holding
torch. *C.* 2. *R.I.C.* 739. *B.M.C.* 706 ..   ..   9·00
1425 R. CONSECRATIO. Peacock stg. r. *C.* 71. *R.I.C.* 744. *B.M.C.* 714   9·00
1426 R. — Large altar. *C.* 75. *R.I.C.* 746. *B.M.C.* 725 ..   ..   ..   9·00
1427 DIVAE FAVSTIN . AVG . MATR . CASTROR. Veiled and dr. bust, r. R. —
Funeral pyre surmounted by biga. *C.* 81. *R.I.C.* 749. *B.M.C.* 701   25·00

1428 **Æ sestertius.** R. CONSECRATIO S . C. Faustina seated l. on peacock **Fine**
flying r. *C.* 69. *R.I.C.* 1702. *B.M.C.* 1570 ..   ..   12·00
1429 R. — Peacock stg. l., tail in splendour. *C.* 72. *R.I.C.* 1703. *B.M.C.*
1573 ..   ..   10·00
1430 R. SIDERIBVS RECEPTA S . C. Diana stg. r., holding torch. *C.* 215.
R.I.C. 1715. *B.M.C.* 1584   ..   ..   12·00
1431 **Æ as.** R. S . C. Crescent and seven stars. *C.* 213. *R.I.C.* 1714.
B.M.C. 1593 ..   ..   7·50

Colonial and Provincial Coinage   Very Fine

1432 *Egypt, Alexandria,* **billon tetradrachm.** Dr. bust, r. R. Bust of
Serapis r. *B.M.C.* G.1323. (*Struck under Antoninus*) ..   ..   8·50
1433 — — Similar. R. Tyche seated l. *B.M.C.* G.1346. (*Struck under
Aurelius*)   ..   ..   7·50
1434 — **Æ 25.** Similar. R. Elpis stg. l. *B.M.C.* G.1336. (*Struck
under Antoninus*)   ..   ..   Fair £2·50

1446

LUCIUS VERUS
A.D. 161-169

    *L. Ceionius Commodus, later known as L. Aurelius Verus, was born in A.D. 130, the son
of Aelius Caesar. In A.D. 138 he was adopted by Antoninus, but unlike M. Aurelius, who
was adopted at the same time, he was not raised to the rank of Caesar. Nevertheless, on the
accession of Aurelius in A.D. 161, Verus was immediately made co-emperor. He was also
betrothed to Aurelius' daughter, Lucilla, whom he married in A.D. 164. He campaigned
in the East from A.D. 163-5 with considerable success, but he was a weak man addicted to
pleasure and his death in 169 was a relief to his senior partner.*

Titles and Powers, A.D. 161-169

A.D.	Tribunician Power	Imperatorial Acclamation	Consulship	Other Titles
161	TR.P. – TR.P.II.	IMP.	COS.II.	AVGVSTVS.
162	TR.P.II. – III.			
163	TR.P.III. – IIII.	IMP.II.		ARMENIACVS.
164	TR.P.IIII. – V.			
165	TR.P.V. – VI.	IMP.III.		PARTH. MAX.
166	TR.P.VI. – VII.	IMP.IIII.		MEDICVS. P.P.
167	TR.P.VII. – VIII.		COS.III.	
168	TR.P.VIII. – VIIII.	IMP.V.		
169	TR.P.VIIII.			

Verus became TR.P.II. on December 10th, A.D. 161, and his tribunician power was subsequently renewed each year on that date.

His first consulship was in A.D. 157.

Mint: Rome.

The following are the commonest forms of obverse legend:

A. L . VERVS AVG . ARMENIACVS.

B. L . VERVS AVG . ARM . PARTH . MAX.

C. L . AVREL . VERVS AVG . ARMENIACVS.

D. IMP . CAES . L . AVREL . VERVS AVG.

There are two main varieties of obverse type:

a. Bare hd., r.

b. Laur. hd., r.

Very Fine

1435 *N* **aureus.** Da. ℞. CONCORDIAE AVGVSTOR . TR . P . COS . II. Aurelius and Verus clasping r. hands. *C.* 44. *R.I.C.* 450. *B.M.C.* 31 £150·00

1435A A. Laur., dr. and cuir. bust, r. ℞. TR . P . IIII . IMP . II . COS . II. Victory stg. r., attaching shield, inscribed VIC . AVG., to palm-tree. *C.* 247 *var.* *R.I.C.* 525. *B.M.C.* 296 note. **Plate 7** .. .. .. 150·00

1436 *N* **quinarius.** L . VERVS AVG. Bare-headed and dr. bust, r. ℞. TR . POT . III . COS . II. Providence stg. l., holding globe and cornucopiae. *C.* 180. *R.I.C.* 497. *B.M.C., p.* 416, * .. .. 350·00

1437 **R denarius.** Aa. ℞. ARMEN. (in ex.) TR . P . III . IMP . II . COS . II. Armenia seated l. on ground amidst arms. *C.* 6. *R.I.C.* 501. *B.M.C.* 239 .. .. 10·00

1438 Bb. ℞. PAX (in ex.) TR . P . VI . IMP . IIII . COS . II. Pax stg. l. *C.* 126. *R.I.C.* 561. *B.M.C.* 426 .. .. 8·00

1439 D. (but without CAES.) a. ℞. PROV . DEOR . TR . P . II . COS . II. As 1436. *C.* 155. *R.I.C.* 482. *B.M.C.* 202 .. .. .. 8·00

1440 Ab. ℞. TR . P . IIII . IMP . II . COS . II. Mars stg. r., holding spear and leaning on shield. *C.* 230. *R.I.C.* 516. *B.M.C.* 287 .. .. 8·00

1441 Bb. ℞. TR . P . V . IMP . III . COS . II. Parthia seated r. on ground, hands tied behind back. *C.* 273. *R.I.C.* 540. *B.M.C.* 385 .. .. 12·50

1442 Bb. ℞. TR . P . VI . IMP . IIII . COS . II. Victory stg. r., attaching shield inscribed VIC . PAR., to palm-tree. *C.* 279. *R.I.C.* 566. *B.M.C.* 431 .. .. 9·00

1443 Bb. ℞. TR . P . VII . IMP . IIII . COS . III. Victory advancing l. *C.* 295. *R.I.C.* 574. *B.M.C.* 450.. .. .. 8·00

1444 Bb. ℞. TR . P . VIII . IMP . V . COS . III. Equity seated l. *C.* 318. *R.I.C.* 595. *B.M.C.* 481 .. .. 8·00

1445 **R quinarius.** L . VERVS AVG. b. ℞. TR . P . VII . COS . III. Victory advancing l. *C.* 290. *R.I.C.* 570. *B.M.C.* 445 .. .. .. 100·00

Fine

1446 **Æ sestertius.** Db. R. CONCORD . AVGVSTOR . TR . P . COS . II . S . C.
       As 1435. *C. 28. R.I.C. 1284. B.M.C. 859. Illustrated on p.* 162 .. £10·00
1447 Da. R. FELIC . AVG . TR . P . III . COS . II . S . C.   Galley travelling l.
       C. 71. R.I.C. 1326. B.M.C. 1047   ..   ..   20·00
1448 Db. R. FORT . RED. (in ex.) TR . POT . III . COS . II . S . C.   Fortune
       seated l. *C. 95. R.I.C. 1346. B.M.C. 1057* ..   ..   10·00
1449 C. Laur. and cuir. bust, r. R. REX ARMEN . DAT. (in ex.) TR . P .
       IIII . IMP . II . COS . II . S . C.   Verus seated l. on platform, accompanied
       by three officers, crowning King Sohaemus who stands l. in front of
       platform. *C. 161. R.I.C. 1371. B.M.C. 1106*   ..   ..   ..   30·00
1450 Bb. R. TR . POT . VI . IMP . IIII . COS . II . S . C.   As 1442. *C. 206.*
       R.I.C. 1456. B.M.C. 1308..   ..   ..   12·00
1451 Cb. R. TR . P . IIII . IMP . II . COS . II . S . C.   Mars advancing r., carrying
       spear and trophy. *C. 224. R.I.C. 1379. B.M.C. 1109*   ..   ..   10·00
1452 Ca. R. VICT . AVG . TR . P . IIII . IMP . II . COS . II . S . C.   Victory stg.
       r., holding trophy, Armenia seated r. at feet. *C. 334. R.I.C. 1409.*
       B.M.C. 1120 note   ..   ..   15·00

1453 **Æ dupondius.** D. Rad. hd., r. R. As 1447. *C. 70. R.I.C.*
       1329. B.M.C. 1059..   ..   ..   8·00
1454 D. — R. As 1448. *C. 99. R.I.C. 1348. B.M.C. 1060*   ..   ..   6·00
1455 B. — R. TR . POT . VI . IMP . IIII . COS . II . S . C.   As 1442. *C. 208.*
       R.I.C. 1458. B.M.C. 1315   ..   ..   6·50

1456 **Æ as.** Aa. R. ARMEN. (in ex.) TR . P . IIII . IMP . II . COS . II . S . C.
       Similar to 1437. *C. 9. R.I.C. 1364. B.M.C. 1135* ..   ..   ..   8·00
1457 Aa. R. TR . P . IIII . IMP . II . COS . II . S . C.   Mars advancing l.,
       holding Victory, trophy and parazonium. *C. 222. R.I.C. 1377.*
       B.M.C. 1127 ..   ..   6·50
1458 Aa. R. — Victory advancing l. *C. 242. R.I.C. 1392. B.M.C.*
       1128 note   ..   ..   6·00
1459 Bb. R. TR . P . VII . IMP . IIII . COS . III . S . C.   Roma seated l. on
       cuirass, clasping r. hands with Verus stg. r. *C. 299. R.I.C. 1463.*
       B.M.C. 1327 ..   ..   9·00

Commemorative Coins struck after his death   Very Fine

1460 **Æ denarius.** DIVVS VERVS. Bare hd., r. R. CONSECRATIO. Eagle
       stg. r., hd. turned. *C. 55. R.I.C. 596a. B.M.C. 503*   ..   ..   14·00
1461 — R. — Funeral pyre surmounted by quadriga. *C. 58. R.I.C. 596b.*
       B.M.C. 505 ..   ..   15·00

Fine

1462 **Æ sestertius.** — R. CONSECRATIO S . C.   Eagle stg. r. on globe, hd.
       turned. *C. 56. R.I.C. 1509. B.M.C. 1359*   ..   ..   ..   12·50
1463 — R. — As 1461. *C. 59. R.I.C. 1511. B.M.C. 1363*   ..   ..   14·00

Colonial and Provincial Coinage   Fair

1464 *Argolis, Argos,* **Æ 23.** Laur. bust, r. R. Hera seated l., holding
       patera and sceptre. *B.M.C. G.159*   ..   ..   3·25
1465 *Pisidia, Selge,* **Æ 20.** Bare hd., r. R. Bow and thunderbolt.
       B.M.C. G.75 ..   ..   2·00
1466 *Egypt, Alexandria,* **billon tetradrachm.** Laur. bust, r. R. Dikaiosyne
       stg. l. *B.M.C. G.1355*   ..   ..   ..   *Very fine* £10·00
1467 — **Æ 35.** Similar. R. Eirene seated l., holding patera. *B.M.C.*
       G.1376   ..   ..   3·75

LUCILLA

1480

The eldest daughter of M. Aurelius and Faustina Junior, Lucilla was married to L. Verus in A.D. *164. After his death, she was married to Pompeianus, a man of comparatively humble origin, and in* A.D. *182 she was involved in an unsuccessful plot against her brother, the emperor Commodus. She was banished to Capreae and soon afterwards put to death.*

There are two main varieties of obverse legend:

A. LVCILLA AVGVSTA.

B. LVCILLAE AVG. ANTONINI AVG . F.

All coins have as obverse type dr. bust of Lucilla r.

All *R.I.C.* and *B.M.C.* references are to the coinage of M. Aurelius.

Very Fine

1468 **N aureus.** B. R. VENVS. Venus stg. l., holding apple and sceptre. C. 69. *R.I.C.* 783. *B.M.C.* 320 .. ..£175·00

1469 **N quinarius.** LVCILLAE AVGVSTAE. R. PIETAS. Pietas stg. l., altar at feet. C. 51. *R.I.C.* 776. *B.M.C.* 316 *note* .. .. .. 400·00

1470 **Æ denarius.** A. R. CONCORDIA. Concord seated l. C. 7. *R.I.C.* 759. *B.M.C.* 333 .. .. 8·00

1471 B. R. IVNONI LVCINAE. Juno stg. l., holding child in swaddling clothes. C. 38. *R.I.C.* 771. *B.M.C.* 313 .. .. .. 10·00

1472 A. R. IVNO REGINA. Juno stg. l., peacock at feet. C. 41. *R.I.C.* 772. *B.M.C.* 339 .. .. 8·00

1473 B. R. As 1469. C. 50. *R.I.C.* 775. *B.M.C.* 317 .. .. .. 8·50

1474 A. R. PVDICITIA. Pudicitia seated l. C. 62. *R.I.C.* 781. *B.M.C.* 349 .. .. 9·00

1475 A. R. VENVS VICTRIX. Venus stg. l., holding Victory and leaning on shield. C. 89. *R.I.C.* 786. *B.M.C.* 353 .. .. 10·00

1475A B. R. VESTA. Vesta stg. l., holding simpulum and palladium, altar at feet. C. 92. *R.I.C.* 788. *B.M.C.* 325. **Plate 6** .. .. .. 9·00

1476 B. R. VOTA PVBLICA in three lines within laurel-wreath. C. 98. *R.I.C.* 791. *B.M.C.* 329 .. .. 15·00

Fine

1477 **Æ sestertius.** A. R. FECVNDITAS S . C. Fecunditas seated r., nursing child, two more children stg. on ground. C. 21. *R.I.C.* 1736. *B.M.C.* 1197 .. .. 10·00

1478 B. R. HILARITAS S . C. Hilaritas stg. l. C. 31. *R.I.C.* 1742. *B.M.C.* 1147 .. .. 7·50

1479 A. R. IVNO S . C. Juno seated l., holding patera and sceptre. C. 35. *R.I.C.* 1746. *B.M.C.* 1204 .. .. 7·50

1480 B. R. PIETAS S . C. As 1469. C. 54. *R.I.C.* 1756. *B.M.C.* 1161 *Illustrated above* .. .. 7·50

1481 B. R. VENVS S . C. Venus seated l., holding Victory and sceptre. C. 81. *R.I.C.* 1772. *B.M.C.* 1174 .. .. 7·50

1482 B. R. VESTA S . C. Vesta stg. l., holding simpulum and palladium, altar at feet. C. 94. *R.I.C.* 1779. *B.M.C.* 1178 .. .. .. 7·50

Fine

1483 **Æ dupondius.** A. ℞. As 1478. *C.* 30. *R.I.C.* 1741. *B.M.C.*
1217 .. .. £5·00

1484 B. ℞. PVDICITIA S . C. Pudicitia seated. l. *C.* 64. *R.I.C.* 1759.
B.M.C. 1185 .. .. 5·00

1485 B. ℞. SALVS S . C. Salus stg. l., feeding serpent arising from altar.
C. 67. *R.I.C.* 1761. *B.M.C.* 1186 .. .. 5·00

1486 As 1482. *C.* 95. *R.I.C.* 1780. *B.M.C.* 1192 .. .. 5·00

1487 **Æ as.** B. ℞. CONCORDIA S . C. Concord stg. l. *C.* 11. *R.I.C.*
1733. *B.M.C.* 1182 .. .. 5·00

1488 A. ℞. As 1481. *C.* 86. *R.I.C.* 1777. *B.M.C.* 1226 .. .. 5·00

1541A

COMMODUS
A.D. 177-192

    L. Aelius Aurelius Commodus was the son of M. Aurelius and Faustina Junior and was born at Lanuvium in A.D. 161. *He was made Augustus and co-emperor in* A.D. 177 *and accompanied his father to the second Germanic War. On the death of Aurelius in 180, Commodus concluded a peace with the German and Sarmatian tribes and hurried back to Rome. There were great hopes that he might continue the fine tradition of Antonine government, but he proved a most unworthy son of a noble father. He soon retired from public life and left the administration of the Empire to a succession of favourites – first Perennis, then Cleander and finally Laetus. During his last years he seems to have become quite insane: he disgraced the purple by fighting wild beasts in the amphitheatre, and his megalomania caused him to believe himself the reincarnation of Hercules and to demand the worship of the people. After numerous unsuccessful plots against his life, he was eventually murdered on the night of December 31st,* A.D. 192.

Mint: Rome.

As Caesar
A.D. 175-177, *under M. Aurelius*

    Unless otherwise stated, the obverse legend is COMMODO CAES . AVG . FIL . GERM . SARM., *and the obverse type, bare hd. r. or bare-headed, dr. and / or cuir. bust r.*

    All *R.I.C.* and *B.M.C.* references are to the coinage of M. Aurelius.

Very Fine

1489 *N* **aureus.** ℞. ADVENTVS CAES. Commodus on horseback r., raising
r. hand. *C.* 1. *R.I.C.* 604. *B.M.C.* 641 .. .. .. 300·00

1490 **Æ denarius.** ℞. PIETAS AVG. Sacrificial implements. *C.* 401.
R.I.C. 613. *B.M.C.* 647 .. .. 12·00

Titles and Powers, A.D. 175-192.

A.D.	Tribunician Power	Imperatorial Acclamation	Consulship	Other Titles
175				CAESAR. GERM. SARM.
176	TR.P. (?)			
177	TR.P. (later TR.P.II.) – TR.P.III.	IMP. IMP.II.	COS.	AVGVSTVS. P.P.
178	TR.P.III. – IIII.			
179	TR.P.IIII. – V.	IMP.III.	COS.II.	
180	TR.P.V. – VI.	IMP.IIII.		P.M.
181	TR.P.VI. – VII.		COS.III.	
182	TR.P.VII. – VIII.	IMP.V.		
183	TR.P.VIII. – VIIII.	IMP.VI.	COS.IIII.	PIVS.
184	TR.P.VIIII. – X.	IMP.VII.		BRIT.
185	TR.P.X. – XI.			FELIX.
186	TR.P.XI. – XII.	IMP.VIII.	COS.V.	
187	TR.P.XII. – XIII.			
188	TR.P.XIII. – XIIII.			
189	TR.P.XIIII. – XV.			
190	TR.P.XV. – XVI.		COS.VI.	
191	TR.P.XVI. – XVII.			
192	TR.P.XVII. – XVIII.		COS.VII.	

Commodus would seem to have received the tribunician power either very late in A.D. 176 (after December 10th) or early in A.D. 177. In any case his coins show him as TR.P. early in 177, but then suddenly he changes to TR.P.II. and advances to TR.P.III. on December 10th.

The only conceivable explanation is that after the TR.P. issue of early A.D. 177 it was decided to put back the date on which he had first received the tribunician power to before December 10th, A.D. 176. By means of this legal fiction Commodus would be able to count his second tribunician year as beginning from this date. Subsequently his tribunician power was renewed each year on December 10th.

Very Fine

1491 **Æ denarius.** R. PRINC . IVVENT. Commodus stg. l. beside trophy, holding branch and sceptre. C. 609. R.I.C. 616. B.M.C. 649 note .. £10·00

1492 R. SPES PVBLICA. Spes advancing l. C. 709. R.I.C. 621-2. B.M.C. 655 ..   .. 9·00

1493 IMP . CAES . L . AVREL . COMMODVS GERM . SARM. Laur. and dr. bust, r. R. TR . POT . II . COS. Salus stg. l., feeding serpent arising from altar. C. 741. R.I.C. 626. B.M.C. 748 note ..   .. 9·00

Fine

1494 **Æ sestertius.** — Laur. hd., r. R. DE GERM. (in ex.) TR . P . II . COS . S . C. Two captives seated on ground either side of trophy. C. 81. R.I.C. 1554. B.M.C., p. 668, * ..   .. 17·50

1495 L . AVREL . COMMODO CAES . AVG . FIL . GERM . SARM. R. PIETAS AVG . S . C. Sacrificial implements. C. 403. R.I.C. 1526. B.M.C. 1526 15·00

1496 L . AVREL . COMMODVS CAES . AVG . FIL . GERM. R. PRINC . IVVENT . S . C. As 1491. C. 610. R.I.C. 1518. B.M.C. 1518 ..   .. 15·00

1497 **Æ dupondius.** R. As 1495. C. 405. R.I.C. 1539. B.M.C. 1533 7·50

1498 **Æ as.** COMMODO CAES . AVG . FIL . GERM . SARM . COS. R. HILARITAS S . C. Hilaritas stg. l. C. 218. R.I.C. 1547. B.M.C. 1644 ..   .. 7·50

1499 R. SPES PVBLICA S . C. Spes advancing l. C. 710. R.I.C. 1544. B.M.C. 1536 ..   .. 7·50

As Augustus

With *M. Aurelius*, A.D. 177-180

The following are the commonest forms of obverse legend:

A. L . AVREL . COMMODVS AVG.
B. L . AVREL . COMMODVS AVG . TR . P . III.
C. L . AVREL . COMMODVS AVG . TR . P . IIII.
D. IMP . L . AVREL . COMMODVS AVG . GERM . SARM.

Unless otherwise stated, the obverse type is laur. hd. r., or laur. bust r., dr. or dr. and cuir.
All *R.I.C.* and *B.M.C.* references are to the coinage of M. Aurelius.

		Very Fine
1500	**N aureus.** A. ℞. TR . P . III . IMP . II . COS . P . P. Castor stg. l., holding horse by bridle. *C.* 760. *R.I.C.* 648. *B.M.C.* 774. **Plate 7**	£200·00
1501	**N quinarius.** A. ℞. TR . POT . II . COS . P . P. Spes advancing l. *C.* 743. *R.I.C.* 644. *B.M.C.* 759	400·00
1502	**R denarius.** A. ℞. COS . P . P. Roma stg. l., holding Victory and spear. *C.* 64. *R.I.C.* 651. *B.M.C.* 763	7·00
1503	D. ℞. TR . P . II . COS . P . P. As 1493. *C.* 746. *R.I.C.* 640. *B.M.C.* 756 *note*	7·00
1504	A. ℞. TR . P . IIII . IMP . III . COS . II . P . P. Fortune seated l. *C.* 771. *R.I.C.* 662. *B.M.C.* 796.	7·00
1505	A. ℞. — Victory seated l., holding patera and palm. *C.* 775. *R.I.C.* 666. *B.M.C.* 801	7·00
1506	**Æ sestertius.** D. ℞. DE SARMATIS (in ex.) TR . P . II . COS . P . P . S . C. Pile of arms. *C.* 96. *R.I.C.* 1577. *B.M.C.* 1665	Fine 17·50
1507	C. ℞. IMP . II . COS . P . P . S . C. Minerva stg. l., sacrificing over altar and leaning on shield. *C.* 228. *R.I.C.* 1599. *B.M.C.* 1699 ..	6·50
1508	B. ℞. LIBERTAS AVG . IMP . II . COS . P . P . S . C. Liberty stg. l. *C.* 331. *R.I.C.* 1588. *B.M.C.* 1684	6·50
1509	B. ℞. VOTA PVBLICA IMP . II . COS . P . P . S . C. Commodus stg. l., sacrificing over tripod-altar to l. of which stands victimarius, about to strike bull with axe. *C.* 980. *R.I.C.* 1594. *B.M.C.* 1688	20·00
1510	**Æ dupondius.** C. Rad. hd., r. ℞. As 1507. *C.* 229. *R.I.C.* 1604. *B.M.C.* 1702	4·50
1511	C. Rad. hd., r. ℞. IMP . III . COS . II . P . P . S . C. Victory advancing l. *C.* 237. *R.I.C.* 1614. *B.M.C.* 1708	4·50
1512	D. (but without IMP.) Rad., dr. and cuir. bust, r. ℞. TR . P . II . IMP . II . COS . P . P . S . C. Roma seated l., holding Victory and parazonium. *C.* 756. *R.I.C.* 1585. *B.M.C.* 1674	5·00
1513	**Æ as.** C. ℞. IMP . II . COS . II . P . P . S . C. Mars advancing r., carrying spear and trophy. *C.* 230. *R.I.C.* 1606. *B.M.C., p.* 679, ‡	4·50
1514	A. ℞. TR . P . II . IMP . II . COS . P . P . S . C. Victory advancing l. *C.* 757. *R.I.C.* 1586. *B.M.C., p.* 673, * *note*	4·50

As Sole Emperor, A.D. 180-192

The following are the commonest forms of obverse legend:

A. L . AEL . AVREL . COMM . AVG . P . FEL.
B. M . COMM . ANT . P . FEL . AVG . BRIT.
C. M . COMM . ANT . P . FEL . AVG . BRIT . P . P.
D. M . COMMOD . ANT . P . FELIX AVG . BRIT . P . P.
E. M . COMMODVS ANT . P . FELIX AVG . BRIT.
F. M . COMMODVS ANTONINVS AVG.
G. M . COMMODVS ANTONINVS AVG . PIVS.

Unless otherwise stated, the obverse type is laur. hd., r.

1515 *N* **aureus.** C. Laur., dr. and cuir. bust, r. ℞. GEN . AVG . FELIC . COS . VI. Genius stg. l., altar at feet. *C.* 171. *R.I.C.* 227*a*. *B.M.C.* 288 .. ..£200·00

1516 *N* **quinarius.** F. Laur. and cuir. bust, r. ℞. TR . P . V . IMP . IIII . COS . II . P . P. Fortune seated l. *C.* 787. *R.I.C.* 6*a*. *B.M.C.* 5 400·00

1517 **Æ denarius.** C. ℞. APOL . MONET . P . M . TR . P . XV . COS . VI. Apollo stg. r., l. arm resting on column. *C.* 22. *R.I.C.* 205. *B.M.C.* 275 .. .. 11·00

1518 A. ℞. FELIC . PERPETVAE AVG. Commodus and Felicity clasping r. hands. *C.* 120. *R.I.C.* 249. *B.M.C.* 337 .. .. 13·00

1519 C. ℞. FIDEI COH . P . M . TR . P . XVI . COS . VI. Fides stg. l., holding corn-ears and standard. *C.* 127. *R.I.C.* 220. *B.M.C.* 298 .. .. 12·00

1520 M . COMM . ANT . AVG . P . BRIT . FEL. ℞. FID . EXERC. (in ex.) P . M . TR . P . X . IMP . VII . COS . IIII . P . P. Commodus stg. l., on platform, haranguing three soldiers. *C.* 140. *R.I.C.* 110*b*. *B.M.C.* 160 *note* .. 20·00

1521 B. ℞. HILAR . AVG . P . M . TR . P . XII . IMP . VIII . COS . V . P . P. Hilaritas stg. l. *C.* 212. *R.I.C.* 150*a*. *B.M.C.* 210 .. .. .. 6·50

1522 B. ℞. IOV . IVVEN . P . M . TR . P . XIIII . COS . V . P . P. Jupiter stg. l., eagle at feet. *C.* 259. *R.I.C.* 173. *B.M.C.* 253 .. .. .. 9·00

1523 A. ℞. LIB . AVG . P . M . TR . P . XVII . COS . VII . P . P. Liberty stg. l. *C.* 288. *R.I.C.* 241. *B.M.C.* 308.. .. .. 6·50

1524 A. ℞. MATRI DEV . CONSERV . AVG. Cybele seated facing on lion springing r. *C.* 354. *R.I.C.* 258. *B.M.C.* 353.. .. .. .. 40·00

1525 B. ℞. OPTIME MAXIME C . V . P . P. Jupiter stg. l. *C.* 387. *R.I.C.* 192. *B.M.C.* 233 .. .. 14·00

1526 G. (but ANTON.) ℞. P . M . TR . P . VIIII . IMP . VI . COS . IIII . P . P. Equity stg. l. *C.* 446. *R.I.C.* 73. *B.M.C.* 121 .. .. .. 6·50

1527 COMM . ANT . AVG . P . BRIT. ℞. P . M . TR . P . X . IMP . VII . COS . IIII . P . P. As 1502. *C.* 476. *R.I.C.* 102. *B.M.C.* 154 .. .. 6·50

1528 B. ℞. P . M . TR . P . XIII . IMP . VIII . COS . V . P . P. Genius stg. l., holding patera and corn-ears. *C.* 532. *R.I.C.* 167. *B.M.C.* 245 .. 6·50

1529 A. ℞. P . M . TR . P . XVII . IMP . VIII . COS . VII . P . P. Pietas seated l., child at feet. *C.* 574. *R.I.C.* 236. *B.M.C.* 326 .. .. .. 6·50

1530 B. ℞. SECVR . ORB . P . M . TR . P . XIIII . COS . V . P . P. Security seated l., holding globe. *C.* 697. *R.I.C.* 179. *B.M.C.* 261 .. .. 6·50

1531 C. ℞. TEMP . FELIC . P . M . TR . P . XV . COS . VI. Winged caduceus between two cornuacopiae. *C.* 719. *R.I.C.* 209. *B.M.C.* 283 .. 9·00

1532 F. ℞. TR . P . VI . IMP . IIII . COS . III . P . P. Providence stg. l., globe at feet. *C.* 804. *R.I.C.* 19. *B.M.C.* 66 .. .. 6·50

1533 G. (but ANTON.) ℞. TR . P . VIII . IMP . VI . COS . IIII . P . P. Salus stg. l., feeding serpent arising from altar. *C.* 903. *R.I.C.* 66. *B.M.C.* 113 .. .. 6·50

1534 — ℞. TR . P . VIIII . IMP . VI . COS . IIII . P . P. Minerva advancing r., brandishing javelin, owl at feet. *C.* 914. *R.I.C.* 82. *B.M.C.* 131 .. 6·50

1535 B. ℞. VOT . SOL . DEC . P . M . TR . P . XI . IMP . VIII . COS . V . P . P. Commodus stg. l., sacrificing over tripod-altar. *C.* 1000. *R.I.C.* 140. *B.M.C.* 206 .. .. 8·00

1536 **Æ quinarius.** B. Laur. and dr. bust, r. ℞. P . M . TR . P . XIII . IMP . VIII . COS . V . P . P. Victory advancing l. *C.* 535. *R.I.C.* 170. *B.M.C.* 251 .. .. 45·00

Fine

1537 **Æ sestertius.** L . AVREL . COMMODVS AVG . TR . P . V. Laur. and cuir. bust, r. ℞. ADVENTVS AVG . IMP . IIII . COS . II . P . P . S . C. Commodus on horseback r., raising r. hand. *C.* 3. *R.I.C.* 294. *B.M.C.* 1728 .. .. 17·50

Fine

1538 **Æ sestertius.** E. ℞. CONC . MIL (in ex.) P . M . TR . P . XI . IMP . VII . COS . V . P . P . S . C. Concord stg. l., holding two standards. *C.* 57. *R.I.C.* 465. *B.M.C.* 576 .. .. £7·50

1539 E. ℞. FOR . RED. (in ex.) P . M . TR . P . XIII . IMP . VIII . COS . V . P . P . S . C. Fortune seated l. *C.* 153. *R.I.C.* 513. *B.M.C.* 618. **Plate 6** 7·50

1540 D. ℞. GEN . AVG . FELIC . P . M . TR . P . XV . IMP . VIII . COS . VI . S . C. Genius stg. l., altar at feet. *C.* 174. *R.I.C.* 561. *B.M.C.* 645 .. 8·50

1541 A. Hd. r., wearing lion's skin. ℞. HERCVL. ROMANO AVGV . S . C. in four lines divided by club; all within laurel-wreath. *C.* 192. *R.I.C.* 637. *B.M.C.* 711 .. 35·00

1541A A. Hd. r., wearing lion's skin. ℞. HERCVLI ROMANO AVGV . S . C. Bow, club, quiver and arrows. *C.* 199. *R.I.C.* 639. *B.M.C.* 717. *Illustrated on p.* 166 .. .. 60·00

1542 M . COMMODVS ANTON . AVG . PIVS BRIT. ℞. ITALIA (in ex.) P . M . TR . P . VIIII . IMP . VII . COS . IIII . P . P . S . C. Italy seated l. on globe, holding cornucopiae and sceptre. *C.* 266. *R.I.C.* 438. *B.M.C.* 549.. 17·50

1543 D. ℞. LIB . AVG . P . M . TR . P . XV . IMP . VIII . COS . VI . S . C. Liberty stg. l. *C.* 285. *R.I.C.* 562. *B.M.C.* 648 .. .. .. 7·50

1544 E. ℞. PACI AETERNAE COS . V . P . P . S . C. Pax seated l. *C.* 390. *R.I.C.* 548. *B.M.C.* 606 .. .. 7·50

1545 E. ℞. PIETATI SENATVS COS . V . P . P . S . C. Commodus and senator clasping r. hands. *C.* 410. *R.I.C.* 549. *B.M.C.* 607 .. .. 12·50

1546 G. ℞. P . M . TR . P . VIIII . IMP . VI . COS . IIII . P . P . S . C. Security seated l., holding sceptre. *C.* 455. *R.I.C.* 406. *B.M.C.* 532 .. .. 7·50

1547 E. ℞. P . M . TR . P . XI . IMP . VII . COS . V . P . P . S . C. Janus stg. facing in shrine consisting of semicircular arch resting on two columns. *C.* 489. *R.I.C.* 460. *B.M.C.* 568.. 17·50

1548 E. ℞. — Commodus seated l., crowned by Victory flying behind him. *C.* 506. *R.I.C.* 463. *B.M.C.* 573.. .. .. 12·50

1549 A. ℞. P . M . TR . P . XVII . IMP . VIII . COS . VII . P . P . S . C. Victory advancing l. *C.* 569. *R.I.C.* 612. *B.M.C.* 702 .. .. .. 7·50

1549A E. Laur. and dr. bust r., P . D. beneath. ℞. PROVID . AVG . P . M . TR . P . XI . IMP . VIII . COS . V . P . P . S . C. Galley sailing r. *C.* 636. *R.I.C.* 486. *B.M.C.* 588 *note* .. .. 40·00

1550 G. ℞. TR . P . VIII . IMP . VI . COS . IIII . P . P . S . C. Felicity stg. l. *C.* 907. *R.I.C.* 370. *B.M.C.* 512.. .. .. 7·50

1551 G. ℞. TR . P . VIIII . IMP . VI . COS . IIII . P . P . S . C. Minerva advancing r., brandishing javelin. *C.* 917. *R.I.C.* 410. *B.M.C.* 533.. 7·50

Fine

1552 **Æ sestertius.** *Obv.* As 1542. ℞. VICT . BRIT. (in ex.) P . M . TR . P . X . IMP . VII . COS . IIII . P . P . S . C. Victory seated r. on shields, about to inscribe oval shield set on l. knee. *C.* 946. *R.I.C.* 452. *B.M.C.* 560 £25·00

1553 **Æ dupondius.** D. (but COMM.) Rad. hd., r. ℞. MINER . VICT . P . M . TR . P . XIIII . IMP . VIII . COS . V . DES . VI . S . C. Minerva stg. l. beside trophy. *C.* 373. *R.I.C.* 546. *B.M.C., p.* 824, *   4·50

1554 G. Rad. hd., r. ℞. P . M . TR . P . VIIII . IMP . VI . COS . IIII . P . P . S . C. Roma seated l. *C.* 442. *R.I.C.* 420. *B.M.C.* 539   4·50

1555 F. Rad. hd., r. ℞. TR . P . VII . IMP . V . COS . III . P . P . S . C. Jupiter seated l. *C.* 841. *R.I.C.* 346. *B.M.C., p.* 780, *   4·50

1556 G. Rad. hd., r. ℞. TR . P . VIII . IMP . VI . COS . IIII . P . P . S . C. Fortune stg. l. *C.* 901. *R.I.C.* 388. *B.M.C.* 522   4·50

1557 **Æ as.** M . ANTONINVS COMMODVS AVG. ℞. ANN . AVG . TR . P . VII . IMP . IIII . COS . III . P . P . S . C. Annona stg. l., modius at feet. *C.* 10. *R.I.C.* 339. *B.M.C., p.* 778, †   4·50

1558 D. (but COMM.) ℞. COL . L . AN . COM . P . M . TR . P . XV . IMP . VIII . COS . VI . S . C. Commodus ploughing r. with two oxen. *C.* 40. *R.I.C.* 570. *B.M.C.* 658   17·50

1559 As 1541, but with *rev.* legend HERCVL . ROMAN . AVGV . S . C. *C.* 193. *R.I.C.* 644. *B.M.C.* 722   15·00

1560 E. (but COMM.) ℞. P . M . TR . P . XIII . IMP . VIII . COS . V . P . P . S . C. Genius stg. l., holding patera and corn-ears. *C.* 533. *R.I.C.* 518. *B.M.C., p.* 817, ‖   4·50

1561 G. ℞. TR . P . VIIII . IMP . VI . COS . IIII . P . P . S . C. Minerva stg. r., holding spear and leaning on shield. *C.* 919. *R.I.C.* 428. *B.M.C.* 545   4·50

Commemorative Coins struck after his death

1562 *Struck by Trajan Decius,* Æ *antoninianus.* DIVO COMMODO. Rad. hd., r. ℞. CONSECRATIO. Eagle stg. on sceptre, hd. l. *C.* 1009. *R.I.C.* (*Dec.*) 93   10·00

1563 — Similar. ℞. — Large altar. *C.* 1010. *R.I.C.* (*Dec.*) 94   10·00

Colonial and Provincial Coinage

1564 *Bithynia, Apameia,* **Æ 20.** Laur. bust, r. ℞. Tunny fish r. *B.M.C. G.*30   3·00

1565 *Mysia, Cyzicus,* **Æ 27.** Laur. hd., r. ℞. KYZ / IKHN / ΩNN / EO within laurel wreath. *B.M.C. G.*230   4·50

1566 *Pamphylia, Attalia,* **Æ 20.** Laur. bust, r. ℞. Bust of Serapis l. *B.M.C. G.*21   4·50

1567 *Commagene, Doliche,* **Æ 21.** Bare-headed and dr. bust, r. ℞. ΔΟΛΙ / XAIWN / A in wreath. *B.M.C. G.*4   8·50

1568 *Samaria, Neapolis,* **Æ 19.** Laur. bust, r. ℞. Tyche stg. l., holding spear. *B.M.C. G.*80   17·50

1569 *Egypt, Alexandria,* **billon tetradrachm.** Laur. hd., r. ℞. Laur. hd. of Zeus r. *B.M.C. G.*1394   2·50

1570 — ℞. Zeus seated l. *B.M.C. G.*1397   2·50

1571 — ℞. Rad. bust of Helios r. *B.M.C. G.*1403   3·75

1572 — ℞. Athena seated l., holding Nike and sceptre. *B.M.C. G.*1406   2·50

1573 — ℞. Nike advancing r. *B.M.C. G.*1414   2·50

1574 — ℞. Serapis seated l., Kerberos at feet. *B.M.C. G.*1420   2·50

1575 — ℞. Bust of Nilus r. *B.M.C. G.*1423   3·75

1576 — ℞. Commodus in triumphal quadriga r. *B.M.C. G.*1429   4·25

1577 — ℞. Eagle stg. r. on thunderbolt. *B.M.C. G.*1437   2·50

1578 — ℞. Pharos with ship to r. *B.M.C. G.*1439   10·00

1589

CRISPINA

Bruttia Crispina, the daughter of L. Fulvius Bruttius Praesens, was married to Commodus in A.D. 177. *Early in her husband's reign she was banished to Capreae and later put to death.*

All coins have the following obverse, unless otherwise stated:

CRISPINA AVGVSTA. Dr. bust, r.

All *R.I.C.* and *B.M.C.* references are to the coinage of Commodus.

Very Fine

1579	A aureus. R. VENVS FELIX. Venus seated l., holding Victory and sceptre. *C.* 39. *R.I.C.* 287. *B.M.C.* 47	£550·00
1580	A quinarius. R. VENVS. Venus stg. l., holding apple. *C.* 34. *R.I.C.* 286a. *B.M.C.* 44 note	750·00
1581	Æ denarius. R. CERES. Ceres stg. l., holding corn-ears and torch. *C.* 1. *R.I.C.* 276. *B.M.C.* 33	12·00
1582	R. CONCORDIA. Clasped hands. *C.*8. *R.I.C.* 279. *B.M.C.* 37	15·00
1583	R. DIS GENITALIBVS. Lighted altar. *C.* 16. *R.I.C.* 281. *B.M.C.* 39. **Plate 7**	25·00
1584	R. IVNO. Juno stg. l., peacock at feet. *C.* 21. *R.I.C.* 283. *B.M.C.* 41	12·00
1585	As 1580. *C.* 35. *R.I.C.* 286a. *B.M.C.* 44	12·00
1586	As 1579. *Cf. C.* 42. *R.I.C.* 288. *B.M.C.* 50	12·00

Fine

1587	Æ sestertius. R. CONCORDIA S . C. Concord seated l. *C.* 6. *R.I.C.* 665. *B.M.C.* 406	12·50
1588	R. PVDICITIA S . C. Pudicitia seated l. *C.* 30. *R.I.C.* 670. *B.M.C.* 419	12·50
1589	CRISPINA AVG . IMP . COMMODI AVG. Dr. bust, r. R. SALVS S . C. Salus seated l., feeding serpent arising from altar. *C.* 32. *R.I.C.* 672b. *B.M.C.* 423 *Illustrated above*	15·00
1590	R. VENVS FELIX S . C. As 1579. *C.* 40. *R.I.C.* 673. *B.M.C.* 424	12·50
1591	Æ dupondius. R. HILARITAS S . C. Hilaritas stg. l. *C.* 20. *R.I.C.* 678. *B.M.C.* 428	8·00
1592	R. LAETITIA S . C. Laetitia stg. l. *C.* 28. *R.I.C.* 683. *B.M.C.* 435	8·00
1593	Æ as. R. IVNO S . C. As 1584. *C.* 23. *R.I.C.* 679. *B.M.C.* 431	8·00
1594	R. IVNO LVCINA S . C. Juno stg. l. *C.* 24. *R.I.C.* 680. *B.M.C.* 433	8·00
1595	R. VENVS FELIX S . C. As 1579. *C.* 41. *R.I.C.* 686. *B.M.C.* 440	8·00

For full details of **all** the silver coins from Tiberius to Commodus see:

ROMAN SILVER COINS, *by H. A. Seaby.*

Volume II, *cloth bound* £2·00

and for the period Pertinax to Balbinus and Pupienus:

Volume III, *cloth bound* £2·40

PERTINAX
A.D. 193

1602

P. Helvius Pertinax was born at Alba Pompeia in A.D. *126, the son of a timber-merchant. He had a successful military career and achieved senatorial rank until, at the death of Commodus, he was prefect of the City of Rome. He reluctantly accepted the throne when it was offered him by the murderers of Commodus, but the reforms and economies which he immediately instituted made him unpopular, particularly with the Praetorians. On March 28th a band of mutinous guards invaded the palace and murdered Pertinax after a reign of only 86 days.*

Mint: Rome.

There are two varieties of obverse legend in this reign:

A. IMP . CAES . P . HELV . PERTIN . AVG.
B. IMP . CAES . P . HELV . PERTINAX AVG.

Unless otherwise stated, the obverse type is laur. hd., r.

Very Fine

1596	*N* **aureus.** A. ℞. AEQVIT . AVG . TR . P . COS . II. Equity stg. l. C. 1. *R.I.C.* 1a. *B.M.C.* 14	£650·00
1597	*R* **denarius.** Similar. *C.* 2. *R.I.C.* 1a. *B.M.C.* 15.. ..	90·00
1598	A. ℞. LAETITIA TEMPOR . COS . II. Laetitia stg. l. *C.* 20. *R.I.C.* 4a. *B.M.C.* 8	90·00
1599	A. ℞. VOT . DECEN . TR . P . COS . II. Pertinax stg. l., sacrificing over tripod-altar. *C.* 56. *R.I.C.* 13a. *B.M.C.* 24	100·00

Fine

1600	Æ **sestertius.** B. ℞. OPI DIVIN . TR . P . COS . II . S . C. Ops seated l., holding corn-ears. *C.* 34. *R.I.C.* 20. *B.M.C.* 42	100·00
1601	B. ℞. PROVIDENTIAE DEORVM COS . II . S . C. Providence stg. l., raising r. hand towards star. *C.* 52. *R.I.C.* 22. *B.M.C.* 28	100·00
1602	Æ **dupondius.** A. Rad. hd., r. ℞. LIB . AVG . TR . P . COS . II . S . C. Liberalitas stg. l. *C.* 26. *R.I.C.* 25A. *B.M.C.* 45. *Illustrated above*	65·00
1603	Æ **as.** A. ℞. LAETITIA TEMPORVM COS . II . S . C. Laetitia stg. l. *C.* 22. *R.I.C.* 33. *B.M.C.* 34	65·00

Commemorative Coins struck after his death

1604	*Struck by Septimius Severus, N* **aureus.** DIVVS PERT . PIVS PATER. Bare hd., r. ℞. CONSECRATIO. Eagle stg. r. on globe, hd. turned. *C.* 7. *R.I.C.* (*Sev.*) 24A. *B.M.C.* (*Wars of Succession*) 37 *note* ..	*Very rare*
1605	*R* **denarius.** Similar. *C.* 6. *R.I.C.* 24A. *B.M.C.* 37 *Very fine* £200·00	
1606	Æ **sestertius.** DIVVS PERT . PIVS PATER. Bare-headed and dr. bust, r. ℞. CONSECRATIO S . C. Funeral pyre. *C.* 12. *R.I.C.* 660C. *B.M.C.* 480	*Very rare*
1607	Æ **as.** DIVVS PERTIN . PIVS PATER. Bare hd., r. ℞. CONSECRATIO S . C. As 1604. *C.* 10. *R.I.C.* 660B(c). *B.M.C.*, *p.* 120, § ..	*Very rare*

174

DIDIUS JULIANUS
A.D. 193

1612

(*M. Didius Julianus.*) *After the murder of Pertinax, the Praetorian guards publicly announced that they would elect as emperor the man who would pay the highest price. In the succeeding auction, Julianus, a wealthy senator, offered the soldiers 25,000 sestertii a man, and was duly declared emperor. The circumstances of his elevation aroused such indignation amongst the populace of Rome that they assembled in the Circus and agreed to send an appeal to Pescennius Niger, the governor of Syria, to come to their assistance. Two other provincial governors, Clodius Albinus in Britain and Septimius Severus in Upper Pannonia, also determined to answer the appeal from Rome. Severus quickly advanced on Rome and Julianus, after several fruitless attempts at negotiation with his rival, was deserted by the Praetorians and deposed by the Senate. He sought refuge in his deserted palace, but was beheaded on June 2nd after a reign of only 66 days.*

Mint: Rome.

There are two varieties of obverse legend in this reign:
   A. IMP . CAES . M . DID . IVLIAN . AVG.
   B. IMP . CAES . M . DID . SEVER . IVLIAN . AVG.

Unless otherwise stated, the obverse type is laur. hd., r.   **Very Fine**

1608 **N aureus.** A. ℞. P . M . TR . P . COS. Fortune stg. l. *C.* 8.
    R.I.C. 2. *B.M.C.* 4   ..   ..£900·00

1609 **Æ denarius.** A. ℞. CONCORD . MILIT. Concord stg. l., holding
    legionary eagle and standard. *C.* 2. *R.I.C.* 1. *B.M.C.* 2   ..   .. 130·00

1610 A. ℞. RECTOR ORBIS. Julianus, togate, stg. l., holding globe. *C.* 15.
    R.I.C. 3. *B.M.C.* 7..   ..   ..   120·00

                                                                   Fine

1611 **Æ sestertius.** B. ℞. CONCORD . MILIT . S . C. As 1609. *C.* 3.
    R.I.C. 14. *B.M.C.* 20   ..   ..   65·00

1612 B. ℞. P . M . TR . P. COS . S . C. Fortune stg. l. *C.* 12. *R.I.C.* 15.
    B.M.C. 24. *Illustrated above*   ..   ..   65·00

1613 **Æ dupondius.** A. Rad. hd., r. ℞. As previous. *C.* 13. *R.I.C.*
    12. *B.M.C.* 17   ..   ..   90·00

MANLIA SCANTILLA
Wife of Didius Julianus

1614

There are two varieties of obverse legend:
   A. MANL . SCANTILLA AVG.
   B. MANLIA SCANTILLA AVG.

The obverse type is dr. bust, r.

All *R.I.C.* and *B.M.C.* references are to the coinage of Didius Julianus.

Very Fine

1614 **N aureus.** A. ℞. IVNO REGINA. Juno stg. l., peacock at feet.
C. 1. *R.I.C.* 7a. *B.M.C.* 10. *Illustrated on p.* 174 .. .. £1500·00

1615 **Æ denarius.** Similar. *C.* 2. *R.I.C.* 7a. *B.M.C.* 11 .. .. 300·00

Fine

1616 **Æ sestertius.** A. ℞. IVNO REGINA S . C. Juno stg. l., peacock at feet. *C.* 3. *R.I.C.* 18b. *B.M.C.* 32 *note* .. .. 150·00

1617 B. ℞. As previous *C.* 6. *R.I.C.* 18a. *B.M.C.* 32 .. .. .. 150·00

1618 **Æ dupondius** or **as.** A. ℞. As previous. *C.* 4. *R.I.C.* 19a. *B.M.C.* 37 *note* .. .. 250·00

DIDIA CLARA

Daughter of Didius Julianus

1621

All *R.I.C.* and *B.M.C.* references are to the coinage of Didius Julianus.

Very Fine

1619 **N aureus.** DIDIA CLARA AVG. Dr. bust, r. ℞. HILAR . TEMPOR. Hilaritas stg. l. *C.* 2. *R.I.C.* 10. *B.M.C.* 13 .. .. 1500·00

1620 **Æ denarius.** Similar. *C.* 3. *R.I.C.* 10. *B.M.C.* 14 .. .. .. 300·00

Fine

1621 **Æ sestertius.** Similar, but with S . C. on *rev.* *C.* 4. *R.I.C.* 20. *B.M.C.* 38. *Illustrated above* .. .. 150·00

1622 **Æ dupondius** or **as.** As previous. *C.* 5. *R.I.C.* 21. *B.M.C.*, p. 18, * .. .. 250·00

PESCENNIUS NIGER

A.D. 193-194

Similar to 1624A

Of humble origin, C. Pescennius Niger was born sometime between A.D. 135 *and* 140 *and had a long and honourable career in the army. In* A.D. 190 *he held the consulship and in the following year was appointed governor of Syria. After the murder of Pertinax he was proclaimed emperor by his troops. Severus, however, having secured Rome, turned his attention to his rival in the East, and thrice defeated the forces of Niger. The latter concentrated the remnants of his army at Issus to make a last stand, but he was again defeated and fled towards the Euphrates only to be overtaken and executed.*

Mint: Antioch.

B.M.C. references are to the coinage of the Wars of Succession   **Fine**

1623 **N aureus.** IMP . CAES . C . PESC . NIGER IVST . AVG. Laur., dr. and
cuir. bust, r. R. IOVI CONSERVATORI. Jupiter seated l., holding
Victory and sceptre, eagle at feet. *C.* 39. *R.I.C.* 42. *B.M.C.* 302
note .. ..   *Extr. rare*

1624 **R denarius.** IMP . CAES . C . PESC . NIGER IVS . AVG . COS . II. Laur.
hd., r. R. FELICITAS TEMPORVM. Basket of fruit. *C.* 16. *R.I.C.* 17.
B.M.C. 293 .. ..£335·00

1624A *Obv.* Similar, but IVSTVS instead of IVS. R. INVICTO IMP . TROPAEA.
Trophy and arms. *C.* 36. *R.I.C.* 38a. *B.M.C.* 296 *note*. *Similar type
illustrated on p.* 175 .. .. 200·00

1625 IMP . CAES . C . PESCEN . NIGER IVST . AVG. Laur. hd., r. R. ROMAE
AETERNAE. Roma seated l., holding Victory and spear. *C.* 60. *R.I.C.*
70*b*. *B.M.C., p.* 80, * *note*.. .. .. 200·00

CLODIUS ALBINUS
A.D. 195-197

1632

(*Decimus Clodius Septimius Albinus*). *Born at Hadrumetum in Africa, Albinus entered
the army at an early age and served with great distinction until, at the death of Pertinax,
he was governor of Britain. Severus, in order to keep the West quiet whilst he consolidated
his position and dealt with Julianus and Niger, offered Albinus the title of Caesar, which he
accepted. However, as soon as Italy and the East were under his control Severus determined
to be absolute master of the Empire, and in* 195 *he had Albinus declared a public enemy.
Albinus, having been saluted as Augustus by his troops, made preparation for the forthcoming
struggle with Severus, but after some initial successes he was ultimately defeated in a great
battle fought on February* 19th, A.D. 197 *near Lugdunum (Lyons). He later committed
suicide and his body, together with those of his wife and children who were put to death, was
thrown into the Rhone.*

Mints: Rome (as Caesar); Lugdunum (as Augustus).

B.M.C. references are to the coinage of the Wars of Succession.

As Caesar
A.D. 193-195, *under Septimius Severus*

Very Fine

1626 **N aureus.** D . CL . SEPT . ALBIN . CAES. Bare hd., r. R. SAECVLO
FRVGIFERO COS . II. Saeculum Frugiferum seated l. on throne flanked
by two sphinxes. *C.* 68. *R.I.C.* 10. *B.M.C.* 103 .. ..   1200·00

1627 **N quinarius.** — R. COS . II. Fortune seated l. *C.* 8. *R.I.C.* 3.
B.M.C. 90 .. ..   *Extr. rare*

1628 **R denarius.** D . CLOD . SEPT . ALBIN . CAES. Bare hd., r. R.
MINER . PACIF . COS . II. Minerva stg. l., holding olive-branch and shield.
C. 48. *R.I.C.* 7. *B.M.C.* 98 .. .. 25·00

Very Fine

1629 **Æ denarius.** D . CLODIVS ALBINVS CAES. Bare hd., r. ℞. PROVID .
AVG . COS. Providence stg. l., globe at feet. *C.* 58. *R.I.C.* 1*a.* *B.M.C.*
38 .. .. £30·00

1630 D . CL . SEPT . ALBIN . CAES. Bare hd., r. ℞. ROMAE AETERNAE.
Roma seated l., holding palladium and spear. *C.* 61. *R.I.C.* 11*a.*
B.M.C. 43 .. .. 30·00

1631 **Æ sestertius.** *Obv.* As 1628. ℞. FELICITAS COS . II . S . C. **Fine**
Felicity stg. l. *C.* 16. *R.I.C.* 52*b.* *B.M.C.* 529 .. .. .. 37·50

1632 — ℞. MINER . PACIF . COS . II . S . C. As 1628. *C.* 49. *R.I.C.* 54*a.*
B.M.C. 536. *Illustrated on p.* 176 .. .. 30·00

1633 *Obv.* As 1626. ℞. SAECVLO FRVGIFERO COS . II . S . C. Saeculum
Frugiferum stg. l., holding caduceus and trident. *C.* 71. *R.I.C.* 56*a.*
B.M.C. 539 .. .. 45·00

1634 **Æ as.** *Obv.* As 1628. ℞. COS . II . S . C. Aesculapius stg. l.,
holding serpent-wreathed rod. *C.* 11. *R.I.C.* 57*a.* *B.M.C.* 543 .. 25·00

1635 — ℞. As 1631. *C.* 17. *R.I.C.* 58. *B.M.C.* 545 .. .. .. 20·00

As Augustus **Very Fine**

1636 **N aureus.** IMP . CAES . D . CLO . ALBIN . AVG. Laur. and dr. bust, l.
℞. GEN . LVG . COS . II. Genius of Lugdunum stg. l., holding sceptre
and cornucopiae, eagle at feet. *C.*—. *R.I.C.* 24. *B.M.C., p.* 63, § *Extr. rare*

1637 **Æ denarius.** IMP . CAES . D . CLO . SEP . ALB . AVG. Laur. hd., r. ℞.
AEQVITAS AVG . COS . II. Equity stg. l. *C.* 1. *R.I.C.* 13*a.* *B.M.C.* 280 40·00

1638 — ℞. FIDES LEGION . COS . II. Clasped hands holding legionary eagle.
C. 24. *R.I.C.* 20*b.* *B.M.C.* 284 .. .. 40·00

1639 **Æ as.** — ℞. FORTVNAE REDVCI COS . II. Fortune seated l. *C.*—.
R.I.C. 64. *B.M.C.* 622 .. .. *Unique*

SEPTIMIUS SEVERUS
A.D. 193-211

1700

(*Lucius Septimius Severus*). *Born in* A.D. 146 *at Leptis Magna in Africa, Severus was a
soldier of outstanding ability, holding a series of increasingly important commands until, at
the death of Commodus, he was governor of Upper Pannonia. He expressed his allegiance
to Pertinax, but on the murder of the latter and the shameful elevation of Didius Julianus,
which caused much indignation in the provinces, Severus was saluted as emperor by the
troops at Carnuntum. He rapidly disposed of Julianus and Niger and later attacked and
defeated his third rival, Clodius Albinus (*A.D. 197*). *Severus spent much of his reign in
campaigning in different parts of the Empire and also visiting many of the provinces. In
A.D. 208 he came to Britain where there was much unrest following a great invasion by the
barbarians of the North in A.D. 197. He repaired Hadrian's Wall, which had been partly
destroyed, and invaded Caledonia, but without much success. The strains of this campaign,
however, proved too much for the old emperor and he died at York on February 4th, A.D. 211.*

Titles and Powers, A.D. 193-211

A.D.	Tribunician Power	Imperatorial Acclamation	Consulship	Other Titles
193	TR.P.	IMP. IMP.II.		AVGVSTVS.
194	TR.P.II.	IMP.III. IMP.IIII.	COS.II.	P.M. P.P.
195	TR.P.III.	IMP.V. IMP.VI. IMP.VII.		PARTHICVS ARABICVS.
				PARTHICVS ADIABENICVS.
196	TR.P.IIII.	IMP.VIII.		
197	TR.P.V.	IMP.VIIII. IMP.X.		
198	TR.P.VI.	IMP.XI.		PART.MAX.
199	TR.P.VII.			
200	TR.P.VIII.			
201	TR.P.VIIII.			
202	TR.P.X.		COS.III.	
203	TR.P.XI.			
204	TR.P.XII.			
205	TR.P.XIII.			
206	TR.P.XIIII.			
207	TR.P.XV.			
208	TR.P.XVI.			
209	TR.P.XVII.			
210	TR.P.XVIII.			BRIT.
211	TR.P.XVIIII.			

Severus became TR.P.II. on January 1st, A.D. 194, and his tribunician power was subsequently renewed each year on that date, thus causing the tribunician year to coincide with the calendar year.

His first consulship was in A.D. 185.

Mints: Rome; Caesarea (?); Laodiceia ad Mare; Emesa (?); Alexandria (?).

The following are the commonest forms of obverse legend:

A.   IMP . CAE . L . SEP . SEV . PERT . AVG.
B.   IMP . CAE . L . SEP . SEV . PERT . AVG . COS . II.
C.   L . SEPT . SEV . AVG . IMP . XI . PART . MAX.
D.   L . SEPT . SEV . PERT . AVG . IMP . II . (-X.)
E.   SEVERVS AVG . PART . MAX.
F.   SEVERVS PIVS AVG.
G.   SEVERVS PIVS AVG . BRIT.

All coins have as obverse type laur. hd. of Severus r., unless otherwise stated.

In the *B.M.C.* this reign is covered in three separate sections, with the numbering starting again from 1 in each: Wars of the Succession; Joint Reign of Severus and Caracalla; and Joint Reign of Severus, Caracalla and Geta. No attempt is made here to differentiate between the three sections in the *B.M.C.* references quoted.

Very Fine

1640   **Ŋ aureus.** D. (IMP . III.) Ŗ. P . M . TR . P . II . COS . II . P . P. Jupiter seated l., holding Victory and sceptre. *C.* 379. *R.I.C.* 34. *B.M.C.* 68. **Plate 7**   ..   ..£200·00

1641   **Ŋ quinarius.** D. (IMP . III.) Ŗ. COS . II . P . P. Victory advancing r. *C.* 93. *R.I.C.* 30. *B.M.C.* 62   ..   .. 400·00

1642   **Ŗ cistophorus.** IMP . C . L . SEP . SEVERVS P . AV. Ŗ. AVGVSTORVM. Legionary eagle between two standards. *C.* 55. *R.I.C.* 528. *B.M.C.* 758   ..   .. 225·00

Very Fine

1643 **Æ denarius.** D. (IMP . VIII.) Ɍ. ADVENTVI AVG . FELICISSIMO. Severus on horseback r., raising r. hand. *C.* 6. *R.I.C.* 74. *B.M.C.* 151 .. .. £7·50

1644 C. Ɍ. AEQVITATI AVGG. Equity stg. l. *C.* 21. *R.I.C.* 122*c.* *B.M.C.* 122 .. .. 3.00

1645 F. Ɍ. AFRICA. Africa stg. r., holding scorpion, lion at feet. *C.* 25. *R.I.C.* 253. *B.M.C.* 309 .. .. 7·00

1646 D. (IMP . IIII.) Ɍ. APOLLINI AVGVSTO. Apollo stg. l., holding patera and lyre. *C.* 42. *R.I.C.* 40. *B.M.C.* 78 .. .. .. 5·00

1647 D. (IMP . VII.) Ɍ. ARAB . ADIAB . COS . II . P . P. Victory advancing l. *C.* 50. *R.I.C.* 64. *B.M.C.* 131 .. .. 4·00

1648 B. Ɍ. BONA SPES. Spes advancing l. *C.* 58. *R.I.C.* 364. *B.M.C.* 340 .. .. 5·00

1649 F. Ɍ. COS . III . P . P. Victory advancing l. *C.* 102. *R.I.C.* 526. *B.M.C.* 732 .. .. 4·50

1650 F. Ɍ. — Front view of the Triumphal Arch of Severus. *C.* 104. *R.I.C.* 259. *B.M.C.* 320 .. .. 150·00

1651 F. Ɍ. FELICITAS AVGG. Felicity stg. l. *C.* 135. *R.I.C.* 261. *B.M.C.* 322 .. .. 3·00

1652 D. (IMP . VIII.) Ɍ. FORTVNAE REDVCI. Fortune seated l. *C.* 188. *R.I.C.* 78*a.* *B.M.C.* 161 .. .. 3·75

1653 F. Ɍ. FVNDATOR PACIS. Severus stg. l., holding olive-branch. *C.* 205. *R.I.C.* 265. *B.M.C.* 330 .. .. 3·25

1654 D. (IMP . VIII.) Ɍ. HERCVLI DEFENS. Hercules stg. r., leaning on club and holding bow. *C.* 210. *R.I.C.* 79. *B.M.C.*, *p.* 47,*.. .. 5·00

1655 — Ɍ. INDVLGENTIA AVG. Indulgence seated l. *C.* 216. *R.I.C.* 80. *B.M.C.* 163 .. .. 5·00

1656 F. Ɍ. INDVLGENTIA AVGG . IN . CARTH. Dea Caelestis seated facing on lion springing r. *C.* 222. *R.I.C.* 266. *B.M.C.* 335 .. .. 5·00

1657 B. Ɍ. INVICTO IMP. Trophy with arms at base. *C.* 232. *R.I.C.* 389. *B.M.C.* 365 .. .. 5·00

1658 F. Ɍ. LAETITIA TEMPORVM. Ship with sail set and gangway to ground; in front, animals; in background, four quadrigae. *C.* 253. *R.I.C.* 274. *B.M.C.* 343 .. .. 65·00

1659 A. Ɍ. LEG . VIII . AVG . TR . P . COS. Legionary eagle between two standards. *C.* 267. *R.I.C.* 11. *B.M.C.* 14 .. .. .. 27·50

1660 A. Ɍ. LEG . XIIII . GEM . M . V . TR . P . COS. As previous. *C.* 272. *R.I.C.* 14. *B.M.C.* 19 .. .. 20·00

1661 D. (IMP . VIIII.) Ɍ. LIBERO PATRI. Bacchus stg. facing, hd. l., holding thyrsus; at feet l., panther. *C.* 304. *R.I.C.* 99. *B.M.C.* 222 5·25

1662 D. (IMP . IIII.) Ɍ. MARS PATER. Mars advancing r., carrying spear and trophy. *C.* 311. *R.I.C.* 46. *B.M.C.* 84 .. .. .. 4·50

1663 D. (IMP . X.) Ɍ. MARTI PACIFERO. Mars stg. l., holding olive-branch and spear. *C.* 315. *R.I.C.* 113. *B.M.C.* 250 .. .. .. 4·25

1664 C. Ɍ. MARTI VICTORI. Mars stg. r., holding spear and leaning on shield set on helmet (?). *C.* 321. *R.I.C.* 509. *B.M.C.* 665 .. .. 4·00

1665 B. Ɍ. MONET . AVG. Moneta stg. l. *C.* 330. *R.I.C.* 411*a.* *B.M.C.* 380 .. .. 3·75

1666 D. (IMP . VIIII.) Ɍ. MVNIFICENTIA AVG. Elephant r., wearing cuirass. *C.* 349. *R.I.C.* 100. *B.M.C.* 224 .. .. .. 10·00

Very Fine

1667 **Æ denarius.** F. ℞. PART . MAX . P . M . TR . P . VIIII. Trophy with
two captives seated at base. *C.* 370. *R.I.C.* 176. *B.M.C.* 256 .. £3·75

1668 D. (IMP . III.) ℞. P . M . TR . P . II . COS . II . P . P. Jupiter seated
l., holding Victory and sceptre. *C.* 380. *R.I.C.* 34. *B.M.C.* 69 .. 3·75

1669 D. (IMP . V.) ℞. P . M . TR . P . III . COS . II . P . P. Minerva stg. l.,
holding spear and shield. *C.* 390. *R.I.C.* 61. *B.M.C.* 114 .. 3·50

1670 — ℞. — As 1662. *C.* 396. *R.I.C.* 52. *B.M.C.* 110 .. .. 3·75

1671 D. (IMP . VIII.) ℞. P . M . TR . P . IIII . COS . II . P . P. Victory
advancing l. *C.* 419. *R.I.C.* 86. *B.M.C.* 146 .. .. 3·25

1672 D. (IMP . VIIII.) ℞. P . M . TR . P . V . COS . II . P . P. Sol stg. l.,
holding whip. *C.* 433. *R.I.C.* 101. *B.M.C.* 227 .. .. .. 3·50

1673 — ℞. — Fortune stg. l. *C.* 442. *R.I.C.* 104. *B.M.C.* 229 .. 3·25

1674 F. ℞. P . M . TR . P . XIII . COS . III . P . P. Jupiter stg. l., eagle at
feet. *C.* 469. *R.I.C.* 196. *B.M.C.* 471 .. .. 4·25

1675 F. ℞. — Mars or Roma stg. l., holding Victory and spear. *C.* 471.
R.I.C. 197. *B.M.C.* 474 .. .. 4·25

1676 F. ℞. P . M . TR . P . XIIII . COS . III . P . P. Genius stg. l., altar at
feet. *C.* 475. *R.I.C.* 201. *B.M.C.* 493 .. .. 4·50

1677 F. ℞. — Annona stg. l., modius at feet. *C.* 476. *R.I.C.* 200.
B.M.C. 489 .. .. 4·25

1678 F. ℞. P . M . TR . P . XV . COS . III . P . P. Africa stg. r., lion at feet.
C. 493. *R.I.C.* 207. *B.M.C.* 531 .. .. 6·50

1679 F. ℞. P . M . TR . P . XVII . COS . III . P . P. Neptune stg. l., r. foot
on rock, holding trident. *C.* 529. *R.I.C.* 228. *B.M.C.* 3 .. .. 4·25

1680 G. ℞. P . M . TR . P . XVIII . COS . III . P . P. Jupiter stg. l., between
two children. *C.* 540. *R.I.C.* 240. *B.M.C.* 25 .. .. .. 5·50

1681 G. ℞. P . M . TR . P . XIX . COS . III . P . P. As previous. *C.* 563.
R.I.C. 243. *B.M.C.* 111 .. .. 8·00

1682 D. (IMP . VIII.) ℞. PROFECTIO AVG. Severus on horseback r.,
holding spear. *C.* 580. *R.I.C.* 106. *B.M.C.* 234 .. .. .. 10·00

1683 E. ℞. PROVID . AVGG. Providence stg. l., globe at feet. *C.* 586.
R.I.C. 166. *B.M.C.* 197 .. .. 3·25

1684 E. ℞. RESTITVTOR VRBIS. Severus stg. l., sacrificing over tripod-altar
and holding spear. *C.* 599. *R.I.C.* 167a. *B.M.C.* 202 .. 3·00

1685 F. ℞. — Roma seated l., holding palladium and sceptre or spear.
C. 606. *R.I.C.* 288. *B.M.C.* 359.. .. .. 3·00

1686 D. (IMP . VIII.) ℞. SECVRITAS PVBLICA. Security seated l., holding
globe. *C.* 647 *R I.C.* 93. *B.M.C.* 174 .. .. 4·50

1687 B. ℞. S . P . Q . R . OPTIMO PRINCIPI. Severus on horseback l., holding
spear. *C.* 652. *R.I.C.* 415. *B.M.C.* 389 .. .. 20·00

1688 E. ℞. VICT . AETERN. Victory flying l., holding wreath over shield
set on base. *C.* 670. *R.I.C.* 170. *B.M.C.* 209.. .. .. .. 4·00

1689 D. (IMP . X.) ℞. VICT . AVGG . COS . II . P . P. Victory advancing l.
C. 694. *R.I.C.* 120c. *B.M.C.* 258 .. .. 3·75

1690 F. ℞. VICTORIAE AVGG. Victory in biga galloping r. *C.* 713.
R.I.C. 299. *B.M.C.* 370 .. .. 10·00

1691 C. ℞. VICTORIAE AVGG . FEL. As 1688. *C.* 719. *R.I.C.* 144b.
B.M.C. 139 .. .. 3·50

1692 G. ℞. VICTORIAE BRIT. Victory advancing r. *C.* 727. *R.I.C.* 332.
B.M.C. 51 .. .. 15·00

1693 G. ℞. — Victory stg. facing, hd. l. *C.* 728. *R.I.C.* 333. *B.M.C.*
59 .. .. 20·00

1694 G. ℞. — Victory seated l., resting shield on r. knee. *C.* 731.
R.I.C. 335. *B.M.C.* 61 .. .. 17·50

Very Fine

1695 **Æ denarius.** C. R. VICT . PARTHICAE. Victory advancing l.,
captive at feet. C. 741. *R.I.C.* 142a. *B.M.C.* 137 .. .. £4·50

1696 E. R. VIRT . AVGG. Roma stg. l., holding Victory, spear and shield.
C. 761. *R.I.C.* 171a. *B.M.C.* 211 .. .. 3·00

1697 D. (IMP . VIII.) R. VOTA PVBLICA. Severus stg. l., sacrificing over
tripod-altar. C. 777. *R.I.C.* 96a. *B.M.C.* 178 .. .. .. 5·00

1698 F. R. VOTA SVSCEPTA XX. As previous. C. 791. *R.I.C.* 308.
B.M.C. 375 .. .. 3·50

1699 **Æ quinarius.** A. R. TR . P . COS. Victory advancing l. C. 657.
R.I.C. 20. *B.M.C.* 26 .. .. 40·00

Fine

1700 **Æ sestertius.** D. (IMP . VIII.) Laur. and cuir. bust, r. R. ADVENTVI
AVG. FELICISSIMO S . C. Severus on horseback, r., preceded by soldier
who leads horse by rein. C. 8. *R.I.C.* 719. *B.M.C.* 596 *note.*
Illustrated on p. 177 .. .. 25·00

1701 L . SEPT . SEVERVS PIVS AVG . BRIT. R. AEQVITATI PVBLICAE S . C. The
three Monetae stg. l., each holding scales and cornucopiae. C. 23.
R.I.C. 833. *B.M.C.,* p. 405, * .. .. 35·00

1702 D. (IMP . III.) R. DIS AVSPICIB . TR . P . II . COS . II . P . P . S . C.
Hercules and Bacchus stg. l., side by side; between them, panther.
C. 119. *R.I.C.* 669. *B.M.C.* 505.. .. .. 35·00

1703 D. (IMP . VII.) R. DIVI M . PII F . P . M . TR . P . III . COS . II . P . P . S .
C. Felicity stg. l., r. foot on prow. C. 124. *R.I.C.* 701. *B.M.C.* 570 15·00

1704 IMP . CAES . L . SEPT . SEV . PERT . AVG. R. FIDEI LEG . TR . P . COS . S . C.
Fides stg. l., holding Victory and standard. C. 147. *R.I.C.* 651.
B.M.C. 469 .. .. 20·00

1705 *Obv.* As 1700. R. FORTVNAE REDVCI S . C. Fortune seated l. C. 193.
R.I.C. 720. *B.M.C.* 599 *note* .. .. 15·00

1706 *Obv.* As 1704. R. LEG . XIIII . GEM . M . V . TR . P . COS . S . C. Legionary eagle between two standards. C. 275. *R.I.C.* 652. *B.M.C.* 471.. 30·00

1707 D. (IMP . VIII.) R. MVNIFICENTIA AVG . S . C. Elephant walking r.
C. 351. *R.I.C.* 721. *B.M.C.* 602.. .. .. 30·00

1708 D. (IMP . V.) Laur. and cuir. bust, r. R. PART . ARAB . PART . ADIAB .
COS . II . P . P . S . C. Trophy with two captives seated at base. C. 366.
R.I.C. 690b. *B.M.C.* 556 .. .. 25·00

1709 D. (IMP . VII.) Laur. and cuir. bust, r. R. P . M . TR . P . IIII . COS .
II . P . P . S . C. Mars stg. r., holding spear and leaning on shield, cuirass
at feet. C. 413. *R.I.C.* 708. *B.M.C.* 584 .. .. .. 15·00

1710 L . SEPT . SEVERVS PIVS AVG. R. VICTORIAE BRITTANNICAE S . C. Two
Victories stg. facing each other, attaching shield to palm-tree at base of
which are two captives seated. C. 732. *R.I.C.* 818. *B.M.C.* 811 .. 50·00

Fine

1711 Æ **sestertius.** D. (IMP . III.) Laur. and dr. bust r. ℞. VIRT . AVG .
TR . P . II . COS . II . P . P . S . C. Roma stg. l., holding Victory and spear.
C. 758. *R.I.C.* 673. *B.M.C.* 512..   ..   ..   £15·00

1712 D. (IMP . VIII.) ℞. VOTA PVBLICA S . C. Severus and Caracalla stg.
either side of tripod-altar, sacrificing. *C.* 782. *R.I.C.* 730. *B.M.C.*
605 ..   ..   25·00

1713 Æ **dupondius.** D. (IMP . IIII.) Rad. hd., r. ℞. AFRICA S . C.
Africa stg. r., lion at feet. *C.* 30. *R.I.C.* 680. *B.M.C.* 523 ..   ..   15·00

1714 D. (IMP . VII.) Rad. hd., r. ℞. As 1703. *C.* 125. *R.I.C.* 712.
B.M.C. 581 ..   ..   10·00

1715 **Æ as.** D. (IMP . IIII.) ℞. APOLLINI AVGVSTO S . C. As 1646. *C.* 44.
R.I.C. 682. *B.M.C.* 525 ..   ..   12·50

1716 F. ℞. VIRTVS AVGVSTOR . S . C. Roma seated l., holding Victory and
parazonium. *C.* 767. *R.I.C.* 830*a*. *B.M.C.* 815   ..   ..   ..   10·00

Commemorative Coins struck after his death   Very Fine

R.I.C. references are to the coinage of Caracalla, and *B.M.C.* references to the
coinage of the Joint Reign of Caracalla and Geta.

1717 *Struck by Caracalla and Geta,* N **aureus.** DIVO SEVERO PIO. Bare hd., r.
℞. CONSECRATIO. Eagle stg. facing on thunderbolt, hd. l. *C.* 81.
R.I.C. 191A. *B.M.C.* 19 ..   ..   400·00

1718 Æ **denarius.** — ℞. — Eagle stg. facing on globe, hd. l. *C.* 84.
R.I.C. 191C. *B.M.C.* 21 ..   ..   17·50

1719 Æ **sestertius.** DIVO SEPTIMIO SEVERO PIO. Bare hd., r. ℞. CONSE-
CRATIO S . C. Funeral pyre surmounted by Severus in quadriga. *C.* 90.
R.I.C. 490B. *B.M.C.* 49 ..   .. *Fine* £50·00

1720 *Struck by Trajan Decius,* Æ **antoninianus.** DIVO SEVERO. Rad. hd., r.
℞. CONSECRATIO. Large altar. *C.* 800. *R.I.C.* (*Dec.*) 96 ..   ..   18·00

Colonial and Provincial Coinage   Fair

1721 *Moesia Inferior, Istrus,* Æ **30.** Laur. hd., r. ℞. Kybele enthroned r.
Pick 495 ..   ..   4·00

1722 — *Marcianopolis,* Æ **26.** Laur. and dr. bust, r. ℞. Kybele enthroned l. between two lions. *Pick* 566 ..   ..   3·75

1723 *Corcyra,* Æ **25.** Laur. bust, r. ℞. Galley r. *B.M.C. G.* 662   ..   3·75

1724 *Megaris, Megara,* Æ **23.** Laur. hd., r. ℞. Demeter stg. r. *B.M.C.*
*G.*48 ..   ..   3·75

1725 *Mysia, Attaea,* Æ **24.** — ℞. Asklepios stg. l. *B.M.C. G.*11 ..   ..   2·50

1726 — *Hadrianeia,* Æ **18.** — ℞. Asklepios advancing r., hd. turned.
Grose 7622 ..   ..   3·25

1727 *Pisidia, Antioch,* Æ **31.** — ℞. Mên stg. r., holding sceptre and Nike.
*B.M.C. G.*20 ..   ..   3·25

1728 *Cappadocia, Caesarea,* Æ **drachm.** — ℞. Mount Argaeus with star
on summit. *B.M.C. G.*219 ..   .. *Fine* £5·00

1729 *Mesopotamia, Edessa,* Æ **22.** Laur. bust, r. ℞. Bust of Abgar VIII r.
*B.M.C. G.*16 ..   ..   1·75

1730 *Egypt, Alexandria,* **billon tetradrachm.** Laur. hd., r. ℞. Eagle
stg. r. on thunderbolt, hd. turned l. *B.M.C. G.*1459 .. *Fine* £7·50

JULIA DOMNA

1757

Born at Emesa in Syria, Julia Domna came to Rome as a young woman and in A.D. 173 *was married to Septimius Severus as his second wife. In* A.D. 188 *she bore him a son, the future emperor Caracalla, and in the following year another son, Geta, who was also destined to become emperor. She was a woman of brilliant intellect and Severus often consulted her on matters of importance and was frequently guided by her counsels. In* A.D. 217, *after the murder of her son, Caracalla, she considered her position to be hopeless and committed suicide by a voluntary abstinence from food.*

Struck under Septimius Severus, A.D. 193-211

Obv. legends are as follows:

A.   IVLIA DOMNA AVG.

B.   IVLIA AVGVSTA

All have as obv. type dr. bust of Julia Domna r.

All *R.I.C.* references are to the coinage of Severus and all *B.M.C.* references to the coinage of the Wars of Succession and that of the Joint Reign of Severus and Caracalla.

Very Fine

1731 **N aureus.** A. R. VENERI VICTR. Venus stg. r., holding apple and palm and leaning on column. *C.* 193. *R.I.C.* 536. *B.M.C.* 47   .. £265·00

1732 **N quinarius.** B. R. IVNO. Juno stg. l., peacock at feet. *C.* 81. *R.I.C.* 559. *B.M.C.* 37 *note*   ..   .. 400·00

1733 **R cistophorus.** B. R. MATRI CASTR. Five corn-ears in bundle. *C.* 130. *R.I.C.* 650. *B.M.C., p.* 305, † ..   .. 250·00

1734 **R denarius.** B. R. CERERI FRVGIF. Ceres seated l., holding corn-ears and torch. *C.* 14. *R.I.C.* 546. *B.M.C.* 10   ..   ..   .. 3·75

1735 B. R. DIANA LVCIFERA. Diana stg. l., holding torch. *C.* 27. *R.I.C.* 548. *B.M.C.* 15   ..   .. 4·00

1736 B. R. FELICITAS. Felicity stg. l. *C.* 47. *R.I.C.* 551. *B.M.C.* 22   3·50

1737 B. R. FORTVNAE FELICI. Fortune stg. l. *C.* 55. *R.I.C.* 552. *B.M.C.* 24   ..   .. 3·50

1738 B. R. — Fortune seated l., child at feet. *C.* 57. *R.I.C.* 554. *B.M.C.* 29   ..   .. 3·75

1739 B. R. HILARITAS. Hilaritas stg. l. *C.* 72. *R.I.C.* 556. *B.M.C.* 31   3·50

1740 B. R. — Hilaritas stg. l. between two children. *C.* 79. *R.I.C.* 557. *B.M.C.* 34   ..   .. 4·00

1741 B. R. IVNO REGINA. As 1732. *C.* 97. *R.I.C.* 560. *B.M.C.* 42 ..   3·75

1742 B. R. LAETITIA. Laetitia stg. l., holding wreath and rudder. *C.* 101. *R.I.C.* 561. *B.M.C.* 45   ..   .. 3·75

1743 B. R. MATER AVGG. Julia Domna, as Cybele, seated l. on car drawn by four lions. *C.* 117. *R.I.C.* 562. *B.M.C.* 48   ..   ..   .. 7·00

                                                        Very Fine

1744 **Æ denarius.** B. Ṝ. MATER DEVM. Cybele seated l. on throne
      flanked by two lions. *C.* 123. *R.I.C.* 564. *B.M.C.* 51 *note* ..   .. £5·50
1745 B. Ṝ. — Cybele stg. l., holding branch and drum, lion at feet.
      C. 128. *R.I.C.* 566. *B.M.C.* 49 ..   .. 7·50
1746 B. Ṝ. PIETAS AVGG. Pietas stg. l., sacrificing over altar. *C.* 150.
      R.I.C. 572. *B.M.C.* 62 ..   .. 3·50
1747 B. Ṝ. PIETAS PVBLICA. Pietas stg. l. at altar, raising both hands.
      C. 156. *R.I.C.* 574. *B.M.C.* 69 ..   .. 3·50
1748 B. Ṝ PVDICITIA. Pudicitia seated l., r. hand on breast *C.* 168.
      R.I.C. 576. *B.M.C.* 614   ..   .. 3·75
1749 B. Ṝ. SAECVLI FELICITAS. Isis stg. r., l. foot on prow, nursing infant
      Horus. *C.* 174. *R.I.C.* 577. *B.M.C.* 75   ..   .. 4·00
1750 As 1731. *C.* 194. *R.I.C.* 536. *B.M.C.* 49   ..   .. 3·50
1751 B. Ṝ. VENVS FELIX. Venus stg. facing, hd. l., holding apple. *C.* 198.
      R.I.C. 580. *B.M.C.* 85   ..   .. 3·75
1752 B. Ṝ. VENVS VICTRIX. Venus stg. l., holding helmet and palm and
      leaning on column. *C.* 215. *R.I.C.* 581. *B.M.C.* 90 ..   ..   .. 4·00
1753 B. Ṝ. VESTAE SANCTAE. Vesta stg. l., holding patera and sceptre.
      C. 246. *R.I.C.* 587. *B.M.C.* 99 ..   .. 6·00
1754 **Æ quinarius.** As 1732. *C.* 83. *R.I.C.* 559. *B.M.C.* 40 ..   .. 60·00

                                                              Fine

1755 **Æ sestertius.** B. Ṝ. HILARITAS S . C. Hilaritas stg. l. *C.* 73.
      R.I.C. 855. *B.M.C.* 768 ..   .. 20·00
1756 B. Ṝ. MATER DEVM S . C. As 1744. *C.* 124. *R.I.C.* 859. *B.M.C.*
      772   ..   .. 25·00
1757 A. Ṝ. VENERI VICTR . S . C. As 1731. *C.* 195. *R.I.C.* 842. *B.M.C.*
      488. *Illustrated on p. 183*   ..   .. 25·00
1758 B. Ṝ. VENVS FELIX S . C. As 1751. *C.* 199. *R.I.C.* 866. *B.M.C.*
      776   ..   .. 20·00
1759 A. Ṝ. VESTA S . C. Vesta seated l., holding palladium and sceptre.
      C. 222. *R.I.C.* 843. *B.M.C.* 491   ..   .. 25·00
1760 B. Ṝ. As previous. *C.* 224. *R.I.C.* 867. *B.M.C.* 778   ..   .. 20·00
1761 **Æ dupondius.** B. Ṝ. VENVS FELIX S . C. As 1751. *C.* 200.
      R.I.C. 887. *B.M.C.* 794 ..   .. 10·00
1762 **Æ as.** B. Ṝ. CERES S . C. Ceres stg. l., holding corn-ears and torch,
      altar at feet. *C.* 19. *R.I.C.* 870. *B.M.C.* 781 ..   .. 10·00
1763 As 1755. *C.* 74. *R.I.C.* 877. *B.M.C.* 786   ..   .. 10·00

Struck under Caracalla, A.D. 211-217

All have obv. legend IVLIA PIA FELIX AVG.

The obv. type is draped bust of Julia Domna r., unless otherwise stated.

All *R.I.C.* references are to the coinage of Caracalla, and all *B.M.C.* references to the
coinage of the Sole Reign of Caracalla.

                                                        Very Fine

1764 **꙳ double aureus.** Diad. and dr. bust. r., resting on crescent. Ṝ.
      VENVS GENETRIX. Venus seated l., holding sceptre. *C.* 202. *R.I.C.*
      389*a note. B.M.C.* 21   ..   .. *Very rare*
1765 **꙳ aureus.** Ṝ. PIETATI. As 1746. *C.* 157. *R.I.C.* 384. *B.M.C.*
      18A ..   .. 300·00
1766 **Æ antoninianus.** *(Double denarius, first introduced by Caracalla at the
      end of A.D.* 214.) *Obv.* As 1764. Ṝ. LVNA LVCIFERA. Luna in biga
      galloping l. *C.* 106. *R.I.C.* 379*a. B.M.C.* 9 ..   .. 12·50

					Very Fine
1767	**Æ antoninianus.** As 1764. *C.* 211. *R.I.C.* 388A. *B.M.C.* 22			..	£12·00
1768	**Æ denarius.** R. As 1735. *C.* 32. *R.I.C.* 373A. *B.M.C.* 1			..	3·50
1769	R. As 1766. *C.* 105. *R.I.C.* 379c. *B.M.C.* 10	..	..	..	8·00

1770   R. MAT . AVGG . MAT . SEN . M . PATR. Julia seated l., holding branch and sceptre. *C.* 111. *R.I.C.* 381. *B.M.C.* 12 ..   ..   6·50

1771   R. MATRI DEVM. Cybele stg. l., holding drum and sceptre and leaning on column, lion at feet. *C.* 137. *R.I.C.* 382. *B.M.C.* 14   ..   ..   5·50

1772   R. VESTA. Vesta seated l., holding simpulum and sceptre. *C.* 226. *R.I.C.* 391. *B.M.C.* 31. **Plate 7**   ..   ..   3·50

1773   R. — Vesta stg. l., holding palladium and sceptre. *C.* 230. *R.I.C.* 390. *B.M.C.* 29   ..   ..   3·50

1774   **Æ quinarius.** R. As 1732. *C.* 84. *R.I.C.* 376. *B.M.C.* 5   ..   65·00

Fine

1775   **Æ sestertius.** R. IVNONEM S . C. As 1732. *C.* 88. *R.I.C.* 585. *B.M.C.* 208 *note*   ..   ..   20·00

1776   R. IVNONI LVCINAE S . C. Juno seated l., holding flower and child in swaddling-clothes. *C.* 93. *R.I.C.* 586. *B.M.C.* 211 ..   ..   ..   20·00

1777   Diad. and dr. bust, r. R. SAECVLI FELICITAS S . C. Felicity stg. l., sacrificing over altar and holding caduceus. *C.* 178. *R.I.C.* 590. *B.M.C.* 215 ..   ..   25·00

1778   — R. VESTA S . C. As 1772. *C.* 228. *R.I.C.* 593. *B.M.C.* 217   20·00

1779   **Æ dupondius.** R. CEREREM S . C. Ceres stg. l., holding corn-ears and sceptre, modius at feet. *C.* 13. *R.I.C.* 596. *B.M.C.* 220   ..   10·00

1780   **Æ as.** R. IVNONEM S . C. As 1732. *C.* 89. *R.I.C.* 599. *B.M.C.* 224 ..   ..   10·00

1781   Diad. and dr. bust, r. R. VESTA S . C. Four Vestals, accompanied by two children, stg. in front of round temple of Vesta; in centre, altar over which two of the Vestals are sacrificing. *C.* 234. *R.I.C.* 607. *B.M.C.* 232 ..   ..   25·00

Commemorative Coins struck after her death
Struck under Elagabalus

1782   **Æ denarius.** DIVA IVLIA AVGVSTA. Veiled and dr. bust, r. R. CONSECRATIO. Peacock walking l., tail in splendour. *C.* 24. *R.I.C.* (*Car.*) 396 and (*Sev. Alex.*) 715. *B.M.C.* (*Elag.*) 9   *Very fine* £60·00

1783   **Æ sestertius.** — R. CONSECRATIO S . C. Julia seated on peacock flying r. *C.* 25. *R.I.C.* (*Car.*) 609 and (*Sev. Alex.*) 716. *B.M.C.* (*Elag.*), *p.* 589, ** ..   ..   100·00

Colonial and Provincial Coinage

1784   *Macedon, Thessalonica*, **Æ 22.** Dr. bust, r. R. Kabeiros stg. l., holding rhyton and hammer. *B.M.C. G.* 94   ..   ..   ..   3·75

1785   *Lycaonia, Parlais*, **Æ 23.** Dr. bust, l. R. Mên stg. l. *B.M.C. G.* 1   8·00

1786   *Phoenicia, Berytus*, **Æ 25.** Dr. bust, r. R. Tetrastyle temple of Astarte. *B.M.C. G.* 132 ..   ..   5·00

1787   *Egypt, Alexandria*, **billon tetradrachm.** — R. Tyche seated l. *B.M.C. G.* 1468 ..   ..   7·50

1788   — — R. Hera stg. l., peacock at feet. *B.M.C. G.* 1470 ..   ..   9·00

CARACALLA
A.D. 198-217

1873A

M. Aurelius Antoninus, originally named Bassianus, was born at Lugdunum on April 6th, A.D. 188, the elder son of Severus and Julia Domna.   In 196 he was given the rank of Caesar and in 198 he was created Augustus, although only ten years of age.   He accompanied his father and brother on the expedition to Britain in 208 and led the campaign of 210 in person. On the death of Severus in 211, Caracalla reigned jointly with his brother Geta, as Severus had arranged.   In 212, however, Geta was assassinated by the orders of Caracalla who also caused many prominent and distinguished Romans to be put to death, so as to consolidate his position as sole ruler.   His reign was marked by extravagance and cruelty and in his wars he achieved more by treachery than by force of arms.   He was finally murdered by the orders of Macrinus, the praetorian prefect, on April 8th, 217, whilst he was travelling between Edessa and Carrhae.

The one notable action which can be attributed to Caracalla was the giving to all free inhabitants of the Empire the name and privileges of Roman citizens.   The name " Caracalla," by which this emperor is commonly known, was a nick-name derived from a long tunic of Gallic origin which he adopted as his favourite dress.

Titles and Powers, A.D. 196-217

A.D.	Tribunician Power	Imperatorial Acclamation	Consulship	Other Titles
196				CAESAR.
197		IMP.DESIG.		PONTIFEX.
198	TR.P.	IMP.		AVGVSTVS.
199	TR.P.II.			
200	TR.P.III.			
201	TR.P.IIII.			
202	TR.P.V.		COS.	
203	TR.P.VI.			
204	TR.P.VII.			
205	TR.P.VIII.		COS.II.	
206	TR.P.VIIII.			
207	TR.P.X.			
208	TR.P.XI.		COS.III.	
209	TR.P.XII.			
210	TR.P.XIII.			BRIT.
211	TR.P.XIIII.			P.M. P.P.
212	TR.P.XV.	IMP.II. (?)		
213	TR.P.XVI.		COS.IIII.	FELIX. GERM.
214	TR.P.XVII.	IMP.III.		
215	TR.P.XVIII.			
216	TR.P.XVIIII.			
217	TR.P.XX.			

Caracalla became TR.P.II. on January 1st, A.D. 199, and his tribunician power was subsequently renewed each year on that date.

Mint (during sole reign): Rome.

The following are the commonest forms of obverse legend:

- A. ANTONINVS AVGVSTVS.
- B. ANTONINVS PIVS AVG.
- C. ANTONINVS PIVS AVG. BRIT.
- D. ANTONINVS PIVS AVG . GERM.
- E. M . AVR . ANTON . CAES . PONTIF.
- F. M . AVR . ANTONINVS CAES.
- G. M . AVREL . ANTONINVS PIVS AVG . BRIT.

Legends E *and* F *belong to the period as Caesar, and the others to the period following his elevation to the rank of Augustus.*

The portraiture of Caracalla on the coins closely follows his physical development from a boy of eight years to a man of twenty-nine, the age at which he was murdered.

As Caesar and in his early years as Augustus, he is depicted as a child, but in the latter half of his joint reign with Severus the portrait becomes that of an adolescent.

He is first shown with a beard in A.D. 209 and from then on the portrait steadily develops to the full maturity of his last years. Harold Mattingly, writing in the fifth volume of the British Museum Catalogue, states that " the mature portrait of Caracalla is rendered with a brutal realism that shocks the eye."

As Caesar

A.D. 196-198, *under Septimius Severus*

There are two varieties of obverse type:

- a. Bare-headed and draped bust, r.
- b. Bare-headed, draped and cuirassed bust, r.

All *B.M.C.* references are to the coinage of the Wars of Succession.

Very Fine

1789 **N aureus.** Fb. ℞. SPEI PERPETVAE. Spes advancing l. C. 593. *R.I.C. 5. B.M.C.* 189 .. ..£300·00

1790 **R denarius.** Eb. ℞. DESTINATO IMPERAT. Sacrificial implements. C. 53. *R.I.C. 6. B.M.C.* 193 .. .. 10·00

1791 Ea. ℞. IMPERII FELICITAS. Felicity stg. l., holding caduceus and child. C. 95. *R.I.C. 9. B.M.C.* 199 .. .. 6·00

1792 Ea. ℞. MARTI VLTORI. Mars advancing r., carrying spear and trophy. C. 154. *R.I.C. 11. B.M.C.* 202 .. .. 5·00

1793 Eb. ℞. PRINCIPI IVVENTVTIS. Caracalla stg. l. beside trophy, holding rod and spear. C. 505. *R.I.C.* 13b. *B.M.C.* 208 .. .. .. 5·00

1794 Fb. ℞. SECVRITAS PERPETVA. Minerva stg. l., leaning on shield and holding spear. C. 562. *R.I.C. 2. B.M.C.* 181 *note* .. .. .. 6·50

1795 Fb. ℞. SEVERI AVG . PII FIL. Sacrificial implements. C. 587. *R.I.C. 4. B.M.C.* 184 .. .. 7·50

1796 As 1789. C. 594. *R.I.C. 5. B.M.C.* 190 .. .. 5·00

1797 **Æ sestertius.** Eb. ℞. PRINCIPI IVVENTVTIS S . C. As 1793. C. 506. *R.I.C.* 398a. *B.M.C.* 618 .. .. **Fine** 20·00

1798 Eb. ℞. SPEI PERPETVAE S . C. Spes advancing l. C. 595. *R.I.C.* 401. *B.M.C.* 613 .. .. 17·50

1799 **Æ as.** Fa. ℞. SEVERI AVG . PII FIL . S . C. Sacrificial implements. C. 586. *R.I.C.* 404. *B.M.C.* 615.. .. .. 12·50

As Augustus

With Septimius Severus, A.D. 198-209

With Septimius Severus and Geta, A.D. 209-211

With Geta, A.D. 211-212

As sole emperor, A.D. 212-217

There are three main varieties of obverse type:

    a. Laureate head, r.

    b. Laureate and draped bust, r.

    c. Laureate, draped and cuirassed bust, r.

In the *B.M.C.* the coinage of this reign is dealt with in four sections, corresponding to the four periods of the reign as listed above.   In each section the numbering starts again from 1, but no attempt is made here to distinguish between the different sections in the *B.M.C.* references quoted.

Very Fine

1800 **N double aureus.** D. Rad., dr. and cuir. bust, r. R. P . M . TR . P . XVIIII . COS . IIII . P . P. Jupiter seated l., holding Victory and sceptre, eagle at feet. *C.* 341. *R.I.C.* 277a. *B.M.C.* 157 .. .. *Very rare*

1801 **N aureus.** Dc. R. — Serapis stg. l., holding sceptre. *C.* 347. *R.I.C.* 280a. *B.M.C.* 164 *note* .. ..£225·00

1802 Bc. R. PONTIF . TR . P . VIII . COS . II. Mars stg. l., r. foot on helmet, holding branch and spear. *C.* 419. *R.I.C.* 80a. *B.M.C.* 476 .. .. 200·00

1803 Ac. R. RECTOR ORBIS. Caracalla, naked, stg. l., holding globe and spear. *C.* 541. *R.I.C.* 39a. *B.M.C.* 163 .. .. 200·00

1804 **N quinarius.** Ca. R. COS . III . P . P. Victory advancing l. *C.* 41. *R.I.C.* 203. *B.M.C.* 108 .. .. 400·00

1805 **R cistophorus.** IM . C . M . AVR . ANTONINVS AVG. a. R. VICTORIA AVGVSTI. Victory advancing l. *C.* 618. *R.I.C.* 358a. *B.M.C.* 762 .. 200·00

1806 **R antoninianus.** (*Double denarius, first introduced at the end of* A.D. 214). D. Rad., dr. and cuir. bust, r. R. P . M . TR . P . XVIII . COS . IIII . P . P. As 1800. *C.* 277. *R.I.C.* 260b. *B.M.C.* 117 .. .. 10·00

1807 — R. — Jupiter stg. r., holding thunderbolt and sceptre. *C.* 279. *R.I.C.* 258a. *B.M.C.* 110 .. .. 10·00

1808 — R. — Diana in biga of bulls prancing l. *C.* 294. *R.I.C.* 256b. *B.M.C.* 121 .. .. 12·50

1809 — R. — Serapis stg. facing, hd. l., holding sceptre. *C.* 295. *R.I.C.* 263d. *B.M.C.* 128 .. .. 10·00

1810 — R. — Lion walking l., holding thunderbolt in jaws. *C.* 322. *R.I.C.* 273d. *B.M.C.* 150 .. .. 15·00

1811 D. Rad. and dr. bust, r. R. P . M . P . XVIIII . COS . IIII . P . P. Sol. stg. l., holding globe. *C.* 358. *R.I.C.* 281a. *B.M.C.* 170 .. .. 10·00

1812 *Obv.* As 1800. R VENVS VICTRIX Venus stg. l., holding Victory and spear and leaning on shield. *C.* 608. *R.I.C.* 311c. *B.M.C.* 79. **Plate 7** .. .. 10·00

1813 — R. VIC . PART. (in ex.) P . M . TR . P . XX . COS . IIII . P . P. Victory seated r. on cuirass, resting shield, inscribed VOT . XX., on l. knee; to r., trophy with two captives seated at base. *C.* 648. *R.I.C.* 297d. *B.M.C.* 199 .. .. 20·00

Very Fine

1814 **Æ denarius.** Bb. ℞. ADVENT . AVGG. Galley travelling l. over waves. *C.* 3. *R.I.C.* 120. *B.M.C.* 267 .. .. £10·00

1815 Ac. ℞. BONVS EVENTVS. Bonus Eventus stg. l., altar at feet. *C.* 19. *R.I.C.* 33. *B.M.C.* 159 .. .. 5·00

1815A Bb. ℞. FELICIA TEMPORA. The Four Seasons as four boys at play. *C.* 58. *R.I.C.* 126. *B.M.C.*, *p.* 207, * .. .. 125·00

1816 Ac. ℞. FELICITAS AVGG. Felicity stg. l. *C.* 61. *R.I.C.* 34. *B.M.C.* 61 *note* .. .. 4·00

1817 IMP . CAE . M . AVR . ANT . AVG . P . TR . P. b. ℞. FIDES PVBLICA. Fides stg. r. *C.* 82. *R.I.C.* 24a. *B.M.C.* 102 .. .. .. 4·00

1818 Bb. ℞. INDVLGENTIA AVGG . IN CARTH. Dea Caelestis seated facing on lion springing r. *C.* 97. *R.I.C.* 130a. *B.M.C.* 280 .. .. 4·50

1819 Ca. ℞. INDVLG . FECVNDAE. Julia Domna (?) seated l. on curule chair, holding sceptre. *C.* 104. *R.I.C.* 214. *B.M.C.* 73 .. .. 8·00

1820 Ba. ℞. LIBERALITAS AVG . VI. Liberalitas stg. l. *C.* 128. *R.I.C.* 158. *B.M.C.* 509 .. .. 3·75

1821 Ba. ℞. LIBERTAS AVG. Liberty stg. l. *C.* 143. *R.I.C.* 161. *B.M.C.* 511 .. .. 3·25

1822 Ca. ℞. MARTI PACATORI. Mars stg. l., holding olive-branch and spear and leaning on shield. *C.* 149. *R.I.C.* 222. *B.M.C.* 81 .. 3·00

1823 Ca. ℞. MARTI PROPVGNATORI. Mars advancing l., carrying spear and trophy. *C.* 150. *R.I.C.* 223. *B.M.C.* 87 .. .. .. 3·00

1824 *Obv.* As 1817. ℞. MINER . VICTRIX. Minerva stg. l. beside trophy, holding Victory and spear. *C.* 159. *R.I.C.* 25a. *B.M.C.* 107 .. 3·25

1825 Ca. ℞. MONETA AVG. Moneta stg. l. *C.* 165. *R.I.C.* 224. *B.M.C.* 90 .. .. 3·00

1826 Bb. ℞. PART . MAX . PONT . TR . P . IIII. Trophy with two captives seated at base. *C.* 175. *R.I.C.* 54b. *B.M.C.* 262 .. .. 3·50

1827 Ac. ℞. P . MAX . TR . P . IIII . COS. Caracalla stg. l., sacrificing over tripod-altar. *C.* 183. *R.I.C.* 344b. *B.M.C.* 727 *note* .. .. 6·00

1828 Ca. ℞. P . M . TR . P . XIIII . COS . III . P . P. Virtus stg. r., l. foot on helmet. *C.* 186. *R.I.C.* 187. *B.M.C.*, *p.* 420, * .. .. 4·00

1829 Ca. ℞. P . M . TR . P . XV . COS . III . P . P. Hercules stg. l., holding olive-branch and club. *C.* 196. *R.I.C.* 192. *B.M.C.* 35 .. 3·25

1830 Ca. ℞. P . M . TR . P . XVI . COS . IIII . P . P. Serapis stg. l., holding sceptre. *C.* 211. *R.I.C.* 208a. *B.M.C.* 50 .. .. .. 3·50

1831 ANTONINVS PIVS FEL . AVG. a. ℞. — As previous. *C.* 212. *R.I.C.* 208b. *B.M.C.* 56 .. .. 4·50

1832 Da. ℞. — As previous. *C.* 213. *R.I.C.* 208c. *B.M.C.* 59 .. 4·00

1833 Ca. ℞. — Liberty stg. l. *C.* 224. *R.I.C.* 209a. *B.M.C.* 53 .. 3·00

1834 Da. ℞. P . M . TR . P . XVII . COS . IIII . P . P. Jupiter stg. l., holding thunderbolt and sceptre, eagle at feet. *C.* 239. *R.I.C.* 240. *B.M.C.* 94 .. .. 3·00

1835   Æ **denarius.** Da. R. P . M . TR . P . XVIII . COS . IIII . P . P.   Apollo
       stg. l., holding branch and resting l. hand on lyre. *C.* 282. *R.I.C.* 254.
       B.M.C. 107 ..   ..   £4·00

1836   Da. R. — Aesculapius stg. facing between Telesphorus and globe,
       holding serpent-wreathed rod. *C.* 307. *R.I.C.* 253. *B.M.C.* 105 ..   5·50

1837   Da. R. — Fides stg. l., holding two standards. *C.* 315. *R.I.C.* 266.
       B.M.C. 143 ..   ..   3·25

1838   Da. R. P . M . TR . P . XVIIII . COS . IIII . P . P.   Sol stg. facing, hd.
       l., holding globe. *C.* 359. *R.I.C.* 281*b*. *B.M.C.* 172 ..   ..   3·00

1839   Da. R. P . M . TR . P . XX . COS . IIII . P . P.   Serapis stg. l., holding
       wreath and sceptre. *C.* 382. *R.I.C.* 289*c*. *B.M.C.* 188   ..   3·50

1840   Ac. R. PONTIF . TR . P . III.   As 1803. *C.* 413. *R.I.C.* 30*a*. *B.M.C.*
       179. **Plate 7**   ..   ..   3·25

1841   Bb. R. PONTIF . TR . P . VIII . COS . II.   Mars stg. l., holding branch
       and spear. *C.* 420. *R.I.C.* 80*b*. *B.M.C.* 480 ..   ..   ..   4·00

1842   Ba. R. PONTIF . TR . P . VIIII . COS . II.   Mars stg. l., holding spear and
       leaning on shield. *C.* 424. *R.I.C.* 83. *B.M.C.* 498 ..   ..   3·25

1843   Ba. R. PONTIF . TR . P . X . COS . II.   Security seated r., holding sceptre.
       C. 434. *R.I.C.* 92. *B.M.C.* 549 ..   ..   3·50

1844   Ba. R. — Caracalla stg. r., holding spear and parazonium. *C.* 440.
       R.I.C. 95. *B.M.C.* 552 ..   ..   4·00

1845   Ba. R. PONTIF . TR . P . XI . COS . III.   Mars, in fighting attitude, stg.
       r., holding spear and shield. *C.* 447. *R.I.C.* 100. *B.M.C.* 569   ..   4·00

1846   Ba. R. PONTIF . TR . P . XII . COS . III.   Virtus stg. r., holding spear and
       parazonium. *C.* 464. *R.I.C.* 112. *B.M.C.* 13   ..   ..   ..   3·25

1847   Ba. R. — Concord seated l. *C.* 465. *R.I.C.* 111. *B.M.C.* 10 ..   3·25

1848   Ba. R. PONTIF . TR . P . XIII . COS . III.   As 1846. *C.* 477. *R.I.C.*
       117*a*. *B.M.C.* 32 ..   ..   3·00

1849   Ca. R. — Concord seated l. *C.* 483. *R.I.C.* 116*b*. *B.M.C.* 34 ..   3·00

1850   Ca. R. PONTIF . TR . P . XIIII . COS . III.   As 1846. *C.* 494. *R.I.C.*
       191. *B.M.C.* 115 ..   ..   4·00

1851   Bb. R. PONT . TR . P . VI . COS.   Roma stg. l., holding Victory and
       spear. *C.* 499. *R.I.C.* 69. *B.M.C.* 435   ..   ..   ..   4·00

1852   Ca. R. PROFECTIO AVG.   Caracalla stg. r., holding spear; to l., two
       standards. *C.* 508. *R.I.C.* 225. *B.M.C.* 97 ..   ..   ..   6·50

1853   Ca. R. PROVIDENTIAE DEORVM.   Providence stg. l., globe at feet.
       C. 529. *R.I.C.* 227. *B.M.C.* 99 ..   ..   3·50

1854   As 1803. *C.* 542. *R.I.C.* 39*a*. *B.M.C.* 165   ..   ..   ..   3·50

1855   Ab. R. SAL . GEN . HVM.   Salus stg. l., raising kneeling figure and
       holding serpent-wreathed sceptre. *C.* 558. *R.I.C.* 42*a*. *B.M.C.* 169   12·00

1856   Ba. R. SECVRIT . IMPERII.   As 1843. *C.* 570. *R.I.C.* 168. *B.M.C.*
       516A ..   ..   5·00

1857   *Obv.* As 1817. R. SPES PVBLICA.   Spes advancing l. *C.* 599.
       R.I.C. 26*a*. *B.M.C.* 114 ..   ..   4·00

1858   Da. R. As 1812. *C.* 606. *R.I.C.* 311*b*. *B.M.C.* 82   ..   ..   3·00

1859   Ab. R. VICT . AETERN.   Victory flying l., holding wreath over shield
       set on base. *C.* 614. *R.I.C.* 47*b*. *B.M.C.* 174 *note* ..   ..   4·50

1860   Ca. R. VICTORIAE BRIT.   Victory advancing r., holding trophy.
       C. 629. *R.I.C.* 231A. *B.M.C.* 102   ..   ..   20·00

1861   Ca. R. — Victory advancing l. *C.* 632. *R.I.C.* 231. *B.M.C.* 105   20·00

Very Fine

1862 **Æ denarius.** Bb. Ŗ. VICT . PART . MAX. Victory advancing l.
C. 658. R.I.C. 144b. B.M.C. 296 .. .. £4·25

1863 Ba. Ŗ. VIRTVS AVGG. Caracalla stg. facing, hd. r., holding spear and
parazonium; at feet l., river-god reclining; at feet r., two captives
seated. C. 670. R.I.C. 175. B.M.C. 520 .. .. 12·00

1864 Ba. Ŗ. VIRTVS AVGVSTOR. Virtus seated l., holding Victory and
parazonium. C. 672. R.I.C. 176. B.M.C. 522 .. .. .. 3·75

1865 Ba. Ŗ. VOTA SVSCEPTA X. Caracalla stg. l., sacrificing over tripod-
altar. C. 689. R.I.C. 179. B.M.C. 524 .. .. 3·50

1866 Ba. Ŗ. VOTA SVSCEPTA XX. Caracalla stg. r., sacrificing over tripod-altar
to r. of which stands attendant; in background, behind altar, flute-player
stg. facing. C. 693. R.I.C. 181. B.M.C. 527 .. .. 30·00

1867 **Æ quinarius.** Ca. Ŗ. COS . IIII . P . P. Victory advancing l. C.
45. R.I.C. 317b. B.M.C. 67 .. .. 50·00

Fine

1868 **Æ sestertius.** Ga. Ŗ. P . M . TR . P . XIIII . COS . III . P . P . S . C.
Security seated r., holding palm. C. 193. R.I.C. 480a. B.M.C. 33 15·00

1869 Ga. Ŗ. P . M . TR . P . XV . COS . III . P . P . S . C. Mars stg. l.,
holding Victory and leaning on shield; at feet l., captive. C. 198.
R.I.C. 490a. B.M.C. 235 .. .. 15·00

1870 G. Laur. and cuir. bust, r. Ŗ. P . M . TR . P . XVI . IMP . II . COS . IIII .
P . P . S . C. The Circus Maximus: in foreground, arcade of thirteen
arches with large arch at each end: down the centre of the circus extends
the *spina,* in middle of which stands tall obelisk. C. 236. R.I.C. 500b.
B.M.C. 251 .. .. 100·00

1871 M . AVREL . ANTONINVS PIVS . AVG . GERM. C. Ŗ. P . M . TR . P . XVII .
IMP . III . COS . IIII . P . P . S . C. As 1869. C. 257. R.I.C. 524a.
B.M.C. 262 .. .. 15·00

1872 — Ŗ. P . M . TR . P . XVIII . IMP . III . COS . IIII . P . P . S . C. Lion
walking l., holding thunderbolt in jaws. C. 335. R.I.C. 548a. B.M.C.
290 .. .. 30·00

1873 Ga. Ŗ. PROVIDENTIAE DEORVM S . C. As 1853. C. 532. R.I.C.
511a. B.M.C. 242 .. .. 15·00

1873A M . AVREL . ANTONINVS PIVS AVG . GERM. Laur., dr. and cuir. bust, l.
Ŗ. As previous. C. 538. R.I.C. 572b. B.M.C. 271 *note.* *Illustrated*
on p. 186 .. .. 35·00

1874 M . AVREL . ANTONINVS PIVS AVG. b. Ŗ. VICTORIAE BRITTANNICAE
S . C. Victory stg. r., erecting trophy to r. of which stands Britannia
facing, captive at feet. C. 639. R.I.C. 464. B.M.C. 819 .. .. 45·00

1875 Ga. Ŗ. VICT . BRIT . P . M . TR . P . XIIII . COS . III . P . P . S . C. As
previous. C. 641. R.I.C. 483a. B.M.C. 36 .. .. 45·00

1876 **Æ dupondius.** C. Rad. hd., r. Ŗ. SECVRITATI PERPETVAE S . C.
Security seated r., holding sceptre, altar at feet. C. 578. R.I.C. 515.
B.M.C. 255 .. .. 10·00

1877 **Æ as.** Ca. Ŗ. P . M . TR . P . XVI . COS . IIII . P . P . S . C. As 1830.
C. 214. R.I.C. 505. B.M.C. 257.. .. .. 10·00

1878 Dc. Ŗ. P . M . TR . P . XX . COS . IIII . P . P . S . C. As 1872. C. 404.
R.I.C. 571b. B.M.C. 312 .. .. 17·50

1879 Ba. Ŗ. PONTIF . TR . P . XII . COS . III . S . C. Victory stg. r., inscribing
shield set on palm-tree. C. 467. R.I.C. 448a. B.M.C. 175 .. .. 12·00

Commemorative Coins struck after his death

Struck under Elagabalus

Fine

1880 **Æ denarius.** DIVO ANTONINO MAGNO. Bare hd., r. R. CONSE-
CRATIO. Eagle stg. l. on globe, wings spread, hd. turned. *C.* 32.
R.I.C. (*Sev. Alex.*) 717. *B.M.C.* (*Elag.*) 7 .. *Very fine* £100·00

1881 **Æ sestertius.** — R. CONSECRATIO S . C. Funeral pyre surmounted
by Caracalla in quadriga. *C.* 34. *R.I.C.* (*Sev. Alex.*) 719. *B.M.C.*
(*Elag.*), *p.* 589, ‖ .. ..£125·00

Colonial and Provincial Coinage

Fair

1882 *Thrace, Pautalia,* **Æ 29.** Laur. hd., r. R. Fish-tailed serpent.
*B.M.C. G.*30 .. .. 3·75

1883 *Moesia Inferior, Tomi,* **Æ 28.** Laur. bust, r. R. Caracalla stg. l.,
altar at feet. *Pick* 2901 .. .. 3·00

1884 *Corcyra,* **Æ 26.** — R. Galley r. *B.M.C. G.*678 .. .. 3·00

1885 *Bithynia, Nicomedia,* **Æ 27.** — R. Octastyle temple. *B.M.C. G.*51 3·00

1886 *Troas, Ilium,* **Æ 26.** — R. Ilos stg. l., sacrificing before statue of
Athena Ilias. *B.M.C. G.*87 .. .. 4·00

1887 *Ionia, Ephesus,* **Æ 17.** Laur. hd., r. R. Boar running r. *B.M.C.*
*G.*280 .. .. 2·00

1888 *Caria, Alabanda,* **Æ 27.** Laur. and dr. bust, r. R. Lyre. *B.M.C.*
*G.*45 .. .. 3·00

1889 *Galatia, Ancyra,* **Æ 17.** Laur. hd., r. R. Palm in prize urn. *B.M.C.*
*G.*27 .. .. 2·25

1890 *Syria, Antioch,* **Æ 20.** — R. S . C. in wreath. *B.M.C. G.*354 .. 1·50

1891 — *Gabala,* **Æ 26.** — R. Tyche seated l. *B.M.C. G.*13 .. .. 5·00

1892 *Phoenicia, Berytus,* **Æ 22.** Laur. bust, r. R. Poseidon stg. l., holding
dolphin and trident. *B.M.C. G.*141 .. .. 1·75

1893 *Mesopotamia, Carrhae,* **Æ 19.** Laur. hd., r. R. Bust of Tyche r.
*B.M.C. G.*17 .. .. 1·75

PLAUTILLA

1905A

The daughter of the powerful praetorian prefect Plautianus, Plautilla was married to
Caracalla in A.D. 202. On the fall of her father in 205, she was banished to the Lipari
Islands where she was murdered by the orders of Caracalla in 211.

There are three varieties of obverse legend:

A.   PLAVTILLA AVG.
B.   PLAVTILLA AVGVSTA.
C.   PLAVTILLAE AVGVSTAE.

All have as obverse type draped bust of Plautilla r.

All *R.I.C.* references are to the coinage of Caracalla, and all *B.M.C.* references to
the coinage of the Joint Reign of Severus and Caracalla.

Very Fine

1894 **N aureus.** B. R. VENVS VICTRIX. Venus stg. l., holding apple and palm and leaning on shield; at feet l., Cupid. *C.* 24. *R.I.C.* 369. *B.M.C.* 427 .. ..£800·00

1895 **R denarius.** B. R. CONCORDIA AVGG. Concord stg. l. *C.* 1. *R.I.C.* 363a. *B.M.C.* 411 .. .. 7·50

1896 C. R. As previous. *C.* 2. *R.I.C.* 359. *B.M.C.* 398 .. .. 9·00

1897 A. R. CONCORDIAE. Concord seated l. *C.* 8. *R.I.C.* 372. *B.M.C.* 739 .. .. 9·00

1898 C. R. CONCORDIAE AETERNAE. Caracalla and Plautilla stg. facing each other, clasping r. hands. *C.* 10. *R.I.C.* 361. *B.M.C.* 401 .. .. 8·50

1899 B. R. CONCORDIA FELIX. As previous. *C.* 12. *R.I.C.* 365a. *B.M.C.* 418 .. .. 10·00

1900 B. R. DIANA LVCIFERA. Diana stg. l., holding torch. *C.* 13. *R.I.C.* 366. *B.M.C.* 420 .. .. 17·50

1901 B. R. PIETAS AVGG. Pietas stg. r., holding sceptre and child. *C.* 16. *R.I.C.* 367. *B.M.C.* 422 .. .. 7·50

1902 C. R. PROPAGO IMPERI. As 1898. *C.* 21. *R.I.C.* 362. *B.M.C.* 406. **Plate 7** .. .. 8·50

1903 As 1894. *C.* 25. *R.I.C.* 369. *B.M.C.* 429 .. .. .. 7·50

1904 **R quinarius.** B. R. VENVS FELIX. Venus stg. l., holding apple. *C.* 23. *R.I.C.* 368. *B.M.C., p.* 238, * .. .. 200·00

Fine

1905 **Æ sestertius.** B. R. VENVS VICTRIX S . C. As 1894. C. 27. *R.I.C.* 579. *B.M.C., p.* 323, ‡ .. .. *Very rare*

1905A **Æ dupondius or as.** C. R. CONCORDIA AVGG . S . C. Concord seated l. *C.* 5. *R.I.C.* 580. *B.M.C., p.* 323, *. *Illustrated on p.* 192 .. 35·00

1906 B. R. PIETAS AVGG . S . C. As 1901. *C.* 18. *R.I.C.* 581. *B.M.C.* 804 .. .. 35·00

GETA
A.D. 209-212

1938A

(L. or P. Septimius Geta). The younger son of Severus and Julia Domna, Geta was born at Rome in A.D. 189. *In 198 he was given the title of Caesar at the same time as his elder brother, Caracalla, was raised to the rank of Augustus. He took part in the British expedition which began in 208, and during the course of this campaign he was created Augustus* (A.D. 209), *it being Severus' clear intention that the brothers should inherit the throne jointly. The savage and jealous nature of Caracalla would, however, admit of no such arrangement, and Geta was murdered in February,* A.D. 212, *after only twelve months of joint-rule. There followed a vigorous persecution of all the adherents of Geta in which, it is said, no less than twenty thousand people met their deaths.*

Titles and Powers, A.D. 198-212

A.D.	Tribunician Power	Imperatorial Acclamation	Consulship	Other Titles
198				CAESAR.
199				
200				PONTIFEX.
201				
202				
203				
204				
205			COS.	
206				
207				
208			COS.II.	
209	TR.P.	IMP.		AVGVSTVS.
210	TR.P.II.			BRIT.
211	TR.P.III.			P.P.
212	TR.P.IIII.			

Geta became TR.P.II. on January 1st, A.D. 210, and his tribunician power was subsequently renewed each year on that date.

Mint (during period as Augustus): Rome.

The following are the commonest forms of obverse legend:

As Caesar:

    A. L . SEPTIMIVS GETA CAES.
    B. P . SEPT . GETA CAES . PONT.
    C. P . SEPTIMIVS GETA CAES.

As Augustus:

    D. IMP . CAES . P . SEPT . GETA PIVS AVG.
    E. P . SEPT . GETA PIVS AVG . BRIT.
    F. P . SEPTIMIVS GETA PIVS AVG . BRIT.

Other obverse legends are given in full.

As in the case of Caracalla, the portraiture of Geta on the coins closely follows his physical development from a young child, through adolescence to early manhood.   Cut short as his life was at the age of twenty-two, his portrait does not reach the full maturity of that of his brother, although he is shown with a beard from A.D. 209.

As Caesar

A.D. 198-209, *under Septimius Severus and Caracalla*

There are two main varieties of obverse type:

    a. Bare-headed and draped bust, r.
    b. Bare-headed, draped and cuirassed bust, r.

All *B.M.C.* references are to the coinage of the Joint Reign of Severus and Caracalla.

Very Fine

1907 **N aureus.** Bb. R. PRINC . IVVENT. Geta stg. l. beside trophy, holding branch and spear. *C.* 156. *R.I.C.* 16a. *B.M.C.* 228..   ..£400·00

1908 **N quinarius.** C. Bare hd., r. R. NOBILITAS. Nobilitas stg. l., holding palladium and sceptre. *R.I.C.* 49. *B.M.C.* 457 ..   .. 600·00

1909 **R denarius.** Ba. R. CASTOR. Castor stg. l. in front of horse which he holds by rein. *C.* 12. *R.I.C.* 6. *B.M.C.* 216 ..   ..   .. 12·00

1910 Ba. R. FELICITAS AVGG. Felicity stg. l., holding caduceus and cornucopiae. *C.* 36. *R.I.C.* 8. *B.M.C.* 218 ..   .. 4·50

Very Fine

1911 **Æ denarius.** Bb. ℞. FELICITAS PVBLICA. As previous. *C.* 38.
R.I.C. 9*b*. *B.M.C.* 220 *note* .. .. £4·50

1912 Aa. ℞. FELICITAS TEMPOR. Felicity and Geta stg. facing each other,
clasping r. hands. *C.* 49. *R.I.C.* 1. *B.M.C.* 146 .. .. .. 7·50

1913 Ca. ℞. MINERVA. Minerva stg. l., holding spear and leaning on shield.
C. 77. *R.I.C.* 46. *B.M.C.* 454 .. .. 6·00

1914 Ba. ℞. NOBILITAS. Nobilitas stg. r., holding sceptre and palladium.
C. 90. *R.I.C.* 13*a*. *B.M.C.* 223 .. .. 5·00

1915 Cb. ℞. PONTIF . COS. As 1913. *C.* 104. *R.I.C.* 34*a*. *B.M.C.*
446 *note* .. .. 4·25

1916 C. Bare hd., r. ℞. PONTIF . COS . II. Genius stg. l., holding patera
and corn-ears, altar at feet. *C.* 114. *R.I.C.* 59*b*. *B.M.C.* 579.. .. 4·25

1917 Ca. ℞. — Geta stg. l., holding globe and sceptre. *C.* 117. *R.I.C.*
61*b*. *B.M.C.* 586 .. .. 4·50

1918 Ba. ℞. PRINC . IVVENTVTIS. As 1907. *C.* 157. *R.I.C.* 18.
B.M.C. 234 .. .. 4·50

1919 Ca. ℞. PROVID . DEORVM. Providence stg. l., globe at feet. *C.* 170.
R.I.C. 51. *B.M.C.* 458 .. .. 4·25

1920 Ba. ℞. SECVRIT . IMPERII. Security seated l., holding globe. *C.* 183.
R.I.C. 20*a*. *B.M.C.* 240. **Plate 7** .. .. 4·00

1921 Aa. ℞. SPEI PERPETVAE. Spes advancing l. *C.* 192. *R.I.C.* 96.
B.M.C. 689 .. .. 5·00

1922 Bb. ℞. VICT . AETERN. Victory flying l., holding wreath over shield
set on base. *C.* 206. *R.I.C.* 23. *B.M.C.* 247 .. .. .. 4·00

1923 GETA CAES . PONT . COS. a. ℞. VOTA PVBLICA. Geta stg. l., sacrificing
over tripod-altar. *C.* 230. *R.I.C.* 38*b*. *B.M.C.* 442 .. .. 5·00

1924 **Æ quinarius.** — ℞. COS. Victory advancing l. *C.* 27. *R.I.C.* 27.
B.M.C. 437 .. .. 150·00

1925 **Æ sestertius.** Ab. ℞. SEVERI PII AVG . FIL . S . C. Sacrificial
implements. *C.* 190. *R.I.C.* 110. *B.M.C.* 797   *Fine* £30·00

1926 **Æ dupondius or as.** Ca. ℞. CONCORDIA MILIT . S . C. Concord
stg. l., amidst six standards. *C.* 20. *R.I.C.* 141*a*. *B.M.C.* 841
Fine £17·50

As Augustus

With Septimius Severus and Caracalla, A.D. 209-211

With Caracalla, A.D. 211-212

All have as obverse type laur. hd. of Geta r., unless otherwise stated.

B.M.C. references are to the coinage of the Joint Reign of Severus, Caracalla and
Geta, and that of the Joint Reign of Caracalla and Geta.

1927 **Æ aureus.** D. ℞. PONTIF . TR . P . II . COS . II. Julia Domna (?)
stg. r., holding sceptre; at feet r., two children. *C.* 132. *R.I.C.* 71.
B.M.C., p. 365, * .. .. 450·00

1928 **Æ denarius.** E. ℞. ADVENTVS AVGVSTI. Geta on horseback l.,
raising r. hand. *C.* 3. *R.I.C.* 84. *B.M.C.* 63 .. .. .. 25·00

1929 E. ℞. FORT . RED . TR . P . III . COS . II. Fortune seated l. *C.* 51.
R.I.C. 75. *B.M.C.* 118 .. .. 8·50

1930 E. ℞. FORT . RED . TR . P . III . COS . II . P . P. Fortune reclining r.,
leaning on wheel and holding cornucopiae. *C.* 62. *R.I.C.* 77. *B.M.C.*
10 .. .. 8·50

1931 E. ℞. LIBERALITAS AVG . V. Liberalitas stg. l. *C.* 68. *R.I.C.* 88.
B.M.C. 65 .. .. 10·00

Very Fine

1932 **Æ denarius.** D. ℞. PONTIF . TR . P . II . COS . II. Felicity stg. l.
C. 137. *R.I.C.* 69a. *B.M.C.* 40 .. .. £8·00
1933 D. ℞. — As 1916. C. 140. *R.I.C.* 70b. *B.M.C.* 43 .. .. 8·00
1934 E. ℞. TR . P . III . COS . II . P . P. Janus stg., holding spear and
thunderbolt. C. 197. *R.I.C.* 79. *B.M.C.* 13 .. .. 12·50
1935 E. ℞. VICTORIAE BRIT. Victory stg. l. C. 219. *R.I.C.* 92. *B.M.C.*
68 .. .. 20·00

1936 **Æ sestertius.** F. ℞. CONCORDIAE AVGG . S . C. Caracalla and Geta   Fine
stg. facing each other, clasping r. hands and holding spears; Caracalla
is crowned by Hercules stg. behind him and Geta, by Bacchus. C. 25.
R.I.C. 184. *B.M.C.* 232 .. .. 35·00
1937 F. ℞. FORT . RED . TR . P . III . COS . II . P . P . S . C. Fortune seated l.
C. 52. *R.I.C.* 168a. *B.M.C.* 40 .. .. 20·00
1938 F. Laur. and dr. bust, r. ℞. VICT . BRIT . TR . P . III . COS . II . S . C.
Victory seated r. on cuirass, inscribing shield set on l. knee. C. 210.
R.I.C. 172b. *B.M.C.* 268 .. .. 45·00
1938A F. ℞. VICTORIAE BRITTANNICAE S . C. Victory stg. r., erecting trophy
to r. of which stands Britannia facing, captive at feet. C. 223. *R.I.C.*
186. *B.M.C.*, p. 407, *. *Illustrated on p.* 193 .. .. 55·00
1939 **Æ dupondius.** E. Rad. hd., r. ℞. PONTIF . TR . P . III . COS . II .
S . C. As 1927. C. 153. *R.I.C.* 174a. *B.M.C.* 272 .. .. .. 12·50
1940 **Æ as.** D. ℞. PONTIF . TR . P . II . COS . II . S . C. Mars stg. l.,
crowning trophy and leaning on shield. C. 134. *R.I.C.* 162a.
B.M.C. 223 .. .. 10·00
1941 F. ℞. VOTA PVBLICA S . C. Geta stg. l., sacrificing over tripod-altar.
C. 233. *R.I.C.* 192. *B.M.C.* 238.. .. .. 10·00

Colonial and Provincial Coinage   Fair

1942 *Thrace, Serdica,* **Æ 18.** Laur. and dr. bust, r. ℞. Hermes stg. l.
Grose 4538 .. .. 2·25
1943 *Bithynia, Heraclea Pontica,* **Æ 22.** — ℞. Asklepios stg. l. *B.M.C.*
G.50 .. .. 2·50
1944 *Ionia, Ephesus,* **Æ 17.** Laur. hd., r. ℞. Cultus-statue of Artemis
between two children. *B.M.C.* G.283 .. .. 2·25
1945 *Coele-Syria, Heliopolis,* **Æ 22.** Laur. bust, r. ℞. Bust of Tyche l.
B.M.C. G.13 .. .. 3·25

MACRINUS
A.D. 217-218

1963

M. *Opelius Macrinus was born of very humble parents at Caesarea in Mauretania in*
A.D. 164. *After holding various appointments in the imperial household, he became prefect
of the Praetorian guards under Caracalla, and was party to the latter's murder. On April
11th, 217, he was saluted Augustus by his troops, and his elevation was confirmed by the*

Senate. A peace was patched up with the Parthians, but the terms were so unfavourable to the Romans that Macrinus lost much of his popularity. A conspiracy, fostered by Julia Maesa, the sister of Julia Domna, in favour of her grandson Bassianus (Elagabalus), caused the Syrian army to break into open revolt. In the ensuing struggle Macrinus was defeated and fled to Chalcedon, but was betrayed, captured and put to death after a reign of fourteen months.

Titles and Powers, A.D. 217-218

A.D.	Tribunician Power	Imperatorial Acclamation	Consulship	Other Titles
217	TR.P.	IMP.	COS. (*ornamenta consularia*)	AVGVSTVS. P.M. P.P.
218	TR.P.II.		COS. (COS.II.)	

Macrinus renewed his tribunician power on January 1st, A.D. 218.

Mints: Rome; Antioch (?).

There are two main varieties of obverse legend, one for gold and silver and the other for aes:

IMP . C . M . OPEL . SEV . MACRINVS AVG. – N and R.

IMP . CAES. M . OPEL . SEV . MACRINVS AVG. – Æ.

All denominations, except the antoninianus and dupondius, have as obverse type laur., dr. and | or cuir. bust, r. Antoniniani and dupondii have rad., dr. and | or cuir. bust, r.

Very Fine

1946	N **aureus.** R. FIDES MILITVM. Fides stg. facing, hd. r., holding standard in each hand. *C.* 21. *R.I.C.* 64. *B.M.C.* 11 .. ..£500·00	
1947	N **quinarius.** M . OPEL . SEV . MACRINVS AVG. R. COS . II. Victory advancing r. *C.* 13. *R.I.C.* 51. *B.M.C., p.* 504, § .. .. .. 850·00	
1948	R **antoninianus.** R. SALVS PVBLICA. Salus seated l., feeding serpent arising from altar. *C.* 115. *R.I.C.* 88. *B.M.C.* 25 *note* .. .. 45·00	
1949	R **denarius.** R. AEQVITAS AVG. Equity stg. l. *C.* 2. *R.I.C.* 53. *B.M.C.* 58 *note* .. .. 12·00	
1950	R. ANNONA AVG. Annona seated l., modius at feet. *C.* 8. *R.I.C.* 55. *B.M.C.* 6 .. .. 12·00	
1951	R. FELICITAS TEMPORVM. Felicity stg. l. *C.* 15. *R.I.C.* 60. *B.M.C.* 63 .. .. 12·00	
1952	As 1946. *C.* 23. *R.I.C.* 66. *B.M.C.* 12 .. .. .. 12·00	
1953	R. IOVI CONSERVATORI. Jupiter stg. l., holding thunderbolt and sceptre; at feet l., small figure of Macrinus. *C.* 37. *R.I.C.* 76. *B.M.C.* 20. **Plate 7** .. .. 14·00	
1954	R. P . M . TR . P . II . COS . P . P. Annona stg. l., modius at feet. *C.* 47. *R.I.C.* 26. *B.M.C.* 44 .. .. 12·00	
1955	R. — Macrinus seated l. on curule chair, holding globe and sceptre. *C.* 51. *R.I.C.* 27. *B.M.C.* 45 .. .. 15·00	
1956	R. PONTIF . MAX . TR . P . COS . P . P. Jupiter stg. l., holding thunderbolt and sceptre. *C.* 55. *R.I.C.* 17. *B.M.C.* 31 *note* .. .. 14·00	
1957	R. PROVIDENTIA DEORVM. Providence stg. l., holding rod and cornucopiae, globe at feet. *C.* 108. *R.I.C.* 80. *B.M.C.* 73 .. 12·00	
1958	R. SALVS PVBLICA. Salus seated l., feeding serpent arising from altar. *C.* 114. *R.I.C.* 85 *B.M.C.* 76 .. .. 12·00	
1959	R. SECVRITAS TEMPORVM. Security stg. l., holding sceptre and leaning on column. *C.* 122. *R.I.C.* 92. *B.M.C.* 79 .. .. 12·00	

1960 **Æ denarius.** ℞. VICTORIA PARTHICA. Victory advancing r. *C*. 134.
R.I.C. 96. *B.M.C.* 81 *note* .. .. £27·50

1961 ℞. VOTA PVBL . P . M . TR . P. Felicity stg. l. *C*. 147. *R.I.C.* 6.
B.M.C. 2 *note* .. .. 17·00

1962 **Æ quinarius.** ℞. SECVRITAS TEMPORVM. Security seated l., holding
sceptre, altar at feet. *R.I.C.* 94A. *B.M.C.* 28 *note* .. .. *Extr. rare*

Fine

1963 **Æ sestertius.** ℞. PONTIF . MAX . TR . P . COS . P . P . S . C. Felicity
stg. l. *C*. 66. *R.I.C.* 139. *B.M.C.* 120 *note*. *Illustrated on p*. 196 .. 35·00

1964 **Æ dupondius.** ℞. SALVS PVBLICA S . C. Salus seated l., feeding
serpent arising from altar and holding sceptre. *C*. 119. *R.I.C.* 199.
B.M.C. 108 .. .. 20·00

1965 **Æ as.** ℞. PONTIF . MAX . TR . P . II . COS . II . P . P . S . C. As 1956.
C. 90. *R.I.C.* 154. *B.M.C.* 131 .. .. 15·00

1966 ℞. VICT . PART . P . M . TR . P . II . COS . II . P . P . S . C. Victory seated
r. on cuirass, resting shield on l. knee. *C*. 140. *R.I.C.* 166. *B.M.C.*
135 .. .. 25·00

Colonial and Provincial Coinage

1967 *Syria, Antioch,* **Æ 19.** Laur. hd., r. ℞. S . C. in wreath. *B.M.C.*
G. 385.. .. .. *Fair* £2·50

DIADUMENIAN
A.D. 218

1974

M. Opelius Diadumenianus, the son of Macrinus, was born in A.D. 208 *and was given
the rank of Caesar at the same time as his father was saluted Augustus. In the following
year he was raised to the rank of Augustus, but after his father's defeat he fled towards
Parthia, only to be overtaken and executed.*

All *R.I.C.* and *B.M.C.* references are to the coinage of Macrinus.

As Caesar

A.D. 217-218, *under Macrinus*

Very Fine

1968 **N aureus.** M . OPEL . ANT . DIADVMENIAN . CAES. Bare-headed and dr.
bust, r. ℞. PRINC . IVVENTVTIS. Diadumenian stg. facing, hd. r.,
holding standard and sceptre; to r., two standards. *C*. 2. *R.I.C.* 101.
B.M.C., p. 509, † .. .. 1750·00

Very Fine

1969 N **quinarius.** — ℞. — Diadumenian stg. facing, hd. r., holding standard and sceptre. *C.* 16. *R.I.C.* 110. *B.M.C.* 83 *note* .. *Extr. rare*

1970 Æ **antoninianus.** M . OPEL . DIADVMENIANVS CAES. Rad. and dr. bust, r. ℞. — Diadumenian stg. l., holding rod and sceptre; to r., two standards. *C.* 11. *R.I.C.* 106. *B.M.C.* 82 *note* .. .. ..£125·00

1970A Æ **denarius.** As 1968. *C.* 3. *R.I.C.* 102. *B.M.C.* 87. **Plate 7** .. 35·00

1971 *Obv.* As 1968. ℞. As 1970. *C.* 14. *R.I.C.* 109. *B.M.C.* 82 *note* 37·50

1972 — ℞. SPES PVBLICA. Spes advancing l. *C.* 21. *R.I.C.* 116. *B.M.C.* 94 .. .. 40·00

1973 Æ **quinarius.** M . OPEL . ANT . DIADVMENIAN . CAES. Bare-headed, dr. and cuir. bust, r. ℞. PRINC . IVVENTVTIS. Diadumenian stg. facing, hd. r., holding standard and sceptre; to r., standard. *C.* 17. *R.I.C.* 111. *B.M.C.* 83 .. .. *Extr. rare*

Fine

1974 Æ **sestertius.** M . OPEL . ANTONINVS DIADVMENIANVS CAES. Bare-headed, dr. and cuir bust, r. ℞. PRINC . IVVENTVTIS S . C. As 1968. *C.* 7. *R.I.C.* 211. *B.M.C.* 150. *Illustrated on p.* 198 .. .. 45·00

1975 Æ **dupondius.** M . OPEL . DIADVMENIANVS CAES. Bare-headed and dr. bust, r. ℞. — As 1970. *C.* 13. *R.I.C.* 216. *B.M.C.* 163 .. 27·50

1976 Æ **as.** As 1974. *C.* 8. *R.I.C.* 212. *B.M.C.* 158 *note* .. .. .. 27·50

As Augustus

1977 Æ **denarius.** IMP . C . M . OPEL . ANT . DIADVMEN . AVG. Laur. and dr. bust, r. ℞. FELICITAS TEMPORVM. Felicity stg. l., holding cornucopiae and caduceus. *R.I.C.* 118. *B.M.C.* 95 .. .. .. *Unique*

Colonial and Provincial Coinage

Fair

1978 *Moesia Inferior, Marcianopolis,* Æ **24.** Bare-headed and dr. bust, r. ℞. Artemis advancing r., holding bow, hound at her side. *B.M.C. G.*39 .. .. 5·00

1979 *Phrygia, Cibyra,* Æ **30.** — ℞. Zeus enthroned l., eagle at feet. *B.M.C. G.*56 .. .. 6·50

2031A

ELAGABALUS
A.D. 218-222

Varius Avitus Bassianus, later known as M. Aurelius Antoninus, was born at Emesa about A.D. 205, *the son of Sextus Varius Marcellus and Julia Soaemias, the daughter of Julia Maesa. In his boyhood he was appointed priest of the Sun-God Elagabalus, and it is by this name that he is best known. On May 16th,* A.D. 218, *he was proclaimed Emperor by the troops stationed in the district around Emesa, and the revolt soon spread to the rest of the Syrian army. Julia Maesa, the grandmother of Elagabalus, was the true instigator of the rebellion: taking advantage of the growing unpopularity of Macrinus she spread the rumour amongst the soldiers that Elagabalus was the son of Caracalla, whose memory the soldiers held dear. Following the defeat of the army of Macrinus, Elagabalus was accepted by the Senate as Emperor and began a leisurely journey to Rome. His reign was notorious for religious fanaticism, for cruelty, bloodshed and excesses of every description, and there was general satisfaction when, on March 6th, 222, Elagabalus and his mother Julia Soaemias were murdered in the praetorian camp. Their bodies were dragged through the streets of Rome and thrown into the Tiber.*

Titles and Powers, A.D. 218-222

A.D.	Tribunician Power	Imperatorial Acclamation	Consulship	Other Titles
218	TR.P.	IMP.	COS.	AVGVSTVS. P.M. P.P.
219	TR.P.II.		COS.II.	
220	TR.P.III.		COS.III.	
221	TR.P.IIII.			
222	TR.P.V.		COS.IIII.	

Elagabalus became TR.P.II. on January 1st, A.D. 219, and his tribunician power was subsequently renewed each year on that date.

Mints: Rome; Antioch (perhaps other Eastern mints too).

The following are the commonest forms of obverse legend:
- A. ANTONINVS PIVS FEL . AVG.
- B. IMP . ANTONINVS AVG.
- C. IMP . ANTONINVS PIVS AVG.
- D. IMP . CAES . ANTONINVS AVG.
- E. IMP . CAES . M . AVR . ANTONINVS AVG.
- F. IMP . CAES . M . AVR . ANTONINVS PIVS AVG.

The normal obverse type for all denominations except the antoninianus and dupondius is laur. bust r., dr. or dr. and cuir. Antoniniani and dupondii have rad. bust r., dr. or dr. and cuir. In his latest issues, Elagabalus is depicted with a small horn, signifying divine power, placed over the forehead. Such coins are denoted by an "h" placed after the obverse legend letter.

Very Fine

1979A **A/ aureus.** C. R. ADVENTVS AVGVSTI. Elagabalus on horseback l., raising r. hand. C. 5. R.I.C. 57. B.M.C. 195. **Plate 7** .. ..£350·00

1980 E. R. VICTOR . ANTONINI AVG. Victory advancing r. C. 288. R.I.C. 154. B.M.C. 30 .. .. 300·00

1981 **Æ antoninianus.** E. R. FIDES EXERCITVS. Fides seated l., holding eagle and standard; to l., standard. C. 31. R.I.C. 70. B.M.C. 11 .. .. 10·00

1982 B. R. FIDES MILITVM. Fides stg. facing, hd. r., holding two standards. C. 39. R.I.C. 72. B.M.C. 131 .. .. 10·00

1983 B. R. IOVI CONSERVATORI. Jupiter stg. l., eagle at feet; to r., two standards. C. 66. R.I.C. 90. B.M.C. 139 .. .. 12·00

1984 B. R. LAETITIA PVBL. Laetitia stg. l., holding wreath and rudder C. 72. R.I.C. 94. B.M.C. 145 .. .. 10·00

1985 E. R. MARS VICTOR. Mars advancing r., carrying spear and trophy. C. 112. R.I.C. 122. B.M.C. 19 .. .. 10·00

1986 **Æ antoninianus.** E. ℞. P . M . TR . P . COS . P . P. Roma seated l., holding Victory and sceptre. *C.* 125. *R.I.C.* 1. *B.M.C.* 4 .. .. £11·00

1987 B. ℞. PROVID . DEORVM. Providence stg. l., holding rod and cornucopiae and leaning on column, globe at feet. *C.* 243. *R.I.C.* 129. *B.M.C.* 155 .. .. 10·50

1988 E. ℞. SALVS ANTONINI AVG. Salus stg. r., feeding serpent held in arms. *C.* 254. *R.I.C.* 138. *B.M.C.* 26 .. .. 10·00

1989 B. ℞. TEMPORVM FELICITAS. Felicity stg. l. *C.* 280. *R.I.C.* 149. *B.M.C.* 166 .. .. 11·00

1990 E. ℞. As 1980. *C.* 291. *R.I.C.* 155. *B.M.C.* 32 .. .. .. 10·00

1991 **Æ denarius.** C. ℞. ABVNDANTIA AVG. Abundance stg. l., emptying cornucopiae. *C.* 1. *R.I.C.* 56. *B.M.C.* 192 .. .. 4·50

1992 A. ℞. CONCORDIA MILIT. Two standards between two legionary eagles. *C.* 15. *R.I.C.* 187. *B.M.C.* 275 .. .. 6·00

1993 C. ℞. CONSERVATOR AVG. Sol advancing l., holding whip. *C.* 19. *R.I.C.* 63. *B.M.C.* 199 .. .. 6·00

1994 B. ℞. CONSVL II . P . P. Equity stg. l. *C.* 23. *R.I.C.* 168. *B.M.C.* 307 *note* .. .. 7·50

1995 A. ℞. FELICITAS TEMP. Galley travelling r. over waves. *C.* 27. *R.I.C.* 188. *B.M.C.* 277 *note* .. .. 12·50

1996 B. ℞. As 1982. *C.* 38. *R.I.C.* 73. *B.M.C.* 137 .. .. .. 3·75

1997 C. ℞. FIDES MILITVM. Legionary eagle between two standards. *C.* 44. *R.I.C.* 78. *B.M.C.* 201 .. .. 6·00

1998 A. ℞. FORTVNAE REDVCI. Fortune stg. l. *C.* 50. *R.I.C.* 83. *B.M.C.* 204 *note* .. .. 6·00

1999 A. ℞. HILARITAS AVG. Hilaritas stg. l. between two children, holding patera and long palm. *C.* 54. *R.I.C.* 190. *B.M.C.* 282 .. 5·00

2000 Ch. ℞. INVICTVS SACERDOS AVG. Elagabalus stg. l., sacrificing over altar and holding club. *C.* 61. *R.I.C.* 88. *B.M.C.* 212 .. .. 4·50

2001 B. ℞. As 1984. *C.* 70. *R.I.C.* 95. *B.M.C.* 147 *note* .. .. 5·00

2002 C. ℞. LIBERALITAS AVG . III. Liberalitas stg. l. *C.* 86. *R.I.C.* 103. *B.M.C.* 216 .. .. 5·00

2003 C. ℞. LIBERTAS AVG. Liberty stg. l. *C.* 92. *R.I.C.* 107. *B.M.C.* 221 .. .. 3·75

2004 D. ℞. As 1985. *C.* 109. *R.I.C.* 121. *B.M.C.* 112 .. .. 3·75

2005 C. ℞. PAX AVGVSTI. Pax advancing l. *C.* 120. *R.I.C.* 125. *B.M.C.* 223 .. .. 4·50

2006 E. ℞. As 1986. *C.* 127. *R.I.C.* 3. *B.M.C.* 6 .. .. .. 5·00

2007 C. ℞. P . M . TR . P . II . COS . II . P . P. Sol stg. l., holding whip. *C.* 134. *R.I.C.* 17. *B.M.C.* 304 .. .. 5·00

2008 B. ℞. — As 1987. *C.* 144. *R.I.C.* 23. *B.M.C.* 102 .. .. 3·75

2009 B. ℞. — Fortune seated l. *C.* 149. *R.I.C.* 19. *B.M.C.* 96 .. 4·00

2010 B. ℞. P . M . TR . P . III . COS . III . P . P. Jupiter seated l., holding Victory and sceptre, eagle at feet. *C.* 151. *R.I.C.* 27. *B.M.C.* 178 .. 5·00

2011 C. ℞. P . M . TR . P . IIII . COS . III . P . P. Victory flying l. between two shields, holding wreath with both hands. *C.* 194. *R.I.C.* 45. *B.M.C.* 253 *note* .. .. 5·00

2012 Ch. ℞. — As 2000. *C.* 196. *R.I.C.* 46. *B.M.C.* 256. **Plate 7** .. 5·00

2013 C. ℞. P . M . TR . P . V . COS . IIII . P . P. As 2000. *C.* 213. *R.I.C.* 53. *B.M.C.* 268 *note* .. .. 6·00

Very Fine

2014 **Æ denarius.** Ch. ℞. SACERD . DEI SOLIS ELAGAB. Elagabalus stg. r., sacrificing over altar and holding club. *C.* 246. *R.I.C.* 131. *B.M.C.* 225 .. .. £5·50

2015 Ch. ℞. — As 2000. *C.* 252. *R.I.C.* 135. *B.M.C.* 227 .. .. 6·50

2016 E. ℞. As 1988. *C.* 256. *R.I.C.* 140. *B.M.C.* 28 .. .. .. 4·50

2017 B. ℞. SALVS AVGVSTI. Salus stg. l., feeding serpent arising from altar and holding rudder. *C.* 264. *R.I.C.* 141. *B.M.C.* 162 .. .. 4·25

2018 ANTONINVS FEL . PIVS AVG. ℞. SANCT . DEO SOLI ELAGABAL. Triumphal car, bearing the stone of Emesa, drawn r. by four horses. *C.* 267. *R.I.C.* 197. *B.M.C.* 287 *note* .. .. 65·00

2019 B. ℞. SPEI PERPETVAE. Spes advancing l. *C.* 273. *R.I.C.* 199. *B.M.C.* 313 .. .. 5·00

2020 Ch. ℞. SVMMVS SACERDOS AVG. As 2000, but branch in place of club. *C.* 276. *R.I.C.* 146. *B.M.C.* 232.. .. .. 5·50

2021 A. ℞. TEMPORVM FEL. Felicity stg. l., holding patera and caduceus. *C.* 278. *R.I.C.* 201. *B.M.C.* 289.. .. .. 5·50

2022 D. ℞. As 1980. *C.* 293. *R.I.C.* 153. *B.M.C.* 124.. .. .. 3·75

2023 C. ℞. VICTORIA AVG. As 2011. *C.* 300. *R.I.C.* 161. *B.M.C.* 235 3·75

2024 B. ℞. — Victory advancing l. *C.* 304. *R.I.C.* 162. *B.M.C.* 169 .. 4·25

2025 A. ℞. VOTA PVBLICA. Elagabalus stg. l., sacrificing over tripod-altar. *C.* 306. *R.I.C.* 202. *B.M.C.* 291 *note* .. .. .. 5·50

2026 **Æ quinarius.** As 2003. *C.* 91. *R.I.C.* 109. *B.M.C.* 222A.. .. 125·00

2027 **Æ sestertius.** F. ℞. LIBERTAS AVGVSTI S . C. Liberty stg. l.   **Fine** *C.* 103. *R.I.C.* 358. *B.M.C.* 352 *note* .. .. .. 17·50

2028 F. ℞. MARS VICTOR S . C. As 1985. *C.* 114. *R.I.C.* 362. *B.M.C.* 357 *note* .. .. 17·50

2029 F. ℞. P . M . TR . P . III . COS . III . P . P . S . C. As 1993. *C.* 156. *R.I.C.* 300. *B.M.C.* 424 .. .. 17·50

2030 Fh. ℞. P . M . TR . P . IIII . COS . III . P . P . S . C. As 2000. *C.* 198. *R.I.C.* 323. *B.M.C.* 446 *note* .. .. 20·00

2031 F. ℞. PONTIF . MAX . TR . P . S . C. As 1986. *C.* 226. *R.I.C.* 284. *B.M.C.* 343 .. .. 17·50

2031A F. ℞. SACERD . DEI SOLIS ELAGAB . S . C. As 2000. *C.* 253. *R.I.C.* 369. *B.M.C.* 359. *Illustrated on p.* 199 .. .. 60·00

2032 F. ℞. VICTORIA ANTONINI AVG . S . C. Victory advancing r. *C.* 297. *R.I.C.* 377. *B.M.C.* 362 .. .. 20·00

2033 **Æ dupondius.** F. ℞. P . M . TR . P . III . COS . III . P . P . S . C. As 1993. *C.* 159. *R.I.C.* 301. *B.M.C.* 430 .. .. .. 12·00

2034 **Æ as.** Fh. ℞. INVICTVS SACERDOS AVG . S . C. As 2000. *C.* 65. *R.I.C.* 351. *B.M.C.* 368 .. .. 10·00

2035 F. ℞. MARS VICTOR S . C. As 1985. *C.* 115. *R.I.C.* 364. *B.M.C.* 371 .. .. 9·00

2036 Fh. ℞. P . M . TR . P . V . COS . IIII . P . P . S . C. Elagabalus in quadriga travelling l., holding branch and sceptre. *C.* 219. *R.I.C.* 338. *B.M.C.* 456 .. .. 17·50

| | | Fine |

2037 **Æ as.** F. ℞. VICTOR . ANTONINI AVG . S . C. Victory advancing r.
C. 296. *R.I.C.* 376. *B.M.C.* 372 *note* .. .. £10·00

Colonial and Provincial Coinage

Fair

2038 *Macedon, Amphipolis,* **Æ 21.** Laur. bust, r. ℞. Tyche seated l.
*B.M.C. G.*131 .. .. 2·25

2039 *Thrace, Philippopolis,* **Æ 18.** Laur. hd., r. ℞. Asklepios stg. facing.
*B.M.C. G.*48 .. .. 2·25

2040 *Cappadocia, Caesarea,* **Æ 26.** Rad. bust, r. ℞. Representation of
Mt. Argaeus on altar. *B.M.C. G.*289 .. .. 2·25

2041 *Syria, Antioch,* **billon tetradrachm.** Laur. hd., r. ℞. Eagle stg.
facing, hd. l., wreath in beak. *B.M.C. G.*416 .. .. *Fine* £7·50

2042 *Phoenicia, Berytus,* **Æ 29.** Laur. bust, r. ℞. Tetrastyle temple of
Astarte. *B.M.C. G.*175 .. .. 2·25

2043 — *Sidon,* **Æ 25.** — ℞. Europa on bull r. *B.M.C. G.*235 .. .. 3·00

2044 — *Tyre,* **Æ 29.** — ℞. Astarte stg. facing between column surmounted by Nike and palm-tree. *B.M.C. G.*397 .. .. .. 3·00

2045 *Mesopotamia, Edessa,* **Æ 24.** Laur. bust, l., holding shield. ℞. Tyche
seated l. *Cf. B.M.C. G.*60 .. .. 2·25

2046 *Egypt, Alexandria,* **billon tetradrachm.** Laur. bust, r. ℞. Zeus
stg. l. *B.M.C. G.*1486 .. .. *Fine* £3·75

2047 — — ℞. Athena seated l. *B.M.C. G.*1493 .. .. *Fine* £3·75

JULIA PAULA

2053

Julia Cornelia Paula was married to Elagabalus in A.D. 219, *but was divorced the
following year.*

The normal obverse legend is IVLIA PAVLA AVG.

There are two main varieties of obverse type:

    a. Dr. bust, r.
    b. Diad. and dr. bust, r.

All *R.I.C.* and *B.M.C.* references are to the coinage of Elagabalus.

Very Fine

2048　*N* **aureus.** a. ℞. CONCORDIA. Concord seated l., holding patera and
cornucopiae. *C.* 4. *R.I.C.* 210. *B.M.C.* 171 *note* .. .. ..£900·00

2049　**Æ denarius.** a. ℞. — Concord seated l., holding patera. *C.* 6.
R.I.C. 211. *B.M.C.* 171 .. .. 20·00

2050　a. ℞. VENVS GENETRIX. Venus seated l., holding apple and sceptre.
C. 21. *R.I.C.* 222. *B.M.C.* 177 .. .. 25·00

2051　**Æ quinarius.** a. ℞. As 2049. *C.* 7. *R.I.C.* 212. *B.M.C.* 176
note .. .. 250·00

Fine

2052　**Æ sestertius.** b. ℞. CONCORDIA S . C. Concord seated l., holding
patera and double cornucopiae. *C.* 8. *R.I.C.* 381. *B.M.C.* 415 .. 65·00

2053　**Æ dupondius** or **as.** b. ℞. As previous. *C.* 9. *R.I.C.* 384.
B.M.C. 421 *note.* *Illustrated on p.* 203 .. .. 25·00

2054　a. ℞. As previous. *C.* 11. *R.I.C.* 385. *B.M.C.* 421 .. .. 25·00

2055　a. ℞. CONCORDIA AETERNA S . C. Concord stg. facing between
Elagabalus and Paula who stand facing each other, clasping r. hands.
C. 15. *R.I.C.* 387. *B.M.C.* 423 .. .. 35·00

2056　*Egypt, Alexandria,* **billon tetradrachm.** Dr. bust, r. ℞. Helmeted
hd. of Athena r. *B.M.C.* G.1526 .. .. 10·00

2057　— — ℞. Elagabalus and Paula clasping r. hands. *B.M.C.* G.1535 .. 12·50

AQUILIA SEVERA

2060

Julia Aquilia Severa, one of the Vestal Virgins, was married to Elagabalus in A.D. 220.
*She was divorced the following year, but, after he had divorced Annia Faustina, Elagabalus
returned to her later in the same year.*

All have obverse legend IVLIA AQVILIA SEVERA AVG.

There are two varieties of obverse type:

　a. Dr. bust, r.
　b. Diad. and dr. bust, r.

R.I.C. and *B.M.C.* references are to the coinage of Elagabalus.

Very Fine

2058　**Æ denarius.** a. ℞. CONCORDIA. Concord stg. l., holding patera
and double cornucopiae, altar at feet. *C.* 2. *R.I.C.* 225. *B.M.C.* 185 30·00

2059　a. ℞. — Elagabalus and Severa stg. facing each other, clasping r.
hands. *C.* 6. *R.I.C.* 228. *B.M.C.* 337 .. .. 37·50

2060 **Æ sestertius.** b. ℞. CONCORDIA S . C. As 2058. *C.* 4. *R.I.C.*
389. *B.M.C.* 434. *Illustrated on p.* 204 .. .. £75·00
2061 **Æ dupondius** or **as.** a. ℞. As previous. *C.* 3. *R.I.C.* 393.
B.M.C. 435 .. .. 30·00
2062 b. ℞. As previous. *C.* 5. *R.I.C.* 391. *B.M.C.* 435 *note* .. .. 30·00
2063 *Egypt, Alexandria,* **billon tetradrachm.** Dr. bust, r. ℞. Bust of
Serapis r. *B.M.C. G.*1544 .. .. 12·50

ANNIA FAUSTINA

2065

Third wife of Elagabalus, married in A.D. 221 *but soon divorced.*

R.I.C. and B.M.C. references are to the coinage of Elagabalus.

2064 **Æ denarius.** ANNIA FAVSTINA AVG. Dr. bust, r. ℞. CONCORDIA.
Elagabalus and Faustina stg. facing each other, clasping r. hands. *C.* 1.
R.I.C. 232. *B.M.C.,* p. 570, † .. .. *Excessively rare*
2065 **Æ sestertius.** ANNIA FAVSTINA AVGVSTA. Diad. and dr. bust, r. ℞.
CONCORDIA S . C. As previous. *C.* 2. *R.I.C.* 399. *B.M.C.* 450.
Illustrated above .. .. *Very rare*
2066 *Egypt, Alexandria,* **billon tetradrachm.** Dr. bust, r. ℞. Ares
stg. l., holding spear and parazonium. *B.M.C. G.*1551.. .. .. 25·00

JULIA SOAEMIAS

2072A

*The daughter of Julia Maesa and mother of Elagabalus, Julia Soaemias was, like her son,
fanatically devoted to the worship of the Sun-God Elagabalus. She was murdered at the
same time as her son in* A.D. 222.

The normal obv. legend is IVLIA SOAEMIAS AVG.

There are two main varieties of obv. type:

    a. Dr. bust, r.
    b. Diad. and dr. bust, r.

All *R.I.C. and B.M.C.* references are to the coinage of Elagabalus.

Very Fine

2067 *N* **aureus.** a. ℞. VENVS CAELESTIS. Venus stg. l., holding apple
and sceptre. *C.* 9. *R.I.C.* 240. *B.M.C.* 46 *note* .. .. 1750·00

Very Fine

2068 **Æ antoninianus.** Dr. bust r., resting on crescent. ℞. — Venus seated l., holding apple and sceptre, child at feet. *C.* 17. *R.I.C.* 245. *B.M.C.* 56 *note* .. .. *Very rare*

2069 **Æ denarius.** IVLIA SOAEMIAS AVGVSTA. a. ℞. IVNO REGINA. Juno stg. r., holding sceptre and palladium. *C.* 3. *R.I.C.* 237. *B.M.C.* 41 £17·50

2070 As 2067. *C.* 8. *R.I.C.* 241. *B.M.C.* 45 .. .. 12·50

2071 a. ℞. As 2068. *C.* 14. *R.I.C.* 243. *B.M.C.* 55 .. .. .. 12·50

2072 **Æ quinarius.** As 2067. *C.* 10. *R.I.C.* 242. *B.M.C.* 54 .. .. 175·00

2072A **Æ sestertius.** *Obv.* As 2069. ℞. MATER DEVM S . C. Cybele **Fine** seated l. on throne flanked by two lions, holding branch. *C.* 4. *R.I.C.* 400. *B.M.C.* 374. *Illustrated on p.* 205 .. .. 55·00

2073 b. ℞. VENVS CAELESTIS S . C. As 2068. *C.* 18. *R.I.C.* 406. *B.M.C.* 379 .. .. 35·00

2074 **Æ dupondius** or **as.** As 2072A. *C.* 5. *R.I.C.* 401. *B.M.C.* 383 .. 25·00

2075 b. ℞. VENVS CAELESTIS S . C. As 2067. *C.* 12. *R.I.C.* 403. *B.M.C.* 385 .. .. 15·00

2076 a. ℞. — As 2068. *C.* 20. *R.I.C.* 408. *B.M.C.* 387 *note* .. .. 15·00

2077 *Egypt, Alexandria,* **billon tetradrachm.** Dr. bust, r. ℞. Homonoia stg. l., holding double cornucopiae. *B.M.C.* G.1560 .. .. .. 12·50

JULIA MAESA

2089

The sister of Julia Domna and grandmother of Elagabalus and Severus Alexander, Julia Maesa was largely responsible for the rebellion which resulted in the overthrow of Macrinus and the restoration of the Severan Dynasty. She survived the assassination of Elagabalus and Soaemias in A.D. 222 and died about three years later during the reign of her younger grandson, Severus Alexander.

There are two varieties of obv. legend:

A. IVLIA MAESA AVG.
B. IVLIA MAESA AVGVSTA

There are two main varieties of obv. type:

a. Dr. bust, r.
b. Diad. and dr. bust, r.

All *R.I.C.* and *B.M.C.* references are to the coinage of Elagabalus.

Very Fine

2078 **N aureus.** Aa. ℞. IVNO. Juno stg. l., holding patera and sceptre. *C.* 15. *R.I.C.* 253. *B.M.C.* 66 .. .. 850·00

2079 **Æ antoninianus.** A. Diad. and dr. bust r., resting on crescent. ℞. PIETAS AVG. Pietas stg. l., altar at feet. *C.* 30. *R.I.C.* 264. *B.M.C.* 70 35·00

2080 **Æ denarius.** Aa. ℞. FECVNDITAS AVG. Fecunditas stg. l., holding cornucopiae, child at feet. *C.* 8. *R.I.C.* 249. *B.M.C.* 61 .. .. 10·00

2081 As 2078. *C.* 16. *R.I.C.* 254. *B.M.C.* 67 .. .. 10·00

Very Fine

2082 **Æ denarius.** Aa. ℞. As 2079. *C.* 29. *R.I.C.* 263. *B.M.C.* 73 £10·00
2083 Aa. ℞. PVDICITIA. Pudicitia seated l., holding sceptre. *C.* 36.
R.I.C. 268. *B.M.C.* 76 .. .. 10·00
2084 Aa. ℞. SAECVLI FELICITAS. Felicity stg. l., holding patera and
caduceus, altar at feet. *C.* 45. *R.I.C.* 271. *B.M.C.* 79. **Plate 7** .. 10·00
2085 **Æ quinarius.** As previous. *C.* 46. *R.I.C.* 273. *B.M.C.* 83.. .. 160·00

Fine

2086 **Æ sestertius.** Bb. ℞. PIETAS AVG . S . C. As 2079. *C.* 31.
R.I.C. 414. *B.M.C.* 390 .. .. 25·00
2087 Bb. ℞. PVDICITIA S . C. As 2083. *C.* 42. *R.I.C.* 420. *B.M.C.* 391 25·00
2088 Aa. ℞. SAECVLI FELICITAS S . C. As 2084. *C.* 47. *R.I.C.* 421.
B.M.C. 397 .. .. 25·00
2089 **Æ dupondius** or **as.** As 2086. *C.* 32. *R.I.C.* 415. *B.M.C.* 403 *note.*
Illustrated on p. 206 .. .. 12·50
2090 As 2088. *C.* 48. *R.I.C.* 423. *B.M.C.* 406 .. .. .. 12·50

Commemorative Coins struck after her death

Struck under Severus Alexander

2091 **Æ denarius.** DIVA MAESA AVG. Dr. bust r. ℞. CONSECRATIO.
Maesa seated l. on peacock flying r. *C.* 3. *R.I.C.* (*Sev. Alex.*) 378.
B.M.C. (*Sev. Alex.*) 217 .. .. *Very fine* £90·00
2092 **Æ sestertius.** DIVA MAESA AVGVSTA. Veiled and dr. bust, r. ℞.
CONSECRATIO S . C. Funeral-pyre of three tiers. *Cf. C.* 6. *R.I.C.* 712.
B.M.C. 218 .. .. 120·00

Colonial and Provincial Coinage

2093 *Egypt, Alexandria,* **billon tetradrachm.** Dr. bust, r. ℞. Bust of
Isis l. *B.M.C. G.*1575 .. .. 10·00

2175

SEVERUS ALEXANDER
A.D. 222-235

M. Aurelius Severus Alexander, originally named Alexianus, was born about A.D. 208,
*the son of Julia Mamaea and Gessius Marcianus. In 221 he was adopted by Elagabalus, his
cousin, and given the title of Caesar. After the murder of Elagabalus, Alexander was at once
acknowledged as emperor by the Praetorian guards, the Senate giving its confirmation the
following day. Alexander ruled the empire wisely and well and the condition of the State
was much improved, but the emperor was very much under the influence of his mother, and this
was greatly resented by the army. For the first nine years of the reign the Empire was
untroubled by foreign wars, but in 232 Alexander had to take the field against the Sassanid
Ardashir who had recently overthrown the Arsacid kingdom of Parthia and who was now
threatening Syria and Cappadocia. This campaign met with only partial success and
Alexander soon had to return to the West where disturbances on the German frontier necessitated his presence. However, before the fighting actually began the soldiers proclaimed
Maximinus, one of their commanders, emperor, and Alexander and Julia Mamaea were
murdered at their camp near Mainz (March 22nd,* A.D. 235).

Titles and Powers, A.D. 221-235

A.D.	Tribunician Power	Imperatorial Acclamation	Consulship	Other Titles
221				CAESAR.
222	TR.P.	IMP.	COS.	AVGVSTVS. P.M. P.P.
223	TR.P.II.			
224	TR.P.III.			
225	TR.P.IIII.			
226	TR.P.V.		COS.II.	
227	TR.P.VI.			
228	TR.P.VII.			
229	TR.P.VIII.		COS.III.	
230	TR.P.VIIII.			
231	TR.P.X.			PIVS.
232	TR.P.XI.			
233	TR.P.XII.			
234	TR.P.XIII.			
235	TR.P.XIIII.			

Alexander became TR.P.II. on January 1st, A.D. 223, and his tribunician power was subsequently renewed each year on that date.

Mints: Rome; Antioch.

As Caesar

A.D. 221-222, *under Elagabalus* **Very Fine**

B.M.C. references are to the coinage of Elagabalus.

2094 **N aureus.** M . AVR . ALEXANDER CAES. Bare-headed and dr. bust, r.
℞. INDVLGENTIA AVG. Spes advancing l. *C.* 66. *R.I.C.* 1. *B.M.C.*
264 *note* .. .. *Extr. rare*

2095 **R denarius.** As previous. *C.* 65. *R.I.C.* 2. *B.M.C.* 264 .. .. £65·00

2096 *Obv.* As previous. ℞. PIETAS AVG. Sacrificial implements. *C.* 198.
R.I.C. 3. *B.M.C.* 266 .. .. 75·00

Fine

2097 **Æ sestertius.** M . AVREL . ALEXANDER CAES. Bare-headed, dr. and
cuir. bust, r. ℞. PIETAS AVG . S . C. Sacrificial implements. *C.* 199.
R.I.C. 383. *B.M.C.* 452 .. .. 50·00

2098 **Æ as.** *Obv.* As 2094. ℞. PRINC . IVVENTVTIS S . C. Alexander stg.
l., holding rod and sceptre; to r., two standards. *C.* 485. *R.I.C.* 386.
B.M.C., p. 614, ‖ .. .. 37·50

As Augustus

The following are the commonest forms of obverse legend:

A. IMP . ALEXANDER PIVS AVG.
B. IMP . C . M . AVR . SEV . ALEXAND . AVG.
C. IMP . CAES . M . AVR . SEV . ALEXANDER AVG.
D. IMP . SEV . ALEXAND . AVG.
E. IMP . SEV . ALEXANDER AVG.

*The normal obv. type for all denominations except the dupondius is laur. hd. r., or laur.,
dr. and / or cuir. bust r. Dupondii have rad. hd. r., or rad. bust r., dr. or dr. and cuir.*

N.B. *No antoniniani were struck during this reign.*

2099　*N* **aureus.** A. ℞. IOVI PROPVGNATORI. Jupiter advancing l., hd.
turned, holding thunderbolt. *C.* 75. *R.I.C.* 234. *B.M.C.* 789 ..£250·00

2100　*N* **quinarius.** B. ℞. ANNONA AVG. Annona stg. l., modius at feet.
C. 22. *R.I.C.* 132. *B.M.C.* 340 *note* .. .. 400·00

2101　**Æ denarius.** D. ℞. ABVNDANTIA AVG. Abundance stg. r., emptying cornucopiae. *C.* 1. *R.I.C.* 184. *B.M.C.* 591 .. .. .. 4·50

2102　B. ℞. AEQVITAS AVG. Equity stg. l. *C.* 9. *R.I.C.* 127. *B.M.C.*
329 .. .. 3·75

2103　As 2100. *C.* 23. *R.I.C.* 133. *B.M.C.* 341 .. .. 3·75

2104　B. ℞. CONCORDIA. Concord seated l. *C.* 38. *R.I.C.* 275. *B.M.C.*
1050 .. .. 4·00

2105　B. ℞. FELICITAS AVG. Felicity stg. l., holding patera and caduceus,
altar at feet. *C.* 44. *R.I.C.* 137. *B.M.C.* 470 .. .. 5·00

2106　D. ℞. FIDES MILITVM. Fides seated l., holding two standards.
C. 51. *R.I.C.* 193. *B.M.C.* 684 .. .. 4·50

2107　A. ℞. FORTVNAE REDVCI. Fortune stg. l. *C.* 64. *R.I.C.* 232.
B.M.C. 765 .. .. 4·50

2108　B. ℞. IOVI CONSERVATORI. Jupiter stg. l., holding thunderbolt and
sceptre. *C.* 70. *R.I.C.* 141. *B.M.C.* 56 .. .. 4·00

2109　D. ℞. — As previous, but with small figure of Alexander at Jupiter's
feet. *C.* 73. *R.I.C.* 200. *B.M.C.* 690 .. .. 5·00

2110　As 2099. *C.* 76. *R.I.C.* 235. *B.M.C.* 790 .. .. .. 4·00

2111　D. ℞. IOVI STATORI. Jupiter stg. facing, hd. r., holding sceptre and
thunderbolt. *C.* 92. *R.I.C.* 202. *B.M.C.* 697 .. .. .. 5·00

2112　B. ℞. IOVI VLTORI. Jupiter seated l., holding Victory and sceptre.
C. 95. *R.I.C.* 144. *B.M.C.* 233 .. .. 4·00

2113　B. ℞. LIBERALITAS AVG. Liberalitas stg. l. *C.* 108. *R.I.C.* 148.
B.M.C. 6 .. .. 5·00

2114　D. ℞. LIBERTAS AVG. Liberty stg. l. *C.* 149. *R.I.C.* 285. *B.M.C.*
1012 .. .. 4·50

2115　A. ℞. MARS VLTOR. Mars advancing r., holding spear and shield.
C. 161. *R.I.C.* 246. *B.M.C.* 833 *note* .. .. 3·50

2116　B. ℞. PAX AETERNA AVG. Pax stg. l. *C.* 183. *R.I.C.* 165. *B.M.C.*
131 .. .. 3·50

2117　B. ℞. PAX AVG. Pax advancing l. *C.* 187. *R.I.C.* 168. *B.M.C.*
363 .. .. 3·50

2118　D. ℞. PERPETVITATI AVG. Perpetuitas (or Security) stg. l., holding
globe and sceptre and leaning on column. *C.* 191. *R.I.C.* 208.
B.M.C. 499 .. .. 6·00

2119　B. ℞. PIETAS AVG. Pietas stg. l., altar at feet. *C.* 196. *R.I.C.* 293.
B.M.C. 1058 .. .. 4·50

2120　B. ℞. P . M . TR . P . COS . P . P. As 2108. *C.* 204. *R.I.C.* 5.
B.M.C. 16 .. .. 3·50

2121　B. ℞. P . M . TR . P . II . COS . P . P. Mars stg. l., holding olive-branch
and spear. *C.* 231. *R.I.C.* 23. *B.M.C.* 92 .. .. .. 3·50

2122　B. ℞. P . M . TR . P . III . COS . P . P. Salus seated l., feeding serpent
arising from altar. *C.* 255. *R.I.C.* 42. *B.M.C.* 176 .. .. .. 3·75

2123　B. ℞. — Alexander stg. l., holding globe and spear. *C.* 256. *R.I.C.*
44. *B.M.C.* 178 .. .. 3·75

2124　B. ℞. P . M . TR . P . V . COS . II . P . P. Alexander stg. l., sacrificing
over tripod-altar. *C.* 289. *R.I.C.* 55. *B.M.C.* 373 .. .. 3·75

2125　B. ℞. P . M . TR . P . VI . COS . II . P . P. Mars advancing r., carrying
spear and trophy. *C.* 305. *R.I.C.* 61. *B.M.C.* 409 .. .. .. 3·75

Very Fine

2126 **Æ denarius.** B. ℞. P . M . TR . P . VII . COS . II . P . P. Equity stg. l. C. 346. *R.I.C.* 78. *B.M.C.* 449 ..   ..   £4·00

2127 D. ℞. — Romulus advancing r., carrying spear and trophy. *C.* 351. *R.I.C.* 85. *B.M.C.* 507 ..   ..   4·00

2128 D. ℞. P . M . TR . P . VIII . COS . III . P . P. Liberty stg. l. *C.* 371. *R.I.C.* 95. *B.M.C.* 568 ..   ..   4·00

2129 A. ℞. P . M . TR . P . X . COS . III . P . P. Sol stg. l., holding globe. *C.* 411. *R.I.C.* 109. *B.M.C.* 807 ..   ..   4·00

2130 A. ℞. P . M . TR . P . XIII . COS . III . P . P. Sol advancing l., holding whip. *C.* 448. *R.I.C.* 123. *B.M.C.* 950 ..   ..   3·75

2131 B. ℞. PROVID . DEORVM. Providence stg. l., globe at feet. *C.* 495. *R.I.C.* 294. *B.M.C.* 1062 ..   ..   4·50

2132 A. ℞. PROVIDENTIA AVG. As 2100. *C.* 501. *R.I.C.* 250. *B.M.C.* 875 ..   ..   4·50

2132A A. ℞. — Annona stg. l., holding corn-ears and anchor, modius at feet. *C.* 508. *R.I.C.* 252. *B.M.C.* 814 *note*. **Plate 7** ..   ..   4·50

2133 B. ℞. SALVS AVGVSTI. Salus stg. r., feeding serpent held in arms. *C.* 528. *R.I.C.* 176. *B.M.C.* 479 ..   ..   5·00

2134 B. ℞. SALVS PVBLICA. As 2122. *C.* 530. *R.I.C.* 178. *B.M.C.* 77   4·00

2135 A. ℞. SPES PVBLICA. Spes advancing l. *C.* 546. *R.I.C.* 254. *B.M.C.* 897 ..   ..   3·50

2136 D. ℞. VICTORIA AVG. Victory stg. l. *C.* 556. *R.I.C.* 212. *B.M.C.* 700 ..   ..   3·75

2137 D. ℞. VICTORIA AVGVSTI. Victory stg. r., inscribing VOT . X. on shield attached to palm-tree. *C.* 566. *R.I.C.* 218. *B.M.C.* 638 *note*   6·00

2138 B. ℞. VIRTVS AVG. Virtus stg. r., holding spear and leaning on shield. *C.* 576. *R.I.C.* 182. *B.M.C.* 278 ..   ..   ..   3·50

2139 D. ℞. — Virtus stg. l., holding Victory and leaning on shield, spear resting against l. arm. *C.* 579. *R.I.C.* 220. *B.M.C.* 709 ..   ..   4·50

2140 D. ℞. — Virtus seated l., holding branch and sceptre. *C.* 580. *R.I.C.* 221. *B.M.C.* 653 ..   ..   4·50

2141 D. ℞. — As 2127. *C.* 584. *R.I.C.* 224. *B.M.C.* 522 ..   ..   5·00

2142 D. ℞. — As 2123. *C.* 586. *R.I.C.* 226. *B.M.C.* 647 ..   ..   4·25

2143 **Æ quinarius.** As 2125. *C.* 306. *R.I.C.* 62. *B.M.C.* 414*   ..   65·00

Fine

2144 **Æ sestertius.** C. ℞. ANNONA AVGVSTI S . C. As 2100. *C.* 35. *R.I.C.* 548. *B.M.C.* 347 ..   ..   5·00

2145 C. ℞. FIDES MILITVM S . C. Fides stg. l., holding two standards. *C.* 54. *R.I.C.* 552. *B.M.C.* 228 *note* ..   ..   5·00

2146 E. ℞. IOVI CONSERVATORI S . C. As 2109. *C.* 74. *R.I.C.* 558. *B.M.C.* 692 *note* ..   ..   6·50

2147 A. ℞. IOVI PROPVGNATORI S. C. As 2099. *C.* 79. *R.I.C.* 628. *B.M.C.* 794 ..   ..   5·00

2148 E. ℞. IVSTITIA AVGVSTI S . C. Justitia seated l., holding patera and sceptre. *C.* 106. *R.I.C.* 563. *B.M.C.* 612 *note* ..   ..   7·50

2149 A. ℞. MARS VLTOR S . C. As 2115. *C.* 163. *R.I.C.* 635c. *B.M.C.* 840 *note* ..   ..   5·00

2150 C. ℞. MARTI PACIFERO S . C. As 2121. *C.* 176. *R.I.C.* 585. *B.M.C.* 74 ..   ..   5·00

2151 C. ℞. MONETA AVGVSTI S . C. Moneta stg. l. *C.* 179. *R.I.C.* 587. *B.M.C.* 204 ..   ..   5·50

Fine

2152 **Æ sestertius.** C. R. PAX AVGVSTI S . C. Pax advancing l. *C.* 189.
R.I.C. 592. *B.M.C.* 369 .. .. £5·00
2153 C. R. P . M . TR . P . COS . P . P . S . C. As 2122. *C.* 220. *R.I.C.* 393.
B.M.C. 39 .. .. 5·00
2154 C. R. P . M . TR . P . IIII . COS . P . P . S . C. As 2125. *C.* 262.
R.I.C. 424. *B.M.C.* 250 .. .. 5·00
2155 C. R. P . M . TR . P . VI . COS . II . P . P . S . C. Equity stg. l. *C.* 313.
R.I.C. 459. *B.M.C.* 399 .. .. 5·00
2156 C. R. P . M . TR . P . VII . COS . II . P . P . S . C. As 2127. *C.* 352.
R.I.C. 481. *B.M.C.* 474 .. .. 6·50
2157 C. R. — As 2124. *C.* 358. *R.I.C.* 484. *B.M.C.* 465 .. .. 6·00

2158   2178

2158 E. R. P . M . TR . P . VIII . COS . III . P . P . S . C. Alexander in quadriga r., holding eagle-tipped sceptre. *C.* 377. *R.I.C.* 495. *B.M.C.* 575 15·00
2159 E. R. P . M . TR . P . X . COS . III . P . P . S . C. Annona stg. l., holding
corn-ears and anchor, modius at feet. *C.* 422. *R.I.C.* 518. *B.M.C.*
739 *note* .. .. 5·00
2160 A. R. P . M . TR . P . XI . COS . III . P . P . S . C. As 2129. *C.* 429.
R.I.C. 528. *B.M.C.* 856 .. .. 5·00
2161 A. R. P . M . TR . P . XIIII . COS . III . P . P . S . C. As 2130. *C.* 454.
R.I.C. 541. *B.M.C.* 964 *note* .. .. 6·00
2162 C. R. PONTIF . MAX . TR . P . II . COS . P . P . S . C. Security seated l.,
holding sceptre, altar at feet. *C.* 463. *R.I.C.* 407. *B.M.C.* 123 *note* .. 5·00
2163 C. R. — View of the Coliseum in Rome, showing two gladiators in
the arena. *C.* 468. *R.I.C.* 410. *B.M.C.* 156 *note* .. .. 200·00
2164 C. R. PONTIF . MAX . TR . P . III . COS . P . P . S . C. As 2123. *C.* 475.
R.I.C. 419. *B.M.C.* 184 *note* .. .. 5·00
2165 A. R. PROVIDENTIA AVG . S . C. As 2159. *C.* 509. *R.I.C.* 645.
B.M.C. 815 .. .. 5·00
2166 C. R. PROVIDENTIA DEORVM S . C. Providence stg. l., holding rod
and cornucopiae and leaning on column, globe at feet. *C.* 513. *R.I.C.*
597. *B.M.C.* 141 *note* .. .. 5·00
2167 C. R. SALVS PVBLICA S . C. As 2122. *C.* 533. *R.I.C.* 608. *B.M.C.*
83 .. .. 5·00
2168 A. R. SPES PVBLICA S . C. Spes advancing l. *C.* 547. *R.I.C.* 648.
B.M.C. 904 *note* .. .. 5·00
2169 E. R. VICTORIA AVGVSTI S . C. As 2137. *C.* 567. *R.I.C.* 616.
B.M.C. 642 .. .. 6·50
2170 E. R. — Victory stg. l. *C.* 569. *R.I.C.* 618. *B.M.C.* 704 *note* .. 5·00
2171 C. R. VIRTVS AVGVSTI S . C. As 2138. *C.* 588. *R.I.C.* 623.
B.M.C. 284 .. .. 5·00

Fine

2172 **Æ dupondius.** A. ℞. IOVI PROPVGNATORI S . C. Jupiter advancing l., hd. turned, holding thunderbolt and eagle. *C.* 88. *R.I.C.* 632. *B.M.C.* 827* ..   ..   £6·50

2173 A. ℞. MARS VLTOR S . C. As 2115. *C.* 164. *R.I.C.* 636. *B.M.C.* 844* ..   ..   6·50

2174 A. ℞. P . M . TR . P . XII . COS . III . P . P . S . C. As 2130. *C.* 444. *R.I.C.* 536. *B.M.C.* 938 *note* ..   ..   8·00

2175 E. ℞. RESTITVTOR MON . S . C. Alexander stg. l., holding sceptre. *C.* 517. *R.I.C.* 601. *B.M.C.* 546. *Illustrated on p.* 207   ..   ..   12·00

2176 **Æ as.** A. ℞. IOVI PROPVGNATORI S . C. As 2099. *C.* 80. *R.I.C.* 630. *B.M.C.* 798 ..   ..   6·50

2177 C. ℞. P . M . TR . P . IIII . COS . P . P . S . C. As 2145. *C.* 264. *R.I.C.* 430. *B.M.C.* 243 ..   ..   6·50

2178 C. ℞. P . M . TR . P . V . COS . II . P . P . S . C. The Thermae of Alexander, represented as an archway set on an arched portico which is flanked on either side by wings; in front is a semicircular basin. *C.* 300. *R.I.C.* 450. *B.M.C.* 325. *Illustrated on p.* 211 ..   ..   ..   65·00

2179 As 2158. *C.* 378. *R.I.C.* 498. *B.M.C.* 582 ..   ..   ..   12·50

2180 C. ℞. PONTIF . MAX . TR . P . II . COS . P . P . S . C. Pax seated l., holding olive-branch and sceptre. *C.* 467. *R.I.C.* 403. *B.M.C.* 109 ..   6·50

2181 As 2166. *C.* 514. *R.I.C.* 599. *B.M.C.* 144* ..   ..   ..   6·50

2182 As 2168. *C.* 550. *R.I.C.* 650. *B.M.C.* 910 ..   ..   ..   6·50

Commemorative Coins struck after his death

Struck under Trajan Decius

2183 **Æ antoninianus.** DIVO ALEXANDRO. Rad. hd., r. ℞. CONSECRATIO. Large altar. *C.* 597. *R.I.C.* (*Dec.*) 98 ..   ..   10·00

2184 — ℞. — Eagle stg. r., hd. turned. *C.* 599. *R.I.C.* (*Dec.*) 97..   ..   10·00

Colonial and Provincial Coinage

2185 *Thrace, Byzantium,* Æ **30.** Laur. hd., r. ℞. Agonistic urn containing two palms. *Cf. B.M.C. G.*98 ..   ..   7·50

2186 *Ionia, Ephesus,* Æ **16.** Laur. bust, r. ℞. Stag stg. r. *B.M.C. G.*321   3·75

2187 — *Magnesia ad Maeandrum,* Æ **24.** Laur. and dr. bust, r. ℞. Eagle stg. r. *B.M.C. G.*71   ..   ..   3·75

2188 *Cilicia, Aegeae,* Æ **24.** — ℞. Bust of Athena l. *B.M.C. G.*36   ..   5·00

2189 *Syria, Seleuceia Pieria,* Æ **30.** Laur. bust, r. ℞. Sacred stone of Zeus Kasios within tetrastyle temple. *B.M.C. G.*58 ..   ..   ..   5·00

2190 *Mesopotamia, Carrhae,* Æ **24.** Rad. bust, r. ℞. Tyche seated l. *B.M.C. G.*52 ..   ..   3·75

2191 — *Nisibis,* Æ **27.** Laur. bust, r. ℞. Bust of Tyche r. *B.M.C. G.*4   5·50

2192 *Egypt, Alexandria,* **billon tetradrachm.** Bare-headed, dr. and cuir. bust, r. ℞. Serapis stg. r. *B.M.C. G.*1585 (*as Caesar*)   ..   8·00

2193 — Laur. dr. and cuir. bust, r. ℞. Laur. hd. of Zeus r. *B.M.C. G.*1591   ..   ..   4·50

2194 — — ℞. Rad. bust of Helios r. *B.M.C. G.*1599   ..   ..   4·50

2195 — — ℞. Dikaiosyne stg. l. *B.M.C. G.*1614 ..   ..   ..   3·25

2196 — Laur. and cuir bust, r. ℞. Jugate busts of Serapis and Isis r. *B.M.C. G.*1666   ..   ..   5·00

2197 — Laur., dr. and cuir. bust, r. ℞. Alexandria stg. l., holding corn-ears and vexillum. *B.M.C. G.*1687   ..   ..   3·75

ORBIANA

2202

Sallustia Barbia Orbiana was married to Severus Alexander about A.D. 225. *Julia Mamaea, however, soon became jealous of her daughter-in-law and compelled Alexander to banish her to Africa.*

All have obv. legend SALL . BARBIA ORBIANA AVG.

All have obv. type Diad. and dr. bust, r.

All *R.I.C.* and *B.M.C.* references are to the coinage of Severus Alexander.

Very Fine

2198	Æ **aureus.** Ŗ. CONCORDIA AVGVSTORVM. Concord seated l., holding patera and double cornucopiae. *C.* 3. *R.I.C.* 321. *B.M.C.* 292	£1500·00
2199	Æ **denarius.** Ŗ. CONCORDIA AVGG. As previous. *C.* 1. *R.I.C.* 319. *B.M.C.* 287. **Plate 7**	45·00
2200	Æ **quinarius.** Ŗ. — As previous. *C.* 2. *R.I.C.* 320. *B.M.C.* 291	300·00

Fine

2201	Æ **sestertius.** Ŗ. CONCORDIA AVGVSTORVM S . C. As previous. *C.* 4. *R.I.C.* 655. *B.M.C.* 293	50·00
2202	Ŗ. — Alexander and Orbiana stg. facing each other, clasping r. hands. *C.* 6. *R.I.C.* 657. *B.M.C.* 299. *Illustrated above*	65·00
2203	Æ **as.** Ŗ. — As 2198. *C.* 5. *R.I.C.* 656. *B.M.C.* 297	30·00

JULIA MAMAEA

2225

The daughter of Julia Maesa and mother of Severus Alexander, Julia Mamaea was, during the reign of her son, the real power behind the throne. She exercised a strict control over the young emperor and even selected a wife for him, but she soon disposed of her protégé when she considered that she was gaining too much influence over Alexander. Julia Mamaea was murdered with her son on March 22nd, A.D. 235.

There are two varieties of obverse legend:

A. IVLIA MAMAEA AVG.

B. IVLIA MAMAEA AVGVSTA.

There are two main varieties of obverse type:
- a.   Dr. bust, r.
- b.   Diad. and dr. bust, r.

All *R.I.C.* and *B.M.C.* references are to the coinage of Severus Alexander.

Very Fine

2204 **Aʹ aureus.** Ab. R. VESTA. Vesta stg. l., holding palladium and sceptre. *C.* 80. *R.I.C.* 359. *B.M.C.* 380 ..   ..£750·00

2205 **Aʹ quinarius.** Ab. R. VENVS VICTRIX. Venus stg. l., holding helmet and sceptre, shield at feet. *C.* 75. *R.I.C.* 357. *B.M.C.* 712*   900·00

2206 **Æ denarius.** Ab. R. FECVND . AVGVSTAE. Fecunditas stg. l., holding cornucopiae, child at feet. *C.* 5. *R.I.C.* 331. *B.M.C.* 917 ..   7·00

2207 Ab. R. FELICITAS PVBLICA. Felicity stg. facing, hd. l., holding caduceus and leaning on column. *C.* 17. *R.I.C.* 335. *B.M.C.* 483   6·50

2208 Ab. R. — Felicity seated l. *C.* 24. *R.I.C.* 338. *B.M.C.* 658   ..   7·00

2209 Ab. R. IVNO AVGVSTAE. Juno seated l., holding flower and child. *C.* 32. *R.I.C.* 341. *B.M.C.* 755 ..   ..   7·50

2210 Aa. R. IVNO CONSERVATRIX. Juno stg. l., peacock at feet. *C.* 35. *R.I.C.* 343. *B.M.C.* 43 ..   ..   6·50

2211 Ab. R. VENERI FELICI. Venus stg. r., holding sceptre and Cupid. *C.* 60. *R.I.C.* 351. *B.M.C.* 189 ..   ..   7·00

2212 Ab. R. VENVS GENETRIX. Venus stg. l., holding apple and sceptre, Cupid at feet. *C.* 72. *R.I.C.* 355. *B.M.C.* 152   ..   ..   ..   7·00

2213 As 2205. *C.* 76. *R.I.C.* 358. *B.M.C.* 713   ..   ..   7·00

2214 As 2204. *C.* 81. *R.I.C.* 360. *B.M.C.* 381   ..   ..   6·50

2215 Ab. R. VESTA. Vesta stg. l., holding patera and sceptre. *C.* 85. *R.I.C.* 362. *B.M.C.* 440 ..   ..   7·00

2216 **Æ quinarius.** As 2207. *C.* 19. *R.I.C.* 336. *B.M.C.* 486 ..   .. 150·00

Fine

2217 **Æ sestertius.** Bb. R. FECVNDITAS AVGVSTAE S . C. As 2206. *C.* 8. *R.I.C.* 608. *B.M.C.* 920 ..   ..   6·50

2218 Bb. R. FELICITAS PVBLICA S . C. As 2207. *C.* 21. *R.I.C.* 676. *B.M.C.* 487. **Plate 8**   ..   ..   6·00

2219 Bb. R. — Felicity seated l. *C.* 26. *R.I.C.* 679. *B.M.C.* 661   ..   6·00

2220 Bb. R. IVNO AVGVSTAE S . C. As 2209. *C.* 33. *R.I.C.* 683. *B.M.C.* 759 ..   ..   7·00

2221 Ab. R. IVNO CONSERVATRIX S . C. As 2210. *C.* 39. *R.I.C.* 685. *B.M.C.* 51 *note*   ..   ..   7·50

2222 Bb. R. VENERI FELICI S . C. As 2211. *C.* 62. *R.I.C.* 694. *B.M.C.* 190 ..   ..   6·00

2223 Bb. R. VENVS FELIX S . C. Venus seated l., holding statuette and sceptre. *C.* 69. *R.I.C.* 701. *B.M.C.* 197   ..   ..   6·00

2224 Bb. R. VENVS GENETRIX S . C. Venus stg. l., holding apple and sceptre, child at feet. *C.* 74. *R.I.C.* 704. *B.M.C.* 154   ..   ..   ..   6·00

2225 Bb. R. VENVS VICTRIX S . C. As 2205. *C.* 78. *R.I.C.* 705. *B.M.C.* 719. *Illustrated on p.* 213 ..   ..   6·00

Fine

2226 **Æ sestertius.** Bb. ℞. VESTA S . C. As 2204. *C.* 83. *R.I.C.* 708.
B.M.C. 389 .. .. £6·00
2227 Bb. ℞. — As 2215. *C.* 88. *R.I.C.* 710. *B.M.C.* 445 .. .. 6·00
2228 **Æ dupondius.** B. Diad. and dr. bust r., resting on crescent. ℞.
FELICITAS PVBLICA S . C. As 2207. *C.* 23. *R.I.C.* 678. *B.M.C.* 493 10·00
2229 **Æ dupondius or as.** As 2223. *C.* 70. *R.I.C.* 702. *B.M.C.* 202 .. 7·50
2230 Bb. ℞. VENVS VICTRIX S . C. As 2205. *C.* 79. *R.I.C.* 706.
B.M.C. 723 .. .. 7·50

Colonial and Provincial Coinage

2231 *Pisidia, Baris,* **Æ 26.** Dr. bust, r. ℞. Tyche seated l. *Grose* 8974 6·50
2232 *Syria, Antioch,* **Æ 30.** — ℞. Tyche of Antioch seated l. *B.M.C.*
G. 491 .. .. 5·50
2233 *Arabia Petraea, Bostra,* **Æ 18.** — ℞. Bust of Tyche l. *B.M.C.*
G. 34 .. .. 6·00
2234 *Egypt, Alexandria,* **billon tetradrachm.** Diad. and dr. bust, r. ℞.
Homonoia stg. l., holding double cornucopiae. *B.M.C. G.* 1737 .. 6·00

MAXIMINUS I
A.D. 235-238

2255

(*C. Julius Verus Maximinus*) *Of Thracian peasant stock, and a man of great stature
and physical strength, Maximinus joined the ranks of the Roman army druing the reign of
Septimius Severus. He gained rapid promotion until, during the reign of Severus Alexander,
he was given the command of a legion and later the governorship of Mesopotamia.* In A.D.
235 *he was in charge of levies of recruits on the Rhine, and on March 22nd he was proclaimed
emperor by the army which had grown impatient of the unwarlike character of Severus
Alexander. He campaigned against the Germans with considerable success, but his reign
was characterized by his hatred of the nobility and ruthless cruelty towards anyone suspected
of conspiring against him. The abortive rebellion of the Gordiani in Africa, in March 238,
was soon followed by a similar defection in Rome, when Balbinus and Pupienus were elected
joint emperors by the Senate. Maximinus thereupon invaded Italy, but his advance was
delayed by an unsuccessful siege of Aquileia and his troops finally mutinied and murdered
both him and his son Maximus on June 24th, 238.*

Titles and Powers, A.D. 235-238

A.D.	Tribunician Power	Imperatorial Acclamation	Consulship	Other Titles
235	TR.P.	IMP.		AVGVSTVS. P.M. P.P.
236	TR.P.II.		COS.	GERM.
237	TR.P.III.			
238	TR.P.IIII.			

Maximinus became TR.P.II. on January 1st, A.D. 236, and his tribunician power was
subsequently renewed each year on that date.

Mint: Rome.

There are two varieties of obverse legend:

    A. IMP . MAXIMINVS PIVS AVG.
    B. MAXIMINVS PIVS AVG . GERM.

The normal obverse type for all denominations except the dupondius is laur., dr. and cuir. bust, r. Dupondii have rad., dr. and cuir. bust, r.

N.B. *No antoniniani were struck during this reign.*

Very Fine

2235 N aureus. A. ℞. VICTORIA AVG. Victory advancing r. *C.* 98.
    R.I.C. 16. *B.M.C.* 104* .. ..£750·00

2236 N quinarius. B. ℞. VICTORIA GERM. Victory stg. l., captive at feet.
    C. 105. *R.I.C.* 23. *B.M.C.* 185 .. .. 900·00

2237 R denarius. A. ℞. FIDES MILITVM. Fides stg. l., holding two
    standards. *C.* 7. *R.I.C.* 7A. *B.M.C.* 1 .. .. 6·00
2238 A. ℞. LIBERALITAS AVG. Liberalitas stg. l. *C.* 19. *R.I.C.* 10.
    B.M.C. 45 .. .. 10·00
2239 A. ℞. PAX AVGVSTI. Pax stg. l. *C.* 31. *R.I.C.* 12. *B.M.C.* 68 .. 6·00
2240 B. ℞. As previous. *C.* 37. *R.I.C.* 19. *B.M.C.* 144 .. .. 6·00
2241 A. ℞. P . M . TR . P . P . P. Maximinus stg. l. between two standards,
    holding spear. *C.* 46. *R.I.C.* 1. *B.M.C.* 11 .. .. 7·50
2242 A. ℞. P . M . TR . P . II . COS . P . P. As previous. *C.* 55. *R.I.C.* 3.
    B.M.C. 77 .. .. 7·50
2243 B. ℞. P . M . TR . P . III . COS . P . P. As previous. *C.* 64. *R.I.C.* 5.
    B.M.C. 161 .. .. 8·50
2244 B. ℞. P . M . TR . P . IIII . COS . P . P. As previous. *C.* 70. *R.I.C.* 6.
    B.M.C. 219 .. .. 10·50
2245 A. ℞. PROVIDENTIA AVG. Providence stg. l., globe at feet. *C.* 77.
    R.I.C. 13. *B.M.C.* 86. **Plate 8** .. .. 6·00
2246 B. ℞. SALVS AVGVSTI. Salus seated l., feeding serpent arising from
    altar. *C.* 91. *R.I.C.* 21. *B.M.C.* 173* .. .. 10·00
2247 As 2235. *C.* 99. *R.I.C.* 16. *B.M.C.* 25 .. .. 7·50
2248 As 2236. *C.* 107. *R.I.C.* 23. *B.M.C.* 186 .. .. 9·00

2249 R quinarius. As 2245. *C.* 78. *R.I.C.* 13. *B.M.C.* 89 .. .. 250·00

Fine

2250 Æ sestertius. A. ℞. FIDES MILITVM S . C. As 2237. *C.* 10.
    R.I.C. 43. *B.M.C.* 2 .. .. 6·00
2251 A. ℞. INDVLGENTIA AVG . S . C. Indulgence seated l., holding sceptre.
    C. 17. *R.I.C.* 46. *B.M.C.* 32* .. .. 10·00
2252 A. ℞. LIBERALITAS AVGVSTI S . C. Liberalitas stg. l. *C.* 26. *R.I.C.*
    53. *B.M.C.* 46 .. .. 7·50
2253 B. ℞. PAX AVGVSTI S . C. Pax stg. l. *C.* 38. *R.I.C.* 81. *B.M.C.*
    148 .. .. 6·00
2254 A. ℞. PROVIDENTIA AVG . S . C. As 2245. *C.* 80. *R.I.C.* 61. *B.M.C.*
    17 .. .. 6·00
2255 B. ℞. SALVS AVGVSTI S . C. As 2246. *C.* 92. *R.I.C.* 85. *B.M.C.*
    175. *Illustrated on p. 215* .. .. 6·00
2256 A. ℞. VICTORIA AVG . S . C. Victory advancing r. *C.* 100. *R.I.C.*
    67. *B.M.C.* 27 .. .. 6·00
2257 B. ℞. VICTORIA GERMANICA S . C. As 2236. *C.* 109. *R.I.C.* 90*.
    B.M.C. 191 .. .. 7·50
2258 B. ℞. — Maximinus stg. l., crowned by Victory who stands beside
    him. *C.* 114. *R.I.C.* 93. *B.M.C.* 198 .. .. 17·50

Fine

2259 **Æ dupondius.** B. ℞. As 2253. *C.* 40. *R.I.C.* 82. *B.M.C.* 153 £9·00

2260 A. ℞. PROVIDENTIA AVG . S . C. As 2245. *C.* 82. *R.I.C.* 62.
B.M.C. 18 .. .. 9·00

2261 A. ℞. SALVS AVGVSTI S . C. As 2246. *C.* 90. *R.I.C.* 65. *B.M.C.*
102 .. .. 9·00

2262 **Æ as.** A. ℞. FIDES MILITVM S . C. As 2237. *C.* 11. *R.I.C.* 45.
B.M.C. 66 .. .. 9·00

2263 As 2256. *C.* 101. *R.I.C.* 69. *B.M.C.* 29 .. .. 9·00

Colonial and Provincial Coinage

2264 *Egypt, Alexandria,* **billon tetradrachm.** Laur., dr. and cuir bust, r.
℞. Bust of Hermanubis r. *B.M.C.* G.1798 .. .. .. 5·00

2265 — — ℞. Nilus reclining l. *B.M.C.* G.1802 .. .. .. 5·00

2266 — — ℞. Trophy between two captives. *B.M.C.* G.1809 .. .. 5·00

PAULINA

2268

The wife of Maximinus, she died either before, or shortly after, his accession, as all her coins are commemorative.

B.M.C. references are to the coinage of Maximinus.

Very Fine

2267 **N aureus.** DIVA PAVLINA. Veiled and dr. bust, r. ℞. CONSECRATIO.
Paulina seated l. on peacock flying r. *R.I.C.* 2. *B.M.C.* 126* .. *Unique*

2268 **Æ denarius.** — ℞. — Peacock stg. facing, hd. l., tail in splendour.
C. 1. *R.I.C.* 1. *B.M.C.* 135. *Illustrated above* .. .. .. 75·00

2269 As 2267. *C.* 2. *R.I.C.* 2. *B.M.C.* 127 .. .. 65·00

2270 **Æ sestertius.** As 2267, but with S . C. added on *rev. C.* 3. *R.I.C.* 3.
B.M.C. 129 .. .. *Fine* £65·00

MAXIMUS

Caesar, A.D. 235-238

2276

(C. Julius Verus Maximus) The son of Maximinus, Maximus was probably given the rank of Caesar at the same time as his father became Augustus. He was murdered with his father near Aquileia on June 24th, 238.

All coins have as obverse type bare-headed and dr. bust, r.

B.M.C. references are to the coinage of Maximinus.

Very Fine

2271 **N aureus.** MAXIMVS CAES . GERM. R. PRINCIPI IVVENTVTIS. Maximus stg. l., holding rod and spear; to r., two standards. *R.I.C.* 5. *B.M.C.* 210* .. .. *Unique*

2272 **Æ denarius.** IVL . VERVS MAXIMVS CAES. R. PIETAS AVG. Sacrificial implements. *C.* 1. *R.I.C.* 1. *B.M.C.* 118 .. .. £27·50

2273 MAXIMVS CAES . GERM. R. As previous. *C.* 3. *R.I.C.* 2. *B.M.C.* 201 32·50

2274 — R. PRINC . IVVENTVTIS. As 2271. *C.* 10. *R.I.C.* 3. *B.M.C.* 211. **Plate 8** .. .. 25·00

2275 **Æ quinarius.** As previous. *R.I.C.* 3. *B.M.C.*— .. .. *Extr. rare*

Fine

2276 **Æ sestertius.** C . IVL . VERVS MAXIMVS CAES. R. PIETAS AVG . S . C. Sacrificial implements. *C.* 5. *R.I.C.* 6. *B.M.C.* 119. *Illustrated on p.* 217 .. .. 15·00

2277 — R. PRINCIPI IVVENTVTIS S . C. As 2271. *C.* 12. *R.I.C.* 9. *B.M.C.* 123 .. .. 12·50

2278 MAXIMVS CAES . GERM. R. As previous. *C.* 14. *R.I.C.* 13. *B.M.C.* 213 .. .. 12·50

2279 **Æ dupondius** or **as.** — R. As 2276. *C.* 8. *R.I.C.* 12. *B.M.C.* 201 *note* .. .. 14·00

2280 C . IVL . VERVS MAXIMVS CAES. R. PRINCIPI IVVENTVTIS S . C. As 2271. *C.* 13. *R.I.C.* 10. *B.M.C.* 125 .. .. 14·00

2281 *Egypt, Alexandria,* **billon tetradrachm.** Bare-headed, dr. and cuir. bust, r. R. Nilus reclining l. *B.M.C. G.*1821 .. .. .. 7·50

GORDIAN I AFRICANUS
A.D. 238

2282

(*M. Antonius Gordianus*). *Born about* A.D. 157, *the elder Gordian was distinguished for intellectual and moral excellence, and in the reign of Maximinus was proconsul in Africa. When, in* A.D. 238, *a rebellion broke out in the province against the tyranny of the emperor, Gordian was petitioned to accept the purple, and, although in his eighty-first year, he agreed (March 22nd). He associated his son with him as joint ruler, and a deputation was sent to Rome to ask for the confirmation of the Senate. This was readily granted and Maximinus declared a public enemy; but before the deputies could return to Africa both the Gordians had perished. Capellianus, the governor of Numidia, had remained faithful to Maximinus and marched upon Carthage which had been chosen as the seat of the new government. The younger Gordian, with such troops as he could muster, went out to meet him, but was killed in the ensuing battle. When the news of his son's death reached the elder Gordian he committed suicide after a reign of only twenty-one days (April 12th).*

Mint: Rome.

2282 **N aureus.** IMP . CAES . M . ANT . GORDIANVS AFR . AVG. Laur., dr. and cuir. bust, r. R. ROMAE AETERNAE. Roma seated l., holding Victory and sceptre. *C.* 7. *R.I.C.* 3. *B.M.C.* 7*. *Illustrated above* .. *Extr. rare*

Very Fine

2283 **Æ denarius.** IMP . M . ANT . GORDIANVS AFR . AVG. Type as previous.
R. P . M . TR . P . COS . P . P. Gordian stg. l., holding branch and
sceptre. *C.* 2. *R.I.C.* 1. *B.M.C.* 1 .. ..£135·00

2284 — R. As 2282. *C.* 8. *R.I.C.* 4. *B.M.C.* 8 .. .. 135·00

Fine

2285 **Æ sestertius.** *Obv.* As 2282. R. VICTORIA AVGG . S . C. Victory
advancing l. *C.* 14. *R.I.C.* 12. *B.M.C.* 14 .. .. 100·00

2286 — R. VIRTVS AVGG . S . C. Virtus stg. l., leaning on shield and
holding spear. *C.* 15. *R.I.C.* 14. *B.M.C.* 17.. .. .. .. 100·00

2287 *Egypt, Alexandria,* **billon tetradrachm.** Laur., dr. and cuir. bust, r.
R. Zeus seated l., eagle at feet. *B.M.C. G.* 1824 .. .. .. 20·00

GORDIAN II AFRICANUS
A.D. 238

2290

(*M. Antonius Gordianus*) *The son of Gordian I, Gordian II was born about* A.D. 192
*and was made co-emperor by his father immediately after the latter's elevation. He was
killed in battle on April 12th, 238, as related above.*

Mint: Rome.

Very Fine

2288 **Æ denarius.** IMP . M . ANT . GORDIANVS AFR . AVG. Laur., dr. and
cuir. bust, r. R. PROVIDENTIA AVGG. Providence stg. l., holding
rod and cornucopiae and leaning on column, globe at feet. *C.* 5.
R.I.C. 1. *B.M.C.* 19 .. .. 150·00

2289 — R. VICTORIA AVGG. Victory advancing l. *C.* 12. *R.I.C.* 2.
B.M.C. 28 .. .. 150·00

Fine

2290 **Æ sestertius.** IMP . CAES . M . ANT . GORDIANVS AFR . AVG. Type as
previous. R. ROMAE AETERNAE S . C. Roma seated l., holding Victory
and sceptre. *C.* 9. *R.I.C.* 5. *B.M.C.* 23. *Illustrated above* .. 110·00

2291 — R. VICTORIA AVGG . S . C. Victory advancing l. *C.* 13. *R.I.C.* 7.
B.M.C. 29* .. .. 110·00

2292 *Egypt, Alexandria,* **billon tetradrachm.** Laur., dr. and cuir. bust, r.
R. Nike seated l. *B.M.C. G.* 1833 .. .. 22·50

Although it is not always easy to distinguish between the coins of Gordian I and
Gordian II, with good specimens there should be no difficulty. The face of the elder
man is somewhat thinner and his hair well on to his forehead; but the younger Gordian
is depicted with a bald forehead, little or no hair showing in front of the laurel wreath.

BALBINUS
A.D. 238

2302

(*Decimus Caelius Balbinus*) *The Senate, having been informed of the deaths of the Gordiani and realizing that they had now incurred the active enmity of Maximinus, elected two of their number, Balbinus and Pupienus, as joint rulers. To the former was given the task of directing the civil administration, whilst the latter gathered troops to oppose Maximinus' advance upon Rome. Although Maximinus was checked, and ultimately murdered by his own men, neither the citizens nor the army had any love for their two new rulers, and after a period of civil strife and disorder the Praetorians invaded the palace, dragged out the two emperors and murdered them, after a reign of ninety-eight days (July 29th 238).*

Mint: Rome.

There are two varieties of obverse legend:
A. IMP . C . D . CAEL . BALBINVS AVG.
B. IMP . CAES . D . CAEL . BALBINVS AVG.

Antoniniani and dupondii have rad., dr. and cuir. bust r., whilst all other denominations have laur., dr. and cuir. bust r.

Very Fine

2293 **N aureus.** B. ℞. VICTORIA AVGG. Victory stg. facing, hd. l.
R.I.C. 9. *B.M.C.* 36* .. .. *Extr. rare*

2294 **Æ antoninianus.** B. ℞. CONCORDIA AVGG. Clasped hands. *C.* 3.
R.I.C. 10. *B.M.C.* 67 .. .. £25·00

2295 B. ℞. FIDES MVTVA AVGG. Clasped hands. *C.* 6. *R.I.C.* 11.
B.M.C. 71 .. .. 25·00

2296 B. ℞. PIETAS MVTVA AVGG. Clasped hands. *C.* 17. *R.I.C.* 12.
B.M.C. 74 .. .. 30·00

2297 **Æ denarius.** A. ℞. P . M . TR . P . COS . II . P . P. Balbinus stg. l.,
holding branch and sceptre. *C.* 20. *R.I.C.* 5. *B.M.C.* 26 .. .. 30·00

2298 A. ℞. PROVIDENTIA DEORVM. Providence stg. l., globe at feet.
C. 23. *R.I.C.* 7. *B.M.C.* 33 .. .. 30·00

2299 A. ℞. VICTORIA AVGG. Victory stg. facing, hd. l. *C.* 27. *R.I.C.* 8.
B.M.C. 37. **Plate 8** .. .. 30·00

2300 **Æ quinarius.** As previous. *C.* 28. *R.I.C.* 8. *B.M.C.* 39 .. *Unique*

Fine

2301 **Æ sestertius.** B. ℞. CONCORDIA AVGG . S . C. Concord seated l.
C. 4. *R.I.C.* 22. *B.M.C.* 18 .. .. 30·00

2302 B. ℞. LIBERALITAS AVGVSTORVM S . C. Balbinus, Pupienus and
Gordian III seated l. on platform, accompanied by Liberalitas and
soldier; to l., citizen mounting steps of platform. *C.* 13. *R.I.C.* 14.
B.M.C. 5. *Illustrated above* .. .. 100·00

Fine

2303 **Æ sestertius.** B. ℞. P . M . TR . P . COS . II . P . P . S . C. As 2297.
C. 21. *R.I.C.* 16. *B.M.C.* 28 .. .. £30·00

2304 B. ℞. PROVIDENTIA DEORVM S . C. As 2298. *C.* 24. *R.I.C.* 19.
B.M.C. 34 .. .. 30·00

2305 **Æ dupondius.** B. ℞. IOVI CONSERVATORI S . C. Jupiter stg. l.,
holding thunderbolt and sceptre. *C.* 9. *R.I.C.* 13. *B.M.C.* 23 .. 75·00

2306 **Æ as.** As 2301. *C.* 5. *R.I.C.* 23. *B.M.C.* 21 .. .. .. 85·00

2307 *Egypt, Alexandria,* **billon tetradrachm.** Laur., dr. and cuir. bust, r.
℞. Tyche stg. l. *B.M.C. G.* 1845 .. .. 20·00

PUPIENUS
A.D. 238

2317

(*M. Clodius Pupienus Maximus*) *Elected joint emperor with Balbinus by the Senate, Pupienus was a man of very considerable military experience, although of humbler origin than his colleague. He was murdered with Balbinus on July 29th, 238, as related above.*

Mint: Rome.

There are three varieties of obverse legend:

A. IMP . C . M . CLOD . PVPIENVS AVG.
B. IMP . CAES . M . CLOD . PVPIENVS AVG.
C. IMP . CAES . PVPIEN . MAXIMVS AVG.

Antoniniani and dupondii have rad., dr. and cuir. bust r., whilst all other denominations have laur., dr. and cuir. bust r.

Very Fine

2308 **N aureus.** B. ℞. VICTORIA AVGG. Victory stg. facing, hd. l.
C. 37. *R.I.C.* 8A. *B.M.C.* 57* .. .. *Extr. rare*

2309 **R antoninianus.** B. ℞. AMOR MVTVVS AVGG. Clasped hands.
C. 1. *R.I.C.* 9a. *B.M.C.* 77 .. .. 25·00

2310 C. ℞. As previous. *C.* 2. *R.I.C.* 9b. *B.M.C.* 82 .. .. .. 25·00

2311 B. ℞. CARITAS MVTVA AVGG. Clasped hands. *C.* 4. *R.I.C.* 10a.
B.M.C. 80. **Plate 8** .. .. 30·00

2312 B. ℞. PATRES SENATVS. Clasped hands. *C.* 19. *R.I.C.* 11a.
B.M.C. 81. *Illustrated on p. 13* .. .. 30·00

2313 **R denarius.** A. ℞. CONCORDIA AVGG. Concord seated l. *C.* 6.
R.I.C. 1. *B.M.C.* 42 .. .. 30·00

2314 A. ℞. IOVI CONSERVATORI. Jupiter stg. l., holding thunderbolt and
sceptre. *C.* 12. *R.I.C.* 2. *B.M.C.* 44* .. .. 75·00

2315 A. ℞. PAX PVBLICA. Pax seated l. *C.* 22. *R.I.C.* 4. *B.M.C.* 46 30·00

2316 A. ℞. P . M . TR . P . COS . II . P . P. Pupienus stg. l., holding branch
and sceptre. *C.* 29. *R.I.C.* 5. *B.M.C.* 50* .. .. .. 65·00

Fine

2317 **Æ sestertius.** C. ℞. PAX PVBLICA S . C. Pax seated l. *C.* 24.
R.I.C. 22. *B.M.C.* 96. *Illustrated above.* .. .. 30·00

Fine

2318   **Æ sestertius.** B.   ℞.   P . M . TR . P . COS . II . P . P . S . C.   Felicity stg.
l., holding caduceus and sceptre.   *C.* 28.   *R.I.C.* 16.   *B.M.C.* 55* .. £30·00

2319   B.   ℞.   VICTORIA AVGG . S . C.   As 2308.   *C.* 38.   *R.I.C.* 23.   *B.M.C.*
58 ..   ..   30·00

2320   **Æ dupondius.** B.   ℞.   IOVI CONSERVATORI S . C.   As 2314.   *C.* 13.
R.I.C. 12.   *B.M.C.* 45* ..   ..   75·00

2321   **Æ as.** C.   ℞.   CONCORDIA AVGG . S . C.   Concord seated l.   *C.* 9.
R.I.C. 21.   *B.M.C.* 95 ..   ..   85·00

2322   *Egypt, Alexandria,* **billon tetradrachm.**   Laur., dr. and cuir. bust, r.
℞.   Nike advancing l.   *B.M.C. G.* 1837 ..   ..   20·00

For full details of **all** the silver coins from Pertinax to Balbinus and Pupienus see:
ROMAN SILVER COINS, *by H. A. Seaby.*

Volume III, *cloth bound* £2·40

Volume IV (Gordian III to Postumus) should be published during 1970

GORDIAN III
A.D. 238-244

2381A

    (*M. Antonius Gordianus*).   *Born about* A.D. 225, *Gordian III was the grandson of Gordian I and the nephew of Gordian II.   He was given the title of Caesar by the joint emperors Balbinus and Pupienus, and after their murders he was proclaimed Augustus by the Praetorian guards.   Little is known about his reign, one of the few recorded events of which was a rebellion in Africa, promptly suppressed, in* A.D. 240.   *In 242 Gordian set off for the East to direct the Persian campaign in person, and his first actions were so successful that the enemy were compelled to evacuate Mesopotamia; but due to treachery on the part of M. Julius Philippus, the praetorian prefect, the loyalty of the troops was undermined, and Gordian was deposed and murdered near Circesium in Mesopotamia* (A.D. 244).

Titles and Powers, A.D. 238-244

A.D.	Tribunician Power	Imperatorial Acclamation	Consulship	Other Titles
238				CAESAR, later
	TR.P.	IMP.		AVGVSTVS. P.M. P.P.
239	TR.P. − TR.P.II.		COS.	
240	TR.P.II. − III.			PIVS. FELIX.
241	TR.P.III. − IIII.		COS.II.	
242	TR.P.IIII. − V.			
243	TR.P.V. − VI.			
244	TR.P.VI. − VII.			

    Gordian received the tribunician power *ca.* end of July, A.D. 238 and, reverting to the custom of the early emperors, renewed it annually on the date of its first conferment.

Mints: Rome; Viminacium (?); Antioch.

As Caesar

A.D. 238, *under Balbinus and Pupienus*   **Very Fine**

2323 **Æ denarius.** M . ANT . GORDIANVS CAES.   Bare-headed and dr. bust, r.
      R. PIETAS AVGG.   Sacrificial implements. *C.* 182. *R.I.C.* 1. *B.M.C.*
      (Bal. and Pup.) 62 . .   . . £35·00

2324 **Æ sestertius.** As previous, but with S . C. added to rev. legend.
      C. 183. *R.I.C.* 3. *B.M.C.* *(Bal. and Pup.)* 64 . .   . . *Fine* £30·00

As Augustus

The following are the commonest forms of obverse legend:

  A. IMP . CAES . GORDIANVS PIVS AVG.
  B. IMP . CAES . M . ANT . GORDIANVS AVG.
  C. IMP . GORDIANVS PIVS FEL . AVG.

The normal obverse type for antoniniani and dupondii is rad. bust r., and for all other denominations, laur. bust r.   The bust is usually depicted dr. and cuir., although very often the cuirass is indistinct and may even be missing on some specimens.   Occasionally, the bust is cuir. only.

2325 **N aureus.** C. R. P . M . TR . P . IIII . COS . II . P . P.   Apollo seated
      l., holding branch and resting l. arm on lyre. *C.* 249. *R.I.C.* 102 . . 200·00

2326 **N quinarius.** C. R. AETERNITATI AVG.   Sol stg. l., holding globe.
      C. 38. *R.I.C.* 109 . .   . . 400·00

2327 **Æ antoninianus.** B. R. AEQVITAS AVG.   Equity stg. l. *C.* 17.
      R.I.C. 34 . .   . .   2·25
2328 A. R. As previous. *C.* 22. *R.I.C.* 51   . .   . .   3·00
2329 C. R. As previous. *C.* 25. *R.I.C.* 63   . .   . .   2·25
2330 C. R. As 2326. *C.* 41. *R.I.C.* 83   . .   . .   1·75
2331 B. R. CONCORDIA AVG.   Concord seated l. *C.* 50. *R.I.C.* 35   . .   2·25
2332 C. R. CONCORDIA MILIT.   Concord seated l. *C.* 62. *R.I.C.* 65   . .   2·25
2333 C. R. FELICIT . TEMP.   Felicity stg. l. *C.* 71. *R.I.C.* 140   . .   2·00
2334 B. R. FIDES MILITVM.   Fides stg. l., holding standard and sceptre.
      C. 86. *R.I.C.* 1 . .   . .   2·25
2335 C. R. FORT. REDVX.   Fortune seated l. *C.* 97. *R.I.C.* 143   . .   2·00
2336 B. R. IOVI CONSERVATORI.   Jupiter stg. l., holding thunderbolt and
      sceptre; at feet l., small figure of Gordian. *C.* 105. *R.I.C.* 2 . . 2·50
2337 C. R. IOVI STATORI.   Jupiter stg. facing, hd. r. *C.* 109. *R.I.C.* 84   1·75
2338 C. R. LAETITIA AVG . N.   Laetitia stg. l., holding wreath and anchor.
      C. 121. *R.I.C.* 86 . .   . .   1·75
2339 B. R. LIBERALITAS AVG . II.   Liberalitas stg. l. *C.* 130. *R.I.C.* 36   2·25
2340 C. R. LIBERALITAS AVG . III.   Liberalitas stg. l. *C.* 142. *R.I.C.* 67   2·25
2341 C. R. MARS PROPVG.   Mars advancing r., holding spear and shield.
      C. 155. *R.I.C.* 145 . .   . .   2·00
2342 C. R. MARTEM PROPVGNATOREM.   As previous. *C.* 160. *R.I.C.* 147   2·50
2343 C. R. MARTI PACIFERO.   Mars advancing l., holding olive-branch,
      shield and spear. *C.* 162. *R.I.C.* 212 . .   . .   4·25
2344 C. R. ORIENS AVG.   As 2326. *C.* 167. *R.I.C.* 213 . .   . .   2·25
2345 C. R. PAX AVGVSTI.   Pax advancing l. *C.* 179. *R.I.C.* 214   . .   3·50
2346 B. R. P . M . TR . P . II . COS . P . P.   As 2336. *C.* 189. *R.I.C.* 16   3·75

				Very Fine
2346A	Æ **antoninianus.** B. Rad., dr. and cuir. bust, l. ℞. — Providence stg. l. *C.* 197. *R.I.C.* 172..			£25·00

2347   B.   ℞. — Pax stg. l.   *C.* 203.   *R.I.C.* 17   ..   ..   ..   2·75

2348   B.   ℞. — As 2334.   C. 205.   *R.I.C.* 15   ..   ..   ..   2·75

2349   B.   ℞. — Gordian stg. l., sacrificing over tripod-altar.   *C.* 210.   *R.I.C.* 37   ..   ..   2·25

2350   A.   ℞. — As previous.   *C.* 212.   *R.I.C.* 54   ..   ..   ..   3·00

2351   C.   ℞.   P . M . TR . P . III . COS . II . P . P.   As 2325.   *C.* 237.   *R.I.C.* 87   ..   ..   3·00

2352   C.   ℞.   P . M . TR . P . IIII . COS . II . P . P.   As 2325.   *C.* 250.   *R.I.C.* 88   ..   ..   2·00

2353   C.   ℞. — Gordian stg. r., holding spear and globe.   *C.* 253.   *R.I.C.* 92   ..   ..   2·25

2354   C.   ℞.   P . M . TR . P . V . COS . II . P . P.   As previous.   *C.* 266.   *R.I.C.* 93   ..   ..   2·25

2355   C.   ℞.   P . M . TR . P . VI . COS . II . P . P.   As 2325.   *C.* 272.   *R.I.C.* 90   ..   ..   3·00

2356   C.   ℞.   P . M . TR . P . VII . COS . II . P . P.   As 2341.   *C.* 280.   *R.I.C.* 167A ..   ..   3·50

2357   C.   ℞.   PROVID . AVG.   Providence stg. l., globe at feet.   *C.* 296.   *R.I.C.* 148   ..   ..   2·25

2358   B.   ℞.   PROVIDENTIA AVG.   Providence stg. l., holding globe and sceptre.   *C.* 302.   *R.I.C.* 4   ..   ..   2·25

2359   B.   ℞.   ROMAE AETERNAE.   Roma seated l., holding Victory and sceptre.   *C.* 312.   *R.I.C.* 38   ..   ..   2·25

2360   C.   ℞.   SAECVLI FELICITAS.   As 2353.   *C.* 319.   *R.I.C.* 216 ..   2·25

2361   C.   ℞.   SECVRIT . PERP.   Security stg. l., holding sceptre and leaning on column.   *C.* 327.   *R.I.C.* 151 ..   ..   2·00

2362   C.   ℞.   SECVRITAS PERPETVA.   As previous.   *C.* 336.   *R.I.C.* 153 ..   2·25

2363   C.   ℞.   VICTORIA AETERNA.   Victory stg. l., leaning on shield set on captive and holding palm.   *C.* 353.   *R.I.C.* 156.   ..   ..   2·25

2364   B.   ℞.   VICTORIA AVG.   Victory advancing l.   *C.* 357.   *R.I.C.* 5   ..   2·25

2365   B.   ℞.   VIRTVS AVG.   Virtus stg. l., leaning on shield and holding spear.   *C.* 381.   *R.I.C.* 6 ..   ..   2·25

2366   B.   ℞. — Mars stg. l., holding olive-branch and spear, shield at feet.   *C.* 383.   *R.I.C.* 39 ..   ..   2·25

2367   A.   ℞. — As previous.   *C.* 386.   *R.I.C.* 56   ..   ..   ..   3·00

2368   C.   ℞.   VIRTVTI AVGVSTI.   Hercules stg. r., leaning on club set on rock.   *C.* 404.   *R.I.C.* 95 ..   ..   2·00

2369   Æ **denarius.**   As 2326.   *C.* 39.   *R.I.C.* 111   ..   ..   4·50

2370   C.   ℞.   DIANA LVCIFERA.   Diana stg. r., holding torch.   *C.* 69.   *R.I.C.* 127   ..   ..   6·00

2371   C.   ℞.   As 2338.   *C.* 120.   *R.I.C.* 113 ..   ..   ..   6·00

Very Fine

2372 **Æ denarius.** C. R. PIETAS AVGVSTI. Pietas stg. l., raising both
hands. *C.* 186. *R.I.C.* 129 .. .. £6·00
2373 C. R. P . M . TR . P . III . COS . P . P. Gordian on horseback l.,
raising r. hand. *C.* 234. *R.I.C.* 81. **Plate 8** .. .. 9·00
2374 C. R. P . M . TR . P . III . COS . II . P . P. As 2325. *C.* 238. *R.I.C.*
114 .. .. 6·50
2375 C. R. SALVS AVGVSTI. Salus stg. r., feeding serpent held in arms.
C. 325. *R.I.C.* 129A .. .. 4·50
2376 C. R. SECVRITAS PVBLICA. Security seated l., holding sceptre.
C. 340. *R.I.C.* 130 .. .. 4·50
2377 C. R. VENVS VICTRIX. Venus stg. l., holding helmet and sceptre and
leaning on shield. *C.* 347. *R.I.C.* 131 .. .. 4·50
2378 C. R. As 2368. *C.* 403. *R.I.C.* 116 .. .. 4·50

2379 **Æ quinarius.** IMP . C . M . ANT . GORDIANVS AVG. R. As 2364.
C. 361. *R.I.C.* 13 .. .. 50·00

Fine

2380 **Æ sestertius.** B. R. ABVNDANTIA AVG . S . C. Abundance stg. r.,
emptying cornucopiae. *C.* 1. *R.I.C.* 274a .. .. .. 4·50
2381 B. R. AEQVITAS AVG . S . C. Equity stg. l. *C.* 19. *R.I.C.* 267a .. 4·50
2381A C. R. AETERNITAS AVGVSTI S . C. Gordian on horseback r. *C.* 36.
R.I.C. 314. *Illustrated on p.* 222 .. .. 60·00
2382 C. R. AETERNITATI AVG . S . C. As 2326. *C.* 43. *R.I.C.* 297a .. 4·50
2383 B. R. CONCORDIA AVG . S . C. Concord seated l. *C.* 51. *R.I.C.* 268 4·50
2384 C. R. FELICITAS AVG . S . C. Felicity stg. l. *C.* 76. *R.I.C.* 310a .. 4·50
2385 B. R. FIDES MILITVM . S . C. As 2334. *C.* 88. *R.I.C.* 254a .. 4·50
2386 B. R. IOVI CONSERVATORI S . C. As 2336. *C.* 106. *R.I.C.* 255a .. 5·00
2387 C. R. IOVI STATORI S . C. As 2337. *C.* 111. *R.I.C.* 298a .. .. 4·50
2388 C. R. LAETITIA AVG . N . S . C. As 2338. *C.* 122. *R.I.C.* 300a .. 4·50
2389 A. R. LIBERALITAS AVG . II . S . C. Liberalitas stg. l. *C.* 134.
R.I.C. 279a .. .. 5·50
2390 B. R. As previous. *C.* 136. *R.I.C.* 269a .. .. .. 5·00
2391 C. R. LIBERTAS AVG . S . C. Liberty stg. l. *C.* 153. *R.I.C.* 318a .. 5·00
2392 C. R. PAX AETERNA S . C. Pax advancing l. *C.* 169. *R.I.C.* 319a .. 4·50
2393 B. R. PAX AVGVSTI S . C. Pax stg. facing, hd. l. *C.* 175. *R.I.C.* 256a 4·50
2394 B. R. P . M . TR . P . II . COS . P . P . S . C. As 2359. *C.* 207. *R.I.C.*
264a .. .. 5·00
2395 B. R. — As 2349. *C.* 211. *R.I.C.* 271 .. .. 5·00
2396 B. R. — Gordian in quadriga l., holding eagle-tipped sceptre.
C. 221. *R.I.C.* 276a .. .. 35·00
2397 C. R. P . M . TR . P . III . COS . P . P . S . C. Gordian seated l. on
curule chair, holding globe and sceptre. *C.* 231. *R.I.C.* 294a .. .. 5·50
2398 C. R. P . M . TR . P . III . COS . II . P . P . S . C. As 2325. *C.* 240.
R.I.C. 301a .. .. 4·50
2399 C. R. P . M . TR . P . IIII . COS . II . P . P . S . C. As 2353. *C.* 254.
R.I.C. 306a. **Plate 7** .. .. 4·50
2400 C. R. P . M . TR . P . V . COS . II . P . P . S . C. As 2325. *C.* 262.
R.I.C. 303a .. .. 4·50
2401 C. R. P . M . TR . P . VII . COS . II . P . P . S . C. As 2341. *C.* 281.
R.I.C. 339a .. .. 5·50
2402 B. R. PROVIDENTIA AVG . S . C. As 2358. *C.* 304. *R.I.C.* 257a .. 4·50
2403 B. R. ROMAE AETERNAE S . C. As 2359. *C.* 316. *R.I.C.* 272a .. 5·00

Fine

2404	**Æ sestertius.** B. ℞. SALVS AVG . S . C. Salus seated l., feeding serpent arising from altar. *C.* 322. *R.I.C.* 261*a*		£4·50
2405	C. ℞. SECVRITAS PERPETVA S . C. As 2361. *C.* 337. *R.I.C.* 336 ..		4·50
2406	C. ℞. VICTORIA AETER . S . C. As 2363. *C.* 351. *R.I.C.* 337*a* ..		4·50
2407	B. ℞. VICTORIA AVG . S . C. Victory advancing l. *C.* 358. *R.I.C.* 258*a* ..		4·50
2408	C. ℞. VIRTVS AVG . S . C. As 2366. *C.* 390. *R.I.C.* 293*a*		4·50
2409	B. ℞. — Gordian advancing r., holding spear and shield. *C.* 393. *R.I.C.* 259*a* ..		5·00
2410	**Æ dupondius.** C. ℞. LAETITIA AVG . N . S . C. As 2338. *C.* 124. *R.I.C.* 300*c* ..		6·00
2411	C. R. As 2392. *C.* 171. *R.I.C.* 319*c* ..		6·00
2412	**Æ as.** C. R. AETERNITATI AVG . S . C. As 2326. *C.* 44. *R.I.C.* 297*b* ..		5·50
2413	C. ℞. FORTVNA REDVX S . C. Fortune seated l. *C.* 100. *R.I.C.* 331*b* ..		5·50
2414	C. ℞. IOVI STATORI S . C. As 2337. *C.* 112. *R.I.C.* 298*b*..		5·50
2415	C. ℞. P . M . TR . P . III . COS . II . P . P . S . C. As 2353. *C.* 245. *R.I.C.* 305*b* ..		5·50
2416	B. ℞. ROMAE AETERNAE S . C. As 2359. *C.* 317. *R.I.C.* 272*b* ..		6·50
2417	IMP . GORDIANVS PIVS FELIX AVG. Laur., dr. and cuir. bust, l. ℞. SECVRIT . PERPET . S . C. As 2361. *C.* 331. *R.I.C.* 335*c*		25·00
2418	C. ℞. VICTORIA AETERNA S . C. As 2363. *C.* 355. *R.I.C.* 338*b* ..		5·50
2419	C. ℞. VIRTVS AVG . S . C. As 2366. *C.* 391. *R.I.C.* 293*b*		5·50

Colonial and Provincial Coinage

2420	*Thrace, Deultum,* **Æ 18.** Laur. bust, l. ℞. Homonoia stg. l. *B.M.C. G.*17		6·00
2421	— *Hadrianopolis,* **Æ 26.** Laur. bust, r. ℞. Zeus enthroned l., eagle at feet. *B.M.C. G.*26.		6·00
2422	*Moesia Superior, Viminacium,* **Æ 23.** Rad. bust, r. ℞. Moesia stg. l. between bull and lion. *B.M.C. G.*12		6·00
2423	*Bithynia, Nicaea,* **Æ 19.** — ℞. Four standards. *B.M.C. G.*119 ..		3·75
2424	*Samos,* **Æ 36.** Laur. bust, r. ℞. Tetrastyle temple. *B.M.C. G.*294		14·00
2425	*Phrygia, Lysias,* **Æ 26.** — ℞. Kybele enthroned l., lion at feet. *B.M.C. G.*6		10·00
2426	*Pamphylia, Side,* **Æ 26.** — ℞. Athena stg. l. *B.M.C. G.*93 ..		6·00
2427	*Pisidia, Antioch,* **Æ 35.** — ℞. Nike advancing l. *B.M.C. G.*96 ..		5·50
2428	*Mesopotamia, Edessa,* **Æ 24.** Laur. hd., r. ℞. Bust of Abgar X r. *B.M.C. G.*148 ..		4·50
2429	— *Nisibis,* **Æ 26.** Rad. hd., r. ℞. Bust of Tyche r. *B.M.C. G.*13 ..		6·50
2430	*Egypt, Alexandria,* **billon tetradrachm.** Bare-headed, dr. and cuir. bust, r. ℞. Athena stg. l. *B.M.C. G.*1848 (*as Caesar*) ..		12·50
2431	— Laur. dr. and cuir. bust, r. ℞. Zeus seated l., holding patera and sceptre. *B.M.C. G.*1857 ..		3·50
2432	— — ℞. Dikaiosyne stg. l. *B.M.C. G.*1869 ..		2·50
2433	— Laur. and cuir. bust, r. ℞. Nike seated l. *B.M.C. G.*1885 ..		2·50
2434	— — ℞. Tyche stg. l. *B.M.C. G.* 1889 ..		2·50
2435	— Laur., dr. and cuir. bust, r. ℞. Nilus reclining l. *B.M.C. G.*1902		3·50
2436	— — ℞. Eagle stg l., hd. turned. *B.M.C. G.*1907		2·50
2437	*Gordian III and Tranquillina: Mesopotamia, Singara,* **Æ 31.** Their busts face to face. ℞. Tyche seated l. on rock. *B.M.C. G.*8		8·00

TRANQUILLINA

2439

(*Furia Sabinia Tranquillina*) *The daughter of the praetorian prefect Timisitheus, Tranquillina was married to Gordian III in* A.D. 241.

All have obverse legend SABINIA TRANQVLLINA AVG.

R.I.C. references are to the coinage of Gordian.

		Very Fine
2438	Æ **antoninianus.** Diad. and dr. bust r., resting on crescent. Ṟ. CONCORDIA AVGG. Concord seated l., holding patera and double cornucopiae. *C.* 1. *R.I.C.* 249	£750·00
2439	— Ṟ. — Gordian and Tranquillina stg. facing each other, clasping r. hands. *C.* 4. *R.I.C.* 250. *Illustrated above*	900·00
2440	Æ **denarius.** Diad. and dr. bust, r. Ṟ. As 2438. *R.I.C.* 252 ..	900·00
2441	Æ **quinarius.** — Ṟ. As 2438. *C.* 2. *R.I.C.* 253	1250·00
2442	Æ **sestertius.** — Ṟ. CONCORDIA AVGVSTORVM S . C. As 2439. *C.* 5. *R.I.C.* 341a	**Fine** 650·00
2443	Æ **dupondius.** *Obv.* As 2438. Ṟ. — As 2439. *C.* 6. *R.I.C.* 341c	300·00
2444	Æ **as.** *Obv.* As 2440. Ṟ. CONCORDIA AVGG . S . C. As 2438. *C.* 3. *R.I.C.* 340b	250·00
2445	*Bithynia, Calchedon,* Æ **25.** Dr. bust, r. Ṟ. Apollo reclining r. on swan swimming l. *B.M.C. G.*35	12·50
2446	*Cilicia, Lyrbe,* Æ **26.** — Ṟ. Tyche stg. l. *B.M.C. G.*8	15·00
2447	*Egypt, Alexandria,* **billon tetradrachm.** Diad. and dr. bust, r. Ṟ. Homonoia stg. l., holding double cornucopiae. *B.M.C. G.*1927.. ..	8·00

PHILIP I

A.D. 244-249

2502

(*M. Julius Philippus*). *A native of Arabia, Philip was appointed to the post of praetorian prefect by Gordian III after the death of Timisitheus. He soon brought about the deposition and murder of the young emperor and, after concluding a satisfactory peace with the Persians, he returned to Rome. The chief event of his reign was the celebration, in 248, of the thousandth anniversary of the foundation of Rome. There were magnificent games with many wild beasts, most of which had been collected by Gordian for his Persian triumph. A series of coins was also struck to commemorate the event. The latter part of Philip's reign was troubled by a number of pretenders, and in 249 he had to take the field in person to deal with the rebellious legions of Decius. The two armies met near Verona and in the ensuing battle Philip was defeated and killed together with his son.*

Titles and Powers, A.D. 244-249

A.D.	Tribunician Power	Imperatorial Acclamation	Consulship	Other Titles
244	TR.P.	IMP.		AVGVSTVS. P.M. P.P.
245	TR.P.II.		COS.	
246	TR.P.III.			
247	TR.P.IIII.		COS.II.	
248	TR.P.V.		COS.III.	
249	TR.P.VI.			

Philip became TR.P.II. on January 1st, A.D. 245, and his tribunician power was subsequently renewed each year on that date.

Mints: Rome; Antioch.

The following are the commonest forms of obverse legend:

    A. IMP . C . M . IVL . PHILIPPVS P . F . AVG . P . M.

    B. IMP . M . IVL . PHILIPPVS AVG.

    C. IMP . PHILIPPVS AVG.

The normal obv. type for antoniniani and dupondii is rad. bust r., and for all other denominations, laur. bust r. The bust is usually depicted dr. and cuir., although very often the cuirass is indistinct and may even be missing on some specimens.

In *R.I.C.* the coinage of Philip I, Otacilia and Philip II is dealt with in one group, numbered 1-272.

Very Fine

2448 **N aureus.** B. R. LAET . FVNDATA. Laetitia stg. l., holding wreath and rudder. *C.* 71. *R.I.C.* 35a. *Illustrated on p.* 229 .. .. ..£400·00

2449 **N quinarius.** B. R. FIDES MILIT. Fides stg. l., holding two standards. *C.* 56. *R.I.C.* 32a .. .. 550·00

2450 **Æ antoninianus.** B. R. ADVENTVS AVGG. Philip on horseback l., raising r. hand. *C.* 3. *R.I.C.* 26b .. .. 3·00

2451 B. R. AEQVITAS AVGG. Equity stg. l. *C.* 9. *R.I.C.* 27b .. .. 2·00

2452 C. R. AETERNITAS AVGG. Elephant walking l., guided by driver. *C.* 17. *R.I.C.* 58 .. .. 4·00

2453 B. R. ANNONA AVGG. Annona stg. l., modius at feet. *C.* 25. *R.I.C.* 28c .. .. 2·00

2454 C. R. FELICITAS IMPP. in three lines within laurel-wreath. *C.* 39. *R.I.C.* 60 .. .. 6·00

2455 B. R. FELICITAS TEMP. Felicity stg. l. *C.* 43. *R.I.C.* 31 .. .. 2·50

2456 C. R. FIDES EXERCITVS. Four standards. *C.* 50. *R.I.C.* 62 .. 3·50

2457 B. R. FIDES MILIT. Fides stg. l., holding sceptre and standard. *C.* 54. *R.I.C.* 33 .. .. 3·25

2458 C. R. FORTVNA REDVX. Fortune seated l. *C.* 65. *R.I.C.* 63b .. 3·25

2459 B. R. As 2448. *C.* 72 *R.I.C.* 35b .. .. 3·50

2460 B. R. LAETIT . FVNDAT. Laetitia stg. l., r. foot on prow, holding patera and rudder. *C.* 81. *R.I.C.* 37b .. .. 3·25

2461 B. R. LIBERALITAS AVGG . II. Liberalitas stg. l. *C.* 87. *R.I.C.* 38b 2·75

2462 C. R. NOBILITAS AVGG. Nobilitas stg. r., holding sceptre and globe. *C.* 98. *R.I.C.* 8 .. .. 4·25

2463 B. R. PAX AETERN. Pax stg. l. *C.* 103. *R.I.C.* 40b .. .. 3·25

2448 2464

Very Fine

2464 **Æ antoninianus.** A. ℞. PAX FVNDATA CVM PERSIS. Pax stg. l. C. 113. *R.I.C.* 69 .. .. £8·00

2465 B. ℞. P . M . TR . P . II . COS . P . P. Philip seated l. on curule chair. C. 120. *R.I.C.* 2b .. .. 3·00

2466 B. ℞. P . M . TR . P . III . COS . P . P. Felicity stg. l. C. 124. *R.I.C.* 3 2·50

2467 B. ℞. ROMAE AETERNAE. Roma seated l., holding Victory and sceptre. C. 169. *R.I.C.* 44b .. .. 2·25

2468 As previous, but Roma has altar at feet. C. 170. *R.I.C.* 45 .. .. 2·75

2469 C. ℞. SAECVLARES AVGG. Lion walking r. C. 173. *R.I.C.* 12 .. 4·25

2470 C. ℞. — She-wolf stg. l., suckling Romulus and Remus. C. 178. *R.I.C.* 15 .. .. 5·00

2471 C. ℞. — Stag walking r. C. 182. *R.I.C.* 19 .. .. .. 4·50

2472 C. ℞. — Antelope walking l. C. 189. *R.I.C.* 21 .. .. .. 4·00

2473 C. ℞. — Cippus inscribed COS . III. C. 193. *R.I.C.* 24c .. .. 3·50

2474 C. ℞. SAECVLVM NOVVM. Roma seated facing in temple of six columns. C. 198. *R.I.C.* 25b .. .. 4·50

2475 B. ℞. SALVS AVG. Salus stg. l., feeding serpent arising from altar and holding rudder. C. 205. *R.I.C.* 47 .. .. 3·25

2476 B. ℞. — Salus stg. r., feeding serpent held in arms. C. 209. *R.I.C.* 46b .. .. 2·50

2477 B. ℞. SECVRIT . ORBIS. Security seated l., holding sceptre. C. 215. *R.I.C.* 48b .. .. 2·50

2478 A. ℞. SPES FELICITATIS ORBIS. Spes advancing l. C. 221. *R.I.C.* 70 .. .. 5·50

2479 C. ℞. TRANQVILLITAS AVGG. Tranquillitas stg. l., holding capricorn (?) and sceptre. C. 223. *R.I.C.* 9 .. .. 4·25

2480 B. ℞. VICTORIA AVG. Victory advancing l. C. 231. *R.I.C.* 50 .. 3·25

2481 C. ℞. VICTORIA CARPICA. Victory advancing r. C. 238. *R.I.C.* 66 15·00

2482 B. ℞. VIRTVS AVG. Virtus stg. l., holding branch and spear. C. 239. *R.I.C.* 52 .. .. 3·00

2483 B. ℞. — Virtus seated l., holding branch and spear. C. 240. *R.I.C.* 53 .. .. 2·75

2484 C. ℞. VIRTVS AVGG. Philip I and Philip II galloping r., side by side. C. 241. *R.I.C.* 10 .. .. 5·00

2485 A. ℞. VIRTVS EXERCITVS. Virtus stg. r., holding spear and leaning on shield. C. 243. *R.I.C.* 71 .. .. 5·00

2486 **Æ denarius.** B. ℞. As 2450. C. 5. *R.I.C.* 26a .. .. .. 100·00

2487 **Æ quinarius.** B. ℞. SALVS AVG. As 2476. C. 210. *R.I.C.* 46a .. 150·00

Fine

2488	**Æ sestertius.** B. ℞. ADVENTVS AVGG . S . C. As 2450. *C.* 6.		
	R.I.C. 165		£8·00
2489	B. ℞. AEQVITAS AVGG . S . C. Equity stg. l. *C.* 10. *R.I.C.* 166a ..		4·50
2490	B. ℞. AETERNITAS AVGG . S . C. As 2452. *C.* 18. *R.I.C.* 167a ..		7·50
2491	B. ℞. ANNONA AVGG . S . C. As 2453. *C.* 26. *R.I.C.* 168a ..		4·50
2492	B. ℞. FELICITAS TEMP . S . C. Felicity stg. l. *C.* 44. *R.I.C.* 169a ..		4·50
2493	B. ℞. FIDES EXERCITVS S . C. Four standards. *C.* 51. *R.I.C.* 171a..		6·00
2494	B. ℞. FIDES MILITVM S . C. As 2449. *C.* 59. *R.I.C.* 172a ..		4·50
2495	B. ℞. LAET . FVNDATA S . C. As 2460. *C.* 76. *R.I.C.* 176a ..		4·50
2496	B. ℞. MILIARIVM SAECVLVM S . C. Cippus inscribed COS . III. *C.* 95.		
	R.I.C. 157a		7·50
2497	B. ℞. P . M . TR . P . II . COS . P . P . S . C. As 2465. *C.* 121. *R.I.C.*		
	148a		6·00
2498	B. ℞. P . M . TR . P . IIII . COS . II . P . P . S . C. Felicity stg. l. *C.* 138.		
	R.I.C. 150a. **Plate 8**		4·50
2499	B. ℞. P . M . TR . P . V . COS . III . P . P . S . C. Mars stg. l., holding		
	branch and leaning on shield. *C.* 146. *R.I.C.* 152		5·00
2500	B. ℞. SAECVLARES AVGG . S . C. As 2470. *C.* 179. *R.I.C.* 159 ..		10·00
2501	B. ℞. — Stag walking r. *C.* 183. *R.I.C.* 160a		7·50
2502	B. ℞. — Antelope walking l. *C.* 190. *R.I.C.* 161. *Illustrated on*		
	p. 227		7·50
2503	B. ℞. — Cippus inscribed COS . III. *C.* 195. *R.I.C.* 162a		7·50
2504	B. ℞. SAECVLVM NOVVM S . C. Roma seated facing in temple of eight		
	columns. *C.* 201. *R.I.C.* 164		7·50
2505	B. ℞. SECVRIT . ORBIS S . C. As 2477. *C.* 216. *R.I.C.* 190 ..		4·50
2506	B. ℞. VICTORIA AVG . S . C. Victory advancing r. *C.* 228. *R.I.C.*		
	191a		4·50
2507	B. ℞. VOTIS DECENNALIBVS S . C. within laurel-wreath. *C.* 246.		
	R.I.C. 195a		12·50
2508	**Æ dupondius.** B. ℞. LAET . FVNDATA S . C. As 2448. *C.* 75.		
	R.I.C. 175c		6·50
2509 | **Æ as.** B. ℞. ANNONA AVGG . S . C. As 2453. *C.* 27. *R.I.C.* 168b | | 5·50 |
2510 | As 2492. *C.* 45. *R.I.C.* 169b .. .. | | 5·50 |
2511 | B. ℞. PAX AETERNA S . C. Pax stg. l. *C.* 106. *R.I.C.* 184b .. .. | | 5·50 |
2512 | As 2503. *C.* 196. *R.I.C.* 162b .. .. | | 6·50 |
2513 | B. ℞. SALVS AVG . S . C. As 2476. *C.* 212 *R.I.C.* 186b .. .. | | 5·50 |

Colonial and Provincial Coinage

2514	*Moesia Superior, Viminacium,* **Æ 29.** Laur. and dr. bust, r. ℞.		
	Moesia stg. l., between bull and lion. *B.M.C. G.*21		6·50
2515	*Phrygia, Hadrianopolis-Sebaste,* **Æ 26.** — ℞. River god, Karmeios,		
	reclining l. *B.M.C. G.* 11		6·00
2516	*Cilicia, Seleuceia ad Calycadnum,* **Æ 35.** Rad. bust, r. ℞. Busts of		
	Apollo and Tyche face to face. *B.M.C. G.*50		12·00
2517	*Commagene, Samosata,* **Æ 30.** Laur. bust, r. ℞. Tyche seated l.		
	*B.M.C. G.*47		5·00
2518	*Syria, Antioch,* **billon tetradrachm.** Rad. bust, r. ℞. Eagle stg.		
	facing, hd. l. *B.M.C. G.*505		4·50
2519	— **Æ 30.** Laur. bust, r. ℞. Bust of Tyche r. *B.M.C. G.*526 ..		3·50
2520	*Egypt, Alexandria,* **billon tetradrachm.** Laur. and cuir. bust, r.		
	℞. Bust of Zeus Ammon r. *B.M.C. G.*1942		3·00
2521 | — ℞. Rad. bust of Helios r. *B.M.C. G.*1946 .. .. .. | | 3·25 |
2522 | — ℞. Tyche stg. l. *B.M.C. G.*1974 .. .. | | 2·50 |
2523 | — ℞. Eagle stg. l., hd. turned. *B.M.C. G.*1993 .. .. .. | | 2·50 |

JULIUS MARINUS
Father of Philip I

Fine

2523A *Arabia, Philippopolis,* Æ **30.** ΘΣΩ ΜΑΡΙΝΩ. Bare-headed bust of
Marinus r., supported by eagle. ℞. ΦΙΛΙΠΠΟΠΟΛΙΤΩΝ ΚΟΛΩΝΙΑC.
Roma seated l., holding two small figures and spear; in field, s . c.
B.M.C. G.— .. .. £120·00

OTACILIA SEVERA
Marcia Otacilia Severa, wife of Philip I

2540

There are four varieties of obverse legend:

A. M . OTACIL . SEVERA AVG.
B. MARC . OTACIL . SEVERA AVG.
C. MARCIA OTACIL . SEVERA AVG.
D. OTACIL . SEVERA AVG.

*The normal obverse type is diad. and dr. bust r., antoniniani and dupondii having a
crescent beneath the bust.*

Very Fine

2524	**N aureus.** A. ℞. CONCORDIA AVGG. Concord seated l., holding patera and double cornucopiae. *C.* 2. *R.I.C.* 125a	450·00
2525	**R antoninianus.** A. ℞. As previous. *C.* 4. *R.I.C.* 125c. **Plate 8**	3·25
2526	C. ℞. As previous. *C.* 9. *R.I.C.* 119b	5·00
2527	D. ℞. CONCORDIA AVGG. Concord seated l., holding patera and cornucopiae, altar at feet. *C.* 16. *R.I.C.* 129	3·75
2528	A. ℞. IVNO CONSERVAT. Juno stg. l., holding patera and sceptre. *C.* 20. *R.I.C.* 127	4·50
2529	D. ℞. PIETAS AVGG. Pietas stg. l., holding box of perfumes, altar at feet. *C.* 39. *R.I.C.* 115	4·50
2530	B. ℞. PIETAS AVG . N. Pietas stg. l., child at feet. *C.* 42. *R.I.C.* 133	6·50
2531	D. ℞. PIETAS AVGVSTAE. As 2529, but without altar. *C.* 43. *R.I.C.* 130	3·75
2532	C. ℞. PVDICITIA AVG. Pudicitia seated l., holding sceptre. *C.* 53. *R.I.C.* 123c	3·75
2533	D. ℞. SAECVLARES AVGG. Hippopotamus stg. r. *C.* 63. *R.I.C.* 116b	5·00

Very Fine

2534 **Æ denarius.** C. R. As 2532. *C.* 52. *R.I.C.* 123*b*   .   . . £120·00

2535 **Æ quinarius.** C. R. As 2524. *C.* 8. *R.I.C.* 119*a*   .   . . 150·00

Fine

2536 **Æ sestertius.** C. R. CONCORDIA AVGG . S . C. As 2524. *C.* 10.
      *R.I.C.*203*a*   ..   ..   5·50
2537 C. R. PIETAS AVG . S . C. As 2529, but without altar. *C.* 31.
      R.I.C. 205*a*   ..   ..   5·50
2538 C. R. PIETAS AVGVSTAE S . C. As previous. *C.* 46. *R.I.C.* 208*a* ..   5·50
2539 C. R. PVDICITIA AVG . S . C. As 2532. *C.* 55. *R.I.C.* 209*a* ..   5·50
2540 C. R. SAECVLARES AVGG . S . C. As 2533. *C.* 65. *R.I.C.* 200*a*.
      Illustrated on p. 231 ..   ..   10·00
2541 **Æ dupondius.** C. R. CONCORDIA AVGG . S . C. As 2524. *C.* 12.
      R.I.C. 203*c*   ..   ..   7·50
2542 **Æ as.** C. R. CONCORDIA AVGG . S . C. As 2524. *C.* 11. *R.I.C.*
      203*b*   ..   ..   6·50
2543 C. R. PIETAS AVGVSTAE S . C. As 2529, but without altar. *C.* 47.
      R.I.C. 208*b*   ..   ..   6·50
2544 C. R. SAECVLARES AVGG . S . C. Cippus. *C.* 69. *R.I.C.* 202*b*   ..   8·00
2545 *Ionia, Ephesus,* **Æ 29.** Dr. bust, r. R. Artemis in biga of stags r.
      *B.M.C. G.*342   ..   ..   7·50
2546 — *Colophon,* **Æ 29.** — R. Homer seated r. *B.M.C. G.*54 ..   ..   8·00
2547 *Egypt, Alexandria,* **billon tetradrachm.** — R. Athena stg. l.,
      holding Nike. *B.M.C. G.*2008   ..   ..   4·50
2548 — R. Eusebeia stg. l., sacrificing at altar. *B.M.C. G.*2015 ..   ..   4·00

2560A

(*M. Julius Philippus*). *The son of Philip I, he was given the title of Caesar on the accession of his father and in* A.D. 247 *was elevated to the rank of Augustus. He was probably killed with his father at the battle of Verona.*

PHILIP II
A.D. 247-249

As Caesar

A.D. 244-247, *under Philip I*

The normal obv. legend is M . IVL . PHILIPPVS CAES.

Very Fine

2549 **Æ aureus.** Bare-headed and dr. bust, r. R. PRINCIPI IVVENT.
      Philip II stg. r., holding spear and globe. *C.* 52 *R.I.C.* 216*a*   .. 500·00
2550 **Æ antoninianus.** Rad. and dr. bust, r. R. IOVI CONSERVAT.
      Jupiter stg. l., holding thunderbolt and sceptre. *C.* 13. *R.I.C.* 213 ..   5·00
2551 — R. PIETAS AVGVSTOR. Sacrificial implements. *C.* 32. *R.I.C.* 215   5·00

Very Fine

2552 **Æ antoninianus.** ℞. PRINCIPI IVVENT. Philip II stg. l., holding
globe and spear. *C.* 48. *R.I.C.* 218*d* .. .. £3·00
2553 — ℞. As 2549. *C.* 54. *R.I.C.* 216*c* .. .. 3·50
2554 — ℞. As 2552, but Philip has captive at feet. *C.* 57. *R.I.C.* 219 .. 3·75
2555 — ℞. As 2549, but Philip is accompanied by soldier who stands
behind him. *C.* 58. *R.I.C.* 217 .. .. 5·00
2556 — ℞. SPES PVBLICA. Spes advancing l. *C.* 84. *R.I.C.* 221 .. 6·50
2557 **Æ denarius.** As 2549. *C.* 53. *R.I.C.* 216*b* .. .. 120·00
2558 **Æ quinarius.** Bare-headed and dr. bust, r. ℞. As 2552. *C.* 47.
R.I.C. 218*c* .. .. 150·00

2559 **Æ sestertius.** — ℞. PRINCIPI IVVENT . S . C. As 2552. *C.* 49. **Fine**
R.I.C. 256*a* .. .. 6·00
2560 — ℞. — As 2549. *C.* 55. *R.I.C.* 255*a* .. .. 6·00
2560A Bare-headed and dr. bust, l. ℞. PRINCIPI IVVENTVTIS S.C. Philip II
stg. l., holding standard and spear. *C.* 65. *R.I.C.* 258*c*. *Illustrated on
p. 232* .. .. 65·00
2561 **Æ dupondius or as.** As 2559. *C.* 50. *R.I.C.* 256*b* .. .. 7·50

As Augustus

There are two main varieties of obverse legend:
A. IMP . M . IVL . PHILIPPVS AVG.
B. IMP . PHILIPPVS AVG.

*Although Philip II uses the same obverse legends as his father, his coins are easily
distinguished by his youthful portrait.*

Very Fine

2562 **Æ aureus.** B. Laur., dr. and cuir. bust, r. ℞. PAX AETERNA.
Pax stg. l. *C.* 21. *R.I.C.* 231*a* .. .. 450·00
2563 **Æ antoninianus.** A. Rad., dr. and cuir. bust, r. ℞. AETERNIT .
IMPER. Sol advancing l., holding whip. *C.* 6. *R.I.C.* 226 .. .. 3·75
2564 B. — ℞. LIBERALITAS AVGG . III. Philip I and Philip II seated l. on
curule chairs, side by side. *C.* 17. *R.I.C.* 230 .. .. .. 4·00
2565 B. — ℞. As 2562. *C.* 23. *R.I.C.* 231*c* .. .. 3·00
2566 A. — ℞. As 2562. *C.* 24. *R.I.C.* 227 .. .. 4·50
2567 A. — ℞. P . M . TR . P . VI . COS . P . P. Philip II stg. l., holding
globe and spear, captive at feet. *C.* 41. *R.I.C.* 237 .. .. 7·00
2568 B. — ℞. SAECVLARES AVGG. Goat walking l. *C.* 72. *R.I.C.* 224 .. 5·00
2569 B. — ℞. VIRTVS AVGG. Mars advancing r. *C.* 88. *R.I.C.* 223 .. 3·75
2570 **Æ quinarius.** B. Laur., dr. and cuir. bust, r. ℞. As 2562. *C.* 22.
R.I.C. 231*b* .. .. 150·00

2571 **Æ sestertius.** A. — ℞. LIBERALITAS AVGG . III . S . C. As 2564. **Fine**
C. 18. *R.I.C.* 267*a* .. .. 7·50
2572 B. — ℞. PAX AETERNA S . C. Pax stg. l. *C.* 25. *R.I.C.* 268*c* .. 6·50
2573 A. — ℞. SAECVLARES AVGG . S . C. Goat walking l. *C.* 73. *R.I.C.*
264*a* .. .. 12·50
2574 A. — ℞ — Cippus inscribed COS . II. *C.* 78. *R.I.C.* 265*a* .. 7·50
2575 A. — ℞. VIRTVS AVGG . S . C. Mars advancing r. *C.* 89. *R.I.C.* 263 6·50
2576 **Æ dupondius.** B. Rad., dr. and cuir. bust, r. ℞. P . M . TR . P .
IIII . COS . II . P . P . S . C. Philip II seated l., holding globe and sceptre.
C. 37. *R.I.C.* 262*b* .. .. 12·50
2577 **Æ as.** As 2572. *C.* 26. *R.I.C.* 268*d* .. .. 7·50
2578 As 2574. *C.* 79. *R.I.C.* 265*b* .. .. 8·00

Colonial and Provincial Coinage   Fine

2579 *Lydia, Saïtta,* Æ **22.** Bare-headed bust, r. R. Athena stg. l.,
      holding phiale. *B.M.C. G.* 70 ..   ..   £6·50
2580 *Pamphylia, Perga,* Æ **21.** Laur. bust, r. R. Three purses on chest.
      B.M.C. G. 60 ..   ..   4·00
2581 *Commagene, Samosata,* Æ **28.** — R. Tyche seated l. *B.M.C. G.* 56   5·00
2582 *Arabia Petraea, Philippopolis,* Æ **26.** — R. Roma seated l. *B.M.C.*
      G. 10 ..   ..   10·00
2583 *Egypt, Alexandria,* **billon tetradrachm.** Bare-headed, dr. and cuir.
      bust, r. R. Eagle stg. l., hd. turned. *B.M.C. G.* 2051 ..   ..   3·50
2584 — Laur., dr. and cuir. bust, r. R. Homonoia stg. l., holding double
      cornucopiae. *B.M.C. G.* 2058 ..   ..   4·00

PACATIAN
ca. A.D. 248

2586

(*Ti. Claudius Marinus Pacatianus*) *This usurper, about whom very little is known,
seized power for a brief period in Upper Moesia and issued coins from the mint of Viminacium.
He was murdered by his own soldiers.*

Very Fine

2585 **Æ antoninianus.** IMP . TI . CL . MAR . PACATIANVS P . F . AVG. Rad.,
      dr. and cuir. bust, r. R. CONCORDIA MILITVM. Concord seated l.,
      holding patera and double cornucopiae. *C.* 1. *R.I.C.* 1b ..   .. 850·00
2586 IMP . TI . CL . MAR . PACATIANVS AVG. — R. ROMAE AETER . AN . MIL .
      ET PRIMO. Roma seated l., holding Victory and spear. *C.* 7. *R.I.C.* 6
      Illustrated above ..   .. 1500·00

JOTAPIAN
ca. A.D. 248

(*M. Fulvius Rufus Iotapianus*). *The oppressive administration in Syria of Priscus, the
brother of Philip I, led to the elevation by the army of a certain Jotapian, who claimed to be
a descendant of Alexander. The revolt covered the provinces of Syria and Cappadocia, but
the usurper was killed by his own men after only a very short reign.*

2587 **Æ antoninianus.** IM . C . M . F . RV . IOTAPIANVS. Rad. and cuir.
      bust, r. R. VICTORIA AVG. Victory advancing l. *C.* 2. *R.I.C.* 2c .. 1500·00

SILBANNACUS

Marcus Silbannacus is an emperor of whom there is no record in history. The style of the unique coin in the British Museum, however, fixes the period of his reign to the later years of Philip.

2588 Æ **antoninianus.** IMP . MAR . SILBANNACVS AVG. Rad. and cuir.
bust, r. ℞. VICTORIA AVG. Mercury stg. facing, hd. l., holding
Victory and caduceus. *R.I.C.* 1 .. .. *Unique*

TRAJAN DECIUS
A.D. 249 – 251

2606

(C. Messius Quintus Traianus Decius). Born about A.D. *201 at Budalia, a village in Lower Pannonia, Decius attained senatorial rank early in his career and was governor of Lower Moesia from* A.D. *234-8. Following the abortive rebellion of Pacatian in Upper Moesia, Philip despatched Decius to restore order; but the rebels forced the latter, under threat of death, to assume the purple and march upon Italy. In the ensuing battle, which was fought near Verona, Philip and his son were slain and Decius was left undisputed master of the empire. Much of his short reign was spent in fighting the barbarians on the Northern frontier, and in a battle against the Goths at Abrittus, late in* A.D. *251, Decius was defeated and killed together with his elder son, Herennius Etruscus. The reign of Decius is, perhaps, best known for his rigorous persecution of the Christians, in which Pope Fabian lost his life.*

Mints: Rome; Milan; Antioch.

The obverse legend is IMP . C . M . Q . TRAIANVS DECIVS AVG., *unless otherwise stated.*

The normal obverse type for antoniniani, double sestertii and dupondii is rad., dr. and/or cuir. bust, r. All other denominations have laur., dr. and/or cuir. bust, r.

Apart from his own coins, and those of his wife and sons, Decius also struck a series of antoniniani commemorating most of the deified emperors from Augustus to Severus Alexander. Most of these coins will be found in this catalogue listed under the emperors concerned.

In *R.I.C.* the coinage of Decius, Etruscilla, Etruscus and Hostilian is dealt with in one group, numbered 1-226.

2589 *N* **aureus.** ℞. ABVNDANTIA AVG. Abundance stg. r., emptying
cornucopiae. *C.* 1. *R.I.C.* 10a .. ..£250·00
2590 Æ **antoninianus.** ℞. As previous. *C.* 2. *R.I.C.* 10b .. .. 3·25
2591 ℞. ADVENTVS AVG. Decius on horseback l., raising r. hand. *C.* 4.
R.I.C. 11b. **Plate 8** .. .. 3·50
2592 IMP . TRAIANVS DECIVS AVG. ℞. As previous. *C.* 6. *R.I.C.* 1b .. 4·25
2593 ℞. DACIA. Dacia stg. l., holding staff surmounted by ass's head.
C. 16. *R.I.C.* 12b .. .. 3·50
2594 IMP . CAE . TRA . DEC . AVG. ℞. DACIA. Dacia stg. l., holding standard.
C. 25. *R.I.C.* 36a .. .. 5·00

Very Fine

2595 **Æ antoninianus.** ℞. DACIA FELIX. As previous. *C.* 34. *R.I.C.*
14*b* .. .. £6·00

2596 IMP . CAE . TRA . DEC . AVG. ℞. GEN . ILLYRICI. Genius stg. l.,
holding patera and cornucopiae. *C.* 43. *R.I.C.* 38*a* .. .. .. 4·50

2597 ℞. GENIVS EXERC. ILLYRICIANI. As previous, but with standard to r.
of Genius. *C.* 49. *R.I.C.* 16*c* .. .. 3·00

2598 IMP . TRAIANVS DECIVS AVG. ℞. PANNONIAE. Pannonia stg. facing,
hd. r., holding standard. *C.* 79. *R.I.C.* 5 .. .. 5·00

2599 ℞. PANNONIAE. The two Pannoniae stg. side by side, each holding
standard. *C.* 86. *R.I.C.* 21*b* .. .. 3·50

2600 ℞. PAX AVGVSTI. Pax stg. l. *C.* 92. *R.I.C.* 27 .. .. .. 5·00

2601 ℞. VBERITAS AVG. Uberitas stg. l., holding purse and cornucopiae.
C. 105. *R.I.C.* 28 .. .. 3·25

2602 ℞. VICTORIA AVG. Victory advancing l. *C.* 113 *var.* *R.I.C.* 29*c* .. 3·25

2603 IMP . TRAIANVS DECIVS AVG. ℞. VIRTVS AVG. Virtus seated l., holding
branch and spear. *C.* 123. *R.I.C.* 8 .. .. 3·50

2604 **Æ denarius.** ℞. As 2597. *R.I.C.* 16*b* .. .. 125·00

2605 **Æ quinarius.** ℞. As 2593. *C.* 17. *R.I.C.* 12*a* .. .. .. 80·00

2606 **Æ double sestertius.** ℞. FELICITAS SAECVLI S . C. Felicity stg. l., **Fine**
holding long caduceus and cornucopiae. *C.* 40. *R.I.C.* 115*c*. *Illustrated on p.* 235 .. .. 65·00

2607 **Æ sestertius.** ℞. DACIA S . C. As 2593. *C.* 18. *R.I.C.* 112 .. 9·00

2608 IMP . CAES . C . MESS . Q . DECIO TRAI . AVG. ℞. As previous. *C.* 22.
R.I.C. 101*b* .. .. 10·00

2609 ℞. GENIVS EXERC . ILLYRICIANI S . C. Genius stg. l., holding patera
and cornucopiae; to r., standard. *C.* 53. *R.I.C.* 117*b* .. .. .. 9·00

2610 IMP . CAES . C . MESS . TRAI . Q . DECIO AVG. ℞. GENIVS EXERCITVS
ILLYRICIANI S . C. As previous. *C.* 65. *R.I.C.* 105*d* .. .. .. 10·00

2611 ℞. LIBERALITAS AVG . S . C. Trajan Decius seated l. on platform,
accompanied by prætorian prefect and Liberalitas; to l., citizen mounting
steps of platform. *C.* 75. *R.I.C.* 121 .. .. 35·00

2612 ℞. PANNONIAE S . C. As 2599. *C.* 87. *R.I.C.* 124*a* .. .. .. 9·00

2613 ℞. PAX AVGVSTI S . C. Pax stg. l. *C.* 93. *R.I.C.* 125*a* .. .. 8·00

2614 ℞. VICTORIA AVG . S . C. Victory advancing l. *C.* 117. *R.I.C.* 126*d* .. 8·00

2615 **Æ dupondius.** ℞. DACIA S . C. As 2593. *C.* 20. *R.I.C.* 112*e* .. 9·00

2616 ℞. LIBERALITAS AVG . S . C. Liberalitas stg. l. *C.* 72. *R.I.C.* 120*c* .. 9·00

2617 **Æ as.** As 2609. *C.* 54. *R.I.C.* 117*c* .. .. 9·00

2618 ℞. As 2616. *C.* 71. *R.I.C.* 120*a* .. .. 9·00

2619 ℞. PANNONIAE S . C. As 2599. *C.* 88. *R.I.C.* 124*c* .. .. .. 9·00

2620 **Æ semis.** ℞. S . C. Mars stg. l., leaning on shield and holding spear.
C. 102. *R.I.C.* 128 .. .. 8·00

Colonial and Provincial Coinage

2621 *Phrygia, Cibyra,* **Æ 24.** Rad. and dr. bust, r. ℞. Distyle shrine
containing wicker basket. *B.M.C. G.*87 .. .. 6·00

2622 — *Philomelium,* **Æ 24.** — ℞. River-god, Gallos, reclining l., holding
cornucopiae. *B.M.C. G.*42 .. .. 6·00

2623 *Syria, Antioch,* **billon tetradrachm.** Laur. bust, r. ℞. Eagle stg.
facing on palm-branch, hd. l. *B.M.C. G.*578 .. .. 5·00

2624 *Samaria, Caesarea,* **Æ 27.** — ℞. Nike advancing l. *B.M.C. G.* 156 15·00

2625 *Egypt, Alexandria,* **billon tetradrachm.** Laur., dr. and cuir. bust, r.
℞. Nike advancing r. *B.M.C. G.*2076 .. .. 3·00

2626 — — ℞. Eagle stg. l., hd. turned. *B.M.C. G.*2083 .. .. .. 3·00

HERENNIA ETRUSCILLA

2632

Descended from an old Italian family, Herennia Etruscilla was the wife of Trajan Decius and the mother of Herennius Etruscus and Hostilian.

There are two varieties of obv. type:
a. Diad. and dr. bust, r.
b. Diad. and dr. bust r., resting on crescent.

		Very Fine
2627	Æ **aureus.** HER . ETRVSCILLA AVG. a. ℞. PVDICITIA AVG. Pudicitia seated l., holding sceptre. C. 18. R.I.C. 59a	£275·00
2628	**Æ antoninianus.** — b. ℞. FECVNDITAS AVG. Fecunditas stg. l., holding cornucopiae, child at feet. C. 8. R.I.C. 55b	5·00
2629	— b. ℞. IVNO REGINA. Juno stg. l., peacock at feet. C. 14. R.I.C. 57	5·00
2630	— b. ℞. PVDICITIA AVG. Pudicitia stg. l., holding sceptre. C. 17. R.I.C. 58b	4·00
2631	— b. ℞. As 2627. C. 19. R.I.C. 59b. **Plate 8**	3·50

		Fine
2632	**Æ double sestertius.** HERENNIA ETRVSCILLA AVG. b. ℞. PVDICITIA AVG . S . C. Pudicitia seated l., holding sceptre. C. 21. R.I.C. 136a *Illustrated above*	150·00
2633	**Æ sestertius.** — a. ℞. FECVNDITAS AVG . S . C. As 2628. C. 9. R.I.C. 134a	12·50
2634	— a. ℞. As 2632. C. 22. R.I.C. 136b	10·50
2635	**Æ dupondius.** — b. ℞. As 2632. C. 24. R.I.C. 136d ..	10·00
2636	**Æ as.** — a. ℞. As 2632. C. 23. R.I.C. 136c	9·00
2637	*Egypt, Alexandria,* **billon tetradrachm.** Diad. and dr. bust, r. ℞. Eusebeia stg. l., sacrificing over altar. B.M.C. G.2089	5·00

HERENNIUS ETRUSCUS
A.D. 251

2650

Q. Herennius Etruscus Messius Decius was the elder son of Trajan Decius, and was given the rank of Caesar in A.D. 250. He was created Augustus the following year, but shortly afterwards he and his father were killed in battle against the Goths, as related above.

As Caesar

A.D. 250-251, *under Trajan Decius*

The obv. legend is Q . HER . ETR . MES . DECIVS NOB . C., *unless otherwise stated.*

Very Fine

2638 A' **aureus.** Bare-headed and dr. bust, r. R. PRINCIPI IVVENTVTIS.
Herennius stg. l., holding standard and spear. *C.* 32. *R.I.C.* 148*a* ..£350·00

2639 R **antoninianus.** Rad. and dr. bust, r. R. CONCORDIA AVGG.
Clasped hands. *C.* 4. *R.I.C.* 138 .. .. 8·50

2640 — R. PIETAS AVGG. Mercury stg. l., holding purse and caduceus.
C. 11. *R.I.C.* 142*b* **Plate 8** .. .. 6·50

2641 — R. PIETAS AVGVSTORVM. Sacrificial implements. *C.* 14. *R.I.C.*
143 .. .. 6·50

2642 — R. PRINC. IVVENTVTIS. Apollo seated l., holding branch and
resting l. elbow on lyre. *C.* 22. *R.I.C.* 145 .. .. .. 7·50

2643 — R. PRINCIPI IVVENTVTIS. Herennius stg. l., holding rod and spear.
C. 26. *R.I.C.* 147*c* .. .. 6·50

2644 — R. SPES PVBLICA. Spes advancing l. *C.* 38. *R.I.C.* 149 .. 6·50

2645 HEREN . ETRV . MES . QV . DECIVS CAESAR. — R. VBERITAS AVG. Uberitas
stg. l., holding purse and cornucopiae. *C.* 40. *R.I.C.* 160*a* .. .. 10·00

2646 R **denarius.** Bare-headed and dr. bust, r. R. PRINC. IVVENT.
As 2642. *R.I.C.* 144*a* .. .. 175·00

2647 R **quinarius.** — R. As 2643. *C.* 27. *R.I.C.* 147*b* .. 175·00

2648 Æ **sestertius.** Bare-headed, dr. and cuir. bust, r. R. PIETAS **Fine**
AVGVSTORVM S . C. Sacrificial implements. *C.* 15. *R.I.C.* 168*a* .. 25·00

2649 — R. PRINC . IVVENTVTIS S . C. As 2642. *C.* 23. *R.I.C.* 169*a* .. 25·00

2650 — R. PRINCIPI IVVENTVTIS S . C. As 2643. *C.* 28. *R.I.C.* 171*a*.
Illustrated on p. 237 .. .. 25·00

2651 Æ **dupondius** or **as.** As previous. *C.* 29. *R.I.C.* 171*b* .. .. 15·00

As Augustus

2652 A' **aureus.** IMP . C . Q . HER . ETR . MES . DECIO AVG. Laur., dr. and
cuir. bust, r. R. PRINC . IVVENT. As 2642. *C.* 18. *R.I.C.* 153*a* *Very rare*

2653 R **antoninianus.** — Rad. and dr. bust, r. R. VICTORIA GERMANICA.
Victory advancing r. *C.* 41. *R.I.C.* 154 .. *Very fine* £65·00

HOSTILIAN
A.D. 251

2671

 C. *Valens Hostilianus Messius Quintus was the younger son of Trajan Decius, and was
given the rank of Caesar in* A.D. 251. *On the death of his father and brother, he was left as
the sole surviving male representative of the old imperial family, and Trebonianus Gallus, the
successor of Decius and Etruscus, raised him to the rank of Augustus. After a short period
of joint rule, Hostilian died of plague.*

As Caesar

A.D. 251, *under* (a) *Trajan Decius,*
                   (b) *Trajan Decius and Herennius Etruscus,*
                   (c) *Trebonianus Gallus* (?)

The obv. legend is C . VALENS HOSTIL . MES . QVINTVS N . C., *unless otherwise stated.*

Very Fine

2654 *N* **aureus.** Bare-headed and dr. bust, r. ℞. PRINCIPI IVVENTVTIS.
      Hostilian stg. l., holding standard and spear. *C.* 33.   *R.I.C.* 181*b* .. £450·00

2655 **Æ antoninianus.** Rad. and dr. bust, r. ℞. MARTI PROPVGNATORI.
      Mars advancing r., holding spear and shield. *C.* 15.   *R.I.C.* 177*b*   10·00

2656 C . VAL . HOS . MES . QVINTVS N . C. — ℞. PIETAS AVGG. Mercury stg.
      l., holding purse and caduceus. *C.* 20.   *R.I.C.* 178*b* ..   ..   ..   10·00

2657 Rad. and dr. bust, r. ℞. PIETAS AVGVSTORVM. Sacrificial implements.
      C. 25.   *R.I.C.* 179 ..   ..   10·00

2658 — ℞. PRINCIPI IVVENTVTIS. Apollo seated l., holding branch and
      resting l. elbow on lyre. *C.* 30.   *R.I.C.* 180 ..   ..   ..   15·00

2659 — ℞. As 2654. *C.* 34.   *R.I.C.* 181*d* ..   ..   10·00

2660 C . OVAL . OSTIL . MES . COVINTVS CAESAR. — ℞. PVDICITIA AVG.
      Pudicitia seated l., holding sceptre. *C.* 43.   *R.I.C.* 196*a*   ..   17·50

2661 C . OVL . OSTIL . MES . COVINTVS CAESAR. — ℞. VBERITAS AVG. Uberitas
      stg. l., holding purse and cornucopiae. *C.* 63.   *R.I.C.* 200*a* ..   15·00

2662 **Æ quinarius.** Bare-headed and dr. bust, r. ℞. PRINCIPI IVVENTVTIS.
      Hostilian stg. l., holding rod and spear. *R.I.C.* 183*c* ..   ..   175·00

Fine

2663 **Æ sestertius.** — ℞. PIETAS AVGG . S . C. As 2656. *C.* 23.   *R.I.C.*
      213 ..   ..   30·00

2664 — ℞. PRINCIPI IVVENTVTIS S . C. As 2658. *C.* 31.   *R.I.C.* 215*a* ..   30·00

2665 — ℞. — As 2654. *C.* 35.   *R.I.C.* 216*a*   ..   ..   ..   30·00

2666 **Æ dupondius** or **as.** — ℞. — As 2658. *C.* 32.   *R.I.C.* 215*b*   ..   25·00

As Augustus

With Trebonianus Gallus

The obverse legend is IMP . CAE . C . VAL . HOS . MES . QVINTVS AVG., *unless otherwise stated.*

Very Fine

2667 **Æ antoninianus.** C . OVAL . OSTIL . MES . COVINTVS AVG. Rad. and dr.
      bust, r. ℞. ROMAE AETERNAE. Roma seated l., holding Victory and
      spear. *C.* 45.   *R.I.C.* 204*a* ..   ..   30·00

2668 Rad. and dr. bust, r. ℞. SECVRITAS AVGG. Security stg. facing, hd.
      r., leaning on column. *C.* 59.   *R.I.C.* 191*a*. **Plate 8** ..   ..   30·00

2669 *Obv.* As 2667. ℞. VICTORIA AVG. Victory stg. r. on globe. *C.* 67.
      R.I.C. 209*a* ..   ..   30·00

Fine

2670 **Æ sestertius.** IMP . CAE . C . VAL . HOS . MES . QVINT . AVG. Laur., dr.
      and cuir. bust, r. ℞. QVINTO FELIX S . C. Pax stg. l. *C.* 44.   *R.I.C.*
      222 ..   ..   100·00

2671 Laur., dr. and cuir. bust, r. ℞. SECVRITAS AVGG . S . C. Security stg.
      facing, hd. r., leaning on column. *C.* 60.   *R.I.C.* 225. *Illustrated on
      p.* 238 ..   ..   40·00

2672 **Æ as.** — ℞. PIETAS AVGVST . S . C. Pietas stg. l., altar at feet. *C.* 24.
      R.I.C. 220 ..   ..   30·00

TREBONIANUS GALLUS
A.D. 251 – 253

2673

(C. Vibius Trebonianus Gallus). *Nothing is known of the early history of this emperor, but he is recorded as having held a high command in the army which was defeated by the Goths at Abrittus.* *After the death of Decius, which may have been due to treachery on the part of Gallus, the latter was chosen by the army to fill the vacant throne, and his first act was the conclusion of a peace with the Goths, the terms of which were felt to be shameful to Rome and an encouragement to future aggression to the Goths.* *The reign of Gallus was troubled by invasions on both the Northern and Eastern frontiers, and the situation was further worsened by a devastating plague which swept the empire and even took the life of the joint-emperor, Hostilian.* *In A.D. 252 Aemilian, the governor of Moesia, inflicted a severe defeat on the Goths and was immediately proclaimed emperor by his troops.* *The following year he invaded Italy, and whilst advancing to deal with the rebels, Gallus and his son Volusian were murdered by their own soldiers.*

Mints: Rome; Milan; Antioch.

There are two main varieties of obverse legend:

A. IMP . CAE . C . VIB . TREB . GALLVS AVG.
B. IMP . CAES . C . VIBIVS TREBONIANVS GALLVS AVG.

The obverse type for heavy aurei, antoniniani and dupondii is rad. bust r., *and for all other denominations, laur. bust* r. *The bust is normally depicted dr. and cuir., although very often the cuirass is indistinct and may be missing on some specimens.*

Gallus made an interesting change in the gold coinage: in place of the aureus, which had been struck by his immediate predecessors at an average weight of 66·5 grains, he introduced two new denominations, one with rad. bust and weighing ca. 90·5 grains, the other with laur. bust and weighing ca. 55·2 grains. *The former is called heavy aureus and the latter, aureus, but the relationship between these two coins and their relationships to other denominations are quite uncertain.*

In *R.I.C.* the coinage of Gallus and Volusian is dealt with in one group, numbered 1-264.

Very Fine

2673 **A′ heavy aureus.** A. R. CONCORDIA AVGG. Concord seated l.
C. 25. *R.I.C.* 7. *Illustrated above* .. ..£300·00

2674 **A′ aureus.** A. R. LIBERTAS AVGG. Liberty stg. l. C. 60. *R.I.C.*
20 .. .. 250·00

2675 **A′ light aureus or quinarius.** As previous. C. 61. *R.I.C.* 24 .. 325·00

2676 **AR antoninianus.** IMP . C . C . VIB . TREB . GALLVS P . F . AVG. R.
AEQVITAS AVGG. Equity stg. l. C. 9. *R.I.C.* 81 .. .. .. 4·25

2677 A. R. AETERNITAS AVGG. Eternity stg. l., holding globe surmounted
by phoenix. C. 13. *R.I.C.* 30 .. .. 5·00

2678 A. R. ANNONA AVGG. Annona stg. r., holding rudder and corn-ears.
C. 17. *R.I.C.* 31 .. .. 4·50

2679 A. R. APOLL . SALVTARI. Apollo stg. l., holding branch and leaning
on lyre set on rock. C. 20. *R.I.C.* 32 .. .. 5·00

2680 *Obv.* As 2676. R. FELICITAS PVBL. Felicity stg. l. C. 34. *R.I.C.*
82 .. .. 4·25

Very Fine

2681 **Æ antoninianus.** A. ℞. FELICITAS PVBLICA. Felicity stg. l. *C*. 37.
R.I.C. 33   ..   ..   £3·75

2682 A. ℞. FELICITAS PVBLICA. Felicity stg. l., leaning on column.
C. 41. *R.I.C.* 34A   ..   ..   4·25

2683 IMP . C . C . VIB . TREB . GALLVS AVG. ℞. IVNO MARTIALIS. Juno
seated l., holding corn-ears (?) and sceptre. *C*. 46. *R.I.C.* 69   ..   5·00

2684 A. ℞. IVNONI MARTIALI. Juno seated facing in circular temple of
two columns. *C*. 49. *R.I.C.* 54 ..   ..   15·00

2685 A. ℞. As 2674. *C*. 63. *R.I.C.* 37   ..   ..   3·75

2686 A. ℞. LIBERTAS AVGG. Liberty stg. l., leaning on column. *C*. 67.
R.I.C. 39. **Plate 9** ..   ..   3·75

2687 *Obv.* As 2683. ℞. LIBERTAS PVBLICA. Liberty stg. l. *C*. 68.
R.I.C. 70   ..   ..   4·25

2688 — ℞. PAX AETERNA. Pax stg. l. *C*. 76. *R.I.C.* 71 ..   ..   ..   4·25

2689 A. ℞. PIETAS AVGG. Pietas stg. l., raising both hands. *C*. 84.
R.I.C. 41   ..   ..   3·75

2690 *Obv.* As 2683. ℞. As previous, but Pietas has altar at feet. *C*. 88.
R.I.C. 72   ..   ..   4·25

2691 A. ℞. SALVS AVGG. Salus stg. l., feeding serpent arising from altar.
C. 117. *R.I.C.* 46*a* ..   ..   7·50

2692 GALLVS PIVS AVG. ℞. As previous. *C*. 118. *R.I.C.* 46*b*   ..   25·00

2693 *Obv.* As 2676. ℞. VBERITAS AVG. Uberitas stg. l., holding purse
and cornucopiae. *C*. 125. *R.I.C.* 92   ..   ..   4·75

2694 A. ℞. VICTORIA AVGG. Victory stg. l. *C*. 128. *R.I.C.* 48*a*   ..   4·00

2695 **Æ quinarius.** IMP . C . GALLVS AVG. ℞. As 2682. *C*. 42. *R.I.C.* 29   75·00

Fine

2696 **Æ sestertius.** B. ℞. AETERNITAS AVGG . S . C. As 2677. *C*. 14.
R.I.C. 102   ..   ..   12·50

2697 B. ℞. APOLL . SALVTARI S . C. As 2679. *C*. 21. *R.I.C.* 103   ..   15·00

2698 B. ℞. CONCORDIA AVGG . S . C. Concord seated l. *C*. 26. *R.I.C.*
106*a* ..   ..   10·00

2699 B. ℞. IVNONI MARTIALI S . C. As 2684. *C*. 50. *R.I.C.* 110*a*   ..   30·00

2700 B. ℞. LIBERALITAS AVGG . S . C. Liberalitas stg. l. *C*. 57. *R.I.C.*
113   ..   ..   12·50

2701 B. ℞. PAX AVGG . S . C. Pax stg. l. *C*. 78. *R.I.C.* 115*a*   ..   ..   10·00

2702 B. ℞. PIETAS AVGG . S . C. As 2689. *C*. 86. *R.I.C.* 116*a* ..   ..   10·00

2703 B. ℞. SALVS AVGG . S . C. Salus stg. r., feeding serpent held in arms.
C. 115. *R.I.C.* 121*a*   ..   ..   10·00

2704 B. ℞. VOTIS DECENNALIBVS S . C. in laurel-wreath. *C*. 137. *R.I.C.*
127*a* ..   ..   30·00

2705 **Æ dupondius.** A. ℞. As previous. *R.I.C.* 127*c* ..   ..   ..   40·00

2706 **Æ as.** A. ℞. LIBERTAS AVGG . S . C. Liberty stg. l. *C*. 65. *R.I.C.*
114*b*   ..   ..   12·50

2707 A. ℞. As 2701. *C*. 79. *R.I.C.* 115*b* ..   ..   12·50

2708 A. ℞. As 2703. *C*. 116. *R.I.C.* 121*b*   ..   ..   12·50

Colonial and Provincial Coinage

2709 *Syria, Antioch,* Æ 29. Laur. hd., r. ℞. Tetrastyle temple containing
statue of the Tyche of Antioch. *B.M.C. G.*654 ..   ..   5·00

2710 *Egypt, Alexandria,* **billon tetradrachm.** Laur., dr. and cuir. bust, r.
℞. Dikaiosyne seated l. *B.M.C. G.*2102   ..   ..   4·50

VOLUSIAN
A.D. 251 – 253

2739

(C. Vibius Afinius Gallus Vendumnianus Volusianus).   The son of Trebonianus Gallus, Volusian was given the rank of Caesar at the time of his father's accession.   On the death of Hostilian, he was immediately created Augustus and ruled jointly with his father until their murders in A.D. 253.

As Caesar

A.D. 251, *under Trebonianus Gallus and Hostilian*

The obv. legend is C . VIBIO VOLVSIANO CAES.

Very Fine

2711   **A' aureus.**   Bare-headed and dr. bust, r.   ℞.   PRINCIPI IVVENTVTIS. Volusian stg. l., holding rod and spear.   *C.* 98.   *R.I.C.* 129   ..   ..£500·00

2712   **A' light aureus** or **quinarius.**   As previous.   *C.* 99.   *R.I.C.* 130 ..   500·00

2713   **Æ antoninianus.**   Rad. and dr. bust, r.   ℞.   As previous.   *C.* 100. *R.I.C.* 134   ..   ..   25·00

2714   **Æ sestertius.**   Bare-headed and dr. bust, r.   ℞.   As previous, but   **Fine** with s . c.   added.   *C.* 103.   *R.I.C.* 241 ..   ..   40·00

2715   **Æ dupondius** or **as.** — ℞.   PAX AVGG . s . c.   Pax stg. l.   *C.* 76. *R.I.C.* 240   ..   ..   30·00

2716   — ℞.   VOTIS DECENNALIBVS s . c. in laurel-wreath.   *C.* 141.   *R.I.C.* 243   40·00

As Augustus

The obv. legend is IMP . CAE . C . VIB . VOLVSIANO AVG., *unless otherwise stated.*

The obverse type for heavy aurei, antoniniani and dupondii is rad. bust r., and for all other denominations, laur. bust r.   The bust is normally depicted dr. and cuir., although very often the cuirass is indistinct and may even be missing on some specimens.

Very Fine

2717   **A' heavy aureus.**   ℞.   PIETAS AVGG.   Pietas stg. l., raising both hands. *C.* 82.   *R.I.C.* 150 ..   ..   500·00

2718   **A' aureus.**   ℞.   VICTORIA AVGG.   Victory stg. l.   *C.* 130.   *R.I.C.* 161   450·00

2719   **A' light aureus** or **quinarius.**   ℞.   As 2717.   *C.* 84.   *R.I.C.* 163 ..   450·00

2720   **Æ antoninianus.**   ℞.   AEQVITAS AVGG.   Equity stg. l.   *C.* 8.   *R.I.C.* 166   ..   ..   6·00

2721   ℞.   CONCORDIA AVGG.   Concord stg. l.   *C.* 20.   *R.I.C.* 167 ..   ..   4·50

2722   ℞. — Concord seated l.   *C.* 25.   *R.I.C.* 168 ..   ..   4·50

2723   IMP . C . C . VIB . VOLVSIANVS AVG.   ℞.   FELICITAS PVBL.   Felicity stg. l. *C.* 32.   *R.I.C.* 205 ..   ..   5·00

2724   ℞.   IVNONI MARTIALI.   Juno seated facing in circular temple of two columns.   *C.* 43.   *R.I.C.* 172   ..   ..   12·50

2725   ℞.   PAX AVGG.   Pax stg. l.   *C.* 70.   *R.I.C.* 179   ..   ..   ..   4·50

2726   ℞.   PIETAS AVGG.   Pietas stg. l., altar at feet.   *C.* 88.   *R.I.C.* 182   ..   5·00

Very Fine

2727 **Æ antoninianus.** R. P . M . TR . P . IIII . COS . II. Volusian stg. l.,
holding branch and sceptre. *C.* 92. *R.I.C.* 140. **Plate 9** .. .. £6·00
2728 R. — Volusian stg. l., sacrificing over tripod-altar. *C.* 94. *R.I.C.* 141 6·00
2729 IMP . C . C . VIB . VOLVSIANVS AVG. R. ROMAE AETERNAE AVG. Roma
seated l., holding Victory and spear. *C.* 113. *R.I.C.* 221 .. .. 7·50
2730 R. SALVS AVGG. Salus stg. r., feeding serpent held in arms. *C.* 118.
R.I.C. 184 .. .. 6·00
2731 IMP . C . V . AF . GAL . VEND . VOLVSIANO AVG. R. VBERITAS AVG.
Uberitas stg. l., holding purse and cornucopiae. *C.* 125. *R.I.C.* 237a 12·50
2732 IMP . C . C . VIB . VOLVSIANVS AVG. R. VIRTVS AVGG. Virtus stg. r.
C. 133. *R.I.C.* 206 .. .. 5·50
2733 R. — Virtus stg. l. *C.* 135. *R.I.C.* 186 .. .. .. 6·00
2734 **Æ quinarius.** IMP . C . VOLVSIANVS AVG. R. As 2730. *C.* 119.
R.I.C. 208B .. .. 125·00

Fine

2735 **Æ sestertius.** R. AEQVITAS AVGG . S . C. Equity stg. l. *C.* 9.
R.I.C. 246 .. .. 12·50
2736 R. CONCORDIA AVGG . S . C. Concord stg. l. *C.* 21. *R.I.C.* 249a .. 12·50
2737 R. — Concord seated l. *C.* 26. *R.I.C.* 250a .. .. .. 12·50
2738 R. FELICITAS PVBLICA S . C. Felicity stg. l., leaning on column. *C.* 35.
R.I.C. 251a .. .. 12·50
2739 R. IVNONI MARTIALI S . C. As 2724. *C.* 46. *R.I.C.* 253a. *Illustrated
on p.* 242 .. .. 30·00
2740 R. PAX AVGG . S . C. Pax stg. l. *C.* 74. *R.I.C.* 256a .. .. 12·50
2741 R. PIETAS AVGG . S . C. As 2717. *C.* 87. *R.I.C.* 257 .. .. 12·50
2742 R. SECVRITAS AVGG . S . C. Security stg. r., leaning on column. *C.* 124.
R.I.C. 261 .. .. 12·50
2743 R. VICTORIA AVGG . S . C. Victory stg. l. *C.* 132. *R.I.C.* 262 .. 12·50
2744 **Æ dupondius.** R. As 2736. *C.* 23. *R.I.C.* 249c .. .. .. 30·00
2745 **Æ as.** As 2736. *C.* 22. *R.I.C.* 249b .. .. 12·00
2746 As 2738. *C.* 36. *R.I.C.* 251b .. .. 12·00
2747 As 2740. *C.* 75. *R.I.C.* 256b .. .. 12·00
2748 R. VIRTVS AVGG . S . C. Virtus stg. l. *C.* 137. *R.I.C.* 263b.. .. 12·00

Colonial and Provincial Coinage

2749 *Pisidia, Antioch,* **Æ 23.** Rad. bust, r. R. Legionary eagle between
two standards. *B.M.C. G.*130 .. .. 4·00
2750 *Egypt, Alexandria,* **billon tetradrachm.** Laur., dr. and cuir. bust, r.
R. Tyche stg. l. *B.M.C. G.*2112 .. .. 5·00

2763

AEMILIAN
A.D. 252 – 253

(*M. Aemilius Aemilianus*). *A native of Mauretania, Aemilian was governor of Moesia
in the reign of Gallus, and having successfully repulsed an invasion of his province by the*

Goths, he was hailed as Augustus by his troops.   He subsequently invaded Italy and the soldiers of Gallus and Volusian, realizing the superiority of their adversary, murdered the joint-emperors and transferred their allegiance to Aemilian.   About three months later, however, a similar fate overtook the new emperor: P. Licinius Valerianus, who had been summoned by Gallus to his assistance, remained faithful to the memory of the late emperors and, after having been proclaimed emperor by his troops, invaded Italy.   Aemilian advanced to meet him, but was murdered by his own men, leaving Valerian master of the Roman World.

Mints: Rome; Balkan mint.

There are two main varieties of obv. legend:
- A.   IMP . AEMILIANVS PIVS FEL . AVG.
- B.   IMP . CAES . AEMILIANVS P . F . AVG.

The obverse type for antoniniani and dupondii is rad., dr. and cuir. bust r., and for all other denominations, laur., dr. and cuir. bust r.

Very Fine

2751	**N aureus.** A. R. ERCVL . VICTORI. Hercules stg. r., leaning on club and holding bow. *C.* 12. *R.I.C.* 3a	*Extr. rare*
2752	**R antoninianus.** A. R. APOL . CONSERVAT. Apollo stg. l., holding branch and leaning on lyre set on rock. *C.* 2. *R.I.C.* 1	£25·00
2753	A. R. DIANAE VICTRI. Diana stg. l., holding arrow and bow. *C.* 10. *R.I.C.* 2b	30·00
2754	A. R. As 2751. *C.* 13. *R.I.C.* 3b	25·00
2755	B. R. IOVI CONSERVAT. Jupiter stg. l., holding thunderbolt and sceptre, small figure of Aemilian at feet. *C.* 17. *R.I.C.* 14	25·00
2756	A. R. MARTI PROPVGT. Mars stg. l., leaning on shield and holding spear. *C.* 25. *R.I.C.* 6	20·00
2757	A. R. PACI AVG. Pax stg. l., leaning on column. *C.* 26. *R.I.C.* 8 ..	20·00
2758	IMP . M . AEMIL . AEMILIANVS P . F . AVG. R. PAXS AVG. Pax advancing l. *C.* 31. *R.I.C.* 23	50·00
2759	B. R. P . M . TR . P . I . P . P. Aemilian stg. l., sacrificing over tripod-altar to l. of which is standard. *C.* 33. *R.I.C.* 16	25·00
2760	A. R. ROMAE AETERN. Roma stg. l., holding phoenix and sceptre. *C.* 41. *R.I.C.* 9	25·00
2761	A. R. SPES PVBLICA. Spes advancing l. *C.* 47. *R.I.C.* 10 ..	20·00
2762	A. R. VICTORIA AVG. Victory advancing l. *C.* 53. *R.I.C.* 11 ..	20·00

Fine

2763	**Æ sestertius.** B. R. VIRTVS AVG . S . C. Virtus stg. l., holding branch and spear. *C.* 62. *R.I.C.* 53. *Illustrated on p. 243*	75·00
2764	B. R. VOTIS DECENNALIBVS S . C. in laurel-wreath. *C.* 67. *R.I.C.* 54a	90·00
2765	**Æ dupondius.** B. R. As previous. *C.* 68. *R.I.C.* 54b	75·00
2766	**Æ as.** B. R. SPES PVBLICA S . C. Spes advancing l. *C.* 50. *R.I.C.* 51b	60·00
2767	*Egypt, Alexandria,* **billon tetradrachm.** Laur. and cuir. bust, r. R. Nike advancing r. *B.M.C.* G.2117	10·00

CORNELIA SUPERA

Although completely unknown to history, this lady is generally accepted as having been the wife of Aemilian.

Very Fine

2768 **Æ antoninianus.** C . CORNEL . SVPERA AVG. Diad. and dr. bust r.,
resting on crescent. R. VESTA. Vesta stg. l., holding patera and
sceptre. C. 5. *R.I.C.* (*Aemilian*) 30 .. ..£600·00

URANIUS ANTONINUS
ca. A.D. 252 – 254

2769

(*L. Julius Aurelius Sulpicius Uranius Antoninus*). *Little is known about this ruler,
who maintained himself for about two years in the mint-city of Emesa, in Syria.*

2769 **Ν aureus.** L . IVL . AVR . SVLP . VRA . ANTONINVS. Laur., dr. and cuir.
bust, r. R. CONSERVATOR AVG. Conical stone, draped and ornamented, between two parasols. C. 1. *R.I.C.* 1. *Illustrated above* .. 1000·00
2770 — R. FECVNDITAS AVG. Fortune (?) stg. l., holding rudder and
cornucopiae. C. 3. *R.I.C.* 3 .. .. 1000·00
2771 L . IVL . AVR . SVP . ANTONINVS. Laur., dr. and cuir. bust, l. R.
P . M . TR . P . XVIIII . COS . IIII . P . P. Lion, rad., walking r. *R.I.C.* 6 .. 1000·00
2772 — R. SAECVLARES AVGG. Cippus inscribed COS . I. *R.I.C.* 7 .. .. 1000·00
2773 **Billon tetradrachm.** Laur. bust, r. R. Eagle stg. facing, hd. l.;
S . C. in field; EMICA in ex. *B.M.C. G.*22 .. .. 500·00

VALERIAN I
A.D. 253 – 260

2811A

(*P. Licinius Valerianus*). *Descended from a good Roman family, Valerian held various
offices in the service of the state until, in the reign of Decius, he was appointed Censor.
When Gallus received news of the revolt of Aemilian, he ordered Valerian to come to his
assistance with an army drawn from the Rhine garrisons, but Aemilian acted too swiftly and
Valerian was still in Raetia when he heard of the death of Gallus. He was immediately
proclaimed emperor by his troops and proceeded to invade Italy, and on the murder of
Aemilian he was left undisputed master of the Empire. He at once associated his son
Gallienus with himself as joint ruler. The reign of Valerian was marked by many frontier
troubles, and in A.D. 256 the emperor left Rome for the East in order to deal with the threat
from Persia. He soon established his headquarters at Antioch and achieved a number of
successes against the Persians. In A.D. 260, however, in the course of an advance through
Mesopotamia, the army of Valerian was surrounded and the emperor himself made prisoner.
He spent the remainder of his life in miserable captivity in Persia, the date of his death being
uncertain.*

Titles and Powers, A.D. 253-260

A.D.	Tribunician Power	Consulship
253	TR.P.	COS.
254	TR.P.II.	COS.II.
255	TR.P.III.	COS.III.
256	TR.P.IIII.	
257	TR.P.V.	COS.IIII.
258	TR.P.VI.	
259	TR.P.VII.	
260	TR.P.VIII.	

Mints: Rome; Lugdunum; Milan; Viminacium; Antioch.

The following are the commonest forms of obverse legend:

A. IMP . C . P . LIC . VALERIANVS AVG.

B. IMP . C . P . LIC . VALERIANVS P . F . AVG.

C. IMP . VALERIANVS AVG.

D. IMP . VALERIANVS P . AVG.

E. VALERIANVS P . F . AVG.

The normal obverse type for antoniniani and dupondii is rad., dr. and cuir. bust, r. Denarii, silver quinarii, sestertii and asses have laur., dr. and/or cuir. bust, r.

The gold coinage of Valerian presents serious difficulties, the irregularity in size and weight of the pieces being so great that it would almost seem that their issue was not governed by any fixed standard. R.I.C. quoting 112 recorded coins of the joint reign of Valerian and Gallienus, give weights ranging from a little over 2 grammes to nearly 6 grammes. These coins they consider to be aurei, the average weight being circa 3·25 grammes. They also quote coins of this period of weights less than 2 grammes and over 6 grammes. The former, they consider to be quinarii and the latter, some higher denomination than the aureus (heavy aureus).

The normal obverse type for all gold coins of Valerian is laur., dr. and/or cuir. bust, r. Occasionally, however, the bust is depicted rad. and cuir., such coins usually being of considerably more than average weight, but not always over 6 grammes.

Towards the end of the joint reign of Valerian and Gallienus, in circa A.D. 258, the silver content of the antoninianus, already very low, was so drastically reduced that the appearance of the coin was that of mere bronze. It therefore became necessary to give the coins a coating of white metal in order to indicate that they belonged to the silver series. This silver wash was, however, very thin and in most cases it soon became very patchy or entirely disappeared. Coins with the silvery coating still intact are therefore quite scarce and worth somewhat more than the prices given in this catalogue. Now that the antoninianus had become little more than a bronze coin itself, the issue of sestertii, dupondii and asses almost ceased, although both Valerian and Gallienus had previously issued these denominations in some quantity.

Very Fine

2774 *N* **heavy aureus.** A. Rad. and cuir. bust, r. ℞. AETERNITAS AVGG.
Valerian advancing r., holding globe. *C.* 6. *R.I.C.* 30 .. ..£450·00

2775 *N* **aureus.** A. Laur. and dr. bust, r. ℞. FIDES MILITVM. Fides
stg. l., holding two standards. *C.* 64. *R.I.C.* 35 .. .. .. 275·00

2776 *N* **light aureus** or **quinarius.** B. — ℞. ORIENS AVGG. Sol stg. l.,
holding whip. *C.* 133. *R.I.C.* 46 .. .. 275·00

Very Fine

2777	**Antoninianus** (*usually base silver*). A. ℞. AEQVITAS AVGG. Equity stg. l. *C.* 3. *R.I.C.* 209 ..	£2·50
2778	B. ℞. APOLINI CONSERVA. Apollo stg. l., holding branch and leaning on lyre set on rock. *C.* 17. *R.I.C.* 72 ..	2·75
2779	A. ℞. APOLINI PROPVG. Apollo stg. r., drawing bow. *C.* 25. *R.I.C.* 74 ..	3·00
2780	A. ℞. CONCORDIA AVGG. Concord stg. l. *C.* 31. *R.I.C.* 80 ..	2·50
2781	E. ℞. DEO VOLKANO. Vulcan stg. l., holding hammer and pincers, in temple of four columns. *R.I.C.* 5. ..	5·00
2782	B. ℞. FELICITAS AVGG. Felicity stg. l. *C.* 53. *R.I.C.* 87 ..	2·50
2783	A. ℞. As 2775. *C.* 65. *R.I.C.* 89 ..	2·50
2784	A. ℞. IOVI CONSERVATORI. Jupiter stg. l., holding thunderbolt and sceptre. *C.* 94. *R.I.C.* 92 ..	2·50
2785	A. ℞. LAETITIA AVGG. Laetitia stg. l., holding wreath and anchor. *C.* 101. *R.I.C.* 215 ..	2·50
2786	D. ℞. LIBERALITAS AVGG. Liberalitas stg. l. *C.* 106. *R.I.C.* 243 ..	2·50
2787	E. ℞. ORIENS AVGG. Sol advancing l., holding whip. *R.I.C.* 12 ..	4·00
2788	C. ℞. PAX AVGG. Pax stg. l. *C.* 146. *R.I.C.* 110 ..	2·50
2789	A. ℞. PIETATI AVGG. Security (?) stg. l., holding sceptre and leaning on column. *C.* 155. *R.I.C.* 219 ..	3·00
2790	B. ℞. P. M. TR. P. V. COS. IIII. P. P. Valerian seated l. on curule chair. *C.* 166. *R.I.C.* 142c ..	5·00
2791	C. ℞. — Valerian and Gallienus stg. facing each other. *C.* 169. *R.I.C.* 277 ..	6·00
2792	D. ℞. PROVID. AVGG. Providence stg. l., holding rod and standard. *C.* 173. *R.I.C.* 247 ..	2·75
2793	B. ℞. PROVIDENTIA AVGG. Providence stg. l., holding rod and cornucopiae. *C.* 175. *R.I.C.* 113..	2·50

2794   2808

2794	A. ℞. RESTITVT. GENER. HVMANI. Valerian advancing r., holding globe. *C.* 179. *R.I.C.* 220 ..	5·00
2795	B. ℞. RESTITVTOR ORBIS. Valerian stg. l., raising kneeling female figure. *C.* 183. *R.I.C.* 117. **Plate 9** ..	4·50
2796	A. ℞. RESTITVT. ORIENTIS. The Orient stg. r., presenting wreath to Valerian who stands l., facing her. *C.* 188. *R.I.C.* 286 ..	4·50
2797	D. ℞. SALVS AVGG. Salus stg. l., feeding serpent arising from altar. *C.* 196. *R.I.C.* 16 ..	2·50
2798	C. ℞. SECVRIT. PERPET. Security stg. l., holding sceptre and leaning on column. *C.* 204. *R.I.C.* 256 ..	2·75
2799	D. ℞. SPES PVBLICA. Spes advancing l. *C.* 208. *R.I.C.* 257 ..	2·50

Very Fine

2800 **Antoninianus.** A. ℞. VICTORIA AVGG. Victory stg. l., leaning on
      shield. *C.* 221. *R.I.C.* 127 .. .. £2·50
2801 A. ℞. — Victory stg. l. *C.* 230. *R.I.C.* 125 .. .. .. 2·50
2802 B. ℞. VICTORIA GERM. As 2800. *C.* 245. *R.I.C.* 132 .. .. 5·00
2803 E. ℞. VICT . PARTICA. Victory advancing l., captive at feet. *R.I.C.*
      22 .. .. 8·50
2804 A. ℞. VIRTVS AVGG. Mars stg. l., leaning on shield and holding
      spear. *C.* 263. *R.I.C.* 133 .. .. 2·50
2805 B. ℞. — Valerian and Gallienus stg. facing each other. *C.* 276.
      R.I.C. 293 .. .. 3·00
2806 A. ℞. VOTA ORBIS. Two Victories attaching shield, inscribed S . C.,
      to palm-tree. *C.* 280. *R.I.C.* 294 .. .. 7·50
2807 **Denarius.** (*base silver*). B. ℞. ORIENS AVGG. Sol stg. l., holding
      whip. *C.* 134. *R.I.C.* 144 .. .. 45·00
2808 **Quinarius.** (*base silver*). B. ℞. IOVI CONSERVAT. As 2784. *C.*
      90. *R.I.C.* 146. *Illustrated on p.* 247 .. .. 45·00

Fine

2809 **Æ sestertius.** B. ℞. APOLINI CONSERVA . S . C. As 2778. *C.* 22.
      R.I.C. 152 .. .. 15·00
2810 B. ℞. FELICITAS AVGG . S . C. Felicity stg. l. *C.* 58. *R.I.C.* 157 .. 15·00
2811 A. ℞. LIBERALITAS AVGG . S . C. Liberalitas stg. l. *C.* 110. *R.I.C.*
      164 .. .. 18·00
2811A A. ℞. VESTA S . C. Vesta stg. l., holding patera and sceptre. *C.* 214.
      R.I.C. 175. *Illustrated on p.* 245 .. .. 20·00
2812 **Æ dupondius.** A. ℞. As 2811. *C.* 112. *R.I.C.* 185 .. .. 15·00
2813 **Æ as.** As 2809. *C.* 23. *R.I.C.* 190 .. .. 12·50
2814 A. ℞. CONCORDIA EXERCIT . S . C. Concord stg. l. *C.* 41. *R.I.C.* 191 12·50
2815 B. ℞. ORIENS AVGG . S . C. Sol stg. l., holding whip. *C.* 138. *R.I.C.*
      198 .. .. 12·50
2816 A. ℞. VICTORIA AVGG . S . C. As 2800. *C.* 229. *R.I.C.* 201.. .. 12·50
2817 A. ℞. VIRTVS AVGG . S . C. Virtus stg. l., leaning on shield and holding
      spear. *C.* 270. *R.I.C.* 204 .. .. 12·50

Colonial and Provincial Coinage

2818 *Bithynia, Nicaea,* **Æ 20.** Laur. bust, r. ℞. Hipparchus the astro-
      nomer seated l.; before him, globe on pedestal. *B.M.C. G.*—.. .. 7·50
2819 *Cilicia, Anazarbus,* **Æ 30.** — ℞. Valerian and Gallienus seated l.
      *B.M.C. G.*39 .. .. 10·00
2820 — *Corycus,* **Æ 27.** Rad. and dr. bust, r. ℞. Artemis advancing r.,
      stag at feet. *Grose* 9061 .. .. 10·00
2821 *Coele-Syria, Heliopolis,* **Æ 24.** Laur. and dr. bust, r. ℞. Palm-branch
      in agonistic urn on table. *Grose* 9440 .. .. 7·50
2822 *Egypt, Alexandria,* **billon tetradrachm.** Laur., dr. and cuir. bust, r.
      ℞. Laur. bust of Zeus r. *B.M.C. G.*2122 .. .. 2·50
2823 — — ℞. Nike advancing r. *B.M.C. G.*2133 .. .. 2·25
2824 — — ℞. Alexandria stg. l., holding hd. of Serapis and sceptre.
      *B.M.C. G.*2140 .. .. 2·25
2825 — Laur. and cuir. bust, r. ℞. Eagle stg. l., hd. turned. *B.M.C.*
      *G.*2143 .. .. 2·00

MARINIANA

2826

The wife of Valerian: it would seem that she died before her husband's accession, as all her coins are commemorative.

The obv. legend is DIVAE MARINIANAE.

Very Fine

2826 **A' aureus.** Diad., veiled and dr. bust, r. R. CONSECRATIO. Peacock stg. facing, hd. l., tail in splendour. *C.* 1. *R.I.C.* 1 *Illustrated above Very rare*

2826A **Antoninianus.** (*base silver*). Diad., veiled and dr. bust r., resting on crescent. R. — As previous. *C.* 2. *R.I.C.* 3. **Plate 9** .. .. £20·00

2827 Veiled and dr. bust r., resting on crescent. R. — As previous. *C.* 3. *R.I.C.* 3 .. .. 20·00

2828 *Obv.* As 2826A. R. — Peacock walking r., tail in splendour. *C.* 11. *R.I.C.* 5 .. .. 25·00

2829 *Obv.* As 2827. R. — Mariniana seated l. on peacock flying r. *C.* 16. *R.I.C.* 6 .. .. 25·00

2830 **Quinarius.** (*base silver*). *Obv.* As 2826. R. — Mariniana seated r. on peacock flying l. *R.I.C.* 8 .. .. 150·00

Fine

2831 **Æ sestertius.** — R. CONSECRATIO s . c. Peacock stg. facing, hd. r., tail in splendour. *C.* 7. *R.I.C.* 9.. .. 65·00

2832 **Æ dupondius.** *Obv.* As 2827. R. — As previous. *C.* 9. *R.I.C.* 11 .. .. 40·00

2833 **Æ as.** *Obv.* As 2826. R. — As previous. *C.* 8. *R.I.C.* 11 .. 35·00

2834 Veiled and dr. bust, r. R. CONSECRATIO. As 2830. *C.* 15. *R.I.C.* 12 .. .. 35·00

GALLIENUS

A.D. 253 – 268

2880

(*P. Licinius Egnatius Gallienus*). *The son of Valerian, Gallienus was made co-emperor soon after his father's elevation, and in* A.D. *254 he was entrusted with the defence of the Rhine frontier. During the following years he achieved considerable success against the German tribes, and when Valerian left Rome for the East in 256, Gallienus was charged with the government of the Western provinces. After the capture of Valerian by the Persians, Gallienus found himself sole ruler of an empire subject not only to fierce barbarian attacks from without, but rent by internal revolts, famine and plagues, and the history of his reign is largely made up of frontier wars and contests with provincial usurpers. Much of the Roman East came under the control of Odenathus of Palmyra, and in A.D. 259 Gaul, Spain and Britain were lost to the central government when Postumus, the commander of the Rhine legions, established an independent empire which was destined to endure for about fifteen years. Although an able soldier, Gallienus was not the man to reconstitute an empire showing every sign of disintegration, and after a succession of campaigns he was eventually murdered at the siege of Milan in March, A.D. 268, being then in his fiftieth year. The future emperors Claudius and Aurelian were both involved in the conspiracy of Illyrian officers which led to the assassination.*

Titles and Powers, A.D. 253-268

A.D.	Tribunician Power	Consulship
253	TR.P.	
254	TR.P.II.	COS.
255	TR.P.III.	COS.II.
256	TR.P.IIII.	
257	TR.P.V.	COS.III.
258	TR.P.VI.	
259	TR.P.VII.	
260	TR.P.VIII.	
261	TR.P.VIIII.	COS.IIII.
262	TR.P.X.	COS.V.
263	TR.P.XI.	
264	TR.P.XII.	COS.VI.
265	TR.P.XIII.	
266	TR.P.XIIII.	COS.VII.
267	TR.P.XV.	
268	TR.P.XVI.	

Mints (during sole reign): Rome; Milan; Siscia; Cyzicus (?); Antioch (?).

The following are the commonest forms of obv. legend:

A. GALLIENVS AVG.

B. GALLIENVS P . F . AVG.

C. IMP . GALLIENVS AVG.

D. IMP . GALLIENVS P . F . AVG.

E. IMP . C . P . LIC . GALLIENVS AVG.

F. IMP . C . P . LIC . GALLIENVS P . F . AVG.

The coins of Gallienus fall into two main divisions: those issued during his joint reign with Valerian, A.D. 253-260, and those of his sole reign, A.D. 260-268. Any coin with a rev. legend ending AVGG, belongs to the joint reign, whilst the rev. legend ending AVG. indicates that the coin was struck during the sole reign. There are also details which allocate other coins to either one or other of these periods, but these cannot be dealt with here. In R.I.C. the coinage is divided into two groups, corresponding to the two periods of the reign, with the numbering commencing from 1 in each. The references quoted here are distinguished by the addition of either J or S, signifying Joint Reign or Sole Reign.

The remarks concerning the irregularity of the gold coinage and the debasement of the antoninianus, made in the introduction to the reign of Valerian, apply equally to the coinage of Gallienus' joint reign. During his sole reign, the latter increased the normal weight of the aureus from ca. 3·25 grammes to ca. 4·50 grammes, and the radiate crown was used more frequently. The antoninianus, already reduced to a bronze coin with a silver wash before the end of the joint reign, continued to decline in size and weight during the sole reign, the last issues of Gallienus being amongst the most miserable examples of this denomination.

Very Fine

2835 **N heavy aureus.** GALLIENAE AVGVSTAE. Hd. l., crowned with reeds.
R. VBIQVE PAX. Victory in biga galloping r. *C.* 1015. *R.I.C.* 74(s) £750·00

2836 A. Rad. hd., r. R. VIRTVS AVG. Mars stg. l., holding globe and
sceptre. *C.* 1220. *R.I.C.* 90(s) .. .. 350·00

2837 **N aureus.** E. Laur., dr. and cuir. bust, r. R. IOVI CONSERVA.
Jupiter stg. l., holding thunderbolt and sceptre. *C.* 349. *R.I.C.* 76(J) .. 300·00

2838 **N light aureus** or **quinarius.** A. Laur. hd., r. R. AETERNITAS
AVG. Sol stg. l., holding globe. *C.* 37. *R.I.C.* 99(s) .. .. .. 275·00

*The following coins, Nos. 2839-2904, have as obverse type rad. hd., r., or rad., dr. and/or
cuir. bust, r., unless otherwise stated.*

2839 **Antoninianus.** (*base silver* or *Æ*). A. R. ABVNDANTIA AVG.
Abundance stg. r., emptying cornucopiae. *C.* 5. *R.I.C.* 157(s) .. 2·25

2840 A. R. AEQVITAS AVG. Equity stg. l. *C.* 24. *R.I.C.* 159(s).. .. 1·75

2841 A. R. As 2838. *C.* 38. *R.I.C.* 160(s) .. .. 2·00

2842 A. R. AETERNITAS AVG. She-wolf stg. r., suckling Romulus and
Remus. *C.* 46. *R.I.C.* 628(s) .. .. 3·50

2843 A. R. ANNONA AVG. Annona stg. l., holding corn-ears and anchor.
C. 56. *R.I.C.* 162(s) .. .. 2·00

2844 A. R. APOLLINI CONS . AVG. Centaur walking r., drawing bow.
C. 72. *R.I.C.* 163(s) .. .. 2·25

2845 A. R. — Gryphon walking r. *C.* 75. *R.I.C.* 166(s).. .. .. 2·25

2846 A. R. COHH . PRAET . VI . P . VI . F. Lion walking r. *C.* 104.
R.I.C. 370(J) .. .. 10·00

2847 E. R. CONCORDIA AVGG. Clasped hands. *C.* 125. *R.I.C.* 131(J) .. 3·50

2848 A. R. CONSERVATOR AVG. Aesculapius stg. l., holding serpent-
wreathed rod. *C.* 140. *R.I.C.* 632(s) .. .. 2·50

2849 B. R. DEO MARTI. Mars stg. l. in temple of four columns, leaning
on shield. *C.* 149. *R.I.C.* 10(J) .. .. 3·50

2850 C. R. DIANAE CONS . AVG. Doe walking r., hd. turned. *C.* 153.
R.I.C. 176(s) .. .. 2·25

2851 A. R. — Stag walking r. *C.* 157. *R.I.C.* 178(s) .. .. .. 2·25

2852 A. R. — Antelope walking r. *C.* 162. *R.I.C.* 181(s) .. .. 2·25

2853 A. R. — Antelope walking l. *C.* 165. *R.I.C.* 181(s) .. .. 2·25

2854 C. R. DIANA FELIX. Diana advancing r., holding bow and drawing
arrow, hound at feet. *C.* 169. *R.I.C.* 380(J) .. .. .. 4·25

2854A A. R. FELICIT . PVBL. Felicity seated l. *C.* 193. *R.I.C.* 192(s).
Plate 9 .. .. 2·00

2855 F. R. FELICITAS AVGG. Felicity stg. l. *C.* 195. *R.I.C.* 135(J) .. 1·75

2856 A. R. FIDES MILITVM. Fides stg. l., holding standard and sceptre.
C. 246. *R.I.C.* 192a(s) .. .. 1·75

2857 B. R. — Eagle stg. l. on globe between two standards. *C.* 250.
R.I.C. 14(J) .. .. 4·00

2858 **Antoninianus.** C. R. FORT . REDVX. Fortune seated l. C. 261.
R.I.C. 483(s) ..   ..   £2·00

2859 A. R. FORTVNA REDVX. Fortune stg. l. C. 269. R.I.C. 193(s)   ..   1·75

2860 A. R. GENIVS AVG. Genius stg. l., holding patera and cornucopiae;
to r., standard. C. 296. R.I.C. 197(s) ..   ..   2·00

2861 B. R. GERMANICVS MAX . V. Two captives seated at foot of trophy.
C. 308. R.I.C. 18(J)   ..   ..   3·00

2862 A. R. HERCVLI CONS . AVG. Wild boar running r. C. 317. R.I.C.
202(s) ..   ..   3·50

2863 A. R. INDVLG . AVG. Spes advancing l. C. 322. R.I.C. 204(s)   ..   2·75

2864 A. R. IO . CANTAB. Jupiter, in military dress, stg. l., holding
thunderbolt and sceptre. C. 339. R.I.C. 573(s)   ..   ..   17·50

2865 A. R. IOVI CONS . AVG. Goat walking l. C. 341. R.I.C. 207(s) ..   2·00

2866 E. R. As 2837. C. 351. R.I.C. 143(J)   ..   ..   2·00

2867 F. R. IOVI CONSERVATORI. Gallienus and Jupiter stg. facing each
other. C. 379. R.I.C. 440(J)   ..   ..   2·25

2868 A. R. IOVIS STATOR. Jupiter stg. facing, hd. r., holding sceptre and
thunderbolt. C. 388. R.I.C. 216(s)   ..   ..   1·75

2869 B. R. IOVI VICTORI. Jupiter stg. facing on cippus inscribed IMP .
C . E . S. C. 399. R.I.C. 23(J)   ..   ..   4·00

2870 A. R. IVBENTVS AVG. Gallienus stg. l., holding Victory and spear.
C. 415. R.I.C. 615(s)   ..   ..   4·00

2871 A. R. LAETITIA AVG. Laetitia stg. l. C. 423. R.I.C. 226(s)   ..   2·00

2872 A. R. LEG . I . ADI . VI . P . VI . F. Capricorn r. C. 446. R.I.C.
315(J) ..   ..   10·00

2873 A. R. LEG . II . ADI . VI . P . VI. F. Pegasus flying r. C. 465. R.I.C.
324(J) ..   ..   10·00

2874 A. R. LEG . II . PART . VI . P . VI . F. Centaur running r., holding
club. C. 483. R.I.C. 336(J)   ..   ..   10·00

2875 A. R. LEG . VII . CL . VI . P . VI . F. Bull walking r. C. 510. R.I.C.
348(J) ..   ..   10·00

2876 A. R. LEG . XIII . GEM . VI . P . VI . F. Victory advancing r., facing
lion walking l. C. 537. R.I.C. 360(J)   ..   ..   ..   15·00

2877 A. R. LIBERAL . AVG. Liberalitas stg. l. C. 563. R.I.C. 227(s) ..   1·75

2878 A. R. LIBERO P . CONS . AVG. Panther walking l. C. 586. R.I.C.
230(s) ..   ..   2·50

2879 A. R. LIBERT . AVG. Liberty stg. l., leaning on column. C. 593.
R.I.C. 232(s) ..   ..   2·00

2880 A. R. MARTI PACIFERO. Mars stg. l., holding olive-branch and
leaning on shield. C. 617. R.I.C. 236(s). *Illustrated on p. 249*   ..   1·75

2881 A. R. MERCVRIO CONS . AVG. Hippocamp r. C. 631. R.I.C. 242(s)   3·50

2882 A. R. NEPTVNO CONS . AVG. Hippocamp r. C. 667. R.I.C. 245(s)   2·50

2883 A. R. ORIENS AVG. Sol stg. l., holding whip. C. 686. R.I.C.
494(s) ..   ..   1·75

2884 A. R. PAX AVG. Pax stg. l. C. 727. R.I.C. 256(s)   ..   1·75

2885 C. R. P . M . TR . P . V . COS . IIII . P . P. Valerian and Gallienus stg.
facing each other. C. 815. R.I.C. 435(J)   ..   ..   3·75

2886 C. R. P . M . TR . P . VII . COS. Gallienus stg. l., sacrificing over
tripod-altar. C. 819. R.I.C. 308(J)   ..   ..   ..   2·50

2887 A. Rad. hd., l. R. P . M . TR . P . XIII . C . VI . P . P. Lion walking l.,
bull's head between paws. C. 847. R.I.C. 602(s)   ..   ..   4·00

Very Fine

2888 **Antoninianus.** A. ℞. PROVID . AVG. Providence stg. l., holding globe and sceptre. *C.* 859. *R.I.C.* 270(s) .. .. £1·75

2889 B. ℞. RESTIT . GALLIAR. Gallienus stg. l., raising kneeling figure of Gaul. *C.* 895. *R.I.C.* 29(J) .. .. 3·50

2890 A. ℞. SALVS AVG. Salus stg. r., feeding serpent held in arms. *C.* 932. *R.I.C.* 274*a*(s) .. .. 1·75

2891 A. ℞. SECVRIT . PERPET. Security stg. l., leaning on column. *C.* 961. *R.I.C.* 280(s) .. .. 2·25

2892 A. ℞. SOLI CONS . AVG. Pegasus springing r. *C.* 979. *R.I.C.* 283(s) .. .. 2·25

2893 A. ℞. SOLI INVICTO. As 2883. *C.* 987. *R.I.C.* 658(s) .. .. 2·25

2894 A. ℞. VBERITAS AVG. Uberitas stg. l., holding bunch of grapes and cornucopiae. *C.* 1008. *R.I.C.* 585(s) .. .. 1·75

2895 B. Rad. and cuir. bust l., holding spear and shield. ℞. VICT . GERMANICA. Victory advancing l., captive at feet. *C.* 1059. *R.I.C.* 44(J) .. .. 3·75

2896 B. ℞. — Victory stg. r. on globe between two captives. *C.* 1062. *R.I.C.* 49(J) .. .. 3·75

2897 A. ℞. VICTORIA AET. Victory stg. l. *C.* 1071. *R.I.C.* 586(s) .. 1·75

2898 F. ℞. VICTORIA AVG. Gallienus and Victory stg. facing each other. *C.* 1109. *R.I.C.* 450(J) .. .. 3·00

2899 A. ℞. VICTORIA AVG . III. Victory advancing l. *C.* 1118. *R.I.C.* 305(s) .. .. 2·00

2900 B. ℞. VIRT . GALLIENI AVG. Gallienus advancing r., captive at feet. *C.* 1206. *R.I.C.* 54(J) .. .. 2·25

2901 A. ℞. VIRTVS AVG. Virtus stg. l. *C.* 1236. *R.I.C.* 325(s) .. .. 1·75

2902 A. ℞. — Gallienus stg. r., holding spear and globe. *C.* 1256. *R.I.C.* 670(s) .. .. 1·75

2903 F. ℞. VIRTVS AVGG. Valerian and Gallienus stg. facing each other. *C.* 1310. *R.I.C.* 456(J) .. .. 2·75

2904 A. ℞. VOTIS X. in laurel-wreath. *C.* 1350. *R.I.C.* 598(s) .. .. 5·00

2905 **Denarius.** (*base silver or Æ*). C. Laur. hd., r. ℞. As 2891. *C.* 964. *R.I.C.* 355(s) .. .. 35·00

2906 **Quinarius.** (*base silver or Æ*). F. Laur. and cuir. bust, r. ℞. VICTORIA AVGG. Victory stg. l. *C.* 1139. *R.I.C.* 192(J) .. 50·00

Fine

2907 **Æ sestertius.** E. Laur. and dr. bust, r. ℞. CONCORDIA EXERCIT . s . c. Concord stg. l. *C.* 132. *R.I.C.* 209(J) .. .. 15·00

2908 F. Laur. and cuir. bust, r. ℞. FELICITAS AVGG . s . c. Felicity stg. l. *C.* 203. *R.I.C.* 211(J) .. .. 15·00

Fine

2909 **Æ sestertius.** F. Laur. and cuir. bust, r. R. FIDES MILITVM S . C.
Fides stg. l., holding two standards. *C.* 240. *R.I.C.* 214(J) .. .. £15·00

2910 — — R. LIBERALITAS AVGG . S . C. Liberalitas stg. l. *C.*572. *R.I.C.*
221(J) .. .. 18·00

2911 E. Laur. and dr. bust, r. R. PAX AVGG . S . C. Pax stg. l. *C.* 759.
R.I.C. 231(J) .. .. 15·00

2912 F. Laur. and cuir. bust, r. R. VICTORIA AVGG . S . C. Victory stg. l.,
leaning on shield. *C.* 1144. *R.I.C.* 242(J) .. .. .. 15·00

2913 E. — R. VIRTVS AVGG . S . C. Virtus stg. l. *C.* 1293. *R.I.C.* 248(J) 15·00

2914 **Æ dupondius.** E. Rad., dr. and cuir. bust, r. R. As previous.
C. 1296. *R.I.C.* 257(J) .. .. 20·00

2915 **Æ as.** As 2907. *C.* 133. *R.I.C.* 265(J).. .. .. .. 12·50

2916 IMP . GALLIENVS P . F . AVG . GERM. Laur., dr. and cuir. bust, r. R.
ORIENS AVGG . S . C. Sol stg. l., holding whip. *C.* 712. *R.I.C.* 273(J) 15·00

2917 E. Laur. and dr. bust, r. R. As 2913. *C.* 1294. *R.I.C.* 286(J) .. 12·50

Colonial and Provincial Coinage

2918 *Troas, Alexandria Troas,* **Æ 19**. Laur. bust, r. R. Wolf and twins.
*B.M.C. G.*184 .. .. 3·75

2919 *Ionia, Ephesus,* **Æ 26**. — R. Leto running r., carrying her children
Apollo and Artemis. *B.M.C. G.*374 .. .. 10·00

2920 *Caria, Aphrodisias,* **Æ 24**. Rad. and dr. bust, l. R. Tetrastyle temple
containing cultus-statue of Aphrodite. *B.M.C. G.*133 .. .. 7·50

2921 *Phrygia, Acmoneia,* **Æ 28**. Laur. bust, r. R. Cultus-statue of
Artemis Ephesia facing. *B.M.C. G.*111 .. .. 6·00

2922 *Pamphylia, Aspendus,* **Æ 31**. Laur. and dr. bust, r. R. River-god
Eurymedon reclining l. *B.M.C. G.*102 .. .. 12·00

2923 *Cilicia, Syedra,* **Æ 30**. — R. Bearded figure seated r. on rock.
*B.M.C. G.*13 .. .. 15·00

2924 *Egypt, Alexandria,* **billon tetradrachm.** Laur. and cuir. bust, r.
R. Laur. bust of Zeus r. *B.M.C. G.*2153 .. .. .. 1·75

2925 — — R. Bust of Selene r.; in front, crescent. *B.M.C. G.*2161 .. 2·50

2926 — — R. Athena seated l. *B.M.C. G.*2168 .. .. .. 1·75

2927 — — R. Elpis stg. l. *B.M.C. G.*2181 .. .. 1·75

2928 — — R. Homonoia stg. l. *B.M.C. G.*2186 .. .. .. 1·75

2929 — Laur., dr. and cuir. bust, r. R. Nike advancing r. *B.M.C.*
*G.*2193 .. .. 1·75

2930 — — R. Tyche stg. l. *B.M.C. G.*2199 .. .. 1·75

2931 — — R. Eagle stg. l., hd. turned. *B.M.C. G.*2220 .. .. 1·25

2932 — — R. Inscription in four lines within laurel-wreath. *B.M.C.*
*G.*2240 .. .. 3·75

SALONINA

2944

Cornelia Salonina was the wife of Gallienus and the mother of Valerian II and Saloninus: she was murdered with her husband in A.D. 268.

There are two main varieties of obverse legend:
A. SALONINA AVG.
B. CORNELIA SALONINA AVG.

There are two main varieties of obverse type:
a. Diad. and dr. bust, r.
b. Diad. and dr. bust r., resting on crescent.

As with the coinage of Gallienus, that of Salonina is divided into two groups in *R.I.C.* In the references quoted, those pieces belonging to the period of the Joint Reign are distinguished by a "J", and those of the Sole Reign by an "S".

Very Fine

2933 **N aureus.** Aa. R. FELICITAS PVBLICA. Felicity seated l. *C.* 49.
R.I.C. 2(J) ..   ..   £600·00

2934 **N light aureus** or **quinarius.** Aa. R. FECVNDITAS AVG. Fecunditas stg. r., holding child, another child at feet. *C.* 42. R.I.C. 15(J) .. 550·00

2935 **Antoninianus.** (*base silver or Æ*). Ab. R. AVG . IN PACE.
Salonina seated l., holding olive-branch and sceptre. *C.* 17. *R.I.C.*
58(s) ..   ..   4·00

2936 Ab. R. CONCORD . AET. Concord seated l. *C.* 25. *R.I.C.* 2(s) ..   2·00

2937 Ab. R. DEAE SEGETIAE. Goddess stg. facing in temple of four columns. *C.* 36. *R.I.C.* 5(J) ..   ..   4·50

2938 Ab. R. DIANAE CONS . AVG. Doe walking r. *C.* 37. *R.I.C.* 4(s) ..   2·25

2939 Ab. R. FECVNDITAS AVG. Fecunditas stg. l., holding cornucopiae, child at feet. *C.* 39. *R.I.C.* 5(s) ..   ..   ..   2·00

2940 Ab. R. IVNO REGINA. Juno stg. l. *C.* 60. *R.I.C.* 13(s) ..   ..   2·00

2941 COR . SALONINA AVG. b. R. IVNONI CONS . AVG. Doe walking l.
C. 70. *R.I.C.* 16(s). **Plate 9**   ..   ..   ..   2·25

2942 Ab. R. PIETAS AVG. Pietas stg. l., holding box of perfumes. *C.* 77.
R.I.C. 22(s) ..   ..   2·00

2943 Ab. R. PVDICITIA. Pudicitia seated l. *C.* 94. *R.I.C.* 25(s) ..   2·00

2944 Ab. R. SALVS AVG. Salus stg. r., feeding serpent held in arms.
C. 105. *R.I.C.* 88(s). *Illustrated on p.* 254   ..   ..   3·50

2945 Ab. R. VENVS FELIX. Venus seated l., holding sceptre, child at feet.
C. 115. R.I.C. 7(J) ..   ..   2·50

2946 Ab. R. VENVS GENETRIX. Venus stg. l., holding apple and sceptre,
Cupid at feet. *C.* 121. *R.I.C.* 30(s) ..   ..   ..   2·00

2947 Ab. R. VENVS VICTRIX. Venus stg. l., holding helmet and sceptre,
shield at feet. *C.* 129. *R.I.C.* 31(s) ..   ..   ..   2·00

2948 Ab. R. VESTA. Vesta seated l., holding patera and sceptre. *C.* 143.
R.I.C. 32(s) ..   ..   2·00

2949 **Æ denarius.** Aa. R. As 2936. *C.* 26. *R.I.C.* 34(s) ..   ..   25·00

2950 **Quinarius.** (*base silver or Æ*). As 2934. *C.* 43. *R.I.C.* 42(s) ..   37·50

Fine

2951 **Æ sestertius.** Ba. R. IVNO REGINA S . C. Juno stg. l. *C.* 62.
R.I.C. 46(J) ..   ..   20·00

2952 Ba. R. VENVS GENETRIX S . C. As 2946. *C.* 122. *R.I.C.* 48(J) ..   20·00

2953 Ba. R. VESTA S . C. As 2948. *C.* 145. *R.I.C.* 48(s) ..   ..   20·00

2954 **Æ dupondius.** CORN . SALONINA AVG. b. R. VENVS GENETRIX S . C.
As 2946. *C.* 124. *R.I.C.* 50(J) ..   ..   20·00

2955 **Æ as.** As 2951. *C.* 63. *R.I.C.* 53(J) ..   ..   17·50

2956 Ba. R. PIETAS AVGG . S . C. Pietas seated l., two children at her feet,
one at her side. *C.* 87. *R.I.C.* 54(J) ..   ..   ..   17·50

2957 As 2952. *C.* 123. *R.I.C.* 55(J) ..   ..   17·50

Colonial and Provincial Coinage   Fine

2958 *Egypt, Alexandria*, **billon tetradrachm.** Diad. and dr. bust, r.
R. Dikaiosyne stg. l. *B.M.C. G.*2246 .. .. £1·75
2959 — R. Elpis stg. l. *B.M.C. G.*2251 .. .. 1·75
2960 — R. Homonoia seated l. *B.M.C. G.*2256 .. .. 1·75
2961 — R. Eagle stg. l., hd. turned. *B.M.C. G.*2272 .. .. .. 1·75

VALERIAN II
Caesar, A.D. 253 – 255

2965

(*P. Cornelius Licinius Valerianus*). *The elder son of Gallienus, Valerian II was given the rank of Caesar at the time of his father's elevation to the throne, but died about two years later.*

A number of the pieces that Cohen gives to this prince are now attributed to Valerian I; and most now attributed to Valerian II, Cohen gave to Saloninus.

Very Fine

2962 **N aureus.** VALERIANVS CAES. Bare-headed and dr. bust, r. R. IOVI
CRESCENTI. Infant Jupiter seated facing on the Amalthaean goat
walking r. *R.I.C.* 1 .. .. 750·00
2963 **Antoninianus.** (*base silver*). — Rad. and dr. bust, r. R. As
previous. *R.I.C.* 3 .. .. 5·00
2964 P . LIC . VALERIANVS CAES. — R. PIETAS AVGG. Sacrificial implements.
R.I.C. 19 .. .. 5·00
2965 P . C . L . VALERIANVS NOB . CAES. — R. PRINCIPI IVVENTVTIS. Valerian
II stg. l., holding standard and spear. *R.I.C.* 23. *Illustrated above* .. 5·00
2966 **Denarius.** (*base silver*). As previous, but with *obv.* type bare-headed
and dr. bust, r. *R.I.C.* 29 .. .. 50·00
2967 **Quinarius.** (*base silver*). As previous. *R.I.C.* 30 .. .. .. 75·00
2968 **Æ sestertius.** As previous, but with *rev.* legend PRINCIPI IVVENT . S . C.
R.I.C. 34 .. .. *Fine* £65·00
2969 **Æ as.** P . C . L . VALERIANVS NOB . C. Bare-headed and dr. bust, r.
R. As 2964. *R.I.C.* 36 .. .. *Fine* £35·00

Commemorative Coins struck after his death
Struck under Valerian and Gallienus

2970 **N aureus.** DIVO CAES . VALERIANO. Bare-head and dr. bust, r. R.
CONSACRATIO. Eagle stg. l., hd. turned. *R.I.C.* 7 .. .. .. 850·00
2971 **Antoninianus.** (*base silver*). DIVO VALERIANO CAES. Rad. and dr.
bust, r. R. — Valerian II seated l. on eagle flying r. *R.I.C.* 9.
Plate 9 .. .. 5·00
2972 DIVO CAES . VALERIANO. Rad. hd., r. R. CONSECRATIO. Large altar.
R.I.C. 24 .. .. 6·00
2973 — — R. — Eagle stg. r., hd. turned. *R.I.C.* 27 .. .. .. 5·00
2974 **Quinarius.** (*base silver*). — Bare hd., r. R. — Eagle stg. l., hd.
turned. *R.I.C.* 31 .. .. 75·00

Fine

2975 **Æ sestertius.** — Bare-headed, dr. and cuir. bust, r. ℞. CONSECRATIO
s . c. Funeral pyre surmounted by Valerian II in biga. *R.I.C.* 35 .. £90·00

2976 **Æ dupondius.** DIVO CAESARI VALERIANO. Bare hd., r. ℞. CONSE-
CRATIO. As 2971. *R.I.C.* 41 .. .. 50·00

2977 **Æ as.** DIVO CAES . VALERIANO. Bare-headed and dr. bust, r. ℞.
As 2975. *R.I.C.* 43 .. .. 40·00

SALONINUS
A.D. 259

2982A

*(P. Licinius Cornelius Saloninus Valerianus). On the death of Valerian II in A.D. 255,
the title of Caesar was conferred upon his younger brother, Saloninus. In A.D. 259 he was
elevated to the rank of Augustus, but soon afterwards he was put to death at Cologne by
Postumus, the commander of the Rhine legions, who had been proclaimed emperor by his
troops.*

As Caesar
A.D. 255-259, *under Valerian I and Gallienus*

Very Fine

2978 **N aureus.** SALON . VALERIANVS CAES. Bare-headed and dr. bust, r.
℞. PRINCIPI IVVENTVTIS. Saloninus stg. l., holding rod and trophy.
R.I.C. 20 .. .. 600·00

2979 **N light aureus or quinarius.** LIC . COR . SAL . VALERIANVS N . CAES.
— ℞. PIETAS AVGG. Sacrificial implements. *C.* 44. *R.I.C.* 21 .. 500·00

2980 **Antoninianus.** *(base silver).* SALON . VALERIANVS CAES. Rad. and
dr. bust, r. ℞. PIETAS AVG. Sacrificial implements. *C.* 41. *R.I.C.* 9 4·50

2981 P . COR . SAL . VALERIANVS CAES. — ℞. DII NVTRITORES. Jupiter and
Saloninus stg. facing each other. *C.* 21. *R.I.C.* 35 .. .. 12·50

2982 SALON . VALERIANVS CAES. — ℞. PRINCIPI IVVENTVTIS. Saloninus
stg. l., holding rod and spear; to r., trophy. *C.* 87. *R.I.C.* 12 .. .. 5·00

2982A — — ℞. SPES PVBLICA. Spes advancing l. *C.* 93. *R.I.C.* 13 .. 5·00

2983 SALON . VALERIANVS NOB . CAES. — ℞. — Saloninus and Spes stg.
facing each other. *C.* 95. *R.I.C.* 36 .. .. 7·50

2984 **Quinarius.** *(base silver).* LIC . COR . SAL . VALERIANVS N . CAES. Bare-
headed and dr. bust, r. ℞. PRINCIPI IVVENTVTIS. Saloninus stg. l.,
holding two standards. *C.* 85. *R.I.C.* 31 .. .. .. 75·00

2985 **Æ sestertius.** — — ℞. — Saloninus stg. l., holding globe and sceptre,
captive at feet. *C.* 89. *R.I.C.* 32.. .. .. *Fine* £90·00

2986 **Æ as.** — — ℞. PRINCIPI IVVENTVTIS S . C. As previous. *C.* 90.
R.I.C. 34 .. .. *Fine* £35·00

As Augustus

2987 **N aureus.** IMP . SALON . VALERIANVS AVG. Laur. and dr. bust, r.
℞. FELICITAS AVGG. Felicity stg. l. *C.* 22. *R.I.C.* 1.. .. *Very rare*

2988 **Antoninianus.** *(base silver).* — Rad. and dr. bust, r. ℞. SPES
PVBLICA. Spes advancing l. *C.* 94. *R.I.C.* 14 .. .. .. 60·00

258

MACRIANUS
A.D. 260 – 261

2990

(Fulvius Julius Macrianus). *Following the capture of Valerian by the Persians, the remnants of the Roman army were rallied by T. Fulvius Macrianus, one of Valerian's generals, and Ballista, the praetorian prefect.* *It was decided that the two sons of the former, namely Fulvius Julius Macrianus and Fulvius Julius Quietus, should be proclaimed emperors, and that vigorous action should be taken to halt the advance of the victorious Persians. Ballista achieved a notable victory over Sapor at Corycus, and the latter was obliged to retreat to the Euphrates.* *This success increased the confidence of the new rulers, and Macrianus and his father set out for Europe in order to challenge Gallienus.* *They only got as far as Illyricum, however, for here they were met by the army of Aureolus, one of Gallienus' generals, and in the ensuing battle the Eastern army was utterly defeated and the emperor and his father both slain.*

This ruler is often referred to as Macrianus II, but it is almost certain that the elder Macrianus was never proclaimed emperor himself, he being content with the elevation of his two sons.

Mint: Antioch.

The obv. legend is IMP . C . FVL . MACRIANVS P . F . AVG.

Very Fine

2989 **A aureus.** Laur. and cuir. bust r., drapery on l. shoulder. ℞. CON-SERVATRICI AVGG. Diana stg. r., holding bow, stag at feet. *C.* 3. *R.I.C.* 1 .. .. *Extr. rare*

2990 **Billon antoninianus.** Rad. and cuir. bust r., drapery on l. shoulder. ℞. APOLINI CONSERVA. Apollo stg. l., holding branch and leaning on lyre. *C.* 2. *R.I.C.* 6. *Illustrated above* .. .. £25·00

2991 — ℞. IOVI CONSERVATORI. Jupiter seated l., holding patera and sceptre, eagle at feet. *C.* 8. *R.I.C.* 9 .. .. 25·00

2992 — ℞. SOL . INVICTO. Sol stg. l., holding globe. *C.* 12. *R.I.C.* 12.. 25·00

2993 — ℞. SPES PVBLICA. Spes advancing l. *C.* 13. *R.I.C.* 13 .. .. 25·00

2994 *Egypt, Alexandria,* **billon tetradrachm.** Laur. and cuir. bust, r. ℞. Homonoia stg. l. *B.M.C.* G.2300 .. .. 20·00

QUIETUS
A.D. 260 – 261

2999

(Fulvius Julius Quietus). *The younger brother of Macrianus, Quietus was left in charge of the Eastern provinces during the attempt of his father and brother to overcome Gallienus. After their defeat, Quietus was attacked by Odenathus, king of Palmyra, and after being besieged in Emesa was captured and killed.*

Mint: Antioch.

The obv. legend is IMP . C . FVL . QVIETVS P . F . AVG.

Very Fine

2995 **N aureus.** Laur., dr. and cuir. bust, r. ℞. VICTORIA AVGG. Victory
   advancing r. *C.* 15. *R.I.C.* 1 ..   ..   *Extr. rare*

2996 **Billon antoninianus.** Rad., dr. and cuir. bust, r. ℞. AEQVTAS AVGG.
   Equity stg. l. *C.* 1. *R.I.C.* 2 ..   ..   £25·00

2997 — ℞. INDVLGENTIAE AVG. Indulgence seated l., holding patera and
   sceptre. *C.* 6. *R.I.C.* 5 ..   ..   25·00

2998 — ℞. ROMAE AETERNAE. Roma seated l., holding Victory and spear.
   C. 11. *R.I.C.* 9 ..   ..   25·00

2999 **Æ as.** Laur., dr. and cuir. bust, r. ℞. As 2996. *C.* 2. *R.I.C.* 13.
   Illustrated on p. 258 ..   ..   *Fine* £250·00

3000 *Egypt, Alexandria,* **billon tetradrachm.** Laur., dr. and cuir. bust, r.
   ℞. Homonoia stg. l. *B.M.C.* G.2302 ..   ..   20·00

REGALIANUS
ca. A.D. 260 – 261

3001A

(*P. Caius Regalianus*). *The circumstances of this usurpation are very obscure, but it
would seem that Regalianus, one of Valerian's generals, seized power in Pannonia after the
latter's downfall, but was murdered by his own soldiers after only a short reign. Regalianus
was a native of Dacia and it is said that he was a descendant of Decebalus, the famous king
of Dacia who was defeated by Trajan.*

   *All the coins of Regalianus are antoniniani and are extremely rare; they are of crude style
and usually over-struck on the coins of earlier emperors.*

3001 **R antoninianus.** IMP . C . P . C . REGALIANVS AVG. Rad. and dr. bust, r.
   ℞. ORIENS AVGG. Sol stg. l., holding whip. *R.I.C.* 7 ..   ..   *Extr. rare*

3001A — — ℞. LIBERTAS AVGG. Liberty stg. l., holding pileus and sceptre.
   C. 3. *R.I.C.* 6. *Illustrated above* ..   ..   *Extr. rare*

DRYANTILLA

   *Sulpicia Dryantilla, the daughter of Sulpicius Pollio and Claudia Ammiana Dryantilla,
was probably the wife of Regalianus.*

3002 **R antoninianus.** SVLP . DRYANTILLA AVG. Diad. and dr. bust r.,
   resting on crescent. ℞. IVNONI REDINE. Juno stg. l., holding patera
   and sceptre. *C.* 1. *R.I.C.* 2 ..   ..   *Extr. rare*

POSTUMUS
A.D. 259 – 268

3003

(*M. Cassianus Latinius Postumus*). *A man of humble origin, Postumus was a soldier of great merit and was appointed commander of the Rhine legions by Valerian. In* A.D. 259, *actuated either by personal ambition or at the desire of his troops, he rebelled against Gallienus, and ruled Gaul, Spain and Britain firmly and wisely for almost a decade. He was completely successful not only in fighting back the German tribes from the Rhine frontier, but also in thwarting the repeated attempts of Gallienus to recover the lost provinces. In* A.D. 268, *however, Ulpius Cornelius Laelianus rebelled against Postumus, and although the usurper was quickly attacked and destroyed, the refusal of Postumus to allow his troops to sack Moguntiacum (Mainz), which had supported the rebel, led to his own assassination.*

Titles and Powers, A.D. 259-268

A.D.	*Tribunician Power*	*Consulship*
259	TR.P.	COS.
260	TR.P.II.	COS.II.
261	TR.P.III.	COS.III.
262	TR.P.IIII.	
263	TR.P.V.	
264	TR.P.VI.	
265	TR.P.VII	
266	TR.P.VIII.	
267	TR.P.VIIII.	COS.IIII.
		(or possibly in previous year)
268	TR.P.X.	COS.V.

Mints: Lugdunum; Cologne; Milan.

The obv. legend is IMP . C . POSTVMVS P . F . AVG., *unless otherwise stated.*

Very Fine

3003 **N aureus.** POSTVMVS AVG. Rad., dr. and cuir. bust, three quarter face.
R. HERCVLI THRACIO. Hercules r., overcoming the horses of Diomedes
C. 138. R.I.C. 275. *Illustrated above* .. .. *Extr. rare*

3004 POSTVMVS PIVS AVG. Laur. hd., r. R. ROMAE AETERNAE. Roma
seated l., holding Victory and spear. C. 327. R.I.C. 36.. .. ..£400·00

3005 **N quinarius.** POSTVMVS AVG. Helmeted and cuir. bust, l. R.
PROVIDENTIA AVG. Providence stg. l., holding globe and sceptre.
C. 294. R.I.C. 49 .. .. 550·00

The following coins, Nos. 3006-3035, have as obverse type rad. bust r., dr. or dr. and cuir., unless otherwise stated.

3006 **Antoninianus.** (*billon or Æ*). IMP . POSTVMVS AVG. R. CONCORD .
AEQVIT. Fortune stg. l., holding patera and rudder. C. 18. R.I.C. 371 3·00

3007 R. COS . V. Victory stg. r. C. 32. R.I.C. 288 .. .. .. 2·00

3008 R. FELICITAS AVG. Felicity stg. l. C. 39. R.I.C. 58 .. .. .. 1·75

3009 R. FIDES EQVIT. Fides seated l., holding patera and standard. C. 59.
R.I.C. 377 .. .. 3·00

3010 **Antoninianus.** ℞. FIDES MILITVM. Fides stg. l., holding two
    standards. *C.* 67. *R.I.C.* 59   ..   ..   £1·75

3011 ℞. HERC . DEVSONIENSI. Hercules stg. r., leaning on club and holding
    bow. *C.* 91. *R.I.C.* 64   ..   ..   2·50

3012 ℞. HERC . PACIFERO. Hercules stg. l., holding olive-branch and club.
    C. 101. *R.I.C.* 67   ..   ..   2·00

3013 ℞. IOVI STATORI. Jupiter stg. facing, hd. r., holding sceptre and
    thunderbolt. *C.* 159. *R.I.C.* 309..   ..   ..   1·75

3014 ℞. LAETITIA AVG. Galley travelling l. *C.* 167. *R.I.C.* 73 ..   ..   3·00

3015 ℞. MINER . FAVTR. Minerva advancing l., holding olive-branch, spear
    and shield. *C.* 195. *R.I.C.* 74   ..   ..   2·50

3016 ℞. MONETA AVG. Moneta stg. l. *C.* 199. *R.I.C.* 75   ..   ..   1·75

3017 ℞. NEPTVNO REDVCI. Neptune stg. l., holding dolphin and trident.
    C. 205. *R.I.C.* 76 ..   ..   3·25

3018 ℞. ORIENS AVG. Sol advancing l., holding whip. *C.* 213. *R.I.C.* 77   2·00

3019 ℞. PACATOR ORBIS. Rad. and dr. bust of Sol r. *C.* 214. *R.I.C.* 317   7·50

3020 ℞. PAX AVG. Pax stg. l. *C.* 215. *R.I.C.* 318   ..   ..   ..   1·75

3021 ℞. P . M . TR . P . COS . II . P . P. Postumus stg. l., holding globe and
    spear. *C.* 243. *R.I.C.* 54 ..   ..   2·25

3022 ℞. P . M . TR . P . III . COS . III . P . P. Mars advancing r., carrying spear
    and trophy. *C.* 269. *R.I.C.* 56 ..   ..   2·75

3023 POSTVMVS AVG. Rad. bust l., holding club, lion's skin on l. shoulder.
    ℞. P . M . TR . P . VIIII . COS . IIII . P . P. Bow, club and quiver. *C.* 282.
    R.I.C. 292   ..   ..   20·00

3024 ℞. As 3005. *C.* 295. *R.I.C.* 80   ..   ..   1·75

3025 ℞. SAECVLI FELICITAS. Postumus stg. r., holding spear and globe.
    C. 331. *R.I.C.* 83 ..   ..   2·25

3026 ℞. SAECVLO FRVGIFERO. Winged caduceus. *C.* 333. *R.I.C.* 84   ..   3·75

3027 ℞. SALVS AVG. Aesculapius stg. facing, hd. l., holding serpent-
    wreathed rod. *C.* 336. *R.I.C.* 86 *and* 326   ..   ..   ..   3·00

3028 ℞. — Salus stg. l., feeding serpent arising from altar. *C.* 339. *R.I.C.*
    85   ..   ..   1·75

3029 ℞. SALVS POSTVMI AVG. Salus stg. r., feeding serpent held in arms.
    C. 350. *R.I.C.* 328 ..   ..   3·00

3030 ℞. SALVS PROVINCIARVM. The Rhine reclining l., resting r. hand on
    forepart of boat. *C.* 355. *R.I.C.* 87   ..   ..   6·00

3031 ℞. SERAPI COMITI AVG. Serapis stg. l., holding sceptre. *C.* 360.
    R.I.C. 329   ..   ..   3·75

3031A ℞. VBERITAS AVG. Uberitas stg. l., holding purse and cornucopiae.
    C. 366. *R.I.C.* 330. **Plate 9**   ..   ..   3·25

Very Fine

3032 **Antoninianus.** ℞. VICTORIA AVG. Victory advancing l., captive at
feet. *C.* 377. *R.I.C.* 89 .. .. £2·00
3033 ℞. VIRTVS AVG. Mars stg. r., holding spear and leaning on shield.
C. 419. *R.I.C.* 93 .. .. 1·75
3034 ℞. — Postumus advancing r., holding spear and shield, captive at feet.
C. 427. *R.I.C.* 331 .. .. 2·25
3035 IMP . POSTVMVS AVG. ℞. VIRTVS EQVIT. Mars advancing r., holding
spear and shield. *C.* 441. *R.I.C.* 388 .. .. 3·25
3036 **Denarius.** (*billon or Æ*). POSTVMVS PIVS AVG. Laur. hd., r. ℞.
PROVIDENTIA AVG. Providence stg. l., leaning on column, globe at feet.
C. 301. *R.I.C.* 101 .. .. 45·00
3037 **Quinarius.** (*billon or Æ*). POSTVMVS AVG. Laur. heads of Postumus
and Hercules, jugate, r. ℞. As 3027. *C.* 337. *R.I.C.* 363 .. .. 150·00

Fine

3038 **Æ sestertius.** IMP . C . M . CASS . LAT . POSTVMVS P . F . AVG. Rad., dr.
and cuir. bust, r. ℞. FELICITAS AVG. Triumphal arch surmounted by
trophy, captives and palms. *C.* 47. *R.I.C.* 118.. .. .. .. 65·00
3039 Laur. and dr. bust, r. ℞. FIDES MILITVM. Fides stg. l., holding two
standards. *C.* 69. *R.I.C.* 124 .. .. 15·00
3040 *Obv.* As 3038. ℞. As previous. *C.* 74. *R.I.C.* 123 .. .. 15·00
3041 IMP . C . M . CASS . LAT . POSTVMVS P . F . AVG. Rad. and dr. bust, r. ℞.
HERCVLI MAGVSANO. Hercules stg. r., leaning on club set on rock.
C. 130. *R.I.C.* 139 .. .. 30·00
3042 — — ℞. LAETITIA AVG . S . C. Galley travelling l. *C.* 179. *R.I.C.*
143 .. .. 20·00
3043 — — ℞. P . M . TR . P . COS . II . P . P . S . C. As 3021. *C.* 246.
R.I.C. 106 .. .. 17·50
3044 — — ℞. RESTITVTOR GALLIAR . S . C. Postumus stg. l., raising kneeling figure of Gaul. *C.* 321. *R.I.C.* 157. *Illustrated on p.* 261 .. 30·00
3045 — — ℞. As 3032. *C.* 379. *R.I.C.* 169 .. .. 15·00
3046 Laur. and dr. bust, r. ℞. VICTORIAE AVG. Two Victories stg. facing
each other, attaching shield to palm-tree at base of which are two captives
seated. *C.* 410. *R.I.C.* 167 .. .. 25·00
3047 **Æ dupondius.** *Obv.* As 3041. ℞. PAX AVG . S . C. Pax advancing
l. *C.* 224. *R.I.C.* 218 .. .. 12·50
3048 — ℞. VICTORIA AVG . S . C. Postumus stg. r., holding spear and leaning
on shield; to l., trophy with two captives seated at base. *C.* 404. *R.I.C.*
235 .. .. 17·50
3049 **Æ as.** Laur. and dr. bust, r. ℞. As 3014. *C.* 170. *R.I.C.* 249 .. 15·00

LAELIANUS
A.D. 268

3050

(*Ulpius Cornelius Laelianus*).   *Little is known of this usurper except that he led a revolt
against Postumus which was speedily suppressed.*

Mint: Moguntiacum.

Very Fine

3050 **N aureus.** IMP . C . LAELIANVS P . F . AVG.   Laur. and cuir. bust, r.
℞. TEMPORVM FELICITAS.   Hispania or Tellus reclining l., holding
branch, rabbit at side.   *C.* 2.   *R.I.C.* 1.   *Illustrated on p.* 262 ..   *Extr. rare*

3051 **Æ antoninianus.** — Rad. and cuir. bust, r.   ℞. VICTORIA AVG.
Victory advancing r.   *C.* 4.   *R.I.C.* 9   ..   .. £65·00

3052 **AR denarius.** — Laur. and cuir. bust, r.   ℞. VIRTVS MILITVM.
Virtus stg. l., holding spear and standard inscribed xxx.   *C.* 10.   *R.I.C.*
10   ..   ..   *Unique*

MARIUS
A.D. 268

3053

(*M. Aurelius Marius*).   *A blacksmith by trade, Marius joined the Roman army and,
by his military qualities, rose from the ranks to the status of an officer.   On the death of
Postumus he seized power, but was murdered by his soldiers after a very short reign which
some authorities say was of only two or three days duration.   It is said that he was despatched
with a sword of his own manufacture.*

Mints: Cologne; unidentified mint.

3053 **N aureus.** IMP . C . M . AVR . MARIVS P . F . AVG.   Laur. and cuir. bust,
r.   ℞. CONCORDIA MILITVM.   Clasped hands.   *C.* 3.   *R.I.C.* 1   *Extr. rare*

3054 **Æ antoninianus.** IMP . C . MARIVS P . F . AVG.   Rad., dr. and cuir.
bust, r.   ℞. CONCORD . MILIT.   Clasped hands.   *C.* 8.   *R.I.C.* 6   ..   20·00

3055 — — ℞. SAEC . FELICITAS.   Felicity stg. l.   *C.* 13.   *R.I.C.* 10.
Plate 9   ..   ..   20·00

3056 IMP . C . M . AVR . MARIVS P . F . AVG. — ℞. VICTORIA AVG.   Victory
stg. l., leaning on shield and holding palm.   *C.* 17.   *R.I.C.* 12..   ..   20·00

3057 IMP . C . M . AVR . MARIVS AVG. — ℞. — Victory advancing r.   *C.* 20.
R.I.C. 18   ..   ..   17·50

DOMITIANUS
? A.D. 268

*This usurper, known only from a single coin found at Cleóns, Loire Inférieure, may have
been the general who actually achieved the victory over Macrianus in A.D. 261.   The style
of the coin is obviously Gallic, and it is possible that Domitianus made a momentary grasp
at power in the troubled period following the assassination of Postumus.*

3058 **Æ antoninianus.** IMP . C . DOMITIANVS P . F . AVG.   Rad., dr. and
cuir. bust, r.   ℞. CONCORDIA MILITVM.   Concord stg. l., holding
patera and cornucopiae.   *R.I.C.* 1   ..   ..   *Unique*

VICTORINUS
A.D. 268 – 270

3060

(*M. Piavvonius Victorinus*). *A soldier of considerable ability, Victorinus succeeded to the throne of the Gallo-Roman Empire after the assassination of Marius. Little is known of the history of his short reign, but it would seem that Spain seceded from his empire soon after his accession, and there were also troubles in Gaul, culminating in a rebellion at Augustodunum (Autun). Victorinus succeeded in taking the city after a siege of seven months, but soon afterwards he was murdered by one of his own officers at Cologne.*

Mints: Cologne; Vienna (?); same unidentified mint as Marius.

The obverse legend is IMP . C . VICTORINVS P . F . AVG., *unless otherwise stated.*

Very Fine

3059 **N aureus.** IMP . CAES . VICTORINVS P . F . AVG. Laur. bust, r. R.
COMES AVG. Victory stg. l. *C.* 16. *R.I.C.* 94 ..   ..   ..£750·00

3060 — R. LEG . XXX . VLP . VICT . P . F. Jupiter stg. facing, hd. l., holding
sceptre and thunderbolt, capricorn at feet. *C.* 70. *R.I.C.* 25 ..   .. 1250·00

3061 **N quinarius.** IMP . VICTORINVS AVG. Laur. and cuir. bust, r. R.
ADIVTRIX AVG. Bust of Diana r., holding bow and drawing arrow from
quiver. *C.* 5. *R.I.C.* 35 ..   .. 1000·00

The following coins, Nos. 3062-3071, have as obverse type rad., dr. and/or cuir. bust, r.

3062 **Æ antoninianus.** R. AEQVITAS AVG. Equity stg. l. *C.* 9. *R.I.C.*
40 ..   ..   1·50

3063 IMP . C . PIAV . VICTORINVS P . F . AVG. R. As 3059. *C.* 18. *R.I.C.*
106 ..   ..   2·00

3064 — R. FIDES MILITVM. Fides stg. l., holding two standards. *C.* 36.
R.I.C. 109 ..   ..   2·00

3065 R. INVICTVS. Sol advancing l., holding whip. *C.* 49. *R.I.C.* 114 .. 1·50

3066 R. PAX AVG. Pax stg. l. *C.* 79. *R.I.C.* 118 ..   ..   .. 1·50

3067 R. PIETAS AVG. Pietas stg. l., altar at feet. *C.* 90. *R.I.C.* 57   .. 1·50

3068 R. PROVIDENTIA AVG. Providence stg. l., globe at feet. *C.* 101.
R.I.C. 61   ..   ..   1·50

3069 R. SALVS AVG. Salus stg. r., feeding serpent held in arms. *C.* 112.
R.I.C. 67   ..   ..   1·50

3070 R. — Salus stg. l., feeding serpent arising from altar. *C.* 118. *R.I.C.*
71   ..   ..   1·50

3071 R. VIRTVS AVG. Virtus stg. r., holding spear and leaning on shield.
C. 131. *R.I.C.* 78 ..   ..   1·50

3072 **Æ denarius.** IMP . VICTORINVS P . F . AVG. Laur. bust, r. R.
VICTORIA AVG. Victory stg. l. *C.* 124. *R.I.C.* 93   ..   ..   60·00

Commemorative Coins struck after his death

Struck under Tetricus I

3073 **Æ antoninianus.** DIVO VICTORINO PIO. Rad. hd., r. R. CONSE-
CRATIO. Eagle stg. r. on globe, hd. turned. *C.* 26. *R.I.C.* 85 ..   .. 7·50

3074 — — R. As 3068. *C.* 103. *R.I.C.* 88   ..   ..   .. 6·00

TETRICUS I

A.D. 270 – 273

3082

(*C. Pius Esuvius Tetricus*).   *At the death of Victorinus, Tetricus was governor of Aquitania and, through the influence of Victoria, the mother of Victorinus, he succeeded to the throne.   The power of the Gallo-Roman Empire declined rapidly under Tetricus and when, in* A.D. *273, Aurelian invaded Gaul, Tetricus abdicated and surrendered to him. Aurelian spared the lives of both Tetricus and his son, and even gave Tetricus a post in the government of Italy.   The ex-emperor spent the rest of his life in Rome, honoured by Aurelian and his successors.*

Mint: Vienna (?).

The obverse legend is IMP . C . TETRICVS P . F . AVG., *unless otherwise stated.*

In *R.I.C.* the coinage of Tetricus I and Tetricus II is dealt with in one group, numbered 1-294.

Very Fine

3075	*N* **aureus.** IMP . TETRICVS P . F . AVG. Laur. bust, r. R. FELICITAS PVBLICA. Felicity stg. l., leaning on column. *C.* 36. *R.I.C.* 11	. . £650·00

The following coins, Nos. 3076-3083, have as obverse type rad., dr. and/or cuir. bust, r.

3076	**Æ antoninianus.** IMP . C . P . ESV . TETRICVS AVG. R. FIDES MILITVM. Fides stg. l., holding two standards. *C.* 39. *R.I.C.* 72 ..	2·00
3077	R. HILARITAS AVGG. Hilaritas stg. l. *C.* 55. *R.I.C.* 79	1·50
3078	R. LAETITIA AVGG. Laetitia stg. l., holding wreath and anchor. *C.* 72. *R.I.C.* 87	1·50
3079	R. PAX AVG. Pax stg. l. *C.* 95. *R.I.C.* 100	1·50
3080	R. SALVS AVGG. Salus stg. l., feeding serpent arising from altar. *C.* 154. *R.I.C.* 126	1·50
3081	R. SPES PVBLICA. Spes advancing l. *C.* 170. *R.I.C.* 136	2·00
3082	IMP . C . C . P . ESVVIVS TETRICVS AVG. R. VICTORIA AVG. Victory advancing l. *C.* 184. *R.I.C.* 140. *Illustrated above*	2·50
3083	R. VIRTVS AVGG. Virtus stg. l., leaning on shield and holding spear. *C.* 207. *R.I.C.* 148	1·50
3084	**Æ** (or white metal) **denarius.** IMP . TETRICVS PIVS AVG. Laur. and cuir. bust, r. R. SPES AVGG. Spes advancing l. *C.* 164. *R.I.C.* 175 ..	65·00

TETRICUS II

Caesar A.D. 270 – 273

3085

(*C. Pius Esuvius Tetricus*).   *The son of Tetricus I, he was given the rank of Caesar at the time of his father's accession and, following the abdication of the latter, his life was spared by Aurelian and he spent the rest of his days as a private citizen.*

The obv. legend is C . PIV . ESV . TETRICVS CAES., *unless otherwise stated.*

Very Fine

3085 **N aureus.** c . p . esv . tetricvs caes. Bare-headed bust r., wearing
imperial mantle. ℞. spes avgg. Spes advancing l. *C.* 85. *R.I.C.*
219. *Illustrated on p.* 265 ..   .. *Very rare*

The following coins, Nos. 3086-3091, have as obverse type rad. and dr. bust, r.

3086 **Æ antoninianus.** ℞. hilaritas avgg. Hilaritas stg. l. *C.* 17.
R.I.C. 232 ..   .. £2·00
3087 ℞. pax avg. Pax stg. l. *C.* 34. *R.I.C.* 248 ..   ..   .. 2·25
3088 c . p . e . tetricvs caes. ℞. pietas avgvstor. Sacrificial implements.
C. 60. *R.I.C.* 259 ..   .. 2·00
3089 ℞. princ . ivvent. Tetricus II stg. l., holding rod and standard.
C. 64. *R.I.C.* 260 ..   .. 2·50
3090 ℞. spes avgg. Spes advancing l. *C.* 88. *R.I.C.* 270   .. 1·75
3091 ℞. spes pvblica. Spes advancing l. *C.* 97. *R.I.C.* 272   .. 1·75

3092 **Æ denarius.** Bare-headed and dr. bust, r. ℞. principi ivventvtis.
Tetricus II stg. r., holding spear and globe. *R.I.C.* 281   ..   .. 75·00

CLAUDIUS II GOTHICUS
A.D. 268 – 270

3126

(*M. Aurelius Claudius*). *A native of Illyricum, Claudius was born about* A.D. 215. *He
obtained the imperial favour by his military talents, and became one of the leading generals
under Valerian and Gallienus.   On the assassination of the latter, in the plot against whom
he is said to have taken part, he was immediately proclaimed emperor and then proceeded to
inflict a crushing defeat on the Alamanni, who had invaded Raetia and even penetrated into
Italy.   In* A.D. 269 *he marched against an immense army of Goths, and though the Roman
army was seemingly hopelessly outnumbered, Claudius won a brilliant victory over the
invaders in a great battle fought at Naissus in Upper Moesia.   Unfortunately, some of the
wandering survivors of the Gothic host contracted plague which spread to the Roman army
and claimed the life of Claudius after a reign of only two years.*

Mints: Rome; Milan; Siscia; Cyzicus; Antioch.

The obv. legend is imp . c . clavdivs avg., *unless otherwise stated.*

3093 **N aureus.** Laur. and cuir. bust, r. ℞. salvs avg. Salus stg. l.,
feeding serpent arising from altar. *C.* 261. *R.I.C.* 8 ..   ..   .. 600·00

*The following coins, Nos. 3094-3124, have as obverse type rad. hd. r., or rad., dr. or cuir.
bust r., unless otherwise stated.*

3094 **Æ antoninianus.** ℞. adventvs avg. Claudius on horseback l.,
raising r. hand. *C.* 3. *R.I.C.* 13 ..   .. 3·75
3095 ℞. aeqvitas avg. Equity stg. l. *C.* 6. *R.I.C.* 14 ..   ..   .. 1·75
3096 imp . clavdivs avg. ℞. aeternit . avg. Sol stg. l., holding globe.
C. 16. *R.I.C.* 16 ..   .. 1·75
3097 ℞. annona avg. Annona stg. l., r. foot on prow. *C.* 21. *R.I.C.* 18 1·75

Very Fine

3098 **Æ antoninianus.** ℞. CONSER . AVG.   Serapis stg. l., holding sceptre.
C. 58.   *R.I.C.* 201 .. .. £3·00
3099 ℞. FELIC . TEMPO.   Felicity stg. l.   C. 73.   *R.I.C.* 146 .. .. 1·75
3100 ℞. FELICITAS AVG.   Felicity stg. l.   C. 79.   *R.I.C.* 32.. .. .. 1·75
3101 ℞. FIDES EXERCI.   Fides stg. r., holding two standards.   C. 84.   *R.I.C.*
34 .. .. 1·75
3102 IMP . CLAVDIVS P . F . AVG.   ℞. FIDES MILIT.   Fides stg. l., holding two
standards.   C. 88.   *R.I.C.* 149 .. .. 1·75
3103 — ℞. FORTVNA REDVX.   Fortune stg. l.   C. 102.   *R.I.C.* 234 .. 1·75
3104 ℞. GENIVS EXERCI.   Genius stg. l.   C. 114.   *R.I.C.* 48 .. .. 2·00
3105 ℞. IOVI STATORI.   Jupiter stg. r., holding sceptre and thunderbolt.
C. 124.   *R.I.C.* 52 .. .. 1·75
3106 ℞. IOVI VICTORI.   As previous, but Jupiter stg. l.   C. 130.   *R.I.C.* 54 1·75

3107 Rad. hd., l.   ℞. IVNO REGINA.   Juno stg. l., peacock at feet.   C. 133.
R.I.C. 212 .. .. 3·50
3108 ℞. IVVENTVS AVG.   Hercules stg. facing, hd. l., leaning on club.   C. 137.
R.I.C. 213 .. .. 3·00
3109 IMP . CLAVDIVS AVG.   ℞. LAETITIA AVG.   Laetitia stg. l.   C. 140.
R.I.C. 56 .. .. 1·75
3110 ℞. LIBERALITAS AVG.   Liberalitas stg. l.   C. 144.   *R.I.C.* 57 .. 2·00
3111 ℞. LIBERT . AVG.   Liberty stg. l.   C. 152.   *R.I.C.* 63 .. .. 2·00
3112 IMP . CLAVDIVS AVG.   ℞. MARTI PACIF.   Mars advancing l., holding
branch, spear and shield.   C. 161.   *R.I.C.* 68 .. .. .. 1·75
3113 ℞. NEPTVN . AVG.   Neptune stg. l., holding dolphin and trident.
C. 183.   *R.I.C.* 214 .. .. 3·25
3114 Rad. hd., l.   ℞. As previous.   C. 184.   *R.I.C.* 214 .. .. .. 5·00
3115 IMP . CLAVDIVS P . F . AVG.   ℞. PAX AVG.   Pax advancing l.   C. 202.
R.I.C. 157 .. .. 1·75
3116 ℞. P . M . TR . P . II . COS . P . P.   Claudius stg. l., holding branch and
sceptre.   C. 114.   *R.I.C.* 10 .. .. 3·00
3117 ℞. PROVIDENT . AVG.   Providence stg. l., leaning on column.   C. 230.
R.I.C. 91 .. .. 1·75
3118 ℞. REGI ARTIS.   Vulcan stg. r., holding hammer and pincers.   C. 239.
R.I.C. 215 .. .. 15·00
3119 ℞. As 3093.   C. 265.   *R.I.C.* 98 .. .. 1·75
3120 ℞. SPES PVBLICA.   Spes advancing l.   C. 281.   *R.I.C.* 102 .. .. 1·75
3121 IMP . CLAVDIVS P . F . AVG.   ℞. VICTOR . GERMAN.   Two captives seated
at foot of trophy.   C. 289.   *R.I.C.* 247 .. .. 10·00
3122 ℞. VICTORIA AVG.   Victory stg. l.   C. 293.   *R.I.C.* 104 .. .. 1·75
3122A IMP . CLAVDIVS P . F . AVG.   ℞. — Victory advancing r.   C. 302.
R.I.C. 171.   **Plate 9** .. .. 1·50
3123 IMP . C . M . AVR . CLAVDIVS AVG.   ℞. VICTORIAE GOTHIC.   As 3121.
C. 309.   *R.I.C.* 251 .. .. 12·50

3124 **Æ antoninianus.** R. VIRTVS AVG. Mars stg. l., holding branch and
spear, shield at feet. *C.* 313. *R.I.C.* 109 .. .. £1·75
3125 **Æ quinarius.** IMP . CLAVDIVS P . F . AVG. Laur. hd., r. R. VICTORIA
AVG. Victory stg. facing, hd. l., between two captives. *C.* 299. *R.I.C.*
119 .. .. 20·00
3126 **Æ as.** Laur., dr. and cuir. bust, r. R. IOVI VICTORI. Jupiter stg. l.,
holding thunderbolt and sceptre. *C.* 128. *R.I.C.* 124. *Illustrated on
p.* 266 .. .. *Fine* £35·00

Commemorative Coins struck after his death

(a) *Struck under Quintillus (and later emperors ?)*

3127 **Æ antoninianus.** DIVO CLAVDIO. Rad. hd., r. R. CONSECRATIO.
Eagle stg. l., hd. turned. *C.* 43. *R.I.C.* 266 .. .. 2·00
3128 — — R. — Large altar. *C.* 50. *R.I.C.* 261 .. .. 2·00
3129 DIVO CLAVDIO GOTHICO. — R. — Large altar. *C.* 53. *R.I.C.* 263 10·00
3130 DIVO CLAVDIO. — R. FORTVNA REDVX. Fortune stg. l. *C.* 105.
R.I.C. 274 .. .. 4·50
3131 — — R. LAETITIA AVG. Laetitia stg. l. *C.* 141. *R.I.C.* 277 .. 4·50

(b) *Struck under Constantine the Great*

3132 **Æ 3.** (*c.* 18 mm.) DIVO CLAVDIO OPTIMO IMP. Laur. and veiled hd., r.
R. REQVIES OPTIMOR . MERIT. Claudius seated l. on curule chair.
C. 243. *R.I.C.* 298 .. .. 5·00
3133 **Æ 4.** (*c.* 16 mm.) DIVO CLAVDIO OPT . IMP. — R. MEMORIAE
AETERNAE. Lion walking r. *C.* 171. *R.I.C.* 293 .. .. .. 4·00
3134 — — R. — Eagle stg., hd. l. *C.* 174. *R.I.C.* 294 .. .. .. 4·00

Colonial and Provincial Coinage

3135 *Pisidia, Sagalassus,* **Æ 35.** Laur. and dr. bust, r. R. Herakles stg. l.,
slaying the Hydra. *B.M.C. G.*49 .. .. .. *Fine* £15·00
3136 *Egypt, Alexandria,* **billon tetradrachm.** Laur., dr. and cuir. bust, r.
R. Poseidon stg. l., r. foot on dolphin. *B.M.C. G.*2307 .. .. 2·50
3137 — — R. Hermes stg. l., holding caduceus. *B.M.C. G.*2315 .. .. 3·00
3138 — Laur. and cuir. bust, r. R. Elpis stg. l. *B.M.C. G.*2317 .. 2·25
3139 — — R. Nike advancing r. *B.M.C. G.*2320 .. .. 2·25
3140 — — R. Eagle stg. r., hd. turned. *B.M.C. G.*2334 .. .. .. 1·75

" BARBAROUS RADIATES "

The *antoniniani* of the late 3rd century, particularly those of the emperors Claudius
Gothicus, Tetricus I and Tetricus II, were frequently imitated in Gaul and Britain.
Some of these copies are almost as good as the originals, but most are very crude productions with badly blundered legends and almost unrecognizable types. They are often
found in this country, and we are usually able to offer a wide selection of types, the price
for a " fine " specimen being about £1·25.

269

QUINTILLUS
A.D. 270

3143

(M. Aurelius Claudius Quintillus.)   A younger brother of Claudius Gothicus, Quintillus was proclaimed emperor by his troops at Aquileia on the death of Claudius.   After only a short period of undisputed power, his position was challenged by Aurelian who was proclaimed emperor by the legions at Sirmium.   Realizing the superiority of their rival, the soldiers of Quintillus deserted him and in desperation he committed suicide.

Mints: Rome; Milan; Siscia; Cyzicus.

There are two main varieties of obv. legend:

    A.   IMP . QVINTILLVS AVG.
    B.   IMP . C . M . AVR . CL . QVINTILLVS AVG.

The obverse type is rad., dr. and/or cuir. bust, r.

                                              Very Fine

3141 **Æ antoninianus.** B. ℞. APOLLINI CONS. Apollo stg. l., holding branch and leaning on lyre set on rock. *C.* 5. *R.I.C.* 9   ..   .. £6·00

3142 A. ℞. CONCO . EXERC. Concord stg. l., holding standard and cornucopiae. *C.* 8. *R.I.C.* 45 ..   ..   5·00

3143 A. ℞. DIANA LVCIF. Diana stg. r., holding torch. *C.* 19. *R.I.C.* 49   5·50

3144 A. ℞. FIDES MILIT. Fides stg. l., holding two standards. *C.* 25. *R.I.C.* 52 ..   ..   5·00

3145 B. ℞. LAETITIA AVG. Laetitia stg. l. *C.* 39. *R.I.C.* 22 ..   ..   5·00

3146 A. ℞. MARTI PACI. Mars advancing l., holding olive-branch and spear. *C.* 48. *R.I.C.* 59 ..   ..   5·00

3147 *Egypt, Alexandria,* **billon tetradrachm.** Laur., dr. and cuir. bust, r. ℞. Eagle stg. r., hd. turned. *B.M.C.* G.2337 ..   .. 8·00

AURELIAN
A.D. 270 – 275

3148

(L. Domitius Aurelianus).   Born of humble parents at Sirmium about A.D. 207, Aurelian adopted a military career, and by his skill, courage and bodily strength he ultimately became one of the Empire's greatest generals, his reputation as a commander of cavalry being particularly high.   Some time after the death of Claudius Gothicus, he was proclaimed emperor by his troops at Sirmium, and after the suicide of Quintillus, he was left as undisputed master of the Empire.   During his short reign of only five years, he completely restored the Roman Empire to its former extent, with the exception of Dacia which was finally abandoned in A.D. 271.   He put an end to the Palmyrene Empire in the East and the Gallo-Roman Empire in the West, and Queen Zenobia of Palmyra and Tetricus both appeared as captives in the magnificent triumph which the emperor celebrated in Rome.   In addition to his military exploits, he gave much attention to domestic affairs, and began the building of a strongly

fortified wall around Rome, which was not completed until the reign of Probus. Whilst proceeding towards the East to attack Persia in the summer of A.D. 275, *Aurelian fell victim to a conspiracy of certain of his chief officers. The assassination took place at Caenophrurium in Thrace, the emperor then being in his sixty-eighth year.*

Mints: Rome; Vienna (?); Lugdunum; Milan; Ticinum ; Siscia; Serdica; Cyzicus; Antioch; Tripolis; unidentified mint.

There are two main varieties of obv. legend:

    A.　IMP . AVRELIANVS AVG.
    B.　IMP . C . AVRELIANVS AVG.

Quite early in his reign Aurelian carried out a reform of the coinage. He increased the size and weight of the antoniniani and there appears to have been an improvement in the technique of applying the silver wash, as specimens still showing the silvery coating are far more frequently encountered than with the pre-reform coins. A mark of value (XXI *or* KA) *was also placed on some of the new antoniniani. This has been taken to mean that Aurelian re-tariffed the antoninianus at* 1/20th *of the aureus, the mark meaning "20 of these equal 1 aureus". There are, however, many other theories as to the meaning of these marks.*

Denarii, sestertii and asses were re-introduced and the average weight of the aurei was increased from 5·54 *grammes to* 6·50 *grammes. No attempt was made, however, to re-introduce the silver coinage, this step not being taken until Diocletian's reform, twenty-five years later.*

Very Fine

3148　*N* **heavy aureus.** (average weight *circa* 8·25 grammes). IMP . C . L . DOM . AVRELIANVS P . F . AVG. Rad. and cuir. bust, r. ℞. ADVENTVS AVG. Aurelian on horseback l., raising r. hand. *C.* 2. *R.I.C.* 9. *Illustrated on p.* 269 .. ..£750·00

3149　*N* **aureus.** (pre-reform). Laur., dr. and cuir. bust, r. ℞. VIRTVS AVG. Mars advancing r., carrying spear and trophy, captive at feet. *C.* 269. *R.I.C.* 15 .. .. 400·00

3150　— (post-reform). B. Rad. and cuir. bust, r. ℞. ORIENS AVG. Sol stg. facing, hd. l., holding globe. *C.* 138. *R.I.C.* 18 .. .. 500·00

The following coins, Nos. 3151-3171, *have as obverse type rad., dr. and/or cuir. bust r., unless otherwise stated.*

3151　**Æ antoninianus.** (pre-reform). IMP . C . L . DOM . AVRELIANVS AVG. ℞. APOLLINI CONS. Apollo stg. l., holding branch and leaning on lyre set on rock. *C.* 14. *R.I.C.* 22 .. .. 2·50

3152　— ℞. CONCORDIA AVG. Concord stg. l., altar at feet. *C.* 33. *R.I.C.* 24 .. .. 2·50

3153　A. ℞. DACIA FELIX. Dacia stg. l., holding staff surmounted by ass's head. *C.* 73. *R.I.C.* 108 .. .. 5·00

3154　A. ℞. GENIVS ILLY. Genius stg. l. beside standard. *C.* 103. *R.I.C.* 110 .. .. 4·25

3155　A. ℞. PANNONIAE. Pannonia stg. facing, hd. r., holding standard. *C.* 166. *R.I.C.* 113 .. .. 5·00

3156　IMP . C . L . DOM . AVRELIANVS AVG. ℞. SECVRIT . AVG. Security stg. l., leaning on column. *C.* 225. *R.I.C.* 38 .. .. 2·50

3157　— ℞. VIRTVS AVG. Virtus stg. l., leaning on shield and holding spear. *C.* 274. *R.I.C.* 41 .. .. 2·50

3158　**Æ antoninianus.** (post-reform). B. ℞. CONCORDIA MILITVM. Aurelian and Concord stg. facing each other, clasping r. hands. *C.* 60. *R.I.C.* 59 .. .. 2·25

3159　A. ℞. FORTVNA REDVX. Fortune seated l. *C.* 95. *R.I.C.* 128 .. 2·25

Very Fine

3160 Æ **antoninianus.** (post-reform). A. ℞. IOVI CONSER. Jupiter
stg. l., presenting globe to Aurelian stg. r. *C.* 105. *R.I.C.* 129 .. £2·25

3161 A. ℞. ORIENS AVG. Sol stg. facing, hd. l., between two captives.
C. 145. *R.I.C.* 63 .. .. 2·25

3162 B. ℞. — Sol advancing l., r. foot on captive; to r., another captive
seated on ground. *C.* 153. *R.I.C.* 61 .. .. 2·25

3163 B. ℞. PACATOR ORBIS. Sol advancing l., holding whip. *C.* 161.
R.I.C. 6 .. .. 2·75

3164 B. ℞. PROVIDEN . DEOR. Fides and Sol stg. facing each other.
C. 183. *R.I.C.* 152. **Plate 9** .. .. 2·75

3165 A. ℞. RESTITVT . ORBIS. Female stg. r., presenting wreath to
Aurelian stg. l. *C.* 192. *R.I.C.* 399 .. .. 2·25

3166 DEO ET DOMINO NATO AVRELIANO AVG. ℞. As previous. *C.* 200.
R.I.C. 306 .. .. 25·00

3167 A. ℞. RESTITVT . ORIENTIS. Aurelian stg. l., raising kneeling female
figure. *C.* 204. *R.I.C.* 351 .. .. 3·00

3168 A. ℞. ROMAE AETER. Aurelian stg. r. before Roma seated l. *C.* 219.
R.I.C. 142 .. .. 3·00

3169 A. ℞. SOLI INVICTO. As 3162. *C.* 236. *R.I.C.* 308 .. .. 2·25

3170 A. ℞. VICTORIA AVG. Victory advancing l., captive at feet. *C.* 253.
R.I.C. 55 .. .. 2·25

3171 A. ℞. VIRT . MILITVM. Aurelian and soldier stg. facing each other.
C. 261. *R.I.C.* 56 .. .. 2·50

3172 Æ **denarius.** A. Laur., dr. and cuir. bust, r. ℞. As 3170. *C.*
255. *R.I.C.* 73 .. .. 10·00

Fine

3173 Æ **sestertius.** (diam. over 30 mm.; average weight *c.* 290 grains).
A. Laur. and cuir. bust, r. ℞. CONCORDIA AVG. Aurelian and
Severina stg. facing each other, clasping r. hands; between them, rad.
hd. of Sol r. *C.* 34. *R.I.C.* 76 .. .. 50·00

3174 Æ **dupondius** or **as.** SOL . DOMINVS IMPERI ROMANI. Bare-headed and
dr. bust of Sol r. ℞. AVRELIANVS AVG . CONS. Aurelian stg. l.,
sacrificing over tripod-altar. *C.* 16. *R.I.C.* 319 .. .. .. 65·00

Fine

3175 **Æ dupondius** or **as.** SOL . DOM . IMP . ROMANI. Rad. and dr. bust of
Sol, three quarter face; beneath, four horses, two to r. and two to l. ℞.
As previous. *R.I.C.* 321 .. .. £75·00

3176 As 3173. *C.* 35. *R.I.C.* 80. **Plate 9** .. .. 10·00

Colonial and Provincial Coinage

Very Fine

3177 *Egypt, Alexandria,* **billon tetradrachm.** Laur. and cuir. bust, r.
℞. Athena seated l. *B.M.C. G.*2341 .. .. 2·25

3178 — — ℞. Dikaiosyne stg. l. *B.M.C. G.*2345 .. .. 2·00

3179 — Laur., dr. and cuir. bust, r. ℞. Nike advancing r. *B.M.C.*
*G.*2350 .. .. 2·00

3180 — — ℞. Eagle stg. l., hd. turned. *B.M.C. G.*2355 .. .. .. 1·75

3181 — — ℞. ЄΤΟΥC/Є in laurel-wreath. *B.M.C. G.*2372 .. .. .. 3·25

SEVERINA
Wife of Aurelian

3188

The obv. legend is SEVERINA AVG.

3182 **Æ aureus.** Diad. and dr. bust r., resting on crescent. ℞. CON-
CORDIAE MILITVM. Concord stg. l., holding two standards. *C.* 6.
R.I.C. 2 .. .. 750·00

3183 **Æ antoninianus.** — ℞ CONCORDIA AVGG. Aurelian and Severina
stg. facing each other, clasping r. hands. *C.* 2. *R.I.C.* 3 .. .. 5·50

3184 — ℞. CONCORD . MILIT. Concord seated l. *C.* 5. *R.I.C* 1. .. 6·50

3185 — ℞. As 3182. *C.* 7. *R.I.C.* 7. **Plate 9** .. .. .. 5·50

3186 — ℞. PROVIDEN . DEOR. Fides and Sol stg. facing each other. *C.* 12.
R.I.C. 9 .. .. 6·00

3187 **Æ denarius.** Diad. and dr. bust, r. ℞. VENVS FELIX. Venus stg. l.,
holding Cupid (?) and sceptre. *C.* 14. *R.I.C.* 6 .. .. .. 12·50

3188 **Æ as.** — ℞. IVNO REGINA. Juno stg. l., peacock at feet. *C.* 9.
R.I.C. 7. *Illustrated above* .. .. *Fine* £12·50

3189 *Egypt, Alexandria,* **billon tetradrachm.** Diad. and dr. bust, r. ℞.
Elpis stg. l. *B.M C. G.*2377 .. .. 4·50

3190 — — ℞. Eagle stg. l., hd. turned. *B.M.C. G.*2381 .. .. .. 4·00

ZENOBIA

(*Septimia Zenobia*). *The wife of Odenathus, she took over the government of Palmyra
on the assassination of her husband in* A.D. 267. *She defeated the attempt of Gallienus to
restore the lost Eastern provinces to his Empire, and in the reign of Claudius Gothicus she*

extended the Palmyrene Empire to include Egypt and part of Asia Minor.   She was defeated, however, by Aurelian who took her as an honoured captive to Rome to adorn his great triumph.   He later gave her a villa near Tibur, where she spent the rest of her days.

Fine

3191   *Egypt, Alexandria,* **billon tetradrachm.** CЄΠΤΙΜ . ZHNOBIA CЄB.
Dr. bust, r.   R.   LЄ.   Bust of Selene r., large crescent in front.
*B.M.C. G.*2398   ..   ..£100·00

VABALATHUS
A.D. 271 – 272

3194

The son of Zenobia, Vabalathus became joint ruler of Palmyra with his mother on the assassination of Odenathus. Gallienus refused to grant him the titles which had been conferred upon Odenathus, and Claudius Gothicus did likewise, though neither emperor was able to challenge the power of Palmyra in the East.   Aurelian, however, did grant Vabalathus these titles, but in A.D. *271 the latter was proclaimed Augustus and Aurelian marched against the rival emperor.   In the ensuing struggle the Palmyrene Empire fell to Aurelian, and Zenobia and Vabalathus were taken as captives to Rome.*

As Vir Clarissimus, Rex, Imperator, Dux Romanorum

A.D. 270-271. *with Aurelian*

3192   **Æ antoninianus.**   VABALATHVS V . C . R . IM . D . R.   His laur., dr. and
cuir bust, r.   R.   IMP . C . AVRELIANVS AVG.   His rad. and cuir. bust, r.
C. 1.   *R.I.C. (Aurelian)* 381   ..   ..   7·50

There have been many theories as to the exact meaning of the letters VCRIMDR *in the obverse legend, but the above seems to be the most satisfactory explanation.*

3193   *Egypt, Alexandria,* **billon tetradrachm.** Laur. and diad. bust of
Vabalathus r.   R.   Laur. bust of Aurelian r.   *B.M.C. G.*2384 ..   ..   3·00

As Augustus

3194   **Æ antoninianus.**   IM . C . VHABALATHVS AVG.   Rad. and dr. bust, r.
R.   VICTORIA AVG.   Victory advancing l.   *C.* 6.   *R.I.C.* 6.   *Illustrated
above* ..   ..   90·00

THE INTERREGNUM
A.D. 275

Lasting for about a month, between the murder of Aurelian in August and the accession of Tacitus in September.

3195   **Æ sestertius.**   GENIVS P . R.   Hd. of the Genius of the Roman People
r., laur. and wearing modius (?).   R.   INT . VRB . S . C. in laurel-wreath.
C. 333 (*Gallienus*).   *R.I.C.* 1   ..   ..   50·00

Fine

3196 **Æ sestertius.** Similar, but hd. of Genius rad. instead of laur. *C.* 334
(*Gallienus*). *R.I.C.* 2 .. .. £45·00

3197 **Æ dupondius.** As previous. *C.* 335 (*Gallienus*). *R.I.C.* 3 .. .. 35·00

TACITUS
A.D. 275 – 276

3216

(*M. Claudius Tacitus*).   *After the murder of Aurelian, the soldiers of the Illyrian army, wishing to dissociate themselves from the assassins, sent a request to Rome that the Senate should nominate the new ruler, and pledged themselves to support the choice.   After some delay the Senate selected Tacitus, an elderly senator who claimed descent from the great historian, and he was proclaimed Augustus.   Although seventy-five years of age, the new ruler soon joined the army in Thrace and succeeded in repelling a Gothic invasion of Asia Minor.   However, the exertions of this campaign and the inclement climate proved too much for the aged emperor, and he died in Cappadocia in April,* A.D. *276.*

Mints: Rome; Lugdunum; Arelate (?); Ticinum; Siscia; Serdica; Cyzicus; Antioch; Tripolis.

The obv. legend is IMP . C . M . CL . TACITVS AVG., *unless otherwise stated.*

Very Fine

3198 **A′ heavy aureus.** (*c.* 6·54 *grammes*). Laur., dr. and cuir. bust, r.
R. ROMAE AETERNAE. Roma seated l., holding Victory and sceptre.
C. 116. *R.I.C* 75 **Plate 9** .. .. 375·00

3199 **A′ aureus.** (*c.* 4·61 *grammes*). Laur. and cuir. bust, r. R. PAX
AVGVSTI. Pax advancing l. *R.I.C.* 71 .. .. 425·00

The following coins, Nos. 3200-3217, have as obverse type rad., dr. and/or cuir. bust r., unless otherwise stated.

3200 **Æ antoninianus.** R. AEQVITAS AVG. Equity stg. l. *C.* 7. *R.I.C.*
82 .. .. 3·75

3201 R. CLEMENTIA TEMP. Clemency stg. l., leaning on column. *C.* 16.
R.I.C. 84 .. .. 3·75

3202 R. — Roma stg. r., receiving globe from Tacitus stg. l. *C.* 19. *R.I.C.*
126 .. .. 3·75

3203 R. — Tacitus stg. r., receiving globe from Jupiter stg. l. *C.* 20.
R.I.C. 190 .. .. 3·75

Very Fine

3204 **Æ antoninianus.** R. CONSERVAT . MILIT. As previous. C. 25.
R.I.C. 133 .. .. £3·75

3205 R. FELICITAS SAECVLI. Felicity stg. l., holding patera and caduceus,
altar at feet. C. 34. R.I.C. 22 .. .. 3·75

3206 IMP . CL . TACITVS AVG. R. FIDES MILITVM. Fides stg. l., holding two
standards. C. 47. R.I.C. 27 .. .. 3·75

3207 R. LAETITIA FVND. Laetitia stg. l. C. 52. R.I.C. 89 .. .. 3·75

3208 IMP . CL . TACITVS AVG. R. PAX AETERNA. Pax stg. l. C. 65. R.I.C.
34 .. .. 3·75

3209 IMP . C . CL . TACITVS AVG. R. PROVID . DEOR. Providence stg. l.,
globe at feet. C. 86. R.I.C. 49 .. .. 3·75

3210 R. PROVIDEN . DEOR. Concord and Sol stg. facing each other. C. 94.
R.I.C. 195 .. .. 4·50

3211 R. SALVS AVG. Salus stg. l., feeding serpent arising from altar. C. 123.
R.I.C. 93 .. .. 3·75

3212 R. SECVRIT . PERP. Security stg. l., leaning on column. C. 131.
R.I.C. 163 .. .. 3·75

3213 R. SPES PVBLICA. Spes advancing l. C. 138. R.I.C. 94 .. .. 3·75

3214 IMP . C . M . CL . TACITVS P . F . AVG. R. TEMPORVM FELICITAS. Felicity
stg. l. C. 145. R.I.C. 63 .. .. 3·75

3215 R. VICTORIA GOTTHI. Victory stg. l. C. 157. R.I.C. 172 .. .. 12·50

3216 IMP . C . M . CL . TACITVS P . F . AVG. Rad. and cuir. bust, l. R. As
previous. C. 159. R.I.C. 171. *Illustrated on p. 274* .. .. .. 15·00

3217 R. VIRTVS AVG. Virtus stg. l., leaning on shield and holding spear.
C. 170. R.I.C. 68 .. .. 3·75

3218 **Æ denarius.** IMP . C . M . CL . TACITVS P . F . AVG. Laur. and cuir.
bust l., holding spear and shield. R. VICTORIA AVG. Victory stg. l.
C. 151. R.I.C. 99 .. .. 65·00

3219 **Æ quinarius.** Laur. and dr. bust, r. R. PROVIDENTIA AVG. Providence stg. l., globe at feet. C. 101. R.I.C. 102.. .. .. .. 37·50

3220 **Æ as.** — R. MARS VLTOR. Mars advancing r., holding spear and
shield. C. 59. R.I.C. 108 .. .. *Fine* £45·00

3221 *Egypt, Alexandria,* **billon tetradrachm.** Laur., dr. and cuir. bust, r.
R. Athena seated l. B.M.C. G.2402 .. .. 3·75

3222 — R. Eagle stg. l., hd. turned. B.M.C. G.2406 .. .. .. 3·25

FLORIANUS
A.D. 276

3224

(*M. Annius Florianus*). *After the death of Tacitus his half-brother, Florianus, immediately assumed the purple, and his rule was recognised by the Senate and the western
provinces. The eastern army, however, proclaimed Probus emperor, and Florianus
immediately marched against him. The two armies met near Tarsus in Cilicia, but before
any serious fighting took place Florianus was murdered by his own soldiers after a reign of
little more than two months.*

Mints: Rome; Lugdunum; Ticinum; Siscia; Serdica; Cyzicus.

Very Fine

3223 **N heavy aureus.** (*c. 6·45 grammes*). IMP . C . FLORIANVS AVG. Laur.,
dr. and cuir. bust, r. ℞. CONSERVATOR AVG. Sol in quadriga galloping
l., holding whip. *R.I.C.* 115 .. ..£750·00

3224 **N aureus.** (*c. 4·61 grammes*). VIRTVS FLORIANI AVG. Laur. and cuir.
bust l., holding sceptre and shield. ℞. VICTORIA PERPET. Victory
stg. r., inscribing xxx. on shield set on palm-tree. *C.* 92. *R.I.C.* 23.
Illustrated on p. 275 .. .. 850·00

The following coins, Nos. 3225-3231, *have as obverse type rad., dr. and/or cuir. bust, r.*

3225 **Æ antoninianus.** IMP . C . M . AN . FLORIANVS P . F . AVG. ℞. AETER-
NITAS AVG. Eternity stg. l., holding globe and rudder. *C.* 3. *R.I.C.* 2 15·00

3226 IMP . C . M . AN . FLORIANVS P . AVG. ℞. FELICITAS AVG. Felicity stg. l.
C. 18. *R.I.C.* 60 .. .. 15·00

3227 IMP . C . FLORIANVS AVG. ℞. LAETITIA FVND. Laetitia stg. l. *C.* 38.
R.I.C. 34. **Plate 9** .. .. 15·00

3228 IMP . C . M . AN . FLORIANVS AVG. ℞. PACATOR ORBIS. Sol advancing l.,
holding whip. *C.* 46. *R.I.C.* 9 .. .. 15·00

3229 — ℞. PROVIDENTIA AVG. Providence stg. l., globe at feet. *C.* 75.
R.I.C. 10 .. .. 15·00

3230 IMP . C . FLORIANVS AVG. ℞. SALVS AVG. Salus stg. l., feeding serpent
arising from altar. *C.* 38. *R.I.C.* 40 .. .. 15·00

3231 — ℞. VIRTVS AVG. Florian stg. r., holding spear and globe. *C.* 97.
R.I.C. 47 .. .. 15·00

3232 **Æ (or white metal) denarius.** *Obv.* As 3224. ℞. VIRTVS AVG.
Florian stg. l., holding globe and sceptre. *C.* 95. *R.I.C.* 49 .. .. 175·00

3233 **Æ quinarius.** IMP . C . FLORIANVS AVG. Laur. and dr. bust, r. ℞.
As 3231. *C.* 100. *R.I.C.* 50 .. .. 75·00

3234 **Æ as.** IMP . C . M . ANN . FLORIANVS AVG. Laur. and dr. bust, r. ℞.
SECVRITAS AVG . S . C. Security stg. l., leaning on column. *C.* 85.
R.I.C. 53 .. .. *Fine* £90·00

PROBUS
A.D. 276-282

3263

(*M. Aurelius Probus*). *Born at Sirmium in* A.D. 232, *Probus adopted the profession of arms and gained rapid promotion until, by the reign of Aurelian, he had become one of the leading generals of the Empire. Soon after the death of Tacitus he was proclaimed emperor by his troops and, following the murder of Florianus, he became undisputed master of the Roman world. His reign was notable not only for his considerable military successes, but also for his attempt to restore the economic life of the Empire. To this end he introduced viticulture into several of the western provinces, and had he been able to carry out all his plans the Roman State might have recovered much of its ancient power and prestige. However, in the autumn of* A.D. 282 *he was murdered at Sirmium by a band of mutinous soldiers who were enraged at having been employed on public works instead of military duties.*

Mints: Rome; Lugdunum; Ticinum; Siscia, Serdica; Cyzicus; Antioch; Tripolis.

The following are the commonest forms of obv. legend:

A. PROBVS P . F . AVG.

B. IMP . C . PROBVS P . F . AVG.

C. IMP . C . M . AVR . PROBVS AVG.

D. IMP . C . M . AVR . PROBVS P . F . AVG.

E. VIRTVS PROBI AVG.

Very Fine

3235 Ν heavy **aureus.** (*c.* 8·20 *grammes*). IMP . C . PROBVS INVICTVS AVG.
Rad., dr. and cuir. bust, r. ℞. FIDES MILITVM. Fides stg. l., holding
two standards. *C.* 250. *R.I.C.* 823 .. ..£750·00

3236 Ν **aureus.** (*c.* 6·25 *grammes*). C. Laur., dr. and cuir. bust, r. ℞.
SECVRITAS SAECVLI. Security seated l., holding sceptre. *Cf. C.* 629.
R.I.C. 594 .. .. 275·00

3237 Ν **quinarius.** (*c.* 2·53 *grammes*). PROBVS P . AVG. Laur. and cuir.
bust, r. ℞. MARS VLTOR. Mars advancing r., holding spear and shield.
C. 348. *R.I.C.* 148 .. .. 400·00

*The following coins, Nos. 3238-3280, have as obverse type rad., dr. and/or cuir. bust r.
unless otherwise stated.*

3238 Æ **antoninianus.** B. ℞. ABVNDANTIA AVG. Abundance stg. r.,
emptying cornucopiae. *C.* 1. *R.I.C.* 60 .. .. .. 1·75

3238A IMP . PROBVS AVG. Cuir. bust l., wearing rad. helmet and holding spear
and shield. ℞. ADVENTVS AVG. Probus on horseback l., raising r.
hand, captive seated in front of horse. *C.* 39. *R.I.C.* 157. **Plate 9** .. 2·50

3239 C. ℞. — As previous, but without captive. *C.* 47. *R.I.C.* 625 .. 2·00

3240 D. ℞. ADVENTVS PROBI AVG. As 3238A. *C.* 55. *R.I.C.* 160 .. 2·25

3241 E. Cuir. bust l., wearing rad. helmet and holding spear and shield.
℞. As previous. *C.* 69. *R.I.C.* 166 .. .. 2·50

3242 C. ℞. AEQVITAS AVG. Equity stg. l. *C.* 74. *R.I.C.* 150 .. .. 1·75

3243 IMP . C . M . AVR . PROBVS P . AVG. Rad. bust l., wearing imperial mantle
and holding eagle-tipped sceptre. ℞. CLEMENTIA TEMP. Probus stg.
r., receiving globe from Jupiter stg. l. *C.* 89. *R.I.C.* 839 .. .. 2·50

3244 D. ℞. As previous. *C.* 91. *R.I.C.* 920 .. .. .. 1·75

3245 B. ℞. COMES AVG. Minerva stg. l., holding olive-branch and leaning
on shield. *C.* 105. *R.I.C.* 65 .. .. 2·00

3246 C. ℞. CONCORD . MILIT. Probus and Concord stg. facing each other,
clasping r. hands. *C.* 137. *R.I.C.* 332 .. .. 1·75

3247 C. ℞. CONSERVAT . AVG. Sol stg. l., holding globe. *C.* 179. *R.I.C.*
348 .. .. 1·75

3248 IMP . C . PROBVS AVG . CONS . II. As 3243. ℞. As previous. *C.* 191.
R.I.C. 352 .. .. 12·50

3249 B. ℞. FELICIT . TEMP. Felicity stg. l. *C.* 210. *R.I.C.* 75 .. .. 1·75

3250 B. ℞. FIDES MILIT. Fides stg. l., holding two standards. *C.* 239.
R.I.C. 365 .. .. 1·75

3251 B. ℞. ERCVLI PACIF. Hercules stg. l., holding olive-branch and club.
C. 278. *R.I.C.* 375 .. .. 2·00

3252 A. ℞. IOVI CONS . PROB . AVG. Jupiter stg. l., holding thunderbolt and
sceptre. *C.* 305. *R.I.C.* 175 .. .. 2·00

Very Fine

3253 **Æ antoninianus.** B. ℞. IOVI CONSERVAT. Probus stg. r., receiving globe from Jupiter stg. l. *C.* 310. *R.I.C.* 387 .. .. £1·75
3254 C. ℞. LAETITIA AVG. Laetitia stg. l., holding wreath and anchor. *Cf. C.* 329. *R.I.C.* 31 .. .. 1·75
3255 B. ℞. MARS VICTOR. Mars advancing r., carrying spear and trophy. *C.* 334. *R.I.C.* 38 .. .. 1·75
3256 A. ℞. MARTI PACIF. Mars advancing l., holding olive-branch, spear and shield. *C.* 350. *R.I.C.* 177 .. .. 1·75
3257 *Obv.* As 3241. ℞. As previous. *C.* 358. *R.I.C.* 509 .. .. 2·50
3258 C. ℞. ORIENS AVG. Sol advancing l. between two captives, holding globe. *C.* 388. *R.I.C.* 44 .. .. 1·75
3259 B. ℞. PAX AVG. Pax stg. l. *C.* 401. *R.I.C.* 91 .. .. .. 1·75
3260 B. ℞. PIETAS AVG. Pietas stg. l., altar at feet. *C.* 437. *R.I.C.* 96 .. 1·75
3261 C. ℞. P . M . TR . P . COS . P . P. Probus stg. l. between two standards, holding sceptre. *C.* 440. *R.I.C.* 607 .. .. 3·75
3262 C. ℞. PROVIDEN . DEOR. Fides and Sol stg. facing each other. *C.* 472. *R.I.C.* 845 .. .. 2·25
3263 IMP . C . PROBVS AVG . CONS . IIII. As 3243. ℞. PROVIDENT . AVG. Providence stg. l., holding globe and sceptre. *C.* 490. *R.I.C.* 495. *Illustrated on p.* 276 .. .. 15·00
3264 D. ℞. RESTITVT . ORBIS. Female stg. r., presenting wreath to Probus stg. l. *C.* 509. *R.I.C.* 925.. .. .. 1·75
3265 A. As 3243. ℞. ROMAE AETER. Roma seated facing in temple of six columns. *C.* 528. *R.I.C.* 187 .. .. 3·25
3266 B. ℞. SALVS AVG. Salus stg. l., feeding serpent arising from altar. *C.* 566. *R.I.C.* 745 .. .. 1·75
3267 *Obv.* As 3241. ℞. — Salus stg. r., feeding serpent held in arms. *C.* 584. *R.I.C.* 558 .. .. 2·50
3268 D. As 3243. ℞. SECVRIT . PERP. Security stg. l., leaning on column. *C.* 615. *R.I.C.* 522 .. .. 2·50

3269 C. ℞. SISCIA PROBI AVG. Siscia seated l., between two river gods, holding diadem. *C.* 635. *R.I.C.* 765 .. .. 25·00
3270 A. As 3243. ℞. SOLI INVICTO. Sol in quadriga galloping l. *C.* 642. *R.I.C.* 203 .. .. 2·50
3271 C. As 3241. ℞. — Sol in galloping quadriga facing. *C.* 675. *R.I.C.* 862 .. .. 3·25
3272 C. ℞. SPES AVG. Spes advancing l. *C.* 702. *R.I.C.* 127 .. .. 1·75
3273 B. ℞. TEMPOR . FELICI. Felicity stg. r. *C.* 713. *R.I.C.* 104 .. 1·75
3274 A. ℞. VICTORIA AVG. Victory advancing l., holding wreath and trophy. *C.* 739. *R.I.C.* 215 .. .. 1·75
3275 A. ℞. VICTORIA GERM. Two captives seated at foot of trophy. *C.* 766. *R.I.C.* 223 .. .. 5·00
3276 B. ℞. VIRTVS AVG. As 3255. *C.* 801. *R.I.C.* 428 .. .. .. 1·75

Very Fine

3277 **Æ antoninianus.** B. ℞. — Virtus stg. l., holding Victory and leaning on shield. *C.* 816. *R.I.C.* 436 .. .. £1·75

3278 *Obv.* As 3243. ℞. VIRTVS PROBI AVG. As 3255. *C.* 894. *R.I.C.*
816 .. .. 2·50

3279 D. As 3241. ℞. — Probus galloping r., spearing enemy. *C.* 919.
R.I.C. 817 .. .. 3·00

3280 C. ℞. — As 3275. *C.* 936. *R.I.C.* 821 .. .. 3·00

3281 **Æ denarius.** IMP . PROBVS AVG. Laur. and cuir. bust, r. ℞. As
3275. *C.* 767. *R.I.C.* 259 .. .. 30·00

3282 **Æ quinarius.** C. — ℞. VIRTVS AVG. Probus stg. r., holding spear
and globe. *C.* 841. *R.I.C.* 279 .. .. 20·00

Fine

3283 **Æ dupondius.** A. Rad. and cuir. bust r. ℞. FIDES MILITVM.
Fides stg. l., holding two standards. *R.I.C.* 290. .. .. 75·00

3284 **Æ as.** (*c.* 26 mm *and* 125 *grains*).*Obv.* As 3281. ℞. VICTORIA AVG.
Victory stg. l. *C.* 736. *R.I.C.* 297 .. .. 45·00

3285 **Æ semis.** (*c.* 22 mm. *and* 75 *grains*). IMP . PROBVS P . F . AVG. Laur.
and dr. bust, r. ℞. VIRTVS AVGVSTI. Mars stg. l., leaning on shield
and holding spear. *C.* 852. *R.I.C.* 304 .. .. 35·00

Colonial and Provincial Coinage

Very Fine

3286 *Egypt, Alexandria,* **billon tetradrachm.** Laur. and cuir. bust, r. ℞.
Athena seated l. *B.M.C. G.*2409 .. .. 1·25

3287 — ℞. Eirene stg. l. *B.M.C. G.*2413 .. .. 1·25

3288 — ℞. Elpis stg. l. *B.M.C. G.*2416 .. .. 1·25

3289 — ℞. Nike advancing r. *B.M.C. G.*2420 .. .. .. 1·25

3290 — ℞. Eagle stg. l., hd. turned. *B.M.C. G.*2430 .. .. 1·25

3291 — ℞. Eagle stg. facing, hd. r. *B.M.C. G.*2433 .. .. 1·25

BONOSUS
ca. A.D. 280

*Of British descent, Bonosus was a general of Probus and, having been unsuccessful against
the Germans, assumed the purple at Cologne in fear of the anger of the emperor. He was
defeated by Probus after a severe struggle.*

3292 **Billon antoninianus.** M . C . BONOSVS VA. Rad. hd., r. ℞. PX . GA.
Equity stg. l. *C.* 2. *R.I.C.* 2 .. .. *Very rare*

SATURNINUS
ca. A.D. 280

*(Sextus Julius Saturninus). A general of Probus, Saturninus was proclaimed emperor
by his soldiers at Alexandria in Egypt, but was murdered soon afterwards.*

3293 **N aureus.** IMP . C . IVL . SATVRNINVS AVG. Laur. and cuir. bust, r.
℞. VICTORIAE AVG. Victory advancing r. *R.I.C.* 1 .. .. *Extr. rare*

CARUS
A.D. 282 – 283

3312

(*M. Aurelius Carus*).   *On the death of Probus, Carus, the praetorian prefect, was proclaimed Emperor by the army.   Having conferred the rank of Caesar on his sons Carinus and Numerian, he set out on an expedition against the Persians, accompanied by Numerian, and leaving Carinus to govern the western provinces.   The Persian forces were defeated and driven back in disorder, but before Carus could follow up his successes he was killed by lightning in his camp near Ctesiphon late in A.D. 283.*

Mints: Rome; Lugdunum; Ticinum; Siscia; Cyzicus; Antioch; Tripolis; unidentified mint.

The following are the commonest forms of obv. legend:

A.   IMP . CARVS P . F . AVG.

B.   IMP . C . M . AVR . CARVS P . F . AVG.

In *R.I.C.* the coinage of Carus, Carinus, Numerian, Magnia Urbica and Nigrinian is dealt with in one group, numbered 1-474.

Very Fine

3294   **A′ aureus.** B.   Laur., dr. and cuir. bust, r.   R.   VICTORIA AVG. Victory stg. l. on globe.   *C.* 84.   *R.I.C.* 95   ..   ..£300·00

3295   **Æ heavy antoninianus.**   (*c.* 75 *grains*).   DEO ET DOMINO CARO INVIC . AVG.   Rad. and cuir. bust, r.   R.   FIDES MILITVM.   Fides stg. l., holding two standards.   *C.* 32.   *R.I.C.* 100   ..   ..   30·00

3296   — Rad. busts of Sol and Carus face to face, the former dr., the latter cuir.   R.   FELICITAS REIPVBLICAE.   Felicity stg. l., leaning on column. *C.* 28.   *R.I.C.* 99   ..   ..   45·00

The following coins, Nos. 3297-3309, have as obverse type rad., dr. and/or cuir. bust, r.

3297   **Æ antoninianus.** B.   (but KARVS).   R.   ABVNDANT . AVG.   Abundance stg. r., emptying cornucopiae.   *C.* 1.   *R.I.C.* 67 ..   ..   ..   6·00
3298   A.   R.   ABVNDANTIA AVG.   As previous.   *C.* 2.   *R.I.C.* 69 ..   ..   5·00
3299   B.   R.   AETERNIT . IMPERI.   Sol advancing l., holding whip.   *C.* 11. *R.I.C.* 35   ..   ..   5·00
3300   A.   R.   FIDES MILIT.   As 3295.   *C.* 29.   *R.I.C.* 70   ..   ..   ..   5·00
3301   B.   R.   IOVI VICTORI.   Jupiter stg. l., holding Victory and sceptre, eagle at feet.   *C.* 37.   *R.I.C.* 38 ..   ..   5·00
3302   B.   R.   PAX AVGG.   Pax stg. l.   *C.* 50.   *R.I.C.* 12   ..   ..   ..   5·00
3303   A.   R.   PAX EXERCITI.   Pax stg. l., holding olive-branch and standard. *C.* 56.   *R.I.C.* 75   ..   ..   5·00
3304   B.   R.   PROVIDENT . AVGG.   Providence stg. l., globe at feet.   *C.* 69. *R.I.C.* 42   ..   ..   5·00
3305   B.   R.   RESTITVT . ORBIS.   Female stg. r., presenting wreath to Carus stg. l.   *C.* 71.   *R.I.C.* 106 ..   ..   5·00
3306   A.   R.   SPES PVBLICA.   Spes advancing l.   *C.* 79.   *R.I.C.* 82.   **Plate 10**   ..   ..   5·00
3307   B.   R.   VICTORIA AVG.   Victory advancing l.   *C.* 93.   *R.I.C.* 84   ..   5·00

Very Fine

3308 Æ **antoninianus.** A. ℞. VIRTVS AVGG. Virtus stg. l., leaning on
      shield and holding spear. *C.* 110. *R.I.C.* 46 ..   .. £5·00

3309 B. ℞. VIRTVS AVGGG. Carus stg. r., receiving Victory on globe from
      Jupiter stg. l. *C.* 117. *R.I.C.* 125 ..   .. 5·50

3310 Æ **denarius.** A. Laur. and cuir. bust, r. ℞. PROVIDE . AVGG.
      As 3304. *R.I.C.* 53 ..   .. 55·00

3311 Æ **quinarius.** — — ℞. As 3308. *C.* 111. *R.I.C.* 56 ..   .. 37·50

3312 Æ **as.** IMP . C . M . AVR . CARVS AVG. — ℞. PAX AVGVSTORVM. Pax
      advancing l. *C.* 55. *R.I.C.* 60. *Illustrated on p.* 280   *Fine* £65·00

3313 Æ **semis.** B. — ℞. PRINCIPI IVVENTVT. Carus stg. l., holding
      standard and spear. *R.I.C.* 61 ..   .. *Fine* £45·00

Commemorative Coins struck after his death

Struck under Carinus and Numerian

3314 *N* **aureus.** DIVO CARO PIO. Laur. hd., r. ℞. CONSECRATIO. Eagle
      stg. r., hd. turned. *C.* 14. *R.I.C.* 4 ..   .. 400·00

3315 Æ **antoninianus.** DIVO CARO. Rad. hd., r. ℞. — Eagle stg. facing,
      hd. l. *C.* 15. *R.I.C.* 28 ..   .. 6·50

3316 DIVO CARO PERS. — ℞. — Eagle stg. facing. *C.* 17. *R.I.C.* 48 .. 10·00

3317 DIVO CARO. — ℞. — Large altar. *C.* 20. *R.I.C.* 49 ..   .. 6·50

3318 DIVO CARO PARTHICO. — ℞. — Large altar. *C.* 23. *R.I.C.* 110 .. 9·00

Colonial and Provincial Coinage

3319 *Egypt, Alexandria,* **billon tetradrachm.** Laur., dr. and cuir. bust, r.
      ℞. Dikaiosyne stg. l. *B.M.C. G.*2441 ..   .. 2·50

3320 — — ℞. Eagle stg. l., hd. turned, between two vexilla. *B.M.C.*
      *G.*2443 ..   .. 2·50

3321 — Laur. hd., r. ℞. Flaming altar. *B.M.C. G.*2446. (*Struck after*
      his death) ..   .. 3·00

bronze medallion, Cohen 91.

(*Marcus Aurelius Numerianus*). *Born about* A.D. 254, *Numerian was the younger son
of Carus and was given the rank of Caesar soon after his father's accession. He accompanied
Carus to the East in* A.D. 283 *and in the course of the Persian campaign he was elevated to
the rank of Augustus* (*September or October*). *Following the death of Carus, he led the
army slowly back to Europe, but as the procession neared Heraclea in Thrace, it was dis-
covered that Numerian had been murdered in his litter* (*November,* A.D. 284). *Arrius Aper,
the praetorian prefect and father-in-law of the late emperor, was accused of the crime and
was immediately executed by Diocletian, the commander of the imperial bodyguards.*

NUMERIAN
A.D. 283 – 284

As Caesar

A.D. 282-283, *under Carus.*

A.D. 283, *under Carus and Carinus.*

Very Fine

3322 **A' aureus.** M . AVR . NVMERIANVS NOB . C. Laur., dr. and cuir. bust, r. ℞. PRINCIPI IVVENT. Numerian stg. l., holding branch and sceptre. *C.* 65. *R.I.C.* 369 .. ..£450·00

3323 **Æ antoninianus.** NVMERIANVS NOB . CAES. Rad. and dr. bust, r. ℞. CLEMENTIA TEMP. Numerian stg. r., receiving Victory on globe from Jupiter stg. l. *C.* 9. *R.I.C.* 372 .. .. 4·50

3324 M . AVR . NVMERIANVS NOB . C. — ℞. MARS VICTOR. Mars advancing r., holding spear and trophy. *C.* 18. *R.I.C.* 353 .. .. .. 4·50

3325 — — ℞. PRINCIPI IVVENTVT. Numerian stg. l., holding globe and sceptre. *C.* 72. *R.I.C.* 356 .. .. 4·50

3326 — — ℞. VIRTVS AVGG. As 3323. *C.* 107. *R.I.C.* 377 .. .. 4·50

As Augustus

There are three main varieties of obv. legend:

A. IMP . NVMERIANVS AVG.
B. IMP . NVMERIANVS P . F . AVG.
C. IMP . C . NVMERIANVS P . F . AVG.

3327 **A' aureus.** B. Laur., dr. and cuir. bust, r. ℞. VIRTVS AVGG. Hercules stg. r., leaning on club set on rock. *C.* 100. *R.I.C.* 407 .. 450·00

The following coins, Nos. 3328-3341, have as obverse type rad., dr. and/or cuir. bust r., unless otherwise stated.

3328 **Æ antoninianus.** C. ℞. As 3323. *C.* 8. *R.I.C.* 463 .. .. 4·50

3329 IMP . C . NVMERIANVS AVG. ℞. FELICITAS AVGG. Felicity stg. l., leaning on column. *C.* 14. *R.I.C.* 384 .. .. 4·50

3330 C. ℞. FIDES EXERCIT . AVGG. Fides seated l., holding patera and standard; in background, two more standards. *C.* 15. *R.I.C.* 460 .. 6·00

3331 A. ℞. IOVI VICTORI. Jupiter stg. l., holding Victory and sceptre, eagle at feet. *C.* 16. *R.I.C.* 410 .. .. 4·50

3331A IMP . C . NVMERIANVS AVG. ℞. As 3324. *C.* 21. *R.I.C.* 388. **Plate 10** .. .. 4·50

3332 A. ℞. ORIENS AVGG. Sol advancing l., holding whip. *C.* 37. *R.I.C.* 412 .. .. 4·50

3333 A. Rad. and cuir. bust l., holding spear and shield. ℞. PAX AVGG. Pax stg. l. *C.* 47. *R.I.C.* 395 .. .. 7·00

3334 A. ℞. PIETAS AVGG. Mercury stg. l., holding purse and caduceus. *C.* 57. *R.I.C.* 416 .. .. 5·00

3335 A. ℞. — Pietas stg. r., altar at feet. *C.* 61. *R.I.C.* 397 .. 4·50

3336 B. ℞. PROVIDENT . AVG. Annona stg. l., holding corn-ears and cornucopiae, modius at feet. *C.* 82. *R.I.C.* 446 .. .. .. 4·50

3337 B. ℞. ROMAE AETERN. Roma seated l., holding Victory and sceptre. *C.* 85. *R.I.C.* 449 .. .. 5·00

3338 B. ℞. SECVRIT . AVG. Security stg. l., leaning on column. *C.* 87. *R.I.C.* 450 .. .. 4·50

3339 C. ℞. VIRTVS AVGG. As 3323. *C.* 110. *R.I.C.* 467 .. .. 4·50

3340 A. ℞. VNDIQVE VICTORES. Numerian stg. l., between two captives, holding globe and sceptre. *C.* 120. *R.I.C.* 423 .. .. .. 10·00

3341 C. ℞. VOTA PVBLICA. Numerian and Carinus stg. facing each other, sacrificing over altar. *C.* 122. *R.I.C.* 461 .. .. .. 5·00

Very Fine

3342 **Æ denarius.** A. Laur. and dr. bust, r. ℞. PAX AVGG. Pax
       advancing l. *R.I.C.* 431 .. .. £45·00
3343 **Æ quinarius.** A. — ℞. As 3327. *C.* 101. *R.I.C.* 439 .. .. 45·00
3344 **Æ as.** C. — ℞. As 3342. *C.* 52. *R.I.C.* 440 *Fine* £75·00

Commemorative Coins struck after his death
Struck under Carinus.

3345 **Æ antoninianus.** DIVO NVMERIANO. Rad. hd., r. ℞. CONSECRATIO.
       Eagle stg. facing, hd. l. *C.* 10. *R.I.C.* 424 .. .. 12·50
3346 — — ℞. — Large altar. *Cf. C.* 12. *R.I.C.* 426 .. .. .. 12·50

Colonial and Provincial Coinage

3347 *Egypt, Alexandria,* **billon tetradrachm.** Laur., dr. and cuir. bust, r.
       ℞. Dikaiosyne stg. l. *B.M.C. G.*2462 (*as Caesar*) .. .. 2·25
3348 — ℞. Athena seated l. *B.M.C. G.*2464 (*as Augustus*) .. .. 2·25
3349 — ℞. Eagle stg. l., hd. turned. *B.M.C. G.*2470 (*as Augustus*) .. 2·25

CARINUS
A.D. 283 – 285

3382

   (*M. Aurelius Carinus*). *The elder son of Carus, Carinus was born about* A.D. 249 *and
was given the rank of Caesar soon after his father's accession. When his father and his
younger brother set out for the Eastern frontier early in 283, Carinus was left in Rome to
look after the government of the Western provinces, and in July or August of the same year
he was raised to the rank of Augustus. Early in 285 he left Rome to meet the challenge of
M. Aurelius Julianus who, after having been proclaimed emperor in Pannonia, was marching
against Italy. Carinus defeated him near Verona, but then had to advance against Diocletian who had been proclaimed emperor by the Eastern army following the death of Numerian. In the ensuing conflict Carinus was victorious, but soon afterwards he was murdered
by one of his own officers, and the Empire fell into the hands of Diocletian (spring,* A.D. 285).

As Caesar
A.D. 282-283, *under Carus.*

The obv. legend is M . AVR . CARINVS NOB . CAES., *unless otherwise stated.*

3350 **N aureus.** Laur., dr. and cuir. bust, r. ℞. PAX AETERNA. Pax
       advancing l. *C.* 62. *R.I.C.* 153 .. .. 450·00
3351 **Æ heavy antoninianus.** Rad. and cuir. bust, r. ℞. FELICITAS
       REIPVBLICAE. Felicity stg. l., leaning on column. *C.* 25. *R.I.C.* 194 20·00

The following coins, Nos. 3352-3356, have as obverse type rad., dr. and/or cuir. bust, r.

3352 **Æ antoninianus.** ℞. CLEMENTIA TEMP. Carinus stg. r., receiving
       Victory on globe from Jupiter (or Carus) stg. l. *C.* 19. *R.I.C.* 202 .. 4·00
3353 ℞. PIETAS AVGG. Sacrificial implements. *C.* 74. *R.I.C.* 155 .. 5·00
3354 ℞. PRINCIPI IVVENTVT. Carinus stg. l., holding globe and sceptre.
       C. 91. *R.I.C.* 161 .. .. 4·00
3355 CARINVS NOBIL . CAES. ℞. SAECVLI FELICITAS. Carinus stg. r.,
       holding spear and globe. *C.* 115. *R.I.C.* 152 .. .. 4·00

Very Fine

3356   **Æ antoninianus.** IMP . C . M . AVR . CARINVS NOB . C. ℞. VIRTVS
       AVGG. As 3352. *C.* 182. *R.I.C.* 206 ..   ..   £4·00
3357   **Æ denarius.** Laur., dr. and cuir. bust, r. ℞. MARS VLTOR. Mars
       advancing r., holding spear and shield. *R.I.C.* 163   ..   ..   ..   37·50
3358   **Æ quinarius.** Laur. hd., r. ℞. As 3350. *C.* 63. *R.I.C.* 167 ..   37·50
3359   **Æ as.** Laur. and dr. bust, r. ℞. PRINCIPI IVVENT. Carinus stg. l.,
       holding standard and sceptre. *C.* 81. *R.I.C.* 174   .. *Fine* £50·00
3360   **Æ semis.** — ℞. PAX AVGVSTORVM. Pax advancing l. *C.* 71.
       R.I.C. 175 ..   .. *Fine* £30·00

As Augustus

The following are the commonest forms of obv. legend:
   A.   IMP . CARINVS P . F . AVG.
   B.   IMP . C . M . AVR . CARINVS AVG.

3361   **A' aureus.** IMP . C . CARINVS P . F . AVG. Laur. and cuir. bust, r. ℞.
       VICTORIA AVGG. Victory advancing l. *C.* 146. *R.I.C.* 313   ..   .. 450·00

*The following coins, Nos. 3362-3378, have as obverse type rad., dr. and/or cuir. bust r.,
unless otherwise stated.*

3362   **Æ antoninianus.** B. ℞. AEQVITAS AVGG. Equity stg. l. *C.* 8.
       R.I.C. 238 ..   ..   4·00
3363   A. ℞. AETERNIT . AVG. Eternity stg. l., holding phoenix on globe.
       C. 10. *R.I.C.* 244 ..   ..   4·00
3364   A. ℞. FELICIT . PVBLICA. Felicity stg. l., leaning on column. *C.* 24.
       R.I.C. 295 ..   ..   4·00
3365   B. ℞. FIDES MILITVM. Fides stg. l., holding two standards. *C.* 30.
       R.I.C. 252 ..   ..   4·00
3366   A. ℞. FORTVNA REDVX. Fortune seated l. *C.* 34. *R.I.C.* 298 ..   4·00
3367   B. ℞. GENIVS EXERCITI. Genius stg. l. *C.* 38. *R.I.C.* 255   ..   5·00
3368   A. ℞. IOVI VICTORI. Jupiter stg. l., holding Victory and sceptre,
       eagle at feet. *C.* 45. *R.I.C.* 258   ..   ..   4·00
3369   A. ℞. LAETITIA FVND. Laetitia stg. l. *C.* 47. *R.I.C.* 261 ..   ..   4·00
3370   A. Rad. bust l., wearing imperial mantle and holding eagle-tipped
       sceptre. ℞. As 3355. *C.* 118. *R.I.C.* 215   ..   ..   7·00
3371   B. ℞. As 3355. *C.* 120. *R.I.C.* 214 ..   ..   4·00
3372   B. ℞. SALVS AVGG. Salus stg. r., feeding serpent held in arms.
       C. 122. *R.I.C.* 216 ..   ..   4·00
3373   A. ℞. VICTORIA AVG. Victory advancing l. *C.* 135. *R.I.C.* 218 ..   4·00
3374   A. ℞. VICTORIA AVGG. Victory advancing l. *C.* 151. *R.I.C.* 220.
       Plate 10   ..   ..   4·00
3375   IMP . C . M . AVR . CARINVS P . F . AVG. ℞. VIRTVS AVGG. As 3357.
       C. 171. *R.I.C.* 270 ..   ..   4·00
3376   A. ℞. — Virtus stg. r., holding spear and parazonium. *C.* 172.
       R.I.C. 224 ..   ..   4·00
3377   IMP . C . M . AVR . CARINVS P . F . AVG. ℞. — As 3352. *C.* 184. *R.I.C.*
       325   ..   ..   4·00
3378   — ℞. VOTA PVBLICA. Carinus and Numerian stg. facing each other,
       sacrificing over tripod-altar. *C.* 194. *R.I.C.* 315   ..   ..   5·00
3379   **Æ denarius.** A. Laur. and cuir. bust, r. ℞. As 3373. *C.* 136.
       R.I.C. 275 ..   ..   37·50
3380   **Æ quinarius.** A. — ℞. VIRTVS AVGG. Mars stg. l., leaning on
       shield and holding spear. *Cf. C.* 169. *R.I.C.* 283   ..   ..   37·50
3381   **Æ as.** A. — ℞. VIRTVS AVGG. As 3355. *C.* 174. *R.I.C.* 288.
                                              Fine £50·00

Very Fine

3382 **Æ semis.** IMP . C . M . AVR . CARINVS P . F . AVG. Laur., dr. and cuir.
bust, r. R. PAX AVGG. Pax advancing l. *C.* 64. *R.I.C.* 289.
Illustrated on p. 283 .. .. *Fine* £30·00

Colonial and Provincial Coinage

3383 *Egypt, Alexandria,* **billon tetradrachm.** Laur. and cuir. bust, r. R.
Eagle stg. facing, hd. r., between two vexilla. *B.M.C. G.*2449 (*as*
Caesar) .. .. £2·00
3384 — R. Elpis stg. l. *B.M.C. G.*2453 (*as Augustus*) .. .. .. 2·00
3385 — R. Homonoia stg. l. *B.M.C. G.*2455 (*as Augustus*) .. .. 2·00
3386 — R. Tyche stg. l. *B.M.C. G.*2458 (*as Augustus*) .. .. .. 2·00
3387 — R. Similar to 3383. *B.M.C. G.*2461 (*as Augustus*) .. .. 2·00

MAGNIA URBICA
Wife of Carinus

3388

3388 **A' aureus.** MAGNIA VRBICA AVG. Diad. and dr. bust, r. R. VENERI
VICTRICI. Venus stg. r., holding apple. *C.* 8. *R.I.C.* 340 *Illustrated*
above .. .. 750·00
3389 **Æ antoninianus.** — Diad. and dr. bust r., resting on crescent. R.
VENVS GENETRIX. Venus stg. l., holding apple and sceptre. *C.* 11.
R.I.C. 337 .. .. 30·00
3390 MAGN . VRBICA AVG. — R. VENVS VICTRIX. Venus stg. l., holding
helmet and sceptre, shield at feet. *C.* 17. *R.I.C.* 343 .. .. .. 30·00
3391 **Æ denarius.** MAGNIA VRBICA AVG. Diad. and dr. bust, r. R. As
3389. *C.* 12. *R.I.C.* 338 .. .. 150·00
3392 **Æ quinarius.** MAG . VRBICA AVG. — R. VENERI VICTRI. As 3388.
R.I.C. 344 .. .. 150·00

NIGRINIAN

3394

Probably a son of Carinus; known only from a few coins struck after his death.

3393 **A' aureus.** DIVO NIGRINIANO. Bare hd., r. R. CONSECRATIO.
Funeral pyre surmounted by Nigrinian in biga. *C.* 1. *R.I.C.* 471 *Extr. rare*
3394 **Æ antoninianus.** — Rad. hd., r. R. — Eagle stg. facing, hd. l.
C. 2. *R.I.C.* 472. *Illustrated above* .. .. 100·00
3395 — — R. — Large altar. *C.* 5. *R.I.C.* 474 .. .. 120·00

JULIAN of Pannonia
A.D. 284 – 285

3396

M. Aurelius Julianus rebelled against Carinus in Pannonia in A.D. 284. *He marched against Rome, but was met by Carinus near Verona early in 285 and was defeated and slain. His coins are all from the mint of Siscia.*

Very Fine

3396 **N aureus.** IMP . C . IVLIANVS P . F . AVG. Laur., dr. and cuir. bust, r.
℞. LIBERTAS PVBLICA. Liberty stg. l., holding pileus and cornucopiae.
C. 3. R.I.C. 1. Illustrated above .. .. £1000·00

3397 **Æ antoninianus.** IMP . C . M . AVR . IVLIANVS P . F . AVG. Rad., dr.
and cuir. bust, r. ℞. FELICITAS TEMPORVM. Felicity stg. l. *C. 1.
R.I.C. 2* .. .. 275·00

3398 — — ℞. PANNONIAE AVG. The two Pannoniae stg. side by side.
C. 5. R.I.C. 4 .. .. 350·00

HISTORY OF THE PERIOD A.D. 285-337

The political history of the late third and early fourth centuries is very complex, with sometimes as many as five or more emperors in power at the same time. Only in A.D. 324, following the victory of Constantine over Licinius, was the Roman Empire united under a single ruler, for the first time since Diocletian's sole rule (A.D. 285-286). Under these circumstances, individual biographical notes for each personality would involve a great deal of repetition of facts, so it has been thought best to give the entire history of the period A.D. 285-337 before dealing with the coinage of each emperor, empress and prince. In order to make the following notes more easy of reference, the names of all personalities who issued coins are given in bold type.

C. Aurelius Valerius Diocletianus was born of humble parents in Dalmatia about A.D. 245 and, having risen from the ranks of the Roman army, was given the governorship of Moesia by **Carus**, who later made him commander of the imperial bodyguard. Following the death of **Numerian**, he was proclaimed emperor by the army and in the spring of A.D. 285 became sole emperor after the assassination of **Carinus**. Although a competent general, the new emperor was far more distinguished as a statesman and reformer than as a soldier, and during his twenty years of rule he introduced numerous reforms which completely transformed the character of the Empire. One of these reforms involved the introduction of a new monetary system, the details of which are given below.

Early in his reign **Diocletian** was faced with a revolt of the Bagaudae, the oppressed peasantry of Gaul, who set up two emperors of their own, Aelianus and **Amandus**. **M. Aurelius Valerius Maximianus,** a fellow-countryman of the emperor, was sent against the rebels and soon defeated them, whereupon he was given the rank of Augustus (April 1st, 286). **Diocletian** realized that the government and defence of such a vast empire was too great a task for one man, and also that the likelihood of the success of local insurrections would be greatly reduced if there were a number of colleagues sharing the imperial power. Accordingly, **Maximianus** was placed in charge of the Western half of the Empire, whilst **Diocletian** reserved for himself the administration of the

Eastern provinces.   Seven years later (A.D. 293) the system of imperial colleagues was further extended with the appointment of two Caesars, **Flavius Valerius Constantius,** a Dardanian nobleman, and **Galerius Valerius Maximianus (Galerius)**, a rough but able soldier whose character resembled **Maximianus** as closely as **Constantius** resembled **Diocletian.**   **Constantius** was made Caesar in the West under **Maximianus,** whilst **Galerius** became **Diocletian's** Caesar in the East.   Each Caesar was allocated several provinces to govern and defend and thus came into being the organization known as the First Tetrarchy.   In order to strengthen the ties between the four rulers, **Constantius** divorced his first wife, **Helena,** the mother of **Constantine the Great,** and married **Theodora,** the step-daughter of **Maximianus,** whilst **Galerius** also divorced his first wife and was married to **Diocletian's** daughter, **Galeria Valeria.**

As **Diocletian** had anticipated, this formidable team was far more effective in dealing with emergencies, such as foreign invasions and local rebellions, than a sole emperor could ever have been.   The most important rebel of the period was **M. Aurelius Mausaeus Carausius,** who was of Menapian origin and was originally a general of **Maximianus.**   Having been appointed commander of the fleet stationed at Gesoriacum (Boulogne), he was instructed to clear the sea of the Frankish and Saxon pirates.   However, he soon turned to piracy himself, and in fear of the anger of **Maximianus** he proclaimed himself emperor and sailed to Britain, where he defeated the forces of the governor and took possession of the province (A.D. 287).   All the attempts of **Maximianus** to recover the lost territory were thwarted by his cunning rival, and **Carausius** even extended his control over part of Gaul.   But in A.D. 293, **Constantius** took over the struggle from **Maximianus** and soon captured Boulogne, which was **Carausius'** main stronghold on the Continent.   Soon after this the British emperor was murdered by his chief minister, **Allectus,** who succeeded to the throne.   **Allectus** lacked the great ability of his predecessor, and when **Constantius** finally invaded Britain in A.D. 296, he recovered the province without much difficulty.   In the same year as **Constantius'** British victory, **Diocletian** had to face a rebellion at Alexandria, in Egypt, where a certain **Achilleus,** otherwise known as **L. Domitius Domitianus,** was proclaimed emperor.   Alexandria was besieged by **Diocletian** and its fall in the early spring of 297 brought the usurpation to an end.

On May 1st, 305, **Diocletian** and **Maximianus** both abdicated, their places being taken by **Galerius** and **Constantius** who were raised to the rank of Augusti.   The two vacant Caesarships were filled by **Flavius Valerius Severus** in the West and **Galerius Valerius Maximinus** in the East.   The former was an able soldier, whilst the latter was merely a young relative of **Galerius,** with neither military nor administrative experience.   As both of the Caesars were the nominees of **Galerius,** he in effect controlled three-quarters of the Roman World, although **Constantius** was technically the senior emperor.

Thus, so far, **Diocletian's** system of two Augusti and two Caesars still remained intact, but complications were soon to set in.   On July 25th, 306, **Constantius** died at York after having repelled an invasion of Britain by the Picts.   His son by his first wife **Helena, Flavius Valerius Constantinus (Constantine the Great),** was with him at his death and was immediately proclaimed emperor by the troops.   **Galerius** was furious at the elevation of this popular figure, but he wanted to avoid civil war so he compromised by elevating **Severus** to the rank of Augustus and allowing **Constantine** to bear the title of Caesar.   But the system was again disrupted, this time by **M. Aurelius Valerius Maxentius,** the son of **Maximianus,** who was proclaimed first Princeps, then Caesar and finally Augustus towards the end of A.D. 306.   This revolt, which took place at Rome, assumed far more alarming proportions when **Maxentius** invited his father to re-assume the purple.   **Maximianus,** who had been very reluctant to relinquish his power in 305, eagerly accepted the opportunity of embarking upon a second reign. Meanwhile, **Galerius** instructed **Severus,** in whose territory the rebellion had occurred, to march against the usurpers, but when he did so in the spring of 307, he was deserted by many of his soldiers and fell into his opponents' hands.   The unfortunate Augustus of the West was at first imprisoned and later put to death.   **Galerius,** enraged at the defeat of **Severus** by the rebels, decided to invade Italy in person, and immediately set about making preparations for the campaign.   Realizing the danger of the situation, **Maximianus** travelled to Gaul to seek an alliance with **Constantine,** and this he succeeded in achieving.   **Constantine** was raised to the rank of Augustus, and at the same time he was married to **Fausta,** the daughter of **Maximianus,** in order to strengthen the new alliance (spring, 307).   Whilst **Maximianus** was still in Gaul, **Galerius** descended upon Italy and advanced upon Rome unopposed.   The Imperial City was, however, strongly defended and well provisioned for a long siege, and when **Maxentius'** agents started distributing bribes to the besieging army, **Galerius** was faced with an open mutiny.   He only saved himself by a hasty retreat to Pannonia, during which he was forced to allow the troops that had remained loyal to him to plunder the countryside.

Late in A.D. 307, **Maximianus** returned to Rome, but in the spring of the following year he quarrelled with his son and was forced to flee from Rome and seek the protection of **Constantine** in Gaul.   Later in the same year (308), **Galerius** decided to call a conference at Carnuntum, to attempt to remedy the present political confusion of the Empire.   **Diocletian,** as the founder of the tetrarchy system, was invited to attend and **Maximianus** was also present.   The outcome of the famous Congress at Carnuntum was as follows: **Maximianus** was forced to abdicate again, whilst **Maxentius** was declared a public enemy; **Constantine** was to be degraded to the rank of Caesar, and the vacant post of Augustus of the West was given to **Valerius Licinianus Licinius,** a comrade-in-arms of **Galerius;** the ranks of **Galerius** and **Maximinus** (respectively, Augustus and Caesar in the East) remained unchanged.   Thus the tetrarchy was re-established, but the new arrangements were destined to be of very short duration. **Constantine** and **Maximinus** were both annoyed at the promotion of **Licinius,** who had never held the intermediate rank of Caesar, and **Constantine** was particularly angry at his own degradation from the rank of Augustus.   In order to placate the two Caesars, **Galerius** granted them both the empty title of *filius Augusti,* but **Constantine** and **Maximinus** were dissatisfied with this and **Galerius** was obliged to recognize them as Augusti early in A.D. 309.   Later in the same year, **Maxentius'** hopes of continuing his dynasty were dashed by the death of his young son, **Romulus.**

In the spring of A.D. 310, **Maximianus,** who had been living at the court of **Constantine** since his second abdication, rebelled against his son-in-law and was proclaimed emperor for the third time.   **Constantine** besieged him in Massilia (Marseilles), and shortly after the fall of the city, the old emperor was put to death, or perhaps committed suicide.

The following year (311), **Galerius** was stricken with a dreadful disease and he died at the beginning of May.   **Maximinus** quickly took advantage of this to extend the territories under his control, and with the passing of **Galerius** he also became the senior Augustus.   The same year also witnessed the rebellion of **L. Domitius Alexander** in Africa against the tyranny of **Maxentius.**   The revolt was quickly suppressed and **Alexander** executed, but a far greater threat to **Maxentius'** position was imminent, as **Constantine** was already planning an invasion of Italy.   In the early spring of 312, after having made an alliance with **Licinius, Constantine** marched against **Maxentius** with an army only about a quarter of the size of that of his opponent.   Nevertheless, the north of Italy soon came under his control, and at the famous battle of the Milvian Bridge on October 28th, **Maxentius** was defeated and killed.

Early in the new year (313), **Constantine** and **Licinius** met at Milan, and after celebrating the marriage of **Licinius** to **Constantia,** the half-sister of **Constantine,** they issued the famous Edict of Milan which granted complete religious toleration to the subjects of the Empire.   **Constantine,** confident that his recent victory over **Maxentius** had been achieved through the divine intervention of the Christian God, was eager to put an end to the fierce persecutions to which the Christians had been subjected in recent years, particularly in the Eastern provinces.   But in the existing political situation, the Edict could bring very little relief to the Church, as most of the Eastern part of the Empire was still in the hands of **Maximinus**, who was an ardent persecutor.   However, whilst **Constantine** and **Licinius** were still at Milan, **Maximinus** crossed over from Asia Minor and invaded **Licinius'** territory, capturing several cities as he advanced through Thrace.   **Licinius** hurried to meet him and in a battle fought on April 30th, 313, **Maximinus** was completely defeated and only made good his escape by disguising himself as a slave.   In the autumn of the same year he fell ill and died at Tarsus, and the whole of the Eastern part of the Empire came under the control of **Licinius**.

There followed a decade of joint-rule by **Constantine** and **Licinius**, but relations between the two Augusti were strained even at the best of times.   As early as A.D. 314 there was an open breach and two battles were fought, with no decisive result.   **Licinius** was so confident of success that before the second battle he proclaimed one of his generals, **Aurelius Valerius Valens**, emperor to take the place of **Constantine**.   However, as one of the terms of the peace which followed the second battle, the unfortunate **Valens** was deposed and put to death.

On March 1st, 317, three new Caesars were appointed, two of them, **Flavius Julius Crispus** and **Flavius Claudius Constantinus** (**Constantine II**), being sons of **Constantine**, whilst the other, **Valerius Licinianus Licinius** (**Licinius II**), was the son of **Licinius**.   However, in A.D. 324 the final breach came, and two battles, one at Hadrianopolis in July and the other at Chrysopolis in September, were sufficient to seal the fate of **Constantine's** rival.   Through the intervention of **Constantia**, the wife of **Licinius** and half-sister of **Constantine**, the lives of **Licinius** and his son were spared and they were permitted to retire into private life.   But **Licinius** soon began to intrigue against **Constantine** and was immediately put to death, together with **Marcus Martinianus** whom he had raised to the rank of Augustus shortly before the battle of Chrysopolis, and who had also been spared by **Constantine**.

Soon after the defeat of **Licinius**, **Flavius Julius Constantius** (**Constantius II**), another son of **Constantine**, was given the rank of Caesar, and at about the same time work was started on transforming the city of Byzantium into **Constantine's** new Christian capital of the Empire.   The work took over five years and the city, renamed Constantinopolis, was dedicated on May 11th, 330.   Meanwhile, in 326, a domestic tragedy occurred in the imperial family.   **Fausta**, the wife of **Constantine**, became jealous of her step-son, **Crispus**, who was the son of **Constantine** by his first wife, Minervina.   **Fausta** saw in the growing popularity of **Crispus** a threat to the future of her own three sons, so she fabricated evidence of treason against the unfortunate Caesar who was imprisoned and executed.   When **Constantine** learned the truth, he immediately condemned his wife to death and she was thrown into a bath of boiling water.

In December, 333, **Flavius Julius Constans**, the youngest son of Constantine, was raised to the rank of Caesar, and in 335 two of the emperor's nephews were also elevated.   These were **Flavius Julius Delmatius** and **Flavius Hanniballianus**, both sons of **Constantine's** half-brother Delmatius, and whilst the former was given the normal rank of Caesar, the latter received the unique title of *Rex*, with authority over Armenia, Pontus and Cappadocia.   The Empire was now divided between the three sons and two of the nephews of the emperor, but the supreme power was still in the hands of **Constantine** himself, who was the sole Augustus.

Whilst preparing to supervise a war against the Persians, **Constantine** fell ill and died at Nicomedia on May 22nd, 337.   Following his death, there was an interregnum of nearly four months, during which the unfortunate **Delmatius** and **Hanniballianus** were both put to death, and it was not until September 9th that the three sons of **Constantine, Constantine II, Constantius II** and **Constans**, were proclaimed Augusti and became joint-rulers of the Empire.

DIOCLETIAN
A.D. 284 – 305

gold medallion, Cohen 247

Mints: London; Clausentum (?); Treveri; Lugdunum; Ticinum; Aquileia; Rome; Carthage; Siscia; Serdica; Thessalonica; Heraclea; Nicomedia; Cyzicus; Antioch; Tripolis; Alexandria.

The details of Diocletian's reform of the coinage are rather obscure and there have been many theories as to its date and the exact nature of the changes made. It seems probable that the reform was not one decisive act but rather a series of changes covering about a decade.

The first step was taken in circa A.D. *286 with the introduction of* aurei *struck at* 60 *to the lb. of gold, an increase in weight of about 12 grains on the earlier coins which were struck at 70 to the lb.*

The next step was the introduction of a silver coin of approximately the same fineness and weight as Nero's denarius. *The name of this new denomination was probably* argenteus, *and its introduction marked a very important step in the restoration of the Roman monetary system, as the Empire had been without a silver coinage since the joint reign of Valerian and Gallienus.*

Finally, in A.D. *295 or 296, a new bronze coin was instituted. This piece, known as the* follis, *was approximately equal in size and weight to the* as *of the earlier empire and was usually silver-washed. Coins resembling* antoniniani *continued to be struck but they contained no trace of silver, whereas the pre-reform* antoniniani *contained about 4% of that metal. The absence of the* XXI *mark on these post-reform radiates and the transference of this mark to the* follis, *which contained a small percentage of silver, lends weight to the theory that the true meaning of the* XXI *mark, introduced by Aurelian, is* 20 *parts of copper to 1 part of silver.*

The relative values of the denominations in Diocletian's new monetary system are by no means certain, but there are strong arguments in favour of the following relationships:—

1 *N* aureus	=	24 *R* argentei
1 *R* argenteus	=	5 Æ folles
1 Æ follis	=	5 Æ denarii
1 Æ antoninianus =	1 post-reform radiate	= 2 Æ denarii

Mint-marks were first used about the middle of the third century but to begin with the practice was not general and right up to the time of Diocletian's reform the marks themselves are seldom self-explanatory. After the reform unmarked coins are the exception and the system of marking is reasonably simple and easy to understand.

*From this point on, therefore, I am including the mint-mark in the description of the
reverse of each coin, but two important points should be noted. Firstly, only the exergual
mark is given whilst quite frequently there are also letters and symbols in the field. Secondly,
many coins were issued from more than one mint, the best example of this being the "Genio
Populi Romani" follis of Diocletian and his colleagues which was struck at almost every
mint of the empire. The mint-mark given, therefore, may be only one of many which occur
on any particular coin. I have endeavoured to give one of the commonest marks in each case.
The immensity of the subject prevents me from going into any greater detail in a work of
this scope.*

*In Volumes VI, VII and IX of R.I.C. a completely different arrangement is adopted
from that used in the earlier volumes: instead of being arranged primarily according to
reigns, with subdivisions for the various mints, the primary classification is according to
mints, a method far better suited to the complex political situation of the Late Empire. Thus,
all R.I.C. references from Diocletian's Reform onwards are to the coinage of the particular
mint in question, and not the reign.*

The following are the commonest forms of obv. legend:

    A. IMP . DIOCLETIANVS AVG.
    B. IMP . DIOCLETIANVS P . F . AVG.
    C. IMP . C . C . VAL . DIOCLETIANVS P . F . AVG.

Very Fine

3399 **GOLD.** *Pre-reform coinage.* **Aureus.** (*c.* 72·2 grains, struck at 70
to the lb.). C. Laur., dr. and cuir. bust, r. ℞. VICTORIA AVG.
Victory advancing r.; in field, 0 (=70). *C.* 469. *R.I.C.* 320 ..   ..£175·00

3400 **Quinarius.** (*c.* 34·5 grains). B. Laur. and dr. bust, r. ℞. IOVI
CONSERVAT . AVGG. Jupiter stg. l., holding thunderbolt and sceptre.
C. 224. *R.I.C.* 152 ..   .. 350·00
3401 *Post-reform coinage.* **Aureus.** (*c.* 84·2 grains, struck at 60 to the lb.).
DIOCLETIANVS AVGVSTVS. Laur. hd., r. ℞. CONSVL IIII . P . P .
PROCOS. Diocletian stg. l., holding globe; in ex., SMA; in field, Ξ (=60).
C. 46. *R.I.C.* 307 ..   .. 175·00
3402 DIOCLETIANVS P . F . AVG. Laur., dr. and cuir. bust, r. ℞. IOVI
CONSERVATORI. Jupiter seated l., holding thunderbolt and sceptre,
eagle at feet; in ex., PR. *C.* 266. *R.I.C.* 142a ..   .. 200·00
    There are larger gold, 2, 4 and 8 *aurei.*

3403 **SILVER. Argenteus.** DIOCLETIANVS AVG. Laur. hd., r. ℞. PRO-
VIDENTIA AVGG. Diocletian, Maximianus, Constantius and Galerius
sacrificing in front of camp-gate; in ex., R. *C.* 412. *R.I.C.* 30a   .. 35·00
3404 — — ℞. VICTORIAE SARMATICAE. Camp-gate surmounted by four
turrets; in ex., SMNF. *C.* 492. *R.I.C.* 22a ..   .. 35·00
3405 — — ℞. VIRTVS MILITVM. As 3403; in ex., *SIS. *C.* 517. *R.I.C.*
59 ..   .. 25·00
3406 — — ℞. XCVI . /AQ. in two lines within laurel-wreath. *C.* 548.
R.I.C. 16a ..   .. 65·00

3407 **BRONZE.** *Pre-reform coinage.* **Antoninianus.** (*All with obv. type
rad., dr. and/or cuir. bust r., unless otherwise stated*). A. ℞. ANNONA
AVG. Annona stg. l., modius at feet. *C.* 14. *R.I.C.* 156   ..   .. 2·25

3408　**Antoninianus.** C. ℞. CLEMENTIA TEMP. Diocletian stg. r., receiving Victory on globe from Jupiter stg. l. *C.* 19. *R.I.C.* 252 .. £2·00

3409　A. ℞. COMES AVGG. Minerva stg. l., holding spear and leaning on shield. *C.* 21. *R.I.C.* 15 .. .. 2·25

3410　C. ℞. CONCORDIA MILITVM. As 3408. *C.* 34. *R.I.C.* 284 .. 2·00

3411　C. ℞. CONSERVATOR AVGG. Diocletian and Jupiter stg. facing each other, sacrificing over tripod-altar. *C.* 42. *R.I.C.* 259 .. .. 2·75

3412　C. ℞. HERCVLI CONSERVAT. Hercules stg. r., leaning on club set on rock. *C.* 136. *R.I.C.* 212 .. .. 2·25

3413　A. Rad. bust l., wearing imperial mantle and holding eagle-tipped sceptre. ℞. IOVI AVGG. Jupiter stg. l., holding Victory on globe and sceptre, eagle at feet. *C.* 153. *R.I.C.* 28 .. .. .. 5·00

3414　C. ℞. IOVI CONSERVAT. Jupiter stg. l., small figure of Diocletian at feet. *C.* 206. *R.I.C.* 220 .. .. 2·25

3415　A. ℞. IOVI CONSERVAT . AVG. As 3400. *C.* 214. *R.I.C.* 161 .. 2·00

3416　A. ℞. As 3400. *C.* 228. *R.I.C.* 162 .. .. .. 2·00

3417　C. ℞. IOVI TVTATORI AVGG. As 3413. *C.* 300. *R.I.C.* 50 .. 2·25

3418　A. ℞. LAETITIA FVND. Laetitia stg. l. *C.* 311. *R.I.C.* 171 .. 2·00

3419　A. ℞. PAX AVGG. Pax stg. l., holding Victory on globe and sceptre. *C.* 366. *R.I.C.* 67 .. .. 2·00

3420　IMP . C . DIOCLETIANVS P . F . AVG. ℞. PAX AVGGG. Pax stg. l.; in field, SP; in ex., MLXXI. *C.* 377. *R.I.C.* (*Car., Dio. & Max.*) 9. (*Struck by Carausius*) .. .. 25·00

3421　C. ℞. PROVIDENTIA AVG. As 3407. *C.* 410. *R.I.C.* 77 .. .. 2·25

3422　A. ℞. SALVS AVGG. Salus stg. r., feeding serpent held in arms. *C.* 442. *R.I.C.* 89 .. .. 2·00

3423　C. ℞. VICTORIA AVG. Victory stg. l. *C.* 466. *R.I.C.* 91 .. 2·00

3424　C. ℞. VICTORIA AVGG. Diocletian and Maximianus stg. facing each other, holding between them globe surmounted by Victory. *C.* 477. *R.I.C.* 277 .. .. 2·25

3425　**Denarius.** B. Laur. and dr. bust, r. ℞. IOVI CONSERVAT . AVG. As 3400. *R.I.C.* 187 .. .. 37·50

3426　**Quinarius.** A. — ℞. As 3400. *C.* 227. *R.I.C.* 193 .. .. 20·00

3427　A. — ℞. As 3423. *C.* 468. *R.I.C.* 195 .. .. .. 30·00

3428　**As.** (*c.* 24·5 *mm. and* 100 *grains*). A. — ℞. IOVI CONSERVATORI AVGG. As 3400. *R.I.C.* 199 .. .. *Fine* £40·00

3429　**Semis.** (*c.* 22 *mm. and* 78 *grains*). As previous. *R.I.C.* 202
　　　　　　　　　　　　　　　　　　　　　　　Fine £35·00

3430　*Post-reform coinage.* **Follis.** (*All with the obv. type laur. hd. r., unless otherwise stated*). B. ℞. FELIX ADVENT . AVGG . NN. Africa stg. l., holding standard and elephant's tusk, lion at feet; in ex., PKP. *C.* 67. *R.I.C.* 19a .. .. 4·50

3431　B. ℞. FORTVNAE REDVCI AVGG . NN. Fortune seated l.; in ex., ATR. *C.* 77. *R.I.C.* 380a .. .. 5·00

3432　B. ℞. FORTVNAE REDVCI CAESS . NN. Fortune stg. l.; in ex., BTR. *C.* 78. *R.I.C.* 400 .. .. 5·00

3433　A. ℞. GENIO POPVLI ROMANI. Genius stg. l.; in ex., TR. *C.* 85. *R.I.C.* 305a .. .. 3·00

3434　IMP . C . DIOCLETIANVS P . F . AVG. ℞. As previous; in ex., ALE. *C.* 101. *R.I.C.* 14a. **Plate 9** .. .. 3·00

3435　— Laur. and cuir. bust, r. ℞. As previous; no mint-mark (attributed to London). *C.* 103. *R.I.C.* 6a .. .. 6·50

Very Fine

3436 **Follis.** B. Laur. and cuir. bust, l. ℞. As previous, but with altar
to l. of Genius; in ex., PLG. *C.* 128. *R.I.C.* 94*a* .. .. .. £4·50

3437 IMP . C . DIOCLETIANVS P . F . AVG. ℞. SACRA MON . VRB . AVGG . ET
CAESS . NN. Moneta stg. l.; in ex., RP. *C.* 434. *R.I.C.* 103*a* .. .. 4·00

3438 B. ℞. SACRA MONET . AVGG . ET CAESS . NOSTR. Moneta stg. l.; in ex.,
AQP. *C.* 435. *R.I.C.* 29*a* .. .. 4·00

3439 B. ℞. SALVIS AVGG . ET CAESS . FEL . KART. Carthage stg. l., holding
fruits in both hands; in ex., A. *C.* 438. *R.I.C.* 29*a* .. .. .. 4·50

3440 **Post-Reform Radiates.** (*Similar in appearance to antoniniani*). C.
Rad., dr. and cuir. bust, r. ℞. CONCORDIA MILITVM. Diocletian stg.
r., receiving Victory on globe from Jupiter stg. l.; in ex., ALE. *C.* 34.
R.I.C. 47 .. .. 1·75

3441 C. — ℞. VOT . /XX . /B. in three lines within laurel-wreath. *C.* 541.
R.I.C. 76*a* .. .. 3·75

Coins struck after his abdication

3442 **Æ follis.** D . N . DIOCLETIANO BAEATIS. Laur. bust r., wearing imperial
mantle and holding branch and mappa. ℞. PROVIDENTIA DEORVM.
Quies and Providence stg. facing each other; in ex., ALE. *C.* 414.
R.I.C. 80 .. .. 5·00

3443 D . N . DIOCLETIANO FELICISSIMO SEN . AVG. — ℞. PROVIDENTIA DEORVM
QVIES AVGG. As previous; in ex., PTR. *C.* 426. *R.I.C.* 676*a* .. 5·00

3444 D . N . DIOCLETIANO P . F . S . AVG. — ℞. QVIES AVGG. Quies stg. l.,
holding branch and sceptre; in ex., PLN. *C.* 428. *R.I.C.* 98 .. .. 8·00

3445 — — ℞. QVIES AVGVSTORVM. As previous; in ex., PTR. *C.* 430.
R.I.C. 699 .. .. 5·50

3446 **Æ half-follis.** D . N . DIOCLETIANO FELICIS. Similar, but r. hand
raised. ℞. As 3442. *C.* 419 *var.* *R.I.C.* 93*a* .. .. .. 3·50

Colonial and Provincial Coinage

3447 *Egypt, Alexandria,* **billon tetradrachm.** Laur., dr. and cuir. bust, r.
℞. Athena seated l. *B.M.C. G.*2485 .. .. 1·25

3448 — — ℞. Dikaiosyne stg. l. *B.M.C. G.*2490 .. .. 1·00

3449 — — ℞. Elpis stg. l. *B.M.C. G.*2503 .. .. 1·00

3450 — — ℞. Nike advancing r. *B.M.C. G.*2517 .. .. 1·00

3451 — — ℞. Tyche stg. l. *B.M.C. G.*2426 .. .. 1·00

3452 — — ℞. Alexandria stg. l., holding hd. of Serapis and sceptre.
*B.M.C. G.*2529 .. .. 1·25

3453 — — ℞. Eagle stg. l., hd. turned. *B.M.C. G.*2532 .. .. .. 1·00

*The billon tetradrachms of Alexandria, the last surviving representatives of the once
extensive Colonial and Provincial coinage of the Roman Empire, were finally discontinued
by Diocletian in* A.D. *296, and the mint of Alexandria subsequently struck the normal Roman
coinage with Latin inscriptions.*

AMANDUS
A.D. 285-286

3454 **Æ antoninianus.** IMP . S . AMANDVS P . F . AVG. Rad., dr. and cuir.
bust, r. ℞. . ALVS AVG. Pax stg. l., holding olive-branch and sceptre.
R.I.C. 2

*Of this piece, which is quoted from the collection of Sir Arthur Evans, R.I.C. write
" The coin does not bear any palpable traces of alterations, and while, as such an extreme
rarity, it must be accepted with reserve, it cannot be disregarded."*

CARAUSIUS
A.D. 287 – 293

3475

Mint of London   **Very Fine**

3455 **N aureus.** CARAVSIVS P . F . AVG. Laur. and cuir. bust, r. ℞. CON-SERVATORI AVGGG. Hercules stg. r., leaning on club and holding bow; in ex., ML. *R.I.C.* 2 ..   ..   *Extr. rare*

3456 **Æ denarius.** IMP . CARAVSIVS P . AVG. Laur. and dr. bust, r. ℞. CONSER . AVG. Neptune seated l. on rock, holding anchor and trident; in ex., ML. *R.I.C.* 8   ..   ..£250·00

3457 **Æ antoninianus.** IMP . CARAVSIVS P . F . AVG. Rad., dr. and cuir. bust, r. ℞. COMES AVG. Victory stg. l.; in ex., ML. *R.I.C.* 15   ..   30·00

3458 — — ℞. HILARITAS AVG. Hilaritas stg. l.; in field, BE; in ex., MLXXI. *R.I.C.* 41   ..   ..   25·00

3459 — — ℞. LAETITIA AVG. Laetitia stg. l.; in field, FO; in ex., ML. *R.I.C.* 50   ..   ..   25·00

3460 — — ℞. LEG . II . AVG. Capricorn l.; in ex., ML. *R.I.C.* 58..   ..   75·00

3461 — — ℞. LEG . II . PARTH. Centaur walking l.; in ex., ML. *R.I.C.* 62   65·00

3462 — — ℞. LEG . VII . CL. Bull stg. r.; in ex., ML. *R.I.C.* 75 ..   ..   60·00

3463 — — ℞. PAX AVG. Pax stg. l.; in field, FO; in ex., ML. *R.I.C.* 101 ..   20·00

3464 — — ℞. SALVS AVG. Salus stg. l., feeding serpent arising from altar; in field, BE; in ex., MLXXI. *R.I.C.* 155   ..   ..   25·00

Mint of Clausentum (?)

3465 **Æ denarius.** IMP . CARAVSIVS P . F . AVG. Laur., dr. and cuir. bust, r. ℞. CONCORDIA MILITVM. Clasped hands; in ex., C. *R.I.C.* 186   ..   300·00

3466 **Æ antoninianus.** — Rad., dr. and cuir. bust, r. ℞. CONCORD . MILIT. Carausius and Concord stg. facing each other, clasping r. hands; in ex., C. *R.I.C.* 205   ..   ..   35·00

3467 — — ℞. LAETITIA AVG. Laetitia stg. l.; in field, SP; in ex., C. *R.I.C.* 258   ..   ..   30·00

3468 — Rad. and dr. bust, r. ℞. LEG . I . MIN. Ram stg. r.; in ex., SMC. *R.I.C.* 268   ..   ..   75·00

3469 — Rad., dr. and cuir. bust, r. ℞. PAX AVG. Pax stg. l.; in field, SC; in ex., C. *R.I.C.* 303   ..   ..   27·50

3470 — — ℞. PROVID . AVG. Providence stg. l., globe at feet; in ex., C. *R.I.C.* 348   ..   ..   30·00

3471 — Rad. and dr. bust, r. ℞. VIRTVS AVG. Mars stg. r., holding spear and leaning on shield; in field, SC; in ex., C. *R.I.C.* 437   ..   ..   37·50

3471A *Carausius, Diocletian & Maximianus:* **Æ antoninianus.** CARAVSIVS ET FRATRES SVI. Jugate busts of the three emperors l. ℞. PAX AVGGG. Pax stg. l.; in field, SP; in ex., C. *R.I.C.* 1..   ..   ..   ..   *Extr. rare*

Mint of Rouen
Very Fine

3472 **N aureus.** IMP . CARAVSIVS AVG. Laur. and dr. bust, r. ℞.
CONCORDIA MILITVM. Carausius and Concord stg. facing each other,
clasping r. hands. *R.I.C.* 624 .. .. *Extr. rare*

3473 **℞ denarius.** IMP . CARAVSIVS P . F. Laur. and cuir. bust l., holding
globe. ℞. VBERITAS AVG. Carausius and Uberitas stg. facing each
other, clasping r. hands; in ex., RSR. *R.I.C.* 626 .. .. ..£350·00

3474 **Æ antoninianus.** IMP . C . CARAVSIVS P . F . AVG. Rad. and dr. bust, r.
℞. FORTVNA AVG. Fortune stg. l. *R.I.C.* 639 .. .. 35·00

Unattributed Coins

3475 **N aureus.** VIRTVS CARAVSI. Helmeted bust l., holding spear and shield.
℞. ROMANO RENOVA. She-wolf stg. r., suckling Romulus and Remus;
in ex., RSR. *R.I.C.* 534. *Illustrated on p. 294* .. .. .. *Extr. rare*

3476 **℞ denarius.** IMP . CARAVSIVS P . F . AVG. Laur. and dr. bust, r. ℞.
EXPECTATE VENI. Britannia and Carausius stg. facing each other,
clasping r. hands; in ex., RSR. *R.I.C.* 554 .. .. 250·00

3477 **Æ antoninianus.** — Rad., dr. and cuir. bust, r. ℞. ADVENTVS AVG.
Carausius on horseback l., r. hand raised; in ex., RSR. *R.I.C.* 598 .. 75·00

3478 — — ℞. MONETA AVG. Moneta stg. l.; no mint-mark. *R.I.C.* 855 .. 25·00

3479 *Obv.* As 3474. ℞. PAX AVG. Pax stg. l.; in field, SP. *R.I.C.* 475
Plate 10 .. .. 17·50

3480 *Obv.* As 3477. ℞. As previous, but no mint-mark. *R.I.C.* 880 .. 17·50

3481 — ℞. PROVID . AVG. Providence stg. l.; no mint-mark. *R.I.C.* 952 .. 25·00

3482 — ℞. SAECVLI FELICITAS. Carausius stg. r., holding spear and globe;
no mint-mark. *R.I.C.* 977 .. .. 32·50

3483 — ℞. TEMPORVM FELIC. Felicity stg. l.; no mint-mark. *R.I.C.* 1013 30·00

3484

ALLECTUS
A.D. 293 – 296

The obv. legend is IMP . C . ALLECTVS P . F . AVG., *unless otherwise stated.*

Mint of London

3484 **N aureus.** Laur. and cuir. bust, r. ℞. PAX AVG. Pax stg. l.;
in ex., ML. *R.I.C.* 6. *Illustrated above* .. .. .. *Extr. rare*

3485 **Billon denarius.** IMP . C . ALLECTVS P . AVG. Laur. and cuir. bust, r.
℞. SALVS AVG. Salus stg. l., feeding serpent held in arms; in ex., ML.
R.I.C. 15 .. .. *Very rare*

3486 **Æ antoninianus.** Rad., dr. and cuir. bust, r. ℞. LAETITIA AVG.
Laetitia stg. l.; in field, SA; in ex., MSL. *R.I.C.* 22 .. .. .. 25·00

3487 — ℞. PAX AVG. Pax stg. l.; in field, SA; in ex., ML. *R.I.C.* 28.
Plate 10 .. .. 25·00

3488 Rad. and dr. bust, r. ℞. PIETAS AVG. Pietas stg. l., altar at feet; in
field, SA; in ex., ML. *R.I.C.* 34 .. .. 35·00

3489 — ℞. PROVIDENTIA AVG. Providence stg. l., globe at feet; in field, SA;
in ex., MSL. *R.I.C.* 35 .. .. 30·00

3490 **Æ "quinarius".** Rad. and cuir. bust, r. ℞. VIRTVS AVG. Galley;
in ex., QL. *R.I.C.* 55 .. .. 12·50

Mint of Clausentum (?)   Very Fine

3491 Æ **antoninianus.** Rad. and cuir. bust, r. ℞. LAETITIA AVG. Laetitia stg. l.; in field, SP; in ex., C. *R.I.C.* 79 .. .. .. £25·00

3492 — ℞. MONETA AVG. Moneta stg. l.; in field, SP; in ex., C. *R.I.C.* 83 35·00

3493 — ℞. PAX AVG. Pax stg. l.; in field, SP; in ex., C. *R.I.C.* 86 .. .. 25·00

3494 — ℞. PROVIDENTIA AVG. Providence stg. l.; in field, SP; in ex., CL. *R.I.C.* 105 .. .. 30·00

3495 Æ **"quinarius".** — ℞. LAETITIA AVG. Galley; in ex., QC. *R.I.C.* 124 .. .. 17·50

3496 — ℞. VIRTVS AVG. Galley; in ex., QC. *R.I.C.* 128 .. .. .. 12·50

DOMITIUS DOMITIANUS
A.D. 296 – 297

3498

Mint: Alexandria.

3497 N **aureus.** DOMITIANVS AVG. Laur. hd., r. ℞. VICTOI (*sic*) AVG. Victory advancing l. *C.* 3. *R.I.C.* 5 .. .. *Extr. rare*

3498 Æ **follis.** IMP . C . L . DOMITIVS DOMITIANVS AVG. Laur. hd., r. ℞. GENIO POPVLI ROMANI. Genius stg. l., eagle at feet; in ex., ALE. *C.* 1. *R.I.C.* 20. *Illustrated above* .. .. 100·00

3499 As previous, but with *obv.* legend IMP . C . LVCIVS DOMITIVS DOMITIANVS AVG. *C.* 2. *R.I.C.* 19 .. .. 120·00

3500 *Egypt, Alexandria,* **billon tetradrachm.** ΔΟΜΙΤΙΑΝΟϹ ϹΕΒ. Laur. bust, r. ℞. LB. Nike stg. facing, hd. l. *B.M.C. G.*2626 .. .. 75·00

MAXIMIANUS
First Reign: A.D. 286-305.
Second Reign: A.D. 306-308
Third Reign: A.D. 310

bronze medallion, Cohen 405

Mints: London; Clausentum (?); Treveri; Lugdunum; Ticinum; Aquileia; Rome; Carthage; Siscia; Serdica; Thessalonica; Heraclea; Nicomedia; Cyzicus; Antioch; Tripolis; Alexandria.

The following are the commonest forms of obv. legend:

A.   IMP . MAXIMIANVS AVG.

B.   IMP . MAXIMIANVS P . F . AVG.

C.   IMP . C . MAXIMIANVS P . F . AVG.

First Reign, A.D. 286-305   Very Fine

3501   **GOLD.** *Pre-reform coinage.* **Aureus.** IMP . C . M . AVR . VAL . MAXIMIANVS P . AVG.   Laur., dr. and cuir. bust, r.   ℞ .   IOVI CONSERVAT . AVGG.   Jupiter stg. l., holding thunderbolt and sceptre.   *C.* 347. *R.I.C.* 493   ..   .. £175·00

3502   **Quinarius.**   B.   Laur. and dr. bust, r.   ℞.   As previous.   *C.* 353. *R.I.C.* 501   ..   .. 350·00

3503   *Post-reform coinage.*   **Aureus.**   MAXIMIANVS AVGVSTVS.   Laur. hd., r. ℞.   COS . II.   Maximianus on horseback r., raising r. hand.   *C* 86. *R.I.C.* 598   ..   .. 175·00

3503A   — Laur., dr. and cuir. bust, r.   ℞.   HERCVLI VICTORI.   Hercules seated facing, holding club and lion's skin; to r., bow and quiver; in ex., PR. *C.* —.   *R.I.C.* —.   **Plate 10**   ..   .. 250·00

3504   — Laur. hd., r.   ℞.   P . M . TR . P . P . P.   Maximianus stg. l., amidst four standards, holding spear.   *C.* 467.   *R.I.C.* 600   ..   ..   .. 200·00

There are *double aurei* and larger.

3505   **SILVER.**   **Argenteus.**   MAXIMIANVS AVG.   Laur. hd., r.   ℞. VICTORIAE SARMATICAE.   Camp-gate surmounted by four turrets; in ex., SMNΓ.   *C.* 553.   *R.I.C.* 22*b*   ..   .. 35·00

3506   — — ℞.   VIRTVS MILITVM.   Diocletian, Maximianus, Constantius and Galerius sacrificing in front of camp-gate; in ex., Є.   *C.* 622.   *R.I.C.* 40*b* 25·00

3507   — — ℞.   XCVI. / T. in two lines within laurel-wreath.   *C.* 698.   *R.I.C.* 20*b*   ..   .. 65·00

3508   **BRONZE.**   *Pre-reform coinage.*   **Antoninianus.**   (*All with obv. type rad., dr. and/or cuir. bust r., unless otherwise stated*).   A.   ℞.   ADVENTVS AVGG.   Diocletian and Maximianus on horseback r., raising r. hands. *C.* 6.   *R.I.C.* 347   ..   .. 7·50

3509   MAXIMIANVS P . F . AVG.   ℞.   AETERNITAS AVGG.   Elephant walking l., guided by driver.   *C.* 22.   *R.I.C.* 349   ..   .. 7·50

3510   A.   ℞.   COMES AVGG.   Minerva stg. l., holding spear and leaning on shield.   *C.* 34.   *R.I.C.* 353   ..   .. 2·25

3511   IMP . C . M . A . MAXIMIANVS P . F . AVG.   ℞.   CONCORDIA MILITVM. Maximianus stg. r., receiving Victory on globe from Jupiter stg. l.   *C.* 54. *R.I.C.* 595   ..   .. 2·00

3512   C.   ℞.   HERCVLI CONSERVAT.   Hercules stg. l., holding branch and club.   *C.* 244.   *R.I.C.* —   ..   .. 2·50

3513   IMP . MAXIMIANVS P . AVG.   Rad. and cuir. bust l., holding club and wearing lion's skin on l. shoulder.   ℞.   HERCVLI PACIFERO.   As previous. *C.* 276.   *R.I.C.* 375 ..   .. 6·50

Very Fine

3514 **Antoninianus.** IMP . C . M . AVR . VAL . MAXIMIANVS P . F . AVG. ℞.
IOV . ET HERCV . CONSER . AVGG. Jupiter and Hercules stg. facing each
other. *C.* 311. *R.I.C.* 624 .. .. £2·00
3515 A. ℞. IOVI AVGG. Jupiter stg. l., eagle at feet. *C.* 313. *R.I.C.* 384 2·00
3516 B. ℞. As 3501. *C.* 355. *R.I.C.* 506 .. .. 2·00
3517 A. ℞. PAX AVGG. Pax stg. l., holding Victory and sceptre. *C.* 438.
R.I.C. 399 .. .. 2·00
3518 A. Rad. bust l., wearing imperial mantle and holding eagle-tipped
sceptre. ℞. As previous. *C.* 442. *R.I.C.* 399 .. .. .. 5·00
3519 C. ℞. PAX AVGG. Pax stg. l.; in field, SP; in ex., MLXXI. *R.I.C.*
(*Car., Dio. & Max.*) 34. (*Struck by Carausius*) .. .. .. 25·00
3520 C. ℞. As previous; in field, SP; in ex., C. *R.I.C.* 42. (*Struck by
Carausius*) .. .. 30·00
3521 A. ℞. SALVS AVGG. Salus stg. r., feeding serpent held in arms.
C. 516. *R.I.C.* 422 .. .. 2·00
3522 C. ℞. VIRTVS AVGG. Hercules stg. r., leaning on club set on rock.
C. 566. *R.I.C.* 439 .. .. 2·25
3523 IMP . C . VAL . MAXIMIANVS P . F . AVG. ℞. VIRTVS AVGG. Jupiter and
Hercules stg. facing each other. *C.* 604. *R.I.C.* 432 .. .. 2·00
3524 C. ℞. VIRTVTI AVGG. Hercules stg. r., strangling lion. *C.* 650.
R.I.C. 454 .. .. 4·00
3525 C. Cuir. bust r., wearing rad. helmet. ℞. As previous. *C.* 651.
R.I.C. 454 .. .. 5·00

3526 **Denarius.** B. Laur. and dr. bust, r. ℞. VIRTVS AVGG. Hercules
stg. r., holding club, bow and lion's skin. *R.I.C.* 518 .. .. .. 37·50

3527 **Quinarius.** B. Laur., dr. and cuir. bust, r. ℞. IOVI CONSERVAT .
AVGG. Jupiter stg. l., holding thunderbolt and sceptre. *C.* 351. *R.I.C.*
519 .. .. 20·00

3528 **As.** (*c.* 23.5 mm. *and* 97 *grains*). B. — ℞. As previous. *R.I.C.* 533
Fine £40·00
3529 **Semis.** (*c.* 22 mm. *and* 83 *grains*). C. — ℞. As 3526. *R.I.C.* 537
Fine £35·00
3530 *Post-reform coinage.* **Follis.** (*All with obv. type laur. hd. r., unless
otherwise stated*). B. ℞. FELIX ADVENT . AVGG . NN. Africa stg. l.,
holding standard and elephant's tusk, lion at feet; in ex., PKS. *C.* 106.
R.I.C. 19*b* .. .. 4·50
3531 A. Laur. and cuir. bust, r. ℞. GENIO POPVLI ROMANI. Genius stg. l.;
no mintmark (attributed to London). *C.* 153. *R.I.C.* 28*b* .. .. 6·50

3532 B. Laur. busts of Maximianus and Hercules, jugate, r., the latter holding club. ℞. As previous; in ex., TR. *C.* 168. *R.I.C.* 276 .. .. 65·00
3533 IMP . C . M . A . MAXIMIANVS P . F . AVG. ℞. As previous; in ex., ANT.
C. 184. *R.I.C.* 48*b* .. .. 3·00

Very Fine

3534 **Follis.** IMP . MAXIMIANVS P . AVG. Laur. and cuir. bust l., holding
sceptre. R. As previous, but with altar to l. of Genius; in ex., PLG.
C. 205. *R.I.C.*—. **Plate 10** .. .. 4·50

3535 B. Laur. and cuir. bust, r. R. MONETA S. AVGG . ET CAESS . NN.
Moneta stg. l.; in ex., ATR. *C*. 418. *R.I.C.* 438*b* .. .. .. 4·50

3536 C. R. SAC . MON . VRB . AVGG . ET CAESS . NN. Moneta stg. l.; in ex.,
RS. *C*. 502. *R.I.C.* 105*b* .. .. 4·00

3537 C. R. SACRA MONET . AVGG . ET CAESS . NOSTR. Moneta stg. l.; in ex.,
TT. *C*. 503. *R.I.C.* 47*b* .. .. 4·00

3538 B. R. SALVIS AVGG . ET CAESS . FEL . KART. Carthage stg. l., holding
fruits in both hands; in ex., B. *C*. 510. *R.I.C.* 31*b* .. .. .. 4·50

3539 **Post-Reform Radiates.** IMP . C . M . A . MAXIMIANVS P . F . AVG.
Rad., dr. and cuir. bust, r. R. As 3511; in field, KA. *C*. 54. *R.I.C.*
16*b* .. .. 1·75

3540 — — R. VOT. / XX . / S. in three lines within laurel-wreath. *C*. 675.
R.I.C. 76*b* .. .. 3·75

Coins struck after his first abdication

3541 Æ **follis.** D . N . MAXIMIANO FELICISSIMO SEN . AVG. Laur. bust r.,
wearing imperial mantle and holding branch and mappa. R. PROVI-
DENTIA DEORVM QVIES AVGG. Quies and Providence stg. facing each
other; in ex., PTR. *C*. 489. *R.I.C.* 676*b* .. .. 5·00

Second Reign, A.D. 306-308

3541A **N aureus.** MAXIMIANVS P . F . AVG. Laur. hd., r. R. FELIX
KARTHAGO. Carthage stg. facing, hd. l., holding fruits in both hands;
in ex., PK. *C*. 108. *R.I.C.* 46 .. .. *Extr. rare*

3542 **R argenteus.** *Obv.* Similar. R. VIRTVS MILITVM. Camp-gate
surmounted by four turrets; in ex., PTR. *C*. 632. *R.I.C.* 637 .. .. 90·00

3543 **R half-argenteus.** IMP . MAXIMIANVS P . F . S . AVG. Laur. and cuir.
bust, r. R. As previous; in ex., TR. *C*. —. *R.I.C.* 761 .. .. 200·00

3544 Æ **follis.** C. Laur. hd., r. R. CONSERV . VRB . SVAE. Roma
seated in temple of six columns; in ex., AQP. *C*. 64. *R.I.C.* 121*b* .. 4·00

3545 C. Laur. hd., r. R. CONSERVATORES VRB . SVAE. As previous; in
ex., TT. *C*. 75. *R.I.C.* 84*b* .. .. 4·50

3546 D . N . MAXIMIANO P . F . S . AVG. Laur. and cuir. bust, r. R. GENIO
POP . ROM. Genius stg. l.; in ex., PLN. *C*. 142. *R.I.C.* 90 .. .. 6·00

3547 — — R. As previous; in ex., PTR. *C*. 142. *R.I.C.* 721 .. .. 3·50

3548 — — R. HERCVLI CONSERVATORI. Hercules stg. l., leaning on club
and holding bow; in ex., PLN. *C*. 251. *R.I.C.* 91 .. .. .. 15·00

3549 — — R. ROMAE AETER. Roma seated in temple of six columns; in ex.,
PLN. *C*. 501. *R.I.C.* 100 .. .. 17·50

Coins struck after his second abdication

3550 Æ **half-follis.** D . N . MAXIMIANO BAEATISS. Laur. bust r., wearing
imperial mantle, r. hand raised. R. PROVIDENTIA DEORVM. Quies
and Providence stg. facing each other; in ex., ALE. *C*. 487 *var*. *R.I.C.*
90*b* .. .. 3·50

Commemorative Coins struck after his death

3551 *Struck under Maxentius.* Æ **follis.** DIVO MAXIMIANO PATRI MAXENTIVS
AVG. Veiled hd., r. R. AETERNAE MEMORIAE. Temple with domed
roof surmounted by eagle; in ex., RES. *C*.—. *R.I.C.* 243 .. .. 10·00

Very Fine

3552 *Struck under Constantine the Great.* Æ **3.** (*c.* 18 mm.). DIVO
MAXIMIANO SEN . FORT . IMP. Laur. and veiled hd., r. ℞. REQVIES
OPTIMOR . MERIT. Maximianus seated l. on curule chair; in ex., RP.
C. 495. *R.I.C.* 104 .. .. £5·00

3553 Æ **4.** (*c.* 16 mm.) — — ℞. MEMORIAE AETERNAE. Eagle stg., hd. l.;
in ex., RS. *C.* 397. *R.I.C.* 110 .. .. 4·00

3554 — — ℞. — Lion walking r.; above, club; in ex., RQ. *C.* 400. *R.I.C.*
120 .. .. 4·00

Colonial and Provincial Coinage
All of the first reign

3555 *Egypt, Alexandria,* **billon tetradrachm.** Laur., dr. and cuir. bust, r.
℞. Herakles stg. l., holding Nike and club. *B.M.C. G.*2543 .. 1·25

3556 — — ℞. Eirene stg. l. *B.M.C. G.*2551 .. .. .. 1·00

3557 — — ℞. Homonoia stg. l. *B.M.C. G.*2560 .. .. .. 1·00

3558 — — ℞. Nike advancing r. *B.M.C. G.*2580 .. .. .. 1·00

3559 — — ℞. Tyche stg. l. *B.M.C. G.*2587 .. .. .. 1·00

3560 — — ℞. Eagle stg. l., hd. turned. *B.M.C. G.*2594 .. .. 1·00

CONSTANTIUS I
A.D. 305–306

gold medallion, Cohen 144.

As Caesar, A.D. 293–305

The obv. legend is CONSTANTIVS NOB . CAES., *unless otherwise stated.*

3561 *N* **aureus.** Laur. hd., r. ℞. HERCVLI CONS . CAES. Hercules stg. l.,
leaning on club and holding apple; in ex., SMAᴣ. *C.* 145. *R.I.C.* 7 .. 250·00
There are larger gold, possibly 2½, 4 and 10 *aurei.*

3562 **Æ argenteus.** CONSTANTIVS CAES. Laur. hd., r. ℞. VIRTVS MILITVM.
Diocletian, Maximianus, Constantius and Galerius sacrificing in front
of camp-gate; in ex., z. *C.* 314. *R.I.C.* 42a .. .. .. 30·00

3563 — — ℞. XC / VI. in two lines within laurel-wreath. *C.* 345. *R.I.C.*
16a .. .. 75·00

3564 **BRONZE.** *Pre-reform coinage.* **Antoninianus.** CONSTANTIVS NOB .
C. Rad. and dr. bust, r. ℞. PAX AVGG. Pax stg. l., holding Victory
and sceptre. *C.* 213. *R.I.C.* 633 .. .. 4·50

3565 FL . VAL . CONSTANTIVS NOB . CAES. — ℞. CONCORDIA MILITVM.
Constantius stg. r., receiving Victory on globe from Jupiter stg. l. *C.* 20.
R.I.C. 672 .. .. 4·50

3566 FL . VAL . CONSTANTIVS NOB . C. — ℞. PRINCIPI IVVENTVT. Constantius
stg. r., holding spear and globe. *C.* 221. *R.I.C.* 659 .. .. 5·00

3567 **Denarius.** CONSTANTIVS NOB . C. Laur., dr. and cuir. bust, r. ℞.
PRINCIPI IVVENT. As previous. *R.I.C.* 663 .. .. .. 55·00

3568 **Quinarius.** Laur. and dr. bust, r. ℞. As 3566. *C.* 224. *R.I.C.*
666 .. .. 30·00

Very Fine

3569   *Post-reform coinage.* **Follis.** (*All with obv. type laur. hd. r., unless
        otherwise stated*). ℞. FELIX ADVENT . AVGG . NN. Africa stg. l.,
        holding standard and elephant's tusk, lion at feet; in ex., PKΓ. *C.* 35.
        R.I.C. 22a   ..   ..   £5·00

3570   FL . VAL . CONSTANTIVS NOB . CAES. ℞. GENIO AVGG . ET CAESARVM
        NN. Genius stg. l.; in ex., KB. *C.* 58. *R.I.C.* 11a   ..   ..   ..   5·50

3571   ℞. GENIO POPVLI ROMANI. Genius stg. l.; in ex., TR. *Cf. C.* 61.
        R.I.C. 357a   ..   ..   3·50

3572   CONSTANTIVS NOB . C. Laur. and cuir. bust, r. ℞. As previous; no
        mint-mark (attributed to London). *C.* 72. *R.I.C.* 16. **Plate 10**   ..   7·50

3573   FL . VAL . CONSTANTIVS NOB . CAES. ℞. As previous; in ex., ANT.
        C. 89. *R.I.C.* 49a   ..   ..   3·50

3574   Laur. and cuir. bust, r. ℞. As previous, but with altar to l. of Genius;
        in ex., PLG. *C.* 125. *R.I.C.* 129a   ..   ..   4·00

3575   ℞. SAC . MON . VRB . AVGG . ET CAESS . NN. Moneta stg. l.; in ex.,
        RT. *C.* 263. *R.I.C.* 106a   ..   ..   4·50

3576   ℞. SACRA MONET . AVGG . ET CAESS . NOSTR. Moneta stg. l.; in ex.,
        *SIS. *C.* 264. *R.I.C.* 133a   ..   ..   4·50

3577   ℞. SALVIS AVGG . ET CAESS . FEL . KART. Carthage stg. l., holding
        fruits in both hands; in ex., Γ. *C.* 271. *R.I.C.* 30a   ..   ..   ..   5·00

3578   **Post-Reform Radiates.** As 3565, but with ALE in exergue. *C.* 20.
        R.I.C. 48a   ..   ..   2·50

3579   Rad. and dr. bust, r. ℞. VOT. / XX. / Γ. in three lines within laurel-
        wreath. *C.* 337. *R.I.C.* 88a   ..   ..   4·50

As Augustus

Mints: London; Treveri; Lugdunum; Ticinum; Aquileia; Rome; Carthage;
Siscia; Serdica; Heraclea; Nicomedia; Cyzicus; Antioch; Alexandria.

3580   **N aureus.** CONSTANTIVS P . F . AVG. Laur. hd., r. ℞. CONCORDIA
        AVGG . NOSTR. Concord seated l.; in ex., AQ. *C.* 19. *R.I.C.* 41a   ..   275·00

3581   **R argenteus.** CONSTANTIVS AVG. Laur. hd., r. .℞. VICTORIA AVGG.
        Camp-gate surmounted by four turrets; in ex., SIS. *C.* 284. *R.I.C.*,
        p. 473 ..   ..   *Unique*

3582   **Æ follis.** IMP . C . CONSTANTIVS P . F . AVG. Laur. hd., r. ℞. FIDES
        MILITVM. Fides seated l.; in ex., ST. *C.* 44. *R.I.C.* 55a   ..   ..   6·50

3583   IMP . CONSTANTIVS AVG. Laur. and cuir. bust, r. ℞. As 3571; in ex.,
        PTR. *C.* 114. *R.I.C.* 657a   ..   ..   4·50

3584   IMP . CONSTANTIVS P . F . AVG. Cuir. bust l., wearing laur. helmet and
        holding spear and shield. ℞. VIRTVS AVGG . ET CAESS . NN. Constantius
        galloping r., spearing kneeling enemy; in ex., AQS. *C.* 305. *R.I.C.* 66a   8·00

3585   **Æ post-reform radiate.** IMP . C . CONSTANTIVS P . F . AVG. Rad.
        and dr. bust, r. ℞. As 3565, but with ALE in exergue. *C.* 22.
        R.I.C. 59a   ..   ..   3·50

Commemorative Coins struck after his death

3586   *Struck under Maxentius.* **Æ follis.** IMP . MAXENTIVS DIVO CONSTANTIO
        ADFINI. Veiled hd., r. ℞. AETERNA MEMORIA. Hexastyle temple
        with domed roof surmounted by eagle; in ex., MOSTP. *C.* 2. *R.I.C.* 29   10·00

3587   IMP . MAXENTIVS DIVO CONSTANTIO COGN. Veiled hd., r. ℞. AETERNAE
        MEMORIAE. As previous; in ex., RET. *C.* 5. *R.I.C.* 245   ..   ..   12·00

3588   DIVO CONSTANTIO AVG. Veiled hd., r. ℞ MEMORIA DIVI CONSTANTI.
        Temple with domed roof surmounted by eagle; in ex., TT. *C.* 171.
        R.I.C. 97   ..   ..   6·00

Very Fine

3589 *Struck under Maxentius.* Æ **follis.** DIVO CONSTANTIO PIO. — ℞. —
Large altar surmounted by eagle; in ex., AQΓ. *C.* 174 *var.* *R.I.C.* 127 £6·00

3590 *Struck under Constantine the Great.* Æ **follis.** DIVO CONSTANTIO PIO.
Laur. hd., r. ℞. CONSECRATIO. Eagle stg. r. on altar, wings spread;
in ex., PLG. *C.* 26 *var.* *R.I.C.* 251 .. .. 8·50

3591 DIVO CONSTANTIO PIO. Laur. and veiled bust, r. ℞. MEMORIA FELIX.
Large altar between two eagles; in ex., PTR. *C.* 179 *var.* *R.I.C.* 789.. 4·50

3592 Æ **half-follis.** As previous. *C.* 181 *var.* *R.I.C.* 790.. .. .. 4·50

3593 Æ **3.** (*c.* 18 mm.) DIVO CONSTANTIO PIO PRINCIP. Laur. and veiled hd., r.
℞. REQVIES OPTIMOR . MERIT. Constantius seated l. on curule chair;
in ex., RS. *C.* 249. *R.I.C.* 105 .. .. 5·00

3594 Æ **4.** (*c.* 16 mm.) DIVO CONSTANTIO PIO PRINC. — ℞. MEMORIAE
AETERNAE. Eagle stg., hd. l.; in ex., RP. *C.* 186. *R.I.C.* 111.. .. 4·00

3595 — — ℞. — Lion walking r.; above, club; in ex., RQ. *C.* 188. *R.I.C.*
121 .. .. 4·00

Colonial and Provincial Coinage
All as Caesar.

3596 *Egypt, Alexandria,* **billon tetradrachm.** Laur., dr. and cuir. bust, r.
℞. Elpis stg. l. *B.M.C. G.* 2606 .. .. 3·75

3597 — — ℞. Homonoia stg. l. *B.M.C. G.*2609 .. .. 3·75

GALERIUS
A.D. 305 – 311

3618

As Caesar, A.D. 293-305
The obv. legend is MAXIMIANVS NOB . CAES., *unless otherwise stated.*

3598 **N aureus.** MAXIMIANVS NOB . C. Laur. hd., r. ℞. IOVI CONSERVAT .
AVGG . ET CAESS . NN. Jupiter seated l., holding thunderbolt and sceptre;
in ex., TR. *C.* 121. *R.I.C.* 53 .. .. 200·00
There is also a *double aureus.*

3599 **Æ argenteus.** MAXIMIANVS NOB . C. Laur. hd., r. ℞. VICTORIA
SARMAT. Diocletian, Maximianus, Constantius and Galerius sacrificing
in front of camp-gate; in ex., D. *C.* 207. *R.I.C.* 105b .. .. 35·00

3599A MAXIMIANVS CAES. Laur. hd., r. ℞. VIRTVS MILITVM. As previous,
but with Γ in exergue. *C.* 219. *R.I.C.* 42b. **Plate 10** .. .. 30·00

3600 MAXIMIANVS CAESAR. Laur. hd., r. ℞. XCVI. / AQ. in two lines within
laurel-wreath. *C.* 250. *R.I.C.* 17b .. .. 75·00

3601 **BRONZE.** *Pre-reform coinage.* **Antoninianus.** GAL . VAL .
MAXIMIANVS NOB . CAES. Rad. and dr. bust, r. ℞. CONCORDIA
MILITVM. Galerius stg. r., receiving Victory on globe from Jupiter stg. l.
C. 22. *R.I.C.* 717 .. .. 3·75

3602 — — ℞. IOVI ET HERCVLI CONS . CAES. Jupiter and Hercules stg.
facing each other. *C.* 127. *R.I.C.* 719 .. .. 4·50

3603 *Obv.* As previous, but NOB . C. ℞. PRINCIPI IVVENTVT. Galerius
stg. r., holding spear and globe. *C.* 169. *R.I.C.* 705 .. .. .. 5·00

Very Fine

3604 **Denarius.** Laur., dr. and cuir. bust, r. ℞. PRINCIPI IVVENTVTI.
As previous. *R.I.C.* 708 .. .. ₤55·00

3605 **Quinarius.** MAXIMIANVS NOB . C. — ℞. PRINCIPI IVVENTVT. Galerius
stg. l., holding two standards. *C.* 171. *R.I.C.* 712 .. .. 30·00

3606 *Post-reform coinage.* **Follis.** (*All with obv. type laur. hd. r., unless
otherwise stated*). ℞. FELIX ADVENT . AVGG . NN. Africa stg. l., holding
standard and elephant's tusk, lion at feet; in ex., PK Δ. *C.* 28. *R.I.C.*
22b .. .. 5·00

3607 GAL . VAL . MAXIMIANVS NOB . CAES. ℞. GENIO AVGG . ET CAESARVM NN.
Genius stg. l.; in ex., KA. *C.* 39. *R.I.C.* 11b .. .. 5·50

3608 Laur. and cuir. bust, r. ℞. GENIO POPVLI ROMANI. Genius stg. l.;
no mintmark (attributed to London). *C.* 57. *R.I.C.* 35. **Plate 10**.. 6·50

3609 GAL . VAL . MAXIMIANVS NOB . CAES. ℞. As previous, but with ALE in
exergue. *C.* 78. *R.I.C.* 15b .. .. 3·50

3610 Laur. and cuir. bust l., holding sceptre. ℞. As previous, but with
altar to l. of Genius and PLG in exergue. *C.* 104. *R.I.C.* 144b.. 5·00

3611 ℞. SACRA MON . VRB . AVGG . ET CAESS . NN. Moneta stg. l.; in ex., RQ.
C. 189. *R.I.C.* 104b .. .. 4·50

3612 ℞. SALVIS AVGG . ET CAESS . FEL . KART. Carthage stg. l., holding fruits
in both hands; in ex., Δ. *C.* 191. *R.I.C.* 32b .. .. .. 5·00

3613 **Post-Reform Radiates.** As 3601, but with HA in field. *C.* 22.
R.I.C. 16 .. .. 2·25

3614 Rad. and dr. bust, r. ℞. VOT. / XX. / Δ. in three lines within laurel-
wreath. *C.* 246. *R.I.C.* 88b .. .. 4·00

As Augustus

Mints: London; Treveri; Lugdunum; Ticinum; Aquileia; Rome; Carthage;
Siscia; Serdica; Thessalonica; Heraclea; Nicomedia; Cyzicus; Antioch; Alexandria.

3615 *N* **aureus.** MAXIMIANVS P . F . AVG. Laur. hd., r. ℞. IOVI CONSER-
VATORI AVGG . ET CAESS . NN. Jupiter stg. l., holding thunderbolt and
sceptre; in ex., TR. *C.*—. *R.I.C.* 625a .. .. 250·00

There is also a *double aureus.*

3616 **Æ argenteus.** MAXIMIANVS AVG. Laur. hd., r. ℞. VICTORIA AVGG.
Camp-gate surmounted by four turrets; in ex., SIS. *C.*—. *R.I.C.*— *Extr. rare*

3616A **Æ half-argenteus.** IMP . MAXIMIANVS P . F . AVG. Laur. and cuir.
bust, r. ℞. VIRTVS MILITVM. As previous; in ex., TR. *C.* —.
R.I.C. 757 .. .. 125·00

During the period of Galerius' reign the size and weight of the follis *declined considerably
at both Eastern and Western mints. A typical example is the mint of Antioch where the
latest* folles *of Galerius are only about 22 mm. in diameter and sometimes less than half the
weight of the coin introduced by Diocletian's reform.*

3617 **Æ follis.** GAL . MAXIMIANVS P . F . AVG. Laur. hd., r. ℞. GENIO
AVGVSTI. Genius stg. l.; in ex., . SM . TS . *C.* 40. *R.I.C.* 40a .. .. 2·50

3618 IMP . C . GAL . VAL . MAXIMIANVS P . F . AVG. Laur. hd., r. ℞. GENIO
AVGVSTI CMH. Genius stg. l.; in ex., SMNA. *C.* 42. *R.I.C.* 54a. *Illustrated on p.* 302 .. .. 3·50

3619 — — ℞. GENIO IMPERATORIS. Genius stg. l.; in ex., ALE. *C.* 48.
R.I.C. 101a .. .. 2·00

3620 — — ℞. GENIO POPVLI ROMANI. Genius stg. l.; in ex., HTB. *C.* 81.
R.I.C. 24b .. .. 3·00

3621 **Æ follis.** IMP . MAXIMIANVS P . F . AVG. Helmeted and cuir. bust l., holding spear and shield. ℞. VIRTVS AVGG . ET CAESS . NN. Galerius galloping r., spearing kneeling enemy; in ex., AQP. *C.* —. *R.I.C.* 66*b*... £7·50

3622 **Æ post-reform radiate.** IMP . C . MAXIMIANVS P . F . AVG. Rad. and dr. bust, r. ℞. As 3601, but with ALE in exergue. *C.* —. *R.I.C.* 59*b* 2·25

Commemorative Coins struck after his death

3623 *Struck under Maxentius.* **Æ follis.** IMP . MAXENTIVS DIVO MAXIMIANO SOCERO. Veiled hd., r. ℞. AETERNA MEMORIA. Temple with domed roof surmounted by eagle; in ex., MOSTQ. *C.* 4. *R.I.C.* 31 .. .. 12·00

3624 *Struck under Licinius.* **Æ follis.** DIVO GAL . VAL . MAXIMIANO. Veiled hd., r. ℞. FORTI FORTVNAE. Fortune stg. l.; in ex., SIS. *C.* 30. *R.I.C.* 221 .. .. 20·00

3625 *Struck under Maximinus II.* **Æ follis.** DIVO MAXIMIANO MAXIMINVS AVG . FIL. Laur. hd., r. ℞. AETERNAE MEMORIAE GAL . MAXIMIANI. Large altar surmounted by eagle; in ex., ALE. *C.* 7. *R.I.C.* 133 .. 35·00

Colonial and Provincial Coinage
All as Caesar.

3626 *Egypt, Alexandria,* **billon tetradrachm.** Laur., dr. and cuir. bust, r. ℞. Elpis stg. l. *B.M.C. G.*2615 .. .. 3·75

3627 — — ℞. Helmeted bust of Roma r., holding shield. *B.M.C. G.*2620 5·00

3628 — Laur. and cuir. bust, r. ℞. Eagle stg. l., hd. turned. *B.M.C. G.*2621 .. .. 3·75

GALERIA VALERIA
Daughter of Diocletian and second wife of Galerius

3630

Mints: Siscia; Serdica; Thessalonica; Heraclea; Nicomedia; Cyzicus; Antioch; Alexandria.

3629 **A/ aureus.** GAL . VALERIA AVG. Diad. and dr. bust, r. ℞. VENERI VICTRICI. Venus stg. l., holding apple; in ex., SMN. *C.* 1. *R.I.C.* 53 1500·00
There is also a *double aureus.*

3630 **Æ follis.** As previous, but with ALE in exergue. *C.* 2. *R.I.C.* 110. **Plate 10** *and illustrated above* .. .. 15·00

3631 GAL . VALERIA AVG. Diad. bust r., wearing imperial mantle. ℞. As previous, but with . SM . TS. in exergue. *C.* 7. *R.I.C.* 36 .. .. 20·00

SEVERUS II

A.D. 306 – 307

3645

As Caesar, A.D. 305-306   Very Fine

3632   *N* **aureus.** SEVERVS NOB . CAES. Laur. hd., r. ℞. FELICITAS CAESS . NOSTR. Felicity seated l.; in ex., AQ. *C.* 10. *R.I.C.* 44   ..   ..£450·00
There is also a *double aureus.*

3633   **Æ follis.** FL . VAL . SEVERVS NOB . CAES. Laur. hd., r. ℞. GENIO AVGG . ET CAESARVM NN. Genius stg. l.; in ex., KA. *C.* 18. *R.I.C.* 20a   17·50

3634   SEVERVS NOBILISSIMVS CAESAR. Laur., dr. and cuir. bust, r. ℞. GENIO POPVLI ROMANI. Genius stg. l.; no mint-mark (attributed to London). *C.* 25. *R.I.C.* 58a   ..   ..   20·00

3635   SEVERVS NOB . C. — ℞. As previous, but with altar to l. of Genius and PLG in exergue. *C.* 43. *R.I.C.* 199a   ..   ..   15·00

3636   SEVERVS NOB . CAES. Laur. hd., r. ℞. SAC . MON . VRB . AVGG . ET CAESS. NN. Moneta stg. l.; in ex., RT. *C.* 62. *R.I.C.* 123a   ..   ..   17·50

3637   *Obv.* As 3633. ℞. SALVIS AVGG . ET CAESS . FEL . KART. Carthage stg. l., holding fruits in both hands; in ex., Γ. *C.* 64. *R.I.C.* 40a   ..   17·50

3638   SEVERVS NOB . CAESAR. Laur. hd., r. ℞. VIRTVS AVGG . ET CAESS . NN. Mars advancing r., carrying spear and trophy; in ex., ST. *C.* 70. *R.I.C.* 58a   ..   ..   20·00

3639   **Æ post-reform radiate.** FL . VAL . SEVERVS NOB . CAES. Rad., dr. and cuir. bust, r. ℞. CONCORDIA MILITVM. Severus stg. r., receiving Victory on globe from Jupiter stg. l.; in ex., ALE. *C.* 7. *R.I.C.* 60a ..   12·50

3640   **Æ denarius.** FL . VAL . SEVERVS NOB . C. Laur. hd., r. ℞. As 3634, but with SIS in exergue. *C.* 32. *R.I.C.* 170a   ..   ..   25·00

3641   **Æ quinarius.** SEVERVS NOB . C. Laur. hd., r. ℞. VOT . X . CAESS. in laurel-wreath. *C.* 68. *R.I.C.* 685a   ..   ..   ..   30·00

As Augustus

Mints: London; Treveri; Lugdunum; Ticinum ; Aquileia; Rome; Carthage; Siscia; Serdica; Heraclea; Nicomedia; Cyzicus; Antioch; Alexandria.

3642   *N* **aureus.** SEVERVS AVGVSTVS. Laur. hd., r. ℞. HERCVLI VICTORI NIK. Hercules stg. r., leaning on club and holding apples; in ex., SMN. *C.* 50. *R.I.C.* 41   ..   ..   500·00

3643   **Æ argenteus.** SEVERVS AVG. Laur. hd., r. ℞. VIRTVS MILITVM. Camp-gate surmounted by three turrets; in ex., . SM . SDA. *C.* —. *R.I.C.* 21   ..   ..   400·00

3644   **Æ follis.** IMP . C . SEVERVS P . F . AVG. Laur. hd., r. ℞. FIDES MILITVM. Fides seated l.; in ex., ST. *C.* 13. *R.I.C.* 73   ..   ..   17·50

3645   — Helmeted and cuir. bust l., holding sceptre and shield. ℞. FIDES MILITVM AVGG . ET CAESS . NN. Fides stg. l.; in ex., AQS. *C.* 17. *R.I.C.* 77b. *Illustrated above*   ..   ..   20·00

3647   *Obv.* As 3644. ℞. VIRTVS AVGG . ET CAESS . NN. Severus galloping r., spearing kneeling enemy; in ex., TT. *C.* 77. *R.I.C.* 81   ..   20·00

3648   **Æ post-reform radiate.** IMP . C . SEVERVS P . F . AVG. Rad. and dr. bust, r. ℞. As 3639. *C.* 9. *R.I.C.* 84   ..   ..   ..   12·50

bronze medallion, Cohen 134.

As Caesar, A.D. 305-308   **Very Fine**

3649 **N aureus.** MAXIMINVS NOB . C. Laur. hd., r. ℞. PRINCIPI IVVENTVTIS. Maximinus stg. l. between two standards, holding sceptre; in ex., SIS. *C.* 144. *R.I.C.* 151 ..   ..£375·00
There is also a *double aureus.*

3650 **R argenteus.** — — ℞. VIRTVS MILITVM. Camp-gate surmounted by three turrets; in ex., . SM . SDΔ. *C.* 206. *R.I.C.* 22   ..   ..   350·00

3651 **R half-argenteus.** MAXIMINVS NOB . CAES. Laur. and cuir. bust, r. ℞. — Camp-gate surmounted by four turrets; in ex., TR. *C.* 208. *R.I.C.* 763   ..   ..   200·00

3652 **Æ follis** (declining from *c.* 27 mm. to *c.* 24 mm.) GAL . VAL . MAXIMINVS NOB . CAES. Laur. hd., r. ℞. GENIO AVGG . ET CAESARVM NN. Genius stg. l.; in ex., KΓ. *C.* 15. *R.I.C.* 20*b*   ..   ..   6·50

3653 — — ℞. GENIO CAESARIS. Genius stg. l.; in ex., ALE. *C.* 40. *R.I.C.* 64. **Plate 11**   ..   ..   2·00

3654 GAL . VAL . MAXIMINVS NOB . C. Laur. and cuir. bust, r. ℞. GENIO POPVLI ROMANI. Genius stg. l.; in ex., PTR. *C.* 92. *R.I.C.* 667*b* ..   5·00

3655 MAXIMINVS NOB . CAES. Laur. hd., r. ℞. SAC. MON . VRB . AVGG . ET CAESS . NN. Moneta stg. l.; in ex., RQ. *C.* 148. *R.I.C.* 123*b*   ..   6·0C

3656 *Obv.* As 3652. ℞. SALVIS AVGG . ET CAESS . FEL . KART. Carthage stg. l., holding fruits in both hands; in ex., Δ. *C.* 150. *R.I.C.* 40*b* ..   7·00

3657 MAXIMINVS NOB . CAESAR. Laur. hd., r. ℞. VIRTVS AVGG . ET CAESS . NN. Mars advancing r., carrying spear and trophy; in ex., TT. *C.* 191. *R.I.C.* 58*b*   ..   ..   7·50

3658 **Æ post-reform radiate.** GAL . VAL . MAXIMINVS NOB . CAES. Rad., dr. and cuir. bust, r. ℞. CONCORDIA MILITVM. Maximinus stg. r., receiving Victory on globe from Jupiter stg. l.; in ex., ALE. *C.* 9. *R.I.C.* 60*b*   ..   ..   4·00

3659 **Æ denarius.** *Obv.* As 3649. ℞. As 3654, but with SIS in exergue. *C.* 84. *R.I.C.* 171*b*   ..   ..   15·00

3660 **Æ quinarius.** — ℞. VOT . X . CAESS. in laurel-wreath. *C.* 217. *R.I.C.* 685*b* ..   ..   20·00

As Filius Augustorum, A.D. 308-309

3661 **Æ follis.** MAXIMINVS FIL . AVGG. Laur. hd., r. ℞. GENIO AVGVSTI. Genius stg. l.; in ex., SIS. *C.* 24. *R.I.C.* 200*a* ..   ..   ..   12·50

MAXIMINUS II
A.D. 309 – 313

As Augustus

Mints: London; Treveri; Ticinum; Aquileia; Rome; Ostia; Siscia; Thessalonica; Heraclea; Nicomedia; Cyzicus; Antioch; Alexandria.

Very Fine

3662 *N* **aureus.** MAXIMINVS AVGVSTVS. Laur. hd., r. ℞. IOVI CON-
SERVATORI AVGG. Jupiter stg. l., eagle at feet; in ex., . SM . TS. *C.* 122.
R.I.C. 44b .. ..£325·00

3663 **Æ follis** (declining from *c.* 24 mm. to *c.* 20 mm.) IMP . C . GALER . VAL .
MAXIMINVS P . F . AVG. Laur. hd., r. ℞. BONO GENIO PII IMPERATORIS.
Genius stg. l.; in ex., ALE. *C.* 2. *R.I.C.* 135b .. .. .. 2·50

3664 *Obv.* As previous, but GAL . VAL. ℞. GENIO AVGVSTI. Genius stg. l.,
holding hd. of Serapis and cornucopiae; in ex., ALE. *C.* 17. *R.I.C.*
149b .. .. 2·00

3665 — ℞. — Genius stg. l., holding Victory and cornucopiae; in ex., ANT.
C. 32. *R.I.C.* 162b .. .. 2·00

3666 IMP . MAXIMINVS P . F . AVG. Laur. and cuir. bust, r. ℞. GENIO
POP . ROM. Genius stg. l.; in ex., PTR. *C.* 58. *R.I.C.* 845a .. .. 2·00

3667 — — ℞. IOVI CONSERVATORI AVGG . NN. Jupiter stg. l., eagle at feet;
in ex., SIS. *C.* 127. *R.I.C.* 233b .. .. 2·00

3668 *Obv.* As 3664. ℞. SOLI INVICTO. Sol stg. l., holding hd. of Serapis;
in ex., SMN. *C.* 161. *R.I.C.* 73b .. .. 3·50

3669 *Obv.* As 3666. ℞. SOLI INVICTO COMITI. Sol stg. l., holding globe;
in ex., MOSTT. *C.* 167. *R.I.C.* 84a .. .. 3·00

MAXENTIUS
A.D. 306 – 312

3680

Mints: Treveri; Ticinum; Aquileia; Rome; Ostia; Carthage.

As Princeps, A.D. 306

3670 *N* **aureus.** MAXENTIVS PRINC . INVICT. Laur. hd., r. ℞. MARTI
CONSERV . AVGG . ET CAESS . NN. Mars advancing r., holding spear and
shield; in ex., PR. *C.* 89. *R.I.C.* 140 .. .. .. *Extr. rare*

3671 **Æ argenteus.** — — ℞. VIRTVS MILITVM. Camp-gate surmounted by
three turrets; in ex., RS. *C.* 134. *R.I.C.* 153 .. .. .. 250·00

3672 **Æ follis.** — — ℞. CONSERVATOR AFRICAE SVAE. Africa stg. l.,
holding standard and elephant's tusk, lion at feet; in ex., B. *C.* 47.
R.I.C. 53 .. .. 30·00

As Caesar, A.D. 306

3672A *N* **aureus.** MAXENTIVS NOB . C. Laur. hd., r. ℞. FELIX KARTHAGO.
Carthage stg. facing, hd. l., holding fruits in both hands; in ex., PK.
C. 66. *R.I.C.* 47 .. .. *Very rare*

3673 **Æ follis.** M . AVR . MAXENTIVS NOB . CAES. Laur. hd., r. ℞. SALVIS
AVGG . ET CAESS . FEL . KART. Carthage stg. l., holding fruits in both
hands; in ex., Δ. *C.* 103. *R.I.C.* 51a .. .. 15·00

As Augustus

Very Fine

3674 **A' aureus.** MAXENTIVS P . F . AVG. Laur. hd., r. ℞. FIDES MILITVM. Fides stg. l., holding two standards; in ex., PR. *C.* 67. *R.I.C.* 180 £1000·00

3675 **R argenteus.** — — ℞. MARTI PROPAG . IMP . AVG . N. Mars stg. r., clasping r. hands with female stg. l.; between them, wolf and twins; in ex., MOSTΓ. *C.* 92. *R.I.C.* 11 .. .. 250·00

3676 **Æ follis.** IMP . C . MAXENTIVS P . F . AVG. Laur. hd., r. ℞. AETER-NITAS AVG . N. The Dioscuri stg. facing each other, each holding horse by bridle; in ex., MOSTP. *C.* 5. *R.I.C.* 35 .. .. 4·50

3677 — — ℞. — As previous, but with wolf and twins between the Dioscuri; in ex., MOSTB. *C.* 10. *R.I.C.* 16 .. .. 6·00

3678 — — ℞. AETERNITAS AVG . N. She-wolf stg. l., suckling Romulus and Remus; in ex., MOSTQ. *C.* 16. *R.I.C.* 41 .. .. 8·50

3679 — — ℞. CONSERV . VRB . SVAE. Roma seated facing in hexastyle temple; in ex., RBQ. *C.* 21. *R.I.C.* 210. **Plate 11** .. .. .. 3·50

3680 IMP . MAXENTIVS P . F . AVG . CONS . II. Laur. bust r., wearing imperial mantle and holding eagle-tipped sceptre. ℞. As previous, but with AQΓ in exergue. *C.* 33. *R.I.C.* 125. *Illustrated on p.* 307 .. .. 10·00

3681 *Obv.* As 3676. ℞. CONSERV . VRB . SVAE. Temple of four columns within which sits Roma l., presenting globe to Maxentius stg. r.; in ex., AQS. *C.* 42. *R.I.C.* 113 .. .. 5·00

3682 — ℞. FIDES MILITVM AVG . N. Fides stg. l.; in ex., MOSTS. *C.* 71. *R.I.C.* 45 .. .. 7·50

3683 — ℞. VICTORIA AETERNA AVG . N. Victory advancing l.; in ex., MOSTT. *C.* 122. *R.I.C.* 54 .. .. 6·50

3684 **Æ half-follis.** MAXENTIVS P . F . AVG. Laur. hd., l. ℞. — Victory stg. r., inscribing VOT . X. on shield set on cippus; in ex., MOSTP. *C.* 117. *R.I.C.* 60 .. .. 10·00

3685 **Æ quarter-follis.** — Laur. hd., r. ℞. VOT . Q . Q . MVL . XX. in laurel-wreath. *C.* 138. *R.I.C.* 281*c* .. .. 7·50

ROMULUS

3686A

Son of Maxentius; he died in A.D. 309 *and all his coins are posthumous.*

3686 **Æ follis.** DIVO ROMVLO N . V . BIS CONS. Bare hd., r. ℞. AETERNAE MEMORIAE. Temple with domed roof surmounted by eagle; in ex., RBP. *C.* 6. *R.I.C.* 207 .. .. 30·00

3686A IMP . MAXENTIVS DIVO ROMVLO N . V . FILIO. Bare hd., r. ℞. — Temple with four columns and domed roof surmounted by eagle; in ex., REP. *C.* 11. *R.I.C.* 249. *Illustrated above* .. .. .. 45·00

3687 **Æ quarter-follis.** DIVO ROMVLO N . V . BIS C. Bare hd., r. ℞. As 3686, but with MOSTT in exergue. *C.* 9. *R.I.C.* 58 .. .. .. 17·50

ALEXANDER
A.D. 311

3689

Mint: Carthage.

Very Fine

3688 N **aureus.** IMP . C . ALEXANDER P . F . AVG. Laur. hd., r. ℞. INVICTA ROMA FEL . KARTHAGO. Carthage stg. l., holding fruits in both hands; in ex., PK. *C.* 3. *R.I.C.* 62 .. .. *Extr. rare*

3689 Æ **follis.** IMP . ALEXANDER P . F . AVG. — ℞. INVICTA ROMA FELIX KARTHAGO. As previous. *C.* 6. *R.I.C.* 68. *Illustrated above* ..£300·00

LICINIUS I
A.D. 308 – 324

3700A

Mints: London; Treveri; Lugdunum; Arelate; Ticinum; Aquileia; Rome; Ostia; Siscia; Serdica; Thessalonica; Heraclea; Nicomedia; Cyzicus; Antioch; Alexandria.

3690 N **aureus.** LICINIVS AVGVSTVS. Laur. hd., r. ℞. IOVI CONSERVATORI AVGG. Jupiter stg. l., eagle at feet; in ex., · SM · TS · *C.* 104. *R.I.C.* 44a .. .. 250·00

3691 N **quinarius.** IMP . LICINIVS AVG. Laur. and cuir. bust, r. ℞. — Jupiter seated l.; in ex., TR. *C.* 103. *R.I.C.* 794 .. .. .. 350·00

3692 Æ **heavy miliarense.** (*c.* 5·4 gm.). IMP . LICINIVS PIVS FELIX AVG. Helmeted and cuir. bust l., holding spear and shield. ℞. VOTA ORBIS ET VRBIS SEN . ET P . R. Flaming cippus, on square basis, inscribed XX / XXX / MVL / FEL.; in field, L; in ex., AQ. *C.* 202. *R.I.C.* 80 *Extr. rare*

3693 Æ **follis** (declining from *c.* 24 mm. to *c.* 20 mm.). IMP . LIC . LICINIVS P F . AVG. Laur. hd., r. ℞. GENIO AVGVSTI. Genius stg. l.; in ex., SIS. *C.* 26. *R.I.C.* 198b .. .. 2·00

3694 IMP . C . LIC . LICINNIVS P . F . AVG. — ℞. — Genius stg. l., holding hd. of Serapis and cornucopiae; in ex., ALE. *C.* 32. *R.I.C.* 149a .. 2·50

3695 IMP . C . VAL . LIC . LICINIVS P . F . AVG. — ℞. GENIO IMPERATORIS. Genius stg. l.; in ex., ALE. *C.* 43. *R.I.C.* 101b .. .. .. 2·00

3696 IMP . LICINIVS P . F . AVG. Laur. and cuir. bust, r. ℞. GENIO POP . ROM. Genius stg. l.; in ex., PTR. *C.* 49. *R.I.C.* 845b .. .. 2·00

3697 As previous, but with PLN (*London*) in exergue. *C.* 49. *R.I.C.* 209c 3·50

3698 *Obv.* As 3693. ℞. IOVI CONSERVATORI. Jupiter stg. l., eagle at feet; in ex., SIS. *C.* 83. *R.I.C.* 222a .. .. 2·00

3699 — ℞. IOVI CONSERVATORI AVGG . NN. Jupiter stg. l., eagle at feet; in ex., · TS · B ·. *C.* 126. *R.I.C.* 57 .. .. 2·00

Very Fine

3700 **Æ follis.** *Obv.* As 3696. ℞. s . p . q . r . OPTIMO PRINCIPI.
Legionary eagle between two standards; in ex., RP. *C.* 165. *R.I.C.*
349c .. .. £3·50

3700A VAL . LICINNIANVS LICINNIVS P . F . AVG. Laur. hd., r. ℞. VIRTVTI
EXERCITVS. Mars advancing r., holding spear, shield and trophy; in ex.,
MKV. *C.* 198. *R.I.C.* 51. *Illustrated on p.* 309.. .. .. 7·50

3701 **Æ 3.** (c. 19 mm.) IMP . LICINIVS AVG. Laur. hd., r. ℞. D . N . LICINI
AVGVSTI. Laurel-wreath around VOT . XX.; in ex., BSIS*. *C.* 15.
R.I.C. 160 .. .. 1·50

3702 As 3696, but with MLL (*London*) in exergue. *C.* 49. *R.I.C.* 23 .. 3·00

3703 IMP . LICINIVS AVG. Laur. and cuir. bust, r. ℞. IOVI CONSERVATORI
AVG. Jupiter seated l. on eagle flying r.; in ex., TARL. *C.* 97. *R.I.C.*
196 .. .. 3·50

3704 — Laur. bust l., wearing imperial mantle and holding mappa, globe
and sceptre. ℞. IOVI CONSERVATORI AVGG. Jupiter stg. l.; in ex.,
SMN. *C.* 116. *R.I.C.* 24. **Plate 10** .. .. 1·75

3705 — Helmeted and cuir. bust, r. ℞. ROMAE AETERNAE. Roma seated
r., inscribing XV. on shield set on knees; in ex., RS. *C.* 150. *R.I.C.* 151 2·00

3706 IMP . LICINIVS P . F . AVG. Laur., dr. and cuir. bust, r. ℞. SOLI
INVICTO COMITI. Sol stg. l., holding globe; in ex., RT. *C.* 163. *R.I.C.*
29 .. .. 1·50

3707 — Laur. and cuir. bust, r. ℞. VICTORIAE LAETAE PRINC . PERP. Two
Victories resting shield, inscribed VOT . P . R., on altar; in ex., TT.
C. 177. *R.I.C.* 92 .. .. 2·00

3708 *Obv.* As 3705. ℞. VIRTVS EXERCIT. Two captives seated at foot
of standard inscribed VOT . XX.; in ex., · TS · A ·. *C.* 188. *R.I.C.* 76 1·75

3709 **Æ 4.** (c. 16 mm.). IMP . LICINIVS P . F . AVG. Bare hd., r. ℞.
SAPIENTIA PRINCIPIS. Altar surmounted by owl; in ex., RP. *C.* 153.
R.I.C. 17 .. .. 7·50

CONSTANTIA

Half-sister of Constantine and wife of Licinius

Mint: Constantinople.

3710 **Æ 3.** (20 mm.) CONSTANTIA N . F. Dr. bust, r. ℞. SOROR CONSTAN-
TINI AVG. around wreath within which is PIET / AS PVB / LICA in three lines;
in ex., CONSB. *C.* 1. *R.I.C.* 15 .. .. *Very rare*

LICINIUS II

Caesar, A.D. 317 – 324

3711

Mints: Treveri; Arelate; Ticinum; Aquileia; Rome; Siscia; Thessalonica; Heraclea;
Nicomedia; Cyzicus; Antioch; Alexandria.

3711 **N aureus.** D . N . VAL . LICIN . LICINIVS NOB . C. Bare-headed and dr.
bust facing. ℞. IOVI CONSERVATORI CAES. Jupiter seated facing on
base inscribed SIC . V . SIC . X.; in ex., SMNΓ. *C.* 28. *R.I.C.* 42 .. .. 500·00
There are larger gold, possibly 1½ and 4 *aurei*.

Very Fine

3712 Æ **quinarius.** LICINIVS IVN . NOB . CAES. Laur. and dr. bust, r. ℞.
PRINCIPI IVVENTVTIS. Licinius stg. r., holding spear and globe. *C.* 34.
R.I.C. —, *but see p.* 179, 199 *note* ..   ..   *Extr. rare*

3713 Æ **3.** (*c.* 19 mm.) — Laur. hd., r. ℞. CAESARVM NOSTRORVM.
Laurel-wreath around VOT . V.; in ex., TSЄVI. *C.* 6. *R.I.C.* 92   .. £2·50

3714 LICINIVS NOB . CAES. — ℞. CAESARVM NOSTRORVM around VOTIS V.;
in ex., QA. *C.* 10. *R.I.C.* 221   ..   ..   2·50

3715 D . N . VAL . LICIN . LICINIVS NOB . C. Helmeted and cuir. bust l., holding
spear and shield. ℞. IOVI CONSERVATORI. Jupiter stg. l. between
eagle and captive; in ex., SMHA. *C.* 21. *R.I.C.* 54   ..   ..   ..   2·50

3716 — — ℞. As previous, but with SMALB in exergue. *C.* 21. *R.I.C.* 30.
Illust. on p. 47   ..   ..   2·50

3717 — Laur. bust l., wearing imperial mantle and holding mappa, globe and
sceptre. ℞. IOVI CONSERVATORI CAESS. Jupiter stg. l., captive at feet;
in ex., SMANT. *C.* 32. *R.I.C.* 29 ..   ..   2·50

3718 — — ℞. PROVIDENTIAE CAESS. Jupiter stg. l., palm at feet; in ex.,
SMN. *Cf. C.* 38. *R.I.C.* 33   ..   ..   2·50

3719 — — ℞. — Camp-gate surmounted by three turrets; in ex., . MHTΔ.
Cf. C. 41. *R.I.C.* 21   ..   ..   2·50

3720 LICINIVS IVN . NOB . C. Laur., dr. and cuir. bust, r. ℞. ROMAE
AETERNAE. Roma seated r., inscribing XV on shield set on knees; in ex.,
RT. *C.* 45. *R.I.C.* 154   ..   ..   3·00

3721 — Laur. and dr. bust, r. ℞. VICTORIAE LAETAE PRINC. PERP. Two
Victories resting shield, inscribed VOT . P.R., on altar; in ex., PT. *C.* 55.
R.I.C. 94   ..   ..   3·25

3722 — Rad. and dr. bust, r. ℞. VIRTVS EXERCIT. Two captives seated at
foot of trophy; in ex., STR. *C.* 60. *R.I.C.* 264 ..   ..   2·50

VALENS
A.D. 314

Mints: Cyzicus; Alexandria.

3723 Æ **3.** (20 mm.) IMP . C . AVR . VAL . VALENS P . F . AVG. Laur. hd., r.
℞. IOVI CONSERVATORI AVGG. Jupiter stg. l., eagle at feet; in ex., ALE.
C. 2. *R.I.C.* 19   ..   ..   *Extr. rare*

MARTINIAN
A.D. 324

Mints: Nicomedia; Cyzicus.

Very Fine

3724   **Æ 3.**   (20 mm.)   D . N . M . MARTINIANO P . F . AVG.   Rad., dr. and cuir.
bust, r.   ℞.   IOVI CONSERVATORI.   Jupiter stg. l. between eagle and
captive; in ex., SMNB.   *C.* 4.   *R.I.C.* 46 ..   ..£300·00

CONSTANTINE I,
the Great

A.D. 307 – 337

bronze medallion, Cohen 269.

Mints: London; Treveri; Lugdunum; Arelate; Ticinum; Aquileia; Rome; Ostia;
Carthage; Siscia; Sirmium; Serdica; Thessalonica; Heraclea; Constantinople; Nicomedia; Cyzicus; Antioch; Alexandria.

*The coinage underwent a considerable number of changes during the reign of Constantine.
Whilst he was still only Caesar he reduced the weight of the* follis *at the mints then under his
control (London, Lugdunum and Treveri) and again reduced it soon after his elevation to
the rank of Augustus (March, 307).   The final reduction to c. 68 grains was made some
months later.*

This was only keeping in line with the reductions of the follis *being made by the other
rulers of the empire, but in 312 Constantine made some important changes on his own
initiative.   In place of the* aureus *($^1/_{60}$ lb. of gold) he introduced a new coin called the* solidus
*which was struck at 72 to the lb.   Other gold denominations introduced were the semis ($\frac{1}{2}$
solidus) of c. 2.27 grammes and the $1\frac{1}{2}$ scripulum of c. 1.70 grammes which stood in no
convenient relationship to the* solidus.   *The aureus continued to be struck in the East until
the defeat of Licinius in 324 when the* solidus *became the standard gold coin of the whole
empire.   The aureus, however, was still occasionally struck up to about the end of the fourth
century.*

Later in the reign a silver piece tariffed at 24 to the solidus *was also struck, but although
it was given the name* siliqua *it appears to be of the same weight as Diocletian's* argenteus
($^1/_{96}$ lb. of silver).   In addition to the siliqua, *a larger silver piece of $^1/_{72}$ lb. was introduced.
The name of this coin was* miliarense *and, as can be seen from the weights, the* siliqua *was
equivalent to $\frac{3}{4}$ of the* miliarense *which was, in turn, equivalent to $^1/_{18}$ of the* solidus.   *We
thus have the following system in the precious metals:—*

1 *N* solidus = 2*N* semisses = 18 Æ miliarensia = 24 Æ siliquae.

*As in the case of the N $1\frac{1}{2}$ scripulum, there is also a silver denomination which appears
to stand in no convenient relationship to the other denominations.   This piece is slightly
heavier than the* miliarense *($^1/_{60}$ lb.) and is usually referred to as a* heavy miliarense.

Soon after the defeat of Maxentius in 312, Constantine and Licinius replaced the follis
*with an Æ 3 denomination of c. 18-20 mm. diameter and c. 48 grains weight.   This module
just survived the introduction of the* GLORIA EXERCITVS *type in 330 but was then reduced to
c. 17 mm. and 30 grains.   A few years later, possibly in 336, there was a further reduction in
weight to c. 20-25 grains.   These bronze coins of the last 7 years of Constantine's reign
occasionally decline to Æ 4 module (under 17 mm.) especially after the weight reduction
in 336.*

As there is so much change in the bronze coinage of the late Roman Empire and so little is known about the names of the denominations, I have adopted the headings Æ 1, Æ 2, Æ 3 *and* Æ 4 *which approximate to Cohen's* GB, MB, PB *and* PBQ. *The following table will give some idea of how these classifications are determined:*

Æ 1	= from 25 millimetres diameter.
Æ 2	= from 21	,,	,,
Æ 3	= from 17	,,	,,
Æ 4	= under 17	,,	,,

Weight, however, is also a determining factor: for example, an Æ 2 *coin may be struck on a thick, heavy flan which is only of* Æ 3 *module. In most cases, however, the above table can be used as a fairly reliable guide.*

As Caesar, A.D. 306-307   Very Fine

3725 **N aureus.** CONSTANTINVS NOB . C. Laur. hd., r. ℞. PRINCIPI IVVENTVT. Constantine stg. l., holding sceptre; to l., standard; in ex., PR. C. 405. R.I.C. 141 .. .. *Very rare*

3726 **R argenteus.** — ℞. CONSERVATOR KART . SVAE. Carthage stg. facing in hexastyle temple, holding fruits in both hands; in ex., XCVI. C. 72. R.I.C. 49 .. .. £325·00

3727 — — ℞. VIRTVS MILITVM. Camp-gate surmounted by four turrets; in ex., PTR. C. 706. R.I.C. 636. **Plate 10** .. .. .. 65·00

3728 **R half-argenteus.** As previous. C. 709. R.I.C. — .. *Very rare*

3729 **Æ follis.** CONSTANTINVS NOB . CAES. Laur. hd., r. ℞. CONSERVA-TORES KART . SVAE. As 3726, but with PKΔ in exergue. C. 73. R.I.C. 61 15·00

3730 — — ℞. CONSERVATORES VRB . SVAE. Roma seated facing in hexastyle temple; in ex., RQ. C. 74. R.I.C. 164 .. .. .. 7·50

3731 FL . VAL . CONSTANTINVS NOB . C. Laur., dr. and cuir. bust, r. ℞. GENIO POP . ROM. Genius stg. l.; in ex., PLN (*London*). C. 196. R.I.C. 89*b* .. .. 10·00

3732 — Laur. and cuir. bust, r. ℞. As previous, but with PTR in exergue. C. 196. R.I.C. 719*b* .. .. 6·50

3733 — Laur. and dr. bust, r. ℞. GENIO POPVLI ROMANI. Genius stg. l.; in ex., PTR. C. 218. R.I.C. 666 .. .. 6·50

3734 — Laur. and cuir. bust, r. ℞. MARTI PATRI CONSERVATORI. Mars stg. r., holding spear and leaning on shield; in ex., PTR. C. 358. R.I.C. 725 .. .. 7·50

3735 FL . VAL . CONSTANTINVS NOB . CAES. Laur. hd., r. ℞. PERPETVITAS AVGG. Roma seated l., holding Victory and spear; in ex., ALE. C. 389. R.I.C. 63 .. .. .. °.. .. .. .. 17·50

3736 — — ℞. SALVIS AVGG . ET CAESS . FEL . KART. Carthage stg. l., holding fruits in both hands; in ex., Δ. C. 479. R.I.C. 44*b* .. 12·50

3737 *Obv.* As 3729. ℞. VIRTVS AVGG . ET CAESS . NN. Mars advancing r., carrying spear and trophy; in ex., PT. C. 670. R.I.C. 70*b* .. 12·50

3738 — ℞. — Constantine galloping r., spearing kneeling enemy; in ex., AQΓ. C. 674. R.I.C. 82*b* .. .. 15·00

3739 **Æ half-follis.** FL . VAL . CONSTANTINVS N . C. Laur. and cuir. bust, r. ℞. MARTI PATRI PROPVG. Mars advancing r., holding spear and shield; in ex., PTR. C.—. R.I.C. 741 .. .. 6·50

3740 **Æ post-reform radiate.** FL . VAL . CONSTANTINVS NOB . CAES. Rad. and dr. bust, r. ℞. CONCORDIA MILITVM. Jupiter stg. r., presenting Victory on globe to Constantine stg. l.; in ex., ALE. C. 68. R.I.C. 85 .. 10·00

3741 **Æ denarius.** *Obv.* As 3739. ℞. VOTIS X. in laurel-wreath. C. 748. R.I.C. 750 .. .. 10·00

Very Fine

3742   **Æ quinarius.** CONSTANTINVS N . C. Laur. hd., r. ℞. VOT . X . CAESS . in laurel-wreath. *C.—. R.I.C.* 748   ..   ..   £7·50

As Filius Augustorum, A.D. 308-309

3743   **N aureus.** CONSTANTINVS FIL . AVGG. Laur. hd., r. ℞. CONSVL DD . NN. Constantine stg. l., holding globe and sceptre; in ex., · SM · TS·. *C.* 115. *R.I.C.* 28   ..   ..   *Very rare*

3744   **Æ follis.** FL . VAL . CONSTANTINVS FIL . AVG. Laur. hd., r. ℞. GENIO CAESARIS. Genius stg. l.; in ex., ALE. *C.* 185. *R.I.C.* 99*b*   ..   10·00

As Augustus

3745   **N aureus.** CONSTANTINVS P . F . AVG. Laur. hd., r. ℞. VICTOR OMNIVM GENTIVM. Constantine stg. l. amidst three captives, holding standard and leaning on shield; in ex., PTR. *C.* 574. *R.I.C.* 818   ..   250·00

3746   **N solidus.** CONSTANTINVS MAX . AVG. Diad. and dr. bust, r. ℞. CONSTANTINVS AVG. Victory advancing l., holding wreath and palm; in ex., CONS. *C.* 98. *R.I.C.* 46. **Plate 11**   ..   ..   150·00
There are larger gold, 1½, 2, 3, 4½ and 9 *solidi.*

3747   **N quinarius.** IMP . CONSTANTINVS P . F . AVG. Laur. and cuir. bust, r. ℞. PRINCIPI IVVENTVTIS. Constantine stg. r., holding spear and globe; in ex., PTR. *C.* 413. *R.I.C.* 822 ..   ..   200·00

3748   **N semissis.** IMP . CONSTANTINVS AVG. Laur. and cuir. bust, r. ℞. VBIQVE VICTORES. As previous, but Constantine stands between two captives; in ex., TR. *R.I.C.* 195   ..   ..   175·00

3749   **N 1½ scripulum.** *Obv.* As 3746. ℞. VICTORIA CONSTANTINI AVG. Victory seated r., inscribing VOT . XXX. on shield held by Genius; in ex., CONS. *C.* 616. *R.I.C.* 117..   ..   ..   125·00

3749A   **R 3 miliarensia.** (*c.* 13·5 gm.) AVGVSTVS. Diad. hd., r. ℞. CAESAR in laurel-wreath; in ex., SIS. *R.I.C.* 259 ..   ..   ..   *Very rare*

3750   **R heavy miliarense.** (*c.* 5·4 gm.) *Obv.* No legend. Diad. hd., r. ℞. CONSTANTINVS AVG. Four standards; in ex., CONS. *C.* 106. *R.I.C.* 99   ..   ..   200·00

3752   **R miliarense.** (*c.* 4·5 gm.) CONSTANTINVS MAX . AVG. Diad. and cuir. bust, r. ℞. FELICITAS ROMANORVM. Semicircular arch resting on two columns beneath which stands Constantine l. between two of his sons; in ex., SMH. *C.* 149. *R.I.C.* 105   ..   ..   ..   300·00

3753   **R siliqua.** (*c.* 3·4 gm.) *Obv.* No legend. Diad. hd., r. ℞. CONSTANTINVS AVG. Victory advancing l.; in ex., SIS. *C.* 97. *R.I.C.* 229   ..   ..   85·00

3754   **R half-argenteus.** *Obv.* As 3747. ℞. VIRTVS MILITVM. Camp-gate, surmounted by four turrets; in ex., TR. *C.* 708. *R.I.C.* 758   ..   45·00

The following are the commonest forms of obv. legend on the bronze coins:—
    A.   CONSTANTINVS AVG.
    B.   CONSTANTINVS P . F . AVG.
    C.   CONSTANTINVS MAX . AVG.
    D.   IMP . CONSTANTINVS P . F . AVG.

The obv. type is laur. hd. r. or laur., dr. and/or cuir. bust r., unless otherwise stated.

3755   **Æ follis** (declining from *c.* 26 mm. to *c.* 20 mm.) B.   ℞. ADVENTVS AVG. Constantine on horseback l.; in ex., PLN (*London*). *C.* 3. *R.I.C.* 133   ..   ..   6·50

3756 **Æ follis.** B. Helmeted and cuir. bust l., holding spear and shield.
R. COMITI AVGG . NN. Sol stg. l., holding globe and whip; in ex., PLN
(*London*). *C*. 45. *R.I.C.* 165A ..   £5·00

3757 B. R. CONSERVATORES VRB . SVAE. Roma seated facing in hexastyle
temple; in ex., R*Q. *C*. 75. *R.I.C.* 197 ..   4·50

3758 IMP . C . CONSTANTINVS P . F . AVG. R. CONSTANTINO P . AVG . B . RP .
NAT. Constantine stg. l., holding globe and sceptre; in ex., PLG. *C*. 93.
R.I.C. 252 ..   10·00

3759 B. R. FELICITAS AVGG . NN. Felicity (?) seated l., holding branch and
globe; in ex., PLN (*London*). *C*. 144. *R.I.C.* 246 ..   7·50

3760 FL . VALER . CONSTANTINVS P . F . AVG. R. GENIO AVGVSTI. Genius
stg. l., holding hd. of Serapis and cornucopiae; in ex., ALE. *C*. 172.
R.I.C. 161 ..   2·25

3761 D. R. GENIO POP . ROM. Genius stg. l.; in ex., PTR. *C*. 199. *R.I.C.*
770 ..   2·00

3762 D. R. IOVI CONSERVATORI AVGG . NN. Jupiter stg. l., eagle at feet;
in ex., SIS. *C*. 312. *R.I.C.* 232b ..   2·00

3763 B. R. MARTI CONSERVATORI. Helmeted and cuir. bust of Mars r.;
no mintmark (attributed to Treveri). *C*. 325. *R.I.C.* 884 ..   4·50

3764 D. R. MARTI PATRI PROPVGNATORI. Mars advancing r., holding
spear and shield; in ex., PTR. *C*. 368. *R.I.C.* 775 ..   3·00

3765 D. R. PRINCIPI IVVENTVTIS. Constantine stg. r., holding spear and
globe; in ex., PLG. *C*. 417. *R.I.C.* 305 ..   3·50

3766 B. R. SECVRITAS AVGG. Security stg. l., leaning on column; in ex.,
PLN (*London*). *C*. 491. *R.I.C.* 277 ..   7·50

3767 B. R. SOLI INVICTO COMITI. Rad. and dr. bust of Sol r.; no mint-
mark (attributed to Treveri). *C*. 514. *R.I.C.* 893 ..   4·00

3768 D. R. — Sol stg. l., holding globe; in ex., PLG. *C*. 536. *R.I.C.* 307   2·00

3769 D. R. S . P . Q . R . OPTIMO PRINCIPI. Legionary eagle between
two standards; in ex., RP. *C*. 558. *R.I.C.* 348a ..   3·50

3770 **Æ 3.** (*c*. 18-20 mm.) A. Laur. bust r., wearing imperial mantle and
holding eagle-tipped sceptre. R. BEATA TRANQVILLITAS. Altar
inscribed VOTIS XX; in ex., . STR . *C*. 17. *R.I.C.* 369 ..   1·50

3771 CONSTANTINVS AG. Helmeted and cuir. bust, r. R. BEAT . TRAN-
QLITAS. Altar inscribed VOTIS XX; in ex., PLON (*London*). *C*.—. *R.I.C.*
268 ..   2·50

3772 *Obv.* No legend. Laur. hd. r. R. CONSTAN / TINVS / AVG. in three
lines; above, wreath; beneath, SMANTΓ. *C*. 110. *R.I.C.* 52 ..   4·50

3773 A. R. D . N . CONSTANTINI MAX . AVG. Laurel-wreath around VOT .
XX; in ex., ASIS. *C*. 123. *R.I.C.* 148 ..   1·25

3774 A. R. As previous, but with VOT . XXX; in ex., TT. *C*. 132. *R.I.C.*
174 ..   1·50

3775 C. Diad. hd., r. R. GLORIA EXERCITVS. Constantine stg. r., holding
spear and leaning on shield; in ex., CONS. *C*. 243. *R.I.C.* 22 ..   2·50

3776 IMP . CONSTANTINVS AVG. Laur. bust l., wearing imperial mantle and
holding mappa, globe and sceptre. R. IOVI CONSERVATORI AVGG.
Jupiter stg. l.; in ex., SMANT. *C*. 306. *R.I.C.* 26 ..   1·50

3777 C. Diad. hd., r. R. LIBERTAS PVBLICA. Victory stg. facing on
galley, holding wreath in each hand; in ex., CONS. *C*. 319. *R.I.C.* 25   5·00

3778 A. R. PROVIDENTIAE AVGG. Camp-gate surmounted by two turrets;
in ex., SMTSA. *C*. 454. *R.I.C.* 153 ..   1·25

3779 A. Helmeted and cuir. bust, r. R. ROMAE AETERNAE. Roma seated
r., inscribing XV on shield set on knees; in ex., RQ. *C*. 470. *R.I.C.* 146   2·00

Very Fine

3780 **Æ 3.** A. ℞. SARMATIA DEVICTA. Victory advancing r., captive at feet; in ex., STR. *C.* 487. *R.I.C.* 429 .. .. £2·25

3781 D. ℞. SOLI INVICTO COMITI. Sol stg. l., holding globe; in ex., RS. *C.* 536. *R.I.C.* 2 .. .. 1·25

3782 IMP . CONSTANTINVS AVG. Helmeted and cuir. bust l., holding spear and shield. ℞. As previous, but with PLN (*London*) in exergue. *C.* 532. *R.I.C.* 11. **Plate 11** .. .. 3·75

3783 A. Helmeted and cuir. bust, r. ℞. VICTORIAE LAETAE PRINC . PERP. Two Victories resting shield, inscribed VOT . P . R., on altar; in ex., PLN (*London*). *C.* 633. *R.I.C.* 173 .. .. 3·75

3784 A. Diad. hd., r. ℞. VIRTVS AVGG. Camp-gate, with open doors, surmounted by four turrets; in ex., ARLS. *C.* 665. *R.I.C.* 314 .. 1·50

3785 A. Helmeted and cuir. bust, r. ℞. VIRTVS EXERCIT. Two captives seated at foot of standard inscribed VOT . XX.; in ex., AQP. *C.* 690. *R.I.C.* 48 .. .. 1·75

3786 **Æ 3/4.** (*c.* 17 mm.) C. Diad., dr. and cuir. bust, r. ℞. GLORIA EXERCITVS. Two soldiers stg. either side of two standards; in ex., TRS. *C.* 254. *R.I.C.* 518 .. .. 1·00

3787 C. Diad. and dr. bust, r. ℞. As previous, but only one standard; in ex., SMALA. *C.* 250. *R.I.C.* 65 .. .. 1·00

Commemorative Coins struck after his death

3788 **Æ 4.** DV . CONSTANTINVS PT . AVGG. Veiled hd., r. ℞. VN . MR . Constantine, veiled, stg. r.; in ex., SMALB. *C.* 716 .. .. .. 1·75

3789 — — ℞. No legend. Constantine in quadriga galloping r.; above, hand of God; in ex., CONS. *C.* 760 .. .. 1·75

COMMEMORATIVE ISSUES OF THE PERIOD A.D. 330-346

3790 *Constantinopolis.* **Æ 3/4.** (*c.* 17 mm.) CONSTANTINOPOLIS. Helmeted bust of Constantinopolis l., wearing imperial mantle and holding sceptre. ℞. No legend. Victory stg. l., r. foot on prow, holding sceptre and leaning on shield; in ex., TRS*. *C.* 21. *R.I.C.* 548 .. .. .. 1·00

3791 **Æ 4.** — — ℞. GLORIA EXERCITVS. Two soldiers stg. either side of standard; in ex., SMHΓ. *C.* 4. *R.I.C.* 157 .. .. 4·50

3792 CONSTANTINOPOLI. — ℞. VOT. / XX. / MVLT. / XXX. in four lines within wreath; in ex., SMKS. *C.* 20 .. .. 6·00

3793 As 3790, but with SMALB in exergue. *C.* 22. *R.I.C.* 71 .. .. 2·25

3794 *Roma.* **Æ 3/4.** (*c.* 17 mm.) VRBS ROMA. Helmeted bust of Roma l., wearing imperial mantle. ℞. No legend. She-wolf stg. l., suckling Romulus and Remus; in ex., SMTSE. *C.* 17. *R.I.C.* 187 .. 1·25

3795 **Æ 4.** — — ℞. As 3791, but with SMHA in exergue. *C.* 1. *R.I.C.* 156 5·00

3796 ROMA. Helmeted and dr. bust of Roma r. ℞. P . R. Soldier stg. r., holding spear and leaning on shield. *C.* 4 .. .. 6·00

3797 *Obv.* As 3794. ℞. As 3792, but with SMNB in exergue. *Cf. C.* 10 .. 6·00

3798 As 3794, but with SMALA in exergue. *C.* 19. *R.I.C.* 70 .. .. 2·50

3799 VRBS ROMA BEATA. Helmeted bust of Roma l., wearing imperial mantle. ℞. As 3794, but with R branch Q in exergue. *C.*—. *R.I.C.* 408 .. 5·00

Very Fine

3800   *Pop. Romanus.* **Æ 4.** POP . ROMANVS. Laur. and dr. bust of the
Roman People l., cornucopiae over l. shoulder. R. No legend.
Bridge with tower at each end and river beneath; between towers, CONS /
A. *C.* 1   ..   ..   £4·00

3801   — — R. Star and CONSS in wreath. *C.* 2   ..   ..   4·00

FAUSTA
*Daughter of Maximianus and wife of
Constantine*

3802

Mints: London; Treveri; Lugdunum; Arelate; Ticinum; Rome; Siscia; Sirmium;
Thessalonica; Heraclea; Constantinople; Nicomedia; Cyzicus; Antioch; Alexandria.

3802   **N solidus.** FLAV . MAX . FAVSTA AVG. Dr. bust, r. R. SALVS
REIPVBLICAE. Fausta stg. facing, hd. l., holding Constantine II and
Constantius II; in ex., P◡T. *C.* 5. *R.I.C.* 182 *var.* *Illustrated above Very rare*

There is also a *double solidus.*

3802A **R half-argenteus.** FAVSTAE NOBILISSIMAE FEMINAE. Dr. bust, l.
R. VENVS FELIX. Venus seated l., holding globe and palm; in ex.,
TR. *C.* 22. *R.I.C.* 756   ..   ..   *Very rare*

3803   **Æ 3.** (*c.* 19 mm.). As 3802, but with STR in exergue. *C.* 6. *R.I.C.*
459   ..   ..   4·50

3804   As previous, but with PLON (*London*) in exergue. *C.* 6. *R.I.C.* 300 ..   15·00

3805   *Obv.* As previous. R. SPES REIPVBLICAE. As 3802, but with SMALA
in exergue. *C.* 15. *R.I.C.* 40   ..   ..   4·50

3806   FAVSTA N . F. Dr. bust, r. R. Star in wreath. *C.* 25. *R.I.C.* 51   50·00

HELENA
*First wife of Constantius and mother of
Constantine*

3808

Mints: London; Treveri; Lugdunum; Arelate; Ticinum; Rome; Siscia; Sirmium;
Thessalonica; Heraclea; Constantinople; Nicomedia; Cyzicus; Antioch; Alexandria.

Very Fine

3807   *N* **solidus.** FL . HELENA AVGVSTA. Diad. and dr. bust, r. R.
SECVRITAS REIPVBLICE. Helena stg. l., holding branch; in ex., SMT.
C. 11.   *R.I.C.* 183 ..   ..   *Very rare*
There is also a *double solidus.*

3808   **Æ 3.** (*c.* 19 mm.).   As previous, but with SMANTB in exergue. *C.* 12.
R.I.C. 80.   **Plate 11** *and illustrated on p.* 317 ..   ..   £3·75

3809   HELENA N . F.   Dr. bust, r.   R.   Star in wreath.   *C.* 14.   *R.I.C.* 50   50·00

Commemorative Coins struck after her death

Struck under Constantine II, Constantius II and Constans, A.D. 337-340

3810   **Æ 4.** FL . IVL . HELENAE AVG. Diad. and dr. bust, r. R. PAX
PVBLICA. Pax stg. l.; in ex., TRP.   *C.* 4 ..   ..   2·50

THEODORA

Step-daughter of Maximianus and second wife of Constantius I

Commemorative Coins struck after her death

Struck under Constantine II, Constantius II and Constans, A.D. 337-340

3811   **Æ 4.** FL . MAX . THEODORAE AVG. Diad. and dr. bust, r. R. PIETAS
ROMANA. Pietas stg. r., holding child in arms; in ex., CONSЄ.   *C.* 4 ..   2·50

CRISPUS

Caesar, A.D. 317 – 326

3812

Mints: London; Treveri; Lugdunum; Arelate; Ticinum; Aquileia; Rome; Siscia;
Sirmium; Thessalonica; Heraclea; Constantinople; Nicomedia; Cyzicus; Antioch;
Alexandria.

3812   *N* **solidus.** *Obv.* No legend. Diad. hd., r.   R.   CRISPVS CAESAR.
Victory advancing l.; in ex., SIRM.   *C.* 59.   *R.I.C.* 63.   *Illustrated above*   400·00

3813   *N* **semissis** or **1½ scripulum.** CRISPVS NOB . CAES. Laur., dr. and cuir.
bust, r.   R.   PRINCIPI IVVENTVTIS. Crispus stg. r., holding spear and
globe; in ex., PTR.   *C.* 89.   *R.I.C.*—, *but see p.* 179, 199 *note* ..   *Extr. rare*

3813A   **Æ heavy miliarense.** (*c.* 5.4 gm.)   FL . IVL . CRISPVS NOB . C.   Rad.,
dr. and cuir. bust l., raising r. hand and holding globe in l.   R.   VOTA
ORBIS ET VRBIS SEN. ET P.R.   Flaming cippus, on square basis, inscribed
XX / XXX / MVL / FEL.; in field, L; in ex., AQ.   *C.*—.   *R.I.C.* 81   *Extr. rare*

The following coins, Nos. 3814-3828, *have obv. legend* CRISPVS NOB . CAES., *unless
otherwise stated.*

3814   **Æ 3.** (*c.* 19 mm.)   FL . IVL . CRISPVS NOB . CAES. Laur. hd., r.   R.
ALAMANNIA DEVICTA. Victory advancing r., l. foot on captive; in ex.,
. SIRM .   *C.* 1.   *R.I.C.* 49 ..   ..   5·00

Very Fine

3815 Æ 3. Laur. hd., r. ℞. BEATA TRANQVILLITAS. Altar inscribed VOTIS
XX.; in ex., PLG. *C.* 5. *R.I.C.* 166 .. .. £1·75

3816 CRISPVS NOBIL . C. Helmeted and cuir. bust, l. ℞. BEAT . TRANQLITAS.
Altar inscribed VOTIS XX.; in ex., PLON (*London.*) *C.* 29. *R.I.C.* 247 3·25

3817 Laur. hd., r. ℞. CAESARVM NOSTRORVM. Laurel-wreath around
VOT . V.; in ex., AQT. *C.* 30. *R.I.C.* 68 .. .. 1·75

3818 IVL . CRISPVS NOB . C. Laur. hd., r. ℞. As previous, but VOT . X.;
in ex., STR⌣. *C.* 44. *R.I.C.* 440. **Plate 11** .. .. 1·75

3819 *Obv.* No legend. Laur., dr. and cuir. bust, l. ℞. CRISPVS / CAESAR
in two lines; above, star; beneath, SMANTE. *C.* 60. *R.I.C.* 53 .. 4·50

3820 D . N . FL . IVL . CRISPVS NOB . CAES. Laur. bust l., wearing imperial
mantle and holding mappa, globe and sceptre. ℞. IOVI CONSERVATORI
CAESS. Jupiter stg. l.; in ex., SMAL. *C.* 79. *R.I.C.* 24 .. 2·50

3821 Laur., dr. and cuir. bust, r. ℞. PRINCIPIA IVVENTVTIS. Mars
advancing r., holding spear and shield; in ex., QARL. *C.* 99. *R.I.C.* 130 2·00

3822 CRISPVS NOBIL . CAES. Bare-headed and cuir. bust, r. ℞. — Crispus
stg. r., holding spear and leaning on shield; in ex., RP. *C.* 107. *R.I.C.*
89 .. .. 2·00

3823 *Obv.* As 3820. ℞. PROVIDENTIAE CAESS. Camp-gate surmounted by
three turrets; in ex., MHTΓ. *C.* 115. *R.I.C.* 18 .. .. .. 2·50

3824 FL . IVL . CRISPVS NOB . CAES. Laur., dr. and cuir. bust, r. ℞. As
previous, but two turrets; in ex., PLON (*London*). *C.* 124. *R.I.C.* 295 3·25

3825 Laur. and cuir. bust, r. ℞. SOLI INVICTO COMITI. Sol stg. l., holding
globe; in ex., PLN (*London*). *C.* 136. *R.I.C.* 115 .. .. 3·75

3826 FL . IVL . CRISPVS NOB . C. Rad. and cuir. bust, r. ℞. VICTORIAE
LAETAE PRINC . PERP. Two Victories resting shield, inscribed VOT . P . R.,
on altar; in ex., TT. *C.* 154. *R.I.C.* 93 .. .. 2·25

3827 IVL . CRISPVS NOB . CAES. Laur. and cuir. bust l., holding spear and
shield. ℞. VIRTVS EXERCIT. Two captives seated at foot of standard
inscribed VOT . X; in ex., BSIS*. *C.* 166. *R.I.C.* 123. **Plate 11** .. 2·00

3828 CRISPVS NOBILISS . CAES. Laur., dr. and cuir. bust, r. ℞. VOT . V . /
MVLT . X . / CAESS . / . TS . Є. in four lines within wreath. *C.* 190.
R.I.C. 38 .. .. 5·00

DELMATIUS
Caesar, A.D. 335 – 337

3829

Mints: Treveri; Lugdunum; Arelate; Aquileia; Rome; Siscia; Thessalonica;
Heraclea; Constantinople; Nicomedia; Cyzicus; Antioch; Alexandria.

3829 *N* **solidus.** FL . DELMATIVS NOB . CAES. Diad., dr. and cuir. bust, r.
℞. PRINCIPI IVVENTVTIS. Delmatius stg. l., holding standard and
sceptre; to r., two standards; in ex., TSЄ. *C.* 15. *R.I.C.* 213. *Illustrated above* .. .. 1000·00

3830 Æ **siliqua.** (*c.* 3·4 gm.). *Obv.* No legend. Diad. hd., r. ℞.
DELMATIVS CAESAR. Victory advancing l.; in ex., SMN. *C.* 3. *R.I.C.*
186. *Illustrated on p. 14* .. .. 400·00

Very Fine

3831 Æ 3/4. (*c.* 17 mm.) FL . DELMATIVS NOB . C. Laur. and cuir. bust, r.
℞. GLORIA EXERCITVS. Two soldiers stg. either side of standard; in
ex., SMALB. *C.* 4. *R.I.C.* 69 .. .. £12·50

3832 FL . IVL . DELMATIVS NOB . C. Laur. and dr. bust, r. ℞. As previous,
but with SMKA in exergue. *C.* 8. *R.I.C.* 132 .. .. 12·50

3833 *Obv.* As 3831. ℞. GLORIA EXERCITVS. Two soldiers stg. either side
of two standards; in ex., SMANI. *C.* 12. *R.I.C.* 90 .. .. .. 12·50

HANNIBALLIANUS
Rex, A.D. 335 – 337

3835

Mint: Constantinople.

3834 Æ siliqua. (*c.* 3.4 gm.) FL . ANNIBALIANO REGI. Bare-headed, dr.
and cuir. bust, r. ℞. FELICITAS PVBLICA. The Euphrates reclining l.,
holding fish and rudder; in ex., CONS. *C.* 1. *R.I.C.* 100 .. .. 750·00

3835 Æ 4. (*c.* 16 mm.) FL . HANNIBALLIANO REGI. — ℞. SECVRITAS
PVBLICA. The Euphrates reclining r., holding sceptre; in ex., CONSS.
C. 2. *R.I.C.* 147. *Illustrated above* .. .. 45·00

CONSTANTINE II
A.D. 337 – 340

3838

(*Flavius Claudius Constantinus*) *The eldest son of Constantine I and Fausta, Constantine
II was born in* A.D. 314. *He was created Caesar in 317, and at the age of eighteen he
distinguished himself in a campaign against the Goths. On the division of the Empire
following the death of Constantine I, he received Spain, Gaul and Britain as his sphere of
government. However, he soon quarrelled with his younger brother, Constans, over the
division of the territories, and early in 340 he crossed the Alps and invaded Italy, only to be
killed in an ambush near Aquileia.*

As Caesar, A.D. 317-337

3836 N solidus. CONSTANTINVS IVN . NOB . C. Diad., dr. and cuir. bust, r.
℞. PRINCIPI IVVENTVTIS. Constantine II stg. l., holding standard and
sceptre; to r., two standards; in ex., TS. *C.* 150. *R.I.C.* 190 .. .. 200·00
There are larger gold, 1½, 2, 3, 4½ and 9 *solidi.*

3837 N semissis. — Laur. and cuir. bust, r. ℞. VICTORIA CONSTANTINI
CAES. Victory seated r., inscribing VOT . XX. on shield set on knee; in
ex., CONS. *C.* 210. *R.I.C.* 120 .. .. 250·00

Very Fine

3837A Æ 3 miliarensia. (c. 13.5 gm.) CAESAR. Bare hd., r. ℞. xx in
laurel-wreath; in ex., CONST. *R.I.C.* 411 .. .. .. *Very rare*

3837B Æ heavy miliarense. (c. 5.4 gm.) CONSTANTINVS IVN . NOB . C.
Rad., dr. and cuir. bust l., raising r. hand and holding globe in l. ℞.
VOTA ORBIS ET VRBIS SEN . ET P.R. Cippus, on square basis, inscribed
XX / XXX / AVG.; in field, two stars; in ex., AQS. C. —. *R.I.C.* 84 .. *Extr. rare*

3838 Æ miliarense. (c. 4.5 gm.) *Obv.* As 3837. ℞. GLORIA EXERCITVS.
Female stg. facing, hd. l., holding branch and sceptre and leaning on
column; in ex., C . Є. C. 112. *R.I.C.* 133. *Illustrated on p.* 320 .. £225·00

3839 Æ siliqua. (c. 3.4 gm.) *Obv.* No legend. Diad. hd., r. ℞.
CONSTANTINVS CAESAR. Victory advancing l.; in ex., R. C. 76. *R.I.C.*
378 .. .. 90·00

There are two main varieties of obv. legend on the bronze coins:

A. CONSTANTINVS IVN . N . C.
B. CONSTANTINVS IVN . NOB . C.

The obv. type is laur. hd. r., or laur., dr. and/or cuir. bust r., unless otherwise stated.

3840 Æ 3. (c. 19 mm.) CONSTANTINVS IVN . NOB . CAES. ℞. ALAMANNIA
DEVICTA. Victory advancing r., l. foot on captive; in ex., SIRM ..
C. 1. *R.I.C.* 50 .. .. 5·00

3841 A. Helmeted and cuir. bust, l. ℞. BEAT . TRANQLITAS. Altar
inscribed VOTIS XX.; in ex., PLON (*London*). C. 10. *R.I.C.* 258 .. .. 3·00

3841A A. Laur. and cuir. bust l., holding globe surmounted by Victory. ℞.
As previous. C. —. *R.I.C.* 288. **Plate 11** .. .. .. 3·75

3842 B. As previous. ℞. BEATA TRANQVILLITAS. Altar inscribed VOTIS
XX.; in ex., PTR. C. 23. *R.I.C.* 312 .. .. 1·50

3843 B. ℞. CAESARVM NOSTRORVM. Laurel-wreath around VOT . X.; in ex.,
ASIS*. C. 38. *R.I.C.* 167 .. .. 1·50

3844 FL . CL . CONSTANTINVS IVN . N . C. ℞. CLARITAS REIPVBLICAE. Sol
stg. l., holding globe; in ex., BTR. C. 53. *R.I.C.* 148 .. .. 2·00

3845 *Obv.* No legend. Laur., dr. and cuir. bust, l. ℞. CONSTAN / TINVS /
CAESAR in three lines; above, star; beneath, SMANTA. C. 83. *R.I.C.* 54 4·50

3846 D . N . FL . CL . CONSTANTINVS NOB . C. ℞. PROVIDENTIAE CAESS.
Jupiter stg. l.; in ex., SMN. C. 161. *R.I.C.* 36 .. .. .. 2·50

3847 — Laur. bust l., wearing imperial mantle and holding mappa, globe and
sceptre. ℞. — Camp-gate surmounted by three turrets; in ex.,
MHTЄ. C. 167. *R.I.C.* 20 .. .. 2·00

3848 B. ℞. — Camp-gate surmounted by two turrets; in ex., PLON
(*London*). C. 164. *R.I.C.* 296 .. .. 3·00

3849 FL . CL . CONSTANTINVS IVN . N . C. ℞. SOLI INVICTO COMITI. Sol. stg.
l., holding globe; in ex., PLN (*London*). C. 185. *R.I.C.* 145 .. .. 3·75

3850 A. Rad., dr. and cuir. bust, l. ℞. VIRTVS EXERCIT. Two captives
seated at foot of trophy; in ex., . PTR. C. 262. *R.I.C.* 253 .. .. 1·75

3851 Æ 3/4. (c. 17 mm.) B. ℞. GLORIA EXERCITVS. Two soldiers stg.
either side of two standards; in ex., RFS. C. 122. *R.I.C.* 328 .. .. 1·00

3852 B. ℞. As previous, but only one standard; in ex., SMALB. C. 114.
R.I.C. 66 .. .. 1·00

As Augustus

Mints: Treveri; Lugdunum; Arelate; Aquileia; Rome; Siscia; Thessalonica;
Heraclea; Constantinople; Nicomedia; Cyzicus; Antioch; Alexandria.

Very Fine

3853 **N solidus.** FL . CL . CONSTANTINVS P . F . AVG. Diad., dr. and cuir. bust, r. ℞. VICTORIA DD . NN . AVGG. Victory advancing l.; in ex., TES. *C.* 212 .. .. £250·00
There are larger gold, 1½ and 2 *solidi*.

3854 **Æ siliqua.** (*c.* 3.4 gm.) *Obv.* No legend. Diad. hd., r. ℞. CONSTANTINVS AVG. Victory advancing l.; in ex., SMN. *C.* 66 .. .. 75·00

3855 **Æ 4.** CONSTANTINVS IVN . AVG. Laur. and cuir. bust, r. ℞. GLORIA EXERCITVS. Two soldiers stg. either side of labarum; in ex., SLG. *C.* 121 6·00

3856 VIC . CONSTANTINVS AVG. — ℞. As previous, but standard instead of labarum; in ex., R*P. *C.* 118 .. .. 4·00

3857 — — ℞. VIRTVS AVGVSTI. Constantine II stg. r., holding spear and leaning on shield; in ex., R*T. *C.* 233 .. .. 4·50

CONSTANS
A.D. 337 – 350

3873

Flavius Julius Constans, the youngest son of Constantine I and Fausta, was born about A.D. 320 *and was raised to the rank of Caesar in 333. On the division of the Empire he received Italy, Africa and the Balkans, though he later surrendered Thrace and Constantinople to his brother Constantius* (A.D. 339). *In* 340 *his brother, Constantine, invaded his territories but was defeated and killed, thus leaving Constans master of the western half of the Empire. During the following decade he campaigned against the barbarians with considerable success, and in* 343 *he visited Britain, the last reigning monarch to do so, in order to repel the Picts and Scots. In* A.D. 350, *however, whilst on a hunting expedition in Gaul, he received word that Magnentius had rebelled at Augustodunum (Autun) and that the legions had joined the revolt. Constans thereupon fled in the direction of Spain, but was overtaken and murdered near the fortress of Helene at the foot of the Pyrenees.*

In A.D. 346 *Constantius II and Constans carried out a reform of the bronze coinage. The Æ* 4 *denomination was discontinued and a piece of Æ* 2 *module (c. 23 mm.) was introduced. The name of this new denomination was probably* centenionalis *and at first it always bore the reverse legend* FEL . TEMP . REPARATIO.

As Caesar, A.D. 333-337

3858 **N solidus.** FL . IVL . CONSTANS NOB . CAES. Laur., dr. and cuir. bust, r. ℞. PRINCIPI IVVENTVTIS. Constans stg. l., holding standard and sceptre; to r., two standards; in ex., TR. *C.* 93. *R.I.C.* 575 .. .. 100·00
There are larger gold, 2 and 4½ *solidi*.

3859 **Æ miliarense.** (*c.* 4.5 gm.) — — ℞. CONSTANS CAESAR. Four standards; in ex., SMTR. *C.* 5. *R.I.C.* 585 .. .. 120·00

3860 **Æ siliqua.** (*c.* 3.4 gm.) *Obv.* No legend. Diad. hd., r. ℞. CONSTANS CAESAR. Victory advancing l.; in ex., SMAN. *C.* 4. *R.I.C.* 107 65·00

3861 **Æ 3/4.** (*c.* 17 mm.) FL . IVL . CONSTANS NOB . C. Laur. and cuir. bust, r. ℞. GLORIA EXERCITVS. Two soldiers stg. either side of two standards; in ex., SMANH. *C.* 75. *R.I.C.* 89 .. .. 1·75

3862 FL . CONSTANS NOB . CAES. Laur., dr. and cuir. bust, l. ℞. As previous, but only one standard; in ex., CONSIA. *Cf. C.* 47. *R.I.C.* 140 2·25

As Augustus

Mints: Treveri; Ludgunum; Arelate; Aquileia; Rome; Siscia; Thessalonica; Heraclea; Constantinople; Nicomedia; Cyzicus; Antioch; Alexandria.

Very Fine

3863 N **solidus.** CONSTANS AVGVSTVS. Diad., dr. and cuir. bust, r. ℞.
VICTORIAE DD . NN . AVGG. Two Victories holding wreath within which
is VOT . X . MVLT . XX; in ex., TES. *C.* 171 .. .. £85·00
There are larger gold, 1½, 2, 3, 4½ and 9 *solidi.*

3864 N **semissis.** CONSTANS P . F . AVG. Diad. and dr. bust, r.; all within
wreath. ℞. As previous, but VOT . XX . MVLT . XXX; in ex., branch SIS*.
C. 175 .. .. 80·00

3865 N **1½ scripulum.** FL . IVL . CONSTANS P . F . AVG. Diad. and dr. bust, r.
℞. FELICITAS PERPETVA. Victory advancing l.; in ex., SMAQ. *C.* 25.. 100·00

3866 ℞ **3 miliarensia.** (*c.* 13.5 gm.) — Diad., dr. and cuir. bust, r. ℞.
TRIVMFATOR GENTIVM BARBARARVM. Constans stg. l., holding labarum
and sceptre; in ex., · SIS ·. *C.* 112 *Very rare*

3867 ℞ **heavy miliarense.** (*c.* 5.4 gm.) — — ℞. VICTORIAE DD . NN . AVGG.
Victory seated r., inscribing VOT . X . MVLT . XV. on shield set on knee;
in ex., *AQ. *C.* 163 .. .. 150·00

3868 ℞ **miliarense.** (*c.* 4.5 gm.) — — ℞. GAVDIVM POPVLI ROMANI.
Laurel-wreath around SIC V. SIC X.; in ex., SIS. *C.* 35 .. .. .. 120·00

3869 ℞ **siliqua.** (*c.* 3.4 gm.) *Obv.* As 3864, but without wreath. ℞.
VICTORIA DD . NN . AVGG. Victory advancing l.; in ex., TES. *C.* 156 .. 35·00

Pre-reform bronze coinage, A.D. 337-346

3870 Æ **4.** CONSTANS AVG. Diad. and dr. bust, r. ℞. GLORIA EXERCITVS.
Two soldiers stg. either side of standard; in ex., SMANI. *C.* 53 .. 1·00

3871 CONSTANS P . F . AVG. — ℞. VICTORIAE DD . AVGG . Q . NN. Two
Victories stg. facing each other; in ex., TRS. *C.* 179 .. .. .. 1·00

3872 D . N . CONSTANS . P . F . AVG. Diad. hd., r. ℞. VOT. / XV. / MVLT. / XX.
in laurel-wreath; in ex., SMANϴ. *C.* 196 .. .. 1·25

Post-reform bronze coinage, A.D. 346-350

The obv. legend is D . N . CONSTANS P . F . AVG.

3873 Æ **centenionalis.** Diad., dr. and cuir. bust, r. ℞. FEL . TEMP .
REPARATIO. Constans stg. l. on galley, holding phoenix and labarum;
in ex., RP. *C.* 9. *Illustrated on p. 322* .. .. 2·50

3874 — ℞. As previous, but Victory instead of phoenix; in ex., TRP. *C.* 13 2·50

3875 Diad., dr. and cuir. bust l., holding globe. ℞. FEL . TEMP . REPARATIO.
Constans stg. l., holding labarum, two captives at feet; in ex., ALEA.
C. 14 .. .. 2·50

<table>
<tbody>
<tr><td></td><td></td><td></td><td></td><td style="text-align:right">Very Fine</td></tr>
</tbody>
</table>

3876 **Æ centenionalis.** ℞. — Soldier advancing r., dragging young barbarian from hut beneath tree; in ex., SLG. *C.* 19 .. .. .. £2·50

3877 **Æ ½ centenionalis.** Diad. and dr. bust, r. ℞. — Phoenix stg. r. on globe; in ex., TRP. *C.* 21 .. .. 3·25

3878 — ℞. — Phoenix stg. r. on pyre; in ex., ΓSIS. *C.* 22 .. .. .. 3·25

CONSTANTIUS II
A.D. 337 – 361

3881

(*Flavius Julius Constantius*).   *The second son of Constantine I and Fausta, Constantius II was born in* A.D. *317 and was given the rank of Caesar in 324, soon after the defeat of Licinius.   On the division of the Empire he received all the eastern territories from Asia Minor to Cyrenaica, and two years later (339) he also acquired Thrace.   Following the death of Constans in 350, he marched against Magnentius, who was now recognized by most of the western provinces, and despite some initial reverses he gained a decisive victory over the usurper in September,* A.D. *351.   Magnentius was finally destroyed in 353, and Constantius spent the next few years campaigning on the Danube frontier.   War with Persia, however, necessitated his return to the East in 359, but early in the following year he received news that his cousin Julian had been proclaimed Augustus at Paris by his troops.   After some delay, due to the Persian War, Constantius set out for the West, but whilst advancing through Cilicia he was attacked by fever and died at Mopsucrene on November 3rd, 361, thus leaving Julian master of the Roman world.*

In A.D. *356 Constantius introduced a new silver coin of c. 2.25 gm., i.e. $^2/_3$ the weight of the siliqua.   There are two main theories as to the significance of the introduction of this piece.*

The first of these suggests that there was a 50 per cent. appreciation in the value of silver.   This would mean that the new coin would have the same value in respect of the solidus as the siliqua had had, i.e. $^1/_{24}$.   It is further suggested that the name siliqua was transferred to the new coin and the old siliqua of $^1/_{96}$ lb., which was still occasionally issued after 356, now became a $1^1/_2$ siliqua.   Consequently, the miliarense was now the equivalent of 2 siliquae and $^1/_{12}$ of the solidus.

These changes would give us the following table of values:—

N solidus $= ^1/_{72}$ lb. of gold

N semis $= ^1/_{144}$ lb. of gold $= ^1/_2$ solidus

Æ miliarense $= ^1/_{72}$ lb. of silver $= ^1/_{12}$ solidus

Æ $1^1/_2$ siliqua (=pre-356 siliqua) $= ^1/_{96}$ lb. of silver $= ^1/_{16}$ solidus

Æ siliqua ($^2/_3$ of pre-356 siliqua) $= ^1/_{144}$ lb. of silver $= ^1/_{24}$ solidus

There is one interesting point which lends weight to this theory. Constantius reached the 30th anniversary of his accession on November 8th, A.D. 354. *After this date his* vota *figures should appear as* XXXV. *or* XXXX. *However, the new silver coin which was not introduced until 356 has the rev. legend* VOTIS XXX . MVLTIS XXXX. *The only conceivable explanation for this apparent anomaly is that Constantius wanted his new "siliqua" to take the place of its heavier predecessor as unobtrusively as possible, so he made it an exact replica of the* siliqua *which had been in issue just before the completion of his* tricennium

The other theory is that the new coin circulated merely as a $^2/_3$ *siliqua or* $^1/_2$ *miliarense (*$^1/_{36}$ *solidus), the value of silver remaining unchanged. This theory, however, offers no explanation of the erroneous* VOTIS XXX . MVLTIS XXXX. *legend.*

As we have already seen, in A.D. 346 *Constantius and Constans introduced a new* Æ 2 *coin called* centenionalis. *In 354, however, this piece was discontinued and in its place an* Æ 3 *denomination was once more introduced.*

As Caesar, A.D. 324-337
Very Fine

3879 **N solidus.** FL . IVL . CONSTANTIVS NOB . C. Diad., dr. and cuir. bust, r. R. PRINCIPI IVVENTVTIS. Constantius stg. l., holding standard and sceptre; to r., two standards; in ex., TS. C. 162. R.I.C. 191 .. .. £75·00
There are larger gold, *double solidi* and heavier.

3880 **N semissis.** — Laur. and dr. bust, l. R. — Constantius stg. r., holding spear and globe; in ex., N. C. 153. R.I.C. 116 .. .. 120·00

3881 **R miliarense.** (*c.* 4.5 gm.) — Laur., dr. and cuir. bust, r. R. CONSTANTIVS CAESAR. Four standards; in ex., · CONSI ·. C. 17. R.I.C. 56 *Illustrated on p. 324* .. .. 100·00

3882 **R siliqua.** (*c.* 3.4 gm.) *Obv.* No legend. Diad hd., r. R. — Victory advancing l.; in ex., TSE. C. 15. R.I.C. 216 .. .. 65·00

3883 **Æ 3.** (*c.* 19 mm.) *Obv.* No legend. Laur., dr. and cuir. bust, l. R. CONSTAN / TIVS / CAESAR in three lines; above, star; beneath, SMANTS. C. 20. R.I.C. 55 .. 4·50

3884 FL . IVL . CONSTANTIVS NOB . C. Laur., dr. and cuir. bust, l. R. PROVIDENTIAE CAESS. Camp-gate surmounted by two turrets; in ex., STR. C. 167. R.I.C. 456 .. 1·50

3885 As previous, but with PLON (*London*) in exergue. C. 167. R.I.C. 298 .. 7·50

3886 **Æ 3/4.** (*c.* 17 mm.) — Laur. and cuir. bust, r. R. GLORIA EXERCITVS. Two soldiers stg. either side of two standards; in ex., SMKA. C. 104. R.I.C. 85 .. 1·00

3887 — Laur., dr. and cuir. bust, r. R. As previous, but only one standard; in ex., SMNΓ. C. 92. R.I.C. 201 .. .. .. 1·00

As Augustus

Mints: Ambianum; Treveri; Lugdunum; Arelate; Aquileia; Rome; Siscia; Sirmium; Thessalonica; Heraclea; Constantinople; Nicomedia; Cyzicus; Antioch; Alexandria.

3888 **N solidus.** FL . IVL . CONSTANTIVS PERP . AVG. Helmeted and cuir. bust facing, holding spear and shield. R. GLORIA REIPVBLICAE. Roma and Constantinopolis seated, holding shield inscribed VOT . XXX . MVLT . XXXX.; in ex., SMNS. C. 112. **Plate 11** .. .. .. 45·00
There are larger gold, 1½, 2, 3, 4½, 9 *solidi* and heavier.

Very Fine

3889 *N* **semissis.** CONSTANTIVS AVG. Diad., dr. and cuir. bust, r. ℞.
VICTORIA AVGVSTORVM. Victory seated r., inscribing VOT . XXX. on shield
presented by winged Genius; in ex., SMAN. *C.* 244 .. .. .. £85·00

3890 *N* **1½ scripulum.** CONSTANTIVS P . F . AVG. — ℞. — Victory advancing l.; in ex., R. *C.* 228 .. .. 85·00

3891 Æ **3 miliarensia.** (*c.* 13.5 gm.) FL . IVL . CONSTANTIVS PIVS FELIX
AVG. — ℞. GAVDIVM POPVLI ROMANI. Laurel-wreath around SIC
XX . SIC XXX.; in ex., TES. *C.* 86 .. .. *Very rare*

3892 Æ **heavy miliarense.** (*c.* 5.4 gm.) FL . IVL . CONSTANTIVS PERP . AVG.
— ℞. CONSTANTIVS AVG. Four standards; in ex., PCON. *C.* 7 .. 100·00

3893 Æ **miliarense.** (*c.* 4.5 gm.) D . N . CONSTANTIVS P . F . AVG. — ℞.
VIRTVS EXERCITVS. Soldier stg. r., holding spear and leaning on shield;
in ex., TES. *C.* 326 .. .. 100·00

3894 Æ **siliqua.** (*c.* 3.4 gm.) *Obv.* No legend. Diad. hd., r. ℞.
CONSTANTIVS AVGVSTVS. Victory advancing l.; in ex., C · Γ. *C.* 12 .. 45·00

3895 CONSTANTIVS P . F . AVG. Diad., dr. and cuir. bust, r. ℞. VICTORIA
DD . NN . AVGG. Victory advancing l.; in ex., TES. *C.* 263 .. .. 25·00

3896 D . N . CONSTANTIVS P . F . AVG. — ℞. VOTIS / XXX. / MVLTIS / XXXX.
in four lines within wreath; in ex., TCON. *C.* 342 .. .. .. 15·00

3897 Æ **siliqua.** (reduced weight, *c.* 2.25 gm.) — — ℞. As previous;
in ex., SCON. *C.* 343 .. .. 7·50

3897A — — ℞. VICTORIA DD . NN . AVG. Victory advancing l.; in ex., LVG.
C. 259. **Plate 11** .. .. 12·50

Pre-reform bronze coinage, A.D. 337-346

3898 Æ **4.** CONSTANTIVS AVG. Diad. hd., r. ℞. GLORIA EXERCITVS. Two
soldiers stg. either side of standard; in ex., SMHЄ. *C.* 95 .. .. 1·00

3899 CONSTANTIVS P . F . AVG. Diad., dr., and cuir. bust, r. ℞. VICTORIAE
DD . AVGG . Q . NN. Two Victories stg. facing each other; in ex., PARL.
C. 293 .. .. 1·00

3900 D . N . CONSTANTIVS P . F . AVG. Diad. hd., r. ℞. VOT. / XX. / MVLT. /
XXX. in four lines within wreath; in ex., SMALA. *C.* 335.. .. .. 1·00

Post-reform bronze coinage, A.D. 346-361

The obv. legend is D . N . CONSTANTIVS P . F . AVG.

First period, A.D. 346-354

3901 Æ **centenionalis.** Diad., dr. and cuir. bust, r. ℞. FEL . TEMP .
REPARATIO. Constantius stg. l. on galley, holding Victory and labarum;
in ex., TRS. *C.* 32 .. .. 2·50

3902 — ℞. — As previous, but phoenix instead of Victory; in ex., RQ. *C.* 35 2·50

3903 — ℞. — Soldier advancing l., spearing fallen horseman; in ex., ALEΔ.
C. 46. **Plate 11** .. .. 2·00

3904 Diad., dr. and cuir. bust l., holding globe. ℞. — Constantius stg. l.,
holding labarum, two captives at feet; in ex., ANZ. *C.* 41 .. .. 2·50

3905 — ℞. — Soldier advancing r., dragging young barbarian from hut
beneath tree; in ex., ALEA. *C.* 53 .. .. 2·50

Very Fine

3906   **Æ centenionalis.** — (but bust r.)   ℞. GLORIA ROMANORVM. Constantius galloping r., spearing kneeling enemy; in ex., RB.   *C.* 140   ..   £3·50

3907   Diad., dr. and cuir. bust, r.   ℞. SALVS AVG . NOSTRI.   Large Christogram between A and ⅃J; in ex., TRP*.   *C.* 176   ..   ..   15·00

3908   **Æ ½ centenionalis.** — ℞. FEL . TEMP . REPARATIO.   Phoenix stg. r. on globe; in ex., TRP.   *C.* 57 ..   ..   3·25

3909   — ℞. — Phoenix stg. r. on pyre; in ex., RP.   *C.* 58   ..   ..   ..   3·25

Second period, A.D. 354-361

3910   **Æ 3.** (*c.* 18 mm.)   Diad., dr. and cuir. bust, r.   ℞. FEL . TEMP . REPARATIO.   Soldier advancing l., spearing fallen horseman; in ex., CPLG. *C.* 47 ..   ..   1·50

3911   **Æ 4.** (*c.* 15 mm.) — ℞. SPES REIPVBLICE.   Constantius stg. l., holding globe and spear; in ex., SMTSB.   *C.* 188   ..   ..   2·00

MAGNENTIUS

A.D. 350–353

3917

(*Flavius Magnus Magnentius*). *Of barbarian origin, Magnentius joined the ranks of the Roman army and soon proved himself to be a soldier of great ability. During the reign of Constans he became one of the Empire's foremost generals, but early in* A.D. 350 *he rebelled against his master and was himself proclaimed emperor. Following the death of Constans, his rule was recognized by most of the western provinces, and he determined to extend his authority over the rest of the Empire also. Accordingly he led his army against Constantius II, but after some initial success he was heavily defeated at Mursa (September, 351). In the following year he was forced to withdraw to Gaul, and after a final defeat near Mount Seleucus he was deserted by his soldiers and committed suicide (August 11th, 353).*

Mints: Ambianum; Treveri; Lugdunum; Arelate; Aquileia; Rome; Siscia.

3912   **N solidus.** IM . CAE . MAGNENTIVS AVG.   Bare-headed, dr. and cuir. bust, r.   ℞. VICTORIA AVG . LIB . ROMANOR.   Victory and Liberty stg. facing each other, holding trophy between them; in ex., TR.   *C.* 46   ..   125·00 There are larger gold, 1½ and 2 *solidi.*

3913   **N 1½ scripulum.** D . N . MAGNENTIVS AVG. — ℞. FELICITAS PERPETVA. Victory advancing l.; in ex., SMAQ.   *C.* 2 ..   ..   200·00

3914   **Æ 3 miliarensia.** (*c.* 13.5 gm.) D . N . MAGNENTIVS P . F . AVG. — ℞. SECVRITAS REIPVBLICAE.   Security stg. facing, hd. r., leaning on column; in ex., TR.   *C.* 34   ..   ..   *Very rare*

3915   **Æ miliarense.** (*c.* 4.5 gm.) — — ℞. VICTORIAE DD . NN . AVGG. Victory seated r., inscribing VOT . V . MVLT . X. on shield resting on knee; in ex., *AQ.   *C.* 73   ..   ..   275·00

Very Fine

3916 **Æ siliqua.** (*c.* 3.4 gm.) — — ℞. VIRTVS EXERCITI. Virtus stg. r., holding spear and leaning on shield; in ex., TR. *C.* 81 .. .. .. £75·00

3917 **Æ double centenionalis.** — — ℞. SALVS DD . NN . AVG . ET . CAES. Large Christogram between A and ധ; in ex., AMB. *C.* 30. *Illustrated on p.* 327 .. .. 25·00

3918 **Æ centenionalis.** IM . CAE . MAGNENTIVS AVG. — ℞. FELICITAS REIPVBLICE. Magnentius stg. l., holding Victory and labarum; in ex., TRP. *C.* 5 .. .. 3·50

3919 D . N . MAGNENTIVS P . F . AVG. Diad., dr. and cuir. bust, r. ℞. As previous; in ex., SAR. *C.* 7 .. .. 4·00

3920 IM . CAE . MAGNENTIVS AVG. Bare-headed, dr. and cuir. bust, r. ℞. FEL . TEMP . REPARATIO. Magnentius stg. l. on galley, holding Victory and labarum; in ex., TRS. *C.* 11 .. .. 4·50

3921 D . N . MAGNENTIVS P . F . AVG. — ℞. GLORIA ROMANORVM. Magnentius galloping r., spearing kneeling enemy; in ex., RPLG. *C.* 20 .. 3·50

3922 — — ℞. As 3917; in ex., TRP. *C.* 31 .. .. 15·00

3923 — — ℞. VICTORIAE DD . NN . AVG . ET CAE. Two Victories stg. facing each other, resting shield, inscribed VOT . V . MVLT . X., on cippus; in ex., TRP. *C.* 70 .. .. 3·00

3924 — — ℞. As previous, but without cippus; in ex., RPLG. *C.* 68. 3·00
Plate 11

3925 IMP . CAE . MAGNENTIVS AVG. — ℞. VICTORIA AVG . LIB . ROMANOR. Magnentius stg. r., l. foot on captive, holding standard and branch; in ex., RS. *C.* 57 .. .. 5·00

3926 **Æ ½ centenionalis.** As 3921. *C.* 21 .. .. 5·00

3927 D . N . MAGNENTIVS P . F . AVG. Bare-headed, dr. and cuir. bust, r. ℞. VICTORIAE DD . NN . AVG . ET CAES. Two Victories stg. facing each other, holding between them shield inscribed VOT . V . MVLT . X; in ex., TR. *C.* 69 .. .. 5·00

DECENTIUS
Caesar, A.D. 351–353

3930

Magnus Decentius was the brother of Magnentius, who gave him the rank of Caesar in 351. On receiving news of his brother's suicide, Decentius also took his own life (August 18th, 353).

3928 **A' solidus.** D . N . DECENTIVS FORT . CAES. Bare-headed, dr. and cuir. bust, r. ℞. VICTORIA CAES . LIB . ROMANOR. Victory and Liberty stg. facing each other, holding trophy between them; in ex., TR. *C.* 31 325·00
There is also a 1½ *solidus.*

3929 **A' 1½ scripulum.** DECENTIVS FOR . CAES. — ℞. VICTORIA DD . NN . AVGG. Victory advancing l.; in ex., TR. *C.* 32 .. .. 300·00

3930 **Æ miliarense.** (*c.* 4·5 gm.) D . N . DECENTIVS NOB . CAES. Bareheaded and cuir. bust, r. ℞. PRINCITI (*sic*) IVVENTVTIS. Decentius stg. r., holding spear and globe; in ex., TR. *C.* 7. *Illustrated above* 550·00

Very Fine

3931 **Æ siliqua.** (*c.* 3·4 gm.) *Obv.* As 3928. ℞. VIRTVS EXERCITI.
Virtus stg. r., holding spear and leaning on shield; in ex., TR. *C.* 49 .. £375·00

3932 **Æ double centenionalis** — ℞. SALVS DD . NN . AVG . ET CAES. Large
Christogram between A and ꟃ; in ex., TRP. *C.* 13 .. .. .. 30·00

3933 **Æ centenionalis.** As previous. *C.* 15 .. .. 17·50

3934 MAG . DECENTIVS NOB . CAES. Bare-headed and cuir. bust, r. ℞. VICT .
DD . NN . AVG . ET CAES. Two Victories stg. facing each other, holding
between them shield inscribed VOT . V . MVLT . X.; in ex., RB. *C.* 21 .. 6·50

3935 *Obv.* As 3930. ℞. VICTORIAE DD . NN . AVG . ET CAE. As previous;
in ex., RSLG. *C.* 33. **Plate 11** .. .. 5·00

3936 D . N . DECENTIVS CAESAR. Bare-headed and cuir. bust, r. ℞. — As
previous; in ex., SAR. *C.* 35 .. .. 5·00

3937 *Obv.* As 3930. ℞. — As previous, but shield rests on cippus; in ex.,
AMB. *C.* 43 .. .. 5·00

3938 **Æ ½ centenionalis.** D . N . DECENTIVS NOB . CAES. Bare-headed, dr. and
cuir. bust, r. ℞. VIRTVS EXERCITVS. Decentius stg. l., holding globe
and spear; in ex., AQS. *C.* 50 .. .. 12·50

VETRANIO
A.D. 350

3939

*After the death of Constans, the soldiers of the Illyrian army were undecided as to
whether they should support Magnentius, or express their allegiance to Constantius II.
Eventually they were persuaded by Constantia, the sister of Constantius, to proclaim their
commander, Vetranio, emperor. Vetranio immediately expressed his loyalty to Constantius,
and held Magnentius in check whilst Constantius was settling the affairs of the East. Towards
the end of the year Constantius arrived to take command of the situation in person, and
Vetranio formally abdicated in his presence. The ex-emperor was granted an estate at
Prusa in Bithynia where he spent the last six years of his life in peace and comfort.*

Mints: Siscia; Thessalonica.

3939 **Ɲ solidus.** D . N . VETRANIO P . F . AVG. Laur., dr. and cuir. bust, r.
℞. SALVATOR REIPVBLICAE. Vetranio stg. l., holding labarum, crowned
by Victory stg. behind him; in ex., SIS. *C.* 7. *Illustrated above* .. 1500·00

3940 **Æ siliqua.** (*c.* 3·4 gm.) — — ℞. VICTORIA AVGVSTORVM. Victory
advancing l.; in ex., SIS dot above crescent. *C.* 8 .. .. .. 500·00

3941 **Æ centenionalis.** — — ℞. CONCORDIA MILITVM. Vetranio stg. l.,
holding two labara; in ex., . ASIS*. *C.* 1 .. .. .. 45·00

3942 — — ℞. HOC SIGNO VICTOR ERIS. As 3939; in ex., . BSIS*. *C.* 4 .. 75·00

3943 — — ℞. VIRTVS EXERCITVM. Vetranio stg. l., holding labarum and
leaning on shield; in ex., TSA. *C.* 12 .. .. 50·00

3944 **Æ ½ centenionalis.** — — ℞. GLORIA ROMANORVM. Vetranio stg. l.,
holding labarum and sceptre; in ex., ꞓSIS. *C.* 3 .. .. 45·00

330

NEPOTIAN
A.D. 350

3945

Flavius Julius Popilius Nepotianus Constantinus, a nephew of Constantine the Great, siezed power in Rome in the troubled period following the death of Constans. After a turbulent reign of only 28 days, he fell into the hands of the soldiers of Magnentius and was killed.

Mint: Rome.

Very Fine

3945 **Aʹ solidus.** D . N . IVL . NEPOTIANVS P . F . AVG. Diad. and dr. bust, r. Ɍ. VRBS ROMA. Roma seated l., holding globe surmounted by Christogram and spear; in ex., RP. *C.* 2. *Illustrated above* .. *Extr. rare*

3946 **Æ centenionalis.** FL . POP . NEPOTIANVS P . F . AVG. Bare-headed and dr. bust, r. Ɍ. GLORIA ROMANORVM. Nepotian galloping r., spearing kneeling enemy; in ex., RS. *C.* 1 .. ..£250·00

3947 FL . NEP . CONSTANTINVS AVG. Diad., dr. and cuir. bust, r. Ɍ. VRBS ROMA. Roma seated l., holding Victory and sceptre; in ex., RS. *C.* 4 300·00

CONSTANTIUS GALLUS
Caesar, A.D. 351–354

3951

(Flavius Claudius Constantius, originally named Gallus). A cousin of Constantius II, Gallus was given the rank of Caesar in March, 351, and at the same time his name was changed to Constantius. He was made Governor of the eastern provinces and took up his residence at Antioch, but his rule was so harsh and oppressive that his subjects complained to the emperor of their treatment. Constantius thereupon wrote to the Caesar, requesting his presence in Milan, and had him arrested on the journey. At Pola, in Istria, he was tried, condemned and put to death (winter, A.D. 354).

Mints: Ambianum; Treveri; Lugdunum; Arelate; Aquileia; Rome; Siscia; Sirmium; Thessalonica; Heraclea; Constantinople; Nicomedia; Cyzicus; Antioch; Alexandria.

3948 **Aʹ solidus.** D . N . FL . CL . CONSTANTIVS NOB . CAES. Bare-headed, dr. and cuir. bust, r. Ɍ. GLORIA REIPVBLICAE. Roma and Constantinopolis seated, holding between them shield inscribed VOTIS V.; in ex., SMNS. *C.* 24 .. .. 200·00
There may be larger gold.

3949 **Aʹ semissis.** CONSTANTIVS CAE. — Ɍ. VICTORIA AVGVSTORVM. Victory seated r., inscribing VOTIS V. on shield presented by winged Genius; in ex., SMAN. *C.* 41 .. .. 250·00

Very Fine

3951 **Æ miliarense.** (*c.* 4.5 gm.) *Obv.* As 3948. ℞. FELICITAS ROMA-
NORVM. Semicircular arch resting on two columns beneath which
stand Constantius II and Constantius Gallus; in ex., SMN. *C.* 19.
Illustrated on p. 330 .. .. £300·00

3952 D . N . CONSTANTIVS NOB . CAES. Bare-headed, dr. and cuir bust., r.
℞. GLORIA EXERCITVS. Four standards; in ex., SMN. *C.* 20 .. .. 250·00

3953 **Æ siliqua.** (*c.* 3.4 gm.) — Bare hd., r. ℞. No legend. Star in
laurel-wreath; in ex., LVG. *C.* 61 .. .. 90·00

3954 **Æ centenionalis.** *Obv.* As 3498. ℞. FEL . TEMP . REPARATIO.
Soldier advancing l., spearing fallen horseman; in ex., SMKϵ. *C.* 11 .. 4·00

3955 *Obv.* As 3952. ℞. As previous; in ex., ALEΔ. *C.* 17 .. .. 4·00

3956 **Æ 3.** (*c.* 18 mm.) D . N . CONSTANTIVS IVN . NOB . C. Bare-headed,
dr. and cuir. bust, r. ℞. As previous; in ex., AQT. *C.* 14 .. .. 3·50

JULIAN II
A.D. 360–363

3968

(*Flavius Claudius Julianus*). Born in Constantinople about A.D. 332, Julian was the
half-brother of Gallus and a nephew of Constantine the Great. He was imprisoned by
Constantius II at the time of Gallus' execution, but his life was spared, and later he was
restored to the Imperial favour and given the rank of Caesar (November 6th, 355): about the
same time he married Constantius' youngest sister, Helena. Having been given the governorship of Gaul, he proved himself a very able commander and campaigned with great success
against the barbarian invaders of his province. However, in the spring of A.D. 360 his troops,
having been ordered to furnish contingents for employment against the Persians, rose in revolt
against Constantius and proclaimed Julian Augustus. The new ruler then set out to meet
Constantius, but the latter died in Cilicia whilst on his way to put down the revolt, leaving
Julian in undisputed possession of the Empire. After less than two years of sole rule, however,
he was killed in battle against the Persians (June 26th, 363).

Julian was a man of considerable literary attainments and some of his writings are still
extant. He strongly favoured the old pagan religion, with which he had far more sympathy
than with the Christian creed which he had been forced to adopt, and this caused the Church
historians of the period to stigmatize him as "the Apostate"; but the title "Philosopher,"
which he was also given, is probably more just.

As Caesar, A.D. 335-360

3957 **N solidus.** FL . CL . IVLIANVS NOB . CAES. Bare-headed, dr. and cuir.
bust, r. ℞. GLORIA REIPVBLICAE. Roma and Constantinopolis seated,
holding between them shield inscribed VOTIS V.; in ex., CONS. *C.* 25 .. 100·00
There is also a *double solidus*.

3958 **N semissis.** — — ℞. VICTORIA AVGVSTORVM. Victory seated r.,
inscribing VOT . V. on shield presented by winged Genius; in ex.,
KONSTAN. *C.* 55. *Illustrated on p.* 332 .. .. 125·00

3958   3959

Very Fine

3959 Æ **siliqua.** (*c.* 3.4 gm.) — — ℞. No legend. Star in laurel-
wreath; in ex., TCON. *C.* 170 .. .. £40·00

3960 Æ **siliqua.** (reduced weight, *c.* 2.25 gm.) — — ℞. VOTIS / V. /
MVLTIS / X. in laurel-wreath; in ex., TR. *C.* 155 .. 8·00

3961 D . N . IVLIANVS NOB . CAES. — ℞. As previous; in ex., TCON. *C.* 154 8·00

3962 As 3959, but with CON in exergue. *C.* 171 .. .. .. 25·00

3963 Æ **3.** (*c.* 17 mm.) D . N . IVLIANVS NOB . C. Bare-headed, dr. and
cuir. bust, r. ℞. FEL . TEMP . REPARATIO. Soldier advancing l.,
spearing fallen horseman; in ex., ΔSIS. *C.* 13 .. .. 3·50

3964 Æ **4.** (*c.* 15 mm.) D . N . IVLIANVS NOB . CAES. — ℞. SPES REIPVBLICE.
Julian stg. l., holding globe and spear; in ex., ALEΔ. *C.* 43 .. .. 3·50

As Augustus

Mints: Lugdunum; Arelate; Aquileia; Rome; Siscia; Sirmium; Thessalonica;
Heraclea; Constantinople; Nicomedia; Cyzicus; Antioch; Alexandria.

The obv. type is diad., dr. and cuir. bust r., unless otherwise stated.

3965 *N* **solidus.** FL . CL . IVLIANVS PERP . AVG. ℞. GLORIA REIPVBLICAE.
Roma and Constantinopolis seated, holding between them shield
inscribed VOT . V . MVLT . X.; in ex., KONSTAN. *C.* 27 .. .. 100·00

3966 FL . CL . IVLIANVS P . F . AVG. ℞. VIRTVS EXERCITVS ROMANORVM.
Julian advancing r., hd. turned, dragging captive by hair and holding
trophy; in ex., ANTI. *C.* 79 .. .. 90·00

3967 *N* **semissis.** FL . CL . IVLIANVS PP . AVG. ℞. VICTORIA DD . NN . AVGG.
Victory seated r., inscribing VOT . X. on shield presented by winged
Genius; in ex., LVG. *C.* 60 .. .. 125·00

3968 Æ **miliarense.** (*c.* 4.5 gm.) FL . CL . IVLIANVS P . F . AVG. ℞. VICTORIA
ROMANORVM. Semicircular arch resting on two columns beneath which
stands Julian facing, crowned by Victory who stands beside him; in ex.,
*SIRM. *C.* 63. *Illustrated on p. 331* .. .. .. 300·00

3969 Æ **1½ siliqua.** (*c.* 3.4 gm.) D . N . CL . IVLIANVS AVG. ℞. VOTIS / V. /
MVLTIS / X. in laurel-wreath; in ex., TR. *C.* 157 .. .. .. 30·00

3970 Æ **siliqua.** (*c.* 2.25 gm.) FL . CL . IVLIANVS PP . AVG. ℞. VOT. /
X. / MVLT. / XX. in laurel-wreath; in ex., SLVG. *C.* 146 .. .. 8·00

3971 As 3969, but with TCON in exergue. *C.* 158. **Plate 12** .. .. 8·00

3972 Æ **1.** (*c.* 28 mm.) D . N . FL . CL . IVLIANVS P . F . AVG. ℞. SECVRITAS
REIPVB. Bull stg. r.; above, two stars; in ex., branch BSISC branch.
C. 38. **Plate 11** .. .. 25·00

3973 — — ℞. As previous, but with eagle before bull; in ex., PCONST.
C. 39 .. .. 30·00

3974 Æ **3.** (*c.* 20 mm.) — Helmeted and cuir. bust l., holding spear and
shield. ℞. As 3970; in ex., VRB . ROM . B. *C.* 151 .. .. 3·50

3975 Æ **4.** (*c.* 15 mm.) FL . CL . IVLIANVS PP . AVG. ℞. As 3964; in ex.,
RPLG. *C.* 50 .. .. 4·50

Anonymous coins attributed to the reign of Julian

Very Fine

3976 **Æ 3.** (*c.* 19 mm.) DEO SERAPIDI. Rad. and dr. bust of Serapis r.,
wearing modius on head. ℞. VOTA PVBLICA. Isis in car drawn l. by
two mules. *C.* 103 ..   ..   £35·00

3976   3977

3977 DEO SARAPIDI. Jugate busts of Serapis and Isis l. ℞. — Isis advancing
l., holding sistrum and bucket. *C.* (*Julian and Helena*) 5   ..   30·00

3978 *Obv.* As previous, but jugate busts r. ℞. — The Nile reclining l.,
holding ship and reed. *C.* (*Julian and Helena*) 16   ..   ..   30·00

3979 ISIS FARIA. Bust of Isis r. ℞ — As previous. *C.* (*Helena*) 38   ..   25·00

3980 **Æ 4.** (*c.* 15 mm.) IOVI CONSERVATORI. Jupiter seated l., holding globe
and sceptre. ℞. VICTORIA AVGG. Victory advancing l.; in ex., ANT.
C. 53 ..   ..   10·00

3981 *Obv.* As 3976. ℞. VOTA PVBLICA. Sphinx r. *C.* 136 *var*...   ..   15·00

JOVIAN
A.D. 363–364

3985

*Flavius Jovianus was the captain of the imperial guard under Julian and, following the
latter's death, he was proclaimed emperor by the army. The new ruler lacked the great
ability of his predecessor and immediately began to withdraw his troops from Persian
territory. In order to ensure a safe retreat he concluded a shameful peace with the Persians by
which the Romans surrendered most of the territories which they had acquired during the
reign of Diocletian. Having reached Roman territory Jovian set out for Constantinople, but
was accidentally suffocated at Dadastana, in Galatia, through a brazier of charcoal having
been left in his bed-chamber (February 16th, 364).*

Mints: Lugdunum; Arelate; Aquileia; Rome; Siscia; Sirmium; Thessalonica;
Heraclea; Constantinople; Cyzicus; Antioch; Alexandria.

3892 **N solidus.** D . N . IOVIANVS PEP . AVG. Diad., dr. and cuir. bust, r. ℞.
SECVRITAS REIPVBLICAE. Roma and Constantinopolis seated, holding
between them shield inscribed VOT . V . MVL . X; in ex., ANTΔ. *C.* 8.
Plate 12 ..   ..   110·00

3983 **Æ miliarense.** (*c.* 4.5 gm.) D . N . IOVIANVS P . F . AVG. — ℞.
RESTITVTOR REIP. Jovian stg. r., holding labarum and Victory; in ex.,
PCONST. *C.* 7 ..   ..   300·00

Very Fine

3984   **Æ siliqua.**   (*c.* 2.25 gm.) — — ℞. VOT. / V. / MVLT. /. X. in laurel-
wreath; in ex., PCONST.   *C.* 33   ..   ..   £40·00

3985   **Æ 1.**   (*c.* 28 mm.)   D . N . IOVIANVS P . F . PP . AVG. — ℞. VICTORIA
ROMANORVM.   As 3983; in ex., TESB.   *C.* 23.   *Illustrated on p.* 333   ..   80·00

3986   **Æ 3.**   (*c.* 19 mm.)   D . N . IOVIANVS P . F . AVG.   Diad., dr. and cuir.
bust, l.   ℞. VOT. / V. in laurel-wreath; in ex., HERACB.   *C.* 32   ..   12·50

3987   — Diad., dr. and cuir. bust, r.   ℞. As 3984; in ex., ASISC.   *C.* 35   ..   10·00

BARBAROUS Æ COINS of the FOURTH and FIFTH CENTURIES

The bronze coinage of the House of Constantine, and also that of later periods, was extensively imitated by unofficial mints, some of which must have been situated in Britain as their products are frequently found on Romano-British sites. Some of these copies are almost as good as the originals, but most are very crude productions with badly blundered legends and almost unrecognizable types. We can usually offer a wide selection of sizes and types, the price for a "fine" specimen being about £1·25.

VALENTINIAN I
A.D. 364–375

4000

(Flavius Valentinianus). Born in Pannonia about A.D. 321, *Valentinian adopted a military career and ultimately rose to high rank under Julian and Jovian. Shortly after the latter's death he was proclaimed emperor at Nicaea, and about a month later he created his younger brother, Valens, co-emperor. The Empire was then divided between the two rulers, Valentinian being content to leave the government of the Eastern provinces to his brother, whilst he himself concentrated on the defence of the Rhine frontier, a task which demanded most of his time and energy. In 367 Britain was overrun by Picts, Scots, Franks and Saxons, and the situation was so critical that it took Count Theodosius, a skilled and experienced general, nearly two years to restore law and order in the province. Late in* A.D. 375, *whilst in residence at Bregetio, in Pannonia, Valentinian granted an audience to a deputation of Quadi: enraged at the impudence of the barbarians, the emperor was seized with an apoplectic fit and died soon afterwards.*

Mints: Treveri; Lugdunum; Arelate; Milan; Aquileia; Rome; Siscia; Sirmium; Thessalonica; Heraclea; Constantinople; Nicomedia; Cyzicus; Antioch; Alexandria.

The obv. legend is D . N . VALENTINIANVS P . F . AVG., *unless otherwise stated.*

The obv. type is diad., dr. and cuir. bust r., unless otherwise stated.

3988   **N solidus.**   ℞. RESTITVTOR REIPVBLICAE. Valentinian stg. facing,
hd. r., holding standard and Victory; in ex., ANTH.   *C.* 28.   *R.I.C.* 2a   35·00

3989   ℞. VICTORIA AVGG. Two emperors enthroned facing, holding globe
between them; in background, Victory stg. facing, wings spread; in ex.,
TROBS.   *C.* 43.   *R.I.C.* 17a.   **Plate 12**   ..   ..   40·00

There are larger gold, *aureus* (5½ gm.), 1½, 2, 3 and 4½ *solidi.*

Very Fine

3990 **N semissis.** D . N . VALENTINIANVS P . F . AV. R. VICTORIA DD . NN .
AVG. Victory advancing l.; in ex., LVG. *C.* 54. *R.I.C.* 2 ..   .. £90·00

3991 **N 1½ scripulum.** VALENTINIANVS AVG. R. VICTORIA AVGVSTORVM.
Victory seated r., inscribing VOT . V . on shield presented by winged
Genius; in ex., ANT. *C.* 47. *R.I.C.* 3a ..   .. 75·00

3992 **R 3 miliarensia.** (*c.* 13.5 gm.) R. TRIVMFATOR GENT . BARB.
Valentinian stg. facing, hd. l., holding labarum and globe; at feet l.,
captive; in ex., SISCP. *C.*—. *R.I.C.* 8 ..   ..   *Very rare*

3993 **R heavy miliarense.** (*c.* 5.4 gm.) R. VOTIS / V. / MVLTIS / X. in
laurel-wreath; in ex., TRPS. *C.* 78. *R.I.C.* 23b ..   .. 120·00

3994 **R miliarense.** (*c.* 4·5 gm.) Diad. and cuir. bust, r. R. VICTORIA
AVGVSTORVM. Victory stg. r., inscribing VOT . V . MVLT . X. on shield
set on cippus; in ex., RT. *C.* 51. *R.I.C.* 8a ..   .. 90·00

3995 **Æ 1½ siliqua.** (*c.* 3·4 gm.) R. VOT. / V. in laurel-wreath; in ex.,
CONSB. *C.* 69. *R.I.C.* 11a ..   .. 25·00

3996 **R siliqua.** (*c.* 2·25 gm.) R. RESTITVTOR REIP. Valentinian stg.
facing, hd. r., holding labarum and Victory; in ex., SLVG. *C.* 18.
R.I.C. 6a ..   .. 15·00

3997 R. As 3995; in ex., CP . A. *C.* 69. *R.I.C.* 13a ..   ..   .. 15·00

3998 R. VOT. / V. / MVLT. / X. in laurel-wreath; in ex., RB. *C.* 70. *R.I.C.*
10a ..   .. 15·00

3999 R. VRBS ROMA. Roma seated l., holding Victory and sceptre; in ex.,
RP. *C.* 81. *R.I.C.* 11a ..   .. 12·50

4000 **Æ 1.** (*c.* 27 mm.) R. As 3988; in ex., RT. *C.* 30. *R.I.C.* 14a.
Illustrated on p. 334 ..   .. 65·00

4001 **Æ 2.** (*c.* 22 mm.) R. GLORIA ROMANORVM. Camp-gate with S
between its two turrets; in ex., SMTR. *C.* 13. *R.I.C.* 29a ..   .. 90·00

4002 **Æ 3.** (*c.* 17 mm.) R. — Valentinian advancing r., dragging captive
and holding labarum; in ex., CONST. *C.* 12. *R.I.C.* 7a ..   .. 2·25

4003 R. SECVRITAS REIPVBLICAE. Victory advancing l.; in ex., ΔSISC.
C. 37. *R.I.C.* 15a ..   .. 2·25

VALENS
A.D. 364–378

4014

*Flavius Valens, the younger brother of Valentinian I, was born at Cibalae in Pannonia
about* A.D. 328, *and was raised to the rank of Augustus on March 28th, 364. Given the
government of the Eastern provinces, much of his reign was spent in campaigning against the
Goths on the Danube frontier and in countering the Persian menace in the East. In* A.D. 376
*the Visigoths, hard pressed by the Huns, sought permission to cross the Danube and settle
on Roman territory. Valens granted this permission, but the Goths were so badly treated by
the Romans that they broke into revolt and devastated the countryside of Moesia and Thrace.
Valens advanced against the barbarians, but in a great battle fought near Hadrianopolis on
August 9th, 378, the Roman army was almost annihilated and the emperor himself was
slain.*

Mints: same as for Valentinian I.

The obv. legend is D . N . VALENS P . F . AVG., *unless otherwise stated.*

The obv. type is diad., dr. and cuir. bust, r.

Very Fine

4004 **A' solidus.** D . N . VALENS PER . F . AVG. ℞. RESTITVTOR REIPVBLICAE. Valens stg. facing, hd. r., holding labarum and Victory; in ex., ANTΘ. *C.* 35. *R.I.C.* 2d .. .. £30·00

4005 ℞. VICTORIA AVGG. Two emperors enthroned facing, holding globe between them; in background, Victory stg. facing, wings spread; in ex., TROBS. *C.* 53. *R.I.C.* 17e. **Plate 12** .. .. .. 35·00
There are larger gold, *aureus* (5½ gm.), 1½, 2 and 4½ *solidi.*

4006 **A' semissis.** ℞. VICTORIA AVGVSTORVM. Victory seated r., inscribing VOT . X . MVL . XX. on shield presented by winged Genius; in ex., ANT. *C.* —. *R.I.C.* 24b .. .. 100·00

4007 **A' 1½ scripulum.** VALENS AVGVS. ℞. As previous, but Victory inscribes VOT . V. on shield. *C.* —. *R.I.C.* 3b .. .. .. 75·00

4008 **Æ 3 miliarensia.** (*c.* 13·5 gm.) ℞. TRIVMFATOR GENT . BARB. Valens stg. facing, hd. l., holding labarum and globe; at feet l., captive; in ex., TRPS. *C.* 50. *R.I.C.* 22 .. .. *Very rare*

4009 **Æ heavy miliarense.** (*c.* 5·4 gm.) ℞. VOTIS / V. / MVLTIS / X. in laurel-wreath; in ex., TRPS. *C.* 103. *R.I.C.* 23c .. .. .. 85·00

4010 **Æ miliarense.** (*c.* 4·5 gm.) ℞. VIRTVS EXERCITVS. Valens stg. facing, hd. l., holding labarum and leaning on shield; in ex., · SISCP. *C.* 71. *R.I.C.* 10b .. .. 75·00

4011 **Æ 1½ siliqua.** (*c.* 3·4 gm.) ℞. VOT. / V. in laurel-wreath; in ex., CONSA. *Cf. C.* 88. *R.I.C.* 11d .. .. 25·00

4012 **Æ siliqua.** (*c.* 2·25 gm.) ℞. As previous; in ex., C · Z. *C.* 88. *R.I.C.* 13d .. .. 12·00

4013 ℞. VRBS ROMA. Roma seated l., holding Victory and sceptre; in ex., TRPS. *C.* 109. *R.I.C.* 27e .. .. 7·50

4014 **Æ 1.** (*c.* 29 mm.) ℞. As 4004, but standard instead of labarum; in in ex., SMAQP. *C.* 40. *R.I.C.* 6b. *Illustrated on p. 335* .. 65·00

4015 **Æ 2.** (*c.* 22 mm.) ℞. GLORIA ROMANORVM. Camp-gate with S between its two turrets; in ex., SMTR. *C.* 20. *R.I.C.* 29b .. .. 90·00

4016 **Æ 3.** (*c.* 17 mm.) ℞. — Victory advancing l.; in ex., TRP. *C.* 4. *R.I.C.* 31b .. .. 3·25

4017 ℞. — Valens advancing r., dragging captive and holding labarum; in ex., · BSISC. *C.* 11. *R.I.C.* 14b .. .. 2·00

4018 ℞. SECVRITAS REIPVBLICAE. Victory advancing l.; in ex., ALEΓ. *C.* 47. *R.I.C.* 3b .. .. 2·00

PROCOPIUS
A.D. 365–366

4020

A kinsman and general of Julian II, Procopius took part in the ill-fated Persian expedition of that emperor, and it was he who bore the corpse of Julian to Tarsus for burial. In September, 365, whilst Valens was on his way to Syria, Procopius led a rebellion at Constantinople and was proclaimed emperor. After initial successes he was eventually defeated by the forces of Valens and later put to death (May 27th, 366).

Mints: Heraclea; Constantinople; Cyzicus; Nicomedia.

Very Fine

4019   **N solidus.** D . N . PROCOPIVS P . F . AVG.   Diad., dr. and cuir. bust, r.
R. REPARATIO FEL . TEMP. Procopius stg. facing, hd. r., holding spear
and leaning on shield; in ex., CONS. *C.* 5. *R.I.C.* 2*a* .. .. £1000·00

4020   **R siliqua.** — — R. VOT. / V. in laurel-wreath; in ex., C.Δ. *C.* 14.
R.I.C. 13*e.* *Illustrated on p.* 336 .. .. 140·00

4021   **Æ 1.** (*c.* 30 mm.) — — R. As 4091; in ex., SMHΓ. *C.* 6. *R.I.C.* 6 250·00

4022   **Æ 2.** — — R. REPARATIO FEL . TEMP. Procopius stg. l., foot on prow,
holding labarum and leaning on shield; in ex., SMKA. *C.* 7 *var.*
R.I.C. 6 .. .. 125·00

4023   **Æ 3.** (*c.* 19 mm.) — Diad., dr. and cuir. bust, l. R — Procopius
stg. facing, hd. r., holding labarum and leaning on shield; in ex., SMHA.
C. 9. *R.I.C.* 7 .. .. 50·00

4024   — — R. — As previous, but with small indeterminate object on
ground to l. of Procopius; in ex., CONSB. *C.* 8. *R.I.C.* 17*a* .. .. 45·00

4025   **Æ 3.** (*c.* 17 mm.) — Diad., dr. and cuir. bust, r. R. — As 4023;
in ex., CONSΔ. *C.* 10. *R.I.C.* 18 .. .. 40·00

GRATIAN
A.D. 367–383

4038

(*Flavius Gratianus*).   The son of Valentinian I and Severa, Gratian was given the rank
of Augustus in A.D. 367, when only seven years of age.   Following his father's death in 375 he
became the sole ruler of the Western division of the Empire, though his four-year-old half-
brother, Valentinian II, was also raised to the rank of Augustus at this time and was nominally associated in the government.   After the catastrophe at Hadrianopolis the Eastern
division of the Empire also passed into Gratian's hands, but he found it expedient to elevate
his general Theodosius to be his colleague in the government of these provinces.   In A.D. 383
Magnus Maximus, the commander of the Roman armies in Britain, was proclaimed Augustus
by his troops and invaded Gaul.   Gratian, deserted by his own soldiers, fled in the direction
of the Alps, but was overtaken and murdered at Lugdunum (August 25th).

Mints: same as for Valentinian I.

The obv. legend is D . N . GRATIANVS P . F . AVG., *unless otherwise stated.*

The obv. type is diad., dr. and cuir. bust r., unless otherwise stated.

4026   **N solidus.** R. VICTORIA AVGG. Two emperors enthroned facing,
holding globe between them; in background, Victory stg. facing, wings
spread ; in ex., TROBC. *C.* 38. *R.I.C.* 17*g.* **Plate 12** .. .. 40·00
There are larger gold, *aureus* (5½ gm.), 1½, 2, 3 and 4½ *solidi.*

4027   **N semissis.** R. VICTORIA AVGVSTORVM. Victory seated r., inscribing
VOT . V . MVLT . X. on shield presented by winged Genius; in ex., TROBT.
C. 50. *R.I.C.* 19 .. .. 175·00

4028   **N 1½ scripulum.** R. — Victory advancing l.; in ex., TROB. *C.* 44.
R.I.C. 21*d* .. .. 75·00

Very Fine

4029 **Æ heavy miliarense.** (*c.* 5.4 gm.) ℞. VOTIS / V. / MVLTIS / X. in laurel-wreath; in ex., TRPS ·. *C.* 80. *R.I.C.* 23*e* .. .. £90·00

4030 **Æ miliarense.** (*c.* 4.5 gm.) ℞. VIRTVS EXERCITVS. Gratian stg. facing, hd. l., holding labarum and leaning on shield; in ex., ·SISCP. *C.* 52. *R.I.C.* 10*c* .. .. 75·00

4031 **Æ 1½ siliqua.** (*c.* 3.4 gm.) ℞. VICTORIA AVGVSTORVM. Victory advancing l.; in ex., AQPS. *C.* 45. *R.I.C.* 24 .. .. 60·00

4032 **Æ siliqua.** (*c.* 2.25 gm.) D . N . GRATIANVS AVG. ℞. VOT. / X. / MVLT. / XX. in laurel-wreath; in ex., ·ANTH. *C.* 70. *R.I.C.* 34*f* .. .. 12·50

4033 ℞. VRBS ROMA. Roma seated l. on throne, holding Victory and sceptre; in ex., TRPS ·. *C.* 86. *R.I.C.* 27*f* .. .. 9·00

4034 ℞. As previous, but Roma is seated on cuirass and holds spear instead of sceptre; in ex., TRPS. *C.* 87. *R.I.C.* 46*b* .. .. 9·00

4035 **Æ half-siliqua.** ℞. VICTORIA AVGGG. Victory advancing l.; in ex., RB. *C.*—. *R.I.C.* 36*a* .. .. 100·00

4036 **Æ 1.** (*c.* 28 mm.) ℞. VRBS ROMA. Roma seated l., holding globe and sceptre; in ex., RT. *C.* 88. *R.I.C.* 42*a* .. .. 100·00

4037 **Æ 2.** (*c.* 22 mm.) ℞. GLORIA ROMANORVM. Camp-gate with s between its two turrets; in ex., SMTR. *C.* 26 *var.* *R.I.C.* 29*d* .. 90·00

4038 Helmeted, dr. and cuir. bust, r. holding spear and shield. ℞. — Gratian stg. on galley travelling l., Victory at helm; in ex., ANTB. *C.* 25. *R.I.C.* 40*a.* *Illustrated on p.* 337 .. .. 3·00

4039 ℞. REPARATIO REIPVB. Gratian stg. l., raising kneeling female figure; in ex., PCON. *C.* 30. *R.I.C.* 20*a* .. .. 3·50

4040 **Æ 3.** (*c.* 17 mm.) ℞. CONCORDIA AVGGG. Constantinopolis seated facing, hd. l., holding globe and spear; in ex., CONSS. *C.* 3. *R.I.C.* 56*a* 2·50

4041 D . N . GRATIANVS AVGG . AVG. ℞. GLORIA NOVI SAECVLI. Gratian stg. facing, hd. l., holding labarum and leaning on shield; in ex., CON*. *C.* 13. *R.I.C.* 15 .. .. 3·25

4042 ℞. GLORIA ROMANORVM. Gratian advancing r., dragging captive and holding labarum; in ex., ΔSISCR. *C.* 23. *R.I.C.* 14*c* .. .. 2·50

4043 D . N . GRATIANVS AVGG . AVG. ℞. SECVRITAS REIPVBLICAE. Victory advancing l.; in ex., LVGP. *C.* 35. *R.I.C.* 21*b* .. .. .. 3·00

4044 ℞. VIRTVS ROMANORVM. Roma seated facing, hd. l., holding globe and spear; in ex., TRP. *C.* 57. *R.I.C.* 71*a* .. .. .. 3·25

4045 **Æ 4.** (*c.* 15 mm.) ℞. VOT. / XV. / MVLT. / XX. in laurel-wreath; in ex., TCON. *C.* 75. *R.I.C.* 24 .. .. 1·75

4046 **Æ 4.** (*c.* 13 mm.) ℞. VOT. / XX. / MVLT. / XXX. in laurel-wreath; in ex., SMKA. *C.* 77. *R.I.C.* 22*a* .. .. 2·00

VALENTINIAN II
A.D. 375–392

4053

(*Flavius Valentinianus*). *The son of Valentinian I and Justina, Valentinian II was born at Acincum in Pannonia in* A.D. *371. Raised to the rank of Augustus a few days after the death of his father, in November of* A.D. *375, he was nominally associated with his half-brother in the government of the Western division of the Empire, but following the usurpation of Magnus Maximus and the death of Gratian in 383, he was only left in possession of Italy. In 387 Maximus invaded this province also, and Valentinian fled to Theodosius in the East, but in the following year the two emperors marched against the usurper and Maximus was defeated and executed. Valentinian was thus restored to the government of the Western division of the Empire, but on May 15th, 392, he was strangled, probably by order of his general Arbogastes who had completely undermined the authority of the young emperor.*

Mints: same as for Valentinian I.

There are two varieties of obv. legend:

A.   D . N . VALENTINIANVS P . F . AVG.

B.   D . N . VALENTINIANVS IVN . P . F . AVG.

The obv. type is diad., dr. and cuir. bust r., unless otherwise stated. The portrait of Valentinian II is always younger looking than his father's and usually narrower.

Very Fine

4047 **N solidus.** B. R. VICTORIA AVGG. Two emperors enthroned facing, holding globe between them; in background, Victory stg. facing, wings spread; in ex., TESOB. *C.* 36. *R.I.C.* 34*b.* **Plate 12** .. .. £50·00

4048 A. R. As previous; in ex., COM; in field, MD. *C.* 37. *R.I.C.* 8*a* .. 40·00
There are larger gold, *aureus* (5⅜ gm.), 1½, 2 and 9 *solidi.*

4049 **N semissis.** A. R. VICTORIA AVGVSTORVM. Victory seated r., inscribing VOT . V . MVL . X. on shield; in ex., CONOB. *C.* 53. *R.I.C.* 73*a* 150·00

4050 **N 1½ scripulum.** (1.70 gm.) B. R. — Victory advancing l.; in ex., AQOB. *C.* 50. *R.I.C.* 22*b* .. .. 75·00

4051 **N tremissis.** (1.50 gm.) A. R. — Victory advancing r., holding wreath and cross on globe; in ex., CONOB. *C.* 51 *var.* *R.I.C.* 75*a* .. 75·00

4052 **R 3 miliarensia.** (*c.* 13.5 gm.) A. R. TRIVMFATOR GENT . BARB. Valentinian stg. facing, hd. l., holding labarum and globe; at feet l., captive; in ex., RP. *C.* 35. *R.I.C.* 32 .. .. *Very rare*

4053 **R heavy miliarense.** (*c.* 5.4 gm.) A. R. GLORIA ROMANORVM. Valentinian, nimbate, stg. facing, hd. l., holding sceptre and leaning on shield; in ex., CON. *C.* 17. *R.I.C.* 84. *Illustrated on p.* 338 .. 120·00

4054 **R miliarense.** (*c.* 4.5 gm.) A. R. — Valentinian, nimbate, stg. facing, hd. l., raising r. hand and holding globe; in ex., AQPS. *C.* 19. *R.I.C.* 56*a* .. .. 100·00

4055 **R 1½ siliqua.** (*c.* 3.4 gm.) A. R. VOT. / XV. / MVLT. / XX. in laurel-wreath; in ex., LVG·. *C.* —. *R.I.C.* 42 .. .. 100·00

4056 **R siliqua.** (*c.* 2.25 gm.) B. R. VICTORIA AVGGG. Victory advancing l.; in ex., TRPS. *C.* 40. *R.I.C.* 57*a.* **Plate 12** .. .. 12·00

4057 A. R. VIRTVS ROMANORVM. Roma seated facing, hd. l., holding globe and spear; in ex., AQPS. *C.* 60. *R.I.C.* 41*a* .. .. .. 14·00

4058 A. R. VRBS ROMA. Roma seated l., holding Victory and spear; in ex., LVGPS. *C.* 76. *R.I.C.* 43*a* .. .. 15·00

4059 **R half-siliqua.** A. R. As 4056; in ex., RP. *C.* 42. *R.I.C.* 36*b*.. 90·00

4060 **Æ 1.** (*c.* 28 mm.) A. R. As 4056; no mint-mark (mint of Rome). *C.* 43. *R.I.C.* 39 .. .. 120·00

4061 **Æ 2.** (*c.* 22 mm.) A. Helmeted, dr. and cuir. bust r., holding spear and shield. R. GLORIA ROMANORVM. Valentinian stg. on galley travelling l., Victory at helm; in ex., SMNA. *C.* 22. *R.I.C.* 25*b*.. .. 3·00

4062 B. R. REPARATIO REIPVB. Valentinian stg. l., raising kneeling female figure; in ex., SCON. *C.* 26. *R.I.C.* 20*c* .. .. 3·50

Very Fine

4063   **Æ 2.**   A.   ℞.   VIRTVS EXERCITI.   Valentinian stg. r., l. foot on captive,
holding labarum and globe; in ex., · SMHB.   *C.* 57.   *R.I.C.* 24*a*   ..   £3·50

4064   **Æ 3.**   (*c.* 17 mm.)   A.   ℞.   CONCORDIA AVGGG.   Constantinopolis
seated facing, hd. l., holding globe and spear; in ex., CONSΔ.   *C.* 9.
R.I.C. 56*b*   ..   ..   3·00

4065   A.   ℞.   SECVRITAS REIPVBLICAE.   Victory advancing l.; in ex., ΓSISCC.
C. 33.   *R.I.C.* 22*c*   ..   ..   3·00

4066   **Æ 4.**   (*c.* 15 mm.)   B.   ℞.   As 4055; in ex., SMRP.   *C.* 74.   *R.I.C.*
51*b*   ..   ..   2·00

4067   **Æ 4.**   (*c.* 13 mm.)   A.   ℞.   SALVS REIPVBLICAE.   Victory advancing l.,
carrying trophy and dragging captive; in ex., ALEA.   *C.* 30.   *R.I.C.* 20*a*   1·50

THEODOSIUS I
A.D. 379–395

4082

Flavius Theodosius was born at Italica in Spain about A.D. *346, the son of the famous
Count Theodosius who cleared Britain of invaders in the reign of Valentinian I.   The son
soon proved that he had inherited all his father's military talents, and he became one of the
Empire's foremost generals.   Finally, a few months after the catastrophe of Hadrianopolis,
Gratian elevated him to the rank of Augustus and he succeeded to the throne of the Eastern
division of the Empire (January, 379).   The new emperor immediately set about rescuing
the Eastern provinces from the Gothic onslaught, but no sooner had he completed this task
than he had to turn his attention to the West, where Magnus Maximus had overthrown
Gratian and was threatening Valentinian II.   In 388 Theodosius finally defeated Maximus,
but six years later he again had to march against a Western usurper, this time Eugenius, the
nominee of Arbogastes.   By his victory over Eugenius, Theodosius extended his rule over the
entire Empire, but less than five months later, on January 17th, 395, he died at Milan, a
victim of dropsy.*

Mints: same as for Valentinian I, with the addition of London (?).

The obv. legend is D . N . THEODOSIVS P . F . AVG.

The obv. type is diad., dr. and cuir. bust r., unless otherwise stated.

4068   **N solidus.**   ℞.   CONCORDIA AVGGG.   Γ.   Constantinopolis seated facing,
hd. r., holding sceptre and shield inscribed VOT . X . MVLT . XV.; in ex.,
CONOB.   *C.* 11.   *R.I.C.* 71*a*   ..   ..   40·00

4069   ℞.   VICTORIA AVGG.   Two emperors enthroned facing, holding globe
between them; in background, Victory stg. facing, wings spread; in ex.,
TROBC.   *C.* 37.   *R.I.C.* 50   ..   ..   45·00
There are larger gold, 4½ and 9 (or 10) *solidi*.

4070   **N 1½ scripulum.**   (1.70 gm.)   ℞.   VICTORIA AVGVSTORVM.   Victory
seated r., inscribing VOT . V . MVL . X. on shield; in ex., CONOB.   *C.* 50.
R.I.C. 73*b*   ..   ..   65·00

4071   **N tremissis.**   (1.50 gm.)   ℞. —   Victory advancing r., holding wreath
and cross on globe; in ex., CONOB.   *C.* 47.   *R.I.C.* 75*b*   ..   ..   45·00

4072 **Æ 3 miliarensia.** (*c.* 13.5 gr.) ℞. TRIVMFATOR GENT . BARB.
Theodosius stg. facing, hd. l., holding labarum and globe; at feet l.,
captive; in ex., RT. *Cf. C.* 34. *R.I.C.* 52*a* .. .. .. *Very rare*

4073 **Æ heavy miliarense.** (*c.* 5.4 gm.) ℞. VICTORIA AVGVSTORVM.
Victory advancing r., dragging captive and holding trophy; in ex., Rϵ.
C.—. *R.I.C.* 33*d* .. ..£145·00

4074 **Æ miliarense.** (*c.* 4.5 gm.) Diad., dr. and cuir. bust, l. ℞. GLORIA
ROMANORVM. Theodosius, nimbate, stg. facing, hd. l., raising r. hand
and holding globe; in ex., MDPS. *C.* 17. *R.I.C.* 25*a* .. .. .. 100·00

4075 **Æ siliqua.** (*c.* 2.25 gm.) ℞. CONCORDIA AVGGG. Constantinopolis
seated facing, hd. r., holding sceptre and cornucopiae; in ex., TRPS.
C. 4. *R.I.C.* 55*a*. **Plate 12** .. .. 14·00

4076 ℞. VIRTVS ROMANORVM. Roma seated l., holding Victory and spear;
in ex., TRPS. *C.* 57. *R.I.C.* 94*b* .. .. 12·00

4077 ℞. — Roma seated facing, hd. l., holding globe and spear; in ex., AQPS.
C. 59. *R.I.C.* 28*d* .. .. 12·00

4078 ℞. VRBS ROMA. As 4076; in ex., R*B. *C.* 71. *R.I.C.* 35*c* .. .. 15·00

4079 **Æ half-siliqua.** ℞. VICTORIA AVGGG. Victory advancing l.; in ex.,
MD. *C.*—. *R.I.C.* 33*a* .. .. 65·00

4080 **Æ 1.** (*c.* 29 mm.) ℞. VIRTVS AVGVSTORVM. Theodosius stg. facing,
hd. l., holding standard and leaning on shield; no mint-mark (mint of
Rome). *C.* 52. *R.I.C.* 41 .. .. 110·00

4081 **Æ 2.** (*c.* 22 mm.) ℞. GLORIA ROMANORVM. Theodosius stg. facing,
hd. r., holding standard and globe; in ex., SMNA. *C.* 18. *R.I.C.* 46*a* .. 3·00

4082 Helmeted, dr. and cuir. bust r., holding spear and shield. ℞. —
Theodosius stg. on galley travelling l., Victory at helm; in ex., · TESB.
C. 19. *R.I.C.* 44*b*. *Illustrated on p.* 340 .. .. 3·00

4083 ℞. REPARATIO REIPVB. Theodosius stg. l., raising kneeling female
figure; in ex., SMAQP. *C.* 27. *R.I.C.* 30*d* .. .. 3·50

4084 ℞. VIRTVS EXERCIT. Theodosius stg. r., l. foot on captive, holding
labarum and globe; in ex., · SMHA. *C.* 54. *R.I.C.* 24*b*.. .. .. 3·00

4085 **Æ 3.** (*c.* 17 mm.) ℞. CONCORDIA AVGGG. Constantinopolis seated
facing, hd. l., holding globe and spear; in ex., CONSB. *C.* 5. *R.I.C.* 57*d* 2·50

4086 ℞. GLORIA ROMANORVM. Theodosius on horseback r., raising r. hand;
in ex., SMKΓ. *C.* 21. *R.I.C.* 29*a* .. .. 4·50

4087 **Æ 4.** (*c.* 15 mm.) ℞. VOT. / V. / MVLT. / X. in laurel-wreath; in ex.,
ASISC. *C.* 65. *R.I.C.* 29*d* .. .. 2·00

4088 **Æ 4.** (*c.* 13 mm.) ℞. SALVS REIPVBLICAE. Victory advancing l.,
carrying trophy and dragging captive; in ex., ANTΔ. *C.* 30. *R.I.C.* 67*b* 1·25

AELIA FLACCILLA

4093

First wife of Theodosius I, and mother of Arcadius and Honorius: died A.D. 386.

Mints: Siscia; Thessalonica; Heraclea; Constantinople; Cyzicus; Nicomedia;
Antioch; Alexandria.

All have obv. as follows:
AEL . FLACCILLA AVG.   *Dr. bust r., with elaborate head-dress and necklace.*

Very Fine

4089 **A/ solidus.** R. SALVS REIPVBLICAE S. Victory seated r., inscribing
Christogram on shield set on knee; in ex., CONOB. *C.* 1. *R.I.C.* 72   £1000·00

4090 **A/ tremissis.** R. No legend. Large Christogram in wreath; no
mint-mark (mint of Constantinople). *C.* 7. *R.I.C.* 76   ..   .. 400·00

4091 **Æ siliqua.** R. As previous; in ex., CONS. *Cf. C.* 8. *R.I.C.* 78 .. 500·00

4092 **Æ 2.** (*c.* 22 mm.) R. SALVS REIPVBLICAE. Victory seated r., inscribing Christogram on shield set on cippus; in ex., CONE. *C.* 4. *R.I.C.*
81   ..   .. 20·00

4093 R. — Flaccilla stg. facing, hd. r., arms folded on breast; in ex., SMHA.
C. 6. *R.I.C.* 25. *Illustrated on p.* 341   ..   .. 20·00

4094 **Æ 4.** (*c.* 13 mm.) R. As 4092; in ex., TESΔ. *C.* 5. *R.I.C.* 47 .. 12·50

MAGNUS MAXIMUS
A.D. 383–388

4099

(*Magnus Clemens Maximus*). *A native of Spain, Maximus held a high command in the
Roman army in Britain under Gratian. In July, 383, his soldiers, discontented with the rule
of Gratian, proclaimed Maximus emperor and he immediately invaded Gaul. Gratian was
deserted by his troops and fled in the direction of Italy, only to be overtaken and assassinated.
Maximus thus became ruler of Britain, Gaul, Spain and Africa, but in 387 his ambition
drove him to add Italy to his dominions. His invasion of the peninsula was at first successful,
Valentinian II fleeing at his approach, but Theodosius took up the cause of the unfortunate
young emperor and marched against Maximus: the usurper was utterly defeated at the
Battle of Poetovio and was later executed near Aquileia (July 28th, 388).*

*A vivid, if slightly inaccurate, portrait of this emperor will be found in Rudyard Kipling's
famous "Puck of Pook's Hill".*

Mints: London (?); Treveri; Lugdunum; Arelate; Milan; Aquileia; Rome;
Constantinople.

All have obv. as follows:
D . N . MAG . MAXIMVS P . F . AVG.   *Diad., dr. and cuir. bust, r.*

4095 **A/ solidus.** R. RESTITVTOR REPVBLICAE. Maximus stg. facing, hd. r.,
holding labarum and Victory; in ex., SMTR. *C.* 4. *R.I.C.* 76 ..   .. 145·00

4096 R. VICTORIA AVGG. Two emperors enthroned facing, holding globe
between them; in background, Victory stg. facing, wings spread; in ex.,
TROB. *C.* 9. *R.I.C.* 77b   ..   .. 145·00

4097 **A/ semissis.** R. VICTORIA AVGVSTORVM. Victory seated r., inscribing
VOT . V . MVLT . X. on shield presented by winged Genius; in ex., SMTR.
C. 17. *R.I.C.* 78   ..   .. 225·00

4098 **A/ tremissis.** R. — Victory advancing l.; in ex., SMTR. *C.* 15.
R.I.C. 79a   ..   .. 145·00

Very Fine

4099 **Æ heavy miliarense.** (*c.* 5.4 gm.) ℞. VOTIS / V. / MVLTIS / X. in laurel-wreath; in ex., TRPS.   *C.* 23.   *R.I.C.* 81. *Illustrated on p.* 342 .. £350·00

4100 **Æ miliarense.** (*c.* 4.5 gm.) ℞. VIRTVS EXERCITVS. Maximus stg. facing, hd. l., holding labarum and leaning on shield; in ex., TRPS. *C.* 19.   *R.I.C.* 82 .. .. 275·00

4101 **Æ siliqua.** (*c.* 2.25 gm.) ℞. VIRTVS ROMANORVM. Roma seated facing, hd. l., holding globe and spear; in ex., TRPS.   *C.* 20.   *R.I.C.* 84*b*. **Plate 12** .. .. 20·00

4102 As previous, but with MDPS in exergue.   *C.* 20.   *R.I.C.* 19*a* .. .. 25·00

4103 **Æ 2.** (*c.* 22 mm.) ℞. REPARATIO REIPVB. Maximus stg. l., raising kneeling female figure; in ex., PCON.   *C.* 3.   *R.I.C.* 26*a* .. .. 17·50

4104 ℞. VICTORIA AVGG. Maximus stg. facing, hd. l., holding Victory and standard; in ex., LVGS.   *C.* 10.   *R.I.C.* 33 .. .. 20·00

4105 **Æ 4.** (*c.* 15 mm.) ℞. — Victory advancing l.; in ex., LVGP.   *C.* 11. *R.I.C.* 34 .. .. 12·50

4106 **Æ 4.** (*c.* 13 mm.) ℞. SPES ROMANORVM. Camp-gate with star between its two turrets; in ex., TCON.   *C.* 7.   *R.I.C.* 29*a* .. .. 12·00

FLAVIUS VICTOR
A.D. 387–388

4107

The son of Magnus Maximus, Victor was raised to the rank of Augustus in A.D. 387*and remained in Gaul whilst his father invaded Italy. Following the death of Maximus, he was taken prisoner and executed by Arbogastes, the general of Theodosius.*

Mints: Treveri; Lugdunum; Arelate; Milan; Aquileia; Rome.

All have obv. as follows:
D . N . FL . VICTOR P . F . AVG.   *Diad., dr. and cuir. bust, r.*

4107 **Æ solidus.** ℞. BONO REIPVBLICE NATI. Two emperors enthroned facing, holding globe between them; in background, Victory stg. facing, wings spread; in ex., TROB.   *C.* 1.   *R.I.C.* 75. *Illustrated above* .. 900·00

4108 **Æ semissis.** ℞. VICTORIA AVGVSTORVM. Victory seated r., inscribing VOT . V . MVLT . X. on shield presented by winged Genius; in ex., MDOB. *C.* 5.   *R.I.C.* 17 .. .. 650·00

4109 **Æ tremissis.** ℞. — Victory advancing l.; in ex., MDOB. *C.*—. *R.I.C.* 18*b* .. .. 400·00

4110 **Æ siliqua.** ℞. VIRTVS ROMANORVM. Roma seated facing, hd. l., holding globe and spear; in ex., MDPS.   *C.* 6.   *R.I.C.* 19*b*. *Illustrated on p.* 15 .. .. 75·00

4111 **Æ 4.** (*c.* 13 mm.) ℞. SPES ROMANORVM. Camp-gate with star between its two turrets; in ex., PCON.   *C.* 3.   *R.I.C.* 29*b* .. .. 20·00

344

EUGENIUS
A.D. 392–394

4113

Following the death of Valentinian II in May, 392, the throne of the Western division of the Empire remained vacant for over three months until, on August 22nd, Arbogastes bestowed the purple upon Eugenius, the Master of Offices. A man of good family and originally a teacher of rhetoric and grammar, Eugenius lacked the strength of character to oppose the will of Arbogastes who was thus the real ruler of the Western provinces. Theodosius, of course, refused to countenance the rule of a barbarian general through a puppet emperor, and in 394 he marched into Italy and defeated his adversaries at the Battle on the Frigidus. Eugenius was put to death (September 6th, 394) and a few days later Arbogastes, who had fled into the mountains, committed suicide.

Mints: Treveri; Lugdunum; Arelate; Milan; Aquileia; Rome.

All have obv. as follows:

D . N . EVGENIVS P . F . AVG.   *Diad., dr. and cuir. bust, r.*

Very Fine

4112   **N solidus.** R. VICTORIA AVGG. Two emperors enthroned facing, holding globe between them; in background, Victory stg. facing, wings spread; in field, TR; in ex., COM. *C.* 6. *R.I.C.* 101 .. .. ..£250·00
There are larger gold, *aureus* (5½ gm.) and *double solidus.*

4113   **N tremissis.** R. VICTORIA AVGVSTORVM. Victory advancing l.; in field, TR; in ex., COM. *C.* 10. *R.I.C.* 103. *Illustrated above* .. .. 175·00

4114   **Æ heavy miliarense.** (*c.* 5.4 gm.) R. VOT. / V. / MVLT. / X. in wreath; in ex., MDPS. *C.* 17. *R.I.C.* 30 .. .. 450·00

4115   **Æ miliarense.** (*c.* 4.5 gm.) R. VIRTVS EXERCITVS. Eugenius stg. facing, hd. l., holding standard and leaning on shield; in ex., TRPS. *C.* 13. *R.I.C.* 105 .. .. 350·00

4116   **Æ siliqua.** R. VIRTVS ROMANORVM. Roma seated l., holding Victory and spear; in ex., TRPS. *Cf. C.* 14. *R.I.C.* 106d .. .. .. 65·00

4117   **Æ half-siliqua.** R. VICTORIA AVGGG. Victory advancing l.; in ex., MD. *C.* —. *R.I.C.* 33b .. .. 200·00

4118   **Æ 4.** (*c.* 13 mm.) R. As previous; in ex., LVGP. *Cf. C.* 8. *R.I.C.* 47a 35·00

ARCADIUS
A.D. 383–408

4129

Flavius Arcadius, the elder son of Theodosius I and Aelia Flaccilla, was born in A.D. 377 and was raised to the rank of Augustus by his father in 383. On the death of Theodosius in 395, the Empire was divided between his two sons, Arcadius taking the Eastern division, and Honorius the Western. The imperial brothers had inherited none of their father's great abilities, and in consequence both were constantly under the influence of the strong personalities *in their courts. During the reign of Arcadius, the government of the Eastern division of the Empire was successively in the hands of Rufinus the Praetorian Prefect, Eutropius the eunuch, Gaïnas the Goth, the Empress Eudoxia and finally the Praetorian Prefect Anthemius. On May 1st, 408, the feeble emperor expired in his palace at Constantinople and was succeeded by his seven-year-old son Theodosius II.*

Mints: Treveri; Lugdunum; Arelate; Milan; Aquileia; Rome; Siscia; Sirmium; Thessalonica; Heraclea; Constantinople; Nicomedia; Cyzicus; Antioch; Alexandria.

The obv. legend is D . N . ARCADIVS P . F . AVG.

The obv. type is diad., dr. and cuir. bust r., unless otherwise stated.

Very Fine

4119 **Ṇ solidus.** Ṛ. CONCORDIA AVGGG. Δ. Constantinopolis seated facing, hd. r., holding sceptre and shield inscribed VOT . V . MVL . X.; in ex., CONOB. *G.* 14. *R.I.C.* 70c .. .. £40·00

4120 Ṛ. VICTORIA AVGGG. Arcadius stg. r., holding standard and Victory, l. foot on captive; in field, MD; in ex., COMOB. *G.* 19. *R.I.C.* 35b. **Plate 12** .. .. 35·00
There are larger gold, 3 and 4½ *solidi.*

4121 **Ṇ semissis.** Ṛ. VICTORIA AVGVSTORVM. Victory seated r., inscribing VOT . X . MVLT . XX. on shield presented by winged Genius; in field, MD; in ex., COM. *G.* 20. *R.I.C.* 22 .. .. 90·00

4122 **Ṇ 1½ scripulum.** (1.70 gm.) Ṛ. — Victory seated r., inscribing VOT . V . MVL . X. on shield set on knee; in ex., CONOB. *G.* —. *R.I.C.* 50c .. .. 80·00

4123 **Ṇ tremissis.** (1.50 gm.) Ṛ. — Victory advancing r., holding wreath and cross on globe; in ex., CONOB. *G.* 22. *R.I.C.* 75c .. .. 50·00

4124 **Ṛ 3 miliarensia.** (c. 13.5 gm.) Ṛ. TRIVMFATOR GENT . BARB. Arcadius stg. facing, hd. l., holding labarum and globe; at feet l., captive; in ex., RE. *G.* 6. *R.I.C.* 52b .. .. *Very rare*

4125 **Ṛ heavy miliarense.** (c. 5.4 gm.) Ṛ. VOT. / X. / MVLT. / XX. in wreath; in ex., MDPS. *G.* 10. *R.I.C.* 24 .. .. .. 120·00

4126 **Ṛ miliarense.** (c. 4.5 gm.) Ṛ. GLORIA ROMANORVM. Arcadius, nimbate, stg. facing, hd. l., raising r. hand and holding globe; in ex., AQPS. *G.* 4. *R.I.C.* 56b .. .. 100·00

4127 **Ṛ siliqua.** Ṛ. VIRTVS ROMANORVM. Roma seated l., holding Victory and spear; in ex., TRPS. *G.* 25. *R.I.C.* 106b .. .. .. 12·50

4128 **Ṛ half-siliqua.** Ṛ. VICTORIA AVGGG. Victory advancing l.; in ex., MD. *G.* 30. *R.I.C.* 39a .. .. 40·00

4129 **Æ 2.** (c. 22 mm.) Diad., dr. and cuir. bust r., holding spear and shield; above, hand holding wreath. Ṛ. GLORIA ROMANORVM. Arcadius stg. facing, hd. l., holding standard and leaning on shield; at feet l., captive; in ex., CONΓ*. *G.* 31. *R.I.C.* 53a. *Illustrated on p. 344* .. .. 4·00

4130 Ṛ. VIRTVS EXERCITI. Arcadius stg. r., l. foot on captive, holding standard and globe; in ex., ALEΓ. *G.* 32. *R.I.C.* 18d .. .. 3·50

4131 Ṛ. GLORIA ROMANORVM. Arcadius stg. facing, hd. r., holding standard and globe; in ex., SMKA. *G.* 33. *R.I.C.* 27b .. .. .. 3·50

4132 **Æ 3.** Ṛ. — Arcadius on horseback r., raising r. hand; in ex., SMKB. *G.* 37. *R.I.C.* 29b .. .. 4·50

4133 Ṛ. VIRTVS EXERCITI. Arcadius stg. facing, hd. r., crowned by Victory stg. l. beside him; in ex., CONSA. *G.* 42 .. .. 3·00

4134 **Æ 4.** (c. 13 mm.) Ṛ. SALVS REIPVBLICAE. Victory advancing l., carrying trophy and dragging captive; in ex., CONSΓ. *G.* 45. *R.I.C.* 86c 1·50

4135 Ṛ. VOT. / X. / MVLT. / XX. in wreath; in ex., ANB. *G.* 48. *R.I.C.* 65c .. 1·75

EUDOXIA

4136

Aelia Eudoxia was the daughter of Bauto the Frank and was married to Arcadius in
A.D. 395. *She exercised considerable influence over her weak husband, and from* A.D. 400
till her death in October, 404, she was the virtual ruler of the Eastern division of the Empire.

Mints: Constantinople; Nicomedia; Cyzicus; Antioch; Alexandria.

Very Fine

4136 **N solidus.** AEL . EVDOXIA AVG. Diad. and dr. bust r.; above, hand
holding wreath. R. SALVS REIPVBLICAE. Victory seated r., inscribing
Christogram on shield set on cippus; in ex., CONOB. *G.* 2. *Illustrated
above* .. ..£150·00

4137 **N semissis.** — Diad. and dr. bust r. R. No legend. Christogram
in wreath; in ex., CONOB. *G.* 5 .. .. 175·00

4138 **N tremissis.** — — R. No Legend. Cross in wreath; in ex., CON.
G. 6 .. .. 75·0 0

4138A **R heavy miliarense.** (*c.* 5.4 gm.) — — R. No legend. Christogram in wreath; in ex., CONS. *G.* —. *Glendining sale,* 21/11/69, *lot* 435 2000·00

4139 **R siliqua.** — — R. As last, but no mint-mark. *G.* 7. .. .. 150·00

4140 **Æ 3.** *Obv.* As 4136. R. GLORIA ROMANORVM. Eudoxia enthroned
facing; above, hand holding wreath; in ex., ANT Δ. *G.* 8 .. .. 20·00

4141 As 4136, but with mint-mark CONSA. *G.* 9 .. .. 17·50

HONORIUS

A.D. 393–423

4147

The younger son of Theodosius I and Aelia Flaccilla, Flavius Honorius was born in
A.D. 384 *and was raised to the rank of Augustus in 393. On the death of Theodosius in 395,
Honorius succeeded to the throne of the Western division of the Empire, but the real power was
in the hands of his guardian Stilicho, whose daughter he later married. The period of
Honorius' reign witnessed the beginning of the final collapse of the Western half of the
Empire; the pressure of the barbarian peoples on the Roman frontiers became greater, and
finally in 406 a host of barbarians, mostly Vandals, crossed the Rhine and proceeded to
devastate Gaul, unopposed by any Roman army. The Visigoths, under the leadership of
Alaric, were also constantly threatening the security of Italy, but they were kept at bay by
Stilicho until 408 when the great general was executed as the result of a palace intrigue.
Italy was then at the mercy of Alaric, and Honorius remained helpless at Ravenna whilst*

Rome was besieged three times by the Goths and finally sacked in August, 410. Alaric died later in the same year and was succeeded by Ataulf who, in the spring of 412, led the Visigoths out of Italy into Gaul. The ensuing years were a period of recovery for the Western division of the Empire, thanks largely to the efforts of the great general Constantius who was raised to the rank of Augustus by Honorius in A.D. 421. The feeble son of Theodosius expired at Ravenna in August, 423, after an inglorious reign of thirty years.

Mints: Treveri; Lugdunum; Arelate; Ravenna; Milan; Aquileia; Rome; Sirmium; Thessalonica; Heraclea; Constantinople; Nicomedia; Cyzicus; Antioch; Alexandria.

The obv. legend is D . N . HONORIVS P . F . AVG.

The obv. type is diad., dr. and cuir. bust r., unless otherwise stated.

Very Fine

4142 *N* **solidus.** Helmeted and cuir. bust facing, holding spear and shield. ℞. CONCORDIA AVGGG. Constantinopolis seated facing, hd. r., holding sceptre and Victory; in ex., TESOB. *C.* 3. .. .. £50·00

4143 Helmeted, dr. and cuir. bust, r. ℞. VICTORIA AVGGG. Honorius stg. facing, r. foot on lion, holding long cross surmounted by P and two spears; above, hand holding wreath; in field, RV; in ex., COB. *C.* 43 .. 70·00

4144 ℞. — Honorius stg. r., holding standard and Victory, l. foot on captive; in field, MD; in ex., COMOB. *C.* 44. *R.I.C.* 35c. **Plate 12** .. .. 35·00
There are larger gold, 2¼ (?) and 4½ (?) *solidi.*

4145 *N* **semissis.** ℞. VICTORIA AVGVSTORVM. Victory seated r., inscribing VOT . X . MVLT . XV. on shield presented by winged Genius; in field, RV; in ex., COMOB. *C.* 50 .. .. 60·00

4146 *N* **tremissis.** ℞. — Victory advancing r., holding wreath and cross on globe; in field, RV; in ex., COM. *C.* 47 .. .. 30·00

4147 *AR* **3 miliarensia** (*c.* 13.5 gm.) ℞. TRIVMFATOR GENT . BARB. Honorius stg. facing, hd. l., holding labarum and globe; at feet l., captive; in ex., MDPS. *C.* 34. *Illustrated on p.* 346 .. *Very rare*

4148 *AR* **heavy miliarense.** (*c.* 5.4 gm.) ℞. VOT. / X. / MVLT. / XX. in wreath; in ex., MDPS. *C.* 64 .. .. 150·00

4149 *AR* **miliarense.** (*c.* 4.5 gm.) ℞. GLORIA ROMANORVM. Honorius stg. facing, holding sceptre and leaning on shield; in ex., CON. *C.* 19 .. 150·00

4150 *AR* **siliqua.** ℞. VIRTVS ROMANORVM. Roma seated l., holding Victory and spear; in ex., MDPS. *C.* 59 .. .. 12·50

4151 *AR* **half-siliqua.** ℞. VICTORIA AVGGG. Victory advancing l.; in ex., MD. *C.* 38. *R.I.C.* 38b .. .. 35·00

4152 *AE* **2.** (*c.* 22 mm.) ℞. GLORIA ROMANORVM. Honorius stg. facing, hd. r., holding standard and globe; in ex., SMNΓ. *C.* 20. *R.I.C.* 46c .. 4·50

4153 *AE* **3.** As 4142, but with *rev.* legend CONCORDIA AVGG. and mint-mark CONSA. *C.* 4 .. .. 4·00

4154 ℞. GLORIA ROMANORVM. Honorius on horseback r., raising r. hand; in ex., SMKA. *C.* 23. *R.I.C.* 29c .. .. 4·50

4155 ℞. — Arcadius, Honorius and Theodosius II stg. side by side; in ex., SMKΓ. *C.* 28 .. .. 5·00

4156 ℞. VIRTVS EXERCITI. Honorius stg. facing, hd. r., crowned by Victory stg. l. beside him; in ex., ANTΓ. *C.* 56 .. .. 4·00

4157 ℞. VRBS ROMA FELIX. Roma stg. facing, hd. r., holding trophy on spear and Victory; in ex., SMROM. *C.* 72. *R.I.C.* 67f .. .. 4·50

4158 *AE* **4.** (*c.* 13 mm.) ℞. SALVS REIPVBLICAE. Victory advancing l., carrying trophy and dragging captive; in ex., ALEA. *C.* 32. *R.I.C.* 23c 2·25

CONSTANTINE III
A.D. 407–411

4159

A common soldier, Constantine was proclaimed emperor by the legions in Britain in A.D. 407, and immediately crossed over to Gaul where he established himself side by side with the barbarian invaders of the province.   The following year he added Spain to his dominions, but in 409 this province was overrun by the Vandals, Alani, and Suevi, due to treachery on the part of Gerontius, one of the usurper's generals.   Constantine was eventually captured by Constantius, the general of Honorius, and was sent to Italy for execution (A.D. 411).

Mints: Treveri; Lugdunum; Arelate; Milan.

Very Fine

4159 **N solidus.**   D . N . CONSTANTINVS P . F . AVG.   Diad., dr. and cuir. bust, r.
R.   VICTORIA AAVGGG.   Constantine stg. r., l. foot on captive, holding
standard and Victory; in ex., TROBS   C. 5.   *Illustrated above* ..   .. £200·00

4160 **N tremissis.** — — R.   VICTORIA AVGGG.   Victory advancing r.,
holding wreath and globe; in field, AR; in ex., CONOB.   C. 2   ..   .. 225·00

4161 **Æ siliqua.** — — R.   VICTORIA AAVGGGG.   Roma seated l., holding
Victory and spear; in ex., SMLD.   C. 7   ..   .. 125·00

CONSTANS
A.D. 408–411

The son of Constantine III, Constans was raised to the rank of Augustus by his father in A.D. 408 and led the invasion of Spain later the same year.   In 411 he was besieged in Vienne by Gerontius who later put him to death.

Mint: Arelate.

4162 **Æ siliqua.**   D . N . CONSTANS P . F . AVG.   Diad., dr. and cuir. bust, r.
R.   VICTORIA AAVGGG.   Roma seated l., holding Victory and spear;
in ex., KONT.   C. 1 ..   .. 250·00

MAXIMUS
A.D. 409–411

A man of obscure origin, Maximus was proclaimed emperor in Spain in A.D. 409 by the general Gerontius, who had rebelled against Constantine III and Constans.   After the death of Gerontius in 411, Maximus was pardoned by Honorius and permitted to retire into private life.

Mint: Barcino.

4163 **Æ siliqua.**   D . N . MAXIMVS P . F . AVG.   Diad., dr. and cuir. bust, r.
R.   VICTORIA AAVGGG.   Roma seated l., holding Victory and spear;
in ex., SMBA.   C. 1 ..   .. 300·00

PRISCUS ATTALUS
A.D. 409–410 and 414–415

4166

A Roman of noble descent, Attalus was Prefect of Rome at the time of Alaric's second siege of the city, in A.D. 409. By threatening to destroy the granaries at Ostia, Alaric forced the Senate to raise Attalus to the rank of Augustus, and the feeble emperor, grateful for his elevation, was content to act as a puppet of the barbarian king. The following year (A.D. 410) he was deposed because of his incompetence, but he remained in the Gothic camp and four years later was again proclaimed emperor, this time by Ataulf, Alaric's successor. He was finally deposed in 415 and shortly afterwards was delivered into the hands of Honorius, who banished him to Lipara.

All the coins of Attalus were struck during his first reign.

Mint: Rome.

Very Fine

4164 **N solidus.** PRISCVS ATTALVS P . F . AVG. Diad., dr. and cuir. bust, r.
R. INVICTA ROMA AETERNA. Roma seated facing, holding Victory and
sceptre; in field, RM; in ex., COMOB. *C. 3* .. ..£750·00

4165 IMP . PRISCVS ATTALVS P . F . AVG. — R. VICTORIA AVGVSTI. Attalus
stg. r., l. foot on captive, holding standard and Victory; in field, RM; in
ex., COMOB. *C. 9* .. .. 750·00

4166 **N tremissis.** As 4164, but with *obv.* legend PRISC . ATTALVS P . F . AVG.
C. 4. Illustrated above .. .. 600·00

4167 **R siliqua.** *Obv.* As 4164. R. INVICTA ROMA AETERNA. Roma
seated l., holding Victory and spear; in ex., PST. *C. 7* .. .. 350·00

4168 **Æ 3.** — R. VICTORIA ROMANORVM. Victory advancing l.; in ex.,
SMVRM. *Cf. C. 14* .. .. 75·00

JOVINUS
A.D. 411–413

4169

A Gaulish noble, Jovinus was proclaimed emperor at Mainz in A.D. 411 by Guntiarius, king of the Burgundians, and Goar, king of the Alani. The usurper maintained his position in Gaul for about two years, but was eventually captured by Ataulf the Visigoth, who was in alliance with Honorius, and taken to Narbonne where he was executed by the order of Dardanus, the Praefect of the Gauls.

Mints: Treveri; Lugdunum; Arelate.

4169 **N solidus.** D . N . IOVINVS P . F . AVG. Diad., dr. and cuir. bust, r. R.
RESTITVTOR REIP. Jovinus stg. r., l. foot on captive, holding standard and
Victory; in field, TR; in ex., COMOB. *C. 1. Illustrated above* .. .. 450·00

4170 **R siliqua.** — — R. — Roma seated l., holding Victory and spear;
in ex., KONT. *C. 2* .. .. 125·00

4171 — — R. VICTORIA AVGG. As previous; in ex., SMLD. *C. 4* .. .. 125·00

4172 **R half-siliqua.** — — R. No legend. Cross between A and ധ; in
ex., SMLD. *C. 8* .. .. 300·00

350

SEBASTIANUS
A.D. 412–413

Sebastianus was the brother of Jovinus, who raised him to the rank of Augustus in
A.D. 412. *The following year, however, he was defeated and slain by Ataulf.*

Mint: Arelate.

4173   **Æ siliqua.**   D . N . SEBASTIANVS P . F . AVG.   Diad., dr. and cuir. bust, r.
    R.   VICTORIA AVGG.   Roma seated l., holding Victory and spear; in ex.,
    KONT.   *C.* 1 ..   ..   *Extr. rare*

CONSTANTIUS III
A.D. 421

4174

*Born of humble parents at Naissus in Dacia, Flavius Constantius adopted a military
career and soon proved himself to be a soldier of outstanding ability.   Eventually, in the later
part of the reign of Honorius, he became the foremost general of the Western division of the
Empire, and achieved considerable success against both usurpers and barbarians.   His
authority was so great that he became the virtual ruler of the Western provinces, and in
A.D. 417 he married Galla Placidia, the half-sister of Honorius.   Finally, on February 8th,
421, he was raised to the rank of Augustus, but the government at Constantinople refused to
recognize the new emperor, and civil war was only averted by the premature death of
Constantius, less than seven months after his elevation.*

Mints: Lugdunum; Ravenna.

Very Fine

4174   **N solidus.**   D . N . CONSTANTIVS P . F . AVG.   Diad., dr. and cuir. bust, r.
    R.   VICTORIA AVGGG.   Constantius stg. r., l. foot on captive, holding
    standard and Victory; in field, RV; in ex., COMOB.   *C.* 1.   *Illustrated
    above* ..   ..£750·00

4175   **N tremissis.** — —   R.   VICTORIA AVGVSTORVM.   Victory advancing r.,
    holding wreath and cross on globe; in field, RV; in ex., COM.   *C.* 2   ..   400·00

4176   **Æ siliqua.**   CONSTANTIVS AVG. —   R.   VOTIS / V. / MVLTIS / X. in laurel-
    wreath; in ex., LVG.   *C.* 5 ..   ..   300·00

GALLA PLACIDIA

4178

*Born about A.D. 388, Galla Placidia was the daughter of Theodosius I and Galla and the
half-sister of Arcadius and Honorius.   Taken prisoner by Alaric during the sack of Rome in
410, she was eventually married to his successor, Ataulf, in 414.   After the death of Ataulf*

she was returned to the Romans in exchange for 600,000 measures of corn, and in January,
417, she was married to the general Constantius. During the first twelve years of the reign of
her son, Valentinian III, she acted as regent of the Western provinces, but her last years were
devoted to the erection of churches and other sacred buildings at Ravenna. She died at
Rome in A.D. *450.*

Mints: Aquileia; Ravenna; Rome; Constantinople.

Very Fine

4177　*N* **solidus.**　D . N . GALLA PLACIDIA P . F . AVG.　Diad. and dr. bust r.;
above, hand holding wreath.　R.　VOT . XX . MVLT . XXX.　Victory stg. l.,
holding long cross; in field, RV; in ex., COMOB.　*C.* 13　..　　..　..£375·00

4178　*N* **semissis.** — Diad. and dr. bust, r.　R.　SALVS REIPVBLICAE.
Christogram in wreath; in ex., COMOB.　*C.* 10.　*Illustrated on p.* 350　..　250·00

4179　*N* **tremissis.** — — R.　No legend.　Christogram in wreath; in ex.,
COMOB.　*C.* 15　..　　　..　　　　..　　　　　..　　..　150·00

4180　— — R.　No legend.　Cross in wreath; in ex., COMOB.　*C.* 17　..　150·00

4181　*R* **siliqua.** — — R.　No legend.　Christogram in wreath; in ex., RV.
C. 16 ..　　..　　..　　..　　　..　　　　..　　..　200·00

4182　Æ **4.** — — R.　SALVS REIPVBLICAE.　Cross; in ex., RM.　*C.* 11　..　75·00

JOHANNES
A.D. 423–425

4183

Born about A.D. *380, Johannes entered the civil service and eventually became the*
principal secretary to Honorius. On the death of the emperor, in August, 423, he immediately
assumed the purple, but Theodosius II refused to recognize his elevation and sent an army to
Italy to champion the cause of the rightful heir to the Western throne, the infant Placidius
Valentinianus. Johannes had very few troops at his disposal and was finally captured at
Ravenna in the early summer of A.D. *425. He was then taken to Aquileia where he was first*
mutilated, then exhibited in the circus mounted on an ass, and finally executed.

Mints: Arelate; Ravenna; Rome.

4183　*N* **solidus.**　D . N . IOHANNES P . F . AVG.　Diad., dr. and cuir. bust, r.
R.　VICTORIA AVGGG.　Johannes stg. r., l. foot on captive, holding
standard and Victory; in field, RV; in ex., COMOB.　*C.* 4.　*Illustrated*
above ..　　..　　..　　..　　..　　..　　..　　..　..　250·00

4184　*N* **tremissis.** — — R.　VICTORIA AVGVSTORVM.　Victory advancing r.,
holding wreath and cross on globe; in field, RV; in ex., COMOB.　*C.* 8 ..　150·00

4185　*R* **siliqua.** — — R.　VRBS ROMA.　Roma seated l., holding Victory
and spear; in ex., RVPS.　*C.* 9　..　　..　..　　..　　..　..　225·00

4186　*R* **half-siliqua.** — — R.　VICTORIA AVGG.　Victory stg. l.; in ex.,
RV.　*C.* 3　..　　..　　..　　..　　..　　..　　..　..　200·00

4187　Æ **4.** — — R.　SALVS REIPVBLICE.　Victory advancing l., holding
trophy and dragging captive; in ex., RM.　*Cf. C.* 1　..　　..　..　60·00

THEODOSIUS II
A.D. 402–450

4188

The son of Arcadius and Eudoxia, Theodosius II was born in A.D. 401 *and was raised to the rank of Augustus at the age of nine months (January,* 402). *At the time of his father's death he was still only seven years of age, and the regency was at first assumed by the Praetorian Prefect, Anthemius. In* A.D. 414 *this task was taken over by the young emperor's sister, Aelia Pulcheria, and she continued to be the* de facto *ruler even after her brother had attained his majority. In contrast to the great political upheavals which were occurring in the West, the Eastern division of the Empire enjoyed comparative peace for most of the long reign of Theodosius, and one of the most notable achievements of the period was the compilation of the legal code known as the Codex Theodosianus. In the last years of the reign, however, the Balkan Peninsula was repeatedly ravaged by the Huns, and the emperor was obliged to conclude several treaties with the great Attila, the terms of which were very humiliating for the Romans. Theodosius II died at Constantinople in July,* 450, *after having injured his spine in a hunting accident.*

Mints: Treveri; Ravenna; Rome; Thessalonica; Heraclea; Constantinople; Nicomedia; Cyzicus; Antioch; Alexandria.

Very Fine

4188 **N solidus.** D . N . THEODOSIVS P . F . AVG. Helmeted and cuir. bust facing, holding spear and shield. R. IMP . XXXXII . COS . XVII . P . P. Roma seated l., holding cross on globe and sceptre; in ex., CONOB. *G.* 8 £30·00

4189 — — R. SALVS REIPVBLICAE Γ. Theodosius II and Valentinian III enthroned facing; in ex., CONOB. *G.* 9 .. .. 40·00

4190 — — R. VOT . XX . MVLT . XXX . I. Victory stg. l., holding long cross; in ex., CONOB. *G.* 12 .. .. 30·00

4191 — Diad., dr. and cuir. bust, r. R. VICTORIA AVGGG. Theodosius stg. r., l. foot on captive, holding standard and Victory; in field, RV; in ex., COMOB. *G.* 10 .. .. 50·00

4192 **N semissis.** — — R. VICTORIA AVGG. Victory seated r., inscribing shield set on l. knee; in ex., CONOB. *G.* 15 .. .. .. 30·00

4193 **N tremissis.** — — R. VICTORIA AVGVSTORVM. Victory advancing r.; in ex., CONOB. *G.* 16 .. .. 20·00

4194 — — R. No legend. Trophy; in ex., CONOB. *G.* 17 .. .. 37·50

4195 **R siliqua.** — — R. VOT. / MVLT. / XXXX. in wreath; in ex., CONS*. *G.* 20 .. .. 45·00

4196 **Æ 3.** *Obv.* As 4188. R. CONCORDIA AVGG. Constantinopolis seated facing, hd. r., holding spear and Victory; in ex., CONSA. *G.* 21 .. 10·00

4197 **Æ 4.** *Obv.* As 4191. R. No legend. Cross in wreath; in ex., SMN Δ. *G.* 25.. .. .. 5·00

4198 — R. Monogram of Theodosius in wreath; in ex., CON. *G.* 26 .. 6·50

EUDOCIA

4199

The daughter of the Athenian sophist Leontius, she was originally named Athenais but changed this to Aelia Eudocia shortly before her marriage to Theodosius II in A.D. 421. For a time she exercised considerable political influence, but in 441 she retired to Jerusalem and devoted the rest of her life to the erection of churches and monasteries. She died on October 20th, 460.

Mint: Constantinople.

Very Fine

4199 **N solidus.** AEL . EVDOCIA AVG. Diad. and dr. bust r.; above, hand holding wreath. R . VOT . XX . MVLT . XXX . I. Victory stg. l., holding long cross; in ex., CONOB. *G.* 3. *Illustrated above* .. .. ..£175·00

4200 **N semissis.** — Diad. and dr. bust, r. R . No legend. Christogram in wreath; in ex., CONOB*. *G.* 5 .. .. 100·00

4201 **N tremissis.** — — R . No legend. Cross in wreath; in ex., CONOB*. *G.* 6 .. .. 60·00

4202 **R siliqua.** — — R . As previous; in ex., CONS*. *G.* 7 .. .. 90·00

4203 **Æ 4.** — — R . CONCORDIA AVG. Eudocia enthroned facing; above, hand holding wreath; in ex., CON. *G.* —.. .. .. 30·00

PULCHERIA

4204

The daughter of Arcadius and Eudoxia, Aelia Pulcheria was born in A.D. 399 and created Augusta on July 4th, 414. Although only fifteen years of age, she immediately assumed the regency on behalf of her younger brother, Theodosius II, and as the young emperor possessed none of the abilities required of a good ruler, she remained in control of the government even after he had attained his majority. The empress maintained her supremacy throughout most of her brother's long reign, and after his death, in 450, it was she who selected a successor. She died in July, 453, leaving all her possessions to the poor.

Mint: Constantinople.

4204 **N solidus.** AEL . PVLCHERIA AVG. Diad. and dr. bust r.; above, hand holding wreath. R . VOT . XX . MVLT . XXX. Victory stg. l., holding long cross; in ex., CONOB. *G.* 4. *Illustrated above* .. .. .. 160·00

4205 **N semissis.** — Diad. and dr. bust, r. R . No legend. Christogram in wreath; in ex., CONOB*. *G.* 6 .. .. 150·00

4206 **N tremissis.** — — R . No legend. Cross in wreath; in ex., CONOB*. *G.* 7 .. .. 50·00

Very Fine

4207 **Æ siliqua.** — — R. No legend. Cross in wreath; in ex., CONS*.
G. 8 .. ..£125·00

4208 **Æ half-siliqua.** — — R. As previous. *G.* — .. .. .. 125·00

4209 **Æ 4.** — — R. SALVS REIPVBLICAE. Victory seated r., inscribing
Christogram on shield set on cippus; in ex., CONЄ. *G.* 9 .. .. 40·00

VALENTINIAN III

A.D. 425–455

4211

Born in A.D. 419, *Placidius Valentinianus was the son of Constantius III and Galla
Placidia. Some time after the death of Constantius, Placidia quarrelled with Honorius,
and the empress and her children fled from Ravenna to Constantinople to seek refuge with
their kindred* (A.D. 423). *Two years later, however, they returned to Italy, and after the
death of the usurper Johannes they travelled to Rome where Valentinian was proclaimed
Augustus* (October 23rd, 425). *For the first twelve years of the reign Placidia acted as
regent, but the control of the government then passed into the hands of the great general
Aetius, and he maintained his supremacy until his assassination in 454. The dissolution of
the Western division of the Empire continued steadily throughout the long reign of Valentinian,
the greatest disaster of the period being the loss of Africa to the Vandals. In 451 Attila
invaded Gaul, but the immediate danger was averted by the victory of Aetius and his
Visigothic allies over the Huns at the famous battle of Mauriacus. Valentinian III was
assassinated in March, 455, the victim of a plot hatched by the senator Petronius Maximus.*

Mints: Treveri; Ravenna; Rome; Constantinople; Cyzicus.

4210 **N solidus.** D . N . PLA . VALENTINIANVS P . F . AVG. Diad., dr. and cuir.
bust, r. R. VICTORIA AVGGG. Valentinian stg. facing, r. foot on
serpent, holding long cross and Victory; in field, RV; in ex., COMOB.
C. 19 .. .. 35·00

4211 — Diad. and mantled bust l., holding mappa and cross. R. VOT . X .
MVLT . XX. Valentinian seated facing, holding mappa and cross; in field,
RM; in ex., COMOB. *C.* 41. *Illustrated above* .. .. .. 100·00

4212 **N semissis.** — Diad., dr. and cuir. bust, r. R. SALVS REIPVBLICAE.
Victory seated r., inscribing VOT . X . MVLT . XX. on shield presented by
winged Genius; in ex., CONOB. *C.* 8 .. .. 75·00

4213 **N tremissis.** — — R. No legend. Cross in wreath; in ex., COMOB.
C. 49 .. .. 30·00

4214 **Æ siliqua.** — — R. VRBS ROMA. Roma seated l., holding Victory
and spear; in ex., RMPS. *C.* 46 .. .. 100·00

4215 **Æ half-siliqua.** — — R. VICTORIA AVGG. Victory stg. l.; in ex.,
RV. *C.* 11 .. .. 85·00

4216 **Æ 4.** — — R. SALVS REIPVBLICE. Victory stg. l.; in ex., RM. *C.* — 25·00

4217 D . N . VALENTINIANVS P . F . AVG. — R. VOT . PVB. Camp-gate; in ex.,
RPM. *C.* — .. .. 25·00

LICINIA EUDOXIA

The daughter of Theodosius II and Eudocia, Licinia Eudoxia was born in A.D. 422 and married to Valentinian III on October 29th, 437. After her husband's death, in 455, she was forced to marry his murderer and successor, Petronius Maximus, but later the same year Rome was sacked by the Vandals and Eudoxia was carried off as a captive to Carthage. In 462 she was released by Gaiseric, the Vandal king, and travelled to Constantinople where she spent the remainder of her life.

Mints: Ravenna; Rome.

Very Fine

4218 *N* **solidus.** LICINIA EVDOXIA P . F . AVG. Dr. bust facing, wearing rad. crown surmounted by cross. R. SALVS REIPVBLICAE. Eudoxia enthroned facing, holding cross on globe and long cross; in field, RV; in ex., COMOB. *C. 1* ..   ..   £1400·00

HONORIA

4219

The daughter of Constantius III and Galla Placidia, Justa Grata Honoria was born in A.D. 417 and was probably created Augusta in 425, soon after the elevation of her brother, Valentinian III, to the Western throne. She died in A.D. 454.

Mints: Ravenna; Rome.

4219 *N* **solidus.** D . N . IVST . GRAT . HONORIA P . F . AVG. Diad. and dr. bust r.; above, hand holding wreath. R. BONO REIPVBLICAE. Victory stg. l., holding long cross; in field, RV; in ex., COMOB. *C. 1.* *Illustrated above* ..   ..   700·00

4220 *N* **semissis.** — Diad. and dr. bust r. R. SALVS REIPVBLICAE. Christogram in wreath; in ex., COMOB. *C. 2* ..   ..   ..   400·00

4221 *N* **tremissis.** — — R. No legend. Cross in wreath; in ex., COMOB. *C. 5* ..   ..   225·00

MARCIAN
A.D. 450–457

4222

Following the death of Theodosius II in 450, the choice of a successor was left to the late emperor's sister, Pulcheria. She selected the senator Marcian, a distinguished soldier of humble origin, and having given him her hand in nominal marriage she crowned him in the

Palace of Hebdomon (August 25th).   Marcian soon proved himself to be a wise and generous emperor, and the period of his rule was a time of peace for the Eastern division of the Empire. In 451 the famous Fourth Ecumenical Council was held at Chalcedon, and it is, perhaps, for this event that the reign of Marcian is best remembered.   The emperor died early in A.D. 457 *at the age of* 67.

Mints: Ravenna; Thessalonica; Heraclea; Constantinople; Nicomedia; Cyzicus; Antioch.

Very Fine

4222 **N solidus.** D . N . MARCIANVS P . F . AVG.   Helmeted and cuir. bust facing, holding spear and shield.   R.   VICTORIA AVGGG . A.   Victory stg. l., holding long cross; in ex., CONOB.   *G.* 4.   *Illustrated on p.* 355 .. £35·00

4223 — Diad., dr. and cuir. bust, r.   R.   VICTORIA AVGGG.   Marcian stg. facing, r. foot on serpent, holding long cross and Victory; in field, RV; in ex., COMOB.   *G.* 5   ..   ..   75·00

4224 **N semissis.** — — R.   VICTORIA AVGG.   Victory seated r., inscribing shield set on l. knee; in ex., CONOB.   *G.* 6   ..   ..   60·00

4225 **N tremissis.** — — R.   VICTORIA AVGVSTORVM.   Victory advancing r., hd. turned; in ex., CONOB.   *G.* 7 ..   ..   30·00

4226 **R siliqua.** — — R.   SAL. / REI / PVI. in wreath; in ex., CONS*.   *G.* 9   120·00

4227 **Æ 4.** — — R.   Monogram of Marcian in wreath; in ex., CON.   *G.* 12   7·50

4228 As previous, but with mint-mark NIC.   *G.* 12   ..   ..   8·50

PETRONIUS MAXIMUS

A.D. 455

Born in A.D. 395, *Petronius Maximus was a member of the great senatorial family of the Anicii, and in the later years of Honorius he became one of the most prominent senators at Rome.   He held a succession of important offices under Honorius and Valentinian III, and in 455 his ambition drove him to make a bid for the throne itself.   He arranged for the assassination of Valentinian III, and the deed having been done he was duly proclaimed emperor* (*March 17th*).   *His position was soon threatened, however, by the Vandal king, Gaiseric, who put out of Carthage with a large fleet and set sail for Rome.   Maximus was panic-stricken and decided to flee from the doomed city, but as he was riding through the streets he was attacked and killed by the mob* (*May 31st*).

Mints: Ravenna; Rome.

4229 **N solidus.** D . N . PETRONIVS MAXIMVS P . F . AVG.   Diad., dr. and cuir. bust, r.   R.   VICTORIA AVGGG.   Maximus stg. facing, r. foot on serpent, holding long cross and Victory; in field, RM; in ex., COMOB.   *C.* 1   ..   750·00

AVITUS

A.D. 455–456

4230

Descended from one of the noble families of Gaul, Marcus Maecilius Flavius Eparchius Avitus was the commander of the troops in his native province at the time of the death of

Petronius Maximus. The Visigothic king, Theodoric II, persuaded him to claim the vacant throne of the West, and on July 10th, 455, he was proclaimed emperor at Toulouse by the Goths. Although popular in Gaul, the new emperor was greatly disliked at Rome, and when he stripped the bronze from the roofs of public buildings in order to pay his Gothic allies, the Romans finally revolted and Avitus fled from the city. He was later defeated at Placentia by the general Ricimer and then deposed from the throne (October 17th, 456). The bishopric of Placentia was immediately bestowed upon him, but he died soon afterwards.

Mints: Arelate; Milan.

Very Fine

4230   **N solidus.**   D . N . AVITVS PERP . F . AVG.   Diad., dr. and cuir. bust, r.
       R.   VICTORIA AVGGG.   Avitus stg. r., l. foot on captive, holding long
       cross and Victory; in field, AR; in ex., COMOB.   *C.* 5.   *Illustrated on
       p.* 356 ..   ..£600·00

4231   **N tremissis.**   D . N . AVITVS PERP . AG.   — R.   No legend.   Cross in
       wreath; in ex., CONOB.   *C.* 11   ..   ..   275·00

4232   **R siliqua.**   D . N . AVTIVS P . F . AVG.   — R.   VRBIS ROMA.   Roma
       seated l., holding Victory and spear.   *C.* 9   ..   ..   ..   500·00

LEO I

A.D. 457–474

4234

A native of Dacia and a man of considerable military experience, though of little education, Leo was proclaimed emperor soon after the death of Marcian, early in A.D. 457. At the time of his accession, the army of the East was composed almost entirely of Germans and other foreigners, and it was the one great achievement of Leo that he succeeded in destroying the immense power of the German military faction which was threatening the security of the State. This he accomplished by recruiting large numbers of Isaurians who, though native subjects of the Empire, were just as fierce and formidable as the German barbarians. In 473 Leo was attacked by a serious illness and he thereupon raised his infant grandson, Leo II, to the rank of Augustus in order to settle the question of succession. He died on February 3rd of the following year, at the age of 63.

Mints: Milan; Rome; Thessalonica; Heraclea; Constantinople; Nicomedia; Cyzicus; Antioch; Alexandria.

4233   **N solidus.**   D . N . LEO PERPET . AVG.   Helmeted and cuir. bust facing,
       holding spear and shield.   R.   VICTORIA AVGGG . Γ.   Victory stg. l.,
       holding long cross; in ex., CONOB.   *G.* 6.   **Plate 12** ..   ..   30·00

4234   — Diad. and mantled bust l., holding mappa and long cross.   R.
       VICTORIA AVGGG.   Leo seated facing, holding mappa and cross; in ex.,
       THSOB.   *G.* 7.   *Illustrated above* ..   ..   90·00

4235   — Diad., dr. and cuir. bust, r.   R. —   Leo stg. facing, r. foot on
       serpent holding, long cross and Victory; in field, MD; in ex., COMOB.
       G. 8 ..   ..   70·00

4236   **N semissis.** — — R.   VICTORIA AVGG.   Victory seated r., inscribing
       shield set on l. knee; in ex., CONOB.   *G.* 10   ..   ..   ..   40·00

4237   **N tremissis.** — — R.   VICTORIA AVGVSTORVM.   Victory advancing r.,
       hd. turned; in ex., CONOB.   *G.* 11 ..   ..   25·00

Very Fine

4238   **Æ siliqua.** — — R.   SAL. / REI / PVI. in wreath; in ex., CONS*.   *G.* 14 £65·00
There is a very large silver piece (40 mm.) and also one of 22 mm.

4239   **Æ 2.** (*c.* 20 mm.) — — R.   SALVS RPVRLICA (*sic*). Leo stg. r., l.
foot on captive, holding standard and globe; in ex., CON.   *G.* 16   ..   50·00

4240   **Æ 4.** — — R. No legend. Lion stg. l., hd. turned; in ex., CON.
G. 21 ..   ..   10·00

4241   D . N . LEO P . F . AVG. — R. No legend. Lion crouching l. within
wreath; in ex., CON.   *G.* 21 ..   ..   10·00

4242   D . N . LEO. — R. Monogram of Leo; in ex., CON.   *G.* 20   ..   ..   8·00

4243

VERINA

A woman of great energy and ambition, Aelia Verina was the wife of Leo I and the mother-in-law of Zeno. After the death of her husband in 474 she continued to play a leading part in political life, and was implicated in two serious revolts against Zeno—that of her brother Basiliscus (475-476) and that of Leontius (484-488). She eventually expired at the Isaurian fortress of Cherris in the autumn of A.D. 484, after having witnessed the failure of the revolt of Leontius.

Mint: Constantinople.

4243   *N* **solidus.** AEL . VERINA AVG. Diad. and dr. bust r.; above, hand
holding wreath. R. VICTORIA AVGGG. Θ. Victory stg. l., holding
long cross; in ex., CONOB. *G.* 1. *Illustrated above*   ..   ..   .. 700·00

4244   *N* **tremissis.** — Diad. and dr. bust, r. R. No legend. Cross in
wreath; in ex., CONOB.   *G.* 2   ..   .. 250·00

4245   **Æ 2.** (*c.* 20 mm.) — — R.   SALVS REIPVBLICAE. Victory seated r.,
inscribing Christogram on shield set on cippus; in ex., CONE. *G.* 3 .. 120·00

LEO II
A.D. 473–474

4246

The son of Zeno and Ariadne, Leo II was born about A.D. 467 and was raised to the rank of Augustus by his grandfather, Leo I, in October, 473. Following the death of Leo I less than four months later, the infant Leo II was left as sole ruler, but he was a sickly child and it was rightly feared that he had not long to live. Accordingly, the empresses Ariadne and Verina instructed him to crown his father co-emperor, and the coronation of Zeno took place in the Hippodrome on February 9th, 474. Leo II died nine months later, and on the evidence of the coins it would seem that at some time during this period he was relegated to the rank of Caesar.

It seems that there were no coins of Leo II issued before the elevation of Zeno on Feb. 9th, A.D. 474. There are two varieties of obv. legend for the joint reign of Leo II and Zeno:

A. D . N . LEO ET ZENO PP . AVG.

B. D . N . ZENO ET LEO NOV . CAES.

The portraits on the coins bearing legend A *might be intended to represent Leo II, but it seems more likely that the emperor depicted is Zeno who was the real ruler. Portraits on coins with legend* B *are almost certainly intended to represent Zeno.*

Mints: Rome; Constantinople.

Very Fine

4246 *N* **solidus.** A. Helmeted and cuir. bust facing, holding spear and shield. ℞. SALVS REIPVBLICAE I. Leo II and Zeno enthroned facing; in ex., CONOB. *G. (Leo II)* 1. *Illustrated on p. 358* .. .. ..£100·00

4247 A. — ℞. VICTORIA AVGGG. Victory stg. l., holding long cross; in ex., CONOB. *G. (Leo II)* 2. .. .. 120·00

4248 B. — ℞. VICTORIA AVGGG . Z. As previous. *G. (Zeno)* 1 .. .. 165·00

4249 *N* **semissis.** A. Diad., dr. and cuir. bust. ℞. VICTORIA AVGG. Victory seated r., inscribing shield set on l. knee; in ex., CONOB. *G. (Leo II)* 3 .. .. 100·00

4250 *N* **tremissis.** A. — ℞. VICTORIA AVGVSTORVM. Victory advancing r., hd. turned; in ex., CONOB. *G. (Leo II)* 4 .. .. 50·00

4251 B. — ℞. As previous. *G. (Zeno)* 2 .. .. 75·00

4252 Æ **1.** (*c.* 31 mm.) B. Laur. hd., r. ℞. INVICTA ROMA. Victory advancing r., holding wreath and trophy; in field, SC; in ex., XL. *G. (Zeno)* 3 .. .. 100·00

4253

MAJORIAN
A.D. 457–461

Following the deposition of Avitus in October, 456, there was an interval of nearly six months before the next emperor, Julius Valerianus Majorianus, came to the throne. Descended from an old Roman family, Majorian had served with distinction under Aetius, and he soon proved himself to be a much worthier emperor than any of his immediate predecessors. He entered Gaul late in 458 and defeated the Visigoths near Arelate, after which he began preparations for an attack on the Vandals in Africa. A great fleet was assembled in the Spanish port of Alicante, but with the aid of treachery the Vandals succeeded in destroying most of the Roman ships before the expedition had even set out (A.D. 460). Majorian returned to Italy the following year, but at Tortona he was arrested, deposed and executed by the order of the general Ricimer.

Mints: Arelate; Milan; Ravenna; Rome.

4253 *N* **solidus.** D . N . IVLIVS MAIORIANVS P . F . AVG. Helmeted, dr. and cuir. bust r., holding spear and shield. ℞. VICTORIA AVGGG. Majorian stg. facing, r. foot on serpent, holding long cross and Victory; in field, AR; in ex., COMOB. *C.* 1. *Illustrated above* .. .. 175·00

4254 *N* **tremissis.** — Diad., dr. and cuir. bust, r. ℞. No legend. Cross in wreath; in ex., COMOB. *C.* 15. **Plate 12** .. .. 90·00

Very Fine

4255 **R siliqua.** — Helmeted, dr. and cuir. bust r., holding spear. R.
VOTIS MVLTIS. Majorian stg. facing, holding spear and shield. *C.* 14. . £200·00

4256 **R half-siliqua.** D . N . MAIORIANVS P . F . AVG. — R. As previous.
C. 13 . .   . .   150·00

4257 **Æ 4.** D . N . IVL . MAIORIANVS P . F . AVG. Diad., dr. and cuir. bust, r.
R. VICTORIA AVGGG. Victory advancing l.; in ex., MD. *C.* 6. .   . .   40·00

SEVERUS III
A.D. 461–465

4258

*Of Lucanian origin, Libius Severus was proclaimed emperor at Ravenna on November
19th, 461, nearly four months after the death of Majorian.   He was, however, a mere puppet-
emperor and was content to leave the administration of the State to the general Ricimer,
who had secured his elevation.   He died after an insignificant reign of four years, the
victim, perhaps, of his patron.   Of him, Edward Gibbon write "History has scarcely
deigned to notice his birth, his elevation, his character, or his death".*

Mints: Arelate; Milan; Ravenna; Rome.

4258 **N solidus.** D . N . LIBIVS SEVERVS P . F . AVG. Diad., dr. and cuir. bust, r.
R. VICTORIA AVGGG. Severus stg. facing, r. foot on serpent, holding long
cross and Victory; in field, AR; in ex., COMOB. *C.* 8.   *Illustrated above* . .   100·00

4259 **N semissis.** — — R. SALVS REIPVBLICAE. Christogram in wreath;
in ex., COMOB. *C.* 2. .   . .   .   120·00

4260 **N tremissis.** D . N . LIB . SEVERVS P . F . AVG. — R. No legend.
Cross in wreath; in ex., COMOB. *C.* 19 . .   . .   60·00

4261 **R siliqua.** — — R. VRBIS ROMA. Roma seated l., holding Victory
and spear; in ex., SMPS. *C.* 15 . .   . .   140·00

4262 **R half-siliqua.** — — R. No legend. Christogram in wreath; in
ex., RM. *C.* 16   . .   . .   100·00

4263 **Æ 4.** — — R. VICTO . AVG. Victory stg. l.; in ex., RM. *Cf. C.* 3 . .   25·00

4264 — — R. Monogram of Severus; no mint-mark. *Cf. C.* 18 . .   . .   25·00

ANTHEMIUS
A.D. 467–472

4266

*For about a year and a half following the death of Severus III the Western throne
remained vacant, but in A.D. 467 Leo selected the patrician Procopius Anthemius to be his
colleague in the government of the Empire.   Anthemius, who was the son-in-law of the
emperor Marcian, immediately travelled to Italy and was proclaimed emperor near Rome on
April 12th.   The marriage between his daughter Alypia and the general Ricimer was celebrated soon afterwards, but despite this union relations between the emperor and his general
became increasingly strained.   Finally, in A.D. 472, Ricimer set up a rival emperor, Anicius
Olybrius, and Anthemius was besieged in Rome.   After a long seige the city finally fell, and
Anthemius, disguised as a beggar, sought refuge in one of the churches.   He was soon recognized however, by Ricimer's nephew, Gundobad, and immediately beheaded (July 11th, 472).*

Mints: Milan; Ravenna; Rome.

Very Fine

4265 **N solidus.** D . N . ANTHEMIVS P . F . AVG.   Helmeted and dr. bust facing, holding spear.   R.   SALVS REIPVBLICAE.   Anthemius and Leo I stg. facing side by side, holding between them cross on globe and each holding spear; in field, ROMA in monogram; in ex., COMOB.   *C.* 6   .. .. £125·00

4266 **N semissis.** D . N . ANTHEMIVS PERPET . AVG.   Diad., dr. and cuir. bust, r.   R. — Christogram in wreath; in ex., COMOB.   *C.* 14.   *Illustrated on p.* 360   .. .. 175·00

4267 **N tremissis.** D . N . ANTHEMIVS P . F . AVG. — R.   No legend. Cross in wreath; in ex., COMOB.   *C.* 21 .. .. 100·00

4268 **R half-siliqua.** — — R.   No legend.   Christogram in wreath; in ex., RM.   *C.* 19 .. .. 125·00

4269 **Æ 4.** — — R.   Monogram of Anthemius in wreath; in ex., RM. *C.* 1 .. .. 30·00

EUPHEMIA

Aelia Marcia Euphemia was the daughter of Marcian and the wife of Anthemius.

Mint: Rome.

4270 **N solidus.** D . N . AEL . MARC . EVFIMIAE AVG.   Diad. and dr. bust, r.   R.   VICTORIA AVGGG*.   Victory stg. l., holding long cross; in ex., COMOB.   *C.* 1 .. .. *Extr. rare*

OLYBRIUS
A.D. 472

4272

(Anicius Olybrius) Descended from the great senatorial family of the Anicii, Olybrius was a senator at Rome at the time of the sack of the city by the Vandals in A.D. 455. He succeeded in escaping to Constantinople where, in 462, he married Placidia, the daughter of Valentinian III. Early in A.D. 472 he returned to Italy and was proclaimed emperor by the general Ricimer soon after his arrival, but he died of dropsy on November 2nd of the same year, having reigned for little more than six months.

Mint: Rome.

4271 **N solidus.** D . N . ANICIVS OLYBRIVS AVG.   Diad., dr. and cuir. bust, r.; above, cross.   R.   SALVS MVNDI.   Cross; in ex., COMOB.   *C.* 1.. .. 800·00

4272 — Helmeted, dr. and cuir. bust facing.   R.   As previous.   *C.* 3 .. 900·00

4273 **N tremissis.** — Diad., dr. and cuir. bust, r.   R.   No legend.   Cross in wreath; in ex., COMOB.   *C.* 5 .. .. 400·00

362

GLYCERIUS
A.D. 473-474

4274

    The throne of the Western division of the Empire remained vacant for over four months following the death of Olybrius in November, 472. A successor was eventually found in the person of Glycerius, Count of the Domestics, who was proclaimed emperor at Ravenna by Gundobad, the Master of Soldiers. The government of Constantinople, however, refused to recognize his elevation and Julius Nepos, the military governor of Dalmatia and a relative by marriage of the Imperial Family, was sent to Italy to depose the usurper and to ascend the Western throne as the successor of the last legitimate emperor, Anthemius. Glycerius, having been deserted by Gundobad, was unable to oppose the advance of his adversary, and at Portus, near the mouth of the Tiber, he was dethroned and forcibly consecrated bishop of Salona (June 24th, 474).

Mints: Milan; Ravenna; Rome.

Very Fine

4274 **A' solidus.** D . N . GLYCERIVS P . F . AVG. Diad., dr. and cuir. bust, r.
    R. VICTORIA AVGGG. Glycerius stg. facing, r. foot on stool, holding
    long cross and Victory; in field, RV; in ex., COMOB. C. 3 .. ..£750·00

4275 **A' tremissis.** — — R. No legend. Cross in wreath; in ex., COMOB.
    C. 7 ..   .. 350·00

4276 **Æ siliqua.** — — R. VICTORIA AVGGG. Victory advancing l.; in ex.,
    RM. C. 4 ..   .. 300·00

JULIUS NEPOS
A.D. 474–475 (480)

4277

    Following the dethronement of Glycerius in June, 474, Julius Nepos was duly proclaimed emperor and once more two Augusti reigned in unison. In the summer of 475, however, the barbarian troops in Italy were incited to rebellion by Orestes, the Master of Soldiers, and Nepos fled from Rome to Ravenna. On August 28th the fugitive left Italy for Dalmatia where he remained as an emperor in exile until his death five years later.

Mints: Arelate; Milan; Ravenna; Rome.

4277 **A' solidus.** D . N . IVL . NEPOS P . F . AVG. Helmeted and cuir. bust
    facing, holding spear and shield. R. VICTORIA AVGGG. Victory stg. l.,
    holding long cross; in field, RV; in ex., COMOB. C. 6. *Illustrated above* 350·00

4278 **A' tremissis.** — Diad., dr. and cuir. bust, r. R. No legend. Cross
    in wreath; in ex., COMOB. C. 16 ..   .. 145·00

4279 **Æ siliqua.** — — ℞. VRBS ROMA. Roma seated facing, hd. l., holding
Victory and sceptre; in ex., RVPS. *C.* 13 ..   ..£325·00

4280 **Æ half-siliqua.** — — ℞. No legend. Figure stg. l., r. foot on prow,
holding spear and cornucopiae; in field, RV. *C.* 15   ..   ..   .. 250·00

4281 **Æ 4.** — — ℞. Monogram of Nepos in wreath; no mint-mark. *C.* 2   65·00

ROMULUS AUGUSTUS

A.D. 475-476

4282

Romulus Augustus, nicknamed Augustulus, was the infant son of the general Orestes who proclaimed him emperor at the end of October, 475, two months after the flight of Nepos. Orestes administered Italy in the name of his son until late August, 476, when his barbarian mercenaries mutinied and proclaimed Odovacar king. Orestes was captured and beheaded at Placentia, and the helpless Augustulus was deposed at Ravenna and permitted by Odovacar to retire to a Campanian villa.

Thus ended the succession of Western Emperors which had begun with Honorius in 395. To the emperor Zeno at Constantinople, Odovacar sent the Imperial insignia which Augustulus had worn, together with a deputation of Roman senators who declared that the West no longer required a separate emperor. Zeno conferred upon Odovacar the title of Patrician and the rank of Master of Soldiers, and the whole Empire was once more united under the rule of one Augustus, though most of the Western provinces had now been conquered by Germanic invaders and had become Teutonic kingdoms.

Mints: Arelate; Ravenna; Rome.

4282 **N solidus.** D . N . ROMVLVS AVGVSTVS P . F . AVG. Helmeted and cuir.
bust facing, holding spear and shield. ℞. VICTORIA AVGGG. Victory
stg. l., holding long cross; in field, RM; in ex., COMOB. *C.* 3 ..   1000·00

4283 **N tremissis.** — Diad., dr. and cuir. bust, r. ℞. No legend. Cross
in wreath; in ex., COMOB. *C.* 10 ..   .. 375·00

4284 **Æ half-siliqua.** D . N . ROM . AVGVSTVS P . F . AVG. — ℞. No legend.
Figure stg. l., r. foot on prow, holding spear and cornucopiae; in field, RV.
C. 7 ..   .. 375·00

ZENO

A.D. 474-491

4285

During the reign of Leo I, the Isaurian chieftain Tarasicodissa came to Constantinople where he changed his name to Zeno and, in A.D. 467, married the emperor's elder daughter, Ariadne. Leo II, the son of Zeno and Ariadne, succeeded Leo I on February 3rd, 474, and six days later the young ruler crowned his father co-emperor. Zeno became sole emperor on the death of Leo II later the same year, but he was very unpopular because of his Isaurian origin, and he had to contend not only with the aggression of the Ostrogoths but also with frequent revolts and usurpations. He died following an attack of epilepsy on April 9th, 491, after a turbulent reign of seventeen years.

For the earliest issues of this reign see under Leo II.

Mints: Milan; Ravenna; Rome; Constantinople.

                                                                        Very Fine

4285 **N solidus.** D . N . ZENO PERP . AVG. Helmeted and cuir. bust facing, holding spear and shield. R. VICTORIA AVGGG . S. Victory stg. l., holding long cross; in ex., CONOB. *G. 4. Illustrated on p. 363 ..* .. £25·00

4286 **N semissis.** — Diad., dr. and cuir. bust, r. R. VICTORIA AVGG. Victory seated r., inscribing shield set on knee; in ex., CONOB. *G. 5 ..* 35·00

4287 **N tremissis.** — — R. VICTORIA AVGVSTORVM. Victory advancing r., hd. turned; in ex., CONOB. *G. 8* .. .. 17·50

4288 **R siliqua.** (*c.* 2 gm.) — — R. VOT. / VMSI / ITIS in wreath; in ex., CONS*. *G. —* .. .. 65·00
There is also a larger silver piece of 22 mm.

4289 **R half-siliqua.** (*c.* 1 gm.) — — R. No legend. Figure stg. l., r. foot on prow, holding spear and cornucopiae; in field, MD. *G. 13 ..* 75·00

4290 D . N . ZENO PERP . F . AV. — R. No legend. Eagle stg. l., hd. turned; no mint-mark. *G. 14* .. .. 90·00

4291 **Æ 1.** (*c.* 27 mm.) INP . ZENO FELICISSIMO SEN . AVG. Laur. hd., r. R. IMVICTA ROMA. Victory advancing r., holding wreath and trophy; in field, SC; in ex., XL. *G. 17* .. .. 75·00

4292 **Æ 4.** D . N . ZENO P . F . AVG. Diad., dr. and cuir. bust, r. R. ZENO. Zeno stg. facing, hd. l., holding long cross and globe; no mint-mark. *Cf. G. 19* .. .. 17·50

4293 — — R. Monogram of Zeno in wreath; no mint-mark. *G. 20* .. 10·00

ARIADNE

4295

The elder daughter of Leo I and Verina, Aelia Ariadne was married to Zeno in A.D. 467. Following the death of her husband in 491, she was called upon to select a successor to the Imperial throne, and her choice fell upon the elderly Anastasius of Dyrrhachium whom she married a few weeks later. She died in A.D. 515.

Mint: Constantinople.

4294 **N solidus.** AEL . ARIAdNE AV. Diad. and dr. bust, r. R. VICTORIA AVGGG. Victory stg. l., holding long cross; in ex., CONOB. *G. 1*   *Extr. rare*

4295 **N tremissis.** AEL . ARIAdNE AVG. — R. No legend. Cross in wreath; in ex., CONO. *G. 2. Illustrated above* .. .. .. *Extr. rare*

BASILISCUS
A.D. 475-476

4296

The brother of the empress Verina, Basiliscus was appointed commander of the great armada which was sent against the Vandals in A.D. 468. Following the failure of the expedition, which was due entirely to the incompetence of its commander, Basiliscus retired in disgrace to Heraclea, but six years later he formed a conspiracy with his sister against the emperor Zeno. On January 9th, 475, Zeno fled from Constantinople and Basiliscus was proclaimed emperor, but the new ruler soon made himself extremely unpopular through his unorthodox religious policy, and in August of the following year Zeno was able to re-enter the capital. Basiliscus was deposed and sent, together with his wife, Zenonis, and his son, Marcus, to Cucusus in Cappadocia, where all three were beheaded.

Marcus had been raised by his father to the rank of Augustus, and his name, but not his portrait, appears on some of the coins.

Mints: Ravenna; Rome; Constantinople.

	Basiliscus alone	**Very Fine**

4296 **N solidus.** D . N . bASILISCVS PP . AVG.   Helmeted and cuir. bust facing, holding spear and shield. R. VICTORIA AVGGG. Victory stg. l., holding long cross; in ex., CONOB. *G.* 1. *Illustrated above* .. .. .. £75·00

4297 **N semissis.** — Diad., dr. and cuir. bust, r. R. VICTORIA AVGGG. Victory seated r., inscribing shield set on knee; in ex., CONOB. *G.* 3 .. 110·00

4298 **N tremissis.** — — R. VICTORIA AVGVSTORVM. Victory advancing r., hd. turned; in ex., CONOB. *G.* 4 .. .. 45·00

4299 D . N . BASILISCVS PERT . AVG. — R. No legend. Cross in wreath; in ex., COMOB. *G.* 5 .. .. 55·00

4299A **R siliqua.** D . N . BASILISCVS PP . AVG. — R. VRBIS ROMA. Roma seated facing, hd. l., holding Victory and sceptre; in ex., PS. *Sabatier* 9 175·00

4300 **R half-siliqua.** D . N . BASILISCVS P . AVG. — R. No legend. Figure stg. l., r. foot on prow, holding spear and cornucopiae; in field, RV. *G.* 6 .. .. 125·00

4301 **Æ 4.** .... . N . bASILI .... — R. Monogram of Basiliscus; in ex., CON. *G.* 7 .. .. 30·00

Basiliscus and Marcus   Very Fine

4302 **N solidus.** D . N . BASILISCI ET MARC . P . AVG.   Helmeted and cuir. bust
of Basiliscus facing, holding spear and shield.   R.   SALVS REIPVBLICAE.
Basiliscus and Marcus enthroned facing; in ex., CONOB.   G. 8   .. £100·00

4303 — — R.   VICTORIA AVGGG . Θ.   Victory stg. l., holding long cross; in
ex., CONOB.   G. 9 ..   .. 90·00

4304 **N tremissis.** — Diad., dr. and cuir. bust of Basiliscus r.   R.   VIC-
TORIA AVGVSTORVM.   Victory advancing r., hd. turned; in ex., CONOB.
G. 10 ..   .. 75·00

ZENONIS

4305

(Aelia Zenonis) Wife of Basiliscus and mother of Marcus.

Mint: Constantinople.

4305 **N solidus.** AEL . ZENONIS AVG.   Diad. and dr. bust r.; above, hand
holding wreath.   R.   VICTORIA AVGGG.   Victory stg. l., holding long
cross; in ex., CONOB.   G. 1   ..   .. *Extr. rare*

4306 **Æ 4.** — Diad. and dr. bust, r.   R.   Monogram of Zenonis.   G. 2 *Very rare*

LEONTIUS
A.D. 484-488

In A.D. 484 *the Isaurian general Illus rebelled against Zeno.   First of all he set up
Marcian, the son of Anthemius, as a rival emperor, but soon afterwards he deposed him and
elevated the patrician Leontius in his place.   Verina, who had been a prisoner of Illus since
479, performed the ceremony of coronation at Tarsus, but in a battle fought soon afterwards
the forces of Zeno were victorious and the rebels fled to the Isaurian fortress of Cherris.   The
siege of the fortress continued for nearly four years, but it was eventually taken by treachery,
and Leontius and Illus were both beheaded* (A.D. 488).

Very Fine

4307   *N* **solidus.**   D . N . LEONTIVS P . F . AVG.   Helmeted and cuir. bust facing,
       holding spear and shield.   ℞.   VICTORIA AVG५.   Victory stg. facing,
       holding long cross surmounted by P and cross on globe; in ex., CONOB.
       G. 1.   *Illustrated on p.* 366 ..   ..   *Extr. rare*

ANASTASIUS I
A.D. 491-518

4309

Born at Dyrrhachium about A.D. 430, *Anastasius was a silentiary* (*usher at the Imperial
Palace*) *at the time of the death of Zeno in 491.   He was selected for the succession by the
widowed empress and crowned by the patriarch on April 11th: six weeks later he married
Ariadne.   Anastasius was a very conscientious ruler, and he paid particular attention to the
finances of the Empire.   Unfortunately, however, he held unorthodox religious opinions, and
this led to frequent riots at Constantinople culminating in an armed rising in Thrace in*
A.D. 513.   *Anastasius died on July 9th, 518, at a very advanced age, having outlived
Ariadne by three years.*

In A.D. 498 *Anastasius carried out a monetary reform by which bronze coins of a respec-
table size were once again issued in quantity.   There were several denominations in this new
series, the largest being the* follis *or* 40 nummia *piece.   Each of these coins bore its mark of
value on the reverse* (*e.g.* M=40 *nummia,* K=20 *nummia,* I=10 *nummia, etc.*) *and
their introduction marked an almost complete break with the traditions of the Roman coinage.*

The reform of A.D. 498 *is, therefore, a convenient point at which to terminate the Roman
coinage and to begin the Byzantine, at least as far as the bronze is concerned.   Thus, in the
following list, only the diminutive pre-498 bronze coins are included.   In the case of gold and
silver, however, it is not possible to differentiate between pre- and post-498 issues.*

Mint (pre-reform): Constantinople.

4308   *N* **solidus.**   D . N . ANASTASIVS PP . AVG.   Helmeted and cuir. bust facing,
       holding spear and shield.   ℞.   VICTORIA AVGGG. H.   Victory stg. l., hold-
       ing long cross surmounted by inverted P; in ex., CONOB.   *G.* 1.   **Plate
       12** ..   ..   £25·00
       There is also an *aureus* ($^1/_{60}$ lb.).

4309   *N* **semissis.** — Diad., dr. and cuir. bust, r.   ℞.   VICTORIA AVGGG.
       Victory seated r., inscribing shield set on knee; in ex., CONOB.   *G.* 2 ..   30·00

4310   *N* **tremissis.** — — ℞.   VICTORIA AVGVSTORVM.   Victory advancing r.,
       hd. turned; in ex., CONOB.   *G.* 4 ..   ..   15·00

4311   Æ **siliqua.** — — ℞.   VOT. / MVLT. / MTI. in wreath; in ex., CONOS*.
       G. 8 ..   ..   50·00
       There is also a larger silver piece of 22 mm.

4312   Æ **4.**   D . N . A . . . . — ℞.   Monogram of Anastasius in wreath;
       no mint-mark.   *G.* 14 ..   ..   15·00

CHRONOLOGICAL LIST OF THE LATER (BYZANTINE) RULERS

(*Based on Wroth "Catalogue of the Imperial Byzantine Coins in the British Museum".*)

Name	Date of reign, A.D.
Justin I	518–527
Justin I and Justinian I ..	527
Justinian I	527–565
Justin II	565–578
Tiberius II	578–582
Maurice Tiberius	582–602
Phocas	602–610
Heraclius	610–613
Heraclius and Heraclius Constantine	613–638
Heraclius, Heraclius Constantine and Heraclonas	638–641
Heraclius Constantine and Heraclonas	641
Heraclonas	641
Constantine III (Constans II)..	641–654
Constantine III and Constantine IV	654–668
Constantine IV, Heraclius and Tiberius	668–680
Constantine IV and Justinian II	680–685
Justinian II	685–695
Leontius	695–698
Tiberius III	698–705
Justinian II (again) and Tiberius	705–711
Philippicus	711–713
Anastasius II	713–716
Theodosius III	716–717
Leo III	717–720
Leo III and Constantine V ..	720–741
Constantine V	741–751
Artavasdes and Nicephorus ..	742–744
Constantine V and Leo IV ..	751–775
Leo IV	775–776
Leo IV and Constantine VI ..	776–780
Constantine VI and Irene ..	780–797
Irene	797–802
Nicephorus I	802–803
Nicephorus I and Stauracius ..	803–811
Stauracius	811
Michael I	811
Michael I and Theophylactus ..	811–813
Leo V	813
Leo V and Constantine ..	813–820
Michael II	820–821

Name	Date of reign, A.D.
Michael II and Theophilus ..	821–829
Theophilus	829–832
Theophilus and Constantine ..	832–839
Theophilus	839–840
Theophilus and Michael III ..	840–842
Michael III	842–866
Michael III and Basil I ..	866–867
Basil I	867–869
Basil I and Constantine ..	869–870
Basil I, Constantine and Leo VI	870–879
Basil I, Leo VI and Alexander ..	879–886
Leo VI and Alexander ..	886–911
Leo VI, Alexander and Constantine VII	911–912
Alexander and Constantine VII	912–913
Constantine VII and Zoe ..	913–919
Constantine VII and Romanus I	919–921
Constantine VII, Romanus I and Christopher	921–924
Constantine VII, Romanus I, Christopher, Stephen and Constantine	924–931
Constantine VII, Romanus I, Stephen and Constantine ..	931–944
Constantine VII, Stephen and Constantine	944–945
Constantine VII	945
Constantine VII and Romanus II	945–959
Romanus II	959–960
Romanus II and Basil II ..	960–961
Romanus II, Basil II and Constantine VIII	961–963
Theophano, Basil II and Constantine VIII	963
Nicephorus II, Basil II and Constantine VIII	963–969
John I, Basil II and Constantine VIII	969–976
Basil II and Constantine VIII	976–1025
Constantine VIII	1025–1028
Romanus III	1028–1034
Michael IV	1034–1041
Michael V	1041–1042
Zoe and Theodora	1042

Name	Date of reign, A.D.	Name	Date of reign, A.D.
Constantine IX	1042–1055	John IV	1258
Theodora (again)	1055–1056	John IV and Michael VIII ..	1258–1261
Michael VI	1056–1057		
Isaac I	1057–1059	*The Restored Empire*	
Constantine X	1059–1067	John IV and Michael VIII ..	1261
Eudocia, Michael VII and Constantine	1067	Michael VIII..	1261–1273
Romanus IV, Michael VII, Constantine and Andronicus	1067–1071	Michael VIII and Andronicus II	1273–1282
		Andronicus II	1282–1295
Michael VII	1071–1078	Andronicus II and Michael IX	1295–1320
Nicephorus III	1078–1081	Andronicus II	1320–1325
Nicephorus Melissenus .	1080–1081	Andronicus II and Andronicus	
Alexius I	1081–1092	III	1325–1328
Alexius I and John II ..	1092–1118	Andronicus III	1328–1341
John II	1118–1143	John V	1341–1347
Manuel I	1143–1180	John V and John VI ..	1347–1353
Alexius II	1180–1183	John V, John VI and Matthew	1353–1354
Alexius II and Andronicus I	1183–1184	John V	1354–1373
Andronicus I	1184–1185	John V and Manuel II ..	1373–1376
Isaac II	1185–1195	Andronicus IV	1376–1379
Alexius III	1195–1203	John V and Manuel II (restored)	1379–1391
Isaac II (again) and Alexius IV	1203–1204	Manuel II	1391–1399
Alexius V	1204	Manuel II and John VII ..	1399–1402
		Manuel II	1402–1421
Empire of Nicaea.		Manuel II and John VIII ..	1421–1423
Theodore I	1204–1222	John VIII	1423–1448
John III	1222–1254	Constantine XI	1448–1453
Theodore II	1254–1258		

BOOKS ON ROMAN COINS.

Letters in brackets preceeding the author's name show the abbreviation used in this book when referring to the work in question.

* Indicates that the book is out of print but that it is sometimes available in our stock.

REPUBLICAN

(*B.*) BABELON, E. **Monnaies de la Republique Romaine.** 2 vols. 1885-6. (Reprint 1964)
cloth £27·50

BELLONI, G. G. **Le Monete Romane dell'età Repubblicana.** 1960 cloth £10·00

CRAWFORD, M. H. **Roman Republican Coin Hoards.** 1969 cloth £3·75

GRUEBER, H. A. **Coins of the Roman Republic in the British Museum.** 3 vols. 1910. (Reprint 1969) cloth £10·00

HAEBERLIN, E. J. **Aes Grave. Das Schwergeld Roms und Mittel Italiens.** 2 vols. 1910. (Reprint 1968) cloth £34·00

ROLLAND, H. **Numismatique de la Republique Romaine.** 1924 cloth *

SEABY, H. A. **Roman Silver Coins.** Vol. I. Republic-Augustus. 2nd edition. 1967
cloth £2·00

SYDENHAM, E. A. **Aes Grave.** 1926 cloth *

(*S.*) SYDENHAM, E. A. **The Coinage of the Roman Republic.** 1952. (A new edition available 1970) cloth *

THOMSEN, R. **Early Roman Coinage. A Study of the Chronology.** 3 vols. 1957-61 paper *

IMPERIAL

AKERMAN, J. Y. **Coins of the Romans relating to Britain.** 1844 cloth *

ASKEW, G. **The Coinage of Roman Britain.** Revised edition, 1967 cloth 90p.

BASTIEN, P. **Le Monnayage de Magnence (350-353).** 1964 paper £7·50

BASTIEN, P. **Le Monnayage de bronze de Postume.** 1967 cloth £10·00

BASTIEN, P. and HUVELIN, H. **Trouvaille de Folles de la Periode Constantinienne (307-317).** 1969 paper £7·50

BASTIEN, P. and VASSELLE, F. **Le Tresor Monetaire de Domqueur (Somme).** 1965
paper £6·30

BREGLIA, L. **Roman Imperial Coins.** 1968
cloth £5·25

BRUCK, G. **Die Spätrömische Kupferprägung.** 1961 cloth *

CARSON, R. A. G., HILL, P. V. and KENT, J. P. C. **Late Roman Bronze Coinage, A.D. 324-498.** 1960 cloth £2·00

(*C.*) COHEN, H. **Description Historique des Monnaies frappées sous l'Empire Romain.** 8 vols. 1880-92. (Reprint 1955, with special dictionary) cloth £55·00

(*B.M.C.*) **Coins of the Roman Empire in the British Museum.**
Vol. I. Augustus-Vitellius, by H. Mattingly. 1923. (Reprint 1965) cloth £3·15
Vol. II. Vespasian-Domitian, by H. Mattingly. 1930. (Reprint 1966)
cloth £4·20
Vol. III. Nerva-Hadrian, by H. Mattingly. 1936. (Reprint 1966) cloth £5·25
Vol. IV. Antoninus Pius-Commodus, by H. Mattingly. 1940. (Reprint, in 2 vols., 1968) cloth £7·35
Vol. V. Pertinax-Elagabalus, by H. Mattingly 2 vols. 1950. (Reprinting) cloth *
Vol. VI. Severus Alexander to Balbinus and Pupienus, by R. A. G. Carson. 1962
cloth £5·65

FRANK, R. and HIRMER, M. **Römische Kaiser-porträts im Münzbild** 1969 boards 90p.

FROEHNER, W. **Medaillons de l'Empire Romain.** 1878 cloth *

GNECCHI, F. **The Coin Types of Imperial Rome.** 1908 cloth *

GNECCHI, F. **I Medaglioni Romani.** 3 vols. 1912. (Reprint 1968) cloth £45·00

GOODACRE, H. **The Bronze Coinage of the Late Roman Empire.** 1922 paper *

(*G.*) GOODACRE, H. **A Handbook of the Coinage of the Byzantine Empire.** 2nd edition, 1957 cloth £5·25

GRANT, M. **Roman Imperial Money.** 1954
cloth *

GRANT, M. **Roman History from Coins: some uses of the imperial coinage to the historian.** 1958. (Reprint 1968)
paper 50p.; cloth £1·25

GRANT, M. **From Imperium to Auctoritas. A historical study of the aes coinage in the Roman Empire, 49 B.C.-A.D. 14.** 1946
cloth *

GRANT, M. **The Six Main Aes Coinages of Augustus.** 1953 cloth *

GRUEBER, H. A. **Roman Medallions in the British Museum.** 1874 cloth *

KRAAY, C. M. **The Aes Coinage of Galba.** 1956 cloth £1·90

MAURICE, J. **Numismatique Constantinienne.** 3 vols. 1908-12 cloth *

MAZZINI, G. **Monete Imperiali Romani.** 5 vols. 1957-8 cloth £85·00

ROBERTSON, A. S. **Roman Imperial Coins in the Hunter Coin Cabinet, University of Glasgow.** Vol. I. Augustus-Nerva. 1962 cloth £7·50

(*R.I.C.*) **Roman Imperial Coinage.**
Vol. I. Augustus-Vitellius, by H. Mattingly and E. A. Sydenham. 1923. (Reprinted) cloth £5·00
Vol. II. Vespasian-Hadrian, by H. Mattingly and E. A. Sydenham. 1926. (Reprinted) cloth £6·00
Vol. III. Antoninus Pius-Commodus, by H. Mattingly and E. A. Sydenham.1930. (Reprinted) cloth £6·00
Vol. IV. Part I. Pertinax-Geta, by H. Mattingly and E. A. Sydenham. 1936. (Reprinted) cloth £6·00
Vol. IV. Part II. Macrinus-Pupienus, by H. Mattingly, E. A. Sydenham and C. H. V. Sutherland. 1938. (Reprinted) cloth £6·00
Vol. IV. Part III. Gordian III-Uranius Antoninus, by H. Mattingly, E. A. Sydenham and C. H. V. Sutherland. 1949. (Reprinted) cloth £6·00
Vol. V. Part I. Valerian-Florian, by P. H. Webb. 1927. (Reprinted) cloth £6·00
Vol. V. Part II. Probus-Amandus, by P. H. Webb. 1933. (Reprinted) cloth £7·00
Vol. VI. Diocletian-Maximinus, by C. H. V. Sutherland. 1967 cloth £12·00
Vol. VII. Constantine and Licinius, by P. M. Bruun. 1966 cloth £12·00
Vol. IX. Valentinian I-Theodosius I, by J. W. E. Pearce. 1951. (Reprinted) cloth £7·00
Vols. VIII and X are in preparation.

SABATIER, J. **Medaillons Contorniates.** 1860 cloth *

SABATIER, J. **Description Générale des Monnaies Byzantines.** 2 vols. 1862. (Reprint 1955) cloth £10·00

SEABY, H. A. **Roman Silver Coins.**
Vol. II. Tiberius-Commodus. 2nd edition, 1968 cloth £2·00
Vol. III. Pertinax-Balbinus and Pupienus. 1969 cloth £2·40
Vol. IV. Gordian III-Postumus in preparation

STRACK, P. L. **Untersuchungen zur Römischen Reichsprägung des Zweiten Jahrhunderts.** 3 vols. 1931-37 cloth *

SUTHERLAND, C. H. V. **Coinage and Currency in Roman Britain.** 1937 cloth *

SUTHERLAND, C. H. V. **Coinage in Roman Imperial Policy, 31 B.C.-A.D. 68.** 1951 cloth *

SYDENHAM, E. A. **The Coinage of Nero.** 1920 cloth *

SYDENHAM, E. A. **Historical References on Coins of the Roman Empire from Augustus to Gallienus.** 1968. (Reprinted edition) cloth £2·10

TOLSTOI, J. **Vizantijskije Monety-Monnaies Byzantines.** 9 parts. 1912-14. (Reprinted 1968 in 2 vols.) cloth £30·00

TOYNBEE, J. M. C. **Roman Medallions.** 1944 paper *

ULRICH-BANSA, O. **Moneta Mediolanensis.** 1947 cloth *

VOETTER, O. **Die Münzen der Römischen Kaiser, Kaiserinnen und Caesaren von Diocletianus bis Romulus (284-476).** 1921. (Reprint *c.* 1960) cloth *

LOCAL

(*B.M.C.G.*) **British Museum Catalogue of Greek Coins.** 29 vols. 1873-1927. (Reprint 1963-5) cloth £10·00 per vol. £225·00 the set

DATTARI, G. **Monete Imperiali Greche. Num. Augg. Alexandrini.** 2 vols. 1901 cloth *

GROSE, S. W. **Catalogue of the McClean Collection of Greek Coins (Fitzwilliam Museum).** 3 vols. 1923-9 cloth *

HEAD, B. V. **Historia Numorum.** 3rd edition, 1911. (Reprint 1963) cloth £9·45

KADMAN, L. **Corpus Nummorum Palestinensium**
Vol. I. The Coins of Aelia Capitolina. 1956 cloth *
Vol. II. The Coins of Caesarea Maritima. 1957 cloth *
Vol. IV. The Coins of Akko Ptolemais. 1961 cloth *

MILNE, J. G. **Catalogue of Alexandrian Coins in the Ashmolean Museum.** 1933 cloth *

PICK, B. **Die Antiken Münzen von Dacien und Moesien.** 2 parts, 1898 and 1910. The second part in collaboration with K. Regling cloth*

STRACK, M. L. **Die Antiken Münzen von Thrakien.** 1912 cloth *

SYDENHAM, E. A. **The Coinage of Caesarea in Cappadocia.** 1933 cloth *

Sylloge Nummorum Graecorum.
Danish Series: The Royal Collection of Coins and Medals, Danish National Museum. In many parts, 1942-1961.
German Series: Deutschland: Sammlung von Aulock. In many parts, from 1957
Some parts available—details and prices on request.

WADDINGTON, W. H. **Recueil Général des Monnaies Grecques d'Asie Mineure.** 4 parts, 1904-12, continued and completed by E. Babelon and Th. Reinach cloth *

GENERAL WORKS

AKERMAN, J. Y. **A Descriptive Catalogue of Rare and Unedited Roman Coins.** 2 vols. 1834 cloth *

BOYNE, W. **A Manual of Roman Coins.** 1965 (reprinted edition) cloth £2·25

BRITISH MUSEUM. **A Guide to the Exhibition of Roman Coins in the British Museum.** 1963 paper 55p.

GNECCHI, F. **Roman Coins: Elementary Manual.** 1903 cloth *

HILL, G. F. **Historical Roman Coins.** 1909. (Reprint 1968) cloth £4·50

HILL, G. F. **Handbook of Greek and Roman Coins.** 1899 cloth *

MATTINGLY, H. **Roman Coins from the Earliest Times to the Fall of the Western Empire.** 2nd edition, 1960. (Reprint 1967) cloth £3·75

MILNE, J. G. **Greek and Roman Coins and the Study of History.** 1939 cloth *

MOMMSEN, TH. **Geschichte des Römischen Münzwesens.** 1956 (reprinted edition) cloth £10·50

STEVENSON, S. W. **A Dictionary of Roman Coins.** 1889. (Reprint 1964) cloth £6·00

GRAMMES-GRAINS CONVERSION TABLE

GRAMMES	GRAINS	GRAMMES	GRAINS	GRAMMES	GRAINS
·06	1	2·00	31	7	108
·13	2	2·25	35	8	123
·19	3	2·50	39	9	139
·26	4	2·75	42	10	154
·32	5	3·00	46	12	185
·39	6	3·25	50	15	231
·45	7	3·50	54	20	309
·52	8	3·75	58	25	386
·58	9	4·00	62	30	463
·65	10	4·25	66	40	617
·78	12	4·50	70	50	772
·90	14	4·75	73	60	926
1·00	15	5·00	77	70	1081
1·25	19	5·25	81	80	1234
1·50	23	5·50	85	90	1388
1·75	27	5·75	89	100	1543
		6·00	93		

INCHES-MILLIMETRES CONVERSION TABLE

INCHES	MM.	INCHES	MM.	INCHES	MM.
0·3	8	0·85	22	1·4	36
0·35	9	0·9	23	1·45	37
0·4	10	0·95	24	1·5	38
0·45	11	1·0	26	1·55	40
0·5	13	1·05	27	1·6	41
0·55	14	1·1	28	1·65	42
0·6	15	1·15	29	1·7	43
0·65	17	1·2	31	1·75	44
0·7	18	1·25	32	1·8	46
0·75	19	1·3	33	1·85	47
0·8	20	1·35	34	1·9	48

£ STERLING CONVERSION TABLE (JANUARY 1970)

£ s. d.	= £ p.		U.S. DOLLARS	SWISS FRANCS	FRENCH FRANCS	GERMAN MARKS	DUTCH FLORINS	ITALIAN LIRE
1/–	=	0·05	·12	·52	·67	·44	·43	75
2/–	=	0·10	·24	1·04	1·34	·88	·86	150
3/–	=	0·15	·36	1·56	2·01	1·32	1·29	225
5/–	=	0·25	·60	2·60	3·34	2·21	2·16	375
7/–	=	0·35	·84	3·64	4·68	3·09	3·02	525
10/–	=	0·50	1·20	5·20	6·68	4·42	4·32	750
12/6	=	0·62½	1·50	6·50	8·35	5·52	5·40	938
15/–	=	0·75	1·80	7·80	10·02	6·63	6·48	1125
1/–/–	=	1·00	2·40	10·39	13·36	8·84	8·64	1500
1/5/–	=	1·25	3·00	12·99	16·70	11·05	10·80	1875
1/10/–	=	1·50	3·60	15·59	20·04	13·26	12·96	2250
2/10/–	=	2·50	6·00	25·98	33·40	22·10	21·60	3750
3/15/–	=	3·75	9·00	39·01	50·10	33·15	32·40	5625
5/–/–	=	5·00	12·00	52·00	66·80	44·20	43·20	7500
10/–/–	=	10·00	24·00	103·90	133·60	88·40	86·40	15000
20/–/–	=	20·00	48·00	207·80	267·20	176·80	172·80	30000
50/–/–	=	50·00	120·00	520·00	668·00	442·00	432·00	75000
100/–/–	=	100·00	240·00	1039·00	1336·00	884·00	864·00	150000

INDEX.

PLATE 1

5

29

49

PLATE   2

72   79   87   92   103

113   131   133   134   135

153   161   162   165   171

PLATE 3

178   182   187   189

199   206   210   213

218   227   238   241   246

PLATE 4

253 255 257 267

271 279 280 282

285 293 295 298

PLATE 5

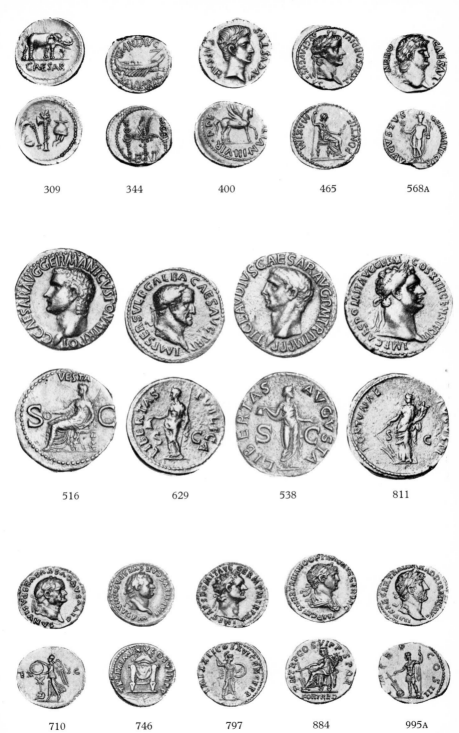

309   344   400   465   568A

516   629   538   811

710   746   797   884   995A

PLATE 6

1008   1155   1539

1036   1299   1417

1201   1250   1318A   1391   1475A

PLATE 7

1435A   1500   1583   1640   1772

1840   1902   1920   1953   1970A

1812   2399

1979A   2012   2084   2132A   2199

PLATE 8

2218

2245

2274

2299   2311   2373   2525   2591

2498

2631   2668   2640

PLATE 9

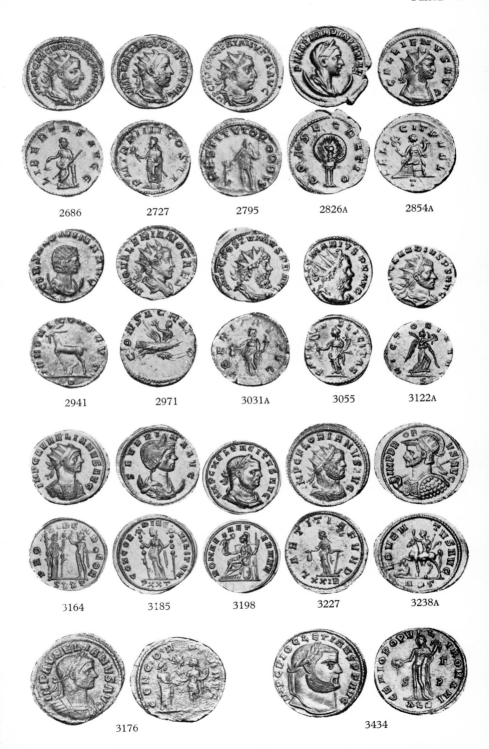

2686   2727   2795   2826A   2854A

2941   2971   3031A   3055   3122A

3164   3185   3198   3227   3238A

3176   3434

PLATE 10

3306   3331A   3374   3479

3487   3503A

3534   3572

3599A   3704   3727

3608   3630

PLATE 11

3653   3679   3746   3782   3808

3818   3827   3841A   3888   3897A

3903   3924   3972   3935

PLATE 12

3971   3982   3989   4005   4026

4047   4056   4075   4101   4254

4120   4144   4233   4308